The Plays of William Shakspeare
by William Shakespeare

Address:
HardPress
8345 NW 66TH ST #2561
MIAMI FL 33166-2626
USA
Email: info@hardpress.net

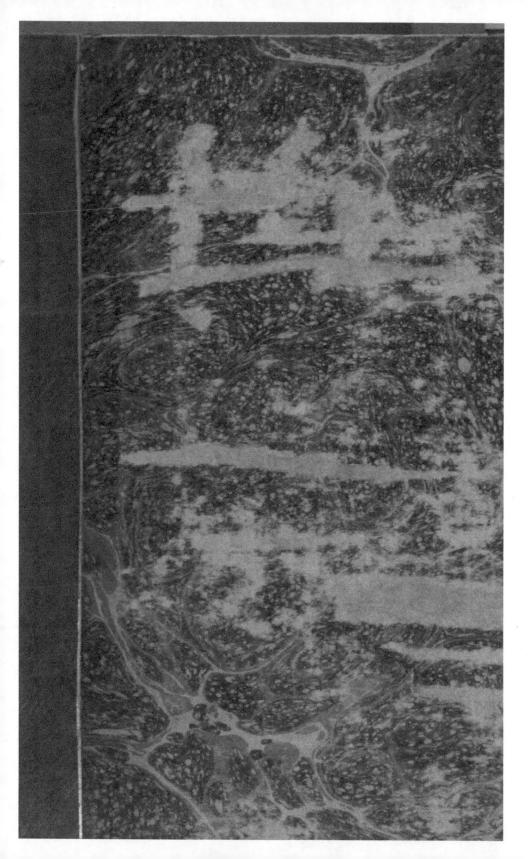

Malone
C. 182.

THE

PLAYS

OF

WILLIAM SHAKSPEARE.

VOLUME THE FOURTH.

THE
PLAYS
OF
WILLIAM SHAKSPEARE.

VOLUME THE FOURTH.

CONTAINING

TWELFTH NIGHT.
MEASURE FOR MEASURE.
MUCH ADO ABOUT NOTHING.

LONDON:

Printed for T. Longman, B. Law and Son, C. Dilly, J. Robson, J. Johnson,
T. Vernor, G. G. J. and J. Robinson, T. Cadell, J. Murray, R. Baldwin,
H. L. Gardner, J. Sewell, J. Nicholls, F. and C. Rivington, W. Goldsmith,
T. Payne, Jun. S. Hayes, R. Faulder, W. Lowndes, B. and J. White,
G. and T. Wilkie, J. and J. Taylor, Scatcherd and Whitaker, T. and J.
Egerton, E. Newbery, J. Barker, J. Edwards, Ogilvy and Speare,
J. Cuthell, J. Lackington, J. Deighton, and W. Miller.

M. DCC. XCIII.

TWELFTH-NIGHT:*

OR,

WHAT YOU WILL.

*Twelfth Night.]   There is great reason to believe, that the serious part of this Comedy is founded on some old translation of the seventh history in the fourth volume of *Belleforest's Histoires Tragiques.*   Belleforest took the story, as usual, from Bandello. The comic scenes appear to have been entirely the production of Shakspeare.   It is not impossible, however, that the circumstances of the Duke sending his Page to plead his cause with the Lady, and of the Lady's falling in love with the Page, &c. might be borrowed from the Fifth Eglog of Barnaby Googe, published with his other original Poems in 1563:

> " A worthy *Knyght* dyd love her longe,
> " And for her sake dyd seale
> " The panges of love, that happen styl
> " By frowning fortune's wheale.
> " He had a *Page,* Valerius named,
> " Whom so muche he dyd truste,
> " That all the secrets of his hart
> " To hym declare he muste.
> " And made hym all the onely meanes
> " To sue for his redresse,
> " And to entreate for grace to her
> " That caused his distresse.
> " *She whan as first she saw his page*
> " *Was straight with hym in love,*
> " *That nothynge coulde Valerius face*
> " *From Claudia's mynde remove.*
> " By hym was Faustus often harde,
> " By hym his sutes toke place,
> " By hym he often dyd aspyre
> " To se his Ladyes face.
> " This passed well, tyll at the length
> " Valerius sore did sewe,
> " With many teares besechynge her
> " His mayster's gryefe to rewe.
> " And tolde her that yf she wolde not
> " Releafe his mayster's payne,
> " *He never wolde attempte her more*
> " *Nor se her ones agayne,*" &c.

Thus also concludes the first scene of the third act of the Play before us:

> " And so adieu, good madam; never more
> " Will I my master's tears to you deplore," &c.

I offer no apology for the length of the foregoing extract, the book from which it is taken, being so uncommon, that only one copy, except that in my own possession, has hitherto occurred.

Even Dr. Farmer, the late Rev. T. Warton, Mr. Reed, and Mr. Malone, were unacquainted with this Collection of Googe's Poetry.

August 6, 1607, a Comedy called *What you Will* (which is the second title of this play), was entered at Stationers' Hall by Tho. Thorpe. I believe, however, it was Marston's play with that name. Ben Jonson, who takes every opportunity to find fault with Shakspeare, seems to ridicule the conduct of *Twelfth-Night* in his *Every man out of his Humour*, at the end of Act III. sc. vi. where he makes *Mitis* say, " That the argument of his comedy might have been of some other nature, as of a duke to be in love with a countess, and that countess to be in love with the duke's son, and the son in love with the lady's waiting maid: *some such cross wooing, with a clown to their serving man*, better than be thus near and familiarly allied to the time." STEEVENS.

I suppose this comedy to have been written in 1614. If however the foregoing passage was levelled at *Twelfth-Night*, my speculation falls to the ground. See *An Attempt to ascertain the order of Shakspeare's plays*, Vol. I. MALONE.

Persons reprefented.

Orfino, *duke of* Illyria.
Sebaftian, *a young gentleman, brother to* Viola.
Antonio, *a fea-captain, friend to* Sebaftian.
A fea-captain, friend to Viola.
Valentine,
Curio,   }   *Gentlemen attending on the duke.*
Sir Toby Belch, *uncle to* Olivia.
Sir Andrew Ague-cheek.
Malvolio, *fteward to* Olivia.
Fabian,
Clown,   }   *fervants to* Olivia.

Olivia, *a rich countefs.*
Viola, *in love with the duke.*
Maria, Olivia's *woman.*

*Lords, Priefts, Sailors, Officers, Muficians, and other
Attendants.*

SCENE, a city in Illyria; *and the fea-coaft near it.*

TWELFTH-NIGHT;

OR,

WHAT YOU WILL.

ACT I.   SCENE I.

An apartment in the Duke's *palace.*

Enter DUKE, CURIO, Lords; *Muſicians attending.*

DUKE. If muſick be the food of love, play on,
Give me exceſs of it; that, ſurfeiting, [2]
The appetite may ſicken, and ſo die.————
That ſtrain again;—it had a dying fall: [3]

[2] *Give me* exceſs *of* it; *that*, ſurfeiting, &c.] So, in *The Two Gentlemen of Verona* :
    "And now *exceſs* of it will make me *ſurfeit.*" STEEVENS.

[3] *That ſtrain again; it had a dying fall :*
    O, it came o'er my ear like the ſweet ſouth,
    That breathes upon a bank of violets,
    Stealing, *and giving odour.*] Milton, in his *Paradiſe Loſt,*
B. IV. has very ſucceſsfully introduced the ſame image :
    "———— now gentle gales,
    "Fanning their odoriferous wings, diſpenſe
    "Native perfumes, and whiſper whence they *ſtole*
    "Thoſe balmy ſpoils." STEEVENS.

That ſtrain *again;—it had* a dying fall :] Hence *Pope*, in his Ode on *Saint Cecilia's Day* :
    "The *ſtrains* decay,
    "And melt away,
    "In *a dying, dying fall.*"
Again, Thomſon, in his *Spring*, v. 722 ; ſpeaking of the nightingale :
    "————Still at every *dying fall*
    "Takes up the lamentable *ſtrain.*" HOLT WHITE.

B 3

O, it came o'er my ear like the sweet south,[4]
That breathes upon a bank of violets,[5]
Stealing, and giving odour.——Enough; no more;
'Tis not so sweet now, as it was before.
O spirit of love, how quick and fresh art thou!
That, notwithstanding thy capacity
Receiveth as the sea, nought enters there,
Of what validity and pitch soever,[6]
But falls into abatement and low price,
Even in a minute! so full of shapes is fancy,
That it alone is high-fantastical.[7]

    Cur. Will you go hunt, my lord?
    Duke.   What, Curio?

---

[4] *——the sweet* south,] The old copy reads——*sweet sound,* which Mr. Rowe changed into *wind,* and Mr. Pope into *south.* The thought might have been borrowed from Sidney's *Arcadia,* Lib. I: " *——*more *sweet* than a *gentle South*-west wind, which comes creeping over *flowery* fields," &c. This work was published in 1590. STEEVENS.

I see no reason for disturbing the text of the old copy, which reads—*Sound.* The wind, from whatever quarter, would produce a sound in breathing on the violets, or else the simile is false. Besides, *sound* is a better relative to the antecedent, *strain.*
                                          DOUCE.

[5] *That breathes upon a bank of* violets,] Here Shakspeare makes the south steal odour from the violet. In his 99th *Sonnet,* the violet is made the thief:
    " The forward violet thus did I chide:
    " Sweet thief, whence didst thou steal thy sweet that smells,
    " If not from my love's breath?" MALONE.

[6] *Of what* validity *and pitch* soever,] *Validity* is here used for *value.* MALONE.
So, in *King Lear:*
    " No less in space, *validity,* and pleasure."
                                      STEEVENS.

[7] *That it alone is* high-fantastical.] High-fantastical, *means* fantastical to the height.
So, in *All's Well that Ends Well:*
    " My *high-repented* blames
    " Dear sovereign, pardon me." STEEVENS.

7

CUR.   The hart.

DUKE. Why, so I do, the noblest that I have:
O, when mine eyes did see Olivia first,
Methought, she purg'd the air of pestilence;
That instant was I turn'd into a hart;.
And my desires, like fell and cruel hounds,
E'er since pursue me.⁸——How now? what news
       from her?

⁸ *That instant was I turn'd into a hart;*
   And my desires, like fell and cruel hounds,
    E'er since pursue me.] This image evidently alludes to the
story of Acteon, by which Shakspeare seems to think men
cautioned against too great familiarity with forbidden beauty.
Acteon, who saw Diana naked, and was torn to pieces by his
hounds, represents a man, who indulging his eyes, or his
imagination, with the view of a woman that he cannot gain,
has his heart torn with incessant longing. An interpretation
far more elegant and natural than that of Sir Francis Bacon,
who, in his *Wisdom of the Ancients*, supposes this story to warn
us against enquiring into the secrets of princes, by shewing,
that those who know that which for reasons of state is to be
concealed, will be detected and destroyed by their own
servants.   JOHNSON.

This thought, (as I learn from an anonymous writer in the
Gentleman's Magazine,) is borrowed from the 5th sonnet of
Daniel:

     "Whilst youth and error led my wand'ring mind,
      " And sette my thoughts in heedles waies to range,
     " All unawares, a goddesse chaste I finde,
      " (Diana like) to worke my suddaine change.
     " For her no sooner had mine eye bewraid,
      " But with disdaine to see mee in that place,
     " With fairest hand the sweet unkindest maid
     '' Casts water-cold disdaine upon my face:
     " *Which turn'd my sport into a hart's despaire,*
      " *Which still is chac'd, while I have any breath,*
     " *By mine own thoughts, sette on me by my faire;*
      " *My thoughts, like hounds, pursue me to my death.*
     " Those that I foster'd of mine own accord,
     " Are made by her to murder thus theyr lord."
See Daniel's *Delia & Rosamond*, augmented, 1594. STEEVENS.

Enter VALENTINE.

VAL. So pleafe my lord, I might not be
     admitted,
But from her hand-maid do return this anfwer:
The element itfelf, till feven years heat, [9]
Shall not behold her face at ample view;
But, like a cloiftrefs, fhe will veiled walk,
And water once a day her chamber round
With eye-offending brine : all this, to feafon
A brother's dead love, which fhe would keep frefh,
And lafting, in her fad remembrance.

DUKE. O, fhe, that hath a heart of that fine
     frame,
To pay this debt of love but to a brother,
How will fhe love, when the rich golden fhaft,
Hath kill'd the flock of all affections [2] elfe
That live in her! [3] when liver, brain, and heart,

---

[9] *The element itfelf, till feven years* heat,] *Heat* for *heated.*
The air, till it fhall have been warmed by feven revolutions of the
fun, fhall not, &c. So, in *King John :*
     " The iron of itfelf, though *beat* red hot—."
Again, in *Macbeth :*
     " ——— And this report
     " Hath fo *exafperate* the king—." MALONE.

[2] ———*the flock of all affections* ———] So, in Sidney's *Arcadia :*
" ———has the *flock* of unfpeakable virtues." STEEVENS.

[3] *O, fhe, that hath a heart of that fine frame,*
     To pay this debt of love but to a brother,
     How will fhe love, when the rich golden fhaft,
     Hath kill'd the flock of all affections elfe
     That live in her!] Dr. Hurd obferves, that *Simo,* in the
Andrian of *Terence,* reafons on his fon's concern for *Chryfis* in the
fame manner :
     " Nonnunquam conlacrumabat : placuit tum id mihi.
     " Sic cogitabam : hic parvæ confuetudinis
     " Causâ mortem hujus tam fert familiariter :
     " Quid fi ipfe amâffet ? quid mihi hic faciet patri ?"
                       STEEVENS.

These sovereign thrones,[4] are all suppl*y*d, and fill'd,
(Her sweet perfections,)[5] with one self king!—[6]
Away before me to sweet beds of flowers;
Love-thoughts lie rich, when canop*y*d with bowers. 　　　　　　　　　　　[*Exeunt.*

SCENE II.

The Sea-coast.

Enter VIOLA,[7] Captain, *and* Sailors.

VIO. What country, friends, is this?
CAP. 　　　　　　　　　　Illyria, lady.[8]

---

[4] These *sovereign thrones,*] We should read—three *sovereign thrones*. This is exactly in the manner of Shakspeare. So, afterwards, in this play, *Thy tongue, thy face, thy limbs, actions, and spirit, do give thee* fivefold *blazon.* WARBURTON.

[5] *Her sweet perfections,*] *Liver, brain,* and *heart,* are admitted in poetry as the residence of *passions, judgment,* and *sentiments.* These are what Shakspeare calls, *her sweet perfections,* though he has not very clearly expressed what he might design to have said. 　　　　　　　　　　　　　STEEVENS.

[6] *—with one self king!*] Thus the original copy. The editor of the second folio, who in many instances appears to have been equally ignorant of our author's language and metre, reads—self-*same* king; a reading, which all the subsequent editors have adopted. The verse is not defective. *Perfections* is here used as a quadrisyllable. So, in a subsequent scene:
"　Methinks I feel this youth's *perfections.*"
Self-king means *self-same* king; one and the same king. So, in *King Richard II:*
"　—— that *self*-mould that fashion'd thee,
"　Made him a man." MALONE.

[7] *Enter Viola,*] *Viola* is the name of a lady in the fifth book of *Gower de Confessione Amantis.* STEEVENS.

[8] *Illyria, lady.*] The old copy reads—" *This is* Illyria, lady." But I have omitted the two first words, which violate the metre, without improvement of the sense. STEEVENS.

Vio. And what fhould I do in Illyria?
My brother he is in Elyfium. *
Perchance, he is not drown'd:——What think you,
     failors?

Cap. It is perchance, that you yourfelf were fav'd.

Vio. O my poor brother! and fo, perchance,
     may he be.

Cap. True, madam: and, to comfort you with
     chance,
Affure yourfelf, after our fhip did fplit,
When you, and that poor number fav'd with you,⁹
Hung on our driving boat, I faw your brother,
Moft provident in peril, bind himfelf
(Courage and hope both teaching him the practice)
To a ftrong maft, that liv'd upon the fea;
Where, like Arion on the dolphin's back,
I faw him hold acquaintance with the waves,
So long as I could fee.

Vio.   For faying fo, there's gold:
Mine own efcape unfoldeth to my hope,
Whereto thy fpeech ferves for authority,
The like of him.   Know'ft thou this country?

Cap. Ay, madam, well; for I was bred and born,
Not three hours travel from this very place.

Vio. Who governs here?

Cap. A noble duke, in nature, ~~as in name.²~~
As *in his name.*

* ——————— *in* Illyria?
   My brother he is in Elyfium.] There is feemingly a play
upon the words—*Illyria* and *Elyfium.* Douce.

   9 ——and that *poor number fav'd with you,*] We fhould rather
read—*this* poor number. The old copy has *thofe.* The failors
who were faved, enter with the captain. Malone.

   ² *A noble duke in nature, as in name.*] I know not whether the
nobility of the name is comprifed in *duke,* or in *Orfino,* which
is, I think, the name of a great Italian family. Johnson.

Vio. What is his name?

Cap. Orfino.

Vio. Orfino! I have heard my father name him:
He was a bachelor then.

Cap.   And fo is now,
Or was fo very late: for but a month
Ago I went from hence; and then 'twas frefh
In murmur, (as, you know, what great ones do,
The lefs will prattle of,) that he did feek
The love of fair Olivia.

Vio.   What's fhe?

Cap. A virtuous maid, the daughter of a count
That dyld fome twelve month fince; then leaving
          her
In the protection of his fon, her brother,
Who fhortly alfo dyd: for whofe dear love,
They fay, fhe hath abjur'd the company
And fight of men.[3]

Vio.   O, that I ferv'd that lady;
And might not be deliver'd to the world,[4]
Till I had made mine own occafion mellow,
What my eftate is!

----

[3] *They fay, fhe hath abjur'd the company*
    And fight of men.
    O, that I ferv'd that lady!]
The old copy reads—
    They fay fhe hath abjur'd the fight
    And company of men.
    O, that I ferv'd that lady;
By the change I have made in the *ordo verborum*, the metre of
three lines is regulated, and an anticlimax prevented. STEEVENS.

[4] *And might not be deliver'd to the world,*] I wifh I might not be
made public to the world, with regard to the *ftate* of my birth and
fortune, till I have gained a *ripe opportunity* for my defign.

Viola feems to have formed a very deep defign with very little
premeditation: fhe is thrown by fhipwreck on an unknown coaft,
hears that the prince is a bachelor, and refolves to fupplant the
lady whom he courts. JOHNSON.

CAP.   That were hard to compafs;
Becaufe fhe will admit no kind of fuit,
No, not the duke's.

VIO. There is a fair behaviour in thee, captain;
And though that nature with a beauteous wall
Doth oft clofe in pollution, yet of thee
I will believe, thou haft a mind that fuits
With this thy fair and outward character.
I pray thee, and I'll pay thee bounteoufly,
Conceal me what I am; and be my aid
For fuch difguife as, haply, fhall become
The form of my intent.   I'll ferve this duke;[5]
Thou fhalt prefent me as an eunuch to him,[6]
It may be worth thy pains; for I can fing,
And fpeak to him in many forts of mufick,

---

[5] —— *I'll ferve this duke;*] Viola is an excellent fchemer,
never at a lofs; if fhe cannot ferve the lady, fhe will ferve the
duke.   JOHNSON.

[6] *Thou fhalt prefent me as an* eunuch *to him,*] This plan of
Viola's was not purfued, as it would have been inconfiftent with
the plot of the play.   She was prefented to the duke as a *page,*
but not as a *eunuch.*   M. MASON.

The ufe of *Evirati,* in the fame manner as at prefent, feems to
have been well known at the time this play was written, about
1600.   BURNEY.

When the practice of caftration (which originated certainly in
the eaft) was firft adopted, folely for the purpofe of improving
the voice, I have not been able to learn.   The firft regular opera,
as Dr. Burney obferves to me, was performed at Florence in 1600:
" till about 1635, mufical dramas were only performed occafionally
in the palaces of princes, and confequently before that time
eunuchs could not abound.   The firft eunuch that was fuffered
to fing in the Pope's chapel, was in the year 1600."
So early, however, as 1604, eunuchs are mentioned by one of
our poet's contemporaries, as excelling in finging:
" Yes, I can fing, fool, if you'll bear the burthen; and I
can play upon inftruments fcurvily, as gentlemen do.   O that I
had been *gelded!* I fhould then have been a fat fool for a chamber,
a fqueaking fool for a tavern, and a private fool for all the ladies."
The Malcontent, by J. Marfton, 1604.   MALONE.

That will allow me very worth his fervice.[7]
What elfe may hap, to time I will commit;
Only fhape thou thy filence to my wit.

Cap. Be you his eunuch, and your mute I'll be:
When my tongue blabs, then let mine eyes not fee!

Vio. I thank thee: Lead me on.   [*Exeunt.*

SCENE III.

A room in Olivia's *houfe.*

Enter Sir Toby Belch, *and* Maria.

Sir To. What a plague means my niece, to take the death of her brother thus? I am fure, care's an enemy to life.

Mar. By my troth, Sir Toby, you muft come in earlier o'nights; your coufin, my lady, takes great exceptions to your ill hours.

Sir To. Why, let her except before excepted.[8]

Mar. Ay, but you muft confine yourfelf within the modeft limits of order.

Sir To. Confine? I'll confine myfelf no finer than I am: thefe clothes are good enough to drink in, and fo be thefe boots too; an they be not, let them hang themfelves in their own ftraps.

Mar. That quaffing and drinking will undo you: I heard my lady talk of it yefterday; and of a foolifh knight, that you brought in one night here, to be her wooer.

---

[7] *That will* allow *me*——] To *allow* is to *approve.* So, in *King Lear,* Act. II. fc. iv:
    " ——if your fweet fway
    " *Allow* obedience——" Steevens.

[8] ——*let her except before excepted.*] A ludicrous ufe of the formal *law phrafe.* Farmer.

Sir To. Who? Sir Andrew Ague-cheek?

Mar. Ay, he.

Sir To. He's as tall [9] a man as any's in Illyria.

Mar. What's that to the purpofe?

Sir To. Why, he has three thoufand ducats a year.

Mar. Ay, but he'll have but a year in all thefe ducats; he's a very fool, and a prodigal.

Sir To. Fie, that you'll fay fo! he plays o'the viol-de-gambo, [2] and fpeaks three or four languages word for word without book, and hath all the good gifts of nature.

Mar. He hath, indeed,—almoft natural: [3] for, befides that he's a fool, he's a great quarreller;

---

[9] ——*as* tall *a man*——] *Tall* means *ftout, courageous.* So, in *Wily Beguiled:*
        " Ay, and he is a *tall fellow*, and a man of his hands too."
Again:
        " If he do not prove himfelf as *tall* a man as he."
                                        STEEVENS.

[2] ——*viol-de-gambo,*] The *viol-de-gambo* feems, in our author's time, to have been a very fafhionable inftrument. In *The Return from Parnaffus,* 1606, it is mentioned, with its proper derivation:
        " Her *viol-de-gambo* is her beft content,
        " For 'twixt ber legs fhe holds her inftrument." COLLINS.
So, in the Induction to the *Mal-content.*   1606.
        " ——come fit *between my legs* here.
        " No indeed, coufin; the audience will then take me for a *viol-de-gambo,* and think that you play upon me."
In the old dramatic writers, frequent mention is made of a *cafe of viols,* confifting of a *viol-de-gambo,* the tenor and the treble.
See Sir John Hawkins's *Hift. of Mufick,* Vol. IV. p. 32, n. 338, wherein is a defcription of a *cafe* more properly termed a *cheft of viols.* STEEVENS.

[3] *He hath indeed,—almoft natural:*] Mr. Upton propofes to regulate this paffage differently:
        He hath indeed, *all, moft* natural. MALONE.

and, but that he hath the gift of a coward to allay the guft he hath in quarrelling, 'tis thought among the prudent, he would quickly have the gift of a grave.

Sir To. By this hand, they are fcoundrels, and fubftractors, that fay fo of him. Who are they?

Mar. They that add moreover, he's drunk nightly in your company.

Sir To. With drinking healths to my niece; I'll drink to her, as long as there's a paffage in my throat, and drink in Illyria: He's a coward, and a coyftril,[4] that will not drink to my niece, till his brains turn o'the toe like a parifh-top.[5] What, wench? Caftiliano vulgo;[6] for here comes Sir Andrew Ague-face.

---

[4] *——a coyftril,*] i. e. a coward cock. It may however be a *keyftril,* or a baftard hawk; a kind of ftone-hawk. So, in *Arden of Feverfham,* 1592:

"   ——as dear
" As ever *coyftril* bought fo little fport." Steevens.

A *coyftril* is a paltry groom, one only fit to carry arms, but not to ufe them. So, in Holinfhed's *Defcription of England,* Vol. I. p. 162: "*Cofterel's,* or bearers of the armes of barons or knights." Vol. III. p. 248: "So that a knight with his efquire and *coiftrell* with his two horfes." P. 272, "women lackies, and *coifterels,* are confidered as the unwarlike attendants on an army." So again, in p. 127, and 217 of his *Hift. of Scotland.* For its etymology, fee *Couftille* and *Couftillier* in Cotgrave's *Dictionary.* Tollet.

[5] *——like a* parifh-top.] This is one of the cuftoms now laid afide. A large top was formerly kept in every village, to be whipped in frofty weather, that the peafants might be kept warm by exercife, and out of mifchief, while they could not work. —— Steevens.

" To fleep like a *town-top,*" is a proverbial expreffion. A top is faid to *fleep,* when it turns round with great velocity, and makes a fmooth humming noife. Blackstone.

[6] *——Caftiliano vulgo;*] We fhould read *volto.* In Englifh, put on your *Caftilian* countenance; that is, your grave, folemn looks. Warburton.

[handwritten note:] be same comparison is brought forward Night-walker of Fletcher: and dances like a town-top, & reels & h.

Enter SIR ANDREW AGUE-CHEEK.

SIR AND. Sir Toby Belch! how now, Sir Toby Belch?

SIR TO. Sweet fir Andrew!

SIR AND. Blefs you, fair fhrew.

MAR. And you too, fir.

SIR TO. Accoft, fir Andrew, accoft.[7]

Caftiliano vulgo;] I meet with the word *Caftilian* and *Caftilians* in feveral of the old comedies. It is difficult to affign any peculiar propriety to it, unlefs it was adopted immediately after the defeat of the Armada, and became a cant term capricioufly expreffive of jollity or contempt. *The Hoft,* in the *M. W.* of *Windfor,* calls Caius a *Caftilian-king Urinal*; and in the *Merry Devil of Edmonton,* one of the characters fays: "Ha! my *Caftilian* dialogues!" In an old comedy called *Look about you,* 1600, it is joined with another toper's exclamation very frequent in Shakefpeare:
      "And *Rivo* will he cry, and *Caftile* too."
So again, in *Marlowe's Jew of Malta,* 1633:
      "Hey, *Rivo Caftiliano,* man's a man."
Again, in the *Stately Moral of the Three Lords of London,* 1590:
      "Three Cavaliero's *Caftilianos* here," &c.
Cotgrave, however, informs us, that *Caftille* not only fignifies the nobleft part of Spain, but *contention, debate, brabling, alterca-tion.* Ils font en *Caftille. There is a jarre betwixt them;* and prendre la *Caftille* pour autruy: To undertake another man's quarrel. STEEVENS.

Mr. Steevens has not attempted to explain *vulgo,* nor perhaps can the proper explanation be given, unlefs fome incidental application of it may be found in connection with *Caftiliano,* where the context defines its meaning. Sir Toby here, having juft de-clared that he would perfift in drinking the health of his niece, as long as there was *a paffage in his throat,* and drink in Illyria, at the fight of Sir Andrew, demands of Maria, with a banter, *Caftiliano vulgo.* What this was, may be probably inferred from a fpeech in the *Shoemaker's Holiday,* 4to, 1610: "—— Away, firke, *fcower thy throat,* thou fhalt wafh it with *Gaftilian licuor.*"
                                          HENLEY.

[7] Accoft, *fir Andrew,* accoft.] To *accoft,* had a fignification in our author's time that the word now feems to have loft. In the fecond part of *The Englifh Dictionary,* by H. C. 1655, in

Sir And. What's that?

Sir To. My niece's chamber-maid.

Sir And. Good miftrefs Accoft, I defire better acquaintance.

Mar. My name is Mary, fir.

Sir And. Good Miftrefs Mary Accoft,———

Sir To. You miftake, knight: accoft, is, front her, board her,[8] woo her, affail her.

---

which the reader " who is defirous of a more refined and elegant fpeech," is furnifhed with *hard* words, " *to draw near*," is explained thus: " To *accoft*, appropriate, appropinquate." See alfo Cotgrave's Dict. in verb. *accofter.* MALONE.

[8] ———board *her*,] " I hinted that *bourd* was the better reading. Mr. Steevens fuppofed it fhould then be *bourd with her*; but to the authorities which I have quoted for that reading in Jonfon, *Catiline*, Act I. fc. iv. we may add the following:

" I'll *board* him ftraight; how now Cornelio?"
    All Fools, Act. V. fc. i.

" He brings in a parafite that flowteth, and *bourdeth* them thus."
        Nafh's Lenten Stuff, 1599.

" I can *bourd* when I fee occafion."
        'Tis pity She's a Whore, p. 38. WHALLEY.

I am ftill unconvinced that *board* (the naval term) is not the proper reading. It is fufficiently familiar to our author in other places. So, in *The Merry Wives of Windfor*, Act II. fc. i:

" ———unlefs he knew fome ftrain in me, that I know not myfelf, he would never have *boarded* me in this fury.

" *Mrs. Ford.* *Boarding*, call you it? I'll be fure to keep him above deck," &c. &c. STEEVENS.

Probably *board her* may mean no more than *falute her*, *fpeak to her*, &c. Sir Kenelm Digby, in his *Treatife of Bodies*, 1643, fo. Paris, p. 253, fpeaking of a blind man fays, " He would at the firft *aboard* of a ftranger, as foone as he fpoke to him, frame a right apprehenfion of his ftature, bulke, and manner of making."
        REED.

To *board* is certainly to *accoft*, or *addrefs*. So, in the *Hiftory of Celeftina the Faire*, 1596: " ———whereat Alderine fomewhat difpleafed for fhe would verie faine have knowne who he was, *boorded* him thus." RITSON.

Sir And. By my troth, I would not undertake her in this company. Is that the meaning of accoſt?

Mar. Fare you well, gentlemen.

Sir To. An thou let part ſo, ſir Andrew, 'would thou might'ſt never draw ſword again.

Sir And. An you part ſo, miſtreſs, I would I might never draw ſword again. Fair lady, do you think you have fools in hand?

Mar. Sir, I have not you by the hand.

Sir And. Marry, but you ſhall have; and here's my hand.

Mar. Now, ſir, thought is free:⁹ I pray you, bring your hand to the buttery-bar, and let it drink.

Sir And. Wherefore, ſweet heart? what's your metaphor?

Mar. It's dry, ſir.²

---

⁹ *Fair lady,* do you think you have fools in hand!——
Mar. *Now, Sir,* thought is free:] There is the ſame pleaſantry in *Lylies Euphues*, 1581: " None (quoth ſhe) can judge of wit but they that have it; why then (quoth he) *doeſt thou think me a fool? Thought is free,* my Lord, quoth ſhe." HOLT WHITE.

² *It's dry, ſir.*] What is the jeſt of *dry hand,* I know not any better than Sir Andrew. It may poſſibly mean, a hand with no money in it; or, according to the rules of phyſiognomy, ſhe may intend to inſinuate, that it is not a lover's hand, a moiſt hand being vulgarly accounted a ſign of an amorous conſtitution.
JOHNSON.

So, in *Monſieur D'Olive*, 1606: " But to ſay you had a dull eye, a ſharp noſe (the viſible marks of a ſhrew); a *dry hand,* which is the *ſign of a bad liver,* as he ſaid you were, being *toward a huſband* too; this was intolerable."
Again, in Decker's *Honeſt Whore,* 1635: " Of all *dry-fiſted* knights, I cannot abide that he ſhould touch me." Again, in *Weſtward-Hoe,* by Decker and Webſter, 1606: " ———Let her marry a man of a melancholy complexion, ſhe ſhall not be much troubled by him. My huſband has a *hand* as *dry* as his brains," &c. The Chief Juſtice likewiſe in the ſecond part of *K. Henry IV.* enumerates a *dry hand* among the characteriſticks of debility and

7

Sir And. Why, I think fo; I am not fuch an afs, but I can keep my hand dry. But what's your jeft?

Mar. A dry jeft, fir.

Sir And. Are you full of them?

Mar. Ay, fir; I have them at my fingers ends: marry, now I let go your hand, I am barren.

[Exit MARIA.

Sir To. O knight, thou lack'ft a cup of canary: When did I fee thee fo put down?

Sir And. Never in your life, I think; unlefs you fee canary put me down: Methinks, fometimes I have no more wit than a Chriftian, or an ordinary man has: but I am a great eater of beef, and, I believe, that does harm to my wit.

Sir To. No queftion.

Sir And. An I thought that, I'd forfwear it. I'll ride home to-morrow, fir Toby.

Sir To. Pourquoy, my dear knight?

Sir And. What is *pourquoy?* do, or not do? I would I had beftowed that time in the tongues, that I have in fencing, dancing, and bear-baiting: O, had I but follow'd the arts!

Sir To. Then hadft thou had an excellent head of hair.

Sir And. Why, would that have mended my hair?

Sir To. Paft queftion; for thou feeft, it will not curl by nature.[3]

age. Again, in *Antony and Cleopatra*, Charmian fays: " ——if an *oily palm* be not *a fruitful prognoftication*, I cannot fcratch mine ear." All thefe paffages will ferve to confirm Dr. Johnfon's latter fuppofition. STEEVENS.

[3] —— *it will not* curl by *nature.*] The old copy reads—*cool my nature.* The emendation was made by Theobald. STEEVENS.

Sir And. But it becomes me well enough, does't not?

Sir To. Excellent; it hangs like flax on a diftaff; and I hope to fee a houfewife take thee between her legs, and fpin it off.

Sir And. 'Faith, I'll home to-morrow, Sir Toby: your niece will not be feen; or, if fhe be, it's four to one fhe'll none of me: the count himfelf, here hard by, wooes her.

Sir To. She'll none o'the count; fhe'll not match above her degree, neither in eftate, years, nor wit; I have heard her fwear it. Tut, there's life in't, man.

Sir And. I'll ftay a month longer. I am a fellow o'the ftrangeft mind i'the world; I delight in mafques and revels fometimes altogether.

Sir To. Art thou good at thefe kick-fhaws, knight?

Sir And. As any man in Illyria, whatfoever he be, under the degree of my betters; and yet I will not compare with an old man. *4*

Sir To. What is thy excellence in a galliard, knight?

Sir And. 'Faith, I can cut a caper.

Sir To. And I can cut the mutton to't.

---

4 —— and yet I will not compare with an old man.] This is intended as a fatire on that common vanity of old men, in pre-ferring their own times, and the paft generation, to the prefent. WARBURTON.

This ftroke of pretended fatire but ill accords with the cha-racter of the foolifh knight. *Ague-cheek*, though willing enough to arrogate to himfelf fuch experience as is commonly the acquifi-tion of age, is yet careful to exempt his perfon from being com-pared with its bodily weaknefs. In fhort, he would fay with Falftaff:—" *I am old in nothing but my underftanding.*" STEEVENS.

Sir And. And, I think, I have the back-trick, fimply as ftrong as any man in Illyria.

Sir To. Wherefore are thefe things hid? wherefore have thefe gifts a curtain before them? are they like to take duft, like miftrefs Mall's picture?[5]

[5] —— *miftrefs* Mall's *picture?*] The real name of the woman whom I fuppofe to have been meant by *Sir Toby*, was *Mary Frith*. The appellation by which fhe was generally known, was *Mall Cut-purfe*. She was at once an *hermaphrodite*, a proftitute, a bawd, a bully, a thief, a receiver of ftolen goods, &c. &c. On the books of the Stationers' Company, Auguft 1610, is entered—" A Booke called the Madde Francks of Merry *Mall* of the Bankfide, with her walks in man's apparel, and to what purpofe. Written by John Day." *Middleton* and *Decker* wrote a comedy, of which fhe is the heroine. In this, they have given a very flattering reprefentation of her, as they obferve in their preface, that " it is the excellency of a writer, to leave things better than he finds them."

The title of this piece is—*The Roaring Girl, or Moll Cut-purfe; as it hath been lately acted on the Fortune Stage, by the Prince his Players*, 1611. The frontifpiece to it contains a full length of her in man's clothes, fmoaking tobacco. *Nathaniel Field*, in his *Amends for Ladies*, (another comedy, 1618,) gives the following character of her:

" ——————Hence lewd impudent,
" I know not what to term thee, man or woman;
" For nature, fhaming to acknowledge thee
" For either, hath produc'd thee to the world
" Without a fex: Some fay, that thou art woman;
" Others, a man: to many thou art both
" Woman and man; but I think rather neither;
" Or, man, or horfe, as Centaurs old were feign'd."

A life of this woman was likewife publifhed, 12mo. in 1662, with her portrait before it in a male habit; an ape, a lion, and an eagle by her. As this extraordinary perfonage appears to have partook of both fexes, the *curtain* which *Sir Toby* mentions, would not have been unneceffarily drawn before fuch a picture of her as might have been exhibited in an age, of which neither too much delicacy or decency was the characterifick. STEEVENS.

In our author's time, I believe, curtains were frequently hung before pictures of any value. So, in *Vittoria Corombona*, a tragedy, by Webfter, 1612:

" I yet but draw the *curtain*;—now to your *picture*."
MALONE.

why doft thou not go to church in a galliard, and come home in a coranto? My very walk should be a jig; I would not so much as make water, but in a fink-a-pace.[6] What doft thou mean? is it a world to hide virtues in? I did think, by the excellent conftitution of thy leg, it was form'd under the ftar of a galliard.

SIR AND. Ay, 'tis ftrong, and it does indifferent well in a flame-colour'd ftock.[7] Shall we fet about fome revels?

. See a further account of this woman in Dodfley's Collection of Old Plays, edition, 1780, Vol. VI. p. 1. Vol. XII. p. 398.
REED.

Mary Frith was born in 1584, and died in 1659. In a MS. letter in the Britifh Mufeum, from John Chamberlain to Mr. Carleton, dated Feb. 11, 1611-12, the following account is given of this woman's doing penance: " This laft Sunday Moll Cutpurfe, a notorious baggage that ufed to go in man's apparel, and challenged the field of diverfe gallants, was brought to the fame place [St. Paul's Crofs], where fhe wept bitterly, and feemed very penitent; but it is fince doubted fhe was maudlin drunk, being difcovered to have tippel'd of three quarts of fack, before fhe came to her penance. She had the daintieft preacher or ghoftly father that ever I faw in the pulpit, one Radcliffe of Brazen-Nofe College in Oxford, a likelier man to have led the revels in fome inn of court, than to be where he was. But the beft is, he did extreme badly, and fo wearied the audience that the beft part went away, and the reft tarried rather to hear Moll Cutpurfe than him." MALONE.

It is for the fake of correcting a miftake of Dr. Grey, that I obferve this is the character alluded to in the fecond of the following lines; and not Mary Carleton, the German Princefs, as he has very erroneoufly and unaccountably imagined:
" A bold virago ftout and tall,
" As Joan of France, or Englifh Mall."
Hudibras, P. I. c. iii.
The latter of thefe lines is borrowed by Swift in his Baucis and Philemon. RITSON.

6 —— a fink-a-pace.] i. e. a cinque-pace; the name of a dance, the meafures whereof are regulated by the number five. The word occurs elfewhere in our author. SIR J. HAWKINS.

7 ——flame-colour'd ftock.] The old copy reads— a dam'd

So, in Sir John Harrington's anatomie of the Metamorphosed ajax:"—the last verse disordered their mouthes, & was like a tricke "VII in a sinkapace."
Steevens.

Sir To. What fhall we do elfe? were we not born under Taurus?

Sir And. Taurus? that's fides and heart.[8]

Sir To. No, fir; it is legs and thighs. Let me fee thee caper: ha! higher: ha, ha!—excellent!

[*Exeunt.*

SCENE IV.

A Room in the Duke's *Palace.*

Enter VALENTINE, *and* VIOLA *in man's attire.*

Val. If the duke continue thefe favours towards you, Cefario, you are like to be much advanced; he hath known you but three days, and already you are no ftranger.

Vio. You either fear his humour, or my negligence, that you call in queftion the continuance of his love: Is he inconftant, fir, in his favours?

Val. No, believe me.

---

colour'd flock. Stockings were in Shakfpeare's time, called *flocks.* So, in *Jack Drum's Entertainment,* 1601:

" Or would my filk *flock* fhould lofe his glofs elfe."

Again, in one of Heywood's *Epigrams,* 1562:

" Thy upper *flocks,* be they ftuft with filke or flocks,

" Never become thee like a nether paire of *flocks.*"

The fame folicitude concerning the furniture of the legs, makes part of mafter Stephen's character in *Every Man in his Humour:*

" I think my leg would fhow well in a filk hofe."

STEEVENS.

The emendation was made by Mr. Pope. MALONE.

[8] Taurus? *that's fides and heart.*] Alluding to the medical aftrology ftill preferved in Almanacks, which refers the affections of particular parts of the body, to the predominance of particular conftellations. JOHNSON.

C 4

Enter DUKE, CURIO, *and Attendants.*

Vio. I thank you.   Here comes the count.

Duke. Who faw Cefario, ho?

Vio. On your attendance, my lord; here.

Duke. Stand you awhile aloof.——Cefario,
Thou know'ft no lefs but all; I have unclafp'd
To thee the book even of my fecret foul:[9]
Therefore, good youth, addrefs thy gait unto
      her;
Be not deny'd accefs, ftand at her doors,
And tell them, there thy fixed foot fhall grow,
Till thou have audience.

Vio.   Sure, my noble lord,
If fhe be fo abandon'd to her forrow
As it is fpoke, fhe never will admit me.

Duke. Be clamorous, and leap all civil bounds,
Rather than make unprofited return.

Vio. Say, I do fpeak with her, my lord; What
      then?

Duke. O, then unfold the paffion of my love,
Surprize her with difcourfe of my dear faith:
It fhall become thee well to act my woes;
She will attend it better in thy youth,
Than in a nuncio of more grave afpect.

Vio. I think not fo, my lord.

Duke.   Dear lad, believe it;
For they fhall yet belie thy happy years,
That fay, thou art a man: Diana's lip
Is not more fmooth, and rubious; thy fmall **pipe**

---

   9   —— *I have* unclafp'd
    To thee the book *even of my* fecret *foul:*]   So, in the Firft
Part of *K. Henry IV:*
      " And now I will *unclafp* a *fecret book.*" · STEEVENS.

Is as the maiden's organ, fhrill, and found,
And all is femblative a woman's part.[a]
I know, thy conftellation is right apt
For this affair :—Some four, or five, attend him;
All, if you will; for I myfelf am beft,
When leaft in company :—Profper well in this,
And thou fhalt live as freely as thy lord,
To call his fortunes thine.

 Vio.   I'll do my beft,
To woo your lady: yet, [*Afide.*] a barful ftrife![a]
Whoe'er I woo, myfelf would be his wife.

             [*Exeunt.*

S C E N E V.

A room in Olivia's *houfe.*

Enter MARIA, *and* CLOWN.[4]

 Mar. Nay, either tell me where thou haft been,
or I will not open my lips, fo wide as a briftle may
enter, in way of thy excufe : my lady will hang thee
for thy abfence.

---

 [a] —— *a woman's part.*] That is, thy proper part in a play
would be a woman's. Women were the nperfonated by boys.
                 JOHNSON.
 [a] —— *a* barrful *ftrife!*] i. e. a conteft full of impediments.
                 STEEVENS.
 [4] *Clown.*] As this is the firft *clown* who makes his appearance
in the plays of our author, it may not be amifs, from a paffage
in *Tarleton's News out of Purgatory*, to point out one of the ancient
dreffes appropriated to the character : " —I faw one attired in
ruffet, with a button'd cap on his head, a bag by his fide, and a
ftrong bat in his hand; fo artificially attired for a *clowne*, as I
began to call Tarleton's woonted fhape to remembrance."
                 STEEVENS.
 Such perhaps was the drefs of the Clown in this Comedy, in
All's well that ends well, &c. The clown however, in *Meafure for*

Clo. Let her hang me: he, that is well hang'd in this world, needs to fear no colours.[5]

Mar. Make that good.

Clo. He shall see none to fear.

Mar. A good lenten answer:[6] I can tell thee where that saying was born, of, I fear no colours.

Clo. Where, good mistress Mary?

Mar. In the wars; and that may you be bold to say in your foolery.

Clo. Well, God give them wisdom, that have it; and those that are fools, let them use their talents.

Mar. Yet you will be hang'd, for being so long absent: or, to be turn'd away;[7] is not that as good as a hanging to you?

Measure, (as an anonymous writer has observed) is only the tapster of a brothel, and probably was not so apparelled. MALONE.

[5] —— *fear no colours.*] This expression frequently occurs in the old plays. So, in Ben Jonson's *Sejanus*. The persons conversing are Sejanus, and Eudemus the physician to the princess Livia:

"   *Sej.* You minister to a royal lady then?
"   *Eud.* She is, my lord, and fair.
"   *Sej.* That's understood
"   Of all their sex, who are or would be so;
"   And those that would be, physick soon can make 'em:
"   For those that are, their beauties *fear no colours.*"

Again, in *The Two Angry Women of Abingdon*, 1599:

"   —— are you disposed, sir?————
"   Yes indeed: I *fear no colours*; change sides, Richard."
                                        STEEVENS.

[6] —— lenten *answer:*] A *lean*, or as we now call it, a *dry* answer. JOHNSON.

Surely a *lenten* answer, rather means a *short* and *spare* one, like the commons in *Lent*. So, in Hamlet: " —— what *lenten* entertainment the players shall receive from you." STEEVENS.

[7] —— or, to *be turn'd away*;] The editor of the second folio omitted the word *to*, in which he has been followed by all subsequent editors. MALONE.

CLO. Many a good hanging prevents a bad marriage; and, for turning away, let summer bear it out.[8]

MAR. You are refolute then?

CLO. Not fo neither; but I am refolv'd on two points.

MAR. That, if one break,[9] the other will hold; or, if both break, your gafkins fall.

CLO. Apt, in good faith; very apt! Well, go thy way; if Sir Toby would leave drinking, thou wert as witty a piece of Eve's flefh as any in Illyria.

MAR. Peace, you rogue, no more o'that; here comes my lady: make your excufe wifely, you were beft.   [*Exit.*

---

[8] —— *and for* turning away, *let* fummer *bear it out.*] This feems to be a pun from the nearnefs in the pronunciation of *turning away* and *turning of whey.*

I found this obfervation among fome papers of the late Dr. Letherland, for the perufal of which, I am happy to have an opportunity of returning my particular thanks to Mr. Glover, the author of *Medea* and *Leonidas,* by whom, before, I had been obliged only in common with the reft of the world.

I am yet of opinion that this note, however fpecious, is wrong. the literal meaning being eafy and appofite. *For turning away, let fummer bear it out.* It is common for unfettled and vagrant ferving-men, to grow negligent of their bufinefs towards fummer; and the fenfe of the paffage is: " *If I am turned away, the advantages of the approaching fummer will bear out, or fupport all the inconveniencies of difmiffion; for I fhall find employment in every field, and lodging under every hedge.*" STEEVENS.

[9] —— *if one* (point) *break,*] *Points* were metal hooks, faftened to the hofe tie breeches (which had then no opening or buttons,) and going into ftraps or eyes fixed to the doublet, and thereby keeping the hofe from falling down. BLACKSTONE.

So, in *King Henry IV.* P. I: " Their *points* being broken,—down fell their hofe." Again, in *Antony and Cleopatra:*
 " —— mingle eyes
 " With one that ties his *points?* STEEVENS.

Enter OLIVIA, *and* MALVOLIO.

Clo. Wit, and't be thy will, put me into good fooling! Thofe wits, that think they have thee, do very oft prove fools; and I, that am fure I lack thee, may pafs for a wife man: For what fays. Quinapalus? Better a witty fool, than a foolifh wit.[2]——God blefs thee, lady!

Oli. Take the fool away.

Clo. Do you not hear, fellows? Take away the lady.

Oli. Go to, you're a dry fool; I'll no more of you: befides, you grow difhoneft.

Clo. Two faults, Madonna,[3] that drink and good counfel will amend: for give the dry fool drink, then is the fool not dry; bid the difhoneft man mend himfelf; if he mend, he is no longer dif-honeft; if he cannot, let the botcher mend him: Any thing, that's mended, is but patch'd:[4] virtue, that tranfgreffes, is but patch'd with fin; and fin, that amends, is but patch'd with virtue: If that this fimple fyllogifm will ferve, fo; if it will not, What remedy? As there is no true cuckold but calamity, fo beauty's a flower:—the lady bade take away the fool; therefore, I fay again, take her away.

Oli. Sir, I bade them take away you.

Clo. Mifprifion in the higheft degree!—Lady,

---

[2] —— *Better a witty fool, than a foolifh wit.*] Hall, in his *Chronicle*, fpeaking of the death of Sir Thomas More, fays, " that he knows not whether to call him a *foolifh wife man*, or a *wife foolifh man.*" JOHNSON.

[3] — *Madonna,*] Ital. miftrefs, dame. So, *La Maddona*, by way of pre-eminence, the *Bleffed Virgin.* STEEVENS.

[4] — *Any thing, that's mended, is but* patch'd:] Alluding to the *patch'd* or particoloured garment of the fool. MALONE.

Cucullus non facit monachum; that's as much as to
fay, I wear not motley in my brain. Good Madonna,
give me leave to prove you a fool.

OLI. Can you do it?

CLO. Dexterioufly, good Madonna.

OLI. Make your proof.

CLO. I muft catechize you for it, Madonna;
Good my moufe of virtue, anfwer me.

OLI. Well, fir, for want of other idlenefs, I'll
bide your proof.

CLO. Good Madonna, why mourn'ft thou?

OLI. Good fool, for my brother's death.

CLO. I think, his foul is in hell, Madonna.

OLI. I know his foul is in heaven, fool.

CLO. The more fool you, Madonna, to mourn for
your brother's foul being in heaven.——Take away
the fool, gentlemen.

OLI. What think you of this fool, Malvolio?
doth he not mend?

MAL. Yes; and fhall do, till the pangs of death
fhake him: Infirmity, that decays the wife, doth
ever make the better fool.

CLO. God fend you, fir, a fpeedy infirmity, for
the better encreafing your folly! Sir Toby will be
fworn, that I am no fox; but he will not pafs his
word for two-pence that you are no fool.

OLI. How fay you to that, Malvolio?

MAL. I marvel your ladyfhip takes delight in
fuch a barren rafcal; I faw him put down the
other day with an ordinary fool, that has no
more brain than a ftone: Look you now, he's
out of his guard already; unlefs you laugh and
minifter occafion to him, he is gagg'd. I proteft,

I take these wife men, that crow fo at these fet kind of fools, no better than the fools' zanies.[5]

OLI. O, you are fick of felf-love, Malvolio, and tafte with a diftemper'd appetite. To be generous, guiltlefs, and of free difpofition, is to take thofe things for bird-bolts, that you deem cannon-bullets: There is no flander in an allow'd fool, though he do nothing but rail; nor no railing in a known difcreet man, though he do nothing but reprove.

CLO. Now Mercury indue thee with leafing, for thou speak'ft well of fools![6]

Re-enter MARIA.

MAR. Madam, there is at the gate a young gentleman, much defires to fpeak with you.

OLI. From the count Orfino, is it?

MAR. I know not, madam; 'tis a fair young man, and well attended.

OLI. Who of my people hold him in delay?

---

[5] —— *no better than the* fools' zanies] i. e. *fools' baubles,* which had upon the top of them the *head of a fool.* DOUCE.

[6] *Now* Mercury *indue thee with* leafing, *for thou fpeak'ft well of fools!*] This is a ftupid blunder. We fhould read, *with* pleafing, i. e. with eloquence, make thee a gracious and powerful fpeaker, for Mercury was the god of orators as well as cheats. But the firft editors, who did not underftand the phrafe, *indue thee with pleafing,* made this foolifh correction; more excufable, however, than the laft editor's, who, when this emendation was pointed out to him, would make one of his own; and fo, in his Oxford edition, reads, *with learning;* without troubling himfelf to fatisfy the reader how the firft editor fhould blunder in a word fo eafy to be underftood as *learning,* though they well might in the word *pleafing,* as it is ufed in this place. WARBURTON.

I think the prefent reading more humourous: *May Mercury teach thee to lie, fince thou lieft in favour of fools!* JOHNSON.

MAR. Sir Toby, madam, your kinfman.

OLI. Fetch him off, I pray you; he fpeaks nothing but madman: Fie on him! [*Exit* MARIA.] Go you, Malvolio: if it be a fuit from the count, I am fick, or not at home; what you will, to difmifs it. [*Exit* MALVOLIO.] Now you fee, fir, how your fooling grows old, and people diflike it.

CLO. Thou haft fpoke for us, Madonna, as if thy eldeft fon fhould be a fool: whofe fcull Jove cram with brains, for here he comes, one of thy kin, has a moft weak *pia mater.*

Enter SIR TOBY BELCH.

OLI. By mine honour, half drunk.—What is he at the gate, coufin?

SIR To. A gentleman.

OLI. A gentleman? What gentleman?

SIR To. 'Tis a gentleman here¹——A plague o'thefe pickle-herrings!—How now, fot?

CLO. Good Sir Toby,——

¹ *'Tis a gentleman* here——] He had before faid it was a gentleman. He was afked, what gentleman? and he makes this reply; which, it is plain, is corrupt, and fhould be read thus:
'*Tis a gentleman*-heir.
i. e. fome lady's eldeft fon juft come out of the nurfery; for this was the appearance Viola made in men's clothes. See the character Malvolio draws of him prefently after. WARBURTON.

Can any thing be plainer than that Sir Toby was going to defcribe the gentleman, but was interrupted by the effects of his *pickle-herring?* I would print it as an imperfect fentence. Mr. Edwards has the fame obfervation. STEEVENS.

Mr. Steevens's interpretation may be right: yet Dr. Warburton's reading is not fo ftrange, as it has been reprefented. In Broome's *Jovial Crew,* Scentwell fays to the gypfies: " We muft find a young *gentlewoman-heir* among you." FARMER.

—— a moft weak pia mater.] The pia mater is the membrane that immediately covers the fubstance of the brain. So in Philemon Holland's Translation of Pliny's Nat. Hift. Book XXIV. Chap. 8." — the fine pellicle called Pia Mater, which lappeth and enfoldeth the brain. Lit. 1601. p. 185.   Steevens

OLI. Coufin, coufin, how have you come fo early by this lethargy?

SIR TO. Lechery! I defy lechery: There's one at the gate.

OLI. Ay, marry; what is he?

SIR TO. Let him be the devil, an he will, I care not: give me faith, fay I. Well, it's all one. [*Exit.*

OLI. What's a drunken man like, fool?

CLO. Like a drown'd man, a fool, and a mad-man: one draught above heat [8] makes him a fool; the fecond mads him; and a third drowns him.

OLI. Go thou and feek the coroner, and let him fit o' my coz; for he's in the third degree of drink, he's drown'd: go, look after him.

CLO. He is but mad yet, Madonna; and the fool fhall look to the madman. [*Exit* CLOWN.

Re-enter MALVOLIO.

MAL. Madam, yond young fellow fwears he will fpeak with you. I told him you were fick; he takes on him to underftand fo much, and therefore comes to fpeak with you: I told him you were afleep; he feems to have a fore-knowledge of that too, and therefore comes to fpeak with you. What is to be faid to him, lady? he's fortified againft any denial.

OLI. Tell him, he fhall not fpeak with me.

MAL. He has been told fo; and he fays, he'll ftand at your door like a fheriff's poft, [9] and be

---

8 ―― *above heat* ――] i. e. above the ftate of being warm in a proper degree. STEEVENS.

9 ―― *ftand at your door like a* fheriff's poft,] It was the cuftom for that officer to have large *pofts* fet up at his door, as an

the supporter to a bench, but he'll speak with you.

OLI. What kind of man is he?

MAL. Why, of man kind.

OLI. What manner of man?

MAL. Of very ill manner; he'll speak with you, will you, or no.

OLI. Of what perfonage, and years, is he?

MAL. Not yet old enough for a man, nor young enough for a boy; as a fquafh is before 'tis a peafcod, or a codling when 'tis almoft an apple:[2] 'tis with him e'en ftanding water,[3] between boy and man. He is very well-favour'd, and he fpeaks

---

indication, of his office. The original of which was, that the king's proclamations, and other public acts, might be affixed thereon, by way of publication. So, Jonfon's *Every Man out of his Humour:*

"———————— put off
" To the lord Chancellor's tomb, or the *Shrives pofts.*"

So again, in the old play called *Lingua:*

" Knows he how to become a fcarlet gown? hath he a pair of frefh *pofts* at his door? WARBURTON.

Dr. Letherland was of opinion, that " by this poft is meant a poft to mount a horfe from, a horfeblock, which, by the cuftom of the city, is ftill placed at the fheriff's door."

In the *Contention for Honour and Riches,* a mafque by Shirley, 1633, one of the competitors fwears

" By the *Shrive's poft,*" &c.

Again, in *A Woman never vex'd,* Com. by Rowley, 1632:

" If e'er I live to fee thee *fheriff* of London,
" I'll gild thy painted *pofts* cum privilegio." STEEVENS.

[2] ————— *or a codling when 'tis almoft an* apple:] A *codling* anciently meant an *immature apple.* So, in Ben Jonfon's *Alchemift:*

" Who is it, Dol?
" A fine young *quodling.*"

The fruit at prefent ftyled a *codling,* was unknown to our gardens in the time of Shakfpeare. STEEVENS.

[3] ————'tis with him e'en ftanding water,] The old copy has—*in.* The emendation was made by Mr. Steevens. In the firft folio *e'en* and *in* are very frequently confounded. MALONE.

very fhrewifhly; one would think, his mother's
milk were fcarce out of him.

Oli. Let him approach: Call in my gentlewoman.

Mal. Gentlewoman, my lady calls.   [*Exit.*

Re-enter MARIA.

Oli. Give me my veil: come, throw it o'er my face;
We'll once more hear Orfino's embafly.

Enter VIOLA.

Vio. The honourable lady of the houfe, which
is fhe?

Oli. Speak to me, I fhall anfwer for her;
Your will?

Vio. Moft radiant, exquifite, and unmatchable
beauty,—I pray you, tell me, if this be the lady of
the houfe, for I never faw her: I would be loth *a/*
to caft away my fpeech; for, befides that it is
excellently well penn'd, I have taken great pains
to con it. Good beauties, let me fuftain no fcorn;
I am very comptible,[4] even to the leaft finifter ufage.

Oli. Whence came you, fir?

Vio. I can fay little more than I have ftudied,
and that queftion's out of my part. Good gentle
one, give me modeft affurance, if you be the lady
of the houfe, that I may proceed in my fpeech.

Oli. Are you a comedian?

Vio. No, my profound heart: and yet, by the

---

[4] ——*I am very* comptible,] *Comptible* for ready to call to
account. WARBURTON.

Viola feems to mean juft the contrary. She begs fhe may not
be treated with fcorn, becaufe fhe is very fubmiffive, even to
lighter marks of reprehenfion. STEEVENS.

very fangs of malice, I fwear, I am not that I play. Are you the lady of the houfe?

OLI. If I do not ufurp myfelf, I am.

VIOL. Moft certain, if you are fhe, you do ufurp yourfelf; for what is yours to beftow, is not yours to referve. But this is from my commiffion: I will on with my fpeech in your praife, and then fhew you the heart of my meffage.

OLI. Come to what is important in't: I forgive you the praife.

VIO. Alas, I took great pains to ftudy it, and 'tis poetical.

OLI. It is the more like to be feign'd; I pray you, keep it in. I heard, you were faucy at my gates; and allow'd your approach, rather to wonder at you than to hear you. If you be not mad, be gone; if you have reafon, be brief:[5] 'tis not that time of moon with me, to make one in fo fkipping[6] a dialogue.

MAR. Will you hoift fail, fir? here lies your way.

VIO. No, good fwabber; I am to hull here[7] a

---

[5] *If you be not mad, be gone; if you have reafon, be brief:*] The fenfe evidently requires that we fhould read,
If you be mad, be gone, &c.
For the words *be mad,* in the firft part of the fentence, are oppofed to *reafon* in the fecond. M. MASON.

[6] —— *fkipping* ——] Wild, frolick, mad. JOHNSON.
So, in *K. Henry IV.* P. I:
" The *fkipping* king, he ambled up and down," &c.
STEEVENS.
Again, in the *Merchant of Venice:*
" ———————— take pain
" To allay, with fome cold drops of modefty,
" Thy *fkipping* fpirit." MALONE.

[7] —— *I am to* hull *here* ——] To *hull* means to drive to and

little longer.——Some mollification for your giant,[7]
sweet lady.

OLI. Tell me your mind.

VIO. I am a meffenger.[8]

OLI. Sure, you have fome hideous matter to deliver, when the courtefy of it is fo fearful. Speak
your office.

VIO. It alone concerns your ear. I bring no
overture of war, no taxation of homage; I hold the
olive in my hand: my words are as full of peace
as matter.

OLI. Yet you began rudely. What are you?
what would you?

VIO. The rudenefs, that hath appear'd in me,

---

fro upon the water, without fails or rudder. So in the *Noble
Soldier*, 1634:
    " That all thefe mifchiefs *bull* with flagging fail."
                             STEEVENS.

[7] ——*fome mollification for your giant*,] Ladies, in romance,
are guarded by giants, who repel all improper or troublefome
advances. Viola, feeing the waiting-maid fo eager to oppofe her
meffage, intreats Olivia to pacify her giant. JOHNSON.

Viola likewife alludes to the diminutive fize of *Maria*, who is
called on fubfequent occafions, *little villain, youngeft wren of nine,*
&c. STEEVENS.

So, Falftaff to his page:
    " Sirrah, you *giant*," &c. *K. Henry IV.* P. II. Act I.
                            MALONE.

[8] Oli. *Tell me your mind.*
    Vio. *I am a meffenger.*] Thefe words (which in the old copy
are part of Viola's laft fpeech) muft be divided between the two
fpeakers.

Viola growing troublefome, Olivia would difmifs her, and therefore cuts her fhort with this command, *Tell me your mind.* The
other, taking advantage of the ambiguity of the word *mind*, which
fignifies either *bufinefs* or *inclination*, replies as if fhe had ufed it in
the latter fenfe, *I am a meffenger.* WARBURTON.

As a *meffenger*, fhe was not to fpeak her own mind, but that of
her employer. M. MASON.

have I learn'd from my entertainment. What I am, and what I would, are as fecret as maiden-head: to your ears, divinity; to any other's, pro-phanation.

Oli. Give us the place alone: we will hear this divinity. [*Exit* MARIA.] Now, fir, what is your text?

Vio. Moft fweet lady,——

Oli. A comfortable doctrine, and much may be faid of it. Where lies your text?

Vio. In Orfino's bofom.

Oli. In his bofom? In what chapter of his bofom?

Vio. To anfwer by the method, in the firft of his heart.

Oli. O, I have read it; it is herefy. Have you no more to fay?

Vio. Good madam, let me fee your face.

Oli. Have you any commiffion from your lord to negotiate with my face? you are now out of your text: but we will draw the curtain, and fhew you the picture. Look you, fir, fuch a one I was this prefent: Is't not well done?[9]   [*Unveiling.*

---

[9] —— *Look you, fir, fuch a one I was this prefent: Is't not well done?*] This is nonfenfe. The change of *was* to *wear*, I think, clears all up, and gives the expreffion an air of gallantry. Viola preffes to fee Olivia's face: The other at length pulls off her veil, and fays: *We will draw the curtain, and fhew you the* picture. I wear this complexion to-day, I may wear another to-morrow; jocularly intimating, that fhe *painted.* The other, vext at the jeft, fays, "Excellently *done*, if God *did* all." Perhaps, it may be true, what you fay in jeft; otherwife 'tis an excellent face. *'Tis in grain*, &c. replies Olivia. WARBURTON.

I am not fatisfied with this emendation. We may read, "Such a one I was." This *prefence*, is't not well done?" i. e. this mien, is it not happily reprefented? Similar phrafeology occurs in *Othello:*—"This fortification, fhall we fee it?" STEEVENS.

Vio. Excellently done, if God did all.

Oli. 'Tis in grain, fir; 'twill endure wind and weather.

Vio. 'Tis beauty truly blent,[2] whofe red and white
Nature's own fweet and cunning hand laid on:
Lady, you are the cruel'ft fhe alive,
If you will lead thefe graces to the grave,
And leave the world no copy.[3]

This paffage is nonfenfe as it ftands, and neceffarily requires fonfe amendment. That propofed by Warburton would make fenfe of it; but then the allufion to a picture would be dropped, which began in the preceding part of the fpeech, and is carried on through thofe that follow. If we read *prefents*, inftead of *prefent*, this allufion will be preferved, and the meaning will be clear. I have no doubt but the line fhould run thus:
    " Look you, Sir, fuch *as once I was, this prefents.*"
Prefents means *reprefents*. So Hamlet calls the pictures he fhews his mother:
    " The counterfeit *prefentment* of two brothers."
She had faid before—" But we will draw the curtain, and fhew you the *picture*;" and concludes with afking him, if it was *well done.* The fame idea occurs in *Troilus and Creffida,* where Pandarus, taking off her veil, fays:
    " Come draw this curtain, and let us fee your *picture.*"
                                        M. MASON.

I fufpect, the author intended that Olivia fhould again cover her face with her veil, before fhe fpeaks thefe words. MALONE.

[2] *'Tis beauty truly* blent,] i. e. blended, mixed together. *Blent* is the ancient participle of the verb to *blend.* So, in a *Looking Glafs for London and England,* 1617:
    " ————the beautiful encreafe
    " Is wholly *blent.*"
Again, in Spenfer's *Fairy Queen,* B. I. c. 6:
    " ————for having *blent*
    " My name with guile, and traiterous intent." STEEVENS.

[3] *If you will lead thefe graces to the grave,*
    And leave the world no copy.] How much more elegantly is this thought expreffed by Shakfpeare, than by Beaumont and Fletcher in their *Philafter!*
    " I grieve fuch virtue fhould be laid in earth,
    " Without an *heir.*"

Oli. O, fir, I will not be fo hard-hearted; I will give out divers fchedules of my beauty: It fhall be inventoried; and every particle, and utenfil, label'd to my will: as, item, two lips indifferent red; item, two grey eyes, with lids to them; item, one neck, one chin, and fo forth. Were you fent hither to 'praife me?'[4]

Vio. I fee you what you are: you are too proud; But, if you were the devil, you are fair. My lord and mafter loves you; O, fuch love Could be but recompens'd, though you were crown'd The nonpareil of beauty!

Shakfpeare has copied himfelf in his 11th Sonnet:
    " She carv'd thee for her feal, and meant thereby
    " Thou fhould'ft print more, nor let that *copy* die."
Again, in the 3d Sonnet:
    " Die fingle, and thine image dies with thee."
                            STEEVENS.
Again, in his 9th Sonnet:
    " Ah! if thou iffuelefs fhalt hap to die,
    " The world will hail thee like a makelefs wife;
    " The world will be thy widow, and ftill weep
    " *That thou no form of thee haft left behind.*"
Again, in the 13th Sonnet:
    " O that you were yourfelf! but, love, you are
    " No longer yours than you yourfelf here live:
    " Againft this coming end you fhould prepare,
    " *And your fweet femblance to fome other give.*" MALONE.

4 ―――― *to* 'praife *me?*] i. e. to *appraife*, or *appretiate* me. The foregoing words, *fchedules*, and *inventoried*, fhew, I think, that this is the meaning. So again, in *Cymbeline*: " I could then have looked on him without the help of admiration; though the *catalogue* of his endowments had been *tabled* by his fide, and I to perufe him by *items*." MALONE.

Malone's conjecture is ingenious, and I fhould have thought it the true reading, if the foregoing words, *fchedule* and *inventoried*, had been ufed by Viola: but as it is Olivia herfelf who makes ufe of them, I believe the old reading is right, though Steevens has adopted that of Malone. Viola has extolled her beauty fo highly, that Olivia afks, whether fhe was fent there on purpofe to praife her. M. MASON.

OLI.   How does he love me?

VIO. With adorations, with fertile tears,[5]
With groans that thunder love, with fighs of fire.[6]

   OLI. Your lord does know my mind, I cannot
        love him:
Yet I suppose him virtuous, know him noble,
Of great estate, of fresh and stainless youth;
In voices well divulg'd,[7] free, learn'd, and valiant,
And, in dimension, and the shape of nature,
A gracious person: but yet I cannot love him;
He might have took his answer long ago.

   VIO. If I did love you in my master's flame,
With such a suffering, such a deadly life,
In your denial I would find no sense,
I would not understand it.

---

[5] —— with *fertile tears*,] *With*, which is not in the old copy,
was added by Mr. Pope to supply the metre. *Tears* is here used
as a diffyllable, like *fire, hour, swear,* &c. " With adoration's
fertile tears," i. e. with the copious tears that unbounded and
adoring love pours forth. MALONE.

To read *tears* as a diffyllable [i. e. tĕ-ārs] at the end of a verse,
is what no ancient examples have authorised, and no human ears
can endure.   STEEVENS.

[6] *With groans that* thunder *love, with fighs of fire.*] This line is
worthy of Dryden's *Almanzor,* and, if not said in mockery of
amorous hyperboles, might be regarded as a ridicule on a passage
in Chapman's translation of the first book of *Homer,* 1598:
   " Jove *thunder'd out a figh*;"
or, on another in *Lodge's Rosalynde,* 1592:
   " The winds of my deepe fighes
   " That *thunder* still for noughts," &c. STEEVENS.

So, in our author's *Lover's Complaint* :
   " O, that forc'd *thunder* from his heart did fly !" MALONE.

[7] *In* voices well divulg'd,] Well spoken of by the world.
                       MALONE.

So, in *Timon* :
   " Is this the Athenian minion, whom the world
   " Voic'd so regardfully ?" STEEVENS.

OLI. Why, what would you?

VIO. Make me a willow cabin at your gate,
And call upon my foul within the houfe;
Write loyal cantons of contemned love,[8]
And fing them loud even in the dead of night;
Holla your name to the reverberate hills,[9]
And make the babbling goffip of the air[2]
Cry out, Olivia! O, you fhould not reft
Between the elements of air and earth,
But you fhould pity me.

OLI. You might do much: What is your parentage?

VIO. Above my fortunes, yet my ftate is well:
I am a gentleman.

OLI. Get you to your lord;
I cannot love him: let him fend no more;
Unlefs, perchance, you come to me again,

---

[8] *Write loyal* cantons *of contemned love,*] The old copy has *cantons*; which Mr. Capell, who appears to have been entirely unacquainted with our ancient language, has changed into *canzons.*—— There is no need of alteration. *Canton* was ufed for *canto* in our author's time. So, in *The London Prodigal*, a Comedy, 1605: " What-do-you-call-him has it there in his third *canton.*" Again, in Heywood's Preface to *Britaynes Troy*, 1609 :——" in the judicial perufal of thefe few *cantons*," &c. MALONE.

[9] *Holla your name to the* reverberate *hills,*] I have corrected, *reverberant.* THEOBALD.

Mr. Upton well obferves, that Shakfpeare frequently ufes the adjective paffive, *actively.* Theobald's emendation is therefore unneceffary. B. Jonfon, in one of his mafques at court, fays:
" ————— which fkill, Pythagoras
" Firft taught to men by a *reverberate* glafs." STEEVENS.

Johnfon, in his Dictionary, adopted Theobald's correction. But the following line from T. Heywood's *Troja Britannica*, 1609, canto 11. ft. ix. fhows that the original text fhould be preferved:
" Give fhrill *reverberat echoes* and rebounds."
HOLT WHITE.

[2] ————— *the babbling goffip of the air*——] A moft beautiful ex-preffion for an *echo.* DOUCE.

To tell me how he takes it.   Fare you well:
I thank you for your pains: spend this for me.

   Vio. I am no fee'd post,[3] lady; keep your purse;
My master, not myself, lacks recompense.
Love make his heart of flint, that you shall love;.
And let your fervour, like my master's, be
Plac'd in contempt! Farewel, fair cruelty.   [*Exit.*

   Oli. What is your parentage?
Above my fortunes, yet my state is well:
I am a gentleman.——I'll be sworn thou art;
Thy tongue, thy face, thy limbs, actions, and spirit,
Do give thee five-fold blazon:——Not too fast:——
       soft! soft!
Unless the master were the man.[4]——How now?
Even so quickly may one catch the plague?
Methinks, I feel this youth's perfections,
With an invisible and subtle stealth,
To creep in at mine eyes.   Well, let it be.——
What, ho, Malvolio!——

Re-enter MALVOLIO.

   Mal.   Here, madam, at your service.
   Oli. Run after that same peevish messenger,
The county's man:[5] he left this ring behind him,

---

   [3] *I am no fee'd* post,] *Post,* in our authour's time, signified a
messenger. MALONE.

   [4] ——*soft! soft!*
   Unless the master were the man.] Unless the dignity of the
master were added to the merit of the servant, I shall go too far,
and disgrace myself. Let me stop in time. MALONE.

   Perhaps she means to check herself by observing,——This is un-
becoming forwardness on my part, *unless I were as much in love
with the master as I am with the man.* STEEVENS.

   [5] *The* county's *man:*] *County* and *count* in old language were
synonymous. The old copy has *countes,* which may be right: the
Saxon genitive case. MALONE.

Would I, or not; tell him, I'll none of it.
Defire him not to flatter with his lord,[6]
Nor hold him up with hopes; I am not for him:
If that the youth will come this way to-morrow,
I'll give him reafons for't.   Hie thee, Malvolio.

MAL. Madam, I will.   [*Exit.*

OLI. I do I know not what; and fear to find
Mine eye[7] too great a flatterer for my mind.
Fate, fhew thy force: Ourfelves we do not owe;[8]
What is decreed, muft be; and be this fo! [*Exit.*

---

[6] — *to flatter* with *his lord*,] This was the phrafeology of the time.
So, in *King Richard II :*
    " Shall dying men flatter *with* thofe that live."
Many more inftances might be added.   MALONE.

[7] *Mine eye,* &c.] I believe the meaning is; I am not miftrefs
of my own actions; I am afraid that my eyes betray me, and
flatter the youth without my confent, with difcoveries of love.
                                            JOHNSON.
Johnfon's explanation of this paffage is evidently wrong.   It
would be ftrange indeed if Olivia fhould fay, that fhe feared her
eyes would betray her paffion, and flatter the youth, without her
confent, with a difcovery of her love, after fhe had actually fent
him a ring, which muft have difcovered her paffion more ftrongly,
and was fent for that very purpofe.——The true meaning appears to
me to be thus :—*She fears that her eyes had formed fo flattering an
idea of Cefario, that fhe fhould not have ftrength of mind fufficient to
refift the impreffion.*   She had juft before faid :
    " Methinks, I feel this youth's perfections,
    " With an invifible and fubtle ftealth,
    " To creep in at mine eyes."
which confirms my explanation of this paffage.   M. MASON.

I think the meaning is, I fear that my eyes will feduce my
underftanding; that I am indulging a paffion for this beautiful
youth, which my reafon cannot approve.   MALONE.

[8] —— *Ourfelves we do not* owe;] i. e. we are not our own
mafters.   We cannot govern ourfelves.   So, in *Macbeth :*
    " —— the difpofition that I *owe*;" i. e. own, poffefs.
                                            STEEVENS.

ACT II.   SCENE I.

The Sea-coaſt.

Enter ANTONIO *and* SEBASTIAN.

ANT. Will you ſtay no longer? nor will you not, that I go with you?

SEB. By your patience, no: my ſtars ſhine darkly over me; the malignancy of my fate might, perhaps, diſtemper yours; therefore I ſhall crave of you your leave, that I may bear my evils alone: It were a bad recompenſe for your love, to lay any of them on you.

ANT. Let me yet know of you, whither you are bound.

SEB. No, 'footh, ſir; my determinate voyage is mere extravagancy. But I perceive in you ſo ex-cellent a touch of modeſty, that you will not extort from me what I am willing to keep in; therefore it charges me in manners the rather to expreſs myſelf.[9] You muſt know of me then, Antonio, my name is Sebaſtian, which I call'd Rodorigo; my father was that Sebaſtian of Meſſaline,[2] whom I know, you have heard of: he left behind him, my-ſelf, and a ſiſter, both born in an hour; If the heavens had been pleas'd, 'would we had ſo ended! but, you, ſir, alter'd that; for, ſome hour before you took me from the breach of the ſea,[3] was my ſiſter drown'd.

---

[9] —— *to expreſs myſelf.*] That is, *to reveal myſelf.* JOHNSON.

[2] —— *Meſſaline,*] Sir Thomas Hanmer very judiciouſly offers to read *Metelin,* an iſland in the Archipelago; but Shakſpeare knew little of geography, and was not at all ſolicitous about orthographical nicety. The ſame miſtake occurs in the concluding ſcene of the play :
    " Of *Meſſaline*; Sebaſtian was my father." STEEVENS.

[3] —— *the* breach *of the ſea,*] i. e. what we now call the *breaking* of the ſea. In Pericles it is ſtyled—" the *rupture* of the ſea." STEEVENS.

Ant. Alas, the day!

Seb. A lady, fir, though it was faid fhe much refembled me, was yet of many accounted beautiful : but, though I could not, with fuch eftimable wonder,[3] over-far believe that, yet thus far I will boldly publifh her, fhe bore a mind that envy could not but call fair : fhe is drown'd already, fir, with falt water,[4] though I feem to drown her remembrance again with more.

Ant. Pardon me, fir, your bad entertainment.

Seb. O, good Antonio, forgive me your trouble.

Ant. If you will not murder me for my love, let me be your fervant.

Seb. If you will not undo what you have done, that is, kill him whom you have recover'd, defire it not. Fare ye well at once : my bofom is full of kindnefs ; and I am yet fo near the manners of my mother,[5] that upon the leaft occafion more, mine eyes will tell tales of me. I am bound to the count Orfino's court : farewel. [*Exit.*

Ant. The gentlenefs of all the gods go with thee!

---

[3] — *with fuch* eftimable wonder,] Thefe words Dr. Warburton calls *an interpolation of the players,* but what did the players gain by it? they may be fometimes guilty of a joke without the concurrence of the poet, but they never lengthen a fpeech only to make it longer. Shakfpeare often confounds the active and paffive adjectives. *Eftimable wonder* is *efteeming wonder,* or *wonder and efteem.* The meaning is, that he could not venture to think fo highly as others of his fifter. JOHNSON.

Thus Milton ufes *unexpreffive* notes, for *unexpreffible,* in his hymn on the Nativity. MALONE.

[4] —*fhe is drown'd already, fir, with falt water,*] There is a refemblance between this and another falfe thought in *Hamlet :*
    " *Too much of water haft thou, poor Ophelia,*
    " *And therefore I forbid my tears.*" STEEVENS.

[5] *I am yet fo near the manners of my* mother,] So, in *King Henry V.* Act IV. fc. vi:
    " And all my *mother* came into my eyes." MALONE.

I have many enemies in Orfino's court,
Elfe would I very fhortly fee thee there:
But, come what may, I do adore thee fo,
That danger fhall feem fport, and I will go. [*Exit.*

S C E N E   II.

A Street.

Enter VIOLA; MALVOLIO *following.*

MAL. Were not you even now with the countefs Olivia?

VIO. Even now, fir; on a moderate pace I have fince arrived but hither.

MAL. She returns this ring to you, fir; you might have faved me my pains, to have taken it away yourfelf. She adds moreover, that you fhould put your lord into a defperate affurance fhe will none of him: And one thing more; that you be never fo hardy to come again in his affairs, unlefs it be to report your lord's taking of this. Receive it fo.[6]

VIO. She took the ring of me; I'll none of it.[7]

---

[6] *Receive it fo.*] One of the modern editors reads, with fome probability, receive it, *fir.* But the prefent reading is fufficiently intelligible. MALONE.

" *Receive it* fo," is, *underfland* it fo. Thus, in the third Act of this play, Olivia fays to Viola—

" ——— To one of your *receiving*

" Enough is fhewn;—" STEEVENS.

[7] *She took* the *ring of me; I'll none of it.*] This paffage has been hitherto thus pointed; which renders it, as it appears to me, quite unintelligible. The following punctuation:

" She took the ring of me!—I'll none of it."

Was fuggefted by an ingenious friend, and certainly renders the line lefs exceptionable: yet I cannot but think there is fome corruption in the text. Had our author intended fuch a mode of fpeech, he would probably have written—

She took *a* ring of me!—I'll none of it.

MAL. Come, fir, you peevifhly threw it to her; and her will is, it fhould be fo return'd: if it be worth ftooping for, there it lies in your eye; if not, be it his that finds it.   [*Exit.*

VIO. I left no ring with her: What means this lady? Fortune forbid, my outfide have not charm'd her! She made good view of me; indeed, fo much, That, fure,[8] methought, her eyes had loft her tongue,[9]

Malvolio's anfwer feems to intimate that Viola had faid fhe had not given any ring. We ought therefore, perhaps, to read,
    She took *no* ring of me;—I'll none of it.
So afterwards: " I left *no* ring with her." Viola exprefsly denies her having given Olivia any ring. How then can fhe affert, as fhe is made to do by the old regulation of the paffage, that the lady had received one from her?

Since I wrote the above, it has occurred to me that the latter part of the line may have been corrupt, as well as the former: our author might have written—
    She took *this* ring of me! *She*'ll none of it!
So before: " —he left *this* ring;—tell him, I'll none of it." And afterwards: " None of my lord's ring!"—Viola may be fuppofed to repeat the fubftance of what Malvolio has faid. Our author is feldom ftudious on fuch occafions to ufe the very words he had before employed. MALONE.

I do not perceive the neceffity of the change recommended. Viola finding the ring fent after her, accompanied by a fiction, is prepared to meet it with another. This lady as Dr. Johnfon has obferved, is an excellent fchemer; fhe is never at a lofs, or taken unprepared. STEEVENS.

[8] *That,* fure,] *Sure,* which is wanting in the old copy, was added, to complete the metre, by the editor of the fecond folio. *Sure* in the prefent inftance is not very likely to have been the word omitted in the firft copy, being found in the next line but one. MALONE.

[9] —— *her eyes had* loft *her tongue,*] We fay a man *lofes* his company when they go one way and he goes another. So Olivia's tongue loft her eyes; her tongue was talking of the duke, and her eyes gazing on his meffenger. JOHNSON.

It rather means that the very fixed and eager view fhe took of Viola, perverted the ufe of her tongue, and made her talk diftractedly. This conftruction of the verb—*loft,* is alfo much in Shakfpeare's manner. DOUCE.

For she did speak in starts distractedly.
She loves me, sure; the cunning of her passion
Invites me in this churlish messenger.
None of my lord's ring! why, he sent her none.
I am the man;—If it be so, (as 'tis)
Poor lady, she were better love a dream.
Disguise, I see, thou art a wickedness,
Wherein the pregnant enemy ² does much.
How easy is it, for the proper-false
In women's waxen hearts to set their forms! ³

---

² —— *the* pregnant *enemy* —] Is, I believe, the dexterous fiend,
or enemy of mankind. JOHNSON.

Pregnant is certainly *dexterous*, or *ready*. So, in *Hamlet:*
"How *pregnant* sometimes his replies are!" STEEVENS.

³ *How easy is it for the* proper-false
In women's waxen hearts to set their forms!] This is obscure.
The meaning is, *how easy is disguise to women!* how easily does
their own falsehood, contained in their *waxen* changeable *hearts*,
enable them to assume deceitful appearances! The two next lines
are perhaps transposed, and should be read thus :
"*For such as we are made, if such we be,*
"*Alas, our frailty is the cause, not we.*" JOHNSON.

I am not certain that this explanation is just. Viola has been
condemning those who disguise themselves, because Olivia had
fallen in love with a specious appearance. How easy is it, she
adds, for those who are at once *proper* (i. e. fair in their appearance) and *false* (i. e. deceitful) to make an impression on the easy
hearts of women?—The *proper-false* is certainly a less elegant
expression than the *fair deceiver*, but seems to mean the same thing.
A *proper man*, was the ancient phrase for a *handsome man:*
"This Ludovico is a *proper* man." *Othello.*
To *set their forms*, means, to plant their images, i. e. to make an
impression on their easy minds. Mr. Tyrwhitt concurs with me
in this interpretation. STEEVENS.

This passage, according to Johnson's explanation of it, is so
severe a satire upon women, that it is unnatural to suppose that
Shakspeare should put it in the mouth of one of the sex, especially
a young one. Nor do I think that the words can possibly express
the sense which he contends for. Steevens's explanation appears to
be the true one. The word *proper* certainly means *handsome*; and
Viola's reflection, how easy it was for those who are handsome and

Alas, our frailty [4] is the caufe, not we;
For, fuch as we are made of, fuch we be. [5]
How will this fadge? [6] My mafter loves her dearly;

deceitful, to make an impreffion on the waxen hearts of women,
is a natural fentiment for a girl to utter who was herfelf in love.
An expreffion fimilar to that of *proper-falfe*, occurs afterwards in
this very play, where Antonio fays:

" Virtue is beauty, but the *beauteous-evil*
" Are empty trunks o'er flourifh'd by the devil."

M. MASON.

Mr. Steevens's explanation is undoubtedly the true one. So, in
our author's *Rape of Lucrece*:

" —— men have marble, *women waxen minds*,
" And therefore are they form'd as marble will;
" The weak opprefs'd, the *impreffion of ftrange kinds*
" Is *form'd* in them by force, by *fraud*, or fkill:
" Then call them not the authors of their ill——."

Again, in *Meafure for Meafure*:

" Nay, call us ten times frail,
" For we are *foft* as our complexions are,
" And *credulous to falfe prints*." MALONE.

[4] —— our *frailty*—] The old copy reads—O frailty.
STEEVENS.
The emendation was made by the editor of the fecond folio.
MALONE.

[5] *For, fuch as we are made of, fuch we be.*] The old copy reads—
made if. Mr. Tyrwhitt obferves, that " inftead of tranfpofing
thefe lines according to Dr. Johnfon's conjecture," he is inclined
to read the latter as I have printed it. So, in the *Tempeft*:

" —— we are fuch ftuff
" As dreams are made *of.*" STEEVENS.

I have no doubt that Mr. Tyrwhitt's conjecture is right. *Of*
and *if* are frequently confounded in the old copies. Thus in the
folio, 1632, *King John*, p. 6: " Lord of our prefence, Angiers, and
if you." [inftead of—*of* you.]
Again, *of.* is printed inftead of *if. Merchant of Venice*, 1623:
" Mine own I would fay, but, *of* mine, then yours."
In *As you like it*, we have a line conftructed nearly like the prefent,
as now corrected:
" Who fuch a one as fhe, fuch is her neighbour."
MALONE.

[6] *How will this* fadge?] To *fadge*, is *to fuit, to fit*, ~ *to go with*. So, in
Decker's comedy of *Old Fortunatus*, 1600:
" I fhall never *fadge* with the humour, becaufe I cannot lie."

VOL. IV. E

And I, poor monster, fond as much on him;
And she, mistaken, seems to dote on me:
What will become of this? As I am man,
My state is desperate for my master's love;
As I am woman, now alas the day!
What thriftless sighs shall poor Olivia breathe?
O time, thou must untangle this, not I;
It is too hard a knot for me to untie.   [*Exit.*

S C E N E   III.

A room in Olivia's *house.*

Enter SIR TOBY BELCH, *and* SIR ANDREW AGUE-
CHEEK.

Sir To. Approach, sir Andrew: not to be a-bed
after midnight, is to be up betimes; and *diluculo
surgere,*[7] thou know'st,———

Sir And. Nay, by my troth, I know not: but
I know, to be up late, is to be up late.

Sir To. A false conclusion; I hate it as an un-
fill'd can: To be up after midnight, and to go
to bed then, is early; so that, to go to bed after
midnight, is to go to bed betimes. Do not our
lives consist of the four elements?[8]

So, in *Mother Bombie,* 1594:
     " I'll have thy advice, and if it *fadge,* thou shalt eat."——
     " But how will it *fadge* in the end?"——
     " All this *fadges* well."——
     " We are about a matter of legerdemain, how will this
        fadge?"——
     " ——in good time it *fadges.*" STEEVENS.

   [7] —— *diluculo surgere,*] *saluberrimum est.* This adage our author
found in Lilly's Grammar, p. 51. MALONE.

   [8] —— *Do not our lives consist of the four elements?*] So, in our
author's 45th Sonnet :

Sir And. 'Faith, so they say; but, I think, it rather consists of eating and drinking.[9]

Sir To. Thou art a scholar; let us therefore eat and drink.—Marian, I say!——a stoop [1] of wine!

Enter Clown.

Sir And. Here comes the fool, i'faith.

Clo. How now, my hearts? Did you never see the picture of we three?[1]

Sir To. Welcome, ass. Now let's have a catch.

Sir And. By my troth, the fool has an excellent breast.[4] I had rather than forty shillings I had

" My
" Sin
So also, in
dull elements
[9] — *I think*
on the medic
consist in the j
the human fram WARBURTON.

[1] —— *a stoop*—] A *stoop*, cadus, à γεoππα, Belgis, *stoop*. Ray's *Proverbs*, p. 111. In Hexham's Low Dutch Dictionary, 1660, a gallon is explained by *een kanne van twee stoopen*. A *stoop*, however, seems to have been something more than half a gallon. In a Catalogue of the rarities in the Anatomy Hall at Leyden, printed there, 4to. 1701, is " The bladder of a man containing four *stoop* (which is something above TWO English gallons) of water."
REED.

[1] —— *Did you never see the picture of* we three?] An allusion to an old print, sometimes pasted on the wall of a country alehouse, representing TWO, but under which the spectator reads—
" *We three* are asses." HENLEY.

I believe Shakspeare had in his thoughts a common sign, in which two wooden heads are exhibited, with this inscription under it: " *We three* loggerheads be." The spectator or reader is supposed to make the third. The clown means to insinuate, that Sir Toby and Sir Andrew had as good a title to the name of *fool* as himself.
MALONE.

[4] *By my troth, the fool has an excellent* breast.] *Breast, voice.*
E 2

Homer, Iliad IX. concurs in opinion with Sir Andrew:
" —— strength consists in spirits & in blood,
" and these are ow'd to generous wine & food."
Steevens

such a leg; and so sweet a breath to sing, as the fool has. In sooth, thou-wast in very gracious fooling last night, when thou spokest of Pigrogromitus, of the Vapians passing the equinoctial of Queubus; 'twas very good, i'faith. I sent thee six-pence for thy leman; Hadst it?[5]

Breath has been here proposed : but many instances may be brought to justify the old reading beyond a doubt. In the statutes of Stoke-College, founded by Archbishop Parker, 1535, *Strype's Parker,* p. 9 : " Which said queristers, after their *breasts* are changed," &c. that is, after their voices are broken. In Fiddes' *Life of Wolsey,* Append. p. 128 : " Singing-men well-*breasted.*" In Tusser's *Husbandrie,* p. 155. edit. P. Short :

    " The better *brest*, the lesser rest,
    " To serve the queer now there now heere."

Tusser, in this piece, called *The Author's Life*, tells us, that he was a choir-boy in the collegiate chapel of Wallingford-castle; and that, on account of the excellence of his *voice*, he was successively removed to various choirs. T. WARTON.

B. Jonson uses the word *breast* in the same manner, in his *Masque of Gypsies*, p. 623, edit. 1692. In an old play called *The 4 P's*, written by J. Heywood, 1569, is this passage :

    " *Poticary.* I pray you, tell me, can you sing?
    " *Pedler.* Sir, I have some sight in singing.
    " *Poticary.* But is your *breast* any thing sweet?
    " *Pedler.* Whatever my *breast* be, my voice is meet."

I suppose this cant term to have been current among the musicians of the age. All professions have in some degree their jargon ; and the remoter they are from liberal science, and the less consequential to the general interests of life, the more they strive to hide themselves behind affected terms and barbarous phraseology.
                  STEEVENS.

    [5] ——— *I sent thee six-pence for thy* leman; *hadst it ?*] The old copy reads—*lemon*. But the Clown was neither pantler, nor butler. The poet's word was certainly mistaken by the ignorance of the printer. I have restored *leman*, i. e. I sent thee six-pence to spend on thy mistress. THEOBALD.

I receive Theobald's emendation, because it throws a light on the obscurity of the following speech.
    Leman is frequently used by the ancient writers, and Spenser in particular. So again, in *The Noble Soldier*, 1634 :
    " Fright him as he's embracing his new *leman.*"

CLo. I did impeticos thy gratillity;[6] for Malvolio's nose is no whipſtock: My lady has a white
hand, and the Myrmidons are no bottle-ale houſes.

The money was given him for his *leman,* i. e. his miſtreſs. We
have ſtill "*Leman*-ſtreet," in Goodman's-fields. He ſays he did
impeticoat the gratuity, i. e. he gave it to his *petticoat companion*;
for (ſays, he) *Malvolio's noſe is no whipſtock*; i. e. Malvolio may
ſmell out our connection, but his ſuſpicion will not prove the
inſtrument of our puniſhment. *My miſtreſs has a white hand, and
the Myrmidons are no bottle-ale houſes,* i. e. my miſtreſs is handſome,
but the houſes kept by officers of juſtice are no places to make
merry and entertain her at. Such may be the meaning of this
whimſical ſpeech. A *whipſtock* is, I believe, the handle of a whip,
round which a ſtrap of leather is uſually twiſted, and is ſometimes
put for the *whip* itſelf. So, in *Albumazar,* 1615 ;
    " —————— out, Carter,
    " Hence dirty *whipſtock*———"
Again, in *The Two Angry Women of Abingdon,* 1599 :
    " —— the coach-man ſit!
    " His duty is before you to ſtand,
    " Having a luſty *whipſtock* in his hand."
The word occurs again in *Jeronymo,* 1605 :
    " Bought you a whiſtle and a *whipſtock* too." STEEVENS.

[6] *I did* impeticos *thy* gratillity;] This, Sir T. Hanmer tells us,
is the ſame with *impocket thy gratuity.* He is undoubtedly right ;
but we muſt read—*I did* impeticoat *thy* gratuity. The fools were
kept in long coats, to which the alluſion is made. There is yet
much in this dialogue which I do not underſtand. JOHNSON.

Figure 12 in the plate of the *Morris-dancers,* at the end of
K. *Henry IV,* P. I. ſufficiently proves that *petticoats* were not
always a part of the dreſs of *fools* or *jeſters,* though they were of
ideots, for a reaſon which I avoid to offer. STEEVENS.

It is a very groſs miſtake to imagine that this character was
habited like an *ideot.* Neither he nor *Touchſtone,* though they wear
a particoloured dreſs, has either *coxcomb* or *bauble,* nor is by any
means to be confounded with the *Fool* in *King Lear,* nor even,
I think, with the one in *All's Well that Ends Well.*—A *Diſſertation
on the Fools of Shakſpeare,* a character he has moſt judiciouſly
varied and diſcriminated, would be a valuable addition to the
notes on his plays. RITSON.

The old copy reads—" I did *impeticos* thy *gratillity.*" The
meaning, I think, is, I did *impeticoat* or *impocket* thy *gratuity;* but

Sir And. Excellent! Why, this is the beſt fooling, when all is done.   Now, a ſong.

Sir To. Come on; there is ſix-pence for you:
let's have a ſong.

Sir And. There's a teſtril of me too: if one
knight give a————

Clo. Would you have a love-ſong, or a ſong of
good life?[7]

Sir To. A love-ſong, a love-ſong.

Sir And. Ay, ay; I care not for good life.

S O N G.

Clo.   *O miſtreſs mine, where are you roaming?*
     O, ſtay and hear; your true love's coming,
       That can ſing both high and low:
     Trip no further, pretty ſweeting;
     Journeys end in lovers' meeting,
       Every wiſe man's ſon doth know.

Sir And. Excellent good, i'faith!

Sir To. Good, good.

———

the reading of the old copy ſhould not, in my opinion, be here
diſturbed.   The clown uſes the ſame kind of fantaſtick language
elſewhere in this ſcene.   Neither *Pigrogromitus*, nor the *Vapians*
would object to it.   MALONE.

[7] ———— *of* good life?]   I do not ſuppoſe that by a ſong of *good*
life, the Clown means a ſong of a *moral turn*; though Sir Andrew
anſwers to it in that ſignification.   *Good life*, I believe, is *harmleſs*
mirth and jollity.   It may be a Galliciſm: we call a jolly fellow a
bon vivant.   STEEVENS.

From the oppoſition of the words in the Clown's queſtion, I
incline to think that *good life* is here uſed in its uſual acceptation.
In *The Merry Wives of Windſor*, theſe words are uſed for a virtuous
character:

   " Defend your reputation, or farewell to your *good life* for ever."
                      MALONE.

CLO. *What is love? 'tis not hereafter;*
Present mirth hath present laughter;
What's to come, is still unsure:
In delay there lies no plenty; [8]
Then come kiss me, sweet-and-twenty, [9]
Youth's a stuff will not endure.

SIR AND. A mellifluous voice, as I am true knight.

SIR TO. A contagious breath.

SIR AND. Very sweet and contagious, i'faith.

SIR TO. To hear by the nose, it is dulcet in contagion. But shall we make the welkin dance [1]

---

[8] *In delay there lies no plenty;*] No man will ever be worth much, who *delays* the advantages offered by the present hour, in hopes that the future will offer more. So, in *K. Richard III.* Act IV. sc. iii:
"*Delay* leads impotent and snail-pac'd beggary."
Again, in *K. Henry VI.* P. I:
"Defer no time, *delays* have dangerous ends."
Again, in a Scots proverb: "After a *delay* comes a let." See Kelly's Collection, p. 52. STEEVENS.

[9] *Then come kiss me, sweet and twenty,*] This line is obscure; we might read:
Come, a kiss then, sweet and twenty,
Yet I know not whether the present reading be not right, for in some counties *sweet and twenty,* whatever be the meaning, is a phrase of endearment. JOHNSON.

indeed? Shall we roufe the night-owl in a catch,[3] that will draw three fouls out of one weaver?[3] fhall we do that?

Sir And. An you love me, let's do't: I am dog at a catch.

Clo. By'r lady, fir, and fome dogs will catch well.

Sir And. Moft certain: let our catch be, *Thou knave.*

---

3 —— *draw three fouls out of one* weaver?] Our author reprefents weavers as much given to harmony in his time. I have fhewn the caufe of it elfewhere. This expreffion of the power of mufick is familiar with our author. *Much ado about Nothing:* " *Now is his foul ravifhed. Is it not ftrange that fheep's-guts fhould hale fouls out of men's bodies?*"——Why, he fays, *three fouls,* is becaufe he is fpeaking of a catch of *three parts*; and the peripatetic philofophy, then in vogue, very liberally gave every man three fouls. The *vegetative* or *plaftic*, the *animal*, and the *rational*. To this, too, Jonfon alludes, in his *Poetafter:* " *What, will I turn fhark upon my friends? or my friends' friends? I fcorn it with my three fouls.*" By the mention of thefe *three*, therefore, we may fuppofe it was Shakfpeare's purpofe, to hint to us thofe furprizing effects of mufick, which the ancients fpeak of, when they tell us of Amphion, who moved *ftones* and *trees*; Orpheus and Arion, who tamed *favage beafts*; and Timotheus, who governed, as he pleafed, the *paffions of his human auditors.* So noble an obfervation has our author conveyed in the ribaldry of this buffoon character. WARBURTON.

In a popular book of the time, Carew's tranflation of Huarte's *Trial of Wits*, 1594, there is a curious chapter concerning the *three fouls*, " *vegetative, fenfitive,* and *reafonable.*" FARMER.

I doubt whether our author intended any allufion to this divifion of fouls. In *The Tempeft*, we have—" *trebles thee o'er*; i. e. makes thee thrice as great as thou wert before. In the fame manner, I believe, he here only means to defcribe Sir Toby's catch as fo harmonious, that it would hale the foul out of a weaver (the warmeft lover of a fong) *thrice over*; or in other words, give him thrice more delight than it would give another man. Dr. Warburton's fuppofition that there is an allufion to the catch being in *three* parts, appears to me one of his unfounded refinements. MALONE.

Clo. Hold *thy peace, thou knave*, knight? I ſhall be conſtrain'd in't to call thee knave, knight. .

Sir And. 'Tis not the firſt time I have conſtrain'd one to call me knave. Begin, fool; it begins, *Hold thy peace.*

Clo. I ſhall never begin, if I hold my peace.

Sir And. Good, i'faith! Come, begin.

[*They ſing a Catch.*⁴

⁴ *They ſing a catch.*] This catch is loſt. JOHNSON.

A *catch* is a ſpecies of vocal harmony to be ſung by three or more perſons; and is ſo contrived, that though each ſings preciſely the ſame notes as his fellows, yet by beginning at ſtated periods of time from each other, there reſults from the performance a harmony of as many parts as there are ſingers. Compoſitions of this kind are, in ſtrictneſs, called *Canons in the uniſon*; and as properly, *Catches*, when the words in the different parts are made to *catch* or anſwer each other. One of the moſt remarkable examples of a true *catch* is that of Purcel, *Let's live good honeſt lives*, in which, immediately after one perſon has uttered theſe words, " What need we fear the Pope?" another in the courſe of his ſinging fills up a reſt which the firſt makes, with the words, " The devil."

The *catch* above-mentioned to be ſung by ſir Toby, ſir Andrew, and the Clown, from the hints given of it, appears to be ſo contrived as that each of the ſingers calls the other *knave* in turn; and for this the clown means to apologize to the knight, when he ſays, that he ſhall be conſtrained to call him *knave*. I have here ſubjoined the very catch, with the muſical notes to which it was ſung in the time of Shakſpeare, and at the original performance of this Comedy:

A 3 voc.

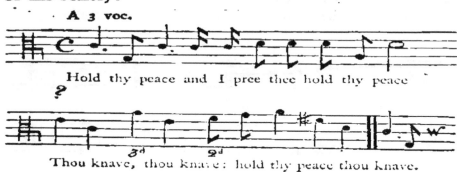

Hold thy peace and I pree thee hold thy peace

Thou knave, thou knave: hold thy peace thou knave.

Enter MARIA.

MAR. What a catterwauling do you keep here! If my lady have not call'd up her ſteward, Malvolio, and bid him turn you out of doors, never truſt me.

SIR To. My lady's a Cataian,⁹ we are politicians; Malvolio's a Peg-a-Ramſey,² and *Three merry men*

The evidence of its authenticity is as follows. There is extant a book entitled, " PAMMELIA, *Muſickes Miſcellanie, or mixed Varietie of pleaſant Roundelays and delightful catches of* 3. 4. 5. 6. 7. 8. 9. 10 *parts in one.*" Of this book there are at leaſt two editions, the ſecond printed in 1618. In 1609, a ſecond part of this book was publiſhed with the title of DEUTEROMELIA, and in this book is contained the catch above given.

SIR J. HAWKINS.

⁹ ———— *a* Cataian,] It is in vain to ſeek the preciſe meaning of this term of reproach. I have already attempted to explain it in a note on *The Merry Wives of Windſor.* I find it uſed again in *Love and Honour,* by Sir W. D'Avenant, 1649:

" Hang him, bold *Cataian.*" STEEVENS.

² ———— *Peg-a-Ramſey,*] In Durfey's *Pills to purge Melancholy* is a very obſcene old ſong, entitled *Peg-a-Ramſey.* See alſo Ward's *Lives of the Profeſſors of Greſham College,* p. 207. PERCY.

Naſh mentions *Peg of Ramſey* among ſeveral other ballads, viz. *Rogero, Baſilino, Turkelony, All the flowers of the Broom, Pepper is black, Green Sleeves,* Peggie Ramſie. It appears from the ſame author, that it was likewiſe a dance performed to the muſic of a ſong of that name. STEEVENS.

Peggy Ramſey, is the name of ſome old ſong; the following is the tune to it :

Peggy Ramſey.

SIR J. HAWKINS.

*be we.*³ Am not I confanguineous? am I not of her

³ *Three merry men,* &c.] *Three merry men be we,* is likewife a fragment of fome old fong, which I find repeated in *Weftward Hoe,* by Decker and Webfter, 1607, and by Beaumont and Fletcher in *The Knight of the Burning Peftle:*
" Three merry men
" And three merry men
" And *three merry men be we.*"
Again, in *The Bloody Brother,* of the fame authors:
" Three merry boys, and three merry boys,
" And three merry boys are we,
" As ever did fing, three parts in a ftring,
" All under the triple tree."
Again, in *Ram-alley,* or *Merry Tricks,* 1611:
" And three merry men, and three merry men,
" And *three merry men be we a.*" STEEVENS.

This is a conclufion common to many old fongs. One of the moft humorous that I can recollect, is the following:
" The wife men were but feaven, nor more fhall be for me;
" The mufes were but nine, the worthies three times three;
" And three merry boyes, and three merry boyes, and three merry boyes are wee.
" The vertues they were feven, and three the greater bee;
" The Cæfars they were twelve, and the fatal lifters three.
" And three merry girles, and three merry girles, and three merry girles are wee."

There are ale-houfes in fome of the villages in this kingdom, that have the fign of *The Three Merry Boys;* there was one at Highgate in my memory. SIR J. HAWKINS.

Three merry men be we, may, perhaps, have been taken originally from the fong of *Robin Hood and the Tanner. Old Ballads.* Vol. I. p. 89:
" Then *Robin Hood* took them by the hands,
" *With a hey,* &c.
" And danced about the oak-tree;
" For three merry men, and three merry men,
" *And three merry men be we.*" TYRWHITT.

But perhaps the following, in *The Old Wives Tale,* by George Peele, 1595, may be the original. *Anticke,* one of the characters, fays: " —— let us rehearfe the old proverb,
" Three merrie men, and three merrie men,
" And three merrie men be wee;
" I in the wood, and thou on the ground,
" And Jack fleepes in the tree." STEEVENS.

blood? Tilly-valley lady![4] *There dwelt a man in Babylon, lady, lady![5]* [*Singing.*

CLO. Beshrew me, the knight's in admirable fooling.

SIR AND. Ay, he does well enough, if he be dis-

See *An Antidote against Melancholy, made up in Pills, compounded of Witty Ballads, Jovial Songs, and merry Catches,* 4to. 1661, p. 69. REED.

[4] *Tilly-valley,* lady!] *Tilly-valley* was an interjection of contempt, which Sir Thomas More's lady is recorded to have had very often in her mouth. JOHNSON.

Tilly-valley is used as an interjection of contempt in the old play of *Sir John Oldcastle;* and is likewise a character in a comedy intituled *Lady Alimony. Tillie-vallie* may be a corruption of the Roman word (without a precise meaning, but indicative of contempt) *Titivilitium.* See the *Casina* of Plautus, z. 5. 39.
STEEVENS.

Tilly-valley is a hunting phrase borrowed from the French. In the *Venerie de Jacques Fouilloux,* 1585, 4to. fo. 12. the following cry is mentioned: " Ty a hillaut & vallecy;" and is set to music in pp. 49 and 50. DOUCE.

[5] *There dwelt a man in Babylon,* lady, lady!] The ballad of *Susanna,* from whence this line [*There dwelt,* &c.] is taken, was licensed by T. Colwell, in 1562, under the title of *The goodly and constant wyfe Susanna.* There is likewise a play on this subject.
T. WARTON.

There dwelt a man in Babylon, lady,] Maria's use of the word *lady* brings the ballad to sir Toby's remembrance: *Lady, lady,* is the *burthen,* and should be printed as such. My very ingenious friend, Dr. Percy, has given a stanza of it in his *Reliques of Ancient Poetry,* Vol. I. p. 204. Just the same may be said, where Mercutio applies it, in *Romeo and Juliet,* Act II. sc. iv. FARMER.

I found what I once supposed to be a part of this song, in *All's lost by Lust,* a tragedy by William Rowley, 1633:
" *There was a nobleman of Spain,* lady, lady,
" *That went abroad, and came not again*
" *To his poor lady.*
" *Oh, cruel age, when one brother,* lady, lady,
" *Shall scorn to look upon another*
" *Of his poor lady.*" STEEVENS.

pos'd, and so do I too; he does it with a better grace, but I do it more natural.

SIR TO. *O, the twelfth day of December,*—[*Singing.*

MAR. For the love o'God, peace.

Enter MALVOLIO.

MAL. My masters, are you mad? or what are you? Have you no wit, manners, nor honesty, but to gabble like tinkers at this time of night? Do ye make an alehouse of my lady's house, that ye squeak out your coziers' catches ⁵ without any mitigation

---

This song, or, at least, one with the same burthen, is alluded to in B. Jonson's *Magnetic Lady*, Vol. IV. p. 449:

"Com. As true it is, *lady, lady* i' the song."
TYRWHITT.

The oldest song that I have seen with this burthen is in the old Morality, entitled *The Trial of Treasure*, 4to. 1567. The following is one of the stanzas:

"Helene may not compared be,
"Nor Cressida that was so bright,
"These cannot stain the shine of thee,
"Nor yet Minerva of great might;
"Thou passest Venus far away,
"Lady, lady;
"Love thee I will, both night and day,
"My dere *lady.*" MALONE.

⁵ ——— coziers' catches ———] A *cozier* is a tailor, from *coudre* to sew, part. *cousu*, Fr. JOHNSON.

Our author has again alluded to their love of vocal harmony in *King Henry IV.* P. I:

"Lady. I will not *sing.*
"Hot. 'Tis the next way to turn *tailor*, or be redbreast teacher."

A *cozier*, it appears from Minshieu, signified a *botcher*, or mender of old clothes, and also a cobler.——Here it means the former.
MALONE.

Minshieu tells us, that *cozier* is a cobler or sowter: and, in Northamptonshire, the waxed thread which a cobler uses in mending shoes, we call a *codger's* end. WHALLEY.

A *coziers' end* is still used in Devonshire for a cobler's end.
HENLEY.

or remorfe of voice? Is there no refpect of place, perfons, nor time, in you?

Sir To. We did keep time, fir, in our catches. Sneck up![6]

Mal. Sir Toby, I muft be round with you. My lady bade me tell you, that, though fhe harbours you as her kinfman, fhe's nothing allied to your diforders. If you can feparate yourfelf and your mifdemeanors, you are welcome to the houfe; if not, an it would pleafe you to take leave of her, fhe is very willing to bid you farewel.

Sir To. *Farewel, dear heart,[7] fince I muft needs be gone.*

Mal. Nay, good fir Toby.

<hr>

[6] —— *Sneck up!*] The modern editors feem to have regarded this unintelligible phrafe as the defignation of a *hiccup*. It is however ufed in Beaumont and Fletcher's *Knight of the Burning Peftle*, as it fhould feem, on another occafion: " let thy father go *fneck up*, he fhall never come between a pair of fheets with me again while he lives."

Again, in the fame play: " —— Give him his money, George, and let him go *fneck up*." Again, in *Wily Beguiled:* " An if my miftrefs would be ruled by him, Sophos might go *fnick up*." Again, in *The Two Angry Women of Abingdon,* 1599: " —— if they be not, let them go *fnick up*." Again, in Heywood's *Fair Maid of the Weft,* 1631, *Blurt Mafter Conftable,* no date, &c.

Perhaps in the two former of thefe inftances, the words may be corrupted. In *King Henry IV.* P. I. Falftaff fays, " The prince is a Jack, a *Sneak-cup*." i. e. one who takes his glafs in a fneaking manner. I think we might fafely read *fneak-cup*, at leaft, in fir Toby's reply to Malvolio. I fhould not however omit to mention that *fneck the door* is a north country expreffion for *latch the door.*

Mr. Malone and others obferve, that from the manner in which this cant phrafe is employed in our ancient comedies, it feems to have been fynonymous to the modern expreffion——*Go hang yourfelf.* Steevens.

[7] *Farewel, dear heart,* &c.] This entire fong, with fome variations, is publifhed by Dr. Percy, in the firft volume of his *Reliques of Ancient Englifh Poetry.* Steevens.

Clo. His eyes do shew his days are almost done.

Mal. Is't even so?

Sir To. But I will never die.

Clo. Sir Toby, there you lie.

Mal. This is much credit to you.

Sir To. Shall I bid him go?　　　　　　[*Singing.*

Clo. What an if you do?

Sir To. Shall I bid him go, and spare not?

Clo. O no, no, no, no, you dare not.

Sir To. Out o'time? sir, ye lie.[8]——Art any more than a steward? Dost thou think, because thou art virtuous, there shall be no more cakes and ale?[9]

Clo. Yes, by Saint Anne; and ginger shall be hot i'the mouth too.

Sir To. Thou'rt i'the right.——Go, sir, rub your chain with crums:[1]——A stoop of wine, Maria!

[8] *Out o'time? sir, ye lie.*] The old copy has—" out o'tune." We should read, " out of *time*," as his speech evidently refers to what Malvolio said before:

　　" Have you no respect of place or *time* in you?
　　" *Sir Toby.* We did keep *time*, sir, in our catches.
　　　　　　　　　　　　　　　　　　　　　M. MASON.

The same correction, I find, had been silently made by Theobald, and was adopted by the three subsequent editors. Sir Toby is here repeating with indignation Malvolio's words.

In the Mss. of our author's age, *tune* and *time* are often quite undistinguishable; the second stroke of the *n* seeming to be the first stroke of the *m*, or *vice versâ*. Hence, in *Macbeth*, Act IV. sc. alt. edit. 1623, we have " This *time*, goes manly," instead of " This *tune* goes manly." MALONE.

[9] *Dost thou think, because thou art virtuous, there shall be no more cakes and ale?*] It was the custom on holidays and saints' days to make cakes in honour of the day. The *Puritans* called this, superstition; and in the next page Maria says, that *Malvolio is sometimes a kind of Puritan.* See, Quarlous's *Account of Rabbi Busy,* Act I. sc. iii. in Ben Jonson's *Bartholomew Fair.*

　　　　　　　　　　　　　　　　　　　　　LETHERLAND.

[1] *—— rub your chain with crums:*] That stewards anciently wore a chain, as a mark of superiority over other servants, may be

7

Mal. Miſtreſs Mary, if you priz'd my lady's favour at any thing more than contempt, you would not give means for this uncivil rule;[3] ſhe ſhall know of it, by this hand.   [*Exit.*

proved from the following paſſage in *The Martial Maid* of Beaumont and Fletcher:

" Doſt thou think I ſhall become the *ſteward's* chair? Will not theſe ſlender haunches ſhew well in a *chain?*"——

Again,

"   *Pia.* Is your *chain* right?
"   *Bob.* It is both right and juſt, ſir;
"   For though I am a *ſteward,* I did get it
"   With no man's wrong."

The beſt method of cleaning any gilt plate, is by *rubbing it with crums.* Naſh, in his piece entitled, *Have with you to Saffron Walden,* 1595, taxes Gabriel Harvey with " *having ſtolen a noble-man's ſteward's chain, at his lord's inſtalling at Windſor.*"

To conclude with the moſt appoſite inſtance of all. See, Web-ſter's *Dutcheſs of Malfy,* 1623:

" Yea, and the chippings of the buttery fly after him, to *ſcouer his gold chain.*" STEEVENS.

[3] —— *rule* ;] *Rule* is method of life; ſo *miſrule* is tumult and riot. JOHNSON.

Rule, on this occaſion, is ſomething leſs than common *method of life.* It occaſionally means the arrangement or conduct of a feſtival or merry-making, as well as behaviour in general. So, in the 27th ſong of Drayton's *Polyolbion:*

"   Caſt in a gallant round about the hearth they go,
"   And at each pauſe they kiſs; was never ſeen ſuch *rule*
"   In any place but here, at bon-fire, or at yeule."

Again, in Heywood's *Engliſh Traveller,* 1633:

"   What gueſts we harbour, and what *rule* we keep."

Again, in Ben Jonſon's *Tale of a Tub:*

"   And ſet him in the ſtocks for his ill *rule.*"

In this laſt inſtance it ſignifies *behaviour.*

There was formerly an officer belonging to the court, called *Lord of Miſrule.* So, in Decker's *Satiromaſtix:* " I have ſome couſins-german at court ſhall beget you the reverſion of the maſter of the king's revels, or elſe be lord of his *Miſrule* now at Chriſt-mas." Again, in *The Return from Parnaſſus,* 1606: " We are fully bent to be lords of *Miſrule* in the world's wild heath." In the country, at all periods of feſtivity, and in the inns of court at their *Revels,* an officer of the ſame kind was elected. STEEVENS.

Mar. Go fhake your ears.

Sir And. 'Twere as good a deed, as to drink when a man's a hungry, to challenge him to the field; and then to break promife with him, and make a fool of him.

Sir To. Do't, knight; I'll write thee a challenge; or I'll deliver thy indignation to him by word of mouth.

Mar. Sweet fir Toby, be patient for to-night; fince the youth of the count's was to-day with my lady, fhe is much out of quiet. For monfieur Malvolio, let me alone with him: if I do not gull him into a nayword,⁴ and make him a common recreation, do not think I have wit enough to lie ftraight in my bed: I know, I can do it.

Sir To. Poffefs us,⁵ poffefs us; tell us fomething of him.

Mar. Marry, fir, fometimes he is a kind of Puritan.

Sir And. O, if I thought that, I'd beat him like a dog.

Sir To. What, for being a Puritan? thy exquifite reafon, dear knight?

Sir And. I have no exquifite reafon for't, but I have reafon good enough.

Mar. The devil a Puritan that he is, or any thing conftantly but a time-pleafer; an affection'd

---

⁴ —— *a* nayword,] A *nayword* is what has been fince called a *byword*, a kind of proverbial reproach. STEEVENS.

⁵ *Poffefs us,*] That is, *inform us, tell us,* make us mafters of the matter. JOHNSON.

So, in *The Merchant of Venice,* Shylock fays:

" I have *poffefs'd* your grace of what I purpofe."

DOUCE.

afs,[6] that cons ftate without book, and utters it by great fwarths:[7] the beft perfuaded of himfelf, fo cramm'd, as he thinks, with excellencies, that it is his ground of faith, that all, that look on him, love him; and on that vice in him will my revenge find notable caufe to work.

Sir To. What wilt thou do?

Mar. I will drop in his way fome obfcure epiftles of love; wherein, by the colour of his beard, the fhape of his leg, the manner of his gait, the expreffure of his eye, forehead, and complexion, he fhall find himfelf moft feelingly perfonated: I can write very like my lady, your niece; on a forgotten matter we can hardly make diftinction of our hands.

Sir To. Excellent! I fmell a device.

Sir And. I have't in my nofe too.

Sir To. He fhall think, by the letters that thou wilt drop, that they come from my niece, and that fhe is in love with him.

Mar. My purpofe is, indeed, a horfe of that colour.

Sir And. And your horfe now would make him an afs.[8]

Mar. Afs, I doubt not.

Sir And. O, 'twill be admirable.

---

[6] —— an affection'd *afs,*] *Affection'd* means *affected.* In this fenfe, I believe, it is ufed in *Hamlet*——"no matter in it that could indite the author of *affection,*" i. e. affectation. STEEVENS.

[7] —— great fwarths:] A *fwarth* is as much grafs as a mower cuts down at one ftroke of his fcythe.] STEEVENS.

[8] Sir And. *And your horfe now,* &c.] This conceit, though bad enough, fhews too quick an apprehenfion for *Sir Andrew.* It fhould be given, I believe, to *Sir Toby;* as well as the next fhort fpeech: *O, 'twill be admirable. Sir Andrew* does not ufually give his own judgement on any thing, till he has heard that of fome other perfon. TYRWHITT.

Pope, in his version of the 18th Iliad:
stretch'd in ranks the levell'd *swarths* are fo

Mar. Sport royal, I warrant you: I know, my physick will work with him. I will plant you two, and let the fool make a third, where he shall find the letter; observe his construction of it. For this night, to bed, and dream on the event. Farewel. [*Exit.*

Sir To. Good night, Penthesilea.[9]

Sir And. Before me, she's a good wench.

Sir To. She's a beagle, true-bred, and one that adores me; What o'that?

Sir And. I was adored once too.

Sir To. Let's to bed, knight.—Thou hadst need send for more money.

Sir And. If I cannot recover your niece, I am a foul way out.

Sir To. Send for money, knight;[2] if thou hast her not i'the end, call me Cut.[3]

Sir And. If I do not, never trust me, take it how you will.

---

[9] —— *Penthesilea.*] i. e. Amazon. STEEVENS.

[2] *Send for money, knight;*] Sir Toby, in this instance, exhibits a trait of Iago:—" Put money in thy purse." STEEVENS.

—— *call me* Cut.] So, in *A Woman's a Weathercock,* 1612: " If I help you not to that as cheap as any man in England, call me Cut."
Again, in *The Two Angry Women of Abingdon,* 1599: " I'll meet you there; if I do not, *call me Cut.*"
This term of contempt, perhaps, signifies only——call me——*gelding.* STEEVENS.

—— *call me* Cut.] i. e. call me horse. So, Falstaff in *King Henry IV.* P. I: " —spit in my face, call me *horse.*" That this was the meaning of this expression is ascertained by a passage in *The Two Noble Kinsmen:* " He'll buy me a white *Cut* forth for to ride."
Again, in *Sir John Oldcastle,* 1600: " But master, 'pray ye, let me ride upon *Cut.*" *Curtal,* which occurs in another of our author's plays, (i. e. a horse, whose tail has been docked,) and *Cut,* were probably synonymous. MALONE.

F 2

Sir To. Come, come; I'll go burn fome fack, 'tis too late to go to bed now: come, knight; come, knight. [*Exeunt.*

SCENE IV.

A room in the Duke's *palace.*

Enter Duke, Viola, Curio, *and Others.*

Duke. Give me fome mufick:——Now, good mor-
row, friends:————
Now, good Cefario, but that piece of fong,
That old and antique fong we heard laft night;
Methought, it did relieve my paffion much;
More than light airs, and recollected * terms,
Of thefe moft brifk and giddy-paced times:————
Come, but one verfe.

Cur. He is not here, fo pleafe your lordfhip, that fhould fing it.

Duke. Who was it?

Cur. Fefte, the jefter, my lord; a fool, that the lady Olivia's father took much delight in: he is about the houfe.

Duke. Seek him out, and play the tune the while.
[*Exit* Curio.——*Mufick.*
Come hither, boy; If ever thou fhalt love,
In the fweet pangs of it, remember me:
For, fuch as I am, all true lovers are;
Unftaid and fkittifh in all motions elfe,
Save, in the conftant image of the creature
That is belov'd.——How doft thou like this tune?

* ——— *recollected* —] Studied. Warburton.

I rather think, that *recollected* fignifies, more nearly to its primitive fenfe, *recalled, repeated,* and alludes to the practice of compofers, who often prolong the fong by repetitions. Johnson.

Thus in Strada's imitation of Claudian
——— *et se*
Multiplicat relegens, ——— Steevens.

Vio. It gives a very echo to the feat
Where Love is thron'd.[5]

Duke. Thou doſt ſpeak maſterly:
My life upon't, young though thou art, thine eye
Hath ſtay'd upon ſome favour that it loves:
Hath it not, boy?

Vio. A little, by your favour.[6]

Duke. What kind of woman is't?

Vio. Of your complexion.

Duke. She is not worth thee then. What years,
            i'faith?

Vio. About your years, my lord.

Duke. Too old, by heaven; Let ſtill the woman
            take
An elder than herſelf; ſo wears ſhe to him,
So ſways ſhe the level in her huſband's heart.
For, boy, however we do praiſe ourſelves,
Our fancies are more giddy and unfirm,
More longing, wavering, ſooner loſt and worn,[7]
Than women's are.

---

5. —— to the feat
Where Love is thron'd.] i. e. to the heart. So, *in Romeo and
Juliet :*
    " My boſom's lord [i. e. *Love*] ſits lightly on his *throne.*"
Again, in *Othello :*
    " Yield up O *Love*, thy crown, and *hearted throne*——."
So before, in the firſt act of this play :
    " —— when liver, brain, and *heart,*
    " Theſe ſovereign *thrones*, are all ſupply'd and fill'd
    " (Her ſweet perfections) with one ſelf-king."
  The meaning is, (as Mr. Heath has obſerved,) " It is ſo con-
ſonant to the emotions of the heart, that they echo it back again."
                                            MALONE.
6 —— *favour,*] The word *favour* ambiguouſly uſed.
                                            JOHNSON.
Favour, in the preceding ſpeech, ſignifies countenance. STEEVENS.
7 —— *loſt and* worn,] Though *loſt and worn* may mean *loſt and
worn out,* yet *loſt and won* being, I think, better, theſe two words
F 3

Vio.   I think it well, my lord.

Duke. Then let thy love be younger than thyself,
Or thy affection cannot hold the bent:
For women are as roses; whose fair flower,
Being once display'd, doth fall that very hour.

Vio. And so they are: alas, that they are so;
To die, even when they to perfection grow!

Re-enter Curio, *and* Clown.

Duke. O fellow, come, the song we had last
                    night:——
Mark it, Cesario; it is old, and plain:
The spinsters and the knitters in the sun,
And the free* maids, that weave their thread with
                    bones,

coming usually and naturally together, and the alteration being
very flight, I would so read in this place with Sir T. Hanmer.
                                                JOHNSON.

   The text is undoubtedly right, and *worn* signifies, *consumed,
worn out.* So Lord Surrey, in one of his Sonnets, describing the
spring, says,
   " Winter is *worn*, that was the flowers' bale."
Again, in *King Henry VI*. P. II:
   " These few days' wonder will be quickly *worn*."
Again, in *The Winter's Tale:*
   " ———— and but infirmity,
   " Which waits upon *worn* times——."   MALONE.

   * ———— *free*—] Is, perhaps, *vacant, unengaged, easy in mind.*
                                                JOHNSON.

   I rather think, that *free* means here—not having yet surrendered
their liberty to man;—unmarried.   MALONE.

   Is not *free*, unreserved, uncontrolled by the restraints of female
delicacy, forward, and such as sing *plain* songs?   HENLEY.

   The precise meaning of this epithet cannot very easily be pointed
out.   As Mr. Warton observes, on another occasion,—" *fair* and
free" are words often paired together in metrical romances.
Chaucer, Drayton, Ben Jonson, and many other poets employ the
epithet *free*, with little certainty of meaning.   *Free*, in the instance
before us, may commodiously signify, *artless, free from art, un-*

Do use to chaunt it; it is silly sooth,[9]
And dallies with the innocence of love,[2]
Like the old age.[3]

    CLO. Are you ready, sir?

    DUKE. Ay; pr'ythee, sing.   [Musick.

SONG.

CLO.   *Come away, come away, death,*
     And in sad cypress let me be laid;[4]
       Fly away, fly away,[5] *breath;*
     I am slain by a fair cruel maid.
     My shroud of white, stuck all with yew,
        O, prepare it;
     My part of death no one so true
        Did share it.[6]

influenced by artificial manners, undirected by false refinement in their choice of ditties. STEEVENS.

  [9] ——*silly sooth,*] It is plain, simple truth. JOHNSON.

  [2] *And* dallies *with the innocence of love,*] To *dally* is to play, to trifle. So, Act III: " They that *dally* nicely with words."
Again, in *Swetnam Arraign'd,* 1620:
    " ——————— he void of fear
    " *Dallied* with danger ———."
Again, in Sir W. D'Avenant's *Albovine,* 1629:
    " Why dost thou *dally* thus with feeble motion?" STEEVENS.

  [3] ——*she* old age.] The *old age* is the *ages past,* the times of simplicity. JOHNSON.

  [4] *And in* sad cypress *let me be laid;*] i. e. in a shroud of *cypress* or *cyprus.* Thus Autolycus, in *The Winter's Tale :*
    " Lawn as white as driven snow,
    " *Cyprus black* as e'er was crow."
These was both black and white *cyprus,* as there is still black and white *crape;* and ancient shrouds were always made of the latter.
                       STEEVENS.

  [5] Fly *away,* fly *away,*] The old copy reads—*Fie away.* The emendation is Mr. Rowe's. MALONE.

  [6] *My part of death no one so true*
  Did share it.] Though *death* is a *part* in which every one acts his *share,* yet of all these actors no one is *so true* as I. JOHNSON.

Not a flower, not a flower sweet,
On my black coffin let there be strown;
Not a friend, not a friend greet
My poor corpse, where my bones shall be thrown:
A thousand thousand sighs to save,
Lay me, O, where
Sad true lover[7] ne'er find my grave,
To weep there.

DUKE. There's for thy pains.

CLO. No pains, sir; I take pleasure in singing, sir.

DUKE. I'll pay thy pleasure then.

CLO. Truly, sir, and pleasure will be paid, one time or another.

DUKE. Give me now leave to leave thee.

CLO. Now, the melancholy god protect thee; and the tailor make thy doublet of changeable taffata, for thy mind is a very opal![8]—I would have

---

[7] *Sad true* lover —] Mr. Pope rejected the word *sad,* and other modern editors have unnecessarily changed true *lover* to—true *love.* By making *never* one syllable the metre is preserved. Since this note was written, I have observed that *lover* is elsewhere used by our poet as a word of one syllable. So, in *A Midsummer-Night's Dream:*
    " Tie up my *lover's* tongue; bring him in silently."
Again, in *King Henry VIII:*
    " Is held no great good *lover* of th' archbishop's."
There is perhaps therefore no need of abbreviating the word *never* in this line.   MALONE.

In the instance produced from *A Midsummer-Night's Dream,* I suppose *lover* to be a misprint for *love*; and in *King Henry VIII.* I know not why it should be considered as a monosyllable.
                                            STEEVENS.

[8] —— *a very* opal!]   A precious stone of almost all colours.
                                            POPE.

So, Milton, describing the walls of heaven:
    " With *opal* tow'rs, and battlements adorn'd."

men of such constancy put to sea, that their business might be every thing, and their intent every
where;[9] for that's it, that always makes a good
voyage of nothing.—Farewel.   [*Exit* Clown.

DUKE. Let all the rest give place.————
       [*Exeunt* CURIO *and Attendants.*
            Once more, Cesario,
Get thee to yon' same sovereign cruelty:
Tell her, my love, more noble than the world,
Prizes not quantity of dirty lands;
The parts that fortune hath bestow'd upon her,
Tell her, I hold as giddily as fortune;
But 'tis that miracle, and queen of gems,
That nature pranks her in,[2] attracts my soul.

The *opal* is a gem which varies its appearance as it is viewed in
different lights. So, in *The Muses' Elizium*, by Drayton:
    " With *opals* more than any one
    " We'll deck'thine altar fuller,
    " For that of every precious stone
    " It doth retain some colour."
" In the *opal* (says P. Holland's translation of Pliny's *Natural
History*, b. xxxviii. c. 6.) you shall see the burning fire of the car-
buncle or rubie, the glorious purple of the amethyst, the green sea
of the emeraud, and all glittering together mixed after an incredible manner." STEEVENS.

   [9] —— *that their business might be every thing, and their intent
every where;*] Both the preservation of the antithesis, and the
recovery of the sense, require we should read,—*and their intent* no
where. Because a man who suffers himself to run with every wind,
and so makes his business every where, cannot be said to have any
intent; for that word signifies a determination of the mind to something. Besides, the conclusion of *making a good voyage* of nothing,
directs to this emendation. WARBURTON.

   An intent *every* where, is much the same as an intent *no where,*
as it hath no one particular place more in view than another. HEATH.

   The present reading is preferable to Warburton's amendment.
We cannot accuse a man of inconstancy who has no intents at all,
though we may the man whose intents are every where; that is,
are continually varying. M. MASON.

   [2] *But 'tis that miracle, and queen of gems,
   That nature pranks her in,*] What is *that miracle, and queen*

VIO. But, if fhe cannot love you, fir?

DUKE. I cannot be fo anfwer'd.[3]

VIO. 'Sooth, but you muft.
Say, that fome lady, as, perhaps, there is,
Hath for your love as great a pang of heart
As you have for Olivia: you cannot love her;
You tell her fo; Muft fhe not then be anfwer'd?

DUKE. There is no woman's fides,
Can bide the beating of fo ftrong a paffion
As love doth give my heart: no woman's heart
So big, to hold fo much; they lack retention.
Alas, their love may be call'd appetite,——
No motion of the liver, but the palate,——
That fuffer furfeit, cloyment, and revolt;[4]

---

of gems? we are not told in this reading. Befides, what is meant by *nature pranking her in a miracle?*——We fhould read:

> But 'tis that miracle, and queen of gems,
> That nature pranks, her mind, ————

i. e. what *attracts my foul*, is not her *fortune*, but *her mind, that miracle and queen of gems that nature pranks*, i. e. fets out, adorns.
WARBURTON.

The *miracle and queen of gems* is her *beauty*, which the commentator might have found without fo emphatical an enquiry. As to her mind, he that fhould be captious would fay, that though it may be formed by nature, it muft be *pranked* by education.

Shakfpeare does not fay that *nature pranks her in a miracle*, but *in the miracle of gems*, that is, *in a gem miraculoufly beautiful.*
JOHNSON.

To *prank* is to deck out, to adorn. See Lye's *Etymologicon.* HEATH.

So, in *The Winter's Tale*:

> "———————— and me,
> "Moft goddefs-like, *prank'd up* ——" STEEVENS.

[3] *I cannot be fo anfwer'd.*] The folio reads——*It* cannot be, &c. The correction by Sir Thomas Hanmer. STEEVENS.

[4] *Alas, their love may be call'd appetite*, &c.
That fuffer furfeit, cloyment, and revolt;] The Duke has changed his opinion of women very fuddenly. It was but a few minutes before, that he faid they had more conftancy in love than men. M. MASON.

But mine is all as hungry as the sea, *
And can digeſt as much: make no compare
Between that love a woman can bear me,
And that I owe Olivia.

Vio.   Ay, but I know,——

Duke. What doſt thou know?

Vio. Too well what love women to men may
          owe:
In faith, they are as true of heart as we.
My father had a daughter lov'd a man,
As it might be, perhaps, were I a woman,
I ſhould your lordſhip.

Duke.   And what's her hiſtory?

Vio. A blank, my lord: She never told her love,
But let concealment, like a worm i'the bud,⁵
Feed on her damaſk cheek: ſhe pin'd in thought;⁶

Mr. Maſon would read—*ſuffers*; but there is no need of change. *Suffer* is governed by *women,* implied under the words, " *their* love." The love of women, &c. *who* ſuffer——.   MALONE.

⁵ —— *like a* worm *i'the* bud,] So, in the 5th Sonnet of Shakſpeare:
          " Which, like a *canker* in the fragrant roſe,
          " Doth ſpot the beauty of thy *budding* name."
                                          STEEVENS.
Again, in our author's *Rape of Lucrece:*
          " Why ſhould the *worm* intrude the maiden *bud?*"
Again, in *King Richard II:*
          " But now will *canker* ſorrow *eat* my *bud,*
          " And chaſe the native beauty from his *cheek*." MALONE.

⁶ —— *ſhe pin'd in* thought;] *Thought* formerly ſignified *melancholy.* So, in *Hamlet:*
          " Is ſicklied o'er. with the pale caſt of *thought.*"
Again, in *The Tragical Hiſtory of Romeus and Juliet,* 1562:
          " The cauſe of this her death was inward care and *thought.*"
                                          MALONE.
Mr. Malone ſays, *thought* means *melancholy.* But why wreſt from this word its plain and uſual acceptation, and make Shakſpeare guilty of tautology? for in the very next line he uſes " *Melancholy.*"   DOUCE.

And, with a green and yellow melancholy,
She sat like patience on a monument,
Smiling at grief.[8]   Was not this love, indeed?

<hr/>

[8] *She sat like patience on a monument,*
    Smiling at grief.] Mr. Theobald suppoſes this might poſſibly
be borrowed from Chaucer:
> " *And har beſidis wonder diſcreetlie*
> " *Dame* pacience *yſitting there I fonde*
> " *With face pale, upon a hill of fonde.*"

And adds: " *If he was indebted, however, for the firſt rude draught,*
how amply has he repaid that debt, in heightening the picture! How
much does the green and yellow melancholy *tranſcend the old bard's*
pale face; *the* monument *his* hill of ſand."—I hope this critic
does not imagine Shakſpeare meant to give us a picture of the *face*
of *patience,* by his *green and yellow melancholy*; becauſe, he ſays,
it tranſcends the *pale face of patience* given us by Chaucer.   To
throw *patience* into a fit of melancholy, would be indeed very
extraordinary.   The *green and yellow* then belonged not to *patience,*
but to *her* who *ſat* like *patience.*   To give *patience* a pale face was
proper: and had Shakſpeare deſcribed *her,* he had done it as
Chaucer did.   But Shakſpeare is ſpeaking of a marble ſtatue of
patience; Chaucer of *patience* herſelf.   And the two repreſentations
of her, are in quite different views.   Our poet, ſpeaking of a
deſpairing lover, judiciouſly compares her to *patience* exerciſed on
the death of friends and relations; which affords him the beautiful
picture of *patience on a monument.*   The old bard, ſpeaking of
patience herſelf, directly, and not by compariſon, as judiciouſly
draws her in that circumſtance where ſhe is moſt exerciſed, and has
occaſion for all her virtue; that is to ſay, under the *loſſes of ſhip-*
wreck.   And now we ſee why ſhe is repreſented as *ſitting on a hill*
of ſand, to deſign the ſcene to be the ſea-ſhore.   It is finely
imagined; and one of the noble ſimplicities of that admirable poet.
But the critic thought, in good earneſt, that Chaucer's invention
was ſo barren, and his imagination ſo beggarly, that he was not
able to be at the charge of a monument for his goddeſs, but left
her, like a ſtroller, ſunning herſelf upon a heap of ſand.
                                                    WARBURTON.

This celebrated image was not improbably firſt ſketched out in
the old play of *Pericles.*   I think, Shakſpeare's hand may be ſometimes ſeen in the latter part of it, and there only.
> " —— thou [*Marina*] doſt look
> " Like Patience, gazing on kings' graves, and ſmiling
> " Extremity out of act." FARMER.

I

We men may fay more, fwear more : but, indeed,
Our fhows are more than will; for ftill we prove
Much in our vows, but little in our love.

So, in our author's *Rape of Lucrece :*
    " So mild, that *Patience feem'd to fcorn his woes.*"

In the paffage in the text, our author perhaps meant to perfonify
GRIEF as well as PATIENCE; for we can fcarcely underftand " *at*
grief" to mean " *in* grief," as no ftatuary could, I imagine, form
a countenance in which fmiles and grief fhould be at once expreffed.
Shakfpeare might have borrowed his imagery from fome ancient
monument on which thefe two figures were reprefented.

The following lines in *The Winter's Tale,* feem to countenance
fuch an idea:
    " I doubt not then, but innocence fhall make
    " Falfe accufation blufh, and TYRANNY
    " Tremble *at* PATIENCE."

Again, in *King Richard III :*
    " ———— like *dumb ftatues,* or unbreathing ftones,
    " Star'd *on each other,* and look'd deadly pale."

In *King Lear,* we again meet with two perfonages introduced in
the text:
    " *Patience* and *Sorrow* ftrove,
    " Who fhould exprefs her goodlieft."

Again, in *Cymbeline,* the fame kind of imagery may be traced:
    " ———— nobly he yokes
    " A *fmiling* with a *figh.*
    " ———————— I do note
    " That *Grief* and *Patience,* rooted in him both,
    " Mingle their fpurs together."

I am aware that Homer's δακρυόεν γελάσασα, and a paffage in
Macbeth,——
    " ———— My plenteous joys
    " Wanton in fullnefs, feek to hide themfelves
    " In drops of forrow——"

may be urged againft this interpretation; but it fhould be remembered, that in thefe inftances it is *joy* which burfts into tears.
There is no inftance, I believe, either in poetry or real life, of
forrow fmiling in anguifh. In *pain* indeed the cafe is different:
the fuffering Indian having been known to fmile in the midft of
torture.——But, however this may be, the fculptor and the painter
are confined to one point of time, and cannot exhibit fucceffive
movements in the countenance.

Dr. Percy however, thinks, that " *grief* may here mean *grievance,*
in which fenfe it is ufed in Dr. Powel's *Hiftory of Wales,* quarto,

Duke. But did thy fifter of her love, my boy?

p. 356. "Of the wrongs and *griefs* done to the noblemen at Stratolyn," &c. In the original, (printed at the end of Wynne's *Hiftory of Wales,* octavo,) it is *gravamina,* i. e. grievances.——The word is often ufed by our author in the fame fenfe, (So, in *King Henry IV.* P. I:

" ——— the king hath fent to know
" The nature of your *griefs* ;)"

but never, I believe, in the fingular number.

In fupport of what has been fuggefted, the authority of Mr. Rowe may be adduced, for in his life of Shakfpeare he has thus exhibited this paffage:

" *She fat like* Patience *on a monument,*
" *Smiling at* Grief."

In the obfervations now fubmitted to the reader, I had once fome confidence, nor am I yet convinced that the objection founded on the particle *at,* and on the difficulty, if not impoffibility, of a fculptor forming fuch a figure as thefe words are commonly fuppofed to defcribe, is without foundation. I have therefore retained my note; yet I muft acknowledge, that the following lines in *K. Richard II.* which have lately occurred to me, render my theory fomewhat doubtful, though they do not overturn it:

" His face ftill combating with *tears* and *fmiles,*
" The badges of his *grief* and *patience.*"

Here we have the fame idea as that in the text; and perhaps Shakfpeare never confidered whether it could be exhibited in marble.

I have expreffed a doubt whether the word *grief* was employed in the fingular number, in the fenfe of *grievance.* I have lately obferved that our author has himfelf ufed it in that fenfe in *King Henry IV.* P. II:

" ———an inch of any ground
" To build a *grief* on."

Dr. Percy's interpretation, therefore, may be the true one.

MALONE.

I am unwilling to fuppofe a monumental image of *Patience* was ever confronted by an emblematical figure of *Grief,* on purpofe that one might fit and fmile at the other; becaufe fuch a reprefentation might be confidered as a fatire on human infenfibility. When *Patience* fmiles, it is to exprefs a chriftian triumph over the common caufe of forrow, a caufe, of which the farcophagus, near her ftation, ought very fufficiently to remind her. True *Patience,* when it is *her cue* to fmile over calamity, knows her office *without a prompter;* knows that ftubborn lamentation difplays *a will moft incorrect to heaven;* and therefore appears content with one of its fevereft difpenfations, the lofs of a relation or a friend. Ancient tombs, in-

Vio. I am all the daughters of my father's house,
And all the brothers too;[8]—and yet I know not:—
Sir, shall I to this lady?

Duke. Ay, that's the theme.
To her in haste; give her this jewel; say,
My love can give no place, bide no denay.[9]

[*Exeunt.*

deed (if we muft conftrue *grief* into *grievance,* and Shakfpeare has certainly ufed the former word for the latter,) frequently exhibit cumbent figures of the deceafed, and over thefe an image of *Patience,* without impropriety, might exprefs a fmile of complacence:

" Her meek hands folded on her modeft breaft,
" With calm fubmiffion lift the adoring eye
" Even to the ftorm that wrecks her."

After all, however, I believe the Homeric elucidation of the paffage to be the true one. Tyrant poetry often impofes fuch complicated tafks as painting and fculpture muft fail to execute.—I cannot help adding, that, to fmile *at* grief, is as juftifiable an expreffion as to rejoice *at* profperity, or repine *at* ill fortune. It is not neceffary we fhould fuppofe the good or bad event, in either inftance, is an objeft vifible, except to the eye of imagination. STEEVENS.

She fat like patience on a monument,
Smiling at grief.] So, in Middleton's *Witch,* Act IV. fc. iii:
" She does not love me now, but painefully
" Like one that's forc'd *to fmile upon a grief.*" DOUCE.

[8] *I am all the daughters of my father's houfe,*
And all the brothers too;] This was the moft artful anfwer that could be given. The queftion was of fuch a nature, that to have declined the appearance of a direct anfwer, muft have raifed fufpicion. This has the appearance of a direct anfwer, *that the fifter died of her love;* fhe (who paffed for a man) faying, fhe was all the daughters of her father's houfe. WARBURTON.

Such another equivoque occurs in Lylly's *Galathea,* 1592:
" —— my father had but one daughter, and therefore I could have no fifter." STEEVENS.

[9] ——*bide no* denay.] *Denay,* is *denial.* To *denay* is an antiquated verb fometimes ufed by Holinfhed: fo, p. 620:
" —— the ftate of a cardinal which was naied and *denaied* him."
Again, in Warner's *Albion's England,* 1602, B. II. ch. 10:
" —— thus did fay
" The thing, friend Battus, you demand, not gladly I *denay.*" STEEVENS.

SCENE V.

Olivia's *Garden.*

Enter SIR TOBY BELCH, SIR ANDREW AGUE-CHEEK, *and* FABIAN.

SIR TO. Come thy ways, signior Fabian.

FAB. Nay, I'll come; if I lose a scruple of this sport, let me be boil'd to death with melancholy.

SIR TO. Would'st thou not be glad to have the niggardly rascally sheep-biter come by some notable shame?

FAB. I would exult, man: you know, he brought me out of favour with my lady, about a bear-baiting here.

SIR TO. To anger him, we'll have the bear again; and we will fool him black and blue:—Shall we not, sir Andrew?

SIR AND. An we do not, it is pity of our lives.

Enter MARIA.

SIR TO. Here comes the little villain:—How now, my nettle of India?[a]

---

[a] ——*my nettle of India?*] The poet must here mean a zoophite, called the *Urtica Marina,* abounding in the Indian seas.

"Quæ tacta totius corporis pruritum quendam excitat, unde nomen *urticæ* est sortita." *Wolfgang Franzii Hist. Animal.* 1665 p. 621

"*Urticæ marinæ* omnes pruritum quendam movent, et acrimoniæ suâ *venerem* extinctam et sopitam excitant."

     Jahnstoni Hist. Nat. de Exang. Aquat. p. 56.

Perhaps the same plant is alluded to by Greene in his *Card of Fancy,* 1608: "the *flower of India* pleasant to be seen, but whoso smelleth to it, *feeleth present smart.*" Again, in his *Mamillia,* 1593: "Consider, the *herb of India* is of pleasant smell, but whoso cometh to it, *feeleth present smart.*" Again, in P. Holland's

Mar. Get ye all three into the box-tree: Malvolio's coming down this walk; he has been yonder
i'the fun, practifing behaviour to his own fhadow,
this half hour: obferve him, for the love of mockery; for, I know, this letter will make a contem-
plative ideot of him. Clofe, in the name of jefting!
[*The men hide themfelves.*] Lie thou there; [*throws
down a letter.*] for here comes the trout that muft
be caught with tickling.[3]   [*Exit* MARIA.

---

tranflation of the 9th book of Pliny's *Natural Hiftory:* " As for
thofe *nettles*, there be of them that in the night raunge to and fro,
and likewife change their colour. Leaves they carry of a flefhy
fubftance, and of flefh they feed. Their qualities is to raife an
itching fmart." Maria had certainly excited a congenial fenfation
in Sir Toby. The folio, 1623, reads—mettle *of India*, which may
mean, my *girl of gold*, my *precious girl.* The change, however,
which I have not difturbed, was made by the editor of the folio,
1632, who, in many inftances, appears to have regulated his text
from more authentic copies of our author's plays than were in the
poffeffion of their firft collective publifhers. STEEVENS.

——*my metal of India?*] So, in *K. Henry IV.* P. I: " Lads,
boys, *hearts of gold*," &c.
Again, *ibidem:*
          " —— and as bountiful
          " As *mines of India.*"
Again, in *K. Henry VIII:*
          " —— To-day the French
          " All clinquant, all *in gold*, like heathen gods,
          " Shone down the Englifh; and to-morrow they
          " Made Britain *India*; every man that ftood,
          " Shew'd like *a mine.*"
So Lily in his *Euphues and his England*, 1580: " I faw that *India*
bringeth gold, but England bringeth goodnefs."
Again, in *Wily Beguil'd*, 1606: " Come, my *heart of gold*, let's
have a dance at the making up of this match."—The perfon there
addreffed, as in *Twelfth-Night*, is a woman. The old copy has
mettle. The two words are very frequently confounded in the
early editions of our author's plays. The editor of the fecond
folio and
fequent e

Cogan,
VOL.

Enter MALVOLIO.

MAL. 'Tis but fortune; all is fortune. Maria
once told me, she did affect me : and I have heard
herself come thus near, that, should she fancy, it
should be one of my complexion. Besides, she uses
me with a more exalted respect, than any one else
that follows her.   What should I think on't ?

SIR TO. Here's an over-weening rogue !

FAB. O, peace ! Contemplation makes a rare tur-
key-cock of him ; how he jets [4] under his advanced
plumes !

SIR AND. 'Slight, I could so beat the rogue :—

SIR TO. Peace, I say.

MAL. To be count Malvolio ;—

SIR TO. Ah, rogue !

SIR AND. Pistol him, pistol him.

SIR TO. Peace, peace !

MAL. There is example for't ; the lady of the
strachy [5] married the yeoman of the wardrobe.

mentator on this passage : " This fish of nature loveth flatterie :
for, being in the water, it will suffer it selfe to be rubbed and
clawed, and so to be taken. Whose example I would wish no maides
to follow, least they repent afterclaps."   STEEVENS.

4 —— *how he* jets——] To *jet* is to strut, to agitate the body by
a proud motion.   So, in *Arden of Feversham*, 1592 :
        " Is now become the steward of the house,
        " And bravely *jets* it in a silken gown."
Again, in *Bussy D'Ambois*, 1607 :
        " To *jet* in others' plumes so haughtily."   STEEVENS.

5 —— *the lady of the* strachy——] We should read *Trachy*, i. e.
Thrace ; for so the old English writers called it.   Mandeville says :
" As Trachye *and Macedoigne, of the which Alisandre was kyng.*"
It was common to use the article *the* before names of places : and
this was no improper instance, where the scene was in Illyria.
                                            WARBURTON.

Sir And. Fie on him, Jezebel!

What we fhould read is hard to fay.   Here is an allufion to fome old ftory which I have not yet difcovered.   Johnson.

Straccio (fee Torriano's and Altieri's dictionaries) fignifies *clown* and *tatters*; and Torriano in his grammar, at the end of his dictionary, fays that *ftraccio* was pronounced *ftratchi*.   So that it is probable that Shakfpeare's meaning was this, that the lady of the queen's wardrobe had married a yeoman of the king's, who was vaftly inferior to her.   Smith.

Such is Mr. Smith's note; but it does not appear that *ftrachy* was ever an Englifh word, nor will the meaning given it by the Italians be of any ufe on the prefent occafion.

Perhaps a letter has been mifplaced, and we ought to read— *ftarchy*; i. e. the room in which linen underwent the once moft complicated operation of *ftarching*.   I do not know that fuch a word exifts; and yet it would not be unanalogically formed from the fubftantive *ftarch*.   In *Harfnet's Declaration*, 1603, we meet with " a yeoman of the *fprucery*;" i. e. wardrobe; and in the *Northumberland Houfehold-Book*, *nurfery* is fpelt *nurcy*.   *Starchy*, therefore, for *ftarchery*, may be admitted.   In *Romeo and Juliet*, the place where *pafte* was made, is called the *paftry*.   The *lady* who had the care of the linen may be fignificantly oppofed to the *yeoman*, i. e. an inferior officer of the wardrobe.   While the *five different coloured ftarches* were worn, fuch a term might have been current.   In the year 1564, a Dutch woman profeffed to teach this art to our fair country-women.   " Her ufual price (fays Stowe) was four or five pounds to teach them how to *ftarch*, and twenty fhillings how to feeth *ftarch*."   The alteration was fuggefted to me by a typographical error in *The World tofs'd at Tennis*, no date, by Middleton and Rowley; where *ftraches* is printed for *ftarches*. I cannot fairly be accufed of having dealt much in conjectural emendation, and therefore feel the lefs reluctance to hazard a guefs on this defperate paffage.   Steevens.

The place in which candles were kept, was formerly called the *chandry*; and in B. Jonfon's *Bartholomew Fair*, a ginger-bread woman is called *lady of the bafket*.—The great objection to this emendation is, that from the *ftarchy* to the *wardrobe* is not what Shakfpeare calls a very " heavy declenfion."   In the old copy the word is printed in Italicks, as the name of a place,—*Strachy*.

The *yeoman of the wardrobe* is not an arbitrary term, but was the proper defignation of the wardrobe-keeper, in Shakfpeare's time.   See Florio's Italian Dictionary, 1598: " *Veftiario*, a ward-robe-keeper, or a *yeoman of a wardrobe*."

The ftory which our poet had in view is perhaps alluded to by

Fab. O, peace! now he's deeply in; look, how imagination blows him.[6]

Mal. Having been three months married to her, sitting in my state,——[7]

Sir To. O, for a stone-bow,[8] to hit him in the eye!

Mal. Calling my officers about me, in my branch'd velvet gown; having come from a day-bed,[9] where I have left Olivia sleeping:

Lily in *Euphues and his England*, 1580: "—— assuring myself there was a certain season when women are to be won; in the which moments they have neither will to deny, nor wit to mistrust. Such a time I have read a young gentleman found to obtain the love of the Dutchefs of Milaine: such a time I have heard that a poor *yeoman* chose, to get the fairest lady in Mantua."   MALONE.

[6] —— *blows him.*] i. e. puffs him up. So, in *Antony and Cleopatra* :
" —————— on her breast
" There is a vent of blood, and something *blown*."
                    STEEVENS.

[7] —— *my* state,——] A *state*, in ancient language, signifies a chair with a canopy over it. So, in *K. Henry IV.* P. I:
" This chair shall be my *state*."   STEEVENS.

[8] —— *stone-bow*,] That is, a crofs-bow, a bow which shoots stones.   JOHNSON.

This instrument is mentioned again in Marston's *Dutch Courtefan*, 1605: "—— whoever will hit the mark of profit, must, like those who shoot in *stone-bows*, wink with one eye." Again, in Beaumont and Fletcher's *King and no King*:
" —————— children will shortly take him
" For a wall, and set their *stone-bows* in his forehead."
                    STEEVENS.

[9] —— *come from a* day-bed,] i. e. a couch. Spenser, in the first canto of the third book of his *Faery Queen*, has dropped a stroke of satire on this lazy fashion:
" So was that chamber clad in goodly wize,
" And round about it many *beds* were dight,
" As whilome was the antique worldes guize,
" Some for *untimely eafe*, some for delight."   STEEVENS.

Eftifania, in *Rule a Wife and have a Wife*, Act I. fays, in answer to Perez:

SIR To. Fire and brimstone!

FAB. O, peace, peace!

MAL. And then to have the humour of state:
and after a demure travel of regard,—telling them,
I know my place, as I would they should do theirs,—
to ask for my kinsman Toby:

SIR To. Bolts and shackles!

FAB. O, peace, peace, peace! now, now.

MAL. Seven of my people, with an obedient start,
make out for him: I frown the while; and, perchance, wind up my watch,² or play with some rich
jewel.³ Toby approaches; court'sies there to me:⁴

> " This place will fit our talk; 'tis fitter far, sir;
> " Above there are *day-beds*, and such temptations
> " I dare not trust, sir." —— REED.

² —— *wind up my* watch,] In our author's time watches were
very uncommon. When Guy Faux was taken, it was urged as a
circumstance of suspicion that a watch was found upon him.
JOHNSON.

Again, in an ancient MS. play, entitled *The Second Maiden's
Tragedy*, written between the years 1610 and 1611:
> " Like one that has a *watche* of curious making;
> " Thinking to be more cunning than the workman,
> " Never gives over tamp'ring with the wheels,
> " 'Till either spring be weaken'd, balance bow'd,
> " Or some wrong pin put in, and so spoils all."

In the *Antipodes*, a comedy, 1638, are the following passages:
> " —————— your project against
> " The multiplicity of pocket-*watches.*"

Again:
> " —————— when every puny clerk can carry
> " The time o' th' day in his breeches."

Again, in *The Alchemist*:
> " And I had lent my *watch* last night to one
> " That dines to-day at the sheriff's." STEEVENS.

Sir To. Shall this fellow live?

Fab. Though our silence be drawn from us with cars,[5] yet peace.

that the manner of paying respect, which is now confined to females, was equally used by the other sex. It is probable, however, that the word *court'sy* was employed to express acts of civility and reverence by either men or women indiscriminately. In an extract from the Black Book of Warwick, *Bibliotheca Topographica Britannica*, p. 4, it is said, " The pulpett being sett at the nether end of the Earle of Warwick's tombe in the said quier, the table was placed where the altar had bene. At the coming into the quier my lord made *lowe curtesie* to the French king's armes." Again, in the *book of kervynge and sewynge*, printed by Wynkyn de Worde, sign. A. I. III: " And whan your Soverayne is set, loke your towell be about your necke, then *make your soverayne curtesy*, then uncover your brede and set it by the salte, and laye your napkyn, knyfe, and spone afore hym, then kneel on your knee," &c. These directions are to male servants. Lord Herbert of Cherbury, in his Life, speaking of dancing, recommends that accomplishment to youth, " that he may know how to come in and go out of a room where company is, how to make *courtesies* handsomely, according to the several degrees of persons he shall encounter." REED.

5 *Though our silence be drawn from us with* cars,] i. e. though it is the greatest pain to us to keep silence. WARBURTON.

I believe the true reading is: *Though our silence be drawn from us with* carts, *yet peace.* In *The Two Gentlemen of Verona*, one of the Clowns says: " *I have a mistress, but who that is*, a team of horses *shall not* pluck from me." So, in this play: " *Oxen and wainropes will not bring them together.*" JOHNSON.

The old reading is *cars*, as I have printed it. It is well known that *cars* and *carts* have the same meaning. STEEVENS.

If I were to suggest a word in the place of *cars*, which I think is a corruption, it should be *cables*. It may be worth remarking, perhaps, that the leading ideas of *Malvolio*, in his *humour of state*, bear a strong resemblance to those of *Alnaschar* in *The Arabian Nights' Entertainments*. Some of the expressions too are very similar. TYRWHITT.

Many Arabian fictions had found their way into obscure Latin and French books, and from thence into English ones, long before any professed version of *The Arabian Nights' Entertainments* had appeared. I meet with a story similar to that of *Alnaschar*, in *The Dialoges of Creatures Moralysed*, bl. l. no date, but probably printed abroad :—" It is but foly to hope to moche of vanyteys.—Wherof

7

[A somewhat similar passage occurs in the old Play "King Leir, 1605." —— ten teame of horses shall no raw me away, till I have full & whole possession: King. I, but one teame & a cart will serve the turn

MAL. I extend my hand to him thus, quenching my familiar smile with an austere regard of control :

SIR TO. And does not Toby take you a blow o'the lips then?

MAL. Saying, *Cousin Toby, my fortunes having cast me on your niece, give me this prerogative of speech ;*—

SIR. TO. What, what?

MAL. *You must amend your drunkenness.*

SIR TO. Out, scab!

FAB. Nay, patience, or we break the sinews of our plot.

MAL. *Besides, you waste the treasure of your time with a foolish knight ;*

SIR AND. That's me, I warrant you.

MAL. *One Sir Andrew :*

SIR AND. I knew, 'twas I ; for many do call me fool.

MAL. What employment have we here? [6]

[*Taking up the letter.*

---

it is tolde in fablys that a lady uppon a tyme delyuered to her mayden a galon of mylke to fell at a cite. And by the waye as she fate and reftid her by a dyche fide, she began to thinke y[t] with with y[e] money of the mylke she wolde bye an henne, the which fhulde bring forth chekyns, and whan they were growyn to hennys she wolde fell them and by piggis, and efchaunge them into shepe, and the shepe into oxen ; and fo whan she was come to richeffe she fholde be maried right worshipfully vnto fome worthy man, and thus she reioycid. And whan she was thus meruelously comfortid, & rauished inwardely in her fecrete folace thinkynge with howe greate ioye she shuld be ledde towarde the churche with her husbond on horsebacke, she fayde to her felf, Goo wee, goo we, fodaynelye she fmote the grounde with her fote, myndynge to fpurre the horfe; but her fote flypped and she fell in the dyche, and there laye all her mylke; and fo she was farre from her pur- pofe, and neuer had that she hopid to haue." Dial. 100. LL. ii. b.
STEEVENS.

[6] *What employment have we here?*] A phrafe of that time, equi- valent to our common fpeech—*What's to do here.* WARBURTON.

Fab. Now is the woodcock near the gin.

Sir To. O, peace! and the fpirit of humours in—timate reading aloud to him!

Mal. By my life, this is my lady's hand: thefe be her very *C*'s, her *U*'s, and her *T*'s; and thus makes fhe her great *P*'s.[7] It is, in contempt of queftion, her hand.

Sir And. Her *C*'s, her *U*'s, and her *T*'s: Why that?

Mal. [*reads*] *To the unknown beloved, this, and my good wifhes:* her very phrafes!—By your leave, wax.—Soft![8]—and the impreffure her Lucrece,

[7] —— *her great* P'*s.*] In the direction of the letter which Malvolio reads, there is neither a C, nor a P, to be found. STEEVENS.

I am afraid fome very coarfe and vulgar appellations are meant to be alluded to by thefe capital letters. BLACKSTONE.

This was perhaps an overfight in Shakfpeare; or rather, for the fake of the allufion hinted at in the preceding note, he chofe not to attend to the words of the direction. It is remarkable, that in the repetition of the paffages in letters, which have been produced in a former part of a play, he very often makes his characters deviate from the words before ufed, though they have the paper itfelf in their hands, and though they appear to recite, not the fubftance, but the very words. So, in *All's well that ends well*, Act V. Helen fays,

  " —— here's your letter; This it fays:
  " *When from my finger you can get this ring,*
  " *And are by me with child;*"——

yet in Act III. fc. ii. fhe reads this very letter aloud; and there the words are different, and in plain profe: " When thou canft get the ring upon my finger, which never fhall come off, and fhew me a child begotten of thy body," &c. Had fhe fpoken in either cafe from memory, the deviation might eafily be accounted for; but in both thefe places, fhe reads the words from Bertram's letter. MALONE.

From the ufual cuftom of Shakfpeare's age, we may eafily fuppofe the whole direction to have run thus:—" *To the Un-known belov'd, this, and my good wifhes, with Care Prefent.*" RITSON.

[8] —— *By your leave, wax.*—Soft!] It was the cuftom in our

with which fhe ufes to feal: 'tis my lady: To whom
fhould this be?

FAB. This wins him, liver and all.

MAL. [*reads.*] *Jove knows, I love :*
                    But who ?
               Lips do not move,
               No man muft know.

No man muft know.——What follows? the numbers
altered!——*No man muft know :*——If this fhould be
thee, Malvolio?

SIR TO. Marry, hang thee, brock![9]

MAL. *I may command, where I adore :*
          But filence, like a Lucrece knife,
     With bloodlefs ftroke my heart doth gore ;
     M, O, A, I, doth fway my life.

poet's time to feal letters with foft wax, which retained its foftnefs
for a good while. The wax ufed at prefent would have been
hardened long before Malvolio picked up this letter. See *Your
Five Gallants*, a comedy, by Middleton : " Fetch a pennyworth
of *foft wax* to feal letters." So, Falftaff, in *King Henry IV*. P. II ;
" I have him already tempering between my finger and my thumb,
and fhortly will I feal with him." MALONE.

I do not fuppofe that—*Soft !* has any reference to the wax ; but
is merely an exclamation equivalent to *Softly !* i. e. be not in too
much hafte. Thus, in *The Merchant of Venice*, Act IV. fc. i:
" *Soft !* no hafte." Again, in *Troilus and Creffida* : " Farewel.
Yet *foft !*"

I may alfo obferve, that though it was anciently the cuftom (as
it ftill is) to feal certain legal inftruments with foft and pliable
wax, familiar letters (of which I have feen fpecimens from the
time of K. Henry VI. to K. James I.) were fecured with wax as
gloffy and firm as that employed in the prefent year.
                                        STEEVENS.

9 ——— *brock !*] i. e. badger. He ufes the word as a term of
contempt, as if he had faid, *hang thee*, cur! *Out* filth! to ftink
like a *brock* being proverbial. RITSON.

Marry, hang thee, brock!] i. e. Marry, hang thee, thou *vain,
conceited coxcomb*, thou over-weening rogue!

Fab. A fuftian riddle!

Sir To. Excellent wench, fay I.

Mal. *M, O, A, I, doth fway my life.*[2]—Nay, but firſt, let me fee,—let me fee,—let me fee.

Fab. What a diſh of poiſon has ſhe dreſs'd him!

Sir To. And with what wing the ftannyel[3] checks at it!

Mal. *I may command where I adore.* Why, ſhe may command me; I ſerve her, ſhe is my lady. Why, this is evident to any formal capacity.[4] There is no obſtruction in this;—And the end;—What ſhould that alphabetical poſition portend? if I could make that reſemble ſomething in me,—Softly!—*M, O, A, I.*—

Brock, which properly fignifies a badger, was uſed in this fenfe in Shakſpeare's time. So, in *The merrie conceited Jeſts of George Peele*, 4to. 1657: "This *felf-conceited brock* had George invited," &c. Malone.

2 ―――― *doth fway my life.*] This phrafe is feriouſly employed in *As you like it*, Act III. fc. ii: "Thy huntrefs name, that *my full life doth fway.*" Steevens.

3 ―――― *ſtannyel* ―] The name of a kind of hawk, is very judiciouſly put here for a *ſtallion*, by Sir Thomas Hanmer. Johnson.

To *check*, fays Latham, in his book of Falconry, is, "when crows, rooks, pies, or other birds, coming in view of the hawk, ſhe forſaketh her natural flight, to fly at them." The *ſtannyel* is the common ſtone-hawk, which inhabits old buildings and rocks; in the North called *ſtanchil*. I have this information from Mr. Lambe's notes on the ancient metrical hiſtory of the battle of Floddon. Steevens.

4 ―*formal capacity.*] i. e. any one in his fenfes, any one whoſe *capacity* is not diſ-arranged, or out of *form*. So, in *The Comedy of Errors*: "Make of him a *formal* man again." Again, in *Meaſure for Meaſure*: "Theſe *informal* women." Steevens.

Sir To. O, ay! make up that:—he is now at a cold scent.

Fab. Sowter' will cry upon't, for all this, though it be as rank as a fox.[6]

Mal. *M,*—Malvolio;—*M,*—why, that begins my name.

Fab. Did not I say, he would work it out? the cur is excellent at faults.

Mal. *M,*—But then there is no consonancy in the sequel; that suffers under probation: *A* should follow, but *O* does.

Fab. And *O* shall end, I hope.[7]

Sir To. Ay, or I'll cudgel him, and make him cry, *O.*

---

[5] *Sowter—*] *Sowter* is here, I suppose, the name of a hound. *Sowterly*, however, is often employed as a term of abuse. So, in *Like will to Like*, &c. 1587:

"You *sowterly* knaves, show you all your manners at once?"
A *sowter* was a cobler. So, in Greene's *Card of Fancy*, 1608:
"—— If Apelles, that cunning painter, suffer the greasy *sowter* to take a view of his curious work," &c. STEEVENS.

I believe the meaning is—This fellow will, notwithstanding, catch at and be duped by our device, though the cheat is so *gross* that any one else would find it out. Our author, as usual, forgets to make his simile answer on both sides; for it is not to be wondered at that a hound should cry or give his tongue, if the scent be as rank as a fox. MALONE.

[6] ——*as rank as a fox.*] Sir Thomas Hanmer reads, "not *as rank.*" The other editions, *though it be as rank*, &c. JOHNSON.

[7] *And O shall end, I hope.*] By *O* is here meant what we now call a *hempen collar.* JOHNSON.

I believe he means only, *it shall end in sighing*, in disappointment. So, in *Romeo and Juliet:*
"Why should you fall into so deep an *O?*"
Again, in Decker's *Honest Whore*, second part, 1630: "—the brick house of castigation, the school where they pronounce no letter well, but *O!*" Again, in *Hymen's Triumph*, by Daniel, 1623:
"Like to an *O*, the character of woe." STEEVENS.

MAL. And then *I* comes behind,

FAB. Ay, an you had any eye behind you, you might fee more detraction at your heels, than fortunes before you.

MAL. M, O, A, I;—This fimulation is not as the former:—and yet, to crufh this a little, it would bow to me, for every one of thefe letters are in my name.   Soft; here follows profe.—*If this fall into thy hand, revolve. In my ftars I am above thee; but be not afraid of greatnefs: Some are born great,*[8] *fome afchieve greatnefs, and fome have greatnefs thruft upon them.   Thy fates open their hands; let thy blood and fpirit embrace them.   And, to inure thyfelf to what thou art like to be, caft thy humble flough, and appear frefh.   Be oppofite*[9] *with a kinfman, furly with fervants: let thy tongue tang arguments of ftate; put thyfelf into the trick of fingularity: She thus advifes thee, that fighs for thee.   Remember who commended thy yellow ftockings;*[a] *and wifh'd to fee thee ever crofs-*

[8] —— *are* born *great,*] The old copy reads—*are* become *great.* The alteration by Mr. Rowe.   STEEVENS.

It is juftified by a fubfequent paffage in which the clown recites from memory the words of this letter.   MALONE.

[9] *Be* oppofite—] That is, be *adverfe, hoftile.* An *oppofite* in the language of our author's age, meant an *adverfary.* See a note on *K. Richard III.* Act V. fc. iv.   To be oppofite *with* was the phrafeology of the time.   So, in Sir T. Overbury's *Character of a Precifian,* 1616: " He will be fure to be in oppofition *with* the papift," &c.   MALONE.

[a] —— *yellow ftockings;*] Before the civil wars, yellow ftockings were much worn. So, in D'Avenant's play, called *The Wits,* Act IV. p. 208.   Works fol. 1673:

" You faid, my girl, Mary Queafie by name, did find your uncle's *yellow ftockings* in a porringer; nay, and you faid fhe ftole them."   PERCY.

So, Middleton and Rowley in their mafque entitled *The World Tofs'd at Tennis,* no date, where the five different-coloured ftarches are introduced as ftriving for fuperiority, *Yellow ftarch* fays to white :

garter'd:[3] *I say, remember. Go to; thou art made, if thou desirest to be so; if not, let me see thee a steward still, the fellow of servants, and not worthy to touch fortune's fingers. Farewel. She, that would alter services with thee,*

The fortunate-unhappy.

Day-light and champian discovers not more:[4] this

> " —— since she cannot
> " Wear her own linen *yellow*, yet she shows
> " Her love to't, and makes him wear *yellow hose*."

Again, in Decker's *Match me in London*, 1631:

> " —— because you wear
> " A kind of *yellow stocking*."

Again, in his *Honest Whore*, second part, 1630: " What *stockings* have you put on this morning, madam? if they be not *yellow*, change them." The yeomen attending the Earl of Arundel, Lord Windsor, and Mr. Fulke Greville, who assisted at an entertainment performed before Queen Elizabeth, on the Monday and Tuesday in Whitsun-week, 1581, were dressed in *yellow worsted stockings*. The book from which I gather this information was published by Henry Goldwell, gent. in the same year. STEEVENS.

[3] —— *cross-garter'd:*] So, in *The Lover's Melancholy*, 1629:

> " As rare an old youth as ever walk'd *cross-gartered*."

Again, in *A Woman's a Weathercock*, 1612:

> " Yet let me say and swear, in a *cross-garter*,
> " Pauls never shew'd to eyes a lovelier quarter."

Very rich garters were anciently worn below the knee. So, in Warner's *Albion's England*, B. IX. ch. 47:

> " *Garters* of listes; but now of *silk*, some edged deep with
>   gold."

It appears, however, that the ancient Puritans affected this fashion. Thus *Barton Holyday*, speaking of the ill success of his TEXNO-ΓAMIA, says:

> " Had there appear'd some sharp *cross-garter'd* man
> " Whom their loud laugh might nick-name *Puritan*;
> " Cas'd up in factious breeches, and small ruffe;
> " That hates the surplice, and defies the cuffe.
> " Then," &c.

In a former scene Malvolio was said to be an affecter of puritanism.

STEEVENS.

[4] *The fortunate-unhappy.*
Day-light and champian discovers not more:] We should read—

is open. I will be proud, I will read politic authors, I will baffle Sir Toby, I will wash off gross acquaintance, I will be point-de-vice, the very man.[5] I do not now fool myself, to let imagination jade me; for every reason excites to this, that my lady loves me. She did commend my yellow stockings of late, she did praise my leg being cross-garter'd; and in this she manifests herself to my love, and, with a kind of injunction, drives me to these habits of her liking. I thank my stars, I am happy. I will be strange, stout, in yellow stockings, and cross-garter'd, even with the swiftness of putting on. Jove, and my stars be praised!—Here is yet a postscript. *Thou canst not choose but know who I am. If thou entertainest my love, let it appear in thy smiling; thy smiles become thee well: therefore in my presence still smile, dear my sweet, I pr'ythee.*—Jove, I thank thee.—I will smile; I will do every thing that thou wilt have me. [*Exit.*

Fab. I will not give my part of this sport for a

" *The fortunate, and happy.*"—*Day-light and champian discovers not more:* i. e. broad day and an open country cannot make things plainer. WARBURTON.

The folio, which is the only ancient copy of this play, reads, *the fortunate-unhappy,* and so I have printed it. *The fortunate-unhappy* is the subscription of the letter. STEEVENS.

[5] —— *I will be* point-de-vice, *the very man.*] This phrase is of French extraction—*a points-devisee.* Chaucer uses it in the *Romaunt of the Rose:*

" Her nose was wrought at *point-device.*"
i. e. with the utmost possible *exactness.*
Again, in *K. Edward I.* 1599:
" That we may have our garments *point-device.*"
Kastril, in *The Alchemist,* calls his sister *Punk-device:* and again, in *The Tale of a Tub,* Act III. sc. vii:
" —— and if the dapper priest
" Be but as cunning *point* in his *devise,*
" As I was in my lie." STEEVENS.

penfion of thoufands to be paid from the Sophy.[6]

Sir To. I could marry this wench for this device:

Sir And. So could I too.

Sir To. And afk no other dowry with her, but fuch another jeft.

Enter MARIA.

Sir And. Nor I neither.

Fab. Here comes my noble gull-catcher.

Sir To. Wilt thou fet thy foot o'my neck?

Sir And. Or o'mine either?

Sir To. Shall I play my freedom at tray-trip,[7] and become thy bond-flave?

[6] —— *a penfion of thoufands to be paid from the Sophy.*] Alluding, as Dr. Farmer obferves, to *Sir Robert Shirley*, who was juft returned in the character of *embaffador from the Sophy.* He boafted of the great rewards he had received, and lived in London with the utmoft fplendor. STEEVENS.

[7] —— *tray-trip.*] *Tray-trip* is mentioned in Beaumont and Fletcher's *Scornful Lady*, 1616:

"Reproving him at *tray-trip*, fir, for fwearing."

Again, in Glapthorne's *Wit in a Conftable*, 1640:

"—— mean time, you may play at *tray-trip* or cockall, for black-puddings."

"My watch are above, at *trea-trip*, for a black-pudding." &c.

Again:

"With lanthorn on ftall, at *trea-trip* we play,
"For ale, cheefe, and pudding, till it be day," &c.
STEEVENS.

The following paffage might incline one to believe that *tray-trip* was the name of fome game at *tables*, or *draughts*: "There is great danger of being taken fleepers at *tray-trip*, if the *king* fweep fuddenly." *Cecil's Correfpondence*, Lett. X. p. 136. Ben Jonfon joins *tray-trip* with *mum-chance*. *Alchemift*, Act V. fc. iv:

"Nor play with cofter-mongers at *mum-chance*, *tray-trip*."
TYRWHITT.

The truth of Mr. Tyrwhitt's conjecture will be eftablifhed by the following extract from *Machiavel's Dogge*, a fatire, 4to. 1617:

Sir And. I'faith, or I either?

Sir To. Why, thou haft put him in fuch a dream, that, when the image of it leaves him, he muft run mad.

Mar. Nay, but fay true; does it work upon him?

Sir To. Like aqua-vitæ [*] with a midwife.

Mar. If you will then fee the fruits of the fport, mark his firft approach before my lady: he will come to her in yellow ftockings, and 'tis a colour fhe abhors; and crofs-garter'd, a fafhion fhe de-tefts;[9] and he will fmile upon her, which will now be fo unfuitable to her difpofition, being addicted to a melancholy as fhe is, that it cannot but turn him into a notable contempt: if you will fee it, follow me.

Sir To. To the gates of Tartar, thou moft excel-lent devil of wit!

Sir And. I'll make one too.   [*Exeunt.*

   " But leaving cardes, lett's goe to dice awhile,
     " To paffage, *treitrippe*, hazarde, or mum-chance:
   " But fubtill males will fimple minds beguile,
     " And blinde their eyes with many a blinking glaunce:
   " Oh, cogges and ftoppes, and fuch like devilifh trickes,
   " Full many a purfe of golde and filver pickes.

   " And therefore firft, for hazard hee that lift,
     " And paffeth not, puts many to a blancke:
   " And *trippe without a treye* makes had I wift
     " To fitte and mourne among the fleeper's ranke:
   " And for mumchance, how ere the chance doe fall,
   " You muft be mum, for fear of marring all."   Reed.

[*] ——— *aqua-vitæ* —]   Is the old name of *ftrong waters.*
                               Johnson.

[9] ——— crofs-garter'd, *a fafhion fhe detefts*;] Sir Thomas Over-bury, in his character of a *footman* without *gards* on his coat, prefents him as more upright than any *croffe-garter'd* gentleman-ufher.   Farmer.

ACT III. SCENE I.

Olivia's *Garden*.

Enter VIOLA, *and* Clown, *with a tabor.*

VIO. Save thee, friend, and thy mufick: Doft thou live by thy tabor?

CLO. No, fir, I live by the church.[a]

VIO. Art thou a churchman?

CLO. No fuch matter, fir; I do live by the church: for I do live at my houfe, and my houfe doth ftand by the church.

VIO. So thou may'ft fay, the king lies by a beggar,[3] if a beggar dwell near him: or, the church ftands by thy tabor, if thy tabor ftand by the church.

CLO. You have faid, fir.——To fee this age!——A fentence is but a cheveril glove[4] to a good wit; How quickly the wrong fide may be turned outward!

---

[a] —— *by thy tabor?*
Clo. No, fir, I live by the church.] The *Clown*, I fuppofe, wilfully miftakes Viola's meaning, and anfwers, as if he had been afked whether he lived by the *fign of the tabor*, the ancient defignation of a mufic fhop. STEEVENS.

It was likewife the fign of an eating-houfe kept by Tarleton, the celebrated clown or fool of the theatre before our author's time; who is exhibited in a print prefixed to his *Jefts*, quarto, 1611, with a *tabor*. Perhaps in imitation of him the fubfequent ftage-clowns ufually appeared with one. MALONE.

[3] —— *the king lies by a beggar,*] *Lies* here, as in many other places in old books, fignifies—*dwells, fojourns.* See *King Henry IV.* P. II. Act III. fc. ii. MALONE.

[4] —— *a* cheveril *glove* —] i. e. a glove made of *kid* leather: *chevreau*, Fr. So, in *Romeo and Juliet*: "——a wit of *cheveril*——" Again, in a proverb in Ray's collection: "He hath a confcience like a *cheveril's* fkin." STEEVENS.

VOL. IV.   H

Vio. Nay, that's certain; they, that dally nicely with words, may quickly make them wanton.

Clo. I would therefore, my fifter had had no name, fir.

Vio. Why, man?

Clo. Why, fir, her name's a word; and to dally with that word, might make my fifter wanton: But, indeed, words are very rafcals, fince bonds difgraced them.

Vio. Thy reafon, man?

Clo. Troth, fir, I can yield you none without words; and words are grown fo falfe, I am loth to prove reafon with them.

Vio. I warrant, thou art a merry fellow, and careft for nothing.

Clo. Not fo, fir, I do care for fomething: but in my confcience, fir, I do not care for you; if that be to care for nothing, fir, I would it would make you invifible.

Vio. Art thou not the lady Olivia's fool?

Clo. No, indeed, fir; the lady Olivia has no folly: fhe will keep no fool, fir, till fhe be married; and fools are as like hufbands, as pilchards are to herrings, the hufband's the bigger: I am, indeed, not her fool, but her corrupter of words.

Vio. I faw thee late at the count Orfino's.

Clo. Foolery, fir, does walk about the orb, like the fun; it fhines every where. I would be forry, fir, but the fool fhould be as oft with your mafter, as with my miftrefs: I think, I faw your wifdom there.

Vio. Nay, an thou pafs upon me, I'll no more with thee. Hold, there's expences for thee.

Clo. Now Jove, in his next commodity of hair, fend thee a beard!

Vio. By my troth, I'll tell thee; I am almoft fick for one; though I would not have it grow on my chin. Is thy lady within?

Clo. Would not a pair of thefe have bred, fir?[5]

Vio. Yes, being kept together, and put to ufe.

Clo. I would play lord Pandarus[6] of Phrygia, fir, to bring a Creffida to this Troilus.

Vio. I underftand you, fir; 'tis well begg'd.

Clo. The matter, I hope, is not great, fir, begging but a beggar; Creffida was a beggar.[7] My lady is within, fir. I will conftrue to them whence you come; who you are, and what you would, are out of my welkin: I might fay, element; but the word is over-worn. [*Exit.*

---

[5] —— *have* bred, *fir?*] I believe our author wrote——have *breed,* fir. The clown is not fpeaking of what a pair *might have* done, had they been kept together, but what they *may* do hereafter in his poffeffion; and therefore covertly folicits another piece from Viola, on the fuggeftion that *one* was ufelefs to him, without another to *breed out of.* Viola's anfwer correfponds with this train of argument: fhe does not fay——" if they *had been* kept together," &c. but, " being kept together," i. e. Yes, they *will* breed, if you keep them together. Our poet has the fame image in his *Venus and Adonis* :

" Foul cank'ring ruft the hidden treafure frets,
" *But gold, that's put to ufe, more gold begets.*"
MALONE.

[6] —— *lord* Pandarus ——] See our author's play of *Troilus and Creffida.* JOHNSON.

[7] —— *Creffida was a* beggar.]
" —— great penurye
" Thou fuffer fhalt, and as a *beggar* dye."
Chaucer's *Teftament of Crefeyde.*
Creffida is the perfon fpoken of. MALONE.

Vio.   This fellow's wise enough to play the
          fool;
And, to do that well, craves a kind of wit:
He muft obferve their mood on whom he jefts,
The quality of perfons, and the time;
And, like the haggard,[8] check at every feather
That comes before his eye.   This is a practice,
As full of labour as a wife man's art:
For folly, that he wifely fhows, is fit;
But wife men, folly-fallen,[9] quite taint their wit.

Again, *ibid:*
     " Thus fhalt thou go *begging* from hous to hous,
     " With cuppe and clappir, like a Lazarous."
                                        THEOBALD.
     [8] —— *the haggard,*] The hawk called the *haggard,* if not well
trained and watched, will fly after every bird without diftinction.
                                        STEEVENS.
     The meaning may be, that he muft catch every opportunity,
as the wild hawk ftrikes every bird.   But perhaps it might be read
more properly:
          Not *like the haggard.*
He muft choofe perfons and times, and obferve tempers; be muft
fly at proper game, like the trained hawk, and not fly at large
like the unreclaimed *haggard,* to feize all that comes in his
way.   JOHNSON.
     [9] *But wife men, folly-*fallen.] Sir Thomas Hanmer reads, *folly
fhewn.* JOHNSON.
     The firft folio reads, *But wife men's folly falne, quite* taint *their
wit.*   From whence I fhould conjecture, that Shakfpeare poffibly
wrote:
          But wife men, folly-fallen, *quite taint their wit.*
i. e. wife men, fallen into folly.   TYRWHITT.
     The fenfe is: *But wife men's folly, when it is once fallen into ex-
travagance, overpowers their difcretion.*   HEATH.
     I explain it thus: The folly which he fhews with proper adap-
tation to perfons and times, *is fit,* has its propriety, and therefore
produces no cenfure; but the folly of wife men when it *falls* or
happens, taints their wit, deftroys the reputation of their judgment.   JOHNSON.
     I have adopted Mr. Tyrwhitt's judicious emendation.
                                        STEEVENS.

Enter SIR TOBY BELCH, *and* SIR ANDREW AGUE-
CHEEK.

Sir To. Save you, gentleman.

Vio. And you, fir.

Sir And. Dieu vous garde, monfieur.

Vio. Et vous auffi ; votre ferviteur.

Sir And. I hope, fir, you are; and I am yours.[2]

Sir To. Will you encounter the houfe? my
niece is defirous you fhould enter, if your trade be
to her.

---

[2] Sir To. *Save you, gentleman.*
Vio. *And you, fir.*
Sir And. *Dieu vous garde, monfieur.*
Vio. *Et vous auffi ; votre ferviteur.*
Sir And. *I hope, fir, you are; and I am yours.*] Thus the old
copy. STEEVENS.

I have ventured to make the two knights change fpeeches in
this dialogue with Viola; and, I think, not without good reafon.
It were a prepofterous forgetfulnefs in the poet, and out of all
probability, to make Sir Andrew not only fpeak French, but underftand what is faid to him in it, who in the firft act did not know
the Englifh of *pourquoi.* THEOBALD.

Mr. Theobald thinks it abfurd that Sir Andrew, who did not
know the meaning of *pourquoi* in the firft act, fhould here fpeak and
underftand French; and therefore has given three of Sir Andrew's
fpeeches to Sir Toby, and *vice versâ,* in which he has been copied
by the fubfequent editors; as it feems to me, without neceffity.
The words,—" Save you, gentleman,—" which he has taken from
Sir Toby, and given to Sir Andrew, are again ufed by Sir Toby
in a fubfequent fcene; a circumftance which renders it the more
probable that they were intended to be attributed to him here
alfo.

With refpect to the improbability that Sir Andrew fhould underftand French here, after having betrayed his ignorance of that
language in a former fcene, it appears from a fubfequent paffage
that he was a picker up of phrafes, and might have learned by
rote from Sir Toby the few French words here fpoken. If we are
to believe Sir Toby, Sir Andrew " could fpeak three or four languages word for word without book." MALONE.

H 3

Vio. I am bound to your niece, fir: I mean, fhe is the lift[2] of my voyage.

Sir To. Tafte your legs, fir,[3] put them to motion.

Vio. My legs do better underftand me, fir, than I underftand what you mean by bidding me tafte my legs.

Sir To. I mean, to go, fir, to enter.

Vio. I will anfwer you with gait and entrance: But we are prevented.[4]

Enter OLIVIA *and* MARIA.

Moft excellent accomplifh'd lady, the heavens rain odours on you!

Sir And. That youth's a rare courtier! *Rain odours!* well.

Vio. My matter hath no voice, lady, but to your own moft pregnant and vouchfafed ear.[5]

Sir And. Odours, pregnant, and *vouchfafed:*—I'll get 'em all three ready.[6]

---

[2] *——the lift—*] is the *bound, limit, fartheft point.* JOHNSON.

[3] Tafte *your legs, fir,* &c.] Perhaps this expreffion was employed to ridicule the fantaftic ufe of a verb, which is many times as quaintly introduced in the old pieces, as in this play, and in *The true Tragedies of Marius and Scilla,* 1594:
"A climbing tow'r that did not *tafte* the wind."
Again, in Chapman's verfion of the 21ft Odyffey:
"——he now began
"To *tafte* the bow, the fharp fhaft took, tugg'd hard."
STEEVENS.

[4] *——prevented.*] i. e. our purpofe is anticipated. So, in the 119th Pfalm:
"Mine eyes *prevent* the night-watches. STEEVENS.

[5] *——moft* pregnant *and vouchfafed ear.*] *Pregnant* for ready; as in *Meafure for Meafure,* Act I. fc. i. STEEVENS.
Vouchfafed for *vouchfafing.* MALONE.

[6] *—— all three* ready.] The old copy has—*all three* already. Mr. Malone reads—" all three *all* ready." STEEVENS.

In the Frogs of Ariftophanes, however, a ar expreffion occurs, v. 466. TEUZAI this oſp te the door, knock gently at it.

OLI. Let the garden door be shut, and leave me to my hearing.

[*Exeunt* SIR TOBY, SIR ANDREW, *and* MARIA.

Give me your hand, fir.

VIO. My duty, madam, and moft humble fervice.

OLI. What is your name?

VIO. Cefario is your fervant's name, fair princefs.

OLI. My fervant, fir! 'Twas never merry world,
Since lowly feigning was call'd compliment:
You are fervant to the count Orfino, youth.

VIO. And he is yours, and his muft needs be yours;
Your fervant's fervant is your fervant, madam.

OLI. For him, I think not on him: for his thoughts,
'Would they were blanks, rather than fill'd with me!

VIO. Madam, I come to whet your gentle thoughts
On his behalf:——

OLI.   O, by your leave, I pray you;
I bade you never fpeak again of him:
But, would you undertake another fuit,
I had rather hear you to folicit that,
Than mufick from the fpheres.

VIO.   Dear lady,——

OLI. Give me leave, I befeech you:[7] I did fend,

The editor of the third folio reformed the paffage by reading only—*ready*. But omiffions ought always to be avoided if poffible. The repetition of the word *all* is not improper in the mouth of Sir Andrew. MALONE.

Præferatur lectio brevior, is a well known rule of criticifm; and in the prefent inftance I moft willingly follow it, omitting the ufelefs repetition—*all*. STEEVENS.

[7] —— I *befeech you:*] The firft folio reads——" 'befeech you." STEEVENS.

This ellipfis occurs fo frequently in our author's plays, that I do not fufpect any omiffion here. The editor of the third folio reads—*I befeech you*; which fupplies the fyllable wanting, but hurts the metre. MALONE.

H 4

After the laſt enchantment you did here,⁸
A ring in chaſe of you; ſo did I abuſe
Myſelf, my ſervant, and, I fear me, you:

I read with the third folio; not perceiving how the metre is injured by the inſertion of the vowel—*I*. STEEVENS.

⁸ ——*you did* here,] The old copy reads—*beare*. STEEVENS. Nonſenſe. Read and point it thus:
  After the laſt enchantment you did here,
i. e. after the enchantment your preſence worked in my affections.
                                                WARBURTON.

The preſent reading is no more nonſenſe than the emendation.
                                                JOHNSON.

Warburton's amendment, the reading. "you did *here*," though it may not perhaps be abſolutely neceſſary to make ſenſe of the paſſage, is evidently right. Olivia could not ſpeak of her ſending him a ring, as a matter he did not know except by hearſay; for the ring was abſolutely delivered to him. It would, beſides, be impoſſible to know what Olivia meant by *the laſt enchantment*, if ſhe had not explained it herſelf, by ſaying—"the laſt enchantment *you did here*." There is not, perhaps, a paſſage in Shakſpeare, where ſo great an improvement of the ſenſe is gained by changing a ſingle letter. M. MASON.

The two words are very frequently confounded in the old editions of our author's plays, and the other books of that age. See the laſt line of *K. Richard III.* quarto, 1613:
    " That ſhe may long live *beare*, God ſay amen."
Again, in *The Tempeſt*, folio, 1623, p. 3, l. 10:
    " *Heare*, ceaſe more queſtions."
Again, in *Love's Labour's Loſt*, 1623, p. 139:
    " Let us complain to them what fools were *beare*."
Again, in *All's well that ends well*, 1623, p. 239:
    " That hugs his kickſey-wickſey *beare* at home."
Again, in Peck's *Deſiderata Curioſa*, Vol. I. p. 205:
    " —— to my utmoſt knowledge, *beare* is ſimple truth and
        verity."
I could add twenty other inſtances, were they neceſſary. Throughout the firſt edition of our author's *Rape of Lucrece*, 1594, which was probably printed under his own inſpection, the word we now ſpell *here*, is conſtantly written *beare*.

Let me add, that Viola had not ſimply *beard* that a ring had been ſent (if even ſuch an expreſſion as—" After the laſt enchantment, you did *beare*," were admiſſible;) ſhe had *ſeen* and *talked* with the bearer of *it*. MALONE.

Under your hard conftruction muft I fit,
To force that on you, in a fhameful cunning,
Which you knew none of yours: What might you
      think?
Have you not fet mine honour at the ftake,
And baited it with all the unmuzzled thoughts
That tyrannous heart can think? To one of your
      receiving[9]
Enough is fhewn; a cyprus,[2] not a bofom,
Hides my poor heart: So let me hear you fpeak.[3]

  Vio. I pity you.

  Oli. That's a degree to love.

  Vio. No, not a grife;[4] for 'tis a vulgar proof,[5]
That very oft we pity enemies.

  Oli. Why, then, methinks, 'tis time to fmile
      again:
O world, how apt the poor are to be proud!
If one fhould be a prey, how much the better
To fall before the lion, than the wolf? [*Clock ftrikes.*
The clock upbraids me with the wafte of time.——
Be not afraid, good youth, I will not have you:

---

[9] *To one of your* receiving —] i. e. to one of your *ready apprehenfion.* She confiders him as an arch page. WARBURTON. *See p. 46. n. 6.*

[2] —— *a cyprus,*] is a tranfparent ftuff. JOHNSON.

[3] *Hides my* poor *heart: So let me* hear *you fpeak.*] The word *hear* is ufed in this line, like *tear, dear, fwear,* &c. as a diffyllable. The editor of the fecond folio, to fupply what he imagined to be a defect in the metre, reads—Hides my *poor* heart; and all the fubfequent editors have adopted his interpolation. MALONE.

I have retained the pathetic and neceffary epithet—*poor.* The line would be barbaroufly diffonant without it. STEEVENS.

[4] —— *a grife;*] is a *ftep,* fometimes written *greefe* from *degres,* French. JOHNSON.

So, in *Othello:* "Which, as a *grife* or ftep, may help thefe lovers."
      STEEVENS.

[5] —— *'tis a* vulgar *proof,*] That is, it is a *common* proof. The experience of every day fhews that, &c. MALONE.

And yet, when wit and youth is come to harveft,
Your wife is like to reap a proper man:
There lies your way, due weft.

    Vio.   Then weftward-hoe:[6]
Grace, and good difpofition 'tend your ladyfhip!
You'll nothing, madam, to my lord by me?

  Oli. Stay:
I pr'ythee, tell me, what thou think'ft of me.

  Vio. That you do think, you are not what you are.

  Oli. If I think fo, I think the fame of you.

  Vio. Then think you right; I am not what I am.

  Oli. I would, you were as I would have you be!

  Vio. Would it be better, madam, than I am,
I wifh it might; for now I am your fool.

  Oli. O, what a deal of fcorn looks beautiful
In the contempt and anger of his lip![7]
A murd'rous guilt fhows not itfelf more foon
Than love that would feem hid: love's night is noon.
Cefario, by the rofes of the fpring,
By maidhood, honour, truth, and every thing,
I love thee fo, that, maugre[8] all thy pride,
Nor wit, nor reafon, can my paffion hide.
Do not extort thy reafons from this claufe,
For, that I woo, thou therefore haft no caufe:

---

  [6] *Then* weftward-hoe:] This is the name of a comedy by T.
Decker, 1607. He was affifted in it by Webfter, and it was
acted with great fuccefs by *the children of Paul's*, on whom Shakfpeare has beftowed fuch notice in *Hamlet*, that we may be fure
they were rivals to the company patronized by himfelf. STEEVENS.

  [7] *O, what a deal of fcorn looks beautiful*
  In the contempt and anger of his lip!] So, in our author's
Venus and Adonis:
    " Which bred more *beauty* in his *angry* eyes." STEEVENS.

  [8] ——— *maugre*——] i. e. in fpite of. So, in *David and Beth-*
fabe, 1599: " *Maugre* the fons of Ammon and of Syria."
                                  STEEVENS.

But, rather, reafon thus with reafon fetter:
Love fought is good, but given unfought, is better.

Vio. By innocence I fwear, and by my youth,
I have one heart, one bofom, and one truth,
And that no woman has;⁹ nor never none
Shall miftrefs be of it, fave I alone.²
And fo adieu, good madam; never more
Will I my mafter's tears to you deplore.

Oli. Yet come again: for thou, perhaps, may'ft
    move
That heart, which now abhors, to like his love.
[*Exeunt.*

SCENE II.

A room in Olivia*'s houfe.*

Enter SIR TOBY BELCH, SIR ANDREW AGUE-CHEEK,
and FABIAN.

Sir And. No, faith, I'll not ftay a jot longer.

Sir To. Thy reafon, dear venom, give thy reafon.

Fab. You muft needs yield your reafon, fir Andrew.

Sir And. Marry, I faw your niece do more favours to the count's ferving man, than ever fhe beftowed upon me; I faw't i'the orchard.

Sir To. Did fhe fee thee the while,³ old boy? tell
me that.

Sir And. As plain as I fee you now.

Fab. This was a great argument of love in her
toward you.

⁹ *And that no woman has;*] And that *heart* and *bofom* I have
never yielded to any woman. JOHNSON.

² ——*fave I alone.*] Thefe three words Sir Thomas Hanmer
gives to Olivia probably enough. JOHNSON.

³ *Did fhe fee thee the while,*] *Thee* is wanting in the old copy.
It was fupplied by Mr. Rowe. MALONE.

Sir And. 'Slight! will you make an afs o' me?

Fab. I will prove it legitimate, fir, upon the oaths of judgement and reafon.

Sir To. And they have been grand jury-men, fince before Noah was a failor.

Fab. She did fhow favour to the youth in your fight, only to exafperate you, to awake your dor-moufe valour, to put fire in your heart, and brim-ftone in your liver: You fhould then have accofted her; and with fome excellent jefts, fire-new from the mint, you fhould have bang'd the youth into dumbnefs. This was look'd for at your hand, and this was baulk'd: the double gilt of this opportu-nity you let time wafh off, and you are now failed into the north of my lady's opinion; where you will hang like an icicle on a Dutchman's beard, unlefs you do redeem it by fome laudable attempt, either of valour, or policy.

Sir And. And't be any way, it muft be with va-lour; for policy I hate: I had as lief be a Brownift,[3] as a politician.

---

[3] —— *as lief be a* Brownift,] The *Brownifts* were fo called from Mr. *Robert Browne*, a noted feparatift in Queen Elizabeth's reign. [See Strype's *Annals of Queen Elizabeth*, Vol. III. p. 15, 16, &c.] In his life of Whitgift, p. 323, he informs us, that *Browne*, in the year 1589, " went off from the feparation, and came into the com-munion of the church."

This *Browne* was defcended from an ancient and honourable family in Rutlandfhire; his grandfather Francis, had a charter granted him by K. Henry VIII. and confirmed by act of parlia-ment; giving him leave " *to put on his hat in the prefence of the king, or his heirs, or any lord fpiritual or temporal in the land, and not to put it off, but for his own eafe and pleafure.*"
Neal's *Hiftory of New-England*, Vol. I. p. 58.   GREY.
The *Brownifts* feem, in the time of our author, to have been the conftant objects of popular fatire. In the old comedy of *Ram-alley*, 1611, is the following ftroke at them:

Sir To. Why then, build me thy fortunes upon the bafis of valour. Challenge me the count's youth to fight with him; hurt him in eleven places; my niece fhall take note of it: and affure thyfelf, there is no love-broker in the world can more prevail in man's commendation with woman, than report of valour.

Fab. There is no way but this, fir Andrew.

Sir And. Will either of you bear me a challenge to him?

Sir To. Go, write it in a martial hand; be curft [4] and brief; it is no matter how witty, fo it be eloquent, and full of invention: taunt him with the licence of ink: if thou *thou'ft* him fome thrice,[5] it

---

" —— of a new feɛ̃t, and the good profeffors will, like the *Brownifɛ̃*, frequent gravel-pits fhortly, for they ufe woods and obfcure holes already."

Again, in *Love and Honour*, by Sir W. D'Avenant:

" Go kifs her:—by this hand, a *Brownifɛ̃* is
" More amorous——." STEEVENS.

[4] —— *in a martial hand*; *be* curft——] *Martial hand*, feems to be a carelefs fcrawl, fuch as fhewed the writer to negleɛ̃t ceremony. *Curft*, is petulant, crabbed. A curft cur, is a dog that with little provocation fnarls and bites. JOHNSON.

[5] —— *taunt him with the licence of ink: if thou* thou'ft *him fome thrice*,] There is no doubt, I think, but this paffage is one of thofe in which our author intended to fhew his refpeɛ̃t for Sir Walter Raleigh, and a deteftation of the virulence of his profecutors. The words quoted, feem to me direɛ̃tly levelled at the Attorney-general Coke, who, in the trial of Sir Walter, attacked him with all the following indecent expreffions:—" *All that he did was by thy inftigation*, thou *viper*; *for I* thou *thee*, thou *traytor!*" (Here, by the way, are the poet's *three* thou's.) " *You are an odious man.*"—" *Is he bafe? I return it into thy throat, on his behalf.*"—" *O damnable atheift.*"—" *Thou art a monfter; thou haft an Englifh face, but a Spanifh heart.*"—" *Thou haft a Spanifh heart, and thyfelf art a fpider of hell.*"—" *Go to, I will lay thee on thy back for the confident'ft traytor that ever came at a bar*," &c. Is not here all the licence of tongue, which the poet fatirically prefcribes to Sir Andrew's ink? And how mean an opinion Shakfpeare had of thefe

shall not be amiss; and as many lies as will lie in thy sheet of paper, although the sheet were big enough for the bed of Ware in England, set 'em down; go, about it. Let there be gall enough in thy ink; though thou write with a goose-pen, no matter: About it.

Sir And. Where shall I find you?

---

petulant invectives, is pretty evident from his close of this speech: *Let there be gall enough in thy ink: though thou write it with a goose-pen, no matter.*——A keener lash at the attorney for a fool, than all the contumelies the attorney threw at the prisoner, as a supposed traytor! THEOBALD.

The same expression occurs in Shirley's *Opportunity*, 1640:

     " ——— Does he *thou* me?
     " How would he domineer, an he were duke!"

The resentment of our author, as Dr. Farmer observes to me, might likewise have been excited by the contemptuous manner in which Lord Coke has spoken of players, and the severity he was always willing to exert against them. Thus, in his *Speech and Charge at Norwich, with a discoverie of the abuses and corruption of officers.* Nath. Butter, 4to. 1607: " Because I must haste unto an end, I will request that you will carefully put in execution the statute against *vagrants*; since the making whereof I have found fewer theeves, and the gaole lesse pestered than before.

" The abuse of *stage-players* wherewith I find the country much troubled, may easily be reformed; they having no commission to play in any place without leave: and therefore, if by your willing-nesse they be not entertained, you may soone be rid of them."

                              STEEVENS.

Though I think it probable Lord Coke might have been in Shakspeare's mind when he wrote the above passage, yet it is by no means certain. It ought to be observed, that the conduct of that great lawyer, bad as it was on this occasion, received too much countenance from the practice of his predecessors, both at the bar and on the bench. The *State Trials* will shew, to the disgrace of the profession, that many other criminals were THOU'D by their prosecutors and judges, besides Sir Walter Raleigh. In Knox's *History of the Reformation*, are eighteen articles exhibited against Master George Wischarde, 1546, every one of which begins——THOU *false heretick*, and sometimes with the addition of *thief, traiter, runagate,* &c. REED.

Sir To. We'll call thee at the *cubiculo:*[6] Go.

[*Exit* SIR ANDREW.

Fab. This is a dear manakin to you, fir Toby.

Sir To. I have been dear to him, lad; fome two thoufand ftrong, or fo.

Fab. We fhall have a rare letter from him: but you'll not deliver it.

Sir To. Never truft me then; and by all means ftir on the youth to an anfwer. I think, oxen and wainropes cannot hale them together. For Andrew, if he were open'd, and you find fo much blood in his liver as will clog the foot of a flea, I'll eat the reft of the anatomy.

Fab. And his oppofite,[7] the youth, bears in his vifage no great prefage of cruelty.

Enter MARIA.

Sir To. Look, where the youngeft wren of nine comes.[8]

[6] —— *at* the *cubiculo:*] I believe we fhould read—at *thy* cubiculo. MALONE.

[7] *And his* oppofite,] *Oppofite* in our author's time was ufed as a fubftantive, and fynonymous to *adverfary.* MALONE.

[8] *Look, where the youngeft* wren *of* nine *comes.*] The women's parts were then acted by boys, fometimes fo low in ftature, that there was occafion to obviate the impropriety by fuch kind of oblique apologies. WARBURTON.

The *wren* generally lays nine or ten eggs at a time, and the laft hatch'd of all birds are ufually the fmalleft and weakeft of the whole brood.

So, in a *Dialogue of the Phœnix,* &c. by R. Chefter, 1601:

" The little *wren* that *many young ones* brings."——
The old copy, however, reads—" *wren* of mine." STEEVENS.

Again, in *Sir Philip Sidney's Ourania,* a poem, by N. Breton, 1606:

" The titmoufe, and the *multiplying wren.*"
The correction was made by Mr. Theobald. MALONE.

7

Again in *A mery play betweene Johan the hus*
& his wyfe &c. Jhō. Raftel, 1533:
"*Syr, that is the left care I have of nyne.*"

Mar. If you defire the fpleen, and will laugh your-felves into ftitches, follow me: yon' gull Malvolio is turned heathen, a very renegado; for there is no Chriftian, that means to be fav'd by believing rightly, can ever believe fuch impoffible paffages of groffnefs. He's in yellow ftockings.

Sir To. And crofs-garter'd?

Mar. Moft villainoufly; like a pedant that keeps a fchool i'the church.—I have dogg'd him, like his murderer: He does obey every point of the letter that I dropp'd to betray him.   He does fmile his face into more lines, than are in the new map, with the augmentation of the Indies: you have not feen fuch a thing as 'tis; I can hardly forbear hurling things at him.   I know, my lady will ftrike him; [9] if fhe do, he'll fmile, and take't for a great favour.

Sir To. Come, bring us, bring us where he is.

[*Exeunt.*

SCENE III.

A Street.

Enter ANTONIO and SEBASTIAN.

Seb. I would not, by my will, have troubled you; But, fince you make your pleafure of your pains, I will no further chide you.

Ant. I could not ftay behind you; my defire, More fharp than filed fteel, did fpur me forth; And not all love to fee you, (though fo much,

---

[9] —— *I know my lady will ftrike him*;] We may fuppofe, that in an age when ladies ftruck their fervants, the box on the ear which Queen Elizabeth is faid to have given to the Earl of Effex, was not regarded as a tranfgreffion againft the rules of common behaviour.

STEEVENS.

As might have drawn one to a longer voyage,)
But jealousy what might befall your travel,
Being skilless in these parts; which to a stranger,
Unguided, and unfriended, often prove
Rough and unhospitable: My willing love,
The rather by these arguments of fear,
Set forth in your pursuit.

SEB.   My kind Antonio,
I can no other answer make, but, thanks,
And thanks, and ever thanks: Often good turns [3]
Are shuffled off with such uncurrent pay:
But, were my worth,[4] as is my conscience, firm,

---

[3] *And thanks, and ever thanks: Often good turns*—] The old copy reads—

" And thankes: and euer oft good turnes"— STEEVENS.
The second line is too short by a whole foot. Then, who ever heard of this goodly double adverb, *ever-oft*, which seems to have as much propriety as *always-sometimes?* As I have restored the passage, it is very much in our author's manner and mode of expression. So, in *Cymbeline:*

" —— Since when I have been debtor to you for courtesies, which I will be *ever* to pay, and yet pay *still.*"
Again, in *All's Well that Ends Well:*

" And let me buy your friendly help thus far,
" Which I will *over-pay*, and *pay again*
" When I have found it." THEOBALD.

I have changed the punctuation. Such liberties every editor has occasionally taken. Theobald has completed the line, as follows:

" And thanks and ever *thanks, and* oft good turns."
STEEVENS.

I would read:—*And thanks again, and ever.* TOLLET.

Mr. Theobald added the word—*and* [*and* oft, &c.] unnecessarily. *Turns* was, I have no doubt, used as a dissyllable.
MALONE.

I wish my ingenious coadjutor had produced some instance of the word—*turns*, used as a dissyllable. I am unable to do it; and therefore have not scrupled to read—*often* instead of *oft*, to complete the measure. STEEVENS.

[4] *But, were my worth.*] *Worth* in this place means *wealth* or *fortune.* So, in *The Winter's Tale:*

You fhould find better dealing. What's to do?
Shall we go fee the reliques of this town?[5]

Ant. To-morrow, fir; beft, firft, go fee your
lodging.

Seb. I am not weary, and 'tis long to night;
I pray you, let us fatisfy our eyes
With the memorials, and the things of fame,
That do renown this city.

Ant.   'Would, you'd pardon me;
I do not without danger walk thefe ftreets:
Once, in a fea-fight, 'gainft the Count his gallies,[6]
I did fome fervice; of fuch note, indeed,
That, were I ta'en here, it would fcarce be anfwer'd.

Seb. Belike, you flew great number of his people.

Ant. The offence is not of fuch a bloody nature;
Albeit the quality of the time, and quarrel,
Might well have given us bloody argument.
It might have fince been anfwer'd in repaying
What we took from them; which, for traffick's fake,
Moft of our city did: only myfelf ftood out:

> " ―――― and he boafts himfelf
> " To have a *worthy* feeding."

Again, in Ben Jonfon's *Cynthia's Revels:*
> " Such as the fatyrift paints truly forth,
> " That only to his crimes owes all his *worth.*"

M. MASON.

5 ―――― *the* reliques *of this town?*] I fuppofe, Sebaftian means,
the *reliques of faints,* or the remains of ancient fabricks.

STEEVENS.

Thefe words are explained by what follows:
> " ―――― Let us fatisfy our eyes
> " With the memorials, and the things of fame,
> " That do renown this city." MALONE.

6 ―――― *the* Count his *gallies,*] I fufpect our author wrote—*county's*
gallies, i. e. the gallies of the county, or count; and that the
tranfcriber's ear deceived him. However, as the prefent reading
is conformable to the miftaken grammatical ufage of the time, I
have not difturbed the text. MALONE.

For which, if I be lapfed in this place,
I fhall pay dear.

Seb.   Do not then walk too open.

Ant. It doth not fit me. Hold, fir, here's my purfe:
In the fouth fuburbs, at the Elephant,
Is beft to lodge : I will befpeak our diet,
Whiles you beguile the time, and feed your know-
          ledge,
With viewing of the town; there fhall you have me.

Seb. Why I your purfe?

Ant. Haply, your eye fhall light upon fome toy
You have defire to purchafe; and your ftore,
I think, is not for idle markets, fir.

Seb. I'll be your purfe-bearer, and leave you for
An hour.

Ant.   To the Elephant.——

Seb.   I do remember.
                              Exeunt.

S C E N E   IV.

Olivia's *Garden.*

Enter OLIVIA, *and* MARIA.

Oli. I have fent after him : He fays, he'll come;[7]
How fhall I feaft him? what beftow on him?[8]
For youth is bought more oft, than begg'd, or bor-
          row'd.
I fpeak too loud.——

---

[7] *He fays, he'll come;*] i. e. I fuppofe now, or admit now, he
fays, he'll come. WARBURTON.

[8] —— *what beftow* on *him?*] The old copy reads—"beftow
of him," a vulgar corruption of—*on.* STEEVENS.

Of, is very commonly, in the North, ftill ufed for *on.* HENLEY.

I 2

Where is Malvolio?——he is fad, and civil,[9]
And fuits well for a fervant with my fortunes;——
Where is Malvolio?

MAR.   He's coming, madam;
But in ftrange manner. He is fure poffefs'd.[2]

OLI. Why, what's the matter? does he rave?

MAR.   No, madam,
He does nothing but fmile: your ladyfhip
Were beft have guard about you, if he come;[3]
For, fure, the man is tainted in his wits.

OLI. Go call him hither.——I'm as mad as he,
If fad and merry madnefs equal be.——

Enter MALVOLIO.

How now, Malvolio?

MAL. Sweet lady, ho, ho. [*Smiles fantaftically.*
OLI. Smil'ft thou?
I fent for thee upon a fad occafion.

---

9 ——*fad, and* civil,] *Civil*, in this inftance, and fome others,
means only, *grave, decent*, or *folemn*.   So, in *As you like it:*
   "Tongues I'll hang on every tree,
   "That fhall *civil* fayings fhow——."
See note on that paffage, Act III. fc. ii.
   Again, in Dekker's *Villanies difcovered by Lanthorne and Candle-
light,* &c. 1616:——"If before fhe ruffled in filkes, now is fhe more
civilly attired than a mid-wife."   Again——"*civilly* fuited, that
they might carry about them fome badge of a fcholler."   Again,
in David Rowland's Tranflation of *Lazarillo de Tormes,* 1586:
"——he throwing his cloake ouer his leaft fhoulder very *civilly*,"
&c.   STEEVENS.

2 *But in ftrange manner. He is fure poffefs'd.*] The old copy reads——
   "But in *very* ftrange manner. He is fure poffefs'd, *madam.*"
For the fake of metre, I have omitted the unneceffary words—*very*,
and *madam.*   STEEVENS.

3 *Were beft have guard about you, if he come;*]   The old copy,
redundantly, and without addition to the fenfe, reads——
   "Were beft *to* have *fome* guard," &c.   STEEVENS.

MAL. Sad, lady? I could be fad: This does make fome obſtruction in the blood, this croſs-gartering; But what of that? if it pleaſe the eye of one, it is with me as the very true fonnet is: *Pleaſe one, and pleaſe all.*

OLI. Why, how doſt thou, man? what is the matter with thee?

MAL. Not black in my mind, though yellow in my legs: It did come to his hands, and commands fhall be executed. I think, we do know the ſweet Roman hand.

OLI. Wilt thou go to bed, Malvolio?

MAL. To bed? ay, ſweet-heart; and I'll come to thee.

OLI. God comfort thee! Why doſt thou ſmile ſo, and kiſs thy hand ſo oft?[4]

MAR. How do you, Malvolio?

MAL. At your requeſt? Yes; Nightingales anſwer daws.

MAR. Why appear you with this ridiculous bold-neſs before my lady?

MAL. *Be not afraid of greatneſs:—*'Twas well writ.

OLI. What meaneſt thou by that, Malvolio?

MAL. *Some are born great,—*

OLI. Ha?

MAL. *Some aſchieve greatneſs,——*

4 —— *kiſs thy hand* ſo oft?] This fantaſtical cuſtom is taken notice of by Barnaby Riche, in *Faults and nothing but Faults*, 4to. 1606, p. 6: " —— and theſe *Flowers of Courteſie*, as they are full of affectation, ſo are they no leſs formall in their ſpeeches, full of fuſtian phraſes, many times delivering ſuch ſentences, as do betray and lay open their maſters' ignorance: and they are ſo frequent *with the kiſſe on the hand*, that word fhall not paſſe their mouthes, till they have clapt their fingers over their lippes." REED.

OLI. What fay'ſt thou?

MAL. And ſome have greatneſs thruſt upon them.

OLI. Heaven reſtore thee!

MAL. Remember, who commended thy yellow ſtock-
ings;——

OLI. Thy yellow ſtockings?

MAL. And wiſh'd to ſee thee croſs-garter'd.

OLI. Croſs-garter'd?

MAL. Go to: thou art made, if thou deſireſt to be ſo;——

OLI. Am I made?

MAL. If not, let me ſee thee a ſervant ſtill.

OLI. Why, this is very midſummer madneſs.[4]

Enter Servant.

SER. Madam, the young gentleman of the count
Orſino's is return'd; I could hardly entreat him back:
he attends your ladyſhip's pleaſure.

OLI. I'll come to him. [*Exit* Servant.]   Good
Maria, let this fellow be look'd to.   Where's my
couſin Toby? Let ſome of my people have a ſpecial
care of him; I would not have him miſcarry for
the half of my dowry.
[*Exeunt* OLIVIA *and* MARIA.

MAL. Oh, ho! do you come near me now? no
worſe man than ſir Toby to look to me? This concurs directly with the letter: ſhe ſends him on purpoſe, that I may appear ſtubborn to him; for ſhe
incites me to that in the letter. *Caſt thy humble*

---

[4] *——midſummer madneſs.*] Hot weather often hurts the brain,
which is, I ſuppoſe, alluded to here.   JOHNSON.

'*Tis midſummer moon with you*, is a proverb in Ray's collection;
ſignifying, you are mad.   STEEVENS.

flough, fays she;—be oppofite with a kinfman, [5] *furly
with fervants,—let thy tongue tang* [6] *with arguments
of ftate,—put thyfelf into the trick of fingularity;——*
and, confequently, fets down the manner how; as,
a fad face, a reverend carriage, a flow tongue, in the
habit of fome fir of note, and fo forth. I have
limed her; [7] but it is Jove's doing, and Jove make
me thankful! And, when fhe went away now, *Let
this fellow be look'd to:* Fellow! [8] not Malvolio, nor
after my degree, but fellow. Why, every thing ad-
heres together; that no dram of a fcruple, no fcruple
of a fcruple, no obftacle, no incredulous or unfafe
circumftance,—What can be faid? Nothing, that
can be, can come between me and the full profpect
of my hopes. Well, Jove, not I, is the doer of this,
and he is to be thanked.

Re-enter MARIA, *with* SIR TOBY BELCH, *and*
FABIAN.

Sir To. Which way is he, in the name of fanctity?
If all the devils in hell be drawn in little, and Legion
himfelf poffeffed him, yet I'll fpeak to him.

---

[5] *—— be oppofite with a kinfman;*] *Oppofite,* here, as in many
other places, means——*adverfe, hoftile.* MALONE.

So, in *King Lear:*
 " —— Thou waft not bound to anfwer
 " An unknown *oppofite.*" STEEVENS.

[6] *—— let thy tongue* tang, &c.] Here the old copy reads——
langer; but it fhould be——*tang,* as I have corrected it from the
letter which Malvolio reads in a former fcene. STEEVENS.

The fecond folio reads——*tang.* TYRWHITT.

[7] *I have limed her;*] I have entangled or caught her, as a bird
is caught with *birdlime.* JOHNSON.

[8] *—— Fellow!*] This word, which originally fignified *companion,* was not yet totally degraded to its prefent meaning; and
Malvolio takes it in the favourable fenfe. JOHNSON.

I 4

Fab. Here he is, here he is:—How is't with you, fir? how is't with you, man?

Mal. Go off; I difcard you; let me enjoy my private; go off.

Mar. Lo, how hollow the fiend fpeaks within him! did not I tell you?—Sir Toby, my lady prays you to have a care of him.

Mal. Ah, ha! does fhe fo?

Sir To. Go to, go to; peace, peace, we muft deal gently with him; let me alone. How do you, Malvolio? how is't with you? What, man! defy the devil: confider, he's an enemy to mankind.[8]

Mal. Do you know what you fay?

Mar. La you, an you fpeak ill of the devil, how he takes it at heart! Pray God, he be not be-witch'd!

Fab. Carry his water to the wife woman.

Mar. Marry, and it fhall be done to-morrow morning, if I live. My lady would not lofe him for more than I'll fay.

Mal. How now, miftrefs?

Mar. O lord!

Sir To. Pr'ythee, hold thy peace; this is not the way: Do you not fee, you move him? let me alone with him.

Fab. No way but gentlenefs; gently, gently: the fiend is rough, and will not be roughly ufed.

Sir To. Why, how now, my bawcock? how doft thou, chuck?

Mal. Sir?

---

[8] —— *enemy to mankind.*]   So, in *Macbeth:*
    "—— mine eternal jewel,
    "Given to the common *enemy of man*," &c. STEEVENS.

Sir To. Ay, Biddy, come with me. What, man!
'tis not for gravity to play at cherry-pit[9] with
Satan: Hang him, foul collier![a]

Mar. Get him to say his prayers; good sir Toby,
get him to pray.

Mal. My prayers, minx?

Mar. No, I warrant you, he will not hear of god-
liness.

Mal. Go, hang yourselves all! you are idle shallow things: I am not of your element; you shall
know more hereafter.   [*Exit.*

Sir To. Is't possible?

Fab. If this were play'd upon a stage now, I
could condemn it as an improbable fiction.

Sir To. His very genius hath taken the infection
of the device, man.

Mar. Nay, pursue him now; lest the device take
air, and taint.

Fab. Why, we shall make him mad, indeed.

Mar. The house will be the quieter.

Sir To. Come, we'll have him in a dark room,

---

[9] —— *cherry-pit* ——] *Cherry-pit* is pitching cherry-stones into
a little hole. Nash, speaking of the paint on ladies' faces, says:
" You may play at *cherry-pit* in their cheeks." So, in a comedy
called *The Isle of Gulls*, 1606: " ——if she were here, I would
have a bout at cobnut or *cherry-pit*." Again, in *The Witch of
Edmonton:* " I have lov'd a witch ever since I play'd at *cherry-pit*."
                                                    STEEVENS.

[a] *Hang him, foul* collier!] *Collier* was, in our author's
time, a term of the highest reproach. So great were the im-
positions practised by the venders of coals, that R. Greene at the
conclusion of his *Notable Discovery of Cozenage*, 1592, has published what he calls, *A pleasant Discovery of the Cosenage of Colliers.*
                                                    STEEVENS.

The devil is called *Collier* for his blackness; *Like will to like,
quoth the Devil to the Collier.* JOHNSON.

and Bound. My niece is already in the belief that he is mad; we may carry it thus, for our pleasure, and his penance, till our very paftime, tired out of breath, prompt us to have mercy on him: at which time, we will bring the device to the bar, and crown thee for a finder of madmen.[3] But fee, but fee.

Enter Sir Andrew Ague-cheek.

Fab. More matter for a May morning.[4]

Sir And. Here's the challenge, read it; I warrant, there's vinegar and pepper in't.

Fab. Is't fo fawcy?

Sir And. Ay, is it, I warrant him: do but read.

Sir To. Give me. [*reads.*] *Youth, whatfoever thou art, thou art but a fcurvy fellow.*

Fab. Good, and valiant.

Sir To. *Wonder not, nor admire not in thy mind, why I do call thee fo, for I will fhow thee no reafon for't.*

---

3 ———— *a finder of madmen.*] This is, I think, an allufion to the witch-finders, who were very bufy. JOHNSON.

If there be any doubt whether a culprit is become *non compos mentis*, after indictment, conviction, or judgement, the matter is tried by a jury; and if he be found either an ideot or *lunatick*, the lenity of the Englifh law will not permit him, in the firft cafe, to be tried, in the fecond, to receive judgement, or in the third, to be executed. In other cafes alfo inquefts are held for the *finding of madmen*. MALONE.

Finders of madmen muft have been thofe who acted under the writ *De lunatico inquirendo*; in virtue whereof they *found* the man mad. It does not appear that a *finder of madmen* was ever a profeffion, which was moft certainly the cafe with *witch-finders*.
RITSON.

4 *More matter for a* May morning.] It was ufual on the firft of May to exhibit metrical interludes of the comic kind, as well as the *morris-dance*, of which a plate is given at the end of the Firft Part of *King Henry IV.* with Mr. Tollet's obfervations on it.
STEEVENS.

*F*A*B*. A good note; that keeps you from the blow of the law.

S*IR* T*O*. *Thou comeſt to the lady Olivia, and in my ſight ſhe uſes thee kindly: but thou lieſt in thy throat, that is not the matter I challenge thee for.*

*F*A*B*. Very brief, and exceeding good ſenſe-leſs.

S*IR* T*O*. *I will way-lay thee going home; where if it be thy chance to kill me,——*

*F*A*B*. Good.

S*IR* T*O*. *Thou kill'ſt me like a rogue and a villain.*

*F*A*B*. Still you keep o'the windy ſide of the law: Good.

S*IR* T*O*. *Fare thee well; And God have mercy upon one of our ſouls! He may have mercy upon mine;[5] but my hope is better, and ſo look to thyſelf. Thy friend, as thou uſeſt him, and thy ſworn enemy,* A*NDREW* A*GUE-CHEEK*.

S*IR* T*O*. If this letter move him not, his legs cannot: I'll give't him.

M*AR*. You may have very fit occaſion for't; he is now in ſome commerce with my lady, and will by and by depart.

---

[5] *He may have mercy upon* mine;] We may read—*He may have mercy upon* thine, *but my hope is better.* Yet the paſſage may well enough ſtand without alteration. It were much to be wiſhed that Shakſpeare, in this, and ſome other paſſages, had not ventured ſo near profaneneſs. J*OHNSON*.

The preſent reading is more humourous than that ſuggeſted by Johnſon. The man on whoſe ſoul he hopes that God will have mercy, is the one that he ſuppoſes will fall in the combat: but Sir Andrew hopes to eſcape unhurt, and to have no preſent occaſion for that bleſſing.

The ſame idea occurs in *Henry V.* where Mrs. Quickly, giving an account of poor Falſtaff's diſſolution, ſays: " Now I, to comfort him, bid him not think of God; I hoped there was no need to trouble himſelf with any ſuch thoughts yet." M. M*ASON*.

Sir To. Go, fir Andrew; fcout me for him at the corner of the orchard, like a bum-bailiff: fo foon as ever thou feeft him, draw; and, as thou draw'ft, fwear horrible:[5] for it comes to pafs oft, that a terrible oath, with a fwaggering accent fharply twang'd off, gives manhood more approbation than ever proof itfelf would have earn'd him.   Away.

Sir And. Nay, let me alone for fwearing. [*Exit.*

Sir To. Now will not I deliver his letter: for the behaviour of the young gentleman gives him out to be of good capacity and breeding; his employment between his lord and my niece confirms no lefs; therefore this letter, being fo excellently ignorant, will breed no terror in the youth, he will find it comes from a clodpole.   But, fir, I will deliver his challenge by word of mouth; fet upon Ague-cheek a notable report of valour; and drive the gentleman, (as, I know, his youth will aptly receive it,) into a moft hideous opinion of his rage, fkill, fury, and impetuofity.   This will fo fright them both, that they will kill one another by the look, like cockatrices.

Enter OLIVIA *and* VIOLA.

Fab. Here he comes with your niece: give them way, till he take leave, and prefently after him.

Sir To. I will meditate the while upon fome horrid meffage for a challenge.

[*Exeunt* SIR TOBY, FABIAN, *and* MARIA.

Oli. I have faid too much unto a heart of ftone, And laid mine honour too unchary out:[6]

----

⁵ ———*fwear* horrible:] Adjectives are often ufed by our author and his contemporaries, adverbially.   MALONE.

⁶ ———*too unchary* out:]   The old copy reads—*on't.*   The emendation is Mr. Theobald's.   MALONE.

There's fomething in me, that reproves my fault;
But fuch a headftrong potent fault it is,
That it but mocks reproof.

Vio. With the fame haviour that your paffion
bears,
Go on my mafter's griefs.

Oli. Here, wear this jewel for me, 'tis my picture;
Refufe it not, it hath no tongue to vex you:
And, I befeech you, come again to-morrow.
What fhall you afk of me, that I'll deny;
That honour, fav'd, may upon afking give?

Vio. Nothing but this, your true love for my
mafter.

Oli. How with mine honour may I give him that
Which I have given to you?

Vio. I will acquit you.

Oli. Well, come again to-morrow: Fare thee
well;
A fiend, like thee, might bear my foul to hell. [*Exit.*

Re-enter Sir Toby Belch, *and* Fabian.

Sir To. Gentleman, God fave thee.

Vio. And you, fir.

Sir To. That defence thou haft, betake thee to't:
of what nature the wrongs are thou haft done him,
I know not; but thy intercepter, full of defpight,
bloody as the hunter, attends thee at the orchard

---

7 —— *wear this* jewel *for me,*] *Jewel* does not properly
fignify a fingle *gem*, but any precious ornament or fuperfluity.
Johnson.
So, in Markham's *Arcadia*, 1607: " She gave him a very fine
jewel, wherein was fet a moft rich diamond." See alfo Mr. T.
Warton's *Hiftory of Englifh Poetry*, Vol. I. p. 121. Steevens.

8 —— *thy* intercepter,] Thus the old copy. Moft of the
modern editors read—*interpreter*. Steevens.

end: difmount thy tuck, be yare in thy preparation, for thy affailant is quick, fkilful, and deadly.

Vio. You miftake, fir; I am fure, no man hath any quarrel to me; my remembrance is very free and clear from any image of offence done to any man.

Sir To. You'll find it otherwife, I affure you: therefore, if you hold your life at any price, betake you to your guard; for your oppofite hath in him what youth, ftrength, fkill, and wrath, can furnifh man withal.

Vio. I pray you, fir, what is he?

Sir To. He is knight, dubb'd with unhack'd rapier, and on carpet confideration;[9] but he is a

---

9 *He is knight, dubb'd with unhack'd rapier, and on carpet confideration*;] That is, he is no foldier by profeffion, not a knight banneret, dubbed in the field of battle, but, *on carpet confideration*, at a feftivity, or on fome peaceable occafion, when knights receive their dignity kneeling, not on the ground, as in war, but on a *carpet*. This is, I believe, the original of the contemptuous term a *carpet knight*, who was naturally held in fcorn by the men of war.   Johnson.

In *Francis Markham's Booke of Honour*, fo. 1625, p. 71, we have the following account of *Carpet Knights*. "Next unto thefe (i. e. thofe he diftinguifhes by the title of *Dunghill or Truck Knights*) in degree, but not in qualitie, (for thefe are truly for the moft part vertuous and worthie) is that rank of Knights which are called *Carpet Knights*, being men who are by the prince's grace and favour made knights at home and in the time of peace by the impofition or laying on of the king's fword, having by fome fpecial fervice done to the commonwealth, or for fome other particular virtues made known to the foveraigne, as alfo for the dignitie of their births, and in recompence of noble and famous actions done by their anceftors, deferved this great title and dignitie." He then enumerates the feveral orders of men on whom this honour was ufually conferred; and adds——"thofe of the vulgar or common fort are called *Carpet Knights*, becaufe (for the moft part) they receive their honour from the king's hand in the court, and upon *carpets*, and fuch like ornaments belonging to the king's ftate and greatneffe; *which howfoever a curious envie may wreft to an ill fenfe*, yet queftionleffe there is no fhadow of dif-

devil in private brawl: souls and bodies hath he
divorced three; and his incensement at this moment is so implacable, that satisfaction can be none
but by pangs of death and sepulchre: hob, nob,* is
his word; give't, or take't.

grace belonging unto it, for it is an honour as perfect as any
honour whatsoever, and the services and merits for which it is
received, as worthy and well deserving both of the king and
country, as that which hath wounds and scarres for his witnesse."
                                                    REED.

Greene uses the term—*Carpet-knights*, in contempt of those of
whom he is speaking; and, in *The Downfal of Robert Earl of
Huntington*, 1601, it is employed for the same purpose:

"   —— soldiers, come away:
" This *Carpet-knight* sits carping at our scars."

In Barrett's *Alvearie*, 1580: "   —— those which do not exercise
themselves with some honest affaires, but serve abhominable and
filthy idlenesse, are, as we use to call them, *Carpet-knights.*"
B. ante O. Again, among sir John Harrington's Epigrams, B. IV.
Ep. 6. *Of Merit and Demerit:*

" That captaines in those days were not regarded,
" That only *Carpet-knights* were well rewarded."

The old copy reads—unhatch'd *rapier,* STEEVENS.

       —— *with* unhatch'd *rapier.*] The modern editors read—
unback'd. It appears from Cotgrave's Dictionary in v. *bacher,* [to
hack, hew, &c.] that to *hatch* the hilt of a sword, was a technical term.—Perhaps we ought to read—with an *hatch'd* rapier,
i. e. with a rapier, the hilt of which was richly *engraved* and
ornamented. Our author, however, might have used *unhatch'd* in
the sense of *unback'd*; and therefore I have made no change.
                                                    MALONE.

* —— *hob, nob.*] This adverb is corrupted from *hap ne hap*;
as *would ne would, will ne will*; that is, *let it happen or not*; and
signifies at random, at the mercy of chance. See Johnson's
Dictionary. So, in Lilly's *Euphues and his England*, 4to. bl. l.
1580: " Thus Philautus determined, *hab nab,* to send his letters,"
&c. STEEVENS.

Is not this the origin of our *hob nob*, or challenge to drink a
glass of wine at dinner? The phrase occurs in Ben Jonson's *Tale
of a Tub:*

"   —— I put it
" Ev'n to your worship's bitterment, *hab nab.*
" I shall have a chance o'the dice for't, I hope."
                                                    M. MASON.

Vio. I will return again into the houfe, and defire fome conduct of the lady. I am no fighter. I have heard of fome kind of men, that put quarrels purpofely on others, to tafte their valour: belike, this is a man of that quirk.

Sir To. Sir, no; his indignation derives itfelf out of a very competent injury; therefore, get you on, and give him his defire. Back you fhall not to the houfe, unlefs you undertake that with me, which with as much fafety you might anfwer him: therefore, on, or ftrip your fword ftark naked; for meddle³ you muft, that's certain, or forfwear to wear iron about you.

Vio. This is as uncivil, as ftrange. I befeech you, do me this courteous office, as to know of the knight what my offence to him is; it is fomething of my negligence, nothing of my purpofe.

Sir To. I will do fo. Signior Fabian, ftay you by this gentleman till my return. [*Exit* Sir Toby.

Vio. Pray you, fir, do you know of this matter?

Fab. I know, the knight is incenfed againft you, even to a mortal arbitrement; but nothing of the circumftance more.

Vio. I befeech you, what manner of man is he?

Fab. Nothing of that wonderful promife, to read him by his form, as you are like to find him in the proof of his valour. He is, indeed, fir, the moft fkilful, bloody, and fatal oppofite that you could

---

So, in Holinfhed's *Hift. of Ireland:* " The citizens in their rage—fhot *habbe or nabbe,* at *random."* Malone.

³ —— *meddle*—] Is here perhaps ufed in the fame fenfe as the French *mêlée.* Steevens.

Afterwards, Sir Andrew fays—" Pox on't, I'll not *meddle* with him." The vulgar yet fay, " I'll neither *meddle* nor make with it." Malone.

poffibly have found in any part of Illyria: Will you walk towards him? I will make your peace with him, if I can.

Vio. I fhall be much bound to you for't: I am one, that had rather go with fir prieft, than fir knight: I care not who knows fo much of my mettle. [*Exeunt.*

Re-enter SIR TOBY, *with* SIR ANDREW.

Sir To. Why, man, he's a very devil;[4] I have not feen fuch a virago.[5] I had a pafs with him, rapier, fcabbard, and all, and he gives me the ftuck-in,[6]

***

[4] *Why, man, he's a very devil,* &c.] Shakfpeare might have taught a hint for this fcene from Ben Jonfon's *Silent Woman*, which was printed in 1609. The behaviour of. Viola and Ague-cheek appears to have been formed on that of Sir John Daw and Sir Amorous La Foole. STEEVENS.

[5] —— *I have not feen fuch a* virago.] *Virago* cannot be properly ufed here, unlefs we fuppofe fir Toby to mean, I never faw one that had fo much the look of woman with the prowefs of man. JOHNSON.

The old copy reads—*firago*. A *virago* always means a female warrior, or, in low language, a fcold, or turbulent woman. In Heywood's *Golden Age*, 1611, *Jupiter* enters "like a nymph or *virago*;" and fays, "I may pafs for a bona-roba, a rounceval, a *virago*, or a good manly lafs." If Shakfpeare (who knew Viola to be a woman, though fir Toby did not) has made no blunder, Dr. Johnfon has fupplied the only obvious meaning of the word. *Firago* may however be a ludicrous term of Shakfpeare's coinage. STEEVENS.

Why may not the meaning be more fimple, "I have never feen the moft furious woman fo obftreperous and violent as he is?"
MALONE.

[6] —— *the* ftuck——] The *ftuck* is a corrupted abbreviation of the *ftoccata*, an Italian term in fencing. So, in *The Return from Parnaffus*, 1606: "Here's a fellow, Judicio, that carried the deadly *ftock* in his pen." Again, in Marfton's *Mal-content*, 1604: "The clofe *ftock*, O mortal," &c. Again, in *Antonio's Revenge*, 1602:

"I would pafs on him with a mortal *ftock*." STEEVENS.

Again, in *The Merry Wives of Windfor*:

"—— thy *ftock*, thy reverfe, thy montánt. MALONE.

VOL. IV.   K

with such a mortal motion, that it is inevitable; and on the answer, he pays you [6] as surely as your feet hit the ground they step on: They say, he has been fencer to the Sophy.

SIR AND. Pox on't, I'll not meddle with him.

SIR. TO. Ay, but he will not now be pacified: Fabian can scarce hold him yonder.

SIR AND. Plague on't; an I thought he had been valiant, and so cunning in fence, I'd have seen him damn'd ere I'd have challeng'd him. Let him let the matter slip, and I'll give him my horse, grey Capilet.

SIR TO. I'll make the motion: Stand here, make a good show on't; this shall end without the perdition of souls: Marry, I'll ride your horse as well as I ride you.   *[Aside.]*

Re-enter FABIAN *and* VIOLA.

I have his horse *[to FAB.]* to take up the quarrel; I have persuaded him, the youth's a devil.

FAB. He is as horribly conceited of him; [7] and pants, and looks pale, as if a bear were at his heels.

SIR TO. There's no remedy, sir; he will fight with you for his oath sake: marry, he hath better bethought him of his quarrel, and he finds that now scarce to be worth talking of: therefore draw, for the supportance of his vow; he protests, he will not hurt you.

VIO. Pray God defend me! A little thing would make me tell them how much I lack of a man. *[Aside.*

FAB. Give ground, if you see him furious.

---

[6] —— *he* pays *you*—] i. e. hits you, does for you. Thus, Falstaff, in the First Part of *K. Henry IV*: " I followed me close, and, with a thought, seven of the eleven I *pay'd*." STEEVENS.

[7] *He is as* horribly conceited *of him*;] That is, he has as horrid an idea or conception of him. MALONE.

Sir To. Come, fir Andrew, there's no remedy; the gentleman will, for his honour's fake, have one bout with you: he cannot by the duello[s] avoid it: but he has promis'd me, as he is a gentleman and a foldier, he will not hurt you. Come on; to't.

Sir And. Pray God, he keep his oath! [*draws.*

Enter ANTONIO.

Vio. I do affure you, 'tis againft my will. [*draws.*

Ant. Put up your fword;—If this young gentleman

Have done offence, I take the fault on me;
If you offend him, I for him defy you. [*drawing.*

Sir To. You, fir? why, what are you?

Ant. One, fir, that for his love dares yet do more
Than you have heard him brag to you he will.

Sir To. Nay, if you be an undertaker,[9] I am for you. [*draws.*

---

[s] —— *by the* duello—] i. e. by the laws of the *duello*, which, in Shakſpeare's time, were ſettled with the utmoſt nicety.
STEEVENS.

[9] *Nay, if you be an* undertaker,] But why was an *undertaker* ſo offenſive a character? I believe this is *a touch upon the times,* which may help to determine the date of this play. At the meeting of the parliament in 1614, there appears to have been a very general perſuaſion, or jealouſy at leaſt, that the King had been induced to call a parliament at that time, by certain perſons, who *had undertaken,* through their influence in the Houſe of Commons, to carry things according to his Majeſty's wiſhes. Theſe perſons were immediately ſtigmatized with the invidious name of *undertakers*; and the idea was ſo unpopular, that the King thought it neceſſary, in two ſet ſpeeches, to deny poſitively (how truly is another queſtion) that there had been any ſuch *undertaking. Parl. Hiſt.* Vol. V. p. 277, and 286. Sir Francis Bacon alſo (then attorney-general) made an artful, apologetical ſpeech in the Houſe of Commons upon the ſame ſubject; *when the houſe* (according to the title of the ſpeech) *was in great heat, and much troubled about the undertakers.* Bacon's Works, Vol. II. p. 236, 4to. edit.
TYRWHITT.

K 2

Enter two Officers.

Fab. O good fir Toby, hold; here come the officers.

Sir To. I'll be with you anon.   [*To* Antonio.

Vio. Pray, fir, put your fword up, if you pleafe.
[*To* Sir Andrew.

Sir And. Marry, will I, fir ;—and, for that I promis'd you, I'll be as good as my word : He will bear you eafily, and reins well.

1 *Off.* This is the man; do thy office.

2 *Off.* Antonio, I arreft thee at the fuit
Of count Orfino.

Ant.   You do miftake me, fir.

1 *Off.* No, fir, no jot; I know your favour well,
Though now you have no fea-cap on your head.—
Take him away; he knows, I know him well.

Ant. I muft obey.—This comes with feeking you;
But there's no remedy; I fhall anfwer it.
What will you do? Now my neceffity
Makes me to afk you for my purfe : It grieves me
Much more, for what I cannot do for you,
Than what befalls myfelf.   You ftand amaz'd;
But be of comfort.

2 *Off.* Come, fir, away.

Ant. I muft entreat of you fome of that money.

Vio. What money, fir?
For the fair kindnefs you have fhow'd me here,
And, part, being prompted by your prefent trouble,
Out of my lean and low ability

Undertakers were perfons employed by the King's purveyors to take up provifions for the royal houfehold, and were no doubt exceedingly odious.   But ftill, I think, the fpeaker intends a quibble ; the fimple meaning of the word being one who undertakes, or takes up the quarrel or bufinefs of another.   Ritson.

I am of Ritson's opinion, that by an undertaker Sir Toby means a man who takes upon himself the quarrel of another. Mr Tyrwhitt's explanation is too learned to be juft, & was probably suggested by his official situation.

M. Mason.

I'll lend you fomething: my having is not much;
I'll make divifion of my prefent with you:
Hold, there is half my coffer.

   Ant.   Will you deny me now?
Is't poffible, that my deferts to you
Can lack perfuafion? Do not tempt my mifery,
Left that it make me fo unfound a man,
As to upbraid you with thofe kindneffes
That I have done for you.

   Vio.   I know of none;
Nor know I you by voice, or any feature:
I hate ingratitude more in a man,
Than lying, vainnefs, babbling, drunkennefs,
Or any taint of vice, whofe ftrong corruption
Inhabits our frail blood.

   Ant.   O heavens themfelves!

   2 *Off.* Come, fir, I pray you, go.

   Ant. Let me fpeak a little. This youth that you
        fee here,
I fnatch'd one half out of the jaws of death;
Reliev'd him with fuch fanctity of love,——
And to his image, which, methought, did promife
Moft venerable worth, did I devotion.

   1 *Off.* What's that to us? The time goes by;
        away.

   Ant. But, O, how vile an idol proves this god!——
Thou haft, Sebaftian, done good feature fhame.——
In nature there's no blemifh, but the mind;
None can be call'd deform'd, but the unkind:
Virtue is beauty; but the beauteous-evil
Are empty trunks, o'erflourifh'd by the devil.[a]

---

  [a] —— *o'erflourifh'd by the devil.*] In the time of Shakfpeare,
trunks, which are now depofited in lumber-rooms, or other obfcure
places, were part of the furniture of apartments in which com-

1 Off. The man grows mad; away with him.
Come, come, fir.

Ant. Lead me on. [*Exeunt* Officers, *with* ANTONIO.

Vio. Methinks, his words do from such paffion fly,
That he believes himfelf; fo do not I.[3]
Prove true, imagination, O, prove true,
That I, dear brother, be now ta'en for you!

Sir To. Come hither, knight; come hither, Fabian; we'll whifper o'er a couplet or two of moft
fage faws.

Vio. He nam'd Sebaftian; I my brother know
Yet living in my glafs;[4] even fuch, and fo,
In favour was my brother; and he went
Still in this fafhion, colour, ornament,
For him I imitate: O, if it prove,
Tempefts are kind, and falt waves frefh in love!
                           [*Exit.*

Sir To. A very difhoneft paltry boy, and more a
coward than a hare: his difhonefty appears, in leaving his friend here in neceffity, and denying him;
and for his cowardfhip, afk Fabian.

pany was received. I have feen more than one of thefe, as old
as the time of our poet. They were richly ornamented on the
tops and fides with fcroll-work, emblematical devices, &c. and
were elevated on feet. Shakfpeare has the fame expreffion in
Meafure for Meafure :
        " ———— your title to him
        " Doth *flourifh* the deceit ————."   STEEVENS.
   Again, in his 60th *Sonnet :*
        " Time doth transfix the *flourifh* fet on youth."   MALONE.

[3] ———— *fo do not I.*] This, I believe, means, I do not yet believe myfelf, when, from this accident, I gather hope of my
brother's life.   JOHNSON.

[4] ———— *I my brother* know
   Yet living in my glafs;] I fuppofe Viola means—*As often as
I behold myfelf in my glafs, I think I fee my brother alive*; i. e.
I *acknowledge* that his refemblance *furvives* in the reflection of my
own figure.   STEEVENS.
     7

Fab. A coward, a moſt devout coward, religious in it.

Sir And. 'Slid, I'll after him again, and beat him.

Sir To. Do, cuff him ſoundly, but never draw thy ſword.

Sir And. An I do not,— [*Exit.*

Fab. Come, let's ſee the event.

Sir To. I dare lay any money, 'twill be nothing yet. [*Exeunt.*

ACT IV.   SCENE I.

The Street before Olivia's *houſe.*

Enter Sebastian *and* Clown.

Clo. Will you make me believe, that I am not ſent for you?

Seb. Go to, go to, thou art a fooliſh fellow; Let me be clear of thee.

Clo. Well held out, i'faith! No, I do not know you; nor I am not ſent to you by my lady, to bid you come ſpeak with her; nor your name is not maſter Ceſario; nor this is not my noſe neither.—— Nothing, that is ſo, is ſo.

Seb. I pr'ythee, vent thy folly ſomewhere elſe; Thou know'ſt not me.

Clo. Vent my folly! He has heard that word of ſome great man, and now applies it to a fool.⁵ Vent

---

⁵ *Vent my folly! He has heard that word of ſome great man, &c.*] This affected word ſeems to have been in uſe in Shakſpeare's time. In *Melvil's Memoirs,* p. 198, we have "My Lord Lindſay *vented himſelf* that he was one of the number," &c. Reed.

my folly! I am afraid this great lubber,[6] the world,
will prove a cockney.[7]—I pr'ythee now, ungird thy
strangenefs, and tell me what I fhall vent to my lady;
Shall I vent to her, that thou art coming?

Seb. I pr'ythee, foolifh Greek,[8] depart from me;
There's money for thee; if you tarry longer,
I fhall give worfe payment.

Clo. By my troth, thou haft an open hand:——
Thefe wife men, that give fools money, get themfelves a good report after fourteen years' purchafe.[9]

---

[6] —— *I am afraid this great lubber*——] That is, affectation
and foppery will overfpread the world. JOHNSON.

[7] —— *prove a* cockney.] So, in *A Knight's Conjuring*, by
Decker: " —— 'tis not their fault, but our mothers', our
cockering mothers, who for their labour make us to be called
Cockneys," &c. STEEVENS.

[8] *I pr'ythee, foolifh* Greek,] Greek, was as much as to fay bawd
or pander. He underftood the Clown to be acting in that office.
A bawdy-houfe was called Corinth, and the frequenters of it
Corinthians, which words occur frequently in Shakfpeare, efpecially in *Timon of Athens*, and *Henry IV*. Yet the Oxford editor
alters it to *Geck*. WARBURTON.

Can our author have alluded to St. Paul's epiftle to the Romans,
c. i. v. 23?
" —— to the *Greeks foolifhnefs*." STEEVENS.

[9] —— *get themfelves a good report after fourteen years' purchafe*.]
This feems to carry a piece of fatire upon *monopolies*, the crying
grievance of that time. The grants generally were for fourteen
years; and the petitions being referred to a committee, it was
fufpected that money gained favourable reports from thence.
WARBURTON.

Perhaps *fourteen years' purchafe* was, in Shakfpeare's time, the
higheft price for land. Lord Bacon's *Effay on Ufury* mentions
fixteen years purchafe. " I will not give more than according to
fifteen years purchafe, faid a dying ufurer to a clergyman, who advifed him to ftudy for a purchafe of the kingdom of heaven."
TOLLET.

Mr. Heath thinks the meaning is, " —— purchafe a good report
[or character] at a very extravagant price." MALONE.

Dr. Warburton's conjecture that there is here a reference to

Enter SIR TOBY, SIR ANDREW, *and* FABIAN.

Sir And. Now, fir, have I met you again? there's for you.   [*Striking* SEBASTIAN.

Seb. Why, there's for thee, and there, and there: Are all the people mad?   [*Beating* SIR ANDREW.

Sir To. Hold, fir, or I'll throw your dagger o'er the houfe.

Clo. This will I tell my lady ftraight: I would not be in fome of your coats for two-pence.
                                [*Exit* Clown.

Sir To. Come on, fir; hold. [*Holding* SEBASTIAN.

Sir And. Nay, let him alone, I'll go another way to work with him; I'll have an action of battery againft him, if there be any law in Illyria: though I ftruck him firft, yet it's no matter for that.

Seb. Let go thy hand.

Sir To. Come, fir, I will not let you go. Come, my young foldier, put up your iron: you are well flefh'd; come on.

Seb. I will be free from thee.   What wouldft
                thou now?
If thou dar'ft tempt me further, draw thy fword.
                                [*draws.*

Sir To. What, what? Nay, then I muft have an ounce or two of this malapert blood from you.
                                [*draws.*

---

monopolies, is, I believe, unfounded.   Mr. Tollet and Mr. Heath are probably right.   Sir Jofiah Child, in his Difcourfe on Trade, fays, "— *certainly* anno 1621, the current price of lands in England was *twelve* years purchafe; and fo I have been affured by many ancient men whom I have queftioned particularly as to this matter; and I find it fo by purchafes made about that time by my own relations and acquaintance."   Sir Thomas Culpepper, fenior, who wrote in 1621, affirms, " that land was then at *twelve* years pur-chafe."   REED.

Enter OLIVIA.

Oli. Hold, Toby; on thy life, I charge thee, hold.

Sir To. Madam?

Oli. Will it be ever thus? Ungracious wretch,
Fit for the mountains, and the barbarous caves,
Where manners ne'er were preach'd! out of my sight!
Be not offended, dear Cesario :———
Rudesby, be gone!—I pr'ythee, gentle friend,

[*Exeunt* Sir Toby, Sir Andrew, *and* Fabian.

Let thy fair wisdom, not thy passion, sway
In this uncivil and unjust extent²
Against thy peace.   Go with me to my house;
And hear thou there how many fruitless pranks
This ruffian hath botch'd up,³ that thou thereby
May'st smile at this: thou shalt not choose but go;
Do not deny: Beshrew his soul for me,
He started one poor heart of mine in thee.⁴

Seb. What relish is in this?⁵ how runs the stream?
Or I am mad, or else this is a dream :——

² *In this uncivil and unjust* extent—] *Extent* is, in law, a writ
of execution, whereby goods are seized for the King.   It is therefore taken here for *violence* in general.   Johnson.

³ *This ruffian hath* botch'd up,] A coarse expression for *made up,*
as a bad tailor is called a *botcher,* and to botch is to make clumsily.
Johnson.

Dr. Johnson is certainly right.   A similar expression occurs in
Antony and Cleopatra :
      "   ——— if you'll *patch* a quarrel,
      "   As matter whole you've not to make it with."
Again, in *King Henry V :*
      "   Do *botch* and bungle up damnation."   Steevens.

⁴ *He started one poor* heart *of mine in thee.*] I know not whether
here be not an ambiguity intended between *heart* and *hart.*   The
sense however is easy enough.   *He that offends thee, attacks one of
my hearts*; or, as the ancients expressed it, *half my heart.* Johnson.

The equivoque suggested by Dr. Johnson was, I have no doubt,
intended.   *Heart* in our author's time was frequently written *hart*;
and Shakspeare delights in playing on these words.   Malone.

⁵ *What relish is in this?*] How does this taste?   What judgement
am I to make of it?   Johnson.

Let fancy ftill my fenfe in Lethe fteep;
If it be thus to dream, ftill let me fleep!

OLI. Nay, come, I pr'ythee: 'Would, thou'dft
be rul'd by me!

SEB. Madam, I will.

OLI. O, fay fo, and fo be!
[*Exeunt.*

SCENE II.

A room in Olivia's *houfe.*

Enter MARIA *and* Clown.

MAR. Nay, I pr'ythee, put on this gown, and
this beard; make him believe, thou art fir Topas[6]
the curate; do it quickly: I'll call fir Toby the
whilft. [*Exit* MARIA.

CLO. Well, I'll put it on, and I will diffemble
myfelf[7] in't; and I would I were the firft that ever
diffembled in fuch a gown. I am not ~~tall~~ enough *fat*
to become the function well;[8] nor lean enough to
be thought a good ftudent: but to be faid, an honeft
man, and a good houfekeeper, goes as fairly, as to

---

[6] —— *fir Topas* —] The name of *fir Topas* is taken from
Chaucer. STEEVENS.

[7] —— *I will* diffemble *myfelf* —] i. e. difguife myfelf.
MALONE.
Shakfpeare has here ftumbled on a Latinifm: Thus Ovid,
fpeaking of Achilles:
" Vefte virum longa *diffimulatus* erat. STEEVENS.

[8] *I am not* ~~tall~~ *enough to become the function well;*] This cant
be right. The word wanted fhould be part of the defcript: vi:
of *a careful man.* I fhould have no objection to read—*pale.*
TYRWHITT

Not tall enough, perhaps means *not of fufficient height to overlook a*
pulpit. STEEVENS.

Dr. Farmer would read *fat* inftead of *tall,* the former of
thefe epithets, in his opinion, being referable to the following words—*a good houfekeeper.* STEEVENS.

say, a careful man, and a great scholar.[8] The competitors enter.[9]

Enter SIR TOBY BELCH, *and* MARIA.

SIR TO. Jove bless thee, master parson.

CLO. *Bonos dies*, sir Toby: for as the old hermit of Prague, that never saw pen and ink, very wittily said to a niece of king Gorboduc, *That, that is, is:*[2] so I, being master parson, am master parson: For what is that, but that and is, but is?

SIR TO. To him, sir Topas.

CLO. What, hoa, I say,—Peace in this prison!

SIR TO. The knave counterfeits well; a good knave.

MAL. [*in an inner chamber.*] Who calls there?

CLO. Sir Topas, the curate, who comes to visit Malvolio the lunatick.

MAL. Sir Topas, sir Topas, good sir Topas, go to my lady.

CLO. Out, hyperbolical fiend! how vexest thou this man? talkest thou nothing but of ladies?

SIR TO. Well said, master parson.

---

[8] —— *as to say, a careful* man, *and a great scholar.*] This refers to what went before: *I am not tall enough to become the function well, nor lean enough to be thought a good student:* it is plain then Shakspeare wrote:—*as to say a* graceful *man,* i. e. comely. To this the Oxford editor says, *recte.* WARBURTON.

A *careful* man, I believe, means a man who has such a regard for his character, as to intitle him to ordination. STEEVENS.

[9] *The* competitors enter.] That is, the confederates or associates. The word *competitor* is used in the same sense in *Richard III.* and in the *Two Gentlemen of Verona.* M. MASON.

[2] —— *very wittily said—That, that is, is:*] This is a very humorous banter of the rules established in the schools, that all reasonings are *ex præcognitis & præconcessis,* which lay the foundation of every science in these maxims, *whatsoever is, is; and it is impossible for the same thing to be and not to be;* with much trifling of the like kind. WARBURTON.

Mal. Sir Topas, never was man thus wrong'd: good fir Topas, do not think I am mad; they have laid me here in hideous darkneſs.

Clo. Fye, thou diſhoneſt Sathan! I call thee by the moſt modeſt terms; for I am one of thoſe gentle ones, that will uſe the devil himſelf with courteſy. Say'ſt thou, that houſe³ is dark?

Mal. As hell, ſir Topas.

Clo. Why, it hath bay windows⁴ tranſparent as barricadoes, and the clear ſtones⁵ towards the ſouth-north are as luſtrous as ebony; and yet complaineſt thou of obſtruction?

Mal. I am not mad, ſir Topas; I ſay to you, this houſe is dark.

³ —— *that* houſe—] That manſion, in which you are now confined. The clown gives this pompous appellation to the ſmall room in which Malvolio, we may ſuppoſe, was confined, to exaſperate him. The word *it* in the clown's next ſpeech plainly means Malvolio's chamber, and confirms this interpretation. MALONE.

⁴ —— *it hath* bay-windows—] A *bay-window* is the ſame as a *bow-window*; a window *in a receſs*, or bay. See *A. Wood's Life,* publiſhed by T. Hearne, 1730, p. 548 and 553. The following inſtances may likewiſe ſupport the ſuppoſition:

Cynthia's Revels, by Ben Jonſon, 1600:

"—— retired myſelf into a *bay-window*," &c.

Again, in Stow's *Chronicle* of King Henry IV:

" As Tho. Montague reſted him at a *bay-window,* a gun was level'd," &c.

Again, in Middleton's *Women beware Women:*

" 'Tis a ſweet recreation for a gentlewoman

" To ſtand in a *bay-window,* and ſee gallants."

Chaucer, in *The Aſſemblie of Ladies,* mentions *bay-windows.* Again, in *King Henry the Sixth's Directions for building the Hall at King's College, Cambridge:*—" on every ſide thereof a *baie-window.*" STEEVENS.

See Minſheu's DICT. in v. " A *bay-window,*—becauſe it is builded in manner of a baie or rode for ſhippes, that is, round. L. *Cava feneſtra.* G. Une feneſtre ſort anthors de la maiſon." MALONE.

⁵ —— *the clear* ſtones—] The old copy has—*ſtores.* The emendation was made by the editor of the ſecond folio. MALONE.

And yet, ſays Mr. Malone, the ſecond folio is not worth three ſhillings. STEEVENS.

Clo. Madman, thou erreft: I fay, there is no darknefs, but ignorance; in which thou art more puzzled, than the Egyptians in their fog.

Mal. I fay, this houfe is as dark as ignorance, though ignorance were as dark as hell; and I fay, there was never man thus abufed: I am no more mad than you are; make the trial of it in any conftant queftion.[6]

Clo. What is the opinion of Pythagoras, concerning wild-fowl?

Mal. That the foul of our grandam might haply inhabit a bird.

Clo. What think'ft thou of his opinion?

Mal. I think nobly of the foul, and no way approve his opinion.

Clo. Fare thee well: Remain thou ftill in darknefs: thou fhalt hold the opinion of Pythagoras, ere I will allow of thy wits; and fear to kill a woodcock,[7] left thou difpoffefs the foul of thy grandam. Fare thee well.

Mal. Sir Topas, fir Topas,—

Sir To. My moft exquifite fir Topas!

Clo. Nay, I am for all waters.[8]

---

[6] —— *conftant queftion.*] A fettled, a determinate, a regular queftion. JOHNSON.

Rather, in any regular *converfation*, for fo generally Shakfpeare ufes the word *queftion.* MALONE.

[7] —— *to kill a* woodcock,] The Clown mentions a woodcock particularly, becaufe that bird was fuppofed to have very little brains, and therefore was a proper anceftor for a man out of his wits. MALONE.

[8] *Nay, I am for all waters.*] A phrafe taken from the aftor's ability of making the audience cry either with mirth or grief. WARBURTON.

I rather think this expreffion borrowed from fportfmen, and relating to the qualifications of a complete fpaniel. JOHNSON.

Mar. Thou might'ft have done this without thy beard, and gown; he fees thee not.

Sir To. To him in thine own voice, and bring me word how thou find'ft him: I would, we were well rid of this knavery. If he may be conveniently deliver'd, I would he were; for I am now fo far in offence with my niece, that I cannot purfue with any fafety this fport to the upfhot. Come by and by to my chamber.

[*Exeunt* Sir Toby *and* Maria.

Clo. *Hey Robin, jolly Robin,*[9]
 Tell me how thy lady does. [*Singing.*

A cloak for all kinds of knavery; taken from the Italian pro-verb, *Tu hai mantillo da ogni acqua.* SMITH.

Nay, I am for all waters.] I can turn my hand to any thing; I can affume any character I pleafe; like a fifh, I can fwim equally well in all waters. Montaigne, fpeaking of Ariftotle, fays, that "he hath *an ear in every water,* and meddleth with all things." Florio's tranflation, 1603. In Florio's *Second Fruites,* 1591, I find an expreffion more nearly refembling that of the text: "*I am a knight for all faddles.*" The equivoque fuggefted in the following note may, however, have been alfo in our author's thoughts. MALONE.

The word *water,* as ufed by jewellers, denotes the colour and the luftre of diamonds, and from thence is applied, though with lefs propriety, to the colour and hue of other precious ftones. I think that Shakfpeare, in this place, alludes to this fenfe of the word *water,* not to thofe adopted either by Johnfon or Warburton. The Clown is complimented by fir Toby, for perfonating fir Topas fo exquifitely; to which he replies, that he can put on all colours, alluding to the word *Topaz,* which is the name of a jewel, and was alfo that of the Curate. M. MASON.

Mr. Henley has adopted the fame idea; and adds,—that "the Clown in his reply plays upon the name of *Topas,* and intimates that he could fuftain as well the character of any other perfon, let him be called by what *gem* he might." STEEVENS.

9 *Hey Robin, jolly Robin,*] This fong fhould certainly begin:
 " Hey, jolly Robin, tell to me
 " How does thy lady do?—
 " My lady is unkind, perdy.—
 " Alas, why is fhe fo? FARMER.
This fong feems to be alluded to in the following paffage of

MAL. Fool,—

CLO. My lady is unkind, perdy.

MAL. Fool,—

CLO. Alas, why is she so?

MAL. Fool, I say ;—

CLO. She loves another——Who calls, ha?

MAL. Good fool, as ever thou wilt deserve well at my hand, help me to a candle, and pen, ink, and paper; as I am a gentleman, I will live to be thankful to thee for't.

CLO. Master Malvolio!

MAL. Ay, good fool.

CLO. Alas, sir, how fell you besides your five wits?⁹

MAL. Fool, there was never man so notoriously abused: I am as well in my wits, fool, as thou art.

CLO. But as well? then you are mad, indeed, if you be no better in your wits than a fool.

MAL. They have here property'd me;² keep me in darkness, send ministers to me, asses, and do all they can to face me out of my wits.

The Merchandises of Popish Priests, 4to. 1629, Sign. F. 2.—— "there is no one so lively and jolly as St. Mathurine.   I can best describe you this arch finger, by such common phrase as we use of him whom we see very lively and pleasantly disposed, we say this, *His head is full of jolly Robbins.*"   REED.

9 ——*your* five wits?] Thus the *five senses* were anciently called.   So, in *King Lear*, Edgar says :
      " Bless thy *five wits !* Tom's a cold."
Again, in the old morality of *Every Man* : " And remember, beaute, *fyve wittes*, strength, and dyscrecyon."   STEEVENS.

'The *Wits*, Dr. Johnson some where observes, were reckoned *five* in analogy to the five senses.   From Stephen Hawes's poem called *Graunde Amoure*, ch. xxiv. edit. 1554, it appears that the *five wits* were—" common wit, imagination, fantasy, estimation, and memory."   *Wit* in our author's time was the general term for the intellectual power.   MALONE.

² ——*property'd me* ;] They have taken possession of me, as of a man unable to look to himself.   JOHNSON.

Clo. Advife you what you fay; the minifter is here.—Malvolio, Malvolio, thy wits the heavens reftore! endeavour thyfelf to fleep, and leave thy vain bibble babble.

Mal. Sir Topas,——

Clo. Maintain no words with him,³ good fellow.—Who, I, fir? not I, fir. God b'w'you, good fir Topas.—Marry, amen.—I will, fir, I will.

Mal. Fool, fool, fool, I fay,——

Clo. Alas, fir, be patient. What fay you, fir? I am fhent⁴ for fpeaking to you.

Mal. Good fool, help me to fome light, and fome paper; I tell thee, I am as well in my wits, as any man in Illyria.

Clo. Well-a-day,—that you were, fir!

Mal. By this hand, I am: Good fool, fome ink, paper, and light, and convey what I will fet down to my lady; it fhall advantage thee more than ever the bearing of letter did.

Clo. I will help you to't. But tell me true, are you not mad indeed? or do you but counterfeit?⁵

---

³ *Maintain no words with him,*] Here the Clown in the dark acts two perfons, and counterfeits, by variation of voice, a dialogue between himfelf and fir Topas.—*I will, fir, I will,* is fpoken after a paufe, as if, in the mean time, fir Topas had whifpered. JOHNSON.

⁴ ——*I am* fhent, *&c.*] i. e. *fcolded, reproved.* So, in *Afcham's Report* and *Difcourfe:* "A wonderfull follie in a great man himfelf, and fome piece of miferie in a whole commonwealth, where fooles chiefly and flatterers may fpeake freely what they will; and wife men, and good men, fhall commonly be *fhent* if they fpeak what they fhould." See alfo note on *Hamlet,* Act III. fc. ii. REED.

⁵ ——*tell me true, are you not mad indeed? or do you but counterfeit?*] If he was not mad, what did he counterfeit by declaring that he was not mad? The fool, who meant to infult him, I think,

Mal. Believe me, I am not; I tell thee true.

Clo. Nay, I'll ne'er believe a madman, till I fee his brains. I will fetch you light, and paper, and ink.

Mal. Fool, I'll requite it in the higheft degree: I pr'ythee, be gone.

Clo.
    I am gone, fir,
    And anon, fir,
   I'll be with you again,
   In a trice,
    Like to the old vice,[6]
   Your need to fuftain;

afks, *are you mad, or do you but counterfeit?* That is, *you look like a madman, you talk like a madman: Is your madnefs real, or have you any fecret defign in it?* This, to a man in poor Malvolio's ftate, was a fevere taunt. JOHNSON.

The meaning of this paffage appears to me to be this. Malvolio had affured the Clown that he was as well in his fenfes as any man in Illyria; and the Clown in reply, afks him this provoking queftion: " Is it true that you are really not mad?" that is, that you are really in your right fenfes, or do you only pretend to be fo? M. MASON.

Dr. Johnfon, in my apprehenfion, misinterprets the words, " —do you but counterfeit?" They furely mean, " do you but counterfeit *madnefs*, or, in other words, " affume the appearance of a madman, though not one." Our author ought, I think, to have written, either, " —are you *mad* indeed, *or do you but* counterfeit?" or elfe, " —are you *not* not mad indeed, *and* do you but counterfeit?" But I do not fufpect any corruption; for the laft I have no doubt was what he *meant*, though he has not expreffed his meaning accurately. He is often carelefs in fuch minute matters. Mr. Mafon's interpretation removes the difficulty; but, confidering the words that immediately precede, is very harfh, and appears to be inadmiffible. MALONE.

[6] *Like to the old* vice,] The *vice* was the fool of the old moralities. Some traces of this character are ftill preferved in puppet-fhows, and by country mummers. JOHNSON.

This character was always acted in a *mafk*; it probably had its name from the old French word *vis*, for which they now ufe *vifage*, though they ftill retain it in *vis à vis*, which is, literally, *face to face.* STEEVENS.

7

Who with dagger of lath,
In his rage and his wrath,
Cries, ah, ha! to the devil:
Like a mad lad,
Pare thy nails, dad,
Adieu, goodman drivel.[7]   [*Exit.*

---

[7] *Adieu, goodman* drivel.] This laft line has neither rhime nor meaning. I cannot but fufpect that the fool tranflates *Malvolio's* name, and fays:

Adieu, goodman mean-evil. JOHNSON.

We have here another old catch; apparently, I think, not of Shakfpeare. I am therefore willing to receive the common reading of the laft line:

Adieu, goodman drivel.

The name of *Malvolio* feems to have been form'd by an accidental tranfpofition in the word, *Malivolo.*

I know not whether a part of the preceding line fhould not be thrown into a queftion, " pare thy nails, dad ?"

In *Henry V.* we again meet with " this roaring devil i'th' old play; every one may *pare his nails* with a wooden dagger."
FARMER.

In the old tranflation of the *Menæchmi*, 1595, Menæchmus fays to Peniculus : " Away, filthie *mad drivell*, away! I will talk no longer with thee." As I cannot fuppofe the author of this ballad defigned that *devil* fhould be the correfponding rhime to *devil*, I read with Dr. Farmer, *drivel.* STEEVENS.

I believe, with Johnfon, that this is an allufion to *Malvolio's* name, but not in his reading, which deftroys the metre. We fhould read—

Adieu, good mean-evil :
that is, *good Malvolio*, literally tranflated. M. MASON.

The laft two lines of this fong have, I think, been mifunderftood. They are not addreffed in the *firft* inftance to Malvolio, but are quoted by the Clown, as the words, *ah, ha!* are, as the ufual addrefs in the old Moralities to the Devil. I do not therefore fufpect any corruption in the words " goodman *Devil.*" We have in *The Merry Wives of Windfor* :—" No *man* means evil but the *devil* ;" and in *Much ado about Nothing*, " God's a good *man.*"

The compound, *good-man*, is again ufed adjectively, and as a word of contempt, in *King Lear* :—" Part (fays Edmund to Kent and the Steward). " With you, (replies Kent,) *good-man boy*, if you pleafe."

SCENE III.

Olivia's *Garden.*

Enter Sebastian.

Seb. This is the air; that is the glorious sun;
This pearl she gave me, I do feel't, and see't:
And though 'tis wonder that enwraps me thus,
Yet 'tis not madness.   Where's Antonio then?
I could not find him at the Elephant:
Yet there he was; and there I found this credit,
That he did range the town to seek me out.[²]

The reason why the Vice exhorts the Devil to pare his nails, is
because the Devil was supposed from choice to keep his nails alway
unpared, and therefore to pare them was an affront.   So, in
Camden's Remaines, 1615:

     " I will follow mine own minde and mine old trade;
     " Who shall let me? *the divel's nailes are unparde.*"
                         Malone.

[²] *Yet there he was; and there I found this* credit,
     That he did range, &c.] i. e. I found it justified, credibly
vouched.   Whether the word *credit* will easily carry this meaning,
I am doubtful.   The expression seems obscure; and though I
have not disturbed the text, I very much suspect that the poet
wrote:

    ——*and there I found this* credent.
He uses the same term again in the very same sense in *The Winter's
Tale:*

     " —— Then 'tis very *credent,*
     " Thou may'st cojoin with something, and thou dost," &c.
                         Theobald.

     Credit, for account, information.   The Oxford editor roundly
alters it to *current;* as he does almost every word that Shakspeare
uses in an anomalous signification.   Warburton.

     Theobald proposes to read *credent,* but *credent* does not signify
justified or vouched; it means probable only, as appears from the
passage he himself has quoted.   Warburton says, that *credit* means
account or information; but as I know no instance of the word's
being used in that acceptation, I believe we should read, *credited*
instead of *credit.*   M. Mason.

His counfel now might do me golden fervice:
For though my foul difputes well with my fenfe,
That this may be fome error, but no madnefs,
Yet doth this accident and flood of fortune
So far exceed all inftance, all difcourfe,[9]
That I am ready to diftruft mine eyes,
And wrangle with my reafon, that perfuades me
To any other truft,[2] but that I am mad,
Or elfe the lady's mad; yet, if 'twere fo,
She could not fway her houfe, command her fol-
        lowers,
Take, and give back, affairs, and their difpatch,
With fuch a fmooth, difcreet, and ftable bearing,
As, I perceive, fhe does: there's fomething in't,
That is deceivable.[3]   But here comes the lady.[4]

Enter OLIVIA, *and a* Prieft.

OLI. Blame not this hafte of mine: If you mean
        well,
Now go with me, and with this holy man,

Credent is creditable, not queftionable.   So, in *Meafure for Meafure,* Angelo fays :
    " For my authority bears a *credent* bulk."   STEEVENS.

Perhaps *credit* is here ufed for *credited.*   So, in the firft fcene of this play, *beat* for *beated;* and in *Hamlet, boift* for *boifted.*
                                                MALONE.

[9] —— *all* inftance, *all* difcourfe,] *Difcourfe,* for reafon.
                                                WARBURTON.

Inftance is *example.* JOHNSON.

[2] *To any other* truft,] To any other belief, or confidence, to any other fixed opinion. JOHNSON.

[3] —— *deceivable.*] Our author licentioufly ufes this word for *deceptious.* MALONE.

[4] *That is deceivable. But here comes the lady.*] The old copy reads:
    " —— *But here the lady comes.*" STEEVENS.

L 3

Into the chantry by :[3] there, before him,
And underneath that confecrated roof,
Plight me the full affurance of your faith;
That my moft jealous and too doubtful foul
May live at peace: He fhall conceal it,
Whiles [4] you are willing it fhall come to note;
What time we will our celebration keep
According to my birth.—What do you fay?

   Seb. I'll follow this good man, and go with you;
And, having fworn truth,[5] ever will be true.

   Oli. Then lead the way, good father;——And
              heavens fo fhine,[6]
That they may fairly note this act of mine! [*Exeunt.*

ACT V.   SCENE I.

The Street before Olivia's *Houfe.*

Enter Clown, *and* Fabian.

Fab. Now, as thou loveft me, let me fee his letter.

---

   [3] *Into the* chantry *by :*] *Chantries* (fays Cowel in his *Law Dictionary*) are ufually little chapels, or particular altars, in fome cathedral or parochial church; and endowed with revenues for the maintenance of one or more priefts, whofe office it is to fing maffes for the fouls of their founders, &c.   STEEVENS.

   [4] *Whiles*——] is *until.* This word is ftill fo ufed in the northern countries. It is, I think, ufed in this fenfe in the preface to the Accidence.   JOHNSON.

   Almoft throughout the old copies of Shakfpeare, *whiles* is given us inftead of *while.* Mr. Rowe, the firft reformer of his fpelling, made the change.   STEEVENS.

   It is ufed in this fenfe in Tarleton's *News out of Purgatorie.* See the novel at the end of *The Merry Wives of Windfor.*   MALONE.

   [5] ——*truth,*] *Truth* is *fidelity.*   JOHNSON.

   [6] ——*heavens fo fhine,* &c.] Alluding perhaps to a fuperftitious fuppofition, the memory of which is ftill preferved in a proverbial faying : " *Happy is the bride upon whom the fun fhines, and bleffed the corpfe upon which the rain falls.*"   STEEVENS.

Clo. Good mafter Fabian, grant me another re-queft.

Fab. Any thing.

Clo. Do not defire to fee this letter.

Fab. That is, to give a dog, and, in recom-pence, defire my dog again.

Enter Duke, Viola, *and Attendants.*

Duke. Belong you to the lady Olivia, friends?

Clo. Ay, fir; we are fome of her trappings.

Duke. I know thee well; How doft thou, my good fellow?

Clo. Truly, fir, the better for my foes, and the worfe for my friends.

Duke. Juft the contrary; the better for thy friends.

Clo. No, fir, the worfe.

Duke. How can that be?

Clo. Marry, fir, they praife me, and make an afs of me; now my foes tell me plainly, I am an afs: fo that by my foes, fir, I profit in the knowledge of myfelf; and by my friends I am abufed: fo that, conclufions to be as kiffes, if your four negatives make your two affirmatives,[7] why, then the worfe for my friends, and the better for my foes.

Duke. Why, this is excellent.

---

[7] —— conclufions *to be as* kiffes, *if your four negatives make your two affirmatives,*] One cannot but wonder, that this paffage fhould have perplexed the commentators. In Marlowe's *Luft's Dominion,* the Queen fays to the Moor:

"—— Come, let's kiffe."

Moor. "Away, away."

Queen. "No, no, fayes, *I*; and *twice away,* fayes *ftay.*" Sir Philip Sidney has enlarged upon this thought in the fixty-third ftanza of his *Aftrophel and Stella.* Farmer.

Clo. By my troth, fir, no; though it pleafe you to be one of my friends.

Duke. Thou fhalt not be the worfe for me; there's gold.

Clo. But that it would be double-dealing, fir, I would you could make it another.

Duke. O, you give me ill counfel.

Clo. Put your grace in your pocket, fir, for this once, and let your flefh and blood obey it.

Duke. Well, I will be fo much a finner to be a double dealer; there's another.

Clo. Primo, fecundo, tertio, is a good play; and the old faying is, the third pays for all: the *triplex,* fir, is a good tripping meafure; or the bells of St. Bennet,[8] fir, may put you in mind; One, two, three.

---

[8] —— or *the bells of St. Bennet, fir, may put you in mind;*] That is, if the other arguments I have ufed are not fufficient, the bells of St. Bennet, &c. MALONE.

We fhould read—" *as* the bells of St. Bennet," &c. inftead of *er.* M. MASON.

When in this play Shakfpeare mentioned the *bed of* Ware, he recollected that the fcene was in Illyria, and added, *in England;* but his fenfe of the fame impropriety could not reftrain him from the bells of St. Bennet. JOHNSON.

Shakfpeare's improprieties and anachronifms are furely venial in comparifon with thofe of contemporary writers. Lodge, in his *True Tragedies of Marius and Sylla,* 1594, has mentioned *the razors of Palermo* and *St. Paul's fteeple,* and has introduced a *Frenchman,* named *Don Pedro,* who, in confideration of receiving *forty crowns,* undertakes to poifon Marius. Stanyhurft, the tranflator of four books of Virgil, in 1582, compares Chorœbus to a *bedlamite,* fays, that old Priam girded on his fword *Morglay;* and makes Dido tell Æneas, that fhe fhould have been contented had fhe been brought to bed even of a *cockney.*

> *Saltem fi qua mibi de te fufcepta fuiffet*
> *Ante fugam foboles——*
> " —— yf yeet foom progenye from me
> " Had crawl'd, by thee father'd, yf a *cockney* dandiprat
> hopthumb." STEEVENS.

Duke. You can fool no more money out of me at this throw: if you will let your lady know, I am here to speak with her, and bring her along with you, it may awake my bounty further.

Clo. Marry, sir, lullaby to your bounty, till I come again. I go, sir; but I would not have you to think, that my desire of having is the sin of co‑vetousness: but, as you say, sir, let your bounty take a nap, I will awake it anon.   [*Exit* Clown.

Enter ANTONIO, *and* Officers.

Vio. Here comes the man, sir, that did rescue me.

Duke. That face of his I do remember well;
Yet, when I saw it last, it was besmear'd
As black as Vulcan, in the smoke of war:
A bawbling vessel was he captain of,
For shallow draught, and bulk, unprizable;
With which such scathful⁹ grapple did he make
With the most noble bottom of our fleet,
That very envy, and the tongue of loss,
Cry'd fame and honour on him.——What's the matter?

1 Off. Orsino, this is that Antonio,
That took the Phœnix, and her fraught, from Candy;
And this is he, that did the Tiger board,
When your young nephew Titus lost his leg:
Here in the streets, desperate of shame, and state,²
In private brabble did we apprehend him.

Vio. He did me kindness, sir; drew on my side;

---

⁹ ———— *scathful* —] i. e. mischievous, destructive. So, in Decker's *If this be not a good Play, the Devil is in it,* 1612:
    " He mickle *scath* hath done me." -
Again, in *The Pinner of Wakefield,* 1599:
    " That offereth *scath* unto the town of Wakefield."
                                    STEEVENS.

² ———— *desperate of shame, and state,*] Unattentive to his cha‑racter or his condition, like a desperate man. JOHNSON.

But, in conclufion, put ftrange fpeech upon me,
I know not what 'twas, but diftraction.

    Duke. Notable pirate! thou falt-water thief!
What foolifh boldnefs brought thee to their mercies,
Whom thou, in terms fo bloody, and fo dear,*
Haft made thine enemies?

    Ant.   Orfino, noble fir,
Be pleas'd that I fhake off thefe names you give me;
Antonio never yet was thief, or pirate,
Though, I confefs, on bafe and ground enough,
Orfino's enemy.   A witchcraft drew me hither:
That moft ingrateful boy there, by your fide,
From the rude fea's enrag'd and foamy mouth
Did I redeem; a wreck paft hope he was:
His life I gave him, and did thereto add
My love, without retention, or reftraint,
All his in dedication: for his fake,
Did I expofe myfelf, pure for his love,
Into the danger of this adverfe town;
Drew to defend him, when he was befet:
Where being apprehended, his falfe cunning,
(Not meaning to partake with me in danger,)
Taught him to face me out of his acquaintance,
And grew a twenty-years-removed thing,
While one would wink; deny'd me mine own purfe,
Which I had recommended to his ufe.
Not half an hour before.

    Vio.   How can this be?

    Duke. When came he to this town?

    Ant. To-day, my lord; and for three months be-
        fore,
(No interim, not a minute's vacancy,)
Both day and night did we keep company.

---

* — *and fo* dear,] *Dear* is *immediate, confequential.* So, in *Hamlet*:
" Would I had met my *deareft* foe in heaven," &c. STEEVENS.

Enter OLIVIA *and Attendants.*

DUKE. Here comes the countefs; now heaven
   walks on earth.———
But for thee, fellow, fellow, thy words are madnefs :
Three months this youth hath tended upon me ;
But more of that anon.———Take him afide.

OLI. What would my lord, but that he may not have,
Wherein Olivia may feem ferviceable ?—
Cefario, you do not keep promife with me.

 VIO. Madam ?

 DUKE. Gracious Olivia,—

 OLI. What do you fay, Cefario ?———Good my
   lord,———

 VIO. My lord would fpeak, my duty hufhes me.

 OLI. If it be aught to the old tune, my lord,.
It is as fat and fulfome[3] to mine ear,
As howling after mufick.

 DUKE.   Still fo cruel ?

 OLI. Still fo conftant, lord.

 DUKE. What ! to perverfenefs ? you uncivil lady,
To whofe ingrate and unaufpicious altars
My foul the faithfull'ft offerings hath breath'd out,
That e'er devotion tender'd.—What fhall I do ?

 OLI. Even what it pleafe my lord, that fhall become him.

 DUKE. Why fhould I not, had I the heart to do it,
Like to the Egyptian thief, at point of death,
Kill what I love;[4] a favage jealoufy,

---

 [3] ——— *as* fat *and* fulfome—] *Fat* means *dull*; fo we fay a *fat-
headed* fellow ; *fat* likewife means *grofs,* and is fometimes ufed for
obfcene. JOHNSON.

 [4] *Why fhould I not, had I the heart to do it,*
  Like to the Egyptian thief, *at point of death,*
  Kill what I love ;] In this *fimile,* a particular ftory is pre-

That fometime favours nobly?——But hear me this:
Since you to non-regardance caft my faith,
And that I partly know the inftrument
That fcrews me from my true place in your favour,
Live you, the marble-breafted tyrant, ftill;
But this your minion, whom, I know, you love,
And whom, by heaven I fwear, I tender dearly,
Him will I tear out of that cruel eye,
Where he fits crowned in his mafter's fpite.——
Come boy, with me; my thoughts are ripe in mif-
　　chief:
I'll facrifice the lamb that I do love,
To fpite a raven's heart within a dove.　　*[Going.*

　　Vio. And I, moft jocund, apt, and willingly,
To do you reft, a thoufand deaths would die.
　　　　　　　　　　　　　　　　[Following.

　　Oli. Where goes Cefario?

　　Vio.　　　　　　　　　　After him I love,
More than I love thefe eyes, more than my life,
More, by all mores, than e'er I fhall love wife:

fuppos'd, which ought to be known to fhow the juftnefs and propriety of the comparifon. It is taken from *Heliodorus's Æthiopics,*
to which our author was indebted for the allufion. This *Egyptian
thief* was Thyamis, who was a native of Memphis, and at the head
of a band of robbers. Theagenes and Chariclea falling into their
hands, Thyamis fell defperately in love with the lady, and would
have married her. Soon after, a ftronger body of robbers coming
down upon Thyamis's party, he was in fuch fears for his miftrefs,
that he had her fhut into a cave with his treafure. It was cuf-
tomary with thofe barbarians, *when they defpaired of their own
fafety, firft to make away with thofe whom they held dear,* and defired
for companions in the next life. Thyamis, therefore, benetted
round with his enemies, raging with love, jealoufy, and anger,
went to his cave; and calling aloud in the Egyptian tongue, fo
foon as he heard himfelf anfwer'd toward the cave's mouth by a
Grecian, making to the perfon by the direction of her voice, he
caught her by the hair with his left hand, and (fuppofing her to
be Chariclea) with his right hand plunged his fword into her
breaft. THEOBALD.

If I do feign, you witneſſes above,
Puniſh my life, for tainting of my love!

OLI. Ah me, deteſted! how am I beguil'd!

VIO. Who does beguile you? who does do you
wrong?

OLI. Haſt thou forgot thyſelf? Is it ſo long?—
Call forth the holy father.   [*Exit an Attendant.*

DUKE.   Come, away. [*To* VIOLA.

OLI. Whither my lord?—Ceſario, huſband, ſtay.

DUKE. Huſband?

OLI.   Ay, huſband; Can he that deny?

DUKE. Her huſband, ſirrah?

VIO.   No, my lord, not I.

OLI. Alas, it is the baſeneſs of thy fear,
That makes thee ſtrangle thy propriety: [5]
Fear not, Ceſario, take thy fortunes up;
Be that thou know'ſt thou art, and then thou art
As great as that thou fear'ſt.—O, welcome, father!

Re-enter Attendant, and Prieſt.

Father, I charge thee, by thy reverence,
Here to unfold (though lately we intended
To keep in darkneſs, what occaſion now
Reveals before 'tis ripe,) what thou doſt know,
Hath newly paſt between this youth and me.

PRIEST. A contract of eternal bond of love, [6]
Confirm'd by mutual joinder of your hands,

---

[5] —— ſtrangle *thy propriety:*] *Suppreſs,* or diſown thy property.
                                        MALONE.

So, in *Macbeth:*
   " And yet dark night *ſtrangles* the travelling lamp." STEEVENS.

[6] *A contract of* eternal bond of love,] So, in *A Midſummer
Night's Dream:*
   " The ſealing day between my love and me,
   " For *everlaſting bond of fellowſhip.*" MALONE.

Attested by the holy close of lips,
Strengthen'd by interchangement of your rings; [6]
And all the ceremony of this compact
Seal'd in my function, by my testimony:
Since when, my watch hath told me, toward my
   grave,
I have travell'd but two hours.

 Duke. O, thou dissembling cub! what wilt thou be,
When time hath sow'd a grizzle on thy case? [7]
Or will not else thy craft so quickly grow,
That thine own trip shall be thine overthrow?
Farewel, and take her; but direct thy feet,
Where thou and I henceforth may never meet.

 Vio. My lord, I do protest,——

 Oli.   O, do not swear;
Hold little faith, though thou hast too much fear.

Enter Sir Andrew Ague-cheek, *with his head broke.*

 Sir And. For the love of God, a surgeon; send
one presently to Sir Toby.

 Oli. What's the matter?

 Sir And. He has broke my head across, and has

---

 [6] —— *interchangement of your rings;*] In our ancient marriage ceremony, the man received as well as gave a ring. This
custom is exemplified by the following circumstance in Thomas
Lupton's *First Booke of Notable Things,* 4°. bl. L. "If a marryed
man bee let or hyndered through inchauntment, sorcery, or witchcraft, from the acte of generation, let him make water through
his maryage ring, and he shall be loosed from the same, and their
doinges shall have no further power in him." Steevens.

 [7] —— *case?*] *Case* is a word used contemptuously for *skin.* We
yet talk of a *fox-case,* meaning the stuffed skin of a fox. Johnson.

 So, in Cary's *Present State of England,* 1626: "Queen Elizabeth
asked a knight named Young, how he liked a company of brave
ladies?——He answered, as I like my silver-haired conies at home;
the *cases* are far better than the bodies." Malone.

*The story perhaps was not unknown
to Burton who, in his Anatomy of Melancholy,
8vo. 1632. p. 460 has the following passage:—
'For generally, as in the rich furred conies,
their cases are far better than their bodies' &c.
Steevens.*

given fir Toby a bloody coxcomb too: for the love of God, your help: I had rather than forty pound, I were at home.

OLI. Who has done this, fir Andrew?

SIR AND. The count's gentleman, one Cefario: we took him for a coward, but he's the very devil incardinate.

DUKE. My gentleman, Cefario?

SIR AND. Od's lifelings, here he is:—You broke my head for nothing; and that that I did, I was fet on to do't by fir Toby.

VIO. Why do you fpeak to me? I never hurt you: You drew your fword upon me, without caufe; But I befpake you fair, and hurt you not.

SIR AND. If a bloody coxcomb be a hurt, you have hurt me; I think, you fet nothing by a bloody coxcomb.

Enter SIR TOBY BELCH, *drunk, led by the* Clown.

Here comes fir Toby halting, you fhall hear more: but if he had not been in drink, he would have tickled you othergates than he did.

DUKE. How now, gentleman? how is't with you?

SIR TO. That's all one; he has hurt me, and there's the end on't.—Sot, did'ft fee Dick furgeon, fot?

CLO. O he's drunk, fir Toby, an hour agone; his eyes were fet at eight i'the morning.

SIR TO. Then he's a rogue. After a paffy-meafure, or a pavin,² I hate a drunken rogue.

---

² *Then he's a rogue. After a* paffy-meafure, *or a* pavin, &c.] The old copy reads—" and a paffy meafures *panyn*." As the *u* in this word is reverfed, the modern editors have been contented to read—" paft-meafure *painim*."

OLI. Away with him: Who hath made this havock with them?

A paffy-meafure pavin may, however, mean a *pavin danced out of
time.* Sir Toby might call the furgeon by this title, becaufe he was
drunk *at a time when he fhould have been fober,* and in a condition
to attend on the wounded knight.

This dance, called the *pavyn,* is mentioned by Beaumont and
Fletcher in *The Mad Lover:*

　　" I'll pipe him fuch a *pavan.*"

And, in *Stephen Goffon's School of Abufe,* containing *a pleafant invective againft Poets, Pipers,* &c. 1579, it is enumerated, as follows,
among other dances:

　" Dumps, *pavins,* galliards, meafures, fancyes, or newe ftreynes."
I do not, at laft, fee how the fenfe will completely quadrate on
the prefent occafion.　Sir W. D'Avenant, in one of his interludes,
mentions " a doleful *pavin.*" In *The Cardinal,* by Shirley, 1652:
" Who then fhall dance the *pavin* with Oforio?"　Again, in *'Tis
pity fhe's a Whore,* by Ford, 1633: " I have feen an afs and a mule
trot the Spanifh *pavin* with a better grace."　Laftly, in *Shadwell's
Virtuofo,* 1676: " A grave *pavin* or almain, at which the black
Tarantula only moved; it danced to it with a kind of grave motion
much like the benchers at the revels.　STEEVENS.

Bailey's Dictionary fays, *pavan* is the loweft fort of inftrumental
mufic; and when this play was written, the *pavin* and the *paffamezzo* might be in vogue only with the vulgar, as with Falftaff and
Doll Tearfheet: and hence fir Toby may mean—he is a rogue, and
a mean low fellow.　TOLLET.

Ben Jonfon alfo mentions the *pavin,* and calls it a Spanifh dance,
Alchemift, p. 97; [Whalley's edition] but it feems to come originally from Padua, and fhould rather be written *pavane,* as a corruption of *paduane.*　A dance of that name (*faltatio paduana*)
occurs in an old writer, quoted by the annotator on *Rabelais,*
B. V. c. 30.

Paffy meafures is undoubtedly a corruption, but I know not how
it fhould be rectified.　TYRWHITT.

The *pavan,* from *pavo* a peacock, is a grave and majeftick dance.
The method of dancing it was anciently by gentlemen dreffed with
a cap and fword, by thofe of the long robe in their gowns, by
princes in their mantles, and by ladies in gowns with long trains,
the motion whereof in the dance, refembled that of a peacock's
tail.　This dance is fuppofed to have been invented by the
Spaniards, and its figure is given with the characters for the ftep,
in the *Orchefographia* of *Thoinet Arbeau.*　Every pavin has its galliard, a lighter kind of air, made out of the former.　The courant,
the jig, and the hornpipe are fufficiently known at this day.

Sir And. I'll help you, fir Toby, becaufe we'll be dreffed together.

Of the *paffamezzo* little is to be faid, except that it was a favourite air in the days of Q. Elizabeth. Ligon, in his Hiftory of Barbadoes, mentions a *paffamezzo* galliard, which in the year 1647, a Padre in that ifland played to him on the lute; the very fame, he fays, with an air of that kind which in Shakfpeare's play of *Henry IV.* was originally played to Sir John Falftaff and Doll Tearfheet, by Sneak, the mufician, there named. This little anecdote Ligon might have by tradition; but his conclufion, that becaufe it was played in a dramatic reprefentation of the hiftory of *Henry IV.* it muft be fo ancient as his time, is very idle and injudicious.——*Paffy-meafure* is therefore undoubtedly a corruption from *paffamezzo.* SIR J. HAWKINS.

With the help of Sir John Hawkins's explanation of *paffy-meafure*, I think I now fee the meaning of this paffage. The fecond folio reads—*after a paffy meafures pavin.*—So that I fhould imagine the following regulation of the whole fpeech would not be far from the truth:

Then he's a rogue. After a paffy-meafure or a *pavin, I hate a drunken rogue,* i. e. *next to a paffy meafure or a pavin,* &c. It is in character, that Sir Toby fhould exprefs a ftrong diflike of *ferious dances,* fuch as the *paffamezzo* and the *pavan* are defcribed to be.
TYRWHITT.

From what has been ftated, I think, it is manifeft that Sir Toby means only by this quaint expreffion, that the furgeon is a rogue, and a *grave folemn coxcomb.* It is one of Shakfpeare's unrivalled excellencies, that his characters are always confiftent. Even in drunkennefs they preferve the traits which diftinguifhed them when fober. Sir Toby, in the firft act of this play, fhewed himfelf well acquainted with the various kinds of the dance. The editor of the fecond folio, who, when he does not underftand any paffage, generally cuts the knot, inftead of untying it, arbitrarily reads—" *after* a paffy-meafures pavyn I hate a drunken rogue." In the fame manner, in the preceding fpeech, not thinking " an hour agone" good Englifh, he reads—" O he's drunk, fir Toby, *above* an hour agone." There is fcarcely a page of that copy in which fimilar interpolations may not be found.
MALONE.

I have followed Mr. Tyrwhitt's regulation, which appears to be well founded on one of the many judicious corrections that ftamp a value on the fecond folio. STEEVENS.

Sir To. Will you help an afs-head, and a coxcomb, and a knave? a thin-faced knave, a gull?[9]

Oli. Get him to bed, and let his hurt be look'd
to.

[*Exeunt* Clown, Sir Toby, *and* Sir Andrew.

Enter Sebastian.

Seb. I am forry, madam, I have hurt your kinf-
man;
But, had it been the brother of my blood,
I muft have done no lefs, with wit, and fafety.
You throw a ftrange regard upon me, and
By that I do perceive it hath offended you;
Pardon me, fweet one, even for the vows
We made each other but fo late ago.

Duke. One face, one voice, one habit, and two
perfons;
A natural perfpective,[2] that is, and is not.

---

[9] —— *an afs-head, and a coxcomb,* &c.]   I believe, Sir Toby
means to apply all thefe epithets either to the furgeon or Sebaftian;
and have pointed the paffage accordingly.   It has been hitherto
printed, " Will you help an afs-head," &c. but why fhould Sir
Toby thus unmercifully-abufe himfelf?   Malone.

As I cannot help thinking that Sir Toby, out of humour with
himfelf, means to difcharge thefe reproaches on the officious Sir
Andrew, who alfo needs the furgeon's *help,* I have left the paffage
as I found it.   Mr. Malone points it thus: " Will you help?—An
afs-head," &c!   Steevens.

[2] *A natural* perfpective,]   A *perfpective* feems to be taken for
fhows exhibited through a glafs with fuch lights as make the pictures appear really protuberant.   The Duke therefore fays, that
nature has here exhibited fuch a fhow, where fhadows feem
realities; where that which *is not* appears like that which is.
                                                        Johnson.

I apprehend this may be explained by a quotation from a duo-
decimo book called *Humane Induftry,* 1661, p. 76 and 77: " It
is a pretty art that in a pleated paper and table furrowed or in-

Seb. Antonio, O my dear Antonio!
How have the hours rack'd and tortur'd me,
Since I have loft thee?

Ant. Sebaftian are you?

Seb.   Fear'ft thou that, Antonio?

Ant. How have you made divifion of yourfelf?—
An apple, cleft in two, is not more twin
Than thefe two creatures.   Which is Sebaftian?

Oli. Moft wonderful!

Seb. Do I ftand there? I never had a brother:
Nor can there be that deity in my nature,
Of here and every where.   I had a fifter,
Whom the blind waves and furges have devour'd:—
Of charity,[3] what kin are you to me?   [*To* Viola.
What countryman? what name? what parentage?

Vio. Of Meffaline: Sebaftian was my father;
Such a Sebaftian was my brother too,

---

dented, men make one picture to reprefent feveral faces——that
being viewed from one place or ftanding, did fhew the head of a
Spaniard, and from another, the head of an afs."——" A picture
of a chancellor of France prefented to the common beholder a
multitude of little faces——but if one did look on it through a
perfpective, there appeared only the fingle pourtraifture of the
chancellor himfelf." Thus that, which is, is not, or in a different pofition appears like another thing. This feems alfo to
explain a paffage in *King Henry V*. Act V. fc. ii: " Yes, my
lord, you fee them *perfpectively*, the cities turn'd into a maid."
                                                        TOLLET.

I believe Shakfpeare meant nothing more by this *natural perfpective*, than a reflection from a glafs or mirror.   M. MASON.

Perfpective certainly means a glafs ufed for optical delufion, or
a glafs generally. In Franck's *Northern Memoirs*, p. 16, Theophilus,
one of the difcourfers, fays—" he that reads his own heart without a *perfpective*, reads all the world." The book was written in
1658.   DOUCE.

[3] *Of charity*,] i. e. out of charity, tell me, &c.   So, in *The
Taming of the Shrew*:
      " Now, let him fpeak; 'tis *charity*, to fhow," &c.
                                                        STEEVENS.

M 2

So went he fuited to his watery tomb:
If fpirits can affume both form and fuit
You come to fright us.

SEB.   A fpirit I am, indeed;
But am in that dimenfion grofsly clad,
Which from the womb I did participate.
Were you a woman, as the reft goes even,
I fhould my tears let fall upon your cheek,
And fay—Thrice welcome, drowned Viola!

VIO. My father had a mole upon his brow.

SEB. And fo had mine.

VIO. And died that day when Viola from her birth
Had number'd thirteen years.

SEB. O, that record is lively in my foul!
He finifhed, indeed, his mortal act,
That day that made my fifter thirteen years.

VIO. If nothing lets to make us happy both,
But this my mafculine ufurp'd attire,
Do not embrace me, till each circumftance
Of place, time, fortune, do cohere, and jump,
That I am Viola: which to confirm,
I'll bring you to a captain in this town,
Where lie my maiden weeds; by whofe gentle help
I was preferv'd, to ferve this noble count:
All the occurrence[2] of my fortune fince
Hath been between this lady, and this lord.

SEB. So comes it, lady, you have been miftook:
                              [*To* OLIVIA.

But nature to her bias drew in that.
You would have been contracted to a maid;
Nor are you therein, by my life, deceiv'd,
You are betroth'd both to a maid and man.

---

[2] —— *occurrence* ——] I believe our author wrote—*occurrents.*
                                        MALONE.

Duke. Be not amaz'd; right noble is his blood.——
If this be fo, as yet the glafs feems true,
I fhall have fhare in this moft happy wreck:
Boy, thou haft faid to me a thoufand times,

[*To* VIOLA.

Thou never fhould'ft love woman like to me.

Vio. And all thofe fayings will I over-fwear;
And all thofe fwearings keep as true in foul,
As doth that orbed continent the fire
That fevers day from night.

Duke. Give me thy hand;
And let me fee thee in thy woman's weeds.

Vio. The captain, that did bring me firft on fhore,
Hath my maid's garments: he, upon fome action,
Is now in durance; at Malvolio's fuit,
A gentleman, and follower of my lady's.

Oli. He fhall enlarge him:——Fetch Malvolio
hither:——
And yet, alas, now I remember me,
They fay, poor gentleman, he's much diftract.

Re-enter Clown, *with a letter.*

A moft extracting frenzy[1] of mine own
From my remembrance clearly banifh'd his.——
How does he, firrah?

---

[1] *A moft extracting frenzy* ——] i. e. a frenzy that drew me away from every thing but its own object. WARBURTON.

So, William de Wyrcefter, fpeaking of King Henry VI. fays "——*fubito cecidit in gravem infirmitatem capitis, ita quod* extractus *à mente videbatur.*" STEEVENS.

I formerly fuppofed that Shakfpeare wrote——*diftracting*; but have fince met with a paffage in *The Hiftorie of Hamblet*, bl. l. 1608, Sig. C 2, that feems to fupport the reading of the old copy: "—— to try if men of great account be *extract* out of their wits." MALONE.

Clo. Truly, madam, he holds Belzebub at the ſtave's end, as well as a man in his caſe may do: he has here writ a letter to you, I ſhould have given it you to-day morning; but as a madman's epiſtles are no goſpels, ſo it ſkills not much, when they are delivered.

Oli. Open it, and read it.

Clo. Look then to be well edified, when the fool delivers the madman.——*By the Lord, madam,*——

Oli. How now! art thou mad?

Clo. No, madam, I do but read madneſs: an your ladyſhip will have it as it ought to be, you muſt allow *vox.*⁴

Oli. Pr'ythee, read i'thy right wits.

Clo. So I do, madonna; but to read his right wits,⁵ is to read thus: therefore perpend, my princeſs, and give ear.

Oli. Read it you, ſirrah. [*To* FABIAN.

---

⁴ —— *you muſt allow* vox.] I am by no means certain that I underſtand this paſſage, which, indeed, the author of *The Reviſal* pronounces to have no meaning. I ſuppoſe the Clown begins reading the letter in ſome fantaſtical manner, on which Olivia aſks him, *if he is mad. No, madam,* ſays he, *I do but barely deliver the ſenſe of this madman's epiſtle; if you would have it read as it ought to be,* that is, with *ſuch a frantic accent and geſture as a madman would read it, you muſt allow* vox, i. e. *you muſt furniſh the reader with a voice,* or, in other words, *read it yourſelf.* But Mr. Malone's explanation, I think, is preferable to mine.

STEEVENS.

The Clown, we may preſume, had begun to read the letter in a very loud tone, and probably with extravagant geſticulation. Being reprimanded by his miſtreſs, he juſtifies himſelf by ſaying, *If you would have it read in character, as ſuch a* mad *epiſtle ought to be read, you muſt permit me to aſſume a* frantick *tone.*

MALONE.

⁵ —— *but to read his right wits,*] To repreſent his preſent ſtate of mind, is to read a madman's letter, as I now do, like a madman. JOHNSON.

F<small>AB</small>. [reads.] *By the Lord, madam, you wrong me, and the world shall know it : though you have put me into darkness, and given your drunken cousin rule over me, yet have I the benefit of my senses as well as your ladyship. I have your own letter that induced me to the semblance I put on ; with the which I doubt not but to do myself much right, or you much shame. Think of me as you please. I leave my duty a little unthought of, and speak out of my injury. The madly-used* Malvolio.

O<small>LI</small>. Did he write this?

C<small>LO</small>. Ay, madam.

D<small>UKE</small>. This favours not much of distraction.

O<small>LI</small>. See him deliver'd, Fabian ; bring him hither.
　　　　　　　　　　　　　　　　[*Exit* F<small>ABIAN</small>.
My lord, so please you, these things further thought
　　　　　　on,
To think me as well a sister as a wife,
One day shall crown the alliance on't, so please
　　　　　　you,[6]
Here at my house, and at my proper cost.

　D<small>UKE</small>. Madam, I am most apt to embrace your
　　　　　　offer.——
Your master quits you ; [*To* V<small>IOLA</small>.] and, for your
　　　　　　service done him,
So much against the mettle of your sex,[7]

---

[6] *One day shall crown the alliance* on't, *so please you,*] The word *on't,* in this place, is mere nonsense. I doubt not the poet wrote :
　　　　—— an't, *so please you.* H<small>EATH</small>.

This is well conjectured ; but *on's* may relate to the double character of sister and wife. J<small>OHNSON</small>.

[7] *So much against the* mettle *of your sex,*] So much against the weak frame and constitution of woman. *Mettle* is used by our author in many other places for *spirit* ; and as *spirit* may be either high or low, mettle seems here to signify natural *timidity*, or *deficiency of spirit.* Shakspeare has taken the same licence in *All's well that ends well:*

So far beneath your soft and tender breeding,
And since you call'd me master for so long,
Here is my hand; you shall from this time be
Your master's mistress.

OLI.   A sister?—you are she.

Re-enter FABIAN, *with* MALVOLIO.

DUKE. Is this the madman?

OLI.   Ay, my lord, this same:
How now, Malvolio?

MAL.   Madam, you have done me wrong,
Notorious wrong.

OLI.   Have I, Malvolio? no.

MAL. Lady, you have.   Pray you, peruse that
              letter:
You must not now deny it is your hand,
Write from it, if you can, in hand, or phrase;
Or say, 'tis not your seal, nor your invention:
You can say none of this: Well, grant it then,
And tell me, in the modesty of honour,
Why you have given me such clear lights of
              favour;
Bade me come smiling, and cross-garter'd to you,
To put on yellow stockings, and to frown
Upon sir Toby, and the lighter⁸ people:
And, acting this in an obedient hope,
Why have you suffer'd me to be imprison'd,
Kept in a dark house, visited by the priest,

" 'Tis only *title* thou disdain'st in her—"
i. e. the *want* of title.   Again, in *King Richard III*:
" The *forfeit*, sovereign, of my servant's life—"
that is, the remission of the forfeit.   MALONE.

• —— *lighter*—] People of less dignity or importance.
                              JOHNSON.

And made the moſt notorious geck,° and gull,
That e'er invention play'd on? tell me why.

   Oli. Alas, Malvolio, this is not my writing,
Though, I confeſs, much like the character:
But, out of queſtion, 'tis Maria's hand.
And now I do bethink me, it was ſhe
Firſt told me, thou waſt mad; then cam'ſt in
       ſmiling,ᵃ
And in ſuch forms which here were preſuppos'dᵇ   \
Upon thee in the letter. Pr'ythee, be content:
This practice hath moſt ſhrewdly paſs'd upon thee;
But, when we know the grounds and authors of it,
Thou ſhalt be both the plaintiff and the judge
Of thine own cauſe.

   Fab.   Good madam, hear me ſpeak;

  ° ——*geck,*] A fool. Johnson.
So, in the viſion at the concluſion of *Cymbeline* :
    " And to become the *geck* and ſcorn
      " Of th' other's villainy."
Again, in *Ane verie excellent and delectabill Treatiſe intitulit*
Philotus, &c. 1603 :
    " Thocht he be auld, my joy, quhat reck,
    " When he is gane give him ane *geck*,
    " And take another be tho neck."
Again :
    " The carle that hecht ſa weill to treat you,
    " I think ſall get ane *geck*." Steevens.

  ᵃ ——*then cam'ſt in ſmiling,*] i. e. then, *that thou* cam'ſt in
ſmiling. Malone.

  I believe the lady means only what ſhe has clearly expreſſed:
" — then thou cameſt in ſmiling;" not *that* ſhe had been informed
of this circumſtance by Maria. Maria's account, in ſhort, was
juſtified by the ſubſequent appearance of Malvolio. Steevens.

  ᵇ ——*here were* preſuppos'd——] *Preſuppos'd,* for impoſed.
                      Warburton.

  Preſuppos'd rather ſeems to mean previouſly pointed out for thy
imitation; or ſuch as it was ſuppoſed thou would'ſt aſſume after
thou hadſt read the letter. The *ſuppoſition* was *previous* to *the act.*
                      Steevens.

And let no quarrel, nor no brawl to come,
Taint the condition of this prefent hour,
Which I have wonder'd at. In hope it fhall not,
Moft freely I confefs, myfelf, and Toby,
Set this device againft Malvolio here,
Upon fome ftubborn and uncourteous parts
We had conceiv'd againft him:[4] Maria writ
The letter, at fir Toby's great importance;[5]
In recompence whereof, he hath married her.
How with a fportful malice it was follow'd,
May rather pluck on laughter than revenge;
If that the injuries be juftly weigh'd,
That have on both fides paft.

OLI. Alas, poor fool![6] how have they baffled
thee?[7]

CLO. Why, *fome are born great, fome atchieve
greatnefs, and fome have greatnefs thrown upon them.
I was one, fir, in this interlude; one fir Topas, fir;
but that's all one:—By the Lord, fool, I am not
mad;—But do you remember?[8] Madam, why laugh*

---

[4] *Upon fome ftubborn and uncourteous parts
We had conceiv'd* againft him:] Surely we fhould rather read
—*conceiv'd* in him. TYRWHITT.

[5] —— *at fir Toby's great* importance;] *Importance* is *importunacy,
importunement.* STEEVENS.

[6] *Alas, poor fool!*] See notes on *King Lear*, Act V. fc. iii.
REED.

[7] —— *how have they* baffled *thee?*] See Mr. Tollet's note on a
paffage in the firft fcene of the firft act of *King Richard II*:
" I am difgrac'd, impeach'd, and *baffled* here."
STEEVENS.

[8] *But do you remember? Madam,*] The old copy points this
paffage erroneoufly:—" But do you remember, madam," &c. I
have followed the regulation propofed in the fubfequent note.
STEEVENS.
As the Clown is fpeaking to Malvolio, and not to Olivia, I
think this paffage fhould be regulated thus—*but do you remember?—
Madam, why laugh you,* &c. TYRWHITT.

*you at fuch a barren rafcal? an you fmile not, he's
gagg'd:* And thus the whirligig of time brings in
his revenges.

MAL. I'll be revenged on the whole pack of you.
　　　　　　　　　　　　　　　　　　　　Exit.

OLI. He hath been moft notorioufly abus'd.

DUKE. Purfue him, and entreat him to a peace:—
He hath not told us of the captain yet;
When that is known, and golden time convents,⁹
A folemn combination fhall be made
Of our dear fouls—Mean time, fweet fifter,
We will not part from hence.—Cefario, come;
For fo you fhall be, while you are a man;
But, when in other habits you are feen,
Orfino's miftrefs, and his fancy's queen.　　*Exeunt.*

S O N G.

*CLO. When that I was and a little tiny boy,*²
　　With hey, ho, the wind and the rain,
A foolifh thing was but a toy,
　　For the rain it raineth every day.

---

⁹ —— *convents*,] Perhaps we fhould read—*confents.* To *convent*,
however, is to *affemble*; and therefore, the count may mean, when
the happy hour *calls us* again *together.* STEEVENS.

—— *convents*,] i. e. fhall ferve, agree, be convenient. DOUCE.

² *When that I was and a little tiny boy,* &c.] Here again we have
an old fong, fcarcely worth correction. 'Gainft *knaves and thieves*
muft evidently be, againft *knave and thief.*—When I was a boy,
my folly and mifchievous actions were little regarded; but when I
came to manhood, men fhut their gates againft me, as a *knave and
a thief.*

Sir Thomas Hanmer rightly reduces the fubfequent words, *beds*
and *heads*, to the fingular number: and a little alteration is ftill
wanting at the beginning of fome of the ftanzas.

Mr. Steevens obferves in a note at the end of *Much ado about
Nothing*, that the play had formerly paffed under the name of

xx —— *and entreat him to a peace*] Thus ʼ
Fletcher's *Two Noble Kinsmen:*
　　" —— Go take her,
" *and fluently perswade her to a peace*"
　　　　　　　　　　　　　　　　　　'Steev

But when I came to man's eftate,
  With hey, ho, the wind and the rain,
'Gainft knave and thief men fhut their gate,
  For the rain it raineth every day.

But when I came, alas! to wive,
  With hey, ho, the wind and the rain,
By fwaggering could I never thrive,
  For the rain it raineth every day.

But when I came unto my bed,
  With hey, ho, the wind and the rain,
With tofs-pots ftill had drunken head,
  For the rain it raineth every day.

A great while ago the world begun,
  With hey, ho, the wind and the rain,
But that's all one, our play is done,
  And we'll ftrive to pleafe you every day.

                                          [Exit.

Benedict and Beatrix. It feems to have been the *court-fafhion* to alter the titles. A very ingenious lady, with whom I have the honour to be acquainted, Mrs. Afkew of Queen's-Square, has a fine copy of the fecond folio edition of Shakfpeare, which formerly belonged to King Charles I. and was a prefent from him to his Mafter of the Revels, Sir Thomas Herbert. Sir Thomas has altered five titles in the lift of the plays, to " *Benedick and Beatrice,—Pyramus and Thifby,—Rofalinde,—Mr. Paroles,* and *Malvolio.* "

It is lamentable to fee how far party and prejudice will carry the wifeft men, even againft their own practice and opinions. Milton, in his Ειχονοχλαςης, cenfures King Charles for reading " one whom (fays he) we well knew was the clofet companion of his folitudes, *William Shakfpeare.* " FARMER.

I have followed the regulations proposed by Sir T. Hanmer and Dr. Farmer; and consequently, instead of knav*es*, thiev*es*, bed*s*, and head*s*, have printed " knave, thief," &c.

Dr. Farmer might have observed, that the alterations of the titles are in his Majesty's own hand-writing, materially differing from Sir Thomas Herbert's, of which the same volume affords more than one specimen. I learn from another manuscript note in it, that *John Lowine* acted *King Henry VIII.* and *John Taylor* the part of *Hamlet*. The book is now in my possession.

To the concluding remark of Dr. Farmer, may be added the following passage from *An Appeal to all rational Men concerning King Charles's Trial*, by John Cooke, 1649: " Had he but studied scripture half so much as *Ben Jonson* or *Shakspeare*, he might have learnt that when Amaziah was settled in the kingdom, he suddenly did justice upon those servants which killed his father Joash," &c. With this quotation I was furnished by Mr. Malone.

A quarto volume of plays attributed to Shakspeare, with the cypher of King Charles II. on the back of it, is preserved in Mr. Garrick's collection.

Though we are well convinced that Shakspeare has written flight ballads for the sake of discriminating characters more strongly, or for other necessary purposes, in the course of his mixed dramas, it is scarce credible, that after he had cleared his stage, he should exhibit his Clown afresh, and with so poor a recommendation as this song, which is utterly unconnected with the subject of the preceding comedy. I do not therefore hesitate to call the nonsensical ditty before us, some buffoon actor's composition, which was accidentally tacked to the Prompter's copy of *Twelfth-Night*, having been casually subjoined to it for the diversion, or at the call, of the lowest order of spectators. In the year 1766, I saw the late Mr. Weston summoned out and obliged to sing *Johnny Pringle and his Pig*, after the performance of Voltaire's *Mahomet*, at the Theatre Royal in Drury-Lane.

STEEVENS.

This play is in the graver part elegant and easy, and in some of the lighter scenes exquisitely humourous. Ague-cheek is drawn with great propriety, but his character is, in a great measure, that of natural fatuity, and is therefore not the proper prey of a satirist. The soliloquy of Malvolio is truly comic; he is betrayed to ridicule merely by his pride. The marriage of Olivia, and the succeeding perplexity, though well enough contrived to divert on the stage, wants credibility, and fails to produce the proper instruction required in the drama, as it exhibits no just picture of life. JOHNSON.

7

MEASURE

FOR

MEASURE.*

* MEASURE FOR MEASURE.] The story is taken from *Cinthio's Novels*, Decad. 8, Novel 5. POPE.

We are sent to Cinthio for the plot of *Measure for Measure*, and Shakspeare's judgment hath been attacked for some deviations from him in the conduct of it, when probably all he knew of the matter was from Madam *Isabella*, in *The Heptameron* of *Whetstone*, Lond. 4to, 1582.——She *reports*, in the fourth dayes Exercise, the rare *Historie of Promos and Cassandra*. A marginal note informs us, that *Whetstone* was the author of the *Comedie* on that subject; which likewise had probably fallen into the hands of Shakspeare.
FARMER.

There is perhaps not one of Shakspeare's plays more darkened than this by the peculiarities of its author, and the unskilfulness of its editors, by distortions of phrase, or negligence of transcription.
JOHNSON.

Dr. Johnson's remark is so just respecting the corruptions of this play, that I shall not attempt much reformation in its metre, which is too often rough, redundant, and irregular. Additions and omissions (however trifling) cannot be made without constant notice of them; and such notices, in the present instance, would so frequently occur, as to become equally tiresome to the commentator and the reader.

Shakspeare took the fable of this play from the *Promos and Cassandra* of George Whetstone, published in 1578. See Theobald's note at the end.

A hint, like a seed, is more or less prolific, according to the qualities of the soil on which it is thrown. This story, which in the hands of Whetstone produced little more than barren insipidity, under the culture of Shakspeare became fertile of entertainment. The curious reader will find that the old play of *Promos and Cassandra* exhibits an almost complete embryo of *Measure for Measure*; yet the hints on which it is formed are so slight, that it is nearly as impossible to detect them, as it is to point out in the acorn the future ramifications of the oak.

Whetstone opens his play thus:

ACT I. Scene i.

" Promos, Mayor, Shirife, Sworde bearer: one with a bunche
of keyes: Phallax, *Promos Man.*
" You officers which now in *Julio* staye,
" Know you your leadge, the King of *Hungarie*,
" Sent me to *Promos*, to joyne with you in sway:
" That styll we may to *Justice* have an eye.

    " And now to fhow my rule and power at lardge,
    " Attentivelie his letters patents heare:
    " *Phallax*, reade out my Soueraignes chardge.
Phal. " As you commaunde I wyll : give heedeful eare.
       Phallax *readeth the Kinges Letters Pattents, which*
         muft be fayre written in parchment, with fome
         great counterfeat zeale.
Pro. " Loe, here you fee what is our Soveraignes wyl,
    " Loe, heare his wiffr, that right, not might, beare fwaye :
    " Loe, heare his care, to weede from good the yll,
    " To fcoorge the wights, good lawes that difobay.
    " Such zeale he beares, unto the common weale,
    " (How fo he byds, the ignoraunt to fave)
    " As he commaundes, the lewde doo rigor feele, &c. &c. &c.

* * *

Pro. " Both fwoorde and keies, unto my princes ufe,
    " I do receyve, and gladlie take my chardge.
    " It refteth now, for to reforme abufe,
    " We poynt a tyme of councell more at lardge,
    " To treate of which, a whyle we wyll depart.
Al. fpeake. " To worke your wyll, we yeelde a willing hart.
                       Exeunt."

    The reader will find the argument of G. Whetftone's *Promos
and Caffandra*, at the end of this play. It is too bulky to be
inferted here. See likewife the piece itfelf among *Six old Plays
on which Shakfpeare founded*, &c. publifhed by S. Leacroft,
Charing-crofs. STEEVENS.

    Meafure for Meafure was, I believe, written in 1603. See *An
Attempt to afcertain the Order of Shakfpeare's Plays*, Vol. I.
                             MALONE.

PERSONS reprefented.

Vincentio, *duke of* Vienna.
Angelo, *lord deputy in the duke's abfence.*
Efcalus, *an ancient lord, joined with* Angelo *in the deputation.*
Claudio, *a young gentleman.*
Lucio, *a fantaftick.*
Two other like gentlemen.
Varrius,* *a gentleman, fervant to the duke.*
Provoft.
Thomas, } *two friars.*
Peter,
A Juftice.
Elbow, *a fimple conftable.*
Froth, *a foolifh gentleman.*
Clown, *fervant to* Mrs. Over-done.
Abhorfon, *an executioner.*
Barnardine, *a diffolute prifoner.*

Ifabella, *fifter to* Claudio.
Mariana, *betrothed to* Angelo.
Juliet, *beloved by* Claudio.
Francifca, *a nun.*
Miftrefs Over-done, *a bawd.*

Lords, Gentlemen, Guards, Officers, *and other Attendants.*

SCENE, Vienna.

* Varrius might be omitted, for he is only once fpoken to, and fays nothing. JOHNSON.

MEASURE

FOR

MEASURE.

ACT I. SCENE I.

An apartment in the Duke's *palace.*

Enter DUKE, ESCALUS, Lords, *and Attendants.*

DUKE. Efcalus,——
ESCAL. My lord.
DUKE. Of government the properties to unfold,
Would feem in me to affect fpeech and difcourfe;
Since I am put to know,[2] that your own fcience,
Exceeds, in that, the lifts[3] of all advice

---

[2] *Since I am* put *to* know,] may mean, *I am compelled to ac-*
knowledge.
So, in *King Henry VI.* P. II. fc. i:
"—— had I firft been *put to* fpeak my mind."
Again, in Drayton's *Legend of Pierce Gaveston:*
"My limbs were *put to* travel day and night."
STEEVENS.

[3] —— *lifts* —] Bounds, limits. JOHNSON.
So, in *Othello:*
" Confine yourfelf within a patient *lift.*"
Again, in *Hamlet:*
" The ocean, over-peering of his *lift,*"——
STEEVENS.

N 2

My ſtrength can give you: Then no more remains,
But that to your ſufficiency, as your worth is able,
And let them work.[4]   The nature of our people,

[4] —— *Then no more remains,*
But *that to your* ſufficiency, *as your worth is able,*
And let them *work.*]   To the integrity of this reading Mr.
Theobald objeſts, and ſays, *What was Eſcalus to put to his ſuf-*
ficiency? why, his ſcience: But his ſcience and ſufficiency were but one
and the ſame thing. On what then does the relative them *depend?*
He will have it, therefore, that a line has been accidentally dropp'd,
which he attempts to reſtore thus:
       But that to your ſufficiency you add
       Due diligence, as your worth is able, &c.
Nodum in ſcirpo quærit.   And all for want of knowing, that by
ſufficiency is meant *authority,* the power delegated by the duke to
Eſcalus.   The plain meaning of the word being this: *Put your*
ſkill in governing (ſays the Duke) *to the power which I give you to*
exerciſe it, and let them work together.   WARBURTON.

   Sir Thomas Hanmer having caught from Mr. Theobald a hint
that a line was loſt, endeavours to ſupply it thus:
       —— *Then no more remains,*
       But that to your ſufficiency you join
       A will to ſerve us, as your worth is able.
— He has, by this bold conjeſture, undoubtedly obtained a meaning, but, perhaps, not even in his own opinion, the meaning of
Shakſpeare.
   That the paſſage is more or leſs corrupt, I believe every
reader will agree with the editors.   I am not convinced that a
line is loſt, as Mr. Theobald conjeſtures, nor that the change of
but to *put,* which Dr. Warburton has admitted after ſome other
editor, [Rowe] will amend the fault.   There was probably ſome
original obſcurity in the expreſſion, which gave occaſion to miſtake
in repetition or tranſcription.   I therefore ſuſpeſt that the author
wrote thus:
       —— *Then no more remains,*
       But that to your ſufficiencies *your worth is* abled,
       And let them work.
Then nothing remains more than to tell you, that your virtue is now
inveſted with power equal to your knowledge and wiſdom.   Let there-
fore your knowledge and your virtue now work together.   It may
eaſily be conceived how *ſufficiencies* was, by an inarticulate ſpeaker,
or inattentive hearer, confounded with *ſufficiency as,* and how *abled,*
a word very unuſual, was changed into *able.*   For *abled,* however,
an authority is not wanting.   Lear uſes it in the ſame ſenſe, or

Our city's inftitutions, and the terms [5]

nearly the fame with the Duke. As for *fufficiencies*, D. Hamilton in his dying fpeech, prays that Charles II. *may exceed both the* virtues *and* fufficiencies *of his father.* JOHNSON.

The uncommon redundancy, as well as obfcurity, of this verfe may be confidered as evidence of its corruption. Take away the ~~unfuft words~~, and the fenfe joins well enough with what went before. *Then* (fays the Duke) *no more remains to fay* :

    And your fufficiency as your worth is able,
      And let them work.

i. e. *Your skill in government is, in ability to ferve me, equal to the integrity of your heart, and let them co-operate in your future miniftry.*

The verfification requires that either fomething fhould be added, or fomething retrenched. The latter is the eafier, as well as the fafer tafk. I join in the belief, however, that a line is loft; and whoever is acquainted with the inaccuracy of the folio, (for of this play there is no other old edition,) will find my opinion juftified.

                       STEEVENS.

Some words feem to be loft here, the fenfe of which, perhaps, may be thus fupplied :

    —— *them no more remains,*

    And let them work.

That is, you are thoroughly acquainted with your duty, fo that nothing more is neceffary to be done, but to inveft you with power equal to your abilities. M. MASON.

    —— *Then no more remains,*
    But that to your fufficiency ** *as your worth is able,*
    And let them work.

I have not the fmalleft doubt that the compofitor's eye glanced from the middle of the fecond of thefe lines to that under it in the MS. and that by this means two half lines have been omitted. The very fame error may be found in *Macbeth*, edit. 1632 :

For common juſtice, you are as pregnant in,[6]
As art and practice hath enriched any

    " —— which, being taught, return,
    " To plague *the ingredients of our poiſon'd chalice*
    " To our own lips.

inſtead of

    " —— which, being taught, return,
    " To plague the *inventor.   This even-handed juſtice*
    " *Commends the* ingredients of our poiſon'd chalice," &c.

Again, in *Much ado about Nothing*, edit. 1623, p. 103:

    " And I will break with her.   Was't not to this end," &c.

inſtead of

    " And I will break with her, *and with her father*,
    " *And thou ſhalt have her.*   Was't not to this end," &c.

The following paſſage, in *King Henry IV*. P. I. which is con-
ſtructed in a manner ſomewhat ſimilar to the preſent when corrected,
appears to me to ſtrengthen the ſuppoſition that two half lines have
been loſt:

    " Send *danger* from the eaſt unto the weſt,
    " So *honour* croſs it from the north to ſouth,
    " *And let them grapple.*"

Sufficiency is ſkill in government; ability to execute his office.
And let them work, a figurative expreſſion; *Let them ferment.*

MALONE.

5 —— *the* terms—] *Terms* mean the technical language of the
courts.   An old book called *Les Termes de la Ley*, (written in
Henry the Eighth's time) was in Shakſpeare's days, and is now,
the accidence of young ſtudents in the law.   BLACKSTONE.

6 —— *the terms*

    For *common juſtice, you are as* pregnant *in*,] The later editions
all give it, without authority,

      —— *the terms*

    Of *juſtice*, ——

and Dr. Warburton makes *terms* ſignify *bounds* or *limits*.   I rather
think the Duke meant to ſay, that Eſcalus was *pregnant*, that is
ready and knowing in all the forms of the law, and, among other
things, in the *terms* or *times ſet apart* for its adminiſtration.

JOHNSON.

The word *pregnant* is uſed with this ſignification in *Ram-Alley*,
or *Merry Tricks*, 1611, where a lawyer is repreſented reading:

    " In triceſſimo primo Alberti Magni——
    " 'Tis very cleare—the place is very *pregnant*."

i. e. very *expreſſive, ready*, or very *big with appoſite meaning*.
Again,

    " —— the proof is moſt *pregnant*."   STEEVENS.

That we remember: There is our commiſſion,
From which we would not have you warp.—Call
       hither,
I ſay, bid come before us Angelo.——

                          [Exit an Attendant.
What figure of us think you he will bear?
For you muſt know, we have with ſpecial ſoul
Elected him our abſence to ſupply; [7]
Lent him our terror, dreſt him with our love;
And given his deputation all the organs
Of our own power: What think you of it?

   ESCAL. If any in Vienna be of worth
To undergo ſuch ample grace and honour,
It is lord Angelo.

               Enter ANGELO.

  DUKE.   Look, where he comes.
  ANG. Always obedient to your grace's will,
I come to know your pleaſure.

---

   [7] *For you muſt know, we have with* ſpecial ſoul
    Elected him our abſence to ſupply;] By the words *with ſpecial
ſoul elected him,* I believe, the poet meant no more than *that he was
the immediate choice of his heart.*
   A ſimilar expreſſion occurs in *Troilus and Creſſida:*
    " —— with *private ſoul,*
    " Did in great Ilion thus tranſlate him to me."
Again, more appoſitely, in *The Tempeſt:*
    " —— for ſeveral virtues
    " Have I lik'd ſeveral women, never any
    " With ſo *full ſoul,* but ſome defect," &c. STEEVENS.

   Steevens has hit upon the true explanation of the paſſage; and
might have found a further confirmation of it in *Troilus and Creſſida,*
where, ſpeaking of himſelf, Troilus ſays,
    " —— ne'er did young man fancy
    " *With ſo eternal, and ſo fix'd a ſoul.*"
To do a thing with all one's *ſoul,* is a common expreſſion.
                            M. MASON.

        N 4

Duke.　　　　　　　　　　　　　　　　Angelo,
There is a kind of character in thy life,
That, to the observer,[8] doth thy history
Fully unfold: Thyself and thy belongings[9]
Are not thine own so proper,[2] as to waste
Thyself upon thy virtues, them on thee.[3]
Heaven doth with us, as we with torches do;

———— *we have with* special soul —] This seems to be only a translation of the usual formal words inserted in all royal grants:—— " De *gratia* nostra *speciali*, et ex mero motu ——." MALONE.

[8] *There is a kind of character in thy life,*
    That, to the observer, &c.] Either this introduction has more solemnity than meaning, or it has a meaning which I cannot discover. What is there peculiar in this, that a man's *life* informs the observer of his *history?* Might it be supposed that Shakspeare wrote this?
    There is a kind of character in thy look.
History may be taken in a more diffuse and licentious meaning, for *future occurrences,* or the part of life yet to come. If this sense be received, the passage is clear and proper. JOHNSON.

Shakspeare must, I believe, be answerable for the unnecessary pomp of this introduction. He has the same thought in *Henry IV*. P. II. which affords some comment on this passage before us.
" There is a history in all men's lives,
" Figuring the nature of the times deceas'd:
" The which observ'd, a man may prophecy
" With a near aim, of the main chance of things
" As yet not come to life," &c. STEEVENS.

On considering this passage, I am induced to think that the words *character* and *history* have been misplaced, and that it was originally written thus:
    There is a kind of history in thy life,
    That to the observer doth thy character
    Fully unfold.
This transposition seems to be justified by the passage quoted by Steevens from the Second Part of *Henry IV*. M. MASON.

[9] ———— *thy belongings* ——] i. e. endowments. MALONE.

[2] *Are not thine own so proper,*] i. e. are not so much thy own property. STEEVENS.

[3] ———— them *on thee.*] The old copy reads—*they* on thee. The emendation was made by Sir T. Hanmer. STEEVENS.

Not light them for themfelves : for if our virtues [4]
Did not go forth of us, 'twere all alike
As if we had them not.   Spirits are not finely
         touch'd,
But to fine iffues : [5] nor nature never lends [6]
The fmalleft fcruple of her excellence,
But, like a thrifty goddefs, fhe determines
Herfelf the glory of a creditor,
Both thanks and ufe. [7]   But I do bend my fpeech
To one that can my part in him advértife ; [8]

[4] —— *for if our virtues*, &c.]
  " *Paulum fepultæ diftat inertiæ*
  " *Celata virtus.*" ——   HOR.   THEOBALD.
Again, in Maffinger's *Maid of Honour :*
  " Virtue, if not in action, is a vice,
  " And, when we move not forward, we go backward."
Thus, in the Latin adage—*Non progredi eft regredi.* STEEVENS.

[5] —— *to fine iffues :*] To great confequences ; for high purpofes. JOHNSON.

[6] —— nor *nature* never *lends* —] Two negatives, not employed
to make an affirmative, are common in our author.
  So, in *Julius Cæfar :*
  " There is no harm intended to your perfon,
  " *Nor* to *no* Roman elfe." STEEVENS.

[7] —— *fhe determines*
  Herfelf *the glory of a creditor,*
  Both thanks and ufe.] i. e. She (Nature) *requires and does to
herfelf* the fame advantages that creditors ufually enjoy,—thanks
for the endowments fhe has beftowed, and extraordinary exertions
in thofe whom fhe hath thus favoured, by way of *intereft* for what
fhe has lent.
  Ufe in the phrafeology of our author's age, fignified *intereft of
money.* MALONE.

[8] —— *I do bend my fpeech,*
  To one that can my part in him advértife ;] This is obfcure.
The meaning is, I direct my fpeech to one who is able to teach
me how to govern ; *my part in him,* fignifying my office, which I
have delegated to him.   *My part in him advertife* ; i. e. who knows
what appertains to the character of a deputy or viceroy.   *Can
advertife my part in him* ; that is, his reprefentation of my perfon.
But all thefe quaintneffes of expreffion, the Oxford editor feems

Hold therefore, Angelo;[9]
In our remove, be thou at full ourfelf;
Mortality and mercy in Vienna
Live in thy tongue and heart: Old Efcalus,
Though firft in queftion,[2] is thy fecondary:
Take thy commiffion.

fworn to extirpate; that is, to take away one of Shakfpeare's cha-
racteriftic marks; which, if not one of the comelieft, is yet one of
the ftrongeft.   So he alters this to,
        To one that can, in my part me advertife.
A better expreffion indeed, but, for all that, none of Shakfpeare's.
                                            WARBURTON.

    I know not whether we may not better read,——
        One that can, my part to him advertife.
One that can *inform himfelf* of that which it would be otherwife
my part to tell him.   JOHNSON.

    To *advertife* is ufed in this fenfe, and with Shakfpeare's ac-
centuation, by Chapman, in his verfion of the 11*th Book of the
Odyffey :*
        " Or, of my father, if thy royal ear
        " Hath been *advértis'd*————."   STEEVENS.

    I believe, the meaning is,——I am talking to one who is himfelf
already fufficiently converfant with the nature and duties of my
office;——of that *office, which I have now delegated to him.*
So, in *Timon of Athens :*
        " It is our *part*, and promife to the Athenians,
        " To fpeak with Timon."   MALONE.

    [9] *Hold therefore, Angelo* ;] That is, continue to be Angelo;
hold as thou art.   JOHNSON.

    I believe that—*Hold therefore, Angelo* ; are the words which the
Duke utters on tendering his commiffion to him.   He concludes
with—*Take thy commiffion.*   STEEVENS.

    If a full point be put after *therefore,* the Duke may be under-
ftood to fpeak of himfelf.   *Hold therefore,* i. e. Let me therefore
hold, or ftop.   And the fenfe of the whole paffage may be this.
——The Duke, who has begun an exhortation to Angelo, checks
himfelf thus :   " But I am fpeaking *to one, that can in him* [in or
by himfelf] apprehend *my part* [all that I have to fay] : I will
therefore fay no more [on that fubject]."   He then merely fignifies to Angelo his appointment.   TYRWHITT.

    [2] ————*firft in queftion,*] That is, firft called for ; firft appointed.
                                            JOHNSON.

Ang.   Now, good my lord,
Let there be fome more teft made of my metal,
Before fo noble and fo great a figure
Be ftamp'd upon it.

Duke.   No more evafion:
We have with a leaven'd and prepared choice[3]
Proceeded to you; therefore take your honours.
Our hafte from hence is of fo quick condition,
That it prefers itfelf, and leaves unqueftion'd
Matters of needful value. We fhall write to you,
As time and our concernings fhall impórtune,
How it goes with us; and do look to know
What doth befal you here. So, fare you well:
To the hopeful execution do I leave you
Of your commiffions.

Ang.   Yet, give leave, my lord,
That we may bring you fomething on the way.[4]

Duke. My hafte may not admit it;
Nor need you, on mine honour, have to do
With any fcruple: your fcope is as mine own;[5]
So to enforce, or qualify the laws,
As to your foul feems good. Give me your hand;

---

[3] *We have with a* leaven'd *and prepared choice* —] *Leaven'd choice*
is one of Shakfpeare's harfh metaphors. His train of ideas feems
to be this: *I have proceeded to you with choice* mature, concocted,
fermented, *leavened.* When bread is *leavened* it is left to ferment:
a *leavened* choice is therefore a choice not hafty, but confiderate;
not declared as foon as it fell into the imagination, but fuffered to
work long in the mind. Thus explained, it fuits better with
prepared than *levelled.* JOHNSON.

[4] —— *bring you fomething on the way.*] i. e. accompany you.
So, in *A Woman kill'd with Kindnefs,* by Heywood, 1617: " She
went very lovingly to *bring him on his way* to horfe." And the
fame mode of expreffion is to be found in almoft every writer of
the times. REED.

[5] —— *your* fcope *is as mine own;*] That is, your amplitude
of power. JOHNSON.

I'll privily away: I love the people,
But do not like to stage me to their eyes: [6]
Though it do well, I do not relish well
Their loud applause, and *aves* vehement;
Nor do I think the man of safe discretion,
That does affect it.   Once more, fare you well.

Ang. The heavens give safety to your purposes!

Escal. Lead forth, and bring you back in happiness!

Duke. I thank you: Fare you well.   [*Exit.*

Escal. I shall desire you, sir, to give me leave
To have free speech with you; and it concerns me
To look into the bottom of my place:
A power I have; but of what strength and nature
I am not yet instructed.

Ang. 'Tis so with me:——Let us withdraw together,
And we may soon our satisfaction have
Touching that point.

Escal.   I'll wait upon your honour.
                                    [*Exeunt.*

SCENE II.

A Street.

Enter Lucio, *and two* Gentlemen.

Lucio. If the duke, with the other dukes, come
not to composition with the king of Hungary, why,
then all the dukes fall upon the king.

---

[6] —— *to stage* me to their eyes:] So, in one of Queen Elizabeth's
speeches to parliament, 1586: " We princes, I tel you, are set on
stages, in the sight and viewe of all the world," &c.   See *The
Copy of a Letter to the Right Honourable the Earle of Leycester*, &c.
4to. 1586.   STEEVENS.

1 Gent. Heaven grant us its peace, but not the king of Hungary's!

2 Gent. Amen.

Lucio. Thou concludeſt like the ſanctimonious pirate, that went to ſea with the ten commandments, but ſcraped one out of the table.

2 Gent. Thou ſhalt not ſteal?

Lucio. Ay, that he razed.

1 Gent. Why, 'twas a commandment to command the captain and all the reſt from their functions; they put forth to ſteal: There's not a ſoldier of us all, that, in the thankſgiving before meat, doth reliſh the petition well that prays for peace.

2 Gent. I never heard any ſoldier diſlike it.

Lucio. I believe thee; for, I think, thou never waſt where grace was ſaid.

2 Gent. No? a dozen times at leaſt.

1 Gent. What? in metre? [7]

Lucio. In any proportion, [8] or in any language.

1 Gent. I think, or in any religion.

Lucio. Ay! why not? Grace is grace, deſpite of all controverſy: [9] As for example; Thou thyſelf art a wicked villain, deſpite of all grace.

---

[7] —— *in metre?*] In the primers there are metrical graces, ſuch as, I ſuppoſe, were uſed in Shakſpeare's time. JOHNSON.

[8] *In any* proportion, &c.] *Proportion* ſignifies *meaſure*; and refers to the queſtion, *What? in metre?* WARBURTON.

This ſpeech is improperly given to *Lucio.* It clearly belongs to the *ſecond Gentleman,* who had heard grace "a dozen times at leaſt." RITSON.

[9] *Grace is grace, deſpite of all controverſy:*] Satirically inſinuating, that the *controverſies* about *grace* were ſo intricate and endleſs, that the diſputants unſettled every thing but this, that *grace was grace*; which, however, in ſpite of controverſy, ſtill remained certain. WARBURTON.

1 *Gent.* Well, there went but a pair of sheers
between us.[2]

Lucio. I grant; as there may between the lists
and the velvet: Thou art the list.

1 *Gent.* And thou the velvet: thou art good
velvet; thou art a three-pil'd piece, I warrant thee:
I had as lief be a list of an English kersey, as be
pil'd, as thou art pil'd, for a French velvet.[3]   Do
I speak feelingly now?

I am in doubt whether Shakspeare's thoughts reached so far
into ecclesiastical disputes.   Every commentator is warped a little
by the tract of his own profession.   The question is, whether the
second gentleman has ever heard grace.   The first gentleman
limits the question to *grace in metre.*   Lucio enlarges it to *grace in
any* form *or language.*   The first gentleman, to go beyond him,
says, or *in any religion,* which Lucio allows, because the nature
of things is unalterable; grace is as immutably grace, as his merry
antagonist is a *wicked villain.*   Difference in religion cannot make
a *grace* not to be *grace,* a *prayer* not to be *holy*; as nothing can
make a *villain* not to be a *villain.*   This seems to be the meaning,
such as it is.   JOHNSON.

[2] —— *there went but a pair of sheers between us.*]   We are both
of the same piece.   JOHNSON.

So, in *The Maid of the Mill,* by Beaumont and Fletcher:——
" There went but a pair of sheers and a bodkin, between them."
STEEVENS.

The same expression is likewise found in Marston's *Malcontent,*
1604: " *There goes but a pair of sheers* betwixt an emperor and the
son of a bagpiper; only the dying, dressing, pressing, and glossing,
makes the difference."   MALONE.

[3] —— *pil'd, as thou art pil'd, for a French velvet.*]   The jest
about the pile of a French velvet, alludes to the loss of hair in the
French disease, a very frequent topick of our author's jocularity.
Lucio finding that the gentleman understands the distemper so well,
and mentions it so *feelingly,* promises to remember to drink his
health, but to forget *to drink after him.*   It was the opinion of
Shakspeare's time, that the cup of an infected person was contagious.   JOHNSON.

The jest lies between the similar sound of the words *pill'd*
and *pil'd.*   This I have elsewhere explained, under a passage in
Henry VIII :
" *Pill'd* priest thou liest."   STEEVENS.

Lucio. I think thou doſt; and, indeed, with moſt painful feeling of thy ſpeech: I will, out of thine own confeſſion, learn to begin thy health; but, whilſt I live, forget to drink after thee.

1 *Gent.* I think, I have done myſelf wrong; have I not?

2 *Gent.* Yes, that thou haſt; whether thou art tainted, or free.

Lucio. Behold, behold, where madam Mitigation comes![4] I have purchaſed as many diſeaſes under her roof, as come to——

2 *Gent.* To what, I pray?

1 *Gent.* Judge.

2 *Gent.* To three thouſand dollars a year.[5]

1. *Gent.* Ay, and more.

Lucio. A French crown more.[6]

---

[4] *Behold, behold, where madam Mitigation comes!*] In the old copy this ſpeech and the next but one, are attributed to Lucio. The preſent regulation was ſuggeſted by Mr. Pope. What Lucio ſays afterwards, "A *French* crown more," proves that it is right. He would not utter a ſarcaſm againſt himſelf. MALONE.

[5] *To three thouſand dollars a-year.*] A quibble intended between *dollars* and *doloxrs*. HANMER.

The ſame jeſt occurred before in *The Tempeſt.* JOHNSON.

[6] *A French crown more.*] Lucio means here not the piece of money ſo called, but that *venereal* ſcab, which among the ſurgeons is ſtyled *corona Veneris.* To this, I think, our author likewiſe makes Quince allude in *A Midſummer Night's Dream*:
"Some of your French crowns have no hair at all; and then you will play bare-faced."
For where theſe eruptions are, the ſkull is carious, and the party becomes bald. THEOBALD.

So, in *The Return from Parnaſſus,* 1606:
" I may chance indeed to give the world a bloody noſe; but it ſhall hardly give me a crack'd crown, though it gives other poets *French crowns.*"

1 *Gent.* Thou art always figuring difeafes in me: but thou art full of error; I am found.

Lucio. Nay, not as one would fay, healthy; but fo found, as things that are hollow: thy bones are hollow;[7] impiety has made a feaft of thee.

Enter Bawd.

1 *Gent.* How now? Which of your hips has the moft profound fciatica?

Bawd. Well, well; there's one yonder arrefted, and carryd to prifon, was worth five thoufand of you all.

1 *Gent.* Who's that, I pray thee?

Bawd. Marry, fir, that's Claudio, fignior Claudio.

1 *Gent.* Claudio to prifon! 'tis not fo.

Bawd. Nay, but I know, 'tis fo: I faw him arrefted; faw him carried away; and, which is more, within thefe three days his head's to be chopped off.

Lucio. But, after all this fooling, I would not have it fo: Art thou fure of this?

Bawd. I am too fure of it: and it is for getting madam Julietta with child.

Lucio. Believe me, this may be: he promifed to meet me two hours fince; and he was ever precife in promife-keeping.

Again, in the Dedication to *Gabriel Harvey's Hunt is up*, 1598:

"———— never metft with any requital, except it were fome few *French crownes*, pil'd friers crownes." &c. STEEVENS.

[7] ———— *thy* bones *are* hollow;] So *Timon*, addreffing himfelf to Phrynia and Timandra:

"Confumptions fow
"In *hollow bones* of man." STEEVENS.

2 GENT. Befides, you know, it draws fomething near to the fpeech we had to fuch a purpofe.

1 GENT. But moft of all, agreeing with the proclamation.

LUCIO. Away; let's go learn the truth of it.

[*Exeunt* LUCIO, *and* Gentlemen.

BAWD. Thus, what with the war, what with the fweat,[7] what with the gallows, and what with poverty, I am cuftom-fhrunk. How now? what's the news with you?

Enter Clown.

CLO. Yonder man is carried to prifon.

BAWD. Well; what has he done?

CLO. A woman.[8]

---

[7] —— *what with the* fweat,] This may allude to the *fweating fickmefs*, of which the memory was very frefh in the time of Shakfpeare: but more probably to the method of cure then ufed for the difeafes contracted in brothels. JOHNSON.

So, in the comedy of *Doctor Dodypoll,* 1600:
" You are very moift, fir: did you *fweat* all this, I pray?
" You have not the *difeafe,* I hope. STEEVENS.

[8] —— *what has he* done?

CLO. A woman.] The ancient meaning of the verb to *do,* (though now obfolete) may be guefs'd at from the following paffages:
" *Chiron.* Thou haft undone our mother.
" *Aaron.* Villain, I've *done* thy mother." *Titus Andronicus.*
Again, in Ovid's *Elegies,* tranflated by Marlowe, printed at Middlebourg, no date:
" The ftrumpet with the ftranger will not *do,*
" Before the room is clear, and door put to."
Again, in *The Maid's Tragedy,* Act II. *Evadne,* while undreffing, fays,—
" I am foon undone.
Dula anfwers, " And as foon *done.*"
Hence the name of Over-*done,* which Shakfpeare has appropriated to his *bawd.* COLLINS.

VOL. IV.　　　　　O

Bawd. But what's his offence?

Clo. Groping for trouts in a peculiar river.⁹

Bawd. What, is there a maid with child by him?

Clo. No; but there's a woman with maid by him: You have not heard of the proclamation, have you?

Bawd. What, proclamation, man?

Clo. All houſes in the ſuburbs ² of Vienna muſt be pluck'd down.

Bawd. And what ſhall become of thoſe in the city?

Clo. They ſhall ſtand for ſeed: they had gone down too, but that a wiſe burgher put in for them.

Bawd. But ſhall all our houſes of reſort in the ſuburbs be pull'd down?³

---

⁹ —— *in a* peculiar *river.*] i. e. a river belonging to an individual; not public property. MALONE.

² All *houſes in the ſuburbs* —] This is ſurely too general an expreſſion, unleſs we ſuppoſe, that *all* the houſes in the ſuburbs were *bawdy-houſes.* It appears too, from what the *bawd* ſays below, " But ſhall *all our houſes of reſort* in the ſuburbs be pulled down?" that the Clown had been particular in his deſcription of the houſes which were to be pulled down. I am therefore inclined to believe that we ſhould read here, *all bawdy-houſes,* or *all houſes of reſort* in the ſuburbs. TYRWHITT.

³ *But ſhall all our houſes of reſort in the* ſuburbs *be pull'd down?*] This will be underſtood from the Scotch law of *James's* time, concerning *huires* (whores): " that comoun women be put at the *utmoſt endes of townes,* queire leaſt perril of fire is." Hence *Urſula* the pig-woman, in *Bartholomew-Fair:* " I, I, gameſters, mock a plain, plump, ſoft *wench of the ſuburbs,* do!" FARMER.

So, in *The Malcontent,* 1604, when *Altofront* diſmiſſes the various characters at the end of the play to different deſtinations, he ſays to *Macquerelle* the bawd:
  " —— thou unto the *ſuburbs.*"
Again, in *Ram-Alley,* or *Merry Tricks,* 1611:
  " Some fourteen bawds; he kept her in *the ſuburbs.*"

Clo. To the ground, miftrefs.

Bawd. Why, here's a change, indeed, in the commonwealth! What fhall become of me?

Clo. Come; fear not you: good counfellors lack no clients: though you change your place, you need not change your trade; I'll be your tapfter ftill. Courage; there will be pity taken on you: you that have worn your eyes almoft out in the fervice, you will be confidered.

Bawd. What's to do here, Thomas Tapfter? Let's withdraw.

Clo. Here comes fignior Claudio, led by the provoft to prifon: and there's madam Juliet.

[*Exeunt.*

SCENE III.

The fame.

Enter Provoft, Claudio, Juliet, *and* Officers; Lucio, *and two* Gentlemen.

Claud. Fellow, why doft thou fhow me thus to
  the world?
Bear me to prifon, where I am committed.

Prov. I do it not in evil difpofition,
But from lord Angelo by fpecial charge.

Claud. Thus can the demi-god, Authority,
Make us pay down for our offence by weight.——

See Martial, where *fummaniana* and *fuburbana* are applied to proftitutes. Steevens.

The licenced houfes of refort at Vienna are at this time all in the fuburbs, under the permiffion of the Committee of Chaftity.
S. W.

The words of heaven;—on whom it will, it will;
On whom it will not, so; yet still 'tis just.[3]

[3] *Thus can the demi-god, Authority,*
   Make us pay down for our offence by weight.—
   The words of heaven;—on whom it will, it will;
   On whom it will not, so; yet still 'tis just.] The sense of the
whole is this: *The demi-god Authority, makes us pay the full penalty
of our offence, and its decrees are as little to be questioned as the words
of heaven, which pronounces its pleasure thus,—I punish and remit
punishment according to my own uncontroulable will; and yet who
can say, what dost thou?—Make us pay down for our offence by
weight,* is a fine expression to signify paying the full penalty. The
metaphor is taken from paying money by *weight,* which is always
exact; not so by *tale,* on account of the practice of diminishing the
species. WARBURTON.

   I suspect that a line is lost. JOHNSON.

   It may be read,—*The sword of heaven.*
      Thus can the demi-god Authority,
      Make us pay down for our offence, by weight ;—
      The sword of heaven :—on whom, &c.
Authority is then poetically called *the sword of heaven,* which will
spare or punish, as it is commanded. The alteration is slight,
being made only by taking a single letter from the end of the
word, and placing it at the beginning.
   This very ingenious and elegant emendation was suggested to
me by the Reverend Dr. Roberts, Provost of Eton; and it may be
countenanced by the following passage in *The Cobler's Prophecy,*
1594:
      " In brief, they are *the swords of heaven* to punish."
   Sir *W. D'Avenant,* who incorporated this play of *Shakspeare*
with *Much ado about Nothing,* and formed out of them a Tragi-
comedy called *The Law against Lovers,* omits the two last lines of
this speech; I suppose, on account of their seeming obscurity.
                                                   STEEVENS.

   The very ingenious emendation proposed by Dr. Roberts, is yet
more strongly supported by another passage in the play before us,
where this phrase occurs, (Act III. sc. last):
      " He who *the sword of heaven* will bear,
      " Should be as holy, as severe."
Yet I believe the old copy is right. MALONE.

   Notwithstanding Dr. Roberts's ingenious conjecture, the text is
certainly right. *Authority,* being absolute in Angelo, is finely
stiled by Claudio, *the demi-god.* To this uncontroulable power,
the poet applies a passage from St. Paul to the Romans, ch. ix.

Lucio. Why, how now, Claudio? whence comes
this reftraint?

Claud. From too much liberty, my Lucio, li-
berty:
As furfeit is the father of much faft,
So every fcope by the immoderate ufe
Turns to reftraint: Our natures do purfue,
(Like rats that ravin down their proper bane,) [4]
A thirfty evil; and when we drink, we die. [5]

Lucio. If I could fpeak fo wifely under an arreft,
I would fend for certain of my creditors: And yet,
to fay the truth, I had as lief have the foppery of
freedom, as the morality [6] of imprifonment.—
What's thy offence, Claudio?

v. 15, 18, which he properly ftyles, *the words of heaven:* "for
he faith to Mofes, I will have mercy on whom I will have mercy,"
&c. And again: "Therefore hath he mercy on whom he will
have mercy," &c. HENLEY.

It fhould be remembered, however, that the poet is here fpeaking
not of *mercy,* but *punifhment.* MALONE.

Mr. Malone might have fpared himfelf this remark, had he
recollected that the words of St. Paul immediately following, and
to which the &c. referred, are—"*and whom he will he hardeneth.*"
See alfo the preceding verfe. HENLEY.

[4] *Like rats that* ravin *down their proper bane,*] To *ravin* was
formerly ufed for eagerly or voracioufly devouring any thing: fo
in *Wilfon's* Epiftle to the Earl of Leicefter, prefixed to his *Difcourfe
upon Ufurye,* 1572: "For thefe bee the greedie cormoraunte wolfes
indeed, that *ravyn* up both beafte and man." REED.

Ravin is an ancient word for *prey.* So, in *Noah's Flood,* by
Drayton:
     "As well of *ravine,* as that chew the cud." STEEVENS.

[5] —— *when we* drink, *we die.*] So, in *Revenge for Honour,* by
Chapman:
     "Like poifon'd rats, which when they've fwallowed
     "The pleafing bane, reft not until they *drink;*
     "And can reft then much lefs, until they burft."
                                        STEEVENS.

[6] —— *as the* morality —] The old copy has *mortality.* It was
corrected by Sir William D'Avenant. MALONE.

O 3

CLAUD. What, but to fpeak of would offend again.

LUCIO. What is it? murder?

CLAUD. No.

LUCIO. Lechery?

CLAUD. Call it fo.

PROV. Away, fir; you muft go.

CLAUD. One word, good friend :——Lucio, a word
         with you.   [*Takes him afide.*

LUCIO. A hundred, if they'll do you any good.——
Is lechery fo look'd after?

CLAUD. Thus ftands it with me :——Upon a true
         contract,
I got poffeffion of Julietta's bed;[7]
You know the lady; fhe is faft my wife,
Save that we do the denunciation lack
Of outward order : this we came not to,
Only for propagation of a dower
Remaining in the coffer of her friends;[8]

---

[7] *I got poffeffion of Julietta's bed, &c.*] This fpeech is furely
too indelicate to be fpoken concerning Juliet, before her face;
for fhe appears to be brought in with the reft, though fhe has nothing to fay.   The Clown points her out as they enter; and yet,
from Claudio's telling Lucio, *that he knows the lady,* &c. one would
think fhe was not meant to have made her perfonal appearance on
the fcene.   STEEVENS.

The little feeming impropriety there is, will be entirely removed, by fuppofing that when Claudio ftops to fpeak to Lucio,
the Provoft's officers depart with Julietta.   RITSON.

Claudio may be fuppofed to fpeak to Lucio apart.   MALONE.

[8] "——— this we came not to,
" *Only for* propagation *of a dower*
" *Remaining in the coffer of her friends*;] This fingular mode
of expreffion certainly demands fome elucidation.   The fenfe
appears to be this.   "*We did not think it proper publickly to celebrate
our marriage; for this reafon, that there might be no hindrance to the
payment of Julietta's portion which was then in the hands of her
friends; from whom, therefore, we judged it expedient to conceal our*

7

From whom we thought it meet to hide our love,
Till time had made them for us. But it chances,
The ſtealth of our moſt mutual entertainment,
With character too groſs, is writ on Juliet.

    Lucio. With child, perhaps?

    Claud. Unhappily, even ſo.
And the new deputy now for the duke,—
Whether it be the fault and glimpſe of newneſs;
Or whether that the body public be
A horſe whereon the governor doth ride,
Who, newly in the ſeat, that it may know
He can command, lets it ſtraight feel the ſpur:
Whether the tyranny be in his place,
Or in his eminence that fills it up,
I ſtagger in:—But this new governor
Awakes me all the enrolled penalties,

love till we had gained their favour." Propagation being here uſed
to ſignify *payment,* muſt have its root in the Italian word *pagare.*
Ediuburgh Magazine for November, 1786.

    I ſuppoſe the ſpeaker means—for the ſake of *getting* ſuch a dower
as her friends might hereafter beſtow on her, when time had reconciled them t

Perhaps w
⁹ —— th
ſo little rela
may read ſt
    Wh
That is, w
glare of new
lines. Joh
   Fault, I
the deputy,
neſs. The f
the meaning
fault ariſing from the mind being attracted by a novel authority, of
which the new governor has yet had only a glimpſe,—*has yet taken*
only a haſty ſurvey; or *whether,* &c. Shakſpeare has many ſimilar
expreſſions. Malone.

         O 4

again, in the fourth Iliad by the same tran
4º.1598. ——— I doubt not but this night
—— to the fleet: to propagate the Greeks' until

Which have, like unfcour'd armour,[2] hung by the
       wall
So long, that nineteen zodiacks have gone round,[3]
And none of them been worn; and, for a name,
Now puts the drowfy and neglected act
Frefhly on me:[4]——'tis, furely, for a name.

    Lucio. I warrant, it is: and thy head ftands fo
tickle[5] on thy fhoulders, that a milk-maid, if fhe
be in love, may figh it off. Send after the duke,
and appeal to him.

    Claud. I have done fo, but he's not to be found.
I pr'ythee, Lucio, do me this kind fervice:

---

  [2] —— *like* unfcour'd armour,] So, in *Troilus and Creffida:*
    " Like *rufty mail* in monumental mockery." Steevens.

  [3] *So long, that* nineteen *zodiacks have gone round,*] The Duke, in
the fcene immediately following, fays:
    Which far thefe fourteen *years we have let flip.*
                    Theobald.

  [4] —— *But this new governor*
  Awakes me all the enrolled penalties
  Which have, like unfcour'd armour, hung by the wall
  So long, ——
  Now puts the drowfy and neglected *act*
  Frefhly on me:] Lord Strafford, in the conclufion of his
Defence in the Houfe of Lords, had, perhaps, thefe lines in his
thoughts:
  " It is now full two hundred and forty years fince any man
was touched for this alledged crime, to this height, before myfelf.
——Let us reft contented with that which our fathers have left
us; and not *awake* thofe *fleeping* lions, to our own deftruction, by
raking up *a few mufty records, that have lain fo many ages by the
walls,* quite *forgotten* and *neglected.*" Malone.

  [5] ——*fo tickle*——] i. e. ticklifh. This word is frequently ufed
by our old dramatic authors. So, in *The true Tragedy of Marius
and Scilla,* 1594:
    " —— lords of Afia
    " Have ftood on *tickle* terms."
Again, in *The Widow's Tears,* by Chapman, 1612:
    " —— upon as *tickle* a pin as the needle of a dial."
                    Steevens.

This day my fifter fhould the cloifter enter,
And there receive her approbation : [6]
Acquaint her with the danger of my ftate ;
Implore her, in my voice, that fhe make friends
To the ftrict deputy ; bid herfelf affay him ;
I have great hope in that : for in her youth
There is a prone and fpeechlefs dialect, [7]

[6] —— *her* approbation :] i. e. enter on her *probation*, or *novi-tiate.* So again, in this play :
"I, in *probation* of a fifterhood."——
Again, in *The Merry Devil of Edmonton*, 1608 :
"Madam, for a twelvemonth's *approbation*,
"We mean to make the trial of our child." MALONE.

[7] —— prone *and fpeechlefs dialect*,] I can fcarcely tell what fignification to give to the word *prone*. Its primitive and tranflated fenfes are well known. The author may, by a *prone* dialect, mean a dialect which men are *prone* to regard, or a dialect natural and unforced, as thofe actions feem to which we are *prone.* Either of thefe interpretations is fufficiently ftrained ; but fuch diftortion of words is not uncommon in our author. For the fake of an eafier fenfe, we may read :
—— *in her youth*
There is a pow'r, *and fpeechlefs dialect,*
Such as moves men ;
Or thus :
There is a prompt *and fpeechlefs dialect.* JOHNSON.

Prone, perhaps, may ftand for *humble*, as *a prone pofture* is *a pofture of fupplication.*
So, in *The Opportunity*, by Shirley, 1640 :
"You have *proftrate* language."
The fame thought occurs in *The Winter's Tale :*
"The filence often of pure innocence
"Perfuades, when fpeaking fails."
Sir *W. D'Avenant*, in his alteration of the play, changes *prone* to *fweet.* I mention fome of his variations, to fhew that what appear difficulties to us, were difficulties to him, who, living nearer the time of Shakfpeare, might be fuppofed to have under-ftood his language more intimately. STEEVENS.

Prone, I believe, is ufed here for *prompt, fignificant, expreffive* (though fpeechlefs), as in our author's *Rape of Lucrece* it means *ardent, head-ftrong*, rufhing forward to its object :
"O that *prone* luft fhould ftain fo pure a bed !"

Such as moves men; beside, she hath prosperous art
When she will play with reason and discourse,
And well she can persuade.

Lucio. I pray, she may: as well for the encouragement of the like, which else would stand under grievous imposition; [8] as for the enjoying of thy life, who I would be sorry should be thus foolishly lost at a game of tick-tack.[9] I'll to her.

Claud. I thank you, good friend Lucio.

Lucio. Within two hours,——

Claud. Come, officer, away.   [*Exeunt.*

S C E N E   IV.

A Monastery.

Enter DUKE, *and* Friar Thomas.

Duke. No; holy father; throw away that
             thought;
Believe not that the dribbling dart of love
Can pierce a cómplete bosom: [2] why I desire thee

Again, in *Cymbeline:* " Unless a man would marry a gallows, and beget young gibbets, I never saw any one so *prone.*"
                                                          MALONE.

  [8] *Under grievous* imposition;] I once thought it should be *inquisition,* but the present reading is probably right. *The crime would be under grievous* penalties imposed. JOHNSON.

  [9] ——*lost at a game of* tick-tack.] *Tick-tack* is a game at tables. " *Jouer au* tric-trac," is used in French, in a wanton sense. MALONE.

  The same phrase, in Lucio's sportive sense, occurs in *Lusty Juventus.* STEEVENS.

  [2] *Believe not that the dribbling dart of love
  Can pierce a cómplete bosom:*] Think not that a breast *compleatly armed* can be pierced by the dart of love, that comes fluttering

To give me fecret harbour, hath a purpofe
More grave and wrinkled than the aims and ends
Of burning youth.

FRI.　　　　　　　May your grace fpeak of it?

DUKE. My holy fir, none better knows than you
How I have ever lov'd the life remov'd;[3]
And held in idle price to haunt affembes,
Where youth, and coft, and witlefs bravery[4] keeps.[5]
I have deliver'd to lord Angelo
(A man of ftricture, and firm abftinence,)[6]

[3] —— *the life* remov'd;] i. e. a life of retirement, a life remote, or removed, from the buftle of the world.

So, in the Prologue to Milton's *Mafque at Ludlow Caftle*: I mean the MS. copy in the Library of Trinity College, Cambridge:

　　" —— I was not fent to court your wonder
　　" With diftant worlds, and ftrange *removed* climes."
　　　　　　　　　　　　　　　　　　STEEVENS.

[4] —— *witlefs* bravery—] *Bravery*, in the prefent inftance, fignifies *fhowy drefs*. So, in *The Taming of a Shrew*:
　　" With fcarfs, and fans, and double change of *bravery*."
　　　　　　　　　　　　　　　　　　STEEVENS.

[5] —— *keeps.*] i. e. dwells, refides. In this fenfe it is ftill ufed at Cambridge, where the ftudents and fellows, referring to their collegiate apartments, always fay they *keep*, i. e. refide there. REED.

[6] *A man of* ftricture, *and firm abftinence,*] *Stricture* makes no fenfe in this place. We fhould read:
　　A man of ftrict ure *and firm abftinence.*
i. e. a man of the *exacteft conduct*, and practifed in the fubdual of his paffions. *Ure* is an old word for ufe, practice: fo *enur'd*, habituated to. WARBURTON.

Stricture may eafily be ufed for *ftrictnefs*; *ure* is indeed an old word, but, I think, always applied to things, never to perfons.
　　　　　　　　　　　　　　　　　　JOHNSON.

Sir W. D'Avenant, in his alteration of this play, reads, *ftrictnefs.* *Ure* is fometimes applied to *perfons*, as well as to things. So, in the Old Interlude of *Tom Tyler and his Wife*, 1661:
　　" So fhall I be fure
　　" To keep him in *ure.*"
The fame word occurs in *Promos and Caffandra*, 1578:
　　" The crafty man oft puts thefe wrongs in *ure.*"
　　　　　　　　　　　　　　　　　　STEEVENS.

My abfolute power and place here in Vienna,
And he fuppofes me travell'd to Poland;
For fo I have ftrew'd it in the common ear,
And fo it is receiv'd: Now, pious fir,
You will demand of me, why I do this?

Fri. Gladly, my lord.

Duke. We have ftrict ftatutes, and moft biting laws,
(The needful bits and curbs for head-ftrong fteeds,)[6]
Which for thefe fourteen years we have let fleep;[7]

---

[6] *The needful* bits *and* curbs *for* head-ftrong fteeds,] In the copies,
The needful bits *and* curbs *for* head-ftrong weeds.
There is no manner of analogy or confonance in the metaphors here: and, though the copies agree, I do not think the author would have talked of *bits* and *curbs* for *weeds*. On the other hand, nothing can be more proper, than to compare perfons of *unbridled licentioufnefs* to head-ftrong *fteeds:* and, in this view, *bridling the paffions* has been a phrafe adopted by our beft poets.
THEOBALD.

[7] *Which for thefe* fourteen *years we have let* fleep;] Thus the old copy; which alfo reads,——
" —— we have let *flip*." STEEVENS.

For *fourteen* I have made no fcruple to replace *nineteen*. The reafon will be obvious to him who recollects what the Duke [Claudio] has faid in a foregoing fcene. I have altered the odd phrafe of " *letting the laws* flip:" for how does it fort with the comparifon that follows, of a lion in his cave that went not out to prey? But letting the laws *fleep*, adds a particular propriety to the thing reprefented, and accords exactly too with the fimile. It is the metaphor too, that our author feems fond of ufing upon this occafion, in feveral other paffages of this play:
The law hath not been dead, though it hath flept;
—— *'Tis now* awake.
And, fo again:
—— *but this new governor*
Awakes *me all the enrolled* penalties;
—— *and for a name,*
Now puts the drowfy *and neglected* act
Frefhly on me. THEOBALD.

Even like an o'er-grown lion in a cave,
That goes not out to prey: Now, as fond fathers
Having bound up the threat'ning twigs of birch,
Only to ftick it in their children's fight,
For terror, not to ufe; in time the rod
Becomes more mock'd, than fear'd: [8] fo our de-
      crees,
Dead to infliction, to themfelves are dead;
And liberty plucks juftice by the nofe;
The baby beats the nurfe,[9] and quite athwart
Goes all decorum.

  Fri.   It refts in your grace
To unloofe this tied-up juftice, when you pleas'd:

The latter emendation may derive fupport from a paffage in *Hamlet*:

    " ——— How ftand I then,
    " That have a father kill'd, a mother ftain'd,
    " Excitements of my reafon and my blood,
    " And *let* all *fleep* ?"

If *flip* be the true reading, (which, however, I do not believe,) the fenfe may be,—which for thefe fourteen years we have fuffered to *pafs unnoticed, unobferved*; for fo the fame phrafe is ufed in *Twelfth Night*:—" Let him *let* this matter *flip*, and I'll give him my horfe, grey Capulet."

  Mr. Theobald altered *fourteen* to *nineteen*, to make the Duke's account correfpond with a fpeech of Claudio's in a former fcene, but without neceffity. *Claudio would naturally reprefent the period during which the law had not been put in practice, greater than it really was.* MALONE.

  Theobald's correction is mifplaced. If any correction is really neceffary, it fhould have been made where Claudio, in a foregoing fcene, fays *nineteen* years. I am difpofed to take the Duke's words. WHALLEY.

  [8] Becomes *more mock'd, than fear'd:*] *Becomes* was added by Mr. Pope, to reftore fenfe to the paffage, fome fuch word having been left out. STEEVENS.

  [9] *The baby beats the nurfe,*] This allufion was borrowed from an ancient print, entitled *The World turn'd upfide down*, where an infant is thus employed. STEEVENS.

And it in you more dreadful would have feem'd,
Than in lord Angelo.

   DUKE.   I do fear, too dreadful:
Sith[9] 'twas my fault to give the people fcope,
'Twould be my tyranny to ftrike, and gall them,
For what I bid them do: For we bid this be done,
When evil deeds have their permiffive pafs,
And not the punifhment.   Therefore, indeed, my
        father,
I have on Angelo impos'd the office;
Who may, in the ambufh of my name, ftrike home,
And yet my nature never in the fight,
To do it flander:[2] And to behold his fway,
I will, as 'twere a brother of your order,
Vifit both prince and people: therefore, I pr'ythee,
Supply me with the habit, and inftruct me
How I may formally in perfon bear[3] me

---

9 *Sith*—] i. e. fince. STEEVENS.

2 To *do* it *flander*:] The text ftood:
     So *do* in *flander:* ———
Sir Thomas Hanmer has very well corrected it thus:
     To *do* it *flander:*
Yet perhaps lefs alteration might have produced the true
reading:
     And yet my nature never, in the fight,
     So *doing flandered:* ———
And yet my nature never fuffer flander, by doing any open acts of
feverity. JOHNSON.

   The old text ftood,
     ————————————in the *fight*
     To do *in* flander:———
Hanmer's emendation is fupported by a paffage in *King Henry IV.*
P. I:
     " *Do me* no *flander*, Douglas, I dare fight." STEEVENS.

   Fight feems to be countenanced by the words *ambufh* and *ftrike.*
Sight was introduced by Mr. Pope. MALONE.

3 ——— in *perfon bear*—] Mr. Pope reads,
     ——— my *perfon bear.*

Like a true friar. More reasons for this action,
At our more leisure shall I render you ;
Only, this one :—Lord Angelo is precise ;
Stands at a guard * with envy ; scarce confesses
That his blood flows, or that his appetite
Is more to bread than stone : Hence shall we see,
If power change purpose, what our seemers be.

[*Exeunt.*

S C E N E V.

A Nunnery.

Enter Isabella *and* Francisca.

Isab. And have you nuns no further privileges ?
Fran. Are not these large enough ?
Isab. Yes, truly : I speak not as desiring more ;
But rather wishing a more strict restraint
Upon the sister-hood, the votarists of saint Clare.
Lucio. Ho! Peace be in this place ! [*Within*]
Isab.   Who's that which calls ?

Perhaps the word which I have inserted in the text, had dropped
out while the sheet was at press. A similar phrase occurs in *The
Tempest* :
" —— some good instruction give
" How I may *bear me* here."
Sir W. D'Avenant reads, in his alteration of the play:
I may in person a true friar seem.
The sense of the passage (as Mr. Henley observes) is—*How I
may demean myself, so as to support the character I have assumed.*

STEEVENS.

* *Stands at a guard*—] Stands on terms of defiance.
JOHNSON.

This rather means, to stand cautiously on his *defence*, than on
terms of defiance. M. MASON.

FRAN. It is a man's voice: Gentle Ifabella,
Turn you the key, and know his bufinefs of him;
You may, I may not; you are yet unfworn:
When you have vow'd, you muft not fpeak with
   men,
But in the prefence of the priorefs:
Then, if you fpeak, you muft not fhow your face;
Or, if you fhow your face, you muft not fpeak.
He calls again; I pray you, anfwer him.
       [*Exit* FRANCISCA.
 ISAB. Peace and profperity! Who is't that calls?

    Enter LUCIO.

 LUCIO. Hail, virgin, if you be; as thofe cheek-
   rofes
Proclaim you are no lefs! Can you fo ftead me,
As bring me to the fight of Ifabella,
A novice of this place, and the fair fifter
To her unhappy brother Claudio?
 ISAB. Why her unhappy brother? let me afk;
The rather, for I now muft make you know
I am that Ifabella, and his fifter.
 LUCIO. Gentle and fair, your brother kindly
   greets you:
Not to be weary with you, he's in prifon.
 ISAB. Woe me! For what?
 LUCIO. For that, which, if myfelf might be his
   judge,[5]
He fhould receive his punifhment in thanks:
He hath got his friend with child.

 [5] For that, which, *if myfelf might be his judge,*] Perhaps thefe
words were tranfpofed at the prefs. The fenfe feems to require—
That, for which, &c. MALONE.

Isab. Sir, make me not your ſtory.[6]

Lucio.   It is true.

I would not [7]—though 'tis my familiar ſin

---

[6] —— make *me not your ſtory.*] Do not, by deceiving me, make me a ſubjeƈt for a tale. JOHNSON.

Perhaps only, *Do not divert yourſelf with me, as you would with a ſtory,* do not make me the ſubjeƈt of your drama. Benedick talks of becoming—the *argument* of his own ſcorn. ✗

Sir W. D'Avenant reads—*ſcorn* inſtead of ſtory.

After all, the irregular phraſe [*me,* &c.] that, perhaps, obſcures this paſſage, occurs frequently in our author, and particularly in the next ſcene, where Eſcalus ſays: " Come *me* to what was done to her."—" Make *me* not your ſtory," may therefore ſignify— *invent not your ſtory on purpoſe to deceive me.* " *It is true,*" in Lucio's reply, means—*What I have already told you, is true.* STEEVENS.

Mr. Ritſon explains this paſſage, " do not make a *jeſt of me.*" REED.

I have no doubt that we ought to read (as I have printed,) Sir, *mock me* not:—your ſtory.

So, in *Macbeth :*

" Thou com'ſt to uſe thy tongue:—*thy ſtory* quickly."

In *King Lear* we have—" Pray, do not *mock* me."

I beſeech you, Sir, (ſays Iſabel) do not play upon my fears; reſerve this idle talk for ſome other occaſion;—proceed at once to your tale. Lucio's ſubſequent words, [" 'Tis true,"—i. e. you are right ; I thank you for reminding me ;] which, as the text has been hitherto printed, had no meaning, are then pertinent and clear. Mr. Pope was ſo ſenſible of the impoſſibility of reconciling them to what preceded in the old copy, that he fairly omitted them.

What Iſabella ſays afterwards, fully ſupports this emendation : " You do blaſpheme the good, in *mocking* me."

I have obſerved that almoſt every paſſage in our author, in which there is either a broken ſpeech, or a ſudden tranſition without a connecting particle, has been corrupted by the careleſſneſs of either the tranſcriber or compoſitor. See a note on *Love's Labour's Loſt,* Aƈt. II. ſc. i :

" A man of—ſovereign, peerleſs, he's eſteem'd."

And another on *Coriolanus,* Aƈt I. ſc. iv :

" You ſhames of Rome! you herd of—Boils and plagues

" Plaſter you o'er!" MALONE.

[7] *I would not —*] i. e. Be aſſured, I would not mock you. So afterwards: " Do not believe it :" i. e. Do not ſuppoſe that I would mock you. MALONE.

I am ſatisfied with the ſenſe afforded by the old punƈtuation.
                                  STEEVENS.

With maids to feem the lapwing,[8] and to jeft,
Tongue far from heart,—play with all virgins fo:[9]
I hold you as a thing enfky'd, and fainted;

---

[8] —— *'tis my familiar fin*
With maids to feem the lapwing,] The Oxford editor's note on
this paffage is in thefe words.: *The lapwings fly, with feeming fright
and anxiety, far from their nefts, to deceive thofe who feek their young.*
And do not all other birds do the fame ? But what has this to do
with the infidelity of a general lover, to whom this bird is compared ?
It is another quality of the lapwing that is here alluded to, viz. its
perpetually flying fo low and fo near the paffenger, that he thinks
he has it, and then is fuddenly gone again. This made it a proverbial expreffion to fignify a lover's falfhood : and it feems to be
a very old one; for Chaucer, in his *Plowman's Tale*, fays:
 " —— And *lapwings* that well conith lie."   WARBURTON.

The modern editors have not taken in the whole fimilitude
here : they have taken notice of the lightnefs of a fpark's behaviour to his miftrefs, and compared it to the *lapwing's* hovering
and fluttering as it flies. But the chief, of which no notice is
taken, is,—" —— *and to jeft.*" (See Ray's *Proverbs*) " The *lapwing* cries, *tongue far* from heart." i. e. moft fartheft from the neft,
i. e. She is, as Shakfpeare has it here,—*Tongue far from heart.*
" The farther fhe is from her neft, where her heart is with her
young ones, fhe is the louder, or perhaps all tongue."   SMITH.

Shakfpeare has an expreffion of the like kind, in his *Comedy of
Errors :*
 " *Adr.* Far from her neft the *lapwing* cries away ;
 " My heart prays for him, though my tongue do curfe."
We meet with the fame thought in Lyly's *Campafpe*, 1584 ; from
whence Shakfpeare might borrow it :
 " *Alex.* —— you refemble the *lapwing*, who crieth moft where
her neft is not, and fo, to lead me from efpying your love for
Campafpe, you cry Timoclea."   GREY.

[9] *I would not—though 'tis my familiar fin*
With maids to feem the lapwing, and to jeft,
Tongue far fromheart,—play with all virgins fo: &c.] This paf-
fage has been pointed in the modern editions thus :
 'Tis true:—I would not (though 'tis my familiar fin
With maids to feem the lapwing, and to jeft,
Tongue far from heart) play with all virgins fo:
I hold you, &c.
According to this punctuation, Lucio is made to deliver a fen-
timent directly oppofite to that which the author intended. *Though*

By your renouncement, an immortal spirit;
And to be talk'd with in sincerity,
As with a saint.

    Isab. You do blaspheme the good, in mocking me.

    Lucio. Do not believe it.   Fewness and truth,[2]
          'tis thus:
Your brother and his lover[3] have embrac'd:
As those that feed grow full; as blossoming time,[4]

'tis my common practice to jest with and to deceive all *virgins, I would
not so play with all virgins.*
    The sense, as I have regulated my text, appears to me clear and
easy. 'Tis very true, (says he) *I ought indeed, as you say, to
proceed at once to my story.* Be *assured*, I would not *mock you,*
Though it is my familiar practice to jest with maidens, and, like
the lapwing, to deceive them by my insincere prattle, *though, I say,
it is my ordinary and habitual practice* to sport in this manner with
all virgins, *yet I should never think of treating you so*; for I consider
you, in consequence of your having renounced the world, as an
immortal spirit, as one to whom I ought to speak with as much
sincerity as if I were addressing a saint. MALONE.
    Mr. Malone complains of a contradiction which I cannot find in
the speech of Lucio.   He has not said that it is his practice to jest
with and deceive *all* virgins.   " Though (says he) it is my
practice with *maids* to seem the lapwing, I would not play with *all*
virgins so;" meaning that she herself is the exception to his usual
practice.   Though he has treated other women with levity, he is
serious in his address to her. STEEVENS.
    [2] *Fewness and truth, &c.*] i. e. in *few words*, and those true
ones. *In few*, is many times thus used by Shakspeare. STEEVENS.
    [3] *Your brother and his* lover—] i. e. his mistress; *lover*, in our
author's time, being applied to the female as well as the male sex.
Thus, one of his poems, containing the lamentation of a deserted
maiden, is entitled, " A *Lover's* Complaint."
    So, in Tarleton's *Newes out of Purgatory*, bl. l. no date: " — he
spide the fetch, and perceived that all this while this was his *lover's*
husband, to whom he had revealed these escapes." MALONE.

    [4] —— as *blossoming time,*
    That from the seedness the bare fallow brings
    To teeming foison; *even so*—] As the sentence now stands, it
is apparently ungrammatical.   I read,
    At *blossoming time, &c.*

That from the feednefs the bare fallow brings
To teeming foifon; even fo her plenteous womb
Expreffeth his full tilth and hufbandry.

 Isab. Some one with child by him?——My coufin
   Juliet?

 Lucio. Is fhe your coufin?

 Isab. Adoptedly; as fchool-maids change their
   names,
By vain though apt affection.

 Lucio.   She it is.

 Isab. O, let him marry her!

 Lucio.   This is the point.
The duke is very ftrangely gone from hence;
Bore many gentlemen, myfelf being one,
In hand, and hope of action:⁶ but we do learn

That is, *As they that feed grow full, fo her womb now* at bloffoming
time, *as that time through which the feed time proceeds to the harveft,*
her womb fhows what has been doing. Lucio ludicroufly calls pregnancy *bloffoming time,* the time when fruit is promifed, though not
yet ripe. JOHNSON.

 Inftead of *that,* we may read—*doth*; and, inftead of *brings,*
bring. Foizon is *plenty.* So, in *The Tempeft:*
  " —— nature fhould bring forth,
  " Of its own kind, all *foizon,*" &c.
Teeming foizon, is abundant produce. STEEVENS.

 The paffage feems to me to require no amendment; and the
meaning of it is this: " As bloffoming time proves the good tillage
of the farmer, fo the fertility of her womb expreffes Claudio's
full tilth and hufbandry." By *bloffoming time* is meant, the time
when the ears of corn are formed. M. MASON.

 This fentence, as Dr. Johnfon has obferved, is apparently ungrammatical. I fufpect two half lines have been loft. Perhaps
however an imperfect fentence was intended, of which there are
many inftances in thefe plays:—or, *as* might have been ufed in
the fenfe of *like. Tilth* is *tillage.*

 So, in our author's 3d Sonnet:
  " For who is fhe fo fair, whofe unear'd *womb*
  " Difdains the *tillage* of thy hufbandry?" MALONE.

 ⁶ *Bore many gentlemen,* ——
  In hand, and hope of action:] *To bear in hand* is a common

By thofe that know the very nerves of ftate,
His givings out were of an infinite diftance
From his true-meant defign.   Upon his place,
And with full line [7] of his authority,
Governs lord Angelo; a man, whofe blood
Is very fnow-broth; one who never feels
The wanton ftings and motions of the fenfe;
But doth rebate and blunt his natural edge
With profits of the mind, ftudy and faft.
He (to give fear to ufe [8] and liberty,
Which have, for long, run by the hideous law,
As mice by lions,) hath pick'd out an act,
Under whofe heavy fenfe your brother's life
Falls into forfeit: he arrefts him on it;
And follows clofe the rigour of the ftatute,
To make him an example: all hope is gone,
Unlefs you have the grace [9] by your fair prayer
To foften Angelo: and that's my pith
Of bufinefs [2] 'twixt you and your poor brother.

ISAB. Doth he fo feek his life?

phrafe for *to keep in expectation and dependance*; but we fhould
read :   —— with *hope of action*. JOHNSON.

So, in *Macbeth*:
   " How you were *borne in hand*," &c.   STEEVENS.

7 ———— *with* full line —] With full extent, with the whole length.
                                                                                JOHNSON.

8 ———— *to give fear to* ufe —] To intimidate *ufe*, that is, practices
long countenanced by *cuftom*.   JOHNSON.

9 *Unlefs you have the grace* —] That is, the acceptablenefs, the
power of gaining favour. So, when fhe makes her fuit, the provoft
fays :
   " Heaven give thee moving *graces!*"   JOHNSON.

2 ——————— *my* pith
   Of bufinefs —] The inmoft part, the main of my meffage.
                                                                                JOHNSON.

So, in *Hamlet* :
   " And enterprizes of great *pith* and moment."   STEEVENS.

P 3

Lucio. Has cenfur'd him[3]
Already; and, as I hear, the provoft hath
A warrant for his execution.

Isab. Alas! what poor ability's in me
To do him good?

Lucio. Affay the power you have.

Isab. My power! Alas! I doubt,——

Lucio. Our doubts are traitors,
And make us lofe the good we oft might win,
By fearing to attempt: Go to lord Angelo,
And let him learn to know, when maidens fue,
Men give like gods; but when they weep and
                    kneel,
All their petitions are as freely theirs[4]
As they themfelves would owe them.[5]

Isab. I'll fee what I can do.

Lucio. But, fpeedily.

---

[3] *Has* cenfur'd *him*——] i. e. fentenced him. So, in *Othello*:
  " —— to you, lord governor,
  " Remains the *cenfure* of this hellifh villain." STEEVENS.

We fhould read, I think, He *has cenfured him*, &c. In the Mfs. of our author's time, and frequently in the printed copy of thefe plays, *he has*, when intended to be contracted, is written—*h'as.* Hence probably the miftake here.

So, in *Othello*, 4to. 1622:
  " And it is thought abroad, that 'twixt my fheets
  " *H'as* done my office."
Again, in *All's well that ends well*, p. 247, folio 1623, we find *H'as* twice, for *He has.* See alfo *Twelfth-Night*, p. 258, edit. 1623: " — *h'as* been told fo," for " *he has* been told fo."
                    MALONE.

[4] *All their petitions are as* freely *theirs*——] All their requefts are as freely granted to them, are granted in as full and beneficial a manner, as they themfelves could wifh. The editor of the fecond folio arbitrarily reads—*as* truly *theirs*; which has been followed in all the fubfequent copies. MALONE.

[5] —— *would* owe *them.*] To *owe*, fignifies in this place, as in many others, to poffefs, to have. STEEVENS.

Isab. I will about it ftraight ;
No longer ftaying but to give the mother [6]
Notice of my affair. I humbly thank you :
Commend me to my brother : foon at night
I'll fend him certain word of my fuccefs.

Lucio. I take my leave of you.

Isab. Good fir, adieu.
[*Exeunt.*

ACT II. SCENE I.

A Hall in ANGELO'S *Houfe.*

Enter ANGELO, ESCALUS, *a* Juftice, Provoft,[7]
Officers, *and other Attendants.*

Ang. We muft not make a fcare-crow of the law,
Setting it up to fear the birds of prey,[8]

[6] —— *the mother* —] The abbefs, or priorefs. JOHNSON.

[7] *Provoft,*] A Provoft martial, *Minfbieu* explains, " Prevoft des mareſchaux: Præfectus *rerum capitalium,* Prætor rerum capitalium." REED.

A *provoft* is generally the executioner of an army. So, in *The Famous Hiftory of Tho. Stukely,* 1605, bl. 1:
" *Provoft,* lay irons upon him, and take him to your charge."
Again, in *The Virgin Martyr,* by Maffinger :
" Thy *provoft,* to fee execution done
" On thefe bafe Chriftians in Cæfarea." STEEVENS.

A prifon for military offenders is at this day, in fome places, called the *Prevôt.* MALONE.

The *Provoft* here, is not a *military officer,* but a kind of fheriff or gaoler, fo called in foreign countries. DOUCE.

[8] —— *to fear the birds of prey,*] To *fear* is to *affright,* to *terrify.* So, in *The Merchant of Venice* :
" —— this afpect of mine
" Hath *fear'd* the valiant." STEEVENS.

P 4

And let it keep one shape, till custom make it
Their perch, and not their terror.

   Escal.   Ay, but yet
Let us be keen, and rather cut a little,
Than fall, and bruise to death: [9] Alas! this gentle-
    man,
Whom I would save, had a most noble father.
Let but your honour know,[2]
(Whom I believe to be most strait in virtue,)
That, in the working of your own affections,
Had time coher'd with place, or place with wishing,
Or that the resolute acting of your blood
Could have attain'd the effect of your own purpose,
Whether you had not sometime in your life
Err'd in this point which now you censure him,[3]
And pull'd the law upon you.

---

   [9] *Than* fall, *and bruise to death*:] I should rather read *fell*,
i. e. strike down. So, in *Timon of Athens:*
      " ——— All save thee,
      " I *fell* with curses."   WARBURTON.

   Fall is the old reading, and the true one.   Shakspeare has used
the same verb active in *The Comedy of Errors:*
      " ——— as easy may'st thou *fall*
      " A drop of water,"———
i. e. let fall.   So, in *As you Like it:*
      " ——— the executioner
      " *Falls* not the axe upon the humbled neck."   STEEVENS.

   Than fall, *and bruise to death*:] i. e. fall *the axe*;—or rather, let
the criminal fall, &c.   MALONE.

   [2] *Let but your honour* know,] To *know* is here to *examine,* to
take cognisance.   So, in *A Midsummer Night's Dream:*
      " Therefore, fair Hermia, question your desires;
      " *Know* of your youth, examine well your blood."   JOHNSON.

   [3] *Err'd in this point, which now you censure him,*] Some word seems
to be wanting to make this line sense.   Perhaps, we should read:
      " Err'd in this point which now you censure him *for.* STEEVENS.

   The sense undoubtedly requires, " ——— which now you censure
him *for,*" but the text certainly appears as the poet left it.   I have
elsewhere shewn that he frequently uses these elliptical expressions.
                                    MALONE.

Ang. 'Tis one thing to be tempted, Efcalus,
Another thing to fall.   I not deny,
The jury, paffing on the prifoner's life,
May, in the fworn twelve, have a thief or two
Guiltier than him they try : What's open made to
   juftice,
That juftice feizes.[4]   What know the laws,
That thieves do pafs on thieves?[5] 'Tis very preg-
   nant,[6]
The jewel that we find, we ftoop and take it,
Becaufe we fee it; but what we do not fee,
We tread upon, and never think of it.
You may not fo extenuate his offence,
For I have had[7] fuch faults; but rather tell me,
When I, that cenfure him, do fo offend,
Let mine own judgement pattern out my death,
And nothing come in partial.   Sir, he muft die.

 Escal. Be it as your wifdom will.

 Ang.   Where is the provoft?

---

 [4] *That juftice feizes.*] For the fake of metre, I think we fhould
read,—feizes *on*; or, perhaps, we fhould regulate the paffage thus:
  Guiltier than him they try : What's open made
  To juftice, juftice feizes.   What know, &c.   STEEVENS.

 [5] —— *What know the laws,*
  That thieves do pafs *on thieves?*] How can the adminiftrators
of the laws take cognizance of what I have juft mentioned? How
can they know, whether the jurymen who *decide* on the life or
death of thieves be themfelves as criminal as thofe whom they try?
To pafs on is a forenfick term.   MALONE.

 So, in *King Lear,* Act III. fc. vii:
   " Though well we may not *pafs upon* his life."
See my note on this paffage.   STEEVENS.

 [6] *'Tis very pregnant,*] "Tis *plain* that we muft act with bad
as with good; we punifh the faults, as we take the advantages that
lie in our way, and what we do not fee we cannot note.
           JOHNSON.

 [7] *For I have had* —] That is, *becaufe, by reafon that* I have had
fuch faults.   JOHNSON.

Prov. Here, if it like your honour.

Ang.   See that Claudio
Be executed by nine to-morrow morning:
Bring him his confeffor, let him be prepar'd;
For that's the utmoft of his pilgrimage.
                          [*Exit* Provoft.

Escal. Well, heaven forgive him! and forgive
                us all!
Some rife by fin, and fome by virtue fall:
Some run from brakes of vice, and anfwer none;
And fome condemned for a fault alone.[8]

---

[8] *Some rife,* &c.] This line is in the firft folio printed in Italics
as a quotation. All the folios read in the next line:
     Some run from brakes of ice, *and anfwer none.*
                                   JOHNSON.

The old reading is, perhaps, the true one, and may mean, *fome
run away from danger, and ftay to anfwer none of their faults,
whilft others are condemned only on account of a fingle frailty.*
If this be the true reading, it fhould be printed:
     Some run from breaks [i. e. fractures] *of ice,* &c.
Since I fuggefted this, I have found reafon to change my opinion.
A *brake* anciently meant not only a *fharp bit,* a *fnaffle,* but alfo the
engine with which farriers confined the legs of fuch unruly horfes
as would not otherwife fubmit themfelves to be fhod, or to have a
cruel operation performed on them. This, in fome places, is ftill
called a fmith's *brake.* In this laft fenfe, Ben Jonfon ufes the word
in his *Underwoods :*
     " And not think he had eat a ftake,
     " Or were fet up in a *brake.*"
And, for the former fenfe, fee *The Silent Woman,* Act IV.
Again, for the latter fenfe, *Buffy d'Ambois,* by Chapman:
     " Or, like a ftrumpet, learn to fet my face
     " In an eternal *brake.*"
Again, in *The Opportunity,* by Shirley, 1640:
     " He is fallen into fome *brake,* fome wench has tied him by the
legs."
Again, in *Holland's Leaguer,* 1633:
     " —— her I'll make
     " A ftale, to catch this courtier in a *brake.*"
I offer thefe quotations, which may prove of ufe to fome more
fortunate conjecturer; but am able myfelf to derive very little from
them to fuit the paffage before us.

Enter ELBOW, FROTH, Clown, Officers, *&c.*

ELB. Come, bring them away : if thefe be good
people in a common-weal, that do nothing but ufe

I likewife find from Holinfhed, p. 670, that the *brake* was an
engine of torture. " The faid Hawkins was caft into the Tower,
and at length brought to the *brake*, called the Duke of Excefter's
daughter, by means of which pain he fhewed many things," &c.

" When the Dukes of Exeter and Suffolk (fays Blackftone, in
his *Commentaries*, Vol. IV. chap. xxv. p. 320, 321,) and other
minifters of Hen VI. had laid a defign to introduce the civil law
into this kingdom as the rule of government, for a beginning
thereof they erected a rack for torture; which was called in de-
rifion the Duke of Exeter's Daughter, and ftill remains in the
Tower of London, where it was occafionally ufed as an engine of
ftate, not of law, more than once in the reign of Queen Elizabeth."
See Coke's Inftit. 35. Barrington, 69, 385. and Fuller's Worthies,
p. 317.

A part of this horrid engine ftill remains in the Tower, and the
following is the figure of it :

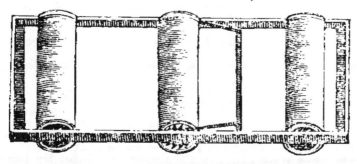

It confifts of a ftrong iron frame about fix feet long, with three
rollers of wood within it. The middle one of thefe, which has iron
teeth at each end, is governed by two ftops of iron, and was,
probably, that part of the machine which fufpended the powers of
the reft, when the unhappy fufferer was fufficiently ftrained by
the cords, &c. to begin confeffion. I cannot conclude this
account of it without confeffing my obligation to Sir Charles
Frederick, who politely condefcended to direct my enquiries, while

their abuses in common houses, I know no law:
bring them away.

his high command rendered every part of the Tower accessible to
my researches.

I have since observed that, in *Fox's Martyrs*, edit. 1596, p. 1843,
there is a representation of the same kind.   To this also, Skelton,
in his *Why come ye not to Court*, seems to allude:

> "   And with a cole rake
> " Bruise them on a *brake*."

If Shakspeare alluded to this engine, the sense of the contested
passage will be: *Some run more than once from engines of punishment,
and answer no interrogatories: while some are condemned to suffer for
a single trespass.*

It should not, however, be dissembled, that yet a plainer meaning may be deduced from the same words.   By *brakes of vice* may
be meant a collection, a number, a *thicket* of vices.   The same
image occurs in Daniel's *Civil Wars*, B. IV:

> "   Rushing into the thickest woods of spears,
> " And *brakes* of swords," &c.

That a *brake* meant a bush, may be known from Drayton's poem
on *Moses and his Miracles*:

> "   Where God unto the Hebrew spake,
> " Appearing from the burning *brake*."

Again, in *The Mooncalf* of the same author:

> "   He brings into a *brake* of briars and thorn,
> " And so entangles."

Mr. Tollet is of opinion that, by *brakes of vice*, Shakspeare means
only the *thorny paths of vice*,

So, in Ben Jonson's *Underwoods*, Whalley's edit. Vol. VI.
p. 367:

> "   Look at the false and cunning man, &c.———
> " Crush'd in the snakey *brakes* that he had past."

STEEVENS.

The words—*answer none* (that is, *make no confession of guilt*)
evidently shew that *brake of vice* here means the *engine of torture*.
The same mode of *question* is again referred to in Act V:

> "   To the *rack* with him: we'll touze you joint by joint,
> " But we will know this purpose."

The name of *brake of vice*, appears to have been given this
machine, from its resemblance to *that used to subdue vicious horses*;
to which Daniel thus refers:

> "   Lyke as the *brake* within the rider's hande
> " Doth *straine* the horse nye *wood* with grief of paine,
> " Not us'd before to come in such a band," &c.

HENLEY.

Ang. How now, fir! What's your name? and what's the matter?

Elb. If it pleafe your honour, I am the poor duke's conftable, and my name is Elbow; I do lean upon juftice, fir, and do bring in here before your good honour two notorious benefactors.

Ang. Benefactors? Well; what benefactors are they? are they not malefactors?

Elb. If it pleafe your honour, I know not well what they are: but precife villains they are, that I am fure of; and void of all profanation in the world, that good chriftians ought to have.

Escal. This comes off well;[9] here's a wife officer.

Ang. Go to: What quality are they of? Elbow is your name? Why doft thou not fpeak, Elbow?[2]

Clo. He cannot, fir; he's out at elbow.

I am not fatisfied with either the old or prefent reading of this very difficult paffage; yet have nothing better to propofe. The modern reading, *vice*, was introduced by Mr. Rowe. In *King Henry VIII.* we have

    " 'Tis but the fate of place, and the rough *brake*
    " That virtue muft go through." MALONE.

[9] *This comes off well*;] This is nimbly fpoken; this is volubly uttered. JOHNSON.

The fame phrafe is employed in *Timon of Athens*, and elfewhere; but in the prefent inftance it is ufed ironically. The meaning of it, when ferioufly applied to fpeech, is—This is well delivered, this ftory is well told. STEEVENS.

[2] *Why doft thou not fpeak*, Elbow?] Says Angelo to the conftable. " He cannot, fir, (quoth the *Clown*,) he's *out at elbow*." I know not whether this quibble be generally underftood: he is *out* at the word *elbow*, and *out* at the *elbow* of his coat. The *Conftable*, in his account of mafter *Froth* and the Clown, has a ftroke at the *Puritans*, who were very zealous againft the ftage about this time: " Precife villains they are, that I am fure of; and void of all profanation in the world, that good Chriftians ought to have." FARMER.

Ang. What are you, fir?

Elb. He, fir? a tapfter, fir; parcel-bawd;[3] one that ferves a bad woman; whofe houfe, fir, was, as they fay, pluck'd down in the fuburbs; and now fhe profeffes a hot-houfe,[4] which, I think, is a very ill houfe too.

Escal. How know you that?

Elb. My wife, fir, whom I deteft[5] before heaven and your honour,—

Escal. How! thy wife?

Elb. Ay, fir; whom, I thank heaven, is an honeft woman;—

Escal. Doft thou deteft her therefore?

Elb. I fay, fir, I will deteft myfelf alfo, as well as fhe, that this houfe, if it be not a bawd's houfe, it is pity of her life, for it is a naughty houfe.

Escal. How doft thou know that, conftable?

Elb. Marry, fir, by my wife; who, if fhe had been a woman cardinally given, might have been accufed in fornication, adultery, and all uncleanlinefs there.

Escal. By the woman's means?

---

[3] —— *a tapfter, fir; parcel-bawd;*] This we fhould now exprefs by faying, *he is* half-tapfter, half-bawd. JOHNSON.

Thus, in *King Henry IV.* P. II: " —— *a parcel*-gilt goblet." STEEVENS.

[4] —— *fhe profeffes a* hot-houfe,] A *hot-houfe* is an Englifh name for a *bagnio.* So, Ben Jonfon:

" Where lately harbour'd many a famous whore,
" A purging bill now fix'd upon the door,
" Tells you it is a *hot-houfe:* fo it may,
" And ftill be a whore-houfe." JOHNSON. ✳ ——

[5] —— *whom I* deteft—] He defigned to fay *proteft.* Mrs. Quickly makes the fame blunder in *The Merry Wives of Windfor,* Act I. fc. iv.—" But, I *deteft,* an honeft maid," &c. STEEVENS.

7

Again, in Goulart's Admirable Hiftories ✳o. 1607. "—hearing that they were together in a hot-houfe of an old woman's that dwelt by him." Steevens

—ink that Ellows, in both inftances detest for atteft; th. —otherof. M. Mason.

ELB. Ay, fir, by miftrefs Overdone's means:[6] but as fhe fpit in his face, fo fhe def✗d him.

CLO. Sir, if it pleafe your honour, this is not fo.

ELB. Prove it before thefe varlets here, thou honourable man, prove it.

ESCAL. Do you hear how he mifplaces?

[*To* ANGELO.

CLO. Sir, fhe came in great with child; and longing (faving your honour's reverence,) for ftew'd prunes;[7] fir, we had but two in the houfe, which at that very diftant time ftood, as it were, in a fruit-difh, a difh of fome three-pence; your honours have feen fuch difhes; they are not China difhes,[8] but very good difhes.

ESCAL. Go to, go to; no matter for the difh, fir.

CLO. No, indeed, fir, not of a pin; you are therein in the right: but, to the point: As I fay, this mif-trefs Elbow, being, as I fay, with child, and being great belly'd, and longing, as I faid, for prunes;

---

[6] *Ay, fir, by miftrefs Overdone's means:*] Here feems to have been fome mention made of Froth, who was to be accufed, and fome words therefore may have been loft, unlefs the irregularity of the narrative may be better imputed to the ignorance of the conftable.   JOHNSON.

[7] ——*ftew'd prunes;*] *Stewed prunes* were to be found in every brothel.

So, in Maroccus *Exftaticus,* or *Bankes's Bay Horfe in a Trance,* 1595: " With this ftocke of wenches will this truftie Roger and his Bettrice fet up, forfooth, with their pamphlet pots and *ftewed prunes,* &c. in a *finful faucer,*" &c.

See a note on the 3d fcene of the 3d Act of the Firft Part of *King Henry IV.* In the old copy *primes* are fpelt, according to vulgar pronunciation, *prewyns.*   STEEVENS.

[8] ——*not China difhes,*] A *China* difh, in the age of Shak-fpeare, muft have been fuch an uncommon thing, that the Clown's exemption of it, as no utenfil in a common brothel, is a ftriking circumftance in his abfurd and tautological depofition.

STEEVENS.

and having but two in the diſh, as I ſaid, maſter Froth here, this very man, having eaten the reſt, as I ſaid, and, as I ſay, paying for them very honeſtly;—for, as you know, maſter Froth, I could not give you three pence again.

Froth. No, indeed.

Clo. Very well : you being then, if you be re-member'd, cracking the ſtones of the foreſaid prunes.

Froth. Ay, ſo I did, indeed.

Clo. Why, very well : I telling you then, if you be remember'd, that ſuch a one, and ſuch a one, were paſt cure of the thing you wot of, unleſs they kept very good diet, as I told you *l*.

Froth. All this is true.

Clo. Why, very well then.

Escal. Come, you are a tedious fool : to the purpoſe.—What was done to Elbow's wife, that he hath cauſe to complain of? Come me to what was done to her.

Clo. Sir, your honour cannot come to that yet.

Escal. No, ſir, nor I mean it not.

Clo. Sir, but you ſhall come to it, by your honour's leave : And, I beſeech you, look into maſter Froth here, ſir ; a man of fourſcore pound a year ; whoſe father died at Hallowmas :—Was't not at Hallowmas, maſter Froth?

Froth. All-hollond eve.

Clo. Why, very well ; I hope here be truths : He, ſir, ſitting, as I ſay, in a lower chair,⁹ ſir ;—

---

⁹ ——*in a* lower chair,] Every houſe had formerly, among its other furniture, what was called——a *low chair*, deſigned for the eaſe of ſick people, and, occaſionally, occupied by lazy ones. Of theſe conveniencies I have ſeen many, though, perhaps, at preſent they are wholly difuſed. STEEVENS.

'twas in the *Bunch of Grapes*, where, indeed, you have a delight to fit: Have you not?

Froth. I have fo; becaufe it is an open room, and good for winter.

Clo. Why, very well then;—I hope here be truths.

Ang. This will laft out a night in Ruffia, When nights are longeft there: I'll take my leave, And leave you to the hearing of the caufe; Hoping, you'll find good caufe to whip them all.

Escal. I think no lefs: Good morrow to your lordfhip.   [*Exit* Angelo.
Now, fir, come on: What was done to Elbow's wife, once more?

Clo. Once, fir? there was nothing done to her once.

Elb. I befeech you, fir, afk him what this man did to my wife.

Clo. I befeech your honour, afk me.

Escal. Well, fir; What did this gentleman to her?

Clo. I befeech you, fir, look in this gentléman's face:—Good mafter Froth, look upon his honour; 'tis for a good purpofe: Doth your honour mark his face?

Escal. Ay, fir, very well.

Clo. Nay, I befeech you, mark it well.

Escal. Well, I do fo.

Clo. Doth your honour fee any harm in his face?

Escal. Why, no.

Clo. I'll be fuppofed * upon a book, his face is the worft thing about him: Good then; if his face be the worft thing about him, how could mafter

---

* *I'll be fuppofed*—] He means *depofed*. Malone.

Froth do the conftable's wife any harm? I would know that of your honour.

Escal. He's in the right: Conftable, what fay you to it?

Elb. Firft, an it like you, the houfe is a refpected houfe; next, this is a refpected fellow; and his miftrefs is a refpected woman.

Clo. By this hand, fir, his wife is a more refpected perfon than any of us all.

Elb. Varlet, thou lieft; thou lieft, wicked varlet: the time is yet to come, that fhe was ever refpected with man, woman, or child.

Clo. Sir, fhe was refpected with him before he married with her.

Escal. Which is the wifer here? Juftice, or Iniquity? [3]—Is this true?

Elb. O thou caitiff! O thou varlet! O thou wicked Hannibal! [4] I refpected with her, before I was married to her? If ever I was refpected with her, or fhe with me, let not your worfhip think me the poor duke's officer:—Prove this, thou wicked Hannibal, or I'll have mine action of battery on thee.

---

[3] *Juftice, or Iniquity?*] Thefe were, I fuppofe, two perfonages well known to the audience by their frequent appearance in the old moralities. The words, therefore, at that time produced a combination of ideas, which they have now loft. JOHNSON.

Juftice or Iniquity?] i. e. The Conftable or the Fool. Efcalus calls the latter *Iniquity*, in allufion to the old *Vice*, a familiar character, in the ancient moralities and dumb-fhews. *Juftice* may have a fimilar allufion, which I am unable to explain. *Iniquitie* is one of the perfonages in the "Worthy interlude of *Kynge Darius*," 4to. bl. l. no date. And in the Firft Part of *King Henry IV.* Prince Henry calls Falftaff,—"that reverend *Vice*, that grey Iniquity." RITSON.

[4] —— *Hannibal!*] Miftaken by the conftable for *Cannibal.*
JOHNSON.

Escal. If he took you a box o' the ear, you might have your action of flander too.

Elb. Marry, I thank your good worfhip for it: What is't your worfhip's pleafure I fhall do with this wicked caitiff?

Escal. Truly, officer, becaufe he hath fome of-fences in him, that thou wouldft difcover if thou couldft, let him continue in his courfes, till thou know'ft what they are.

Elb. Marry, I thank your worfhip for it:—Thou feeft, thou wicked varlet now, what's come upon thee; thou art to continue now, thou varlet; thou art to continue.⁵

Escal. Where were you born, friend? [*To* Froth.

Froth. Here in Vienna, fir.

Escal. Are you of fourfcore pounds a year?

Froth. Yes, and't pleafe you, fir.

Escal. So.—What trade are you of, fir?
[*To the* Clown.

Clo. A tapfter; a poor widow's tapfter.

Escal. Your miftrefs's name?

Clo. Miftrefs Over-done.

Escal. Hath fhe had any more than one hufband?

Clo. Nine, fir; Over-done by the laft.

Escal. Nine!—Come hither to me, mafter Froth. Mafter Froth, I would not have you ac-quainted with tapfters; they will draw you,⁶ mafter

---

⁵ —— *thou to* continue.] Perhaps Elbow, mifinterpreting the language of Efcalus, fuppofes the Clown is to *continue in confinement*; at leaft, he conceives fome fevere punifhment or other to be implied by the word—*continue*. STEEVENS.

⁶ —— *they will* draw *you*,] *Draw* has here a clufter of fenfes. As it refers to the tapfter, it fignifies *to drain, to empty*; as it is

Froth, and you will hang them: Get you gone, and let me hear no more of you.

FROTH. I thank your worſhip: For mine own part, I never come into any room in a taphouſe, but I am drawn in.

ESCAL. Well; no more of it, maſter Froth: farewell. [*Exit* FROTH.]——Come you hither to me, maſter tapſter; what's your name, maſter tapſter?

CLO. Pompey.[6]

ESCAL. What elſe?

CLO. Bum, ſir.

ESCAL. 'Troth, and your bum is the greateſt thing about you;[7] ſo that, in the beaſtlieſt ſenſe, you are

related to *hang*, it means *to be conveyed to execution on a hurdle.* In Froth's anſwer, it is the ſame as *to bring along by ſome motive or power.* JOHNSON.

[6] *Pompey.*] His miſtreſs, in a preceding ſcene, calls him *Thomas.* RITSON.

[7] —— *greateſt thing about you;*] Greene, in one of his pieces, mentions the "*great bumme of Paris.*"

Again, in *Tyro's Roaring Megge,* 1598:
   " Tyro's round breeches have a *cliffe* behind."
                                                        STEEVENS.

Harriſon, in his *Deſcription of Britain,* prefixed to Holinſhed's Chronicle, condemns the exceſs of apparel amongſt his countrymen, and thus proceeds: " Neither can we be more juſtly burdened with any reproche than inordinate behaviour in apparell, for which moſt nations deride us; as alſo for that *we men doe ſeeme to beſtowe moſt coſt upon our arſes,* and much more than upon all the reſt of our bodies, as women do likewiſe upon their heads and ſhoulders." Should any curious reader wiſh for more information upon this ſubject, he is referred to " Strutt's Manners and Cuſtoms of the Engliſh," Vol. III. p. 86. DOUCE.

But perhaps an ancient MS. ballad, entitled, *A lamentable complaint of the pore country men againſte* great hoſe, *for the loſſe of there cattelles tailes,* Muſ. Brit. MS. Harl. 367. may throw further light on the ſubject. This ballad conſiſts of 41 ſtanzas. From theſe the following are ſelected :

Pompey the great. Pompey, you are partly a bawd,
Pompey, howfoever you colour it in being a tap-

5. " For proude and paynted parragenns,
   " And *monstrous breched* beares,
   " This realme almoft hath cleane diftroy'd,
   " Which I reporte with teares.——

9. " And chefely thofe of eache degree
   " Who *monftrous hofe* delyght,
   " As monfters fell, have done to us
   " Moft grevus hurte and fpyte.——

11. " As now of late in leffer thinges
    " To furnyfhe forthe theare pryde,
    " With woole, with flaxe, with hare alfo,
    " To make theare *bryches wyde*.

12. " What hurte and damage doth enfew
    " And fall upon the poore,
    " For want of woll and flax of late
    " Which *monnftrus hofe* devore.——

14. " But heare hath fo poffeffed of late
    " The *bryche of every knave*,
    " That none one beaft nor horfe can tell
    " Which waye his tale to faufe.——

23. " And that with fpeede to take awaye
    " *Great bryches* as the caufe
    " Of all this hurte, or ealfe to make
    " Some fharpe and houlfome lawes,——

39. " So that in fyne the charytie
    " Whiche Chryften men fhoulde fave,
    " By dyvers wayes is blemyfhed,
    " To *boulfter breaches* brave.

40. " But now for that noe remedye
    " As yet cann wel be founde,
    " I wolde that fuche as weare this heare
    " Weare well and trewly bounde,

41. " With every heare a loufe to have,
    " To *ftuffe their breyches* oute ;
    " And then I truft they wolde not weare
    " Nor beare *fuche baggs* about.''

                    Finis.

                    Q 3

*lfo the Perfones Tale of Chaucer: " a
ftokkes of heare behinde, that fervn as
under part of a fhe ape in the full of the.*

fter. Are you not? come, tell me true; it fhall be the better for you.

Clo. Truly, fir, I am a poor fellow, that would live.

Escal. How would you live, Pompey? by being a bawd? What do you think of the trade Pompey? is it a lawful trade?

Clo. If the law would allow it, fir.

Escal. But the law will not allow it, Pompey; nor it fhall not be allowed in Vienna.

Clo. Does your worfhip mean to geld and fpay all the youth in the city?

Escal. No, Pompey.

Clo. Truly, fir, in my poor opinion, they will to't then: If your worfhip will take order[7] for the drabs and the knaves, you need not to fear the bawds.

Escal. There are pretty orders beginning, I can tell you: it is but heading and hanging.

Clo. If you head and hang all that offend that way but for ten year together, you'll be glad to give out a commiffion for more heads. If this law held in Vienna ten year, I'll rent the faireft houfe in it, after three pence a bay:[8] If you live to fee this come to pafs, fay, Pompey told you fo.

In confequence of a diligent infpection of ancient pictures and prints, it may be pronounced that this ridiculous fafhion appeared in the early part of Queen Elizabeth's reign, then declined, and re-commenced at the beginning of that of James the Firft. STEEVENS.

[7] ——*take order*—] i. e. *take meafures.* So, in *Othello:*
" Honeft Iago hath *ta'en order* for't." STEEVENS.

[8] *I'll rent the faireft houfe in it, after three pence a bay:*] A *bay* of building is, in many parts of England, a common term; of which the beft conception that ever I could obtain, is, that it is the fpace between the main beams of the roof; fo that a barn croffed twice with beams is a barn of three *bays.* JOHNSON.

Escal. Thank you, good Pompey: and, in requital of your prophecy, hark you,—I advise you, let me not find you before me again upon any complaint whatsoever, no, not for dwelling where you do; if I do, Pompey, I shall beat you to your tent, and prove a shrewd Cæsar to you; in plain dealing, Pompey, I shall have you whipt: so for this time, Pompey, fare you well.

Clo. I thank your worship for your good counsel; but I shall follow it, as the flesh and fortune shall better determine.
Whip me? No, no; let carman whip his jade;
The valiant heart's not whipt out of his trade.

             [*Exit.*

Escal. Come hither to me, master Elbow; come hither, master constable. How long have you been in this place of constable?

Elb. Seven year and a half, sir.

Escal. I thought, by your readiness[9] in the office, you had continued in it some time: You say, seven years together?

Elb. And a half, sir.

Escal. Alas! it hath been great pains to you! They do you wrong to put you so oft upon't: Are there not men in your ward sufficient to serve it?

  " ——— that by the yearly birth
  " The large-*bay'd* barn doth fill," &c.
I forgot to take down the title of the work from which this instance is adopted. Again, in Hall's *Virgidemiarum*, Lib. IV:
  " His rent in faire respondence must arise,
  " To double trebles of his one yeares price;
  " Of *ewe bayes* breadth, God wot, a silly cote
  " Whose thatched spars are furr'd with sluttish soote." STEEVENS.

 9 ——— *by your readiness*—] Old copy—*the* readiness. Corrected by Mr. Pope. In the MSS. of our author's age, *y^e* and *y^r* (for so they were frequently written) were easily confounded. MALONE.

Elb. Faith, fir, few of any wit in fuch matters: as they are chofen, they are glad to choofe me for them; I do it for fome piece of money, and go through with all.

Escal. Look you, bring me in the names of fome fix or feven, the moft fufficient of your parifh.

Elb. To your worfhip's houfe, fir?

Escal. To my houfe: Fare you well. [*Exit* El-bow.] What's o'clock, think you?

Just. Eleven, fir.

Escal. I pray you home to dinner with me.

Just. I humbly thank you.

Escal. It grieves me for the death of Claudio; But there's no remedy.

Just. Lord Angelo is fevere.

Escal.   It is but needful: Mercy is not itfelf, that oft looks fo; Pardon is ftill the nurfe of fecond woe: But yet,——Poor Claudio!——There's no remedy. Come, fir.   [*Exeunt.*

SCENE II.

Another Room in the fame.

Enter Provoft, *and a* Servant.

Serv. He's hearing of a caufe; he will come straight. I'll tell him of you.

Prov. Pray you, do. [*Exit* Servant.] I'll know His pleafure; may be, he will relent: Alas, He hath but as offended in a dream! All fects, all ages fmack of this vice; and he To die for it!——

Enter ANGELO.

ANG.　　　　Now, what's the matter, provoſt?

PROV. Is it your will Claudio ſhall die to-morrow?

ANG. Did I not tell thee, yea? hadſt thou not
　　　order?
Why doſt thou aſk again?

PROV.　　　　　Leſt I might be too raſh:
Under your good correction, I have ſeen,
When, after execution, judgement hath
Repented o'er his doom.

ANG.　　　　　Go to; let that be mine:
Do you your office, or give up your place,
And you ſhall well be ſpar'd.

PROV.　　　　I crave your honour's pardon.—
What ſhall be done, ſir, with the groaning Juliet?
She's very near her hour.

ANG.　　　　Diſpoſe of her
To ſome more fitter place; and that with ſpeed.

Re-enter Servant.

SERV. Here is the ſiſter of the man condemn'd,
Deſires acceſs to you.

ANG.　　　　Hath he a ſiſter?

PROV. Ay, my good lord; a very virtuous maid,
And to be ſhortly of a ſiſterhood,
If not already.

ANG.　　　Well, let her be admitted.
　　　　　　　　　　　　[*Exit* Servant.
See you, the fornicatreſs be remov'd;
Let her have needful, but not laviſh, means;
There ſhall be order for it.

Enter LUCIO *and* ISABELLA.

PROV. Save your honour! [9]   [*Offering to retire.*

ANG. Stay a little while. [2]——[*To* ISAB.] You are
welcome : What's your will ?

ISAB. I am a woeful fuitor to your honour,
Pleafe but your honour hear me.

ANG.   Well; what's your fuit?

ISAB. There is a vice, that moft I do abhor,
And moft defire fhould meet the blow of juftice;
For which I would not plead, but that I muft;
For which I muft not plead, but that I am
At war, 'twixt will, and will not. [3]

[9] *Save* your honour!] *Your honour*, which is fo often repeated
in this fcene, was in our author's time the ufual mode of addrefs
to a *lord.* It had become antiquated after the Reftoration; for Sir
William D'Avenant in his alteration of this play has fubftituted
your excellence in the room of it. MALONE.

[2] *Stay a little while.*] It is not clear why the Provoft is bidden
to ftay, nor when he goes out. JOHNSON.

The entrance of Lucio and Ifabella fhould not, perhaps, be made
till after Angelo's fpeech to the Provoft, who had only announced
a lady, and feems to be detained as a witnefs to the purity of the
deputy's converfation with her. His *exit* may be fixed with that
of Lucio and Ifabella. He cannot remain longer, and there is no
reafon to think he departs before. RITSON.

Stay a little while, is faid by Angelo, in anfwer to the words,
" *Save your honour*;" which denoted the Provoft's intention to
depart. Ifabella ufes the fame words to Angelo, when fhe *goes out*,
near the conclufion of this fcene. So alfo, when fhe offers to retire,
on finding her fuit ineffectual : " Heaven keep your honour !"
MALONE.

[3] *For which I muft not plead, but that I am*
At war, 'twixt will, *and* will not.] This is obfcure; perhaps
it may be mended by reading :
    For which I muft now plead; but yet I am
    At war, 'twixt will, and will not.
Yet and *yt* are almoft undiftinguifhable in an ancient manufcript.

7

Ang.   Well; the matter?

Isab. I have a brother is condemn'd to die:
I do befeech you, let it be his fault,
And not my brother.[4]

Prov.   Heaven give thee moving graces!

Ang. Condemn the fault, and not the actor of it!
Why, every fault's condemn'd, ere it be done:
Mine were the very cypher of a function,
To find the faults,[5] whofe fine ftands in record,
And let go by the actor.

Isab.   O juft, but fevere law!
I had a brother then.—Heaven keep your honour!
                                    [*Retiring.*

Lucio. [*To* Isab.] Give't not o'er fo: to him
          again, intreat him;
Kneel down before him, hang upon his gown;
You are too cold: if you fhould need a pin,
You could not with more tame a tongue defire it:
To him, I fay.

Yet no alteration is neceffary, fince the fpeech is not unintelligible
as it now ftands. JOHNSON.

For which I muft not plead, but that I am
At war, 'twixt will, and will not.] i. e. for which I muft not
plead, but that there is a conflict in my breaft betwixt my affection
for my brother, which induces me to plead for him, and my regard
to virtue, which forbids me to intercede for one guilty of fuch a
crime; and I find the former more powerful than the latter. MALONE.

[4] —— *let it be his fault,*
And not my brother.] i. e. let his fault be condemned, or extir-
pated, but let not my brother himfelf fuffer. MALONE.

[5] *To* find *the faults,*] The old copy reads—To *fine,* &c.
                                        STEEVENS.
To *fine* means, I think, to pronounce the *fine* or fentence of the
law, appointed for certain crimes. Mr. Theobald, without neceffity,
reads *find.* The repetition is much in our author's manner. MALONE.

Theobald's emendation may be juftified by a paffage in *King Lear:*
    " All's not *offence* that indifcretion *finds,*
    " And dotage terms fo." STEEVENS.

Isab. Muft he needs die?

Ang.   Maiden, no remedy.

Isab. Yes; I do think that you might pardon him,
And neither heaven, nor man, grieve at the mercy.

Ang. I will not do't.

Isab.   But can you, if you would?

Ang. Look, what I will not, that I cannot do.

Isab. But might you do't, and do the world no
                    wrong,
If fo your heart were touch'd with that remorfe [6]
As mine is to him?

Ang.   He's fentenc'd; 'tis too late.

Lucio. You are too cold   [*To* Isabella.

Isab. Too late? why, no; I, that do fpeak a word,
May call it back again : [7] Well believe this, [8]
No ceremony that to great ones 'longs,
Not the king's crown, nor the deputed fword,
The marfhal's truncheon, nor the judge's robe,
Become them with one half fo good a grace,
As mercy does.   If he had been as you,
And you as he, you would have flipt like him;
But he, like you, would not have been fo ftern.

---

[6] —— *touch'd with that* remorfe ——] *Remorfe,* in this place, as
in many others, fignifies *pity*.
    So, in the 5th Act of this play :
        " My fifterly *remorfe* confutes my honour,
        " And I did yield to him."
Again, in Heywood's *Iron Age*, 1632:
        " The perfect image of a wretched creature,
        " His fpeeches beg *remorfe*."
See *Othello*, Act III.   Steevens.

[7] *May call it* back *again :*] The word *back* was inferted by the
editor of the fecond folio, for the fake of the metre.   Malone.

    Surely, it is added for the fake of *fenfe* as well as *metre.* Steevens.

[8] —— Well *believe this,*] Be thoroughly affured of this.
                                        Theobald.

Ang. Pray you, begone.

Isab. I would to heaven I had your potency,
And you were Ifabel! fhould it then be thus?
No; I would tell what 'twere to be a judge,
And what a prifoner.

Lucio. Ay, touch him: there's the vein. [*Afide.*

Ang. Your brother is a forfeit of the law,
And you but wafte your words.

Isab. Alas! alas!
Why, all the fouls that were,[9] were forfeit once;
And He that might the vantage beft have took,
Found out the remedy: How would you be,
If he, which is the top of judgement, fhould
But judge you as you are? O, think on that;
And mercy then will breathe within your lips,
Like man new made.[2]

---

[9] *——all the fouls that* were,] This is falfe divinity. We
fhould read—*are.* WARBURTON.

I fear, the player, in this inftance, is a better divine than the
prelate. The *fouls that* WERE, evidently refer to Adam and Eve,
whofe tranfgreffion rendered them obnoxious to the penalty of
annihilation, but for the remedy which the author of their being
moft gracioufly provided. The learned Bifhop, however, is more
fuccefsful in his next explanation. HENLEY.

[2] *And mercy then will breathe within your lips,*
Like man new made.] This is a fine thought, and finely expreffed. The meaning is, that *mercy will add fuch a grace to your
perfon, that you will appear as amiable as a man come frefh out of the
hands of his Creator.* WARBURTON.

I rather think the meaning is, *You will then change the feverity
of your prefent character.* In familiar fpeech, *You would be quite
another man.* JOHNSON.

And mercy then will breathe within your lips,
Like man new made.] You will then appear as tender-hearted
and merciful as the firft man was in his days of innocence, immediately after his creation. MALONE.

I incline to a different interpretation :—*And you, Angelo, will
breathe new life into Claudio, as the Creator animated Adam, by
" breathing into his noftrils the breath of life."* HOLT WHITE.

Ang.   Be you content, fair-maid;
It is the law, not I, condemns your brother:
Were he my kinfman, brother, or my fon,
It fhould be thus with him;—he muft die to-morrow.

Isab. To-morrow? O, that's fudden! Spare him,
                  fpare him;
He's not prepar'd for death! Even for our kitchens
We kill the fowl of feafon;² fhall we ferve heaven
With lefs refpect than we do minifter
To our grofs felves? Good, good my lord, bethink
                  you:
Who is it that hath died for this offence?
There's many have committed it.

Lucio.   Ay, well faid.

Ang. The law hath not been dead, though it hath
                  flept:³
Thofe many had not dar'd to do that evil,
If the firft man that did the edict infringe,⁴
Had anfwer'd for his deed: now, 'tis awake;
Takes note of what is done; and, like a prophet,
Looks in a glafs,⁵ that fhows what future evils,

---

² —— *of feafon;*] i. e. when it is in feafon. So, in *The Merry
Wives of Windfor*: " —— back; and *of the feafon* too it fhall
appear." STEEVENS.

³ *The law hath not been dead, though it hath flept:*] *Dormiunt ali-
quando leges, moriuntur nunquam*, is a maxim in our law. HOLT WHITE.

⁴ *If the firft man*, &c.] The word *man* has been fupplied by
the modern editors. I would rather read——
          If he, the firft, &c. TYRWHITT.
Man was introduced by Mr. Pope. MALONE.

⁵ —— *like a prophet,*
     Looks in a glafs,] This alludes to the fopperies of the *beril*,
much ufed at that time by cheats and fortune-tellers to predict by.
                                              WARBURTON.
See *Macbeth*, Act IV. fc. i.
So again, in *Vittoria Corombona*, 1612:
     " How long have I beheld the devil *in chryftal?*" STEEVENS.
The *beril*, which is a kind of cryftal, hath a weak tincture of

(Either now,[6] or by remissness new–conceiv'd,
And so in progress to be hatch'd and born,)
Are now to have no successive degrees,
But, where they live, to end.[7]

   Isab.   Yet show some pity.

   Ang. I show it most of all, when I show justice;
For then I pity those I do not know,[8]

red in it. Among other tricks of astrologers, the discovery of past or future events was supposed to be the consequence of looking into it. See *Aubrey's Miscellanies*, p. 165. edit. 1721. REED.

  [6] *Either now,*] Thus the old copy. Modern editors read— *Or new*— STEEVENS.

  [7] *But,* where *they live, to end.*] The old copy reads—But, *here* they live, to end. Sir Thomas Hanmer substituted *ere* for *here*; but *where* was, I am persuaded, the author's word.
So, in *Coriolanus*, Act V. sc. v :
    " —— but *there to end,*
    " WHERE he was to begin, and give away
    " The benefit of our levies," &c.
Again, in *Julius Cæsar* :
    " And WHERE *I did begin, there shall I end.*"
The prophecy is not, that future evils should end, *ere*, or before they are born ; or, in other words, that there should be no more evil in the world (as Sir T. Hanmer by his alteration seems to have understood it ;) but, that they should *end* WHERE they *began* i. e. with the criminal ; who being punished for his first offence, could not proceed by *successive degrees* in wickedness, nor excite others, by his impunity, to vice. So, in the next speech :
    " And do him right, that, answering *one* foul wrong,
    " Lives not to act *another.*"
It is more likely that a letter should have been omitted at the press, than that one should have been added.
The same mistake has happened in *The Merchant of Venice*, folio, 1623, p. 173, col. 2 :—" ha, ha, *here* in Genoa."—instead of— " *where?* in Genoa ?" MALONE.

  Dr. Johnson applauds Sir Thomas Hanmer's emendation. I prefer that of Mr. Malone. STEEVENS.

  [8] ——*show some pity.*
    Ang. I show it most of all, when I show justice ;
    For then I pity those I do not know,] This was one of Hale's memorials. *When I find myself swayed to mercy, let me remember, that there is a mercy likewise due to the country.* JOHNSON.

Which a difmifs'd offence would after gall ;
And do him right, that, anfwering one foul wrong,
Lives not to act another.   Be fatisfied ;
Your brother dies to-morrow ; be content.

  Isab. So you muft be the firft, that gives this
    fentence ;
And he, that fuffers : O, it is excellent
To have a giant's ftrength ; but it is tyrannous,
To ufe it like a giant.[8]

  Lucio.   That's well faid.

  Isab. Could great men thunder
As Jove himfelf does, Jove would ne'er be quiet,
For every pelting,[9] petty officer,
Would ufe his heaven for thunder ; nothing but
    thunder.——
Merciful heaven !
Thou rather, with thy fharp and fulphurous bolt,
Split'ft the unwedgeable and gnarled oak,[2]
Than the foft myrtle ;—O, but man, proud man ![3]

---

[8] *To ufe it* like a giant.] Ifabella alludes to the favage conduct of *giants* in ancient romances. STEEVENS.

[9] —— *pelting.*] i. e. paltry.
 This word I meet with in *Mother Bombie*, 1594:
  " — will not fhrink the city for a *pelting* jade." STEEVENS.

[2] ——gnarled *oak*,] *Gnarre* is the old Englifh word for a *knot in wood.*
So, in *Antonio's Revenge*, 1602 :
  " Till by degrees the tough and *gnarly* trunk
  " Be riv'd in funder."
Again, in Chaucer's *Knight's Tale*, Tyrwhitt's edit. v. 1979 :
  " With knotty *knarry* barrein trees old." STEEVENS.

[3] *Than the foft myrtle ;—O, but man, proud man !*] The defective metre of this line fhews that fome word was accidentally omitted at the prefs ; probably fome additional epithet to *man* ; perhaps *weak*,—" but man, *weak*, proud man—" The editor of the fecond folio, to fupply the defect, reads—O, but man, &c. which, like almoft all the other emendations of that copy, is the worft and the moft improbable that could have been chofen. MALONE.

 I am content with the emendation of the fecond folio, which I conceive to have been made on the authority of fome manufcript, or corrected copy. STEEVENS.

Dreſt in a little brief authority;
Moſt ignorant of what he's moſt aſſur'd,
His glaſſy eſſence,—like an angry ape,
Plays ſuch fantaſtick tricks before high heaven,
As make the angels weep;[4] who, with our ſpleens,
Would all themſelves laugh mortal.[5]

Lucio. O, to him, to him, wench: he will relent;
He's coming; I perceive't.

Prov.   Pray heaven ſhe win him!

Isab. We cannot weigh our brother with ourſelf:[6]
Great men may jeſt with ſaints: 'tis wit in them;
But, in the leſs, foul profanation.

Lucio. Thou'rt in the right, girl; more o' that.

***

[4] *As make the angels weep;*] The notion of angels weeping for the ſins of men is rabbinical.—*Ob peccatum flentes angelos inducunt Hebræorum magiſtri.*—Grotius ad S. Lucam. THEOBALD.

[5] *——who, with our ſpleens,*
    Would all themſelves laugh mortal.] Mr. Theobald ſays the meaning of this is, *that if they were endowed with our ſpleens and periſhable organs, they would laugh themſelves out of immortality;* or, as we ſay in common life, laugh themſelves dead; which amounts to this, that if they were mortal, they would not be immortal. Shakſpeare meant no ſuch nonſenſe. By *ſpleens,* he meant that peculiar turn of the human mind, that always inclines it to a ſpiteful, unſeaſonable mirth. Had the angels *that,* ſays Shakſpeare, they would laugh themſelves out of their immortality, by indulging a paſſion which does not deſerve that prerogative. The ancients thought, that immoderate laughter was cauſed by the bigneſs of the ſpleen. WARBURTON.

[6] *We cannot weigh our brother with* ourſelf:] *We* mortals, proud and fooliſh, cannot prevail on our paſſions to *weigh* or compare *our brother,* a being of like nature and like frailty, *with ourſelf.* We have different names and different judgements for the ſame faults committed by perſons of different condition.
                                                        JOHNSON.

The reading of the old copy, *ourſelf,* which Dr. Warburton changed to *yourſelf,* is ſupported by a paſſage in the fifth Act:
    " ——If he had ſo offended,
    " He would have *weigh'd* thy *brother* by *himſelf,*
    " And not have cut him off." MALONE.

Isab. That in the captain's but a cholerick word,
Which in the soldier is flat blasphemy.

Lucio. Art advis'd o' that? more on't.

Ang. Why do you put these sayings upon me?

Isab. Because authority, though it err like others,
Hath yet a kind of medicine in itself,
That skins the vice o' the top:[6] Go to your bosom;
Knock there; and ask your heart, what it doth know
That's like my brother's fault: if it confess
A natural guiltiness, such as is his,
Let it not sound a thought upon your tongue
Against my brother's life.

Ang.   She speaks, and 'tis
Such sense, that my sense breeds with it.[7]——Fare
              you well.

[6] *That* skins *the vice o' the top:*] Shakspeare is fond of this indelicate metaphor. So, in *Hamlet:*
    " It will but *skin* and film the ulcerous place." STEEVENS.

[7] —— *that my sense* breeds *with it.*] Thus all the folios. Some later editor has changed *breeds* to *bleeds,* and Dr. Warburton blames poor Theobald for recalling the old word, which yet is certainly right. *My sense* breeds *with her sense,* that is, new thoughts are stirring in my mind, new conceptions are *hatched* in my imagination. So we say, to *breed* over thought. JOHNSON.

Sir William D'Avenant's alteration favours the sense of the old reading—*breeds,* which Mr. Pope had changed to *bleeds.*
    —— *She speaks such sense*
    As with my reason breeds *such images*
    As she has excellently form'd.—— STEEVENS.

I rather think the meaning is,—She delivers her sentiments with such propriety, force, and elegance, that my *sensual desires* are inflamed by what she says. *Sense* has been already used in this play with the same signification:
    "   —— one who never feels
    " The wanton stings and motions of the *sense.*"
The word *breeds* is used nearly in the same sense in *The Tempest:*
    "   —— Fair encounter
    " Of two most rare affections! Heavens rain grace
    " On that which *breeds* between them!" MALONE.

Isab. Gentle my lord, turn back.

Ang. I will bethink me :—Come again to-mor-
    row.

Isab. Hark, how I'll bribe you : Good my lord,
    turn back.

Ang. How! bribe me?

Isab. Ay, with such gifts, that heaven shall share
    with you.

Lucio. You had marr'd all else.

Isab. Not with fond shekels ² of the tested gold,⁹
Or stones, whose rates are either rich, or poor,
As fancy values them : but with true prayers,
That shall be up at heaven, and enter there,
Ere sun-rise; prayers from preserved souls,²

The sentence signifies, Isabella does not utter *barren* words, but
speaks such sense as *breeds or produces a consequence* in Angelo's
mind. Those truths which *generate* no conclusion are often termed
barren truths. HOLT WHITE.

I understand the passage thus :—Her arguments are enforced
with so much good sense, as to increase that stock of sense which
I already possess. DOUCE.

² —— fond *shekels*—] *Fond* means very frequently in our
author, *foolish*. It signifies in this place *valued* or *prized by folly.*
    STEEVENS.

⁹ —— tested *gold*,] i. e. attested, or marked with the standard
stamp. WARBURTON.

Rather cupelled, brought to the *test*, refined. JOHNSON.

All gold that is *tested* is not marked with the standard stamp.
The verb has a different sense, and means tried by the cuppel,
which is called by the refiners a *test*. Vide Harris's Lex. Tech.
Voce CUPPELL. SIR J. HAWKINS.

² —— preserved *souls*,] i. e. preserved from the corruption
of the world. The metaphor is taken from fruits preserved in
sugar. WARBURTON.

So, in *The Amorous War*, 1648:
    " You do not reckon us 'mongst marmalade,
    " Quinces and apricots ? or take us for
    " Ladies *preserved?*" STEEVENS.

R 2

From fasting maids, whose minds are dedicate
To nothing temporal.

 Ang.   Well: come to me
To-morrow.

 Lucio. Go to; it is well; away. [*Aside to* Isabel.

 Isab. Heaven keep your honour safe!

 Ang.   Amen: for I
Am that way going to temptation,   [*Aside.*
Where prayers cross.[3]

<hr>

[3] —— *I am that way going to temptation,*
Where prayers cross.] Which way Angelo is going to temptation, we begin to perceive; but how *prayers cross* that way, or cross each other, at that way, more than any other, I do not understand.

Isabella prays that his *honour* may be safe, meaning only to give him his title: his imagination is caught by the word *honour:* he feels that his *honour* is in danger, and therefore, I believe, answers thus:

 I am that way going to temptation,
 Which your *prayers cross.*

That is, I am tempted to lose that honour of which thou implorest the preservation. The temptation under which I labour is that which thou hast unknowingly *thwarted* with thy prayer. He uses the same mode of language a few lines lower. Isabella, parting, says:

 Save your honour!

Angelo catches the word—*Save it! From what?*
 From thee; even from thy virtue!—— Johnson.

The best method of illustrating this passage will be to quote a similar one from *The Merchant of Venice,* Act. III. sc. i:

 " *Sal.* I would it might prove the end of his losses!
 " *Sola.* Let me say *Amen* betimes, *lest the devil cross thy*
  prayer."

For the same reason Angelo seems to say *Amen* to Isabella's prayer; but, to make the expression clear, we should read perhaps—Where prayers *are crossed.* Tyrwhitt.

The petition of the Lord's Prayer—" lead us not into temptation"—is here considered as crossing or intercepting the onward way in which Angelo was going; this appointment of his for the morrow's meeting, being a premeditated exposure of himself to temptation, which it was the general object of prayer to thwart.
               Henley.

Isab. At what hour to-morrow
Shall I attend your lordſhip?

Ang. At any time 'fore noon.

Isab. Save your honour!

    [*Exeunt* Lucio, Isabella, *and* Provoſt.

Ang. From thee; even from thy virtue!——
What's this? what's this? Is this her fault, or mine?
The tempter or the tempted, who ſins moſt? Ha![4]
Not ſhe; nor doth ſhe tempt: but it is I,
That lying by the violet, in the ſun,[5]
Do, as the carrion does, not as the flower,
Corrupt with virtuous ſeaſon. Can it be,
That modeſty may more betray our ſenſe
Than woman's lightneſs?[6] Having waſte ground
          enough,
Shall we deſire to raze the ſanctuary,

---

[4] —— *Ha!*] This tragedy—*Ha!* (which clogs the metre) was certainly thrown in by the player editors. STEEVENS.

[5] —— *it is I,*
That lying by the violet, in the ſun, &c.] I am not corrupted by her, but my own heart, which excites foul deſires under the ſame benign influences that exalt her purity, as the carrion grows putrid by thoſe beams which increaſe the fragrance of the violet.
          JOHNSON.

[6] —— *Can it be,*
That modeſty may more betray our ſenſe
Than woman's lightneſs?] So, in *Promos and Caſſandra,* 1578:

    " I do proteſt her modeſt wordes hath wrought in me a
      maze,
    " Though ſhe be faire, ſhe is not deackt with gariſh ſhewes
      for gaze.
    " Hir bewtie lures, her lookes cut off fond ſuits with chaſt
      diſdain.
    " O God, I feele a ſodaine change, that doth my freedome
      chayne.
    " What didſt thou ſay? fie, *Promos* fie, &c. STEEVENS.

Senſe has in this paſſage the ſame ſignification as in that above
" —that my *ſenſe* breeds with it." MALONE.

R 3

And pitch our evils there?[a]   O, fie, fie, fie!
What doſt thou? or what art thou, Angelo?
Doſt thou deſire her foully, for thoſe things
That make her good? O, let her brother live:
Thieves for their robbery have authority,
When judges ſteal themſelves.   What? do I love
      her,
That I deſire to hear her ſpeak again,
And feaſt upon her eyes? What is't I dream on?
O cunning enemy, that, to catch a ſaint,
With ſaints doſt bait thy hook! Moſt dangerous
Is that temptation, that doth goad us on
To ſin in loving virtue: never could the ſtrumpet,
With all her double vigour, art, and nature,
Once ſtir my temper; but this virtuous maid

---

[a] *And pitch our evils there?*]   So, in *King Henry VIII:*
  " Nor build their *evils* on the graves of great men."
Neither of theſe paſſages appears to contain a very elegant alluſion.

  Evils, in the preſent inſtance, undoubtedly ſtand for *jakes*. Dr. Farmer aſſures me he has ſeen the word *evil* uſed in this ſenſe by our ancient writers; and it appears from *Harrington's Metamorphoſis of Ajax*, &c. that privies were originally ſo ill-contrived, even in royal palaces, as to deſerve the title of *evils* or nuiſances.
                          STEEVENS.

  One of Sir John Berkenhead's queries confirms the foregoing obſervation:
  " Whether, ever ſince the Houſe of Commons has been locked up, the ſpeaker's chair has not been a *cloſe-ſtool?*"
  " Whether it is not ſeaſonable to ſtop the noſe of my *evil?*"
Two CENTURIES OF PAUL's CHURCH-YARD, 8vo. no date.
                          MALONE.

  No language could more forcibly expreſs the aggravated profligacy of Angelo's paſſion, which the purity of Iſabella but ſerved the more to inflame.——The deſecration of edifices devoted to religion, by converting them to the moſt abject purpoſes of nature, was an eaſtern method of expreſſing contempt. See 2 Kings, x. 27.
                          HENLEY.

a Brahmin is forbid to drop his faces even on "the ruins of a temple." So Sir W. Jones's Translation of Institutes of the Hindu Law, or the Ordinances of Menu, London edit. p. 95.
                          Steevens

Subdues me quite;—Ever, till now,
When men were fond, I fmil'd, and wonder'd how.[7]

[*Exit.*

SCENE III.

A Room in a Prifon.

Enter DUKE, *habited like a Friar, and* Provoft.

DUKE. Hail to you, provoft! fo, I think you are.
PROV. I am the provoft: What's your will, good
    friar?
DUKE. Bound by my charity, and my blefs'd order,
I come to vifit the afflicted fpirits
Here in the prifon:[8] do me the common right
To let me fee them; and to make me know
The nature of their crimes, that I may minifter
To them accordingly.
PROV. I would do more than that, if more were
    needful.

Enter JULIET.

Look, here comes one; a gentlewoman of mine,
Who falling in the flames of her own youth,
Hath blifter'd her report:[9] She is with child;

---

[7] —— *I fmil'd, and wonder'd how.*] As a day muft now inter-
vene between this conference of Ifabella with Angelo, and the
next, the act might more properly end here; and here, in my
opinion, it was ended by the poet. JOHNSON.

[8] *I come to vifit the afflicted fpirits
  Here* in the *prifon:*] This is a fcriptural expreffion, very
fuitable to the grave character which the Duke affumes. "By
which alfo he went and preached unto the *fpirits in prifon.*" 1 Pet.
iii. 19. WHALLEY.

[9] *Who falling in the* flames *of her own youth,
  Hath* blifter'd *her report:*] The old copy reads—*flaws.* STEEVENS.

R 4

And he that got it, ſentenc'd : a young man
More fit to do another ſuch offence,
Than die for this.

　　Duke.　　　　　　　When muſt he die ?

　　Prov. As I do think, to-morrow.——
I have provided for you ; ſtay a while, [*To* Juliet.
And you ſhall be conducted.

　　Duke. Repent you, fair one, of the ſin you carry?

Who doth not ſee that the integrity of the metaphor requires
we ſhould read :
　　　　—— flames *of her own youth ?*　Warburton.

Who does not ſee that, upon ſuch principles, there is no end of
correction ?　Johnson.

Dr. Johnſon did not know, nor perhaps Dr. Warburton either,
that Sir William D'Avenant reads *flames* inſtead of *flaws* in his
Law againſt Lovers, a play almoſt literally taken from *Meaſure for*
Meaſure, and *Much ado about Nothing.*　Farmer.

Shakſpeare has *flaming youth* in *Hamlet* ; and Greene, in his
Never too Late, 1616, ſays——" he meaſured the *flames of youth* by
his own dead cinders.''　*Bliſter'd her report,* is *disfigur'd her fame.*
Bliſter ſeems to have reference to the *flames* mentioned in the pre-
ceding line.　A ſimilar uſe of this word occurs in *Hamlet :*
　　　" —— takes the roſe
　　　" From the fair forehead of an innocent love,
　　　" And ſets a *bliſter* there."　Steevens.

In ſupport of this emendation, it ſhould be remembered, that
flaws (for ſo it was anciently ſpelled) and *flames* differ only by a
letter that is very frequently miſtaken at the preſs.　The ſame miſtake is found in *Macbeth,* Act II. ſc. i. edit. 1623 :
　　　" —— my ſteps, which *may* they walk,''——
inſtead of—which *way.*　Again, in this play of *Meaſure for*
Meaſure, Act V. ſc. i. edit. 1623 :——" give *we* your hand ;'' inſtead
of *me.*——In a former ſcene of the play before us we meet with——
" *burning* youth.''　Again, in *All's Well that ends Well :*
　　　" —— Yet, in his idle *fire,*
　　　" To buy his will, it would not ſeem too dear."
To *fall* in, (not *into*) was the language of the time.　So, in
Cymbeline :
　　　" —— almoſt ſpent with hunger,
　　　" I am fallen *in* offence.''　Malone.

Juliet. I do; and bear the shame most patiently.

Duke. I'll teach you how you shall arraign your conscience,
And try your penitence, if it be found,
Or hollowly put on:

Juliet.   I'll gladly learn.

Duke. Love you the man that wrong'd you?

Juliet. Yes, as I love the woman that wrong'd him.

Duke. So then, it seems, your most offenceful act
Was mutually committed?

Juliet.   Mutually.

Duke. Then was your sin of heavier kind than his.

Juliet. I do confess it, and repent it, father.

Duke. 'Tis meet so daughter: But lest you do repent,[2]
As that the sin hath brought you to this shame,—
Which sorrow is always toward ourselves, not heaven;
Showing, we'd not spare heaven,[3] as we love it,
But as we stand in fear,—

---

[2] —— *But lest you do repent,*] Thus the old copy. The modern editors, led by Mr. Pope, read:
" —— *But repent you not.*"
But lest you do repent is only a kind of negative imperative—*Ne te pœniteat,*—and means, repent not on this account. STEEVENS.

I think that a line at least is wanting after the first of the Duke's speech. It would be presumptuous to attempt to replace the words; but the sense, I am persuaded, is easily recoverable out of Juliet's answer. I suppose his advice, in substance, to have been nearly this: " Take care, *lest you repent* [not so much of your fault, as it is an evil,] *as that the sin hath brought you to this shame.*" Accordingly, Juliet's answer is explicit to this point:
I do repent me, as it is an evil,
And take the shame with joy. TYRWHITT.

[3] *Showing, we'd not spare heaven,*] The modern editors had changed this word into *seek.* STEEVENS.

Juliet. I do repent me, as it is an evil;
And take the shame with joy.

Duke.   There rest.[4]
Your partner, as I hear, must die to-morrow,
And I am going with instruction to him.——
Grace go with you! *Benedicite!*[5]   [*Exit.*

Juliet. Must die to-morrow! O, injurious
          love,[6]

Showing, we'd not spare heaven,] i. e. spare to offend heaven.
                                              MALONE.

[4] *There rest.*] Keep yourself in this temper. JOHNSON.

[5] *Grace go with you!* Benedicite!] The former part of this line
evidently belongs to Juliet. *Benedicite* is the Duke's reply.
                                              RITSON.

This regulation is undoubtedly proper: but I suppose Shakspeare
to have written,——
     Juliet. May *grace go with you!*
     Duke.   Benedicite! STEEVENS.

[6] —— *O, injurious love,*] Her execution was respited on account of her pregnancy, the effects of her love; therefore she
calls it *injurious*; not that it brought her to shame, but that it
hindered her freeing herself from it. Is not this all very natural? yet the Oxford editor changes it to *injurious law.*
                                              JOHNSON.

I know not what circumstance in this play can authorise a supposition that Juliet was respited *on account of her pregnancy*; as her
life was in no danger from the law, the severity of which was
exerted only on the seducer. I suppose she means that a parent's
love for the child she bears, is *injurious*, because it makes her
careful of her life in her present shameful condition.

Mr. Tollet explains the passage thus: "O, love, that is injurious in expediting Claudio's death, and that respites me a life,
which is a burthen to me worse than death!" STEEVENS.

Both Johnson's explanation of this passage, and Steevens's refu-
tation of it, prove the necessity of Hanmer's amendment, which
removes every difficulty, and can scarcely be considered as an
alteration, the trace of the letters in the words *law* and *love* being
so nearly alike.——The law affected the life of the man only, not
that of the woman; and this is the injury that Juliet complains of,
as she wished to die with him. M. MASON.

That refpites me a life, whofe very comfort
Is ftill a dying horror!

PROV.   'Tis pity of him. [*Exeunt.*

SCENE IV.

A Room in ANGELO's *Houfe.*

Enter ANGELO.[7]

ANG. When I would pray and think, I think and
pray
To feveral fubjects : heaven hath my empty words;
Whilft my invention,[8] hearing not my tongue,

---

[7] *Enter* Angelo.] *Promos,* in the play already quoted, has likewife a foliloquy previous to the fecond appearance of *Caffandra.*
It begins thus :
    " Do what I can, no reafon cooles defire :
    " The more I ftrive my fond affectes to tame,
    " The hotter (oh) I feele a burning fire
    " Within my breaft, vaine thoughts to forge and frame," &c.
                            STEEVENS.

[8] *Whilft my* invention,] Nothing can be either plainer or
exacter than this expreffion. [Dr. Warburton means—*intention,* a
word fubftituted by himfelf.] But the old blundering folio having
it, *invention,* this was enough for Mr. Theobald to prefer authority to fenfe. WARBURTON.

Intention (if it be the true reading) has, in this inftance more
than its common meaning, and fignifies eagernefs of defire.
So, in *The Merry Wives of Windfor* :
    " — courfe o'er my exteriors, with fuch greedinefs of *intention.*"
By *invention,* however, I believe the poet means *imagination.*
                       STEEVENS.
So, in our author's 103d fonnet :
    " ————— a face,
    " That overgoes my blunt *invention* quite."
Again, in *King Henry V* :
    " O for a mufe of fire, that would afcend
    " The brighteft heaven of *invention !*" MALONE.

  Steevens fays that *intention,* in this place, means eagernefs of
defire ;——but I believe it means *attention* only, a fenfe in which the

    7

Anchors on Isabel : [9] Heaven in my mouth,
As if I did but only chew his name ;
And in my heart, the strong and swelling evil
Of my conception : The state, whereon I studied,
Is like a good thing, being often read,
Grown fear'd and tedious ; [2] yea, my gravity,
Wherein (let no man hear me). I take pride,
Could I, with boot,[3] change for an idle plume,
Which the air beats for vain. O place ! O form ![4]

word is frequently used by Shakspeare and the other writers of his
time.——Angelo says, he *thinks* and prays to several subjects ; that
Heaven has his prayers, but his thoughts are fixed on Isabel.——
So, in *Hamlet*, the King says :

    " My words fly up, my thoughts remain below :
    " Words, without thoughts, never to Heaven go."
                              M. MASON.

[9] Anchors *on Isabel :*] We have the same singular expression in
Antony and Cleopatra :

    " There would he *anchor* his aspect, and die
    " With looking on his life." MALONE.

The same phrase occurs again in *Cymbeline :*

    " Posthumus *anchors* upon Imogen." STEEVENS.

[2] *Grown* fear'd *and tedious* ;] We should read *seared*. i. e. old.
So, Shakspeare uses *in the sear*, to signify old age. WARBURTON.

I think *fear'd* may stand. What we go to with reluctance may
be said to be *fear'd*. JOHNSON.

[3] —— *with* boot,] *Boot* is profit, advantage, gain. So, in
M. Kyffin's translation of *The Andria of Terence*, 1588 : " You obtained this at my hands, and I went about it while there was any *boot*."

Again, in *The Pinner of Wakefield*, 1599 :

    " Then lift to me : Saint Andrew be my *boot*,
    " But I'll raze thy castle to the very ground." STEEVENS.

[4] —— *change for an idle plume*,
   Which the air beats for vain. *O place ! O form !* &c.] There
is, I believe, no instance in Shakspeare, or any other author, of
" *for* vain" being used for " *in* vain." Besides ; has the air or
wind *less* effect on a feather than on twenty other things ? or rather,
is not the reverse of this the truth ? An *idle plume* assuredly is not
that " ever-fixed mark," of which our author speaks elsewhere,
" that looks on tempests, and is never shaken." The old copy
has *vaine*, in which way a *vane* or weather-cock was formerly
spelt. [*See Minsheu's* DICT. 1617, *in verb.*——So also, in *Love's*

How often doſt thou with thy caſe,⁵ thy habit,

Labour's Loſt, Act IV. ſc. i. edit. 1623: " What *vaine?* what weathercock?"] I would therefore read—*vane*.—I would exchange my gravity, ſays Angelo, for an idle feather, which being driven along by the wind, ſerves, to the ſpectator, for a *vane* or weathercock. So, in *The Winter's Tale*:

" I am a *feather* for each *wind* that blows."

And in *The Merchant of Venice* we meet with a kindred thought:

"———I ſhould be ſtill

" Plucking the *graſs, to know where ſits the wind.*"

The omiſſion of the article is certainly awkward, but not without example. Thus, in *King Lear*:

" Hot queſtriſts after him met him *at gate*."

Again, in *Coriolanus*:

" Go, ſee him out *at gates*."

Again, in *Titus Andronicus*:

" Aſcend, fair queen, *Pantheon*:

Again, in *The Winter's Tale*:

" 'Pray heartily, he be *at palace!*"

Again, in *Cymbeline*:

" Nor tent, to *bottom*, that."

The author, however, might have written:

———*an idle plume,*

Which the air beats for vane o' the place.—*O form,*

How often doſt thou—&c.

The pronoun *thou*, referring to only *one* antecedent, appears to me ſtrongly to ſupport ſuch a regulation. MALONE.

I adhere to the old reading.—— As *fair* is known to have been repeatedly uſed by Shakſpeare, Marſton, &c. for *fairneſs, vain* might have been employed on the preſent occaſion, inſtead of *vanity*. *Pure* is alſo ſubſtituted for *purity* in *England's Helicon*. See likewiſe notes on *The Midſummer Night's Dream*, Act I. ſc. i. and *The Comedy of Errors*, Act II. ſc. i. Again, in *Love's Labour's Loſt, foul* is given, as a ſubſtantive, to expreſs *foulneſs*.

The air is repreſented by Angelo as chaſtiſing the plume for being vain. A feather is exhibited by many writers as the emblem of vanity. Shakſpeare himſelf, in *K. Henry VIII*. mentions *fool* and *feather*, as congenial objects.

That the air beats the plume for its vainneſs, is a ſuppoſition fanciful enough; and yet it may be parallel'd by an image in *K. Edward III*. 1599, where flags are made the aſſailants, and " cuff the air, and beat the wind" that ſtruggles to kiſs them.

The pronoun *thou*, referring to the double antecedents *place* and *form*, ought to be no objection, for, a little further on, the Duke ſays:

Wrench awe from fools, and tie the wiser souls
To thy false seeming? [6] Blood, thou still art blood: [7]
Let's write good angel on the devil's horn,
'Tis not the devil's crest. [8]

" O *place* and *greatness!* millions of false eyes
" Are stuck upon *thee.*"
We have all heard of *Town-balls, Town-halls, Town-clocks,* and
Town-tops; but the *vane o' the place* (meaning a thing of general
property, and proverbially distinct from private ownership) is, to
me at least, an idea which no example has hitherto countenanced.——
I may add, that the *plume* could be no longer *idle,* if it served as
an index to the wind:——and with whatever propriety the *vane* in
some petty market-town might be distinguished, can we conceive
there was only a single weathercock in so large a city as Vienna,
where the scene of this comedy is laid? STEEVENS.

5 ———— *case,*] For outside; garb; external shew. JOHNSON.

6 *Wrench awe from fools, and tie the wiser souls*
To thy false seeming?] Here Shakspeare judiciously distinguishes
the different operations of high place upon different minds. Fools
are frighted, and wise men are allured. Those who cannot judge
but by the eye, are easily awed by splendour; those who consider
men as well as conditions, are easily persuaded to love the appearance of virtue dignified with power. JOHNSON.

7 ———— *Blood, thou still art blood:*] The old copy reads——*Blood,*
thou art blood. Mr. Pope, to supply the syllable wanting to
complete the metre, reads——*Blood, thou art our blood!* But the
word now introduced appears to me to agree better with the context, and therefore more likely to have been the author's.——*Blood*
is used here, as in other places, for *temperament of body.*
MALONE.

8 *Let's write good angel on the devil's horn,*
'Tis not the devil's crest.] i. e. Let the most wicked thing have
but a virtuous pretence, and it shall pass for innocent. This was
his conclusion from his preceding words:
————*O form!*
How often dost thou with thy case, thy habit,
Wrench awe from fools, and tie the wiser souls
To thy false seeming? ————
But the Oxford editor makes him conclude just counter to his own
premises; by altering it to,
Is't not the devil's crest?
So that, according to this alteration, the reasoning stands thus:——
False seeming, wrenches awe from fools, and deceives the wise.

Enter Servant.

How now, who's there?

   Serv.   One Isabel, a sister,
Desires access to you.

   Ang.   Teach her the way. [*Exit* Serv.
O heavens!

Therefore, *Let us but write good angel on the devil's horn,* (i. e. give him the appearance of an angel;) and what then? *Is't not the devil's crest?* (i. e. he shall be esteemed a devil.) WARBURTON.

I am still inclined to the opinion of the Oxford editor. Angelo, reflecting on the difference between his seeming character, and his real disposition, observes, that he *could change his gravity for a plume.* He then digresses into an apostrophe, *O dignity, how dost thou impose upon the world!* then returning to himself, *Blood* (says he) *thou art but blood,* however concealed with appearances and decorations. Title and character do not alter nature, which is still corrupt, however dignified:

    Let's write good angel on the devil's horn;
    Is't *not?*—or rather—'*Tis yet the devil's crest.*

It may however be understood, according to Dr. Warburton's explanation. O place, how dost thou impose upon the world by false appearances! so much, that if we *write good angel on the devil's horn,* 'tis *not* taken any longer to be the *devil's crest.* In this sense,

    Blood, thou art but blood!

is an interjected exclamation. JOHNSON.

A Hebrew proverb seems to favour Dr. Johnson's reading:

    " —— 'Tis *yet* the devil's crest."

" A nettle standing among myrtles, doth notwithstanding retain the name of a nettle." STEEVENS.

This passage, as it stands, appears to me to be right, and Angelo's reasoning to be this: " O place! O form! though you wrench awe from fools, and tie even wiser souls to your false seeming, yet you make no alteration in the minds or constitutions of those who possess, or assume you.—Though we should write good angel on the devil's horn, it will not change his nature, so as to give him a right to wear that crest." It is well known that the crest was formerly chosen either as emblematical of some quality conspicuous in the person who bore it, or as alluding to some remarkable incident of his life; and on this circumstance depends the justness of the present allusion. M. MASON.

It should be remembered, that the devil is usually represented with *horns* and cloven feet. The old copy appears to me to require no alteration. MALONE.

[My explanation of these words is confirmed by a passage in Lily's Midas, quoted by Warton in his marks on King John. "Melancholy! is melancholy a word for a barber's mouth? Thou shouldst say, heavy, d doltish: melancholy is the crest *of courtiers."*

Why does my blood thus muster to my heart;[a]
Making both it unable for itself,
And dispossessing all my other parts
Of necessary fitness?
So play the foolish throngs with one that swoons;
Come all to help him, and so stop the air
By which he should revive: and even so
The general, subject to a well—wish'd king,[b]

[a] —— *to my heart* ;] Of this speech there is no other trace in *Promos and Cassandra*, than the following:
    " Both hope and dreade at once my harte doth tuch."
                                                        STEEVENS.

[b] *The general,* subject *to a well-wish'd king*,] The later editions have—" subjects;" but the old copies read:
        The general subject *to a well-wish'd king.*——
The *general subject* seems a harsh expression, but *general subjects* has no sense at all, and *general* was, in our author's time, a word for *people*; so that the *general* is the *people*, or *multitude, subject* to a king. So, in *Hamlet:* " The play pleased not the *million:* 'twas caviare to the *general.*" JOHNSON.

    Mr. Malone observes, that the use of this phrase " *the general,*" for the people, continued so late as to the time of Lord Clarendon :—— " as rather to be consented to, than that *the general* should suffer." Hist. B. V. p. 530, 8vo. I therefore adhere to the old reading, with only a slight change in the punctuation.
        The general, subject to a well-wish'd king,
            Quit, &c.
i. e. the *generality* who are *subjects*, &c.
Twice in *Hamlet* our author uses *subject* for *subjects:*
    " So nightly toils the *subject* of the land." Act I. sc. i.
Again, Act I. sc. ii :
    " The lifts and full proportions, all are made
    " Out of his *subject.*"——
The *general subject* however may mean the *subjects in general.*
So, in *As you like it*, Act II. sc. vii :
    " Wouldst thou disgorge into the *general world.*"
                                                        STEEVENS.
    So the Duke had before (Act I. sc. ii.) expressed his dislike of popular applause :
        " I'll privily away. I love the people,
        " But do not like to stage me to their eyes.
        " Though it do well, I do not relish well
        " Their loud applause and *aves* vehement:

VI. [Quit their own part, and in obfequious fondnefs
Crowd to his prefence, where their untaught love
73. Muft needs appear offence.

Enter ISABELLA.

How now, fair maid?

ISAB.   I am come to know your pleafure.

ANG. That you might know it, would much better
pleafe me,
Than to demand what 'tis. Your brother cannot live.

ISAB. Even fo?—Heaven keep your honour!
                                    [*Retiring.*

ANG. Yet may he live a while; and, it may be,
As long as you, or I: Yet he muft die.

ISAB. Under your fentence?

     " Nor do I think the man of fafe difcretion,
     " That does affect it."

I cannot help thinking that Shakfpeare, in thefe two paffages,
intended to flatter the unkingly weaknefs of James the Firft, which
made him fo impatient of the crowds that flocked to fee him, efpecially upon his firft coming, that, as fome of our hiftorians fay,
he reftrained them by a proclamation. Sir Symonds D'Ewes, in
his Memoirs of his own Life,* has a remarkable paffage with
regard to this humour of James. After taking notice, that the
King going to parliament, on the 30th of January, 1620-1, " fpake
lovingly to the people, and faid, God blefs ye, God blefs ye,"
he adds thefe words, " contrary to his former hafty and paffionate
cuftom, which often, in his fudden diftemper, would bid a pox or
a plague on fuch as flocked to fee him." TYRWHITT.

     Mr. Tyrwhitt's appofite remark might find fupport, if it
needed any, from the following paffage in a *True Narration of the
Entertainment of his Royall Majeftie, from the Time of his Departure
from Edinbrogh, till his receiving in London,* &c. &c. 1603, " — he
was faine to publifh an inhibition againft the inordinate and dayly
acceffe of peoples comming," &c. STEEVENS.

         * A Manufcript in the Britifh Mufeum.

Ang. Yea.

Isab. When, I befeech you? that in his reprieve,
Longer, or fhorter, he may be fo fitted,
That his foul ficken not.

Ang. Ha! Fie, thefe filthy vices! It were as good
To pardon him, that hath from nature ftolen
A man already made,⁴ as to remit
Their fawcy fweetnefs, that do coin heaven's image,
In ftamps that are forbid:⁵ 'tis all as eafy
Falfely to take away a life true made,⁶
As to put mettle in reftrained means,⁷
To make a falfe one.

⁴ —— *that hath from nature ftolen
A man already made.*] i. e. that hath killed a man. MALONE.

⁵ *Their fawcy* fweetnefs, *that do coin* heaven's image
In ftamps that are forbid :] We meet with nearly the fame words
in *King Edward III.* a tragedy, 1596, certainly prior to this play :

 " —— And will your facred felf
 " Commit high treafon 'gainft the *king of heaven,*
 " To *ftamp* his *image* in *forbidden metal?*"

These lines are fpoken by the countefs of Salifbury, whofe
(chaftity like Ifabel's) was affailed by her fovereign.

 Their *fawcy fweetnefs* Dr. Warburton interprets, *their fawcy
indulgence of their appetite.* Perhaps it means nearly the fame as
what is afterwards called *fweet unchaftnefs.* MALONE.

 Sweetnefs, in the prefent inftance has, I believe, the fame fenfe
as—*lickerifhnefs.* STEEVENS.

⁶ Falfely *to take away a life true made,*] *Falfely* is the fame with
difhoneftly, illegally: fo *falfe,* in the next line but one, is *illegal,
illegitimate.* JOHNSON.

⁷ —— *mettle in reftrained means,*] In forbidden moulds. I fufpect
means not to be the right word, but I cannot find another.
JOHNSON.

 I fhould fuppofe that our author wrote,
 —— *in reftrained mints,*
as the allufion may be ftill to *coining.* Sir W. D'Avenant omits
the paffage. STEEVENS.

 Mettle, the reading of the old copy, which was changed to *metal*
by Mr. Theobald, (who has been followed by the fubfequent
editors,) is fupported not only by the general purport of the paffage,
 I

Isab. 'Tis set down so in heaven, but not in earth.[2]

Ang. Say you so? then I shall poze you quickly.

(in which our author having already illustrated the sentiment he has attributed to Angelo by an allusion to coining, would not give the same image a second time,) but by a similar expression in *Timon* :

 " —— thy father, that poor rag,
 " Must be thy subject; who in spite *put stuff*
 " To some she-beggar, and compounded thee,
 " Poor rogue hereditary."

Again, in *The Winter's Tale* :

 " As rank as any flax-wench, that *puts* to,
 " Before her troth-plight."

The controverted word is found again in the same sense in *Macbeth* :

 " —— thy undaunted *mettle* should compose
 " Nothing but males."

Again, in *K. Richard II* :

 " —— that bed, that womb,
 " That *mettle*, that self mould that fashion'd thee,
 " Made him a man."

Again, in *Timon of Athens* :

 " —— Common mother, thou,
 " Whose womb unmeasurable, and infinite breast,
 " Teems and feeds all; whose self-same *mettle*,
 " Whereof thy proud child, arrogant man, is puff'd,
 " Engenders the black toad," &c.

Means is here used for *medium*, or *object*, and the sense of the whole is this: '*Tis as easy wickedly to deprive a man born in wedlock of life, as to have unlawful commerce with a maid, in order to give life to an illegitimate child.* The thought is simply, that murder is as easy as fornication; and the inference which Angelo would draw, is, that it is as improper to pardon the latter as the former. The words—*to make a false one*—evidently referring to *life*, shew that the preceding line is to be understood in a natural, and not in a metaphorical, sense. MALONE.

[2] *'Tis set down so in heaven, but not in earth.*] I would have it considered, whether the train of the discourse does not rather require Isabel to say:

 'Tis so set down in earth, but not in heaven.

When she has said this, *Then*, says Angelo, *I shall poze you quickly.* Would you, who, for the present purpose, declare your brother's crime to be less in the sight of heaven, than the law has made it; would you commit that crime, light as it is, to save your brother's life ? To this she answers, not very plainly in either reading, but more appositely to that which I propose :

 I had rather give my body than my soul. JOHNSON.

S 2

Which had you rather, That the moſt juſt law
Now took your brother's life; or, to redeem him,[8]
Give up your body to ſuch ſweet uncleanneſs,
As ſhe that he hath ſtain'd?

  Isab.   Sir, believe this,
I had rather give my body than my ſoul.[9]

  Ang. I talk not of your ſoul; Our compell'd ſins
Stand more for number than accompt.[2]

  Isab.   How ſay you?

  Ang. Nay, I'll not warrant that; for I can ſpeak
Againſt the thing I ſay. Anſwer to this;——
I, now the voice of the recorded law,
Pronounce a ſentence on your brother's life:

What you have ſtated is undoubtedly the divine law: murder
and fornication are both forbid by the *canon of ſcripture*;—but on
earth the latter offence is conſidered as leſs heinous than the former.
               MALONE.

So, in *King John:*
  " Some ſins *do bear their privilege on earth,*
  " And ſo doth yours." STEEVENS.

 [8] ——— or, *to redeem him,*] The old copy has—*and* to redeem him.
The emendation was made by Sir William D'Avenant. MALONE.

 [9] *I had rather* give my body *than my ſoul.*] Iſabel, I believe,
uſes the words, " give my body," in a different ſenſe from that in
which they had been employed by Angelo. She means, I think, *I
had rather die, than forfeit my eternal happineſs by the proſtitution of
my perſon.* MALONE.

 She may mean—I had rather *give up my body to impriſonment, than
my ſoul to perdition.* STEEVENS.

 [2] ——— *Our compell'd ſins*
 Stand more for number *than* accompt.] Actions to which we
are compelled, however *numerous,* are not *imputed* to us by heaven as crimes. If you cannot ſave your brother but by the loſs
of your chaſtity, it is not a voluntary but compelled ſin, for which
you cannot be *accountable.* MALONE.

 The old copy reads——
  " Stand more for number than *for* accompt."
I have omitted the ſecond *for,* which had been caſually repeated by
the compoſitor. STEEVENS.

Might there not be a charity in fin,
To fave this brother's life?

Isab.   Pleafe you to do't,
I'll take it as a peril to my foul,
It is no fin at all, but charity.

Ang. Pleas'd you to do't, at peril of your foul,[3]
Were equal poize of fin and charity.

Isab. That I do beg his life, if it be fin,
Heaven, let me bear it! you granting of my fuit,
If that be fin, I'll make it my morn prayer
To have it added to the faults of mine,
And nothing of your, anfwer.[4]

Ang.   Nay, but hear me:
Your fenfe purfues not mine: either you are ignorant,
Or feem fo, craftily;[5] and that's not good.

Isab. Let me be ignorant,[6] and in nothing good,
But gracioufly to know I am no better.

---

[3] *Pleas'd you to do't, at peril, &c.*] The reafoning is thus: Angelo afks, whether there might *not be a charity in fin to fave this brother.* Ifabella anfwers, that *if Angelo will fave him, fhe will flake her foul that it were charity, not fin.* Angelo replies, that if Ifabella would *fave him at the bazard of her foul, it would be not indeed no fin, but a fin to which the charity would be equivalent.* JOHNSON.

[4] *And nothing of your, anfwer.*] I think it fhould be read,

And nothing of yours, anfwer.

You, and whatever is *yours*, be exempt from penalty. JOHNSON.

And nothing of your anfwer, means, *and make no part of thofe fins for which you fhall be called to anfwer.* STEEVENS.

This paffage would be clear, I think, if it were pointed thus:

To have it added to the faults of mine,
And nothing of your, anfwer.

So that the fubftantive *anfwer* may be underftood to be joined in conftruction with *mine* as well as *your*. The faults *of mine anfwer* are the faults *which I am to anfwer for.* TYRWHITT.

[5] —— *craftily;*] The old copy reads—*crafty.* Corrected by Sir William D'Avenant. MALONE.

[6] *Let me be ignorant,*] *Me* is wanting in the original copy. The emendation was made by the editor of the fecond folio. MALONE.

Ang. Thus wisdom wishes to appear most bright,
When it doth tax itself: as these black masks
Proclaim an enshield beauty[6] ten times louder

---

[6] *Proclaim an* enshield *beauty* —] An *enshield beauty* is a *shielded beauty, a beauty covered or protected as with a shield.* STEEVENS.

——— *as these black masks*
Proclaim an enshield *beauty, &c.*
This should be written *en-shell'd,* or *in-shell'd,* as it is in *Coriolanus,* Act IV. sc. vi :
  " 'Thrusts forth his horns again into the world
  " 'That were *in-shell'd* when Marcius stood for Rome."
These *Masks* must mean, I think, the *Masks of the audience;* however improperly a compliment to them is put into the mouth of Angelo. As Shakspeare would hardly have been guilty of such an indecorum to flatter a common audience, I think this passage affords ground for supposing that the play was written to be acted at court. Some strokes of particular flattery to the King I have already pointed out; and there are several other general reflections, in the character of the Duke especially, which seem calculated for the royal ear. TYRWHITT.

I do not think so well of the conjecture in the latter part of this note, as I did some years ago; and therefore I should wish to withdraw it. Not that I am inclined to adopt the idea of Mr. Ritson, as I see no ground for supposing that Isabella *had* any *mask in her hand.* My notion at present is, that the phrase *these black masks* signifies nothing more than *black masks;* according to an old idiom of our language, by which the demonstrative pronoun is put for the prepositive article. See the *Glossary to Chaucer,* edit. 1775 : *This, Thise.* Shakspeare seems to have used the same idiom not only in the passage quoted by Mr. Steevens from *Romeo and Juliet,* but also in *King Henry IV.* Part I. Act I. sc. iii :
  " ——— and, but for *these* vile guns,
  " He would himself have been a soldier."
With respect to the former part of this note, though Mr. Ritson has told us that " *enshield* is CERTAINLY put by contraction for *enshielded,*" I have no objection to leaving my conjecture in its place, till some authority is produced for such an usage of *enshield* or *enshielded.* TYRWHITT.

There are instances of a similar contraction or elision, in our author's plays. Thus, *bloat* for *bloated, ballast* for *ballasted,* and *wast* for *wasted,* with many others. RITSON.

Sir William D'Avenant reads——*as a black mask;* but I am afraid

Than beauty could difplayed.—But mark me;
To be received plain, I'll fpeak more grofs:
Your brother is to die.

ISAB. So.

ANG. And his offence is fo, as it appears
Accountant to the law upon that pain.[6]

ISAB. True.

ANG. Admit no other way to fave his life,
(As I fubfcribe not that,[7] nor any other,
But in the lofs of queftion,)[8] that you, his fifter,
Finding yourfelf defir'd of fuch a perfon,
Whofe credit with the judge, or own great place,
Could fetch your brother from the manacles

Mr. Tyrwhitt is too well fupported in his firft fuppofition, by a
paffage at the beginning of *Romeo and Juliet:*
  " *Thefe* happy *mafks* that kifs fair ladies' brows,
  " Being *black*, put us in mind they hide the fair." STEEVENS.

[6] *Accountant to the law upon that* pain.] *Pain* is here for *penalty,
punifhment.* JOHNSON.

[7] *As I* fubfcribe *not that*,] To *fubfcribe* means, to *agree to*.
Milton ufes the word in the fame fenfe.
  So alfo, in Marlowe's *Luft's Dominion*, 1661 :
    " *Subfcribe* to his defires." STEEVENS.

[8] *But in the* lofs *of queftion*,] The *lofs* of queftion I do not
well underftand, and fhould rather read :
    But in the tofs *of queftion.*
In the *agitation*, in the *difcuffion* of the queftion. To *tofs* an argument is a common phrafe. JOHNSON.

  This expreffion, I believe, means, *but in idle fuppofition*, or *converfation that tends to nothing*, which may therefore, in our author's language,
be called *the lofs of queftion*. Thus, in *Coriolanus*, Act III. fc. i:
    " The which fhall turn you to no other harm,
    " Than fo much *lofs of time*."
Queftion, in Shakfpeare, often bears this meaning. So, in his
Tarquin and Lucrece :
    " And after fupper, long he *queftioned*
    " With modeft Lucrece," &c. STEEVENS.

Queftion is ufed here, as in many other places, for *converfation*.
                                        MALONE.

Of the all-binding law;[9] and that there were
No earthly mean to fave him, but that either
You muft lay down the treafures of your body
To this fuppofed, or elfe let him fuffer;[2]
What would you do?

Isab. As much for my poor brother, as myfelf:
That is, Were I under the terms of death,
The impreffion of keen whips I'd wear as rubies,
And ftrip myfelf to death, as to a bed
That longing I have been fick for, ere I'd yield
My body up to fhame.

Ang. Then muft your brother die.

Isab. And 'twere the cheaper way:
Better it were, a brother died at once,[3]
Than that a fifter, by redeeming him,
Should die for ever.

Ang. Were not you then as cruel as the fentence
That you have flander'd fo?

---

[9] *Of the* all-binding *law;*] The old editions read:
———— all-building *law.* JOHNSON.
The emendation is Theobald's. STEEVENS.

[2] ———— *or elfe let him fuffer;*] The old copy reads—"or elfe
to let him," &c. STEEVENS.

Sir Thomas Hanmer reads more grammatically—"or elfe let
him fuffer." But our author is frequently inaccurate in the conftruction of his fentences. I have therefore adhered to the old copy.
You muft be under the neceffity [to let, &c.] muft be underftood.
So, in Holinfhed's *Hiftory of Scotland,* p. 150: "——afleep they
were fo faft, that a man might have removed the chamber over
them, fooner than *to* have awaked them out of their drunken fleep."
MALONE.

The old copy reads—fuppofed, not fuppos'd. The fecond *to* in
the line might therefore be the compofitor's accidental repetition of
the firft. Being unneceffary to fenfe, and injurious to meafure, I
have omitted it.—The pages of Holinfhed will furnifh examples of
every blunder to which printed works are liable. STEEVENS.

[3] ———— *a brother died at once,*] Perhaps we fhould read :
Better it were, a brother died for *once,* &c. JOHNSON.

Isab. Ignomy in ranſom,[4] and free pardon,
Are of two houſes: lawful mercy is
Nothing akin[5] to foul redemption.

Ang. You ſeem'd of late to make the law a tyrant;
And rather prov'd the ſliding of your brother
A merriment than a vice.

Isab. O, pardon me, my lord; it oft falls out,
To have what we'd have, we ſpeak not what we mean:
I ſomething do excuſe the thing I hate,
For his advantage that I dearly love.

Ang. We are all frail.

Isab.   Elſe let my brother die,
If not a feodary, but only he,[6]

---

[4] *Ignomy in ranſom,*] So the word *ignominy* was formerly written. Thus, in *Troilus and Creſſida*, Act V. ſc. iii:

     "Hence, brother lacquey! *ignomy* and ſhame," &c. REED.

Sir William D'Avenant's alteration of theſe lines may prove a reaſonably good comment on them:

     "Ignoble ranſom no proportion bears
     "To pardon freely given." MALONE.

The ſecond folio reads—*ignominy*; but whichſoever reading we take, the line will be inharmonious, if not defective. STEEVENS.

[5] *Nothing akin*—] The old copy reads—*kin*. For this trivial emendation I am anſwerable. STEEVENS.

[6] *If not a* feodary, *but only he*, &c.] This is ſo obſcure, but the alluſion ſo fine, that it deſerves to be explained. A *feodary* was one that in the times of vaſſalage held lands of the chief lord, under the tenure of paying rent and ſervice: which tenures were called *feuda* amongſt the Goths. Now, ſays Angelo, "we are all frail;"—"Yes, replies Iſabella; if all mankind were not *feodaries*, who owe what they are to this tenure of *imbecility*, and who ſucceed each other by the ſame tenure, as well as my brother, I would give him up." The comparing mankind, lying under the weight of original ſin, to a *feodary*, who owes *ſuit* and *ſervice* to his lord, is, I think, not ill imagined. WARBURTON.

Shakſpeare has the ſame alluſion in *Cymbeline*:

     "———————— ſenſeleſs bauble,
     "Art thou a *feodarie* for this act?"

Again, in the prologue to Marſton's *Sophoniſba*, 1606:

     "For ſeventeen kings were Carthage *feodars*."

Owe,[6] and succeed by weakness.[7]

Ang.   Nay, women are frail too.

Isab. Ay, as the glasses where they view themselves;
Which are as easy broke as they make forms.[8]

Mr. M. Mason censures me for not perceiving that *feodary* signifies an *accomplice*. Of this I was fully aware, as it supports the
sense contended for by Warburton, and seemingly acquiesced in by
Dr. Johnson.——Every *vassal* was an *accomplice* with his lord ; i. e. was
subject to be executor of the mischief he did not contrive, and
was obliged to follow in every bad cause which his superior led.
STEEVENS.

I have shewn in a note on *Cymbeline*, that *feodary* was used by
Shakspeare in the sense of an *associate*, and such undoubtedly is its
signification here. Dr. Warburton's note therefore is certainly
wrong, and ought to be expunged.

After having ascertained the true meaning of this word, I must
own, that the remaining part of the passage before us is extremely
difficult. I would, however, restore the original reading *thy*, and
the meaning should seem to be this :——We are all frail, says Angelo. Yes, replies Isabella ; if he has not one *associate* in his crime,
if no other person own and follow the same criminal courses which
you are now pursuing, let my brother suffer death.

I think it, however, extremely probable that something is
omitted. It is observable, that the line " —— Owe, and succeed thy
weakness," does not, together with the subsequent line,——" Nay,
women are frail too,——make a perfect verse : from which it may
be conjectured that the compositor's eye glanced from the word
succeed to *weakness* in a subsequent hemistich, and that by this over-
sight the passage is become unintelligible. MALONE.

[6] *Owe*,] To *owe* is, in this place, to *own*, to *hold*, to have
possession. JOHNSON.

[7] —— by *weakness*.] The old copy reads——*thy* weakness.
STEEVENS.

The emendation was made by Mr. Rowe. I am by no means
satisfied with it. *Thy* is much more likely to have been printed by
mistake for *this*, than the word which has been substituted. Yet *this*
weakness and *by* weakness are equally to be understood. Sir W.
D'Avenant omitted the passage in his *Law against Lovers*, probably
on account of its difficulty. MALONE.

[8] —————— *glasses* ——————
Which are as easy broke as they make *forms*.] Would it not be
better to read ?
—————— take *forms*. JOHNSON.

Women!—Help heaven! men their creation mar
In profiting by them.[9] Nay, call us ten times frail;
For we are soft as our complexions are,
And credulous to falfe-prints.[2]

Ang.   I think it well:
And from this teftimony of your own fex,
(Since, I fuppofe, we are made to be no ftronger
Than faults may fhake our frames,) let me be bold;—
I do arreft your words; Be that you are,
That is, a woman; if you be more, you're none;
If you be one, (as you are well exprefs'd
By all external warrants,) fhow it now,
By putting on the deftin'd livery.

Isab. I have no tongue but one: gentle my lord,
Let me intreat you fpeak the former language.[3]

---

9 *In profiting by them.*] In imitating them, in taking them for examples. JOHNSON.

If men mar their own creation, by taking women for their example, they cannot be said to *profit* much by them.——Isabella is deploring the condition of woman-kind, formed fo frail and credulous, that men prove the deftruction of the whole fex, by taking advantage of their weaknefs, and ufing them for their own purpofes. She therefore calls upon Heaven to affift them. This, though obfcurely expreffed, appears to me to be the meaning of this paffage. M. MASON.

Dr. Johnfon does not feem to have underftood this paffage. Ifabella certainly does not mean to fay that men mar their own creation by taking women for examples. Her meaning is, that *men debafe their nature by taking advantage of fuch weak pitiful creatures.*——Edinburgh Magazine, Nov. 1785. STEEVENS.

[2] *For we are foft as our complexions are,*
And credulous to falfe prints.] i. e. take any impreffion.
                                                        WARBURTON.

So, in *Twelfth Night* :
    " How eafy is it for the proper *falfe*
    " *In women's waxen hearts* to fet their *forms* !
    " Alas! our frailty is the caufe, not we;
    " For, fuch as we are made of, fuch we be." MALONE.

[3] ——*fpeak the* former *language.*] Ifabella anfwers to his circumlocutory courtfhip, that fhe has but *one tongue*, fhe does not

Ang. Plainly conceive, I love you.

Isab. My brother did love Juliet; and you tell me,
That he fhall die for it.

Ang. He fhall not, Ifabel, if you give me love.

Isab. I know, your virtue hath a licence in't,[3]
Which feems a little fouler than it is,[4]
To pluck on others.

Ang.   Believe me, on mine honour,
My words exprefs my purpofe.

Isab. Ha! little honour to be much believ'd,
And moft pernicious purpofe!—Seeming, feem-
                                ing![5]—
I will proclaim thee, Angelo; look for't:
Sign me a prefent pardon for my brother,
Or, with an out-ftretch'd throat, I'll tell the world
Aloud, what man thou art.

Ang.   Who will believe thee, Ifabel?
My unfoil'd name, the aufterenefs of my life,

---

understand this new phrafe, and defires him to talk his *former
language,* that is, to talk as he talked before.   JOHNSON.

[3] *I know your virtue hath a* licence *in't,*] Alluding to the licences
given by minifters to their fpies, to go into all fufpected companies,
and join in the language of malcontents.   WARBURTON.

I fufpect Warburton's interpretation to be more ingenious than
juft.   The obvious meaning is—*I know your virtue affumes an air
of licentioufnefs which is not natural to you, on purpofe to try me.*—
Edinburgh Magazine, Nov. 1786.   STEEVENS.

[4] *Which feems a little fouler,* &c.] So, in *Promos and Caffandra:*
        " *Caf.* Renowned lord, you ufe this fpeech (I hope) your
                thrall to trye,
        " If otherwife, my brother's life fo deare I will not bye."
        " *Pro.* Fair dame, my outward looks my inward thoughts
                bewray;
        " If you miftruft, to fearch my harte, would God you
                had a kaye."   STEEVENS.

[5] ———*Seeming, feeming!*] Hypocrify, hypocrify; counterfeit
virtue.   JOHNSON.

My vouch againſt you,[6] and my place i'the ſtate,
Will ſo your accuſation over‡weigh,
That you ſhall ſtifle in your own report,
And ſmell of calumny.[7] I have begun ;
And now I give my ſenſual race the rein :[8]
Fit thy conſent to my ſharp appetite ;
Lay by all nicety, and prolixious bluſhes,[9]
That baniſh what they ſue for ; redeem thy brother
By yielding up thy body to my will ;
Or elſe he muſt not only die the death,[2]

[6] *My* vouch *againſt you,*] The calling his denial of her charge his *vouch*, has ſomething fine. *Vouch* is the teſtimony one man bears for another. So that, by this, he inſinuates his authority was ſo great, that his *denial* would have the ſame credit that a *vouch* or teſtimony has in ordinary caſes. WARBURTON.

I believe this beauty is merely imaginary, and that *vouch againſt* means no more than denial. JOHNSON.

[7] *That you ſhall ſtifle in your own report,*
And ſmell of calumny.] A metaphor from a lamp or candle extinguiſhed in its own greaſe. STEEVENS.

[8] *And now I give my ſenſual race the rein :*] And now I give my ſenſes the rein, in the race they are now actually running. HEATH.

[9] ——— *and* prolixious *bluſhes.*] The word *prolixious* is not peculiar to Shakſpeare. I find it in *Moſes his Birth and Miracles,* by Drayton :
   " Moſt part by water, more *prolixious* was," &c.
Again, in the Dedication to *Gabriel Harvey's Hunt is Up,* 1598 :
   " ——— rariſier of *prolixious* rough barbariſm," &c.
Again, in Naſh's *Lenten Stuff,* &c. 1599 :
   " ——— well known unto them by his *prolixious* ſea-wandering."
Prolixious bluſhes mean what Milton has elegantly called
   " ———ſweet reluctant *delay.*" STEEVENS.

[2] ——— *die the death,*] This ſeems to be a ſolemn phraſe for death inflicted by law. So, in *A Midſummer Night's Dream :*
   " *Prepare* to die the death." JOHNSON.

It is a phraſe taken from ſcripture, as is obſerved in a note on *The Midſummer Night's Dream.* STEEVENS.

The phraſe is *a good phraſe,* as Shallow ſays, but I do not conceive it to be either of *legal* or *ſcriptural* origin. Chaucer uſes it frequently. See *Cant. Tales,* ver. 607.
   " They were adradde of him, as of *the deth.*" ver. 1222.

But thy unkindnefs fhall his death draw out
To lingering fufferance : anfwer me to-morrow,
Or, by the affection that now guides me moft,
I'll prove a tyrant to him : As for you,
Say what you can, my falfe o'erweighs your true.

                                            [Exit.

   Isab. To whom fhould I complain? Did I tell
            this,
Who would believe me? O perilous mouths,
That bear in them one and the felf-fame tongue,
Either of condemnation or approof!
Bidding the law make court'fy to their will;
Hooking both right and wrong to the appetite,
To follow, as it draws! I'll to my brother:
Though he hath fallen by prompture [3] of the blood,
Yet hath he in him fuch a mind of honour,[4]
That had he twenty heads to tender down
On twenty bloody blocks, he'd yield them up,
Before his fifter fhould her body ftoop
To fuch abhorr'd pollution.
Then Ifabel, live chafte, and, brother, die:
More than our brother is our chaftity.
I'll tell him yet of Angelo's requeft,
And fit his mind to death, for his foul's reft.

                                            [Exit.

    " *The deth* he feleth thurgh his herte fmite." It feems to have been originally a miftaken tranflation of the French *La Mort.*
                                     TYRWHITT.

   3 ——— *prompture* —] Suggeftion, temptation, inftigation.
                                        JOHNSON.

   4 ——— *fuch a mind of honour,*] This, in Shakfpeare's language, may mean, *fuch an honourable mind,* as he ufes " *mind of love,*" in *The Merchant of Venice,* for *loving mind.* Thus alfo, in *Philafter :*
       " ——— I had thought, thy *mind*
       " Had been *of honour.*" STEEVENS.

ACT III. SCENE I.

A Room in the Prifon.

Enter DUKE, CLAUDIO, *and* Provoft.

DUKE. So, then you hope of pardon from lord
    Angelo?

CLAUD. The miferable have no other medicine,
But only hope:
I have hope to live, and am prepar'd to die.

  DUKE. Be abfolute for death;[5] either death, or
    life,
Shall thereby be the fweeter. Reafon thus with life,——
If I do lofe thee, I do lofe a thing
That none but fools would keep:[7] a breath thou art,

---

[5] *Be abfolute for death*;] Be determined to die, without any hope
of life.   *Horace,*——
    " —— The hour which exceeds expectation will be welcome."
                              JOHNSON.

[6] *That none but fools would keep*:] But this reading is not only
contrary to all fenfe and reafon, but to the drift of this moral
difcourfe. The Duke, in his affumed character of a friar, is
endeavouring to inftil into the condemned prifoner a refignation
of mind to his fentence; but the fenfe of the lines in this reading,
is a direct perfuafive to *fuicide*: I make no doubt, but the poet
wrote,
    That none but fools would reck :——
i. e. care for, be anxious about, regret the lofs of. So, in the
tragedy of *Tancred and Gifmund,* Act IV. fc. iii :
    " —— Not that fhe *recks* this life."——
And Shakfpeare, in *The Two Gentlemen of Verona :*
    " *Recking* as little what betideth me."——
                         WARBURTON.

The meaning feems plainly this, that *none but fools* would wifh
to *keep life*; or, *none but fools would keep* it, if choice were allowed.
A fenfe which, whether true or not, is certainly innocent.
                            JOHNSON.

Vol. VI.
289.

(Servile to all the fkiey influences,)
That doft this habitation, where thou keep'ft,[7]
Hourly afflict: merely, thou art death's fool;
For him thou labour'ft by thy flight to fhun,
And yet run'ft toward him ftill:[8] Thou art not
noble;

Keep, in this place, I believe, may not fignify *preferve*, but *care for*. " No lenger for to liven I ne *kepe*," fays Æneas in Chaucer's *Dido, Queen of Carthage*; and elfewhere: " That I *kepe not* rehearfed be:" i. e. which I *care not* to have rehearfed.

Again, in *The Knightes Tale*, Tyrwhitt's edit. ver. 2240:

" I *kepe* nought of armes for to yelpe."

Again, in *A Mery Jefte of a Man called Howleglafs*, bl. 1. no date.

" Then the parfon bad him remember that he had a foule for to *kepe*, and he preached and teached to him the ufe of confeffion," &c. STEEVENS.

Mr. Steevens's explanation is confirmed by a paffage in *The Dutchefs of Malfy*, by Webfter, (1623) an author who has frequently imitated Shakfpeare, and who perhaps followed him in the prefent inftance:

" Of what is't *fools* make fuch vain *keeping*?
" Sin their conception, their birth weeping;
" Their *life* a general mift of error;
" Their death a hideous ftorm of terror."

See the Gloffary to Mr. Tyrwhitt's edit. of *The Canterbury Tales of Chaucer*. v. *kepe*. MALONE.

[7] *That* doft *this* habitation, *where* thou keep'ft,] Sir T. Hanmer changed *doft* to *do* without neceffity or authority. The conftruction is not, " the fkiey influences that do," but, " a breath thou art, that doft," &c. If " Servile to all the fkiey influences" be inclofed in a parenthefis, all the difficulty will vanifh. PORSON.

[8] ——— *merely, thou art* death's fool;
For him thou labour'ft by thy flight to fhun,
And yet run'ft toward him ftill:] In thofe old farces called *Moralities*, the *fool* of the piece, in order to fhow the inevitable approaches of death, is made to employ all his ftratagems to avoid him; which, as the matter is ordered, bring the *fool* at every turn, into his very jaws. So that the reprefentations of thefe fcenes would afford a great deal of good *mirth* and *morals* mixed together. And from fuch circumftances, in the genius of our anceftors' publick diverfions, I fuppofe it was, that the old proverb arofe, of *being merry and wife*. WARBURTON.

For all the accommodations that thou bear'ft,
Are nurs'd by bafenefs : [9] Thou art by no means
   valiant;
For thou doft fear the foft and tender fork

Such another expreffion as *death's fool*, occurs in *The Honeft Lawyer*, a comedy, by S. S. 1616:
  " Wilt thou be a *fool of fate?* who can
  " Prevent the deftiny decreed for man?"
          STEEVENS.

It is obferved by the Editor of *The Sad Shepherd*, 8vo. 1783, p. 154. that the initial letter of Stow's Survey, contains a reprefentation of a ftruggle between *Death* and the *Fool*; the figures of which were moft probably copied from thofe characters as formerly exhibited on the ftage. REED.

There are no fuch characters as *Death* and *the Fool*, in any old *Morality* now extant. They feem to have exifted only in the *dumb Shows*. The two figures in the initial letter of Stow's *Survey*, 1603, which have been miftaken for thefe two perfonages, have no allufion whatever to the ftage, being merely one of the fet known by the name of *Death's Dance*, and actually copied from the margin of an old Miffal. The fcene in the modern pantomime of *Harlequin Skeleton*, feems to have been fuggefted by fome playhoufe tradition of *Death and the Fool*. RITSON. *See Vol. XIII. p. 498. n. 2. Steevens.*

[9] *Are nurs'd by* bafenefs :] Dr. Warburton is undoubtedly miftaken in fuppofing that by *bafenefs* is meant *felf-love*, here affigned as the motive of all human actions. Shakfpeare only meant to obferve, that a minute analyfis of life at once deftroys that fplendour which dazzles the imagination. Whatever grandeur can difplay, or luxury enjoy, is procured by *bafenefs*, by offices of which the mind fhrinks from the contemplation. All the delicacies of the table may be traced back to the fhambles and the dunghill, all magnificence of building was hewn from the quarry, and all the pomp of ornament dug from among the damps and darknefs of the mine. JOHNSON.

This is a thought which Shakfpeare delights to exprefs. So, in *Antony and Cleopatra:*
  " ———— our *dungy earth* alike
  " Feeds man as beaft."
Again :
  " Which fleeps, and never palates more the *dung*,
  " *The beggar's nurfe, and Cæfar's.*" STEEVENS.

Of a poor worm:[2] Thy beſt of reſt is ſleep,
And that thou oft provok'ſt; yet groſsly fear'ſt
Thy death, which is no more.[3] Thou art not thyſelf;[4]
For thou exiſt'ſt on many a thouſand grains
That iſſue out of duſt: Happy thou art not:
For what thou haſt not, ſtill thou ſtriv'ſt to get;
And what thou haſt, forget'ſt: Thou art not certain;

[2] —— *the ſoft and tender* fork
Of a poor worm:] *Worm* is put for any creeping thing or
ſerpent. Shakſpeare ſuppoſes falſely, but according to the vulgar
notion, that a ſerpent wounds with his tongue, and that his tongue
is *forked.* He confounds reality and fiction; a ſerpent's tongue is
ſoft, but not *forked* nor hurtful. If it could hurt, it could not be
ſoft. In *A Midſummer Night's Dream* he has the ſame notion:
     " With *doubler* tongue
     " Than thine, O ſerpent, never adder *ſtung.*" JOHNSON.

   Shakſpeare mentions the " adder's *fork*" in *Macbeth;* and might
have caught this idea from old tapeſtries or paintings, in which
the tongues of ſerpents and dragons always appear barbed like the
point of an arrow. STEEVENS.

[3] —— *Thy beſt of reſt is ſleep,*
   And that thou oft provok'ſt; yet groſsly fear'ſt
   Thy death, which is no more.] Evidently from the following
paſſage of Cicero: " *Habes ſomnum imaginem mortis, eamque quotidie
induis, & dubitas quin ſenſus in morte nullus fit, cum in ejus ſimulacro
videas eſſe nullum ſenſum.*" But the Epicurean inſinuation is, with
great judgement, omitted in the imitation. WARBURTON.

   Here Dr. Warburton might have found a ſentiment worthy of
his animadverſion. I cannot without indignation find Shakſpeare
ſaying, that *death is only ſleep,* lengthening out his exhortation by
a ſentence which in the friar is impious, in the reaſoner is fooliſh,
and in the poet trite and vulgar. JOHNSON.

   This was an overſight in Shakſpeare; for in the ſecond ſcene of
the fourth act, the Provoſt ſpeaks of the deſperate Barnardine, as
one who regards death only as a *drunken ſleep.* STEEVENS.

   I apprehend Shakſpeare means to ſay no more, than that the
paſſage from this life to another is as eaſy as ſleep; a poſition in
which there is ſurely neither folly nor impiety. MALONE.

[4] *Thou art not thyſelf;*] Thou art perpetually repaired and re-
novated by external aſſiſtance, thou ſubſiſteſt upon foreign matter,
and haſt no power of producing or continuing thy own being.
                        JOHNSON.

For thy complexion shifts to strange effects,[5]
After the moon: If thou art rich, thou art poor;
For, like an ass, whose back with ingots bows,[6]
Thou bear'st thy heavy riches but a journey,
And death unloads thee: Friend hast thou none;
For thine own bowels, which do call thee sire,
The mere effusion of thy proper loins,
Do curse the gout, serpigo,[7] and the rheum,
For ending thee no sooner: Thou hast nor youth,
          nor age;
But, as it were, an after-dinner's sleep,
Dreaming on both:[8] for all thy blessed youth
Becomes as aged, and doth beg the alms
Of palsied eld;[9] and when thou art old, and rich,

[5] ——strange effects,] For effects read affects; that is, affections, passions of mind, or disorders of body variously affected. So, in Othello:

    " The young

[6] —— like an ass,
is far more ancient
Churchyard's Discourse
    " Rebellion th
    " Leads out pc
    " Who beares

[7] —— serpigo,] Th
[8] —— Thou hast nor
    But, as it were, a   sleep,
    Dreaming on both:] This is exquisitely imagined. When we
are young, we busy ourselves in forming schemes for succeeding
time, and miss the gratifications that are before us; when we are
old, we amuse the languor of age with the recollection of youthful pleasures or performances; so that our life, of which no part
is filled with the business of the present time, resembles our dreams
after dinner, when the events of the morning are mingled with the
designs of the evening. JOHNSON.

[9] ——palsied eld;] Eld is generally used for old age, decrepitude.
It is here put for old people, persons worn with years.
    So, in Marston's Dutch Courtesan, 1604:
    " Let colder eld their strong objections move."

T 2

Thou haſt neither heat,[2] affection, limb, nor beauty,[3]
To make thy riches pleaſant.   What's yet in this,

Again, in our author's *Merry Wives of Windſor:*
 " The ſuperſtitious idle-headed *eld.*"
Gower uſes it for *age* as oppoſed to *youth :*
 " His *elde* had turned into youth."
   De Confeſſione Amantis, Lib. V. fol. 106.   STEEVENS.

[2] ———*for all thy bleſſed youth*
 Becomes as aged, and doth beg the alms
 Of palſied eld ; and when thou art old, and rich,
 Thou haſt neither heat, &c.]   The drift of this period is to
prove, that neither youth nor age can be ſaid to be really enjoyed,
which, in poetical language, is,——*We have neither youth nor age.*
But how is this made out? That *age* is not enjoyed, he proves by
recapitulating the infirmities of it, which deprive that period of
life of all ſenſe of pleaſure. To prove that youth is not enjoyed, he
uſes theſe words :
    ———*for all thy bleſſed youth*
  Becomes as aged, and doth beg the alms
  Of palſied eld ; ———
Out of which, he that can deduce the concluſion, has a better
knack at logic than I have. I ſuppoſe the poet wrote,
    ——— *For* pall'd, *thy* blazed *youth*
  Becomes aſſuaged ; *and doth beg the alms*
  Of palſied eld ; ———
i. e. when thy youthful appetite becomes palled, as it will be in
the very enjoyment, the blaze of youth is at once aſſuaged, and
thou immediately contracteſt the infirmities of old age ; as particularly the palſy and other nervous diſorders, conſequent on the
inordinate uſe of ſenſual pleaſures. This is to the purpoſe ; and
proves *youth* is not enjoyed, by ſhewing the ſhort duration of it.
                          WARBURTON.

  Here again I think Dr. Warburton totally miſtaken. Shakſpeare
declares that man has *neither youth nor age* ; for in *youth,* which is
the *happieſt* time, or which might be the happieſt, he commonly
wants means to obtain what he could enjoy ; he is dependent on
palſied eld : muſt beg alms from the coffers of hoary avarice ; and
being very niggardly ſupplied, *becomes as aged,* looks, like an old
man, on happineſs which is beyond his reach. And, when *be is
old and rich,* when he has wealth enough for the purchaſe of all
that formerly excited his deſires, he has no longer the powers of
enjoyment ;
    ——— *has neither heat, affection, limb, nor beauty,*
  To make his riches pleaſant. ———

That bears the name of life? Yet in this life
Lie hid more thousand deaths:[4] yet death we fear,
That makes these odds all even.

   CLAUD.   I humbly thank you.
To sue to live, I find, I seek to die;
And, seeking death, find life:[5] Let it come on.

I have explained this passage according to the present reading,
which may stand without much inconvenience; yet I am willing to
persuade my reader, because I have almost persuaded myself, that
our author wrote,
      —— *for all thy* blasted *youth*
    Becomes as aged—— JOHNSON.

   The sentiment contained in these lines, which Dr. Johnson has
explained with his usual precision, occurs again in the forged
letter that Edmund delivers to his father, as written by Edgar;
K. Lear, Act I. sc. ii: " This policy, and reverence of age, makes
the world bitter to *the best of our times*; keeps our fortunes from us
till our oldness cannot relish them." The words above, printed in
Italicks, support, I think, the reading of the old copy,——" *blessed*
youth," and shew that any emendation is unnecessary.
                                      MALONE.

   [3] —— *heat, affection, limb, nor* beauty,] But how does beauty
make *riches pleasant?* We should read *bounty*, which completes the
sense, and is this; thou hast neither the pleasure of enjoying riches
thyself, for thou wantest vigour; nor of seeing it enjoyed by others,
for thou wantest *bounty*. Where the making the want of *bounty* as
inseparable from old age as the want of *health*, is extremely satirical,
though not altogether just. WARBURTON.

   I am inclined to believe, that neither man nor woman will have
much difficulty to tell how *beauty makes riches pleasant*. Surely
this emendation, though it is elegant and ingenious, is not such as
that an opportunity of inserting it should be purchased by declaring
ignorance of what every one knows, by confessing insensibility of
what every one feels. JOHNSON.

   By " heat" and " affection" the poet meant to express *appetite*,
and by " limb" and " beauty" *strength*. EDWARDS.

   [4] —— more *thousand deaths*:] For this Sir T. Hanmer reads:
      —— *a thousand deaths*: ——
The meaning is, not only *a thousand deaths*, but *a thousand deaths*
besides what have been mentioned. JOHNSON.

   [5] *To sue to live, I find, I seek to die*;
    And, seeking death, find life:] Had the Friar, in reconciling

Enter ISABELLA.

Isab. What, ho! Peace here; grace and good
    company!

Prov. Who's there? come in: the wish deserves
    a welcome.

Duke. Dear sir, ere long I'll visit you again.

Claud. Most holy sir, I thank you.

Isab. My business is a word or two with Claudio.

Prov. And very welcome. Look, signior, here's
    your sister.

Duke. Provost, a word with you.

Prov.   As many as you please.

Duke. Bring them to speak, where I may be con-
    ceal'd,

Yet hear them.[6]   [*Exeunt* DUKE *and* Provost.

Claud.   Now, sister, what's the comfort?

Claudio to death, urged to him the certainty of happiness hereafter,
this speech would have been introduced with more propriety; but
the Friar says nothing of that subject, and argues more like a philosopher, than a Christian divine. M. MASON.

  Mr. M. Mason seems to forget that no actual Friar was the speaker,
but the Duke, who might reasonably be supposed to have more of
the philosopher than the divine in his composition. STEEVENS.

  [6] *Bring them to speak, where I may be conceal'd,*
   Yet hear them.] The first copy, published by the players, gives
the passage thus:
   Bring them to hear me speak, where I may be conceal'd.
Perhaps we should read:
   Bring me to hear them speak, where I, &c. STEEVENS.

  The second folio authorizes the reading in the text. TYRWHITT.

  The alterations made in that copy do not deserve the smallest
credit. There are undoubted proofs that they were merely arbitrary;
and in general they are also extremely injudicious. MALONE.

  I am of a different opinion, in which I am joined by Dr. Farmer;
and consequently prefer the reading of the second folio to my own
attempt at emendation, though Mr. Malone has done me the honour
to adopt it. STEEVENS.

Isab. Why, as all comforts are; most good in deed: [7]
Lord Angelo, having affairs to heaven,
Intends you for his swift embaffador,
Where you shall be an everlasting leiger:
Therefore your best appointment [8] make with speed;
To-morrow you set on.

[7] —— *as all comforts are; most good* in deed:] If this reading be right, Isabella must mean that she brings something better than *words* of comfort, she brings an affurance of *deeds*. This is harsh and constrained, but I know not what better to offer. Sir Thomas Hanmer reads:
—— in *speed*. JOHNSON.

The old copy reads:

As all comforts are : most good, most good indeede. Why,

I believe the present reading, as explained by Dr. Johnson, is the true one. So, in *Macbeth:*
"We're yet but young *in deed*." STEEVENS.

I would point the lines thus:
"*Clau.* Now, sister, what's the comfort?
"*Isab.* Why, as all comforts are, most good. Indeed Lord Angelo," &c.
Indeed is the same as *in truth*, or *truly*, the common beginning of speeches in Shakspeare's age. See Charles the First's Trial. The King and Bradshaw seldom say any thing without this preface:
"Truly, Sir ——." BLACKSTONE.

[8] —— *an everlasting* leiger :
Therefore your best appointment —] *Leiger* is the same with resident. *Appointment*; preparation; act of fitting, or state of being fitted for any thing. So in old books, we have a knight well *appointed*; that is, well armed and mounted, or fitted at all points. JOHNSON.

The word *leiger* is thus used in *The Comedy of Look about You*, 1600:
"Why do you stay, Sir?—
"Madam, as *leiger* to solicit for your absent love."
Again, in *Leicester's Commonwealth*, "a special man of that hasty king, who was his *Ledger*, or Agent, in London," &c. STEEVENS.

—— *your best* appointment—] The word *appointment*, on this occasion, should seem to comprehend confeffion, communion, and absolution. "Let him (says Escalus) be furnished with divines, and have all charitable preparation." The King in *Hamlet*, who was cut off prematurely, and without such preparation, is

T 4

CLAUD.   Is there no remedy?

ISAB. None, but such remedy, as, to save a head,
To cleave a heart in twain.

CLAUD.   But is there any?

ISAB. Yes, brother, you may live;
There is a devilish mercy in the judge,
If you'll implore it, that will free your life,
But fetter you till death.

CLAUD.   Perpetual durance?

ISAB. Ay, just, perpetual durance; a restraint,
Though all the world's vastidity [2] you had,
To a determin'd scope. [3]

CLAUD.   But in what nature?

ISAB. In such a one as (you consenting to't)
Would bark your honour [4] from that trunk you bear,
And leave you naked.

CLAUD.   Let me know the point.

ISAB. O, I do fear thee, Claudio; and I quake,
Lest thou a feverous life should'st entertain,
And six or seven winters more respect
Than a perpetual honour.   Dar'st thou die?
The sense of death is most in apprehension;

---

said to be dif-*appointed*. *Appointment*, however, may be more
simply explained by the following passage in *The Antipodes*,
1638:

       " ————— your lodging
       " Is decently *appointed*." i. e. prepared, furnished.
                                                    STEEVENS.

     [2] Though *all the world's vastidity* —] The old copy reads——
Through all, &c.   Corrected by Mr. Pope. MALONE.

     [3] ——— *a restraint* ———
     To a determin'd scope.] A confinement of your mind to one
painful idea; to ignominy, of which the remembrance can neither
be suppressed nor escaped. JOHNSON.

     [4] *Would* bark *your honour* —] A metaphor from stripping trees
of their *bark*. DOUCE.

And the poor beetle, that we tread upon,
In corporal fufferance finds a pang as great
As when a giant dies.[5]

 CLAUD.   Why give you me this fhame?
Think you I can a refolution fetch
From flowery tendernefs? If I muft die,
I will encounter darknefs as a bride,
And hug it in mine arms.[6]

 ISAB. There fpake my brother; there my father's
    grave
Did utter forth a voice! Yes, thou muft die:
Thou art too noble to conferve a life
In bafe appliances. This outward-fainted de-
    puty,—
Whofe fettled vifage and deliberate word
Nips youth i'the head, and follies doth enmew,[7]

---

5 —— *the poor beetle,* &c.] The reafoning is, *that death is no more than every being muft fuffer, though the dread of it is peculiar to man;* or perhaps, *that* we are inconfiftent with ourfelves, when we fo much dread that which we careleßly inflict on other creatures, that feel the pain as acutely as we. JOHNSON.

The meaning is—fear is the principal fenfation in death, which has no pain; and the giant when he dies feels no greater pain than the beetle.—This paßage, however, from its arrangement, is liable to an oppofite conftruction, but which would totally deftroy the illuftration of the fentiment. DOUCE.

6 *I will encounter darknefs as a bride,*
 And hug it in mine arms.] So, in the firft part of *Jeronimo, or The Spanifh Tragedy,* 1605 :
  " ———— *night*
  " That yawning Beldam, with her jetty fkin,
  " 'Tis fhe I *hug* as mine effeminate bride."
           STEEVENS.

Again, in *Antony and Cleopatra* :
  " ———— I will be
  " *A bridegroom* in my *death*; and run into 't,
  " As to a lover's bed." MALONE.

7 —— *follies doth* enmew,] Forces follies to lie in cover, with-out daring to fhow themfelves. JOHNSON.

As falcon doth the fowl,[8]—is yet a devil;
His filth within being cast,[9] he would appear
A pond as deep as hell.

CLAUD.   The princely Angelo?

ISAB. O, 'tis the cunning livery of hell,
The damned'st body to, invest and cover
In princely guards![2] Dost thou think, Claudio,

---

[8] *As falcon doth the fowl,*] In whose presence the follies of youth are afraid to show themselves, as the fowl is afraid to flutter while the falcon hovers over it.
So, in the Third Part of *King Henry VI*:
   " —— not he that loves him best,
   " The proudest he that holds up Lancaster,
   " Dares *stir a wing*, if Warwick shakes his bells."
To *enmew* is a term in falconry, also used by Beaumont and Fletcher, in *The Knight of Malta*:
   " —— I have seen him scale,
   " As if a falcon had run up a train,
   " Clashing his warlike pinions, his steel'd cuirass,
   " And, at his pitch, *enmew* the town below him." STEEVENS.

[9] *His filth within being cast,*] To *cast* a pond is to empty it of mud.
Mr. Upton reads:
   His pond *within being cast, he would appear*
   A filth *as deep as hell.* JOHNSON.

[2] *The* princely *Angelo?* ——
   —— princely *guards!*] The stupid editors, mistaking *guards* for satellites, (whereas it here signifies *lace*,) altered *priestly*, in both places, to *princely*. Whereas Shakspeare wrote it *priestly*, as appears from the words themselves:
   —— 'Tis the cunning livery *of hell*,
   The damned'st body to invest and cover
   With priestly *guards.* ——
In the first place we see that *guards* here signifies *lace*, as referring to *livery*, and as having no sense in the signification of *satellites*. Now *priestly guards* means *sanctity*, which is the sense required. But *princely guards* means nothing but *rich lace*, which is a sense the passage will not bear. Angelo, indeed, as *deputy*, might be called the *princely* Angelo: but not in this place, where the immediately preceding words of,
   This outward-sainted deputy,
demand the reading I have restored. WARBURTON.

   The first folio has, in both places, *prenzie*, from which the other folios made *princely*, and every editor may make what he can. JOHNSON.

If I would yield him my virginity,
Thou might'ft be freed?

 Claud.   O, heavens! it cannot be.

 Isab. Yes, he would give it thee, from this rank
    offence,[3]
So to offend him ftill: This night's the time
That I fhould do what I abhor to name,
Or elfe thou dieft to-morrow.

 Claud.   Thou fhalt not do't.

 Isab. O, were it but my life,
I'd throw it down for your deliverance
As frankly as a pin.[4]

 Claud.   Thanks, dear Ifabel.

 Isab. Be ready, Claudio, for your death to-morrow.

Princely is the judicious correction of the fecond folio. *Princely*
guards mean no more than the badges of royalty, (laced or bordered
robes,) which Angelo is fuppofed to affume during the abfence of the
Duke. The ftupidity of the firft editors is fometimes not more injurious to Shakfpeare, than the ingenuity of thofe who fucceeded them.

In the old play of *Cambyfes* I meet with the fame expreffion.
Sifamnes is left by *Cambyfes* to diftribute juftice while he is abfent;
and in a foliloquy fays:

   " Now may I wear the brodered *garde*,
   " And lye in downe-bed foft."

Again, the queen of *Cambyfes* fays:

   " I do forfake thefe broder'd *gardes*,
   " And all the facions new."   Steevens.

A guard, in old language, meant a welt or border of a garment;
" becaufe (faysMinfhieu) it *gards* and keeps the garment from tearing."
Thefe borders were fometimes of lace. So, in *The Merchant of Venice*:

   " —— Give him a livery
   " More

[3] —— from
my committing
fafety. The ad
fecret of his in
on account of the

[4] —— *as a pi*
   " I do n

CLAUD. Yes.—Has he affections in him,
That thus can make him bite the law by the nose,
When he would force it?[5] Sure it is no sin;
Or of the deadly seven it is the least.[6]

ISAB. Which is the least?

CLAUD. If it were damnable,[7] he, being so wise,
Why, would he for the momentary trick
Be perdurably fin'd?[8]—O Isabel!

[5] *Has he affections, &c.*] *Is he actuated by passions that impel him to transgress the law, at the very moment that he is* enforcing *it against others?* [I find, he is.] *Surely then,* since this is so general a propensity, since the judge is as criminal as he whom he condemns, it is no sin, or at least a venial one. So, in the next Act:

" —— A deflower'd maid,
" And by an eminent body that *enforc'd*
" *The law* against it."

Force is again used for *enforce* in *King Henry VIII:*

" If you will now unite in your complaints,
" And *force* them with a constancy."

Again, in *Coriolanus:*

" Why *force* you this?" MALONE.

[6] *Or of the deadly* seven, *&c.*] It may be useful to know which they are; the reader is therefore presented with the following catalogue of them, viz. Pride, Envy, Wrath, Sloth, Covetousness, Gluttony, and Lechery. To recapitulate the punishments hereafter for these sins, might have too powerful an effect upon the weak nerves of the present generation; but whoever is desirous of being particularly acquainted with them, may find information in some of the old monkish systems of divinity, and especially in a curious book entitled *Le Kalendrier des Bergiers,* 1500. folio, of which there is an English translation. DOUCE.

[7] *If it were damnable,* &c.] Shakspeare shows his knowledge of human nature in the conduct of Claudio. When Isabella first tells him of Angelo's proposal, he answers, with honest indignation, agreeably to his settled principles,

Thou shalt not do't.

But the love of life being permitted to operate, soon furnishes him with sophistical arguments; he believes it cannot be very dangerous to the soul, since Angelo, who is so wise, will venture it.

JOHNSON.

[8] *Be* perdurably *fin'd?*] *Perdurably* is lastingly. So, in *Othello:*

" ——cables of *perdurable* toughness." STEEVENS.

Isab. What says my brother?

Claud. . Death is a fearful thing.

Isab. And shamed life a hateful.

Claud. Ay, but to di⸺

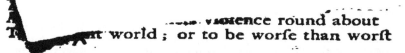

⸺⸺ violence round about
⸺⸺ world; or to be worse than worst

⸺⸺ *delighted spirit*⸺] i. e. the spirit accustomed here to ease and delights. This was properly urged as an aggravation to the sharpness of the torments spoken of. The Oxford editor not apprehending this, alters it to *dilated*. As if, because the spirit in the body is said to be imprisoned, it was *crowded together* likewise; and so by death not only set free, but expanded too; which, if true, would make it the less sensible of pain.
WARBURTON.

This reading may perhaps stand, but many attempts have been made to correct it. The most plausible is that which substitutes
⸺⸺ *the* benighted *spirit*,
alluding to the darkness always supposed in the place of future punishment.

Perhaps we may read:
⸺⸺ *the* delinquent *spirit*,
a word easily changed to *delighted* by a bad copier, or unskilful reader. *Delinquent* is proposed by Thirlby in his manuscript.
JOHNSON.

I think with Dr. Warburton, that by the *delighted* spirit is meant, *the soul once accustomed to delight*, which of course must render the sufferings, afterwards described, less tolerable. Thus our author calls youth, *blessed*, in a former scene, before he proceeds to show its wants and its inconveniencies.

Mr. Ritson has furnished me with a passage which I leave to those who can use it for the illustration of the foregoing epithet. "Sir Thomas Herbert, speaking of the death of Mirza, son to Shah Abbas, says that he gave a period to his miseries in this world, by supping a *delighted* cup of extreame poyson." *Travels*, 1634. p. 104. STEEVENS.

⸺⸺ *viewless winds*] i. e. invisible. So *Comus*, v. 92: "⸺⸺ I must be viewless ⸺ unseen,
STE.

Of those, that lawless and incertain thoughts [2]
Imagine howling!—'tis too horrible!
The weariest and most loathed worldly life,
That age, ach, penury, [3] and imprisonment
Can lay on nature, is a paradise
To what we fear of death. [4]

---

[2] —— *lawless and incertain thoughts* —] Conjecture sent out to wander without any certain direction, and ranging through possibilities of pain. JOHNSON.

[3] —— *penury,*] The old copy has—*pejury*. Corrected by the editor of the second folio. MALONE.

[4] *To what we fear of death.*] Most certainly the idea of the "spirit bathing in fiery floods," or of residing "in thrilling regions of thick-ribbed ice," is not original to our poet; but I am not sure that they came from the Platonick hell of Virgil. The monks also had their hot and their cold hell; "the fyrste is fyre that ever brenneth, and never gyveth lighte," says an old homily :—"The seconde is passying cold, that yf a greate hylle of fyre were cast therin, it shold torne to yce." One of their legends, well remembered in the time of Shakspeare, gives us a dialogue between a bishop and a soul tormented in a piece of ice which was brought to cure a *brenning heate* in his foot; take care, that you do not interpret this the *gout*, for I remember Menage quotes a canon upon us :

"*Si quis dixerit episcopum* podagrâ *laborare, anathema fit.*"

Another tells us of the soul of a monk fastened to a rock, which the winds were to blow about for a twelvemonth, and purge of its enormities. Indeed this doctrine was before now introduced into poetick fiction, as you may see in a poem, "where the lover declareth his pains to exceed far the pains of hell," among the many miscellaneous ones subjoined to the works of Surrey : of which you will soon have a beautiful edition from the able hand of my friend Dr. Percy. Nay, a very learned and inquisitive brother-antiquary hath observed to me, on the authority of Blefkenius, that this was the ancient opinion of the inhabitants of Iceland, who were certainly very little read either in the poet or philosopher.
FARMER.

Lazarus, in *The Shepherd's Calendar*, is represented to have seen these particular modes of punishment in the infernal regions :

"Secondly, I have seen in hell a floud frozen as ice, wherein the envious men and women were plunged unto the navel, and then suddainly came over them a right cold and great wind that grieved and pained them right sore," &c. STEEVENS.

Isab. Alas! alas!

Claud. Sweet fifter, let me live:
What fin you do to fave a brother's life,
Nature difpenfes with the deed fo far,
That it becomes a virtue.

Isab. O, you beaft!
O, faithlefs coward! O, difhoneft wretch!
Wilt thou be made a man out of my vice?
Is't not a kind of inceft,[5] to take life
From thine own fifter's fhame? What fhould ·I
     think?
Heaven fhield, my mother play'd my father fair!
For fuch a warped flip of wildernefs[6]
Ne'er iffu'd from his blood. Take my defiance:[7]
Die; perifh! might but my bending down
Reprieve thee from thy fate, it fhould proceed:
I'll pray a thoufand prayers for thy death,
No word to fave thee.

Claud. Nay, hear me, Ifabel.

Isab. O, fie, fie, fie!

---

[5] *Is't not a kind of inceft,*] In Ifabella's declamation there is
fomething harfh, and fomething forced and far-fetched. But her
indignation cannot be thought violent, when we confider her not
only as a virgin, but as a nun. JOHNSON.

[6] —— *a warped flip of* wildernefs——] *Wildernefs* is here ufed
for *wildnefs,* the ftate of being diforderly. So, in *The Maid's
Tragedy:*
    " And throws an unknown *wildernefs* about me."
Again, in *Old Fortunatus,* 1600:
    " But I in *wildernefs* totter'd out my youth."
The word, in this fenfe, is now obfolete, though employed by
Milton:
    " The paths, and bowers, doubt not, but our joint hands
    " Will keep from *wildernefs* with eafe."
                    STEEVENS.

[7] ——*Take my* defiance:] *Defiance* is *refufal.* So, in *Romeo
and Juliet :*
    " I do *defy* thy commiferation." STEEVENS.

3

Thy fin's not accidental, but a trade:[a]
Mercy to thee would prove itfelf a bawd:
'Tis beft that thou dieft quickly.   [*Going.*

CLAUD.   O hear me, Ifabella.

Re-enter DUKE.

DUKE. Vouchfafe a word, young fifter, but one
word.

ISAB. What is your will?

DUKE. Might you difpenfe with your leifure, I
would by and by have fome fpeech with you : the
fatisfaction I would require, is likewife your own
benefit.

ISAB. I have no fuperfluous leifure; my ftay muft
be ftolen out of other affairs; but I will attend you
a while.

DUKE. [*To* CLAUDIO, *afide.*] Son, I have overheard what hath paft between you and your fifter.
Angelo had never the purpofe to corrupt her; only
he hath made an affay of her virtue, to practice his
judgement with the difpofition of natures: fhe,
having the truth of honour in her, hath made him
that gracious denial which he is moft glad to receive: I am confeffor to Angelo, and I know this
to be true; therefore prepare yourfelf to death: Do
not fatisfy your refolution with hopes that are fallible:[9] to-morrow you muft die; go to your knees,
and make ready.

─────

[a] ──── *but a* trade :] A cuftom; a practice; an eftablifhed habit.
So we fay of a man much addicted to any thing, *be makes* a trade
of it.   JOHNSON.

9 *Do not* fatisfy *your refolution with hopes that are fallible:*] A
condemned man, whom his confeffor had brought to bear death
with decency and refolution, began anew to entertain hopes of life.
This occafioned the advice in the words above.   But how did

Claud. Let me afk my fifter pardon. I am fo out of love with life, that I will fue to be rid of it.

Duke. Hold you there:[2] Farewell.

[*Exit* Claudio.

Re-enter Provoft.

Provoft, a word with you.

Prov. What's your will, father?

Duke. That now you are come, you will be gone: Leave me a while with the maid; my mind promifes with my habit, no lofs fhall touch her by my company.

Prov. In good time.[3]   [*Exit* Provoft.

Duke. The hand that hath made you fair, hath made you good: the goodnefs, that is cheap in beauty, makes beauty brief in goodnefs; but grace, being the foul of your complexion, fhould keep the body of it ever fair. The affault, that Angelo hath made to you, fortune hath convey'd to my underftanding; and, but that frailty hath examples for

---

thefe hopes *fatisfy* his refolution? or what harm was there, if they did? We muft certainly read, *Do not* falfify *your refolution with hopes that are* fallible. And then it becomes a reafonable admonition. For hopes of life, by drawing him back into the world, would naturally elude or weaken the virtue of that *refolution* which was raifed only on motives of religion. And this his confeffor had reafon to warn him of. The term *falfify* is taken from fencing, and fignifies the pretending to aim a ftroke, in order to draw the adverfary off his guard. So, Fairfax:

" Now ftrikes he out, and now he *falfifieth.*" WARBURTON.

The fenfe is this:—Do not reft with fatisfaction on *hopes that are fallible.* There is no need of alteration. STEEVENS.

Perhaps the meaning is, Do not fatisfy or content yourfelf with that kind of refolution, which acquires ftrength from a latent hope that it will not be put to the teft; a hope, that in your cafe, if you rely upon it, will deceive you. MALONE.

[2] *Hold you there:*] Continue in that refolution. JOHNSON.

[3] *In good time.*] i. e. *à la bonne heure,* fo be it, very well. STEEVENS.

his falling, I fhould wonder at Angelo. How would you do to content this fubftitute, and to fave your brother?

Isab. I am now going to refolve him : I had rather my brother die by the law, than my fon fhould be unlawfully born. But O, how much is the good duke deceived in Angelo! If ever he return, and I can fpeak to him, I will open my lips in vain, or difcover his government.

Duke. That fhall not be much amifs : Yet, as the matter now ftands, he will avoid your accufation; he made trial of you only.⁴——Therefore faften your ear on my advifings ; to the love I have in doing good, a remedy prefents itfelf. I do make myfelf believe, that you may moft uprighteoufly do a poor wronged lady a merited benefit ; redeem your brother from the angry law ; do no ftain to your own gracious perfon ; and much pleafe the abfent duke, if, peradventure, he fhall ever return to have hearing of this bufinefs.

Isab. Let me hear you fpeak further ; I have fpirit to do any thing that appears not foul in the truth of my fpirit.

Duke. Virtue is bold, and goodnefs never fearful. Have you not heard fpeak of Mariana the fifter of Frederick, the great foldier, who mifcarried at fea?

Isab. I have heard of the lady, and good words went with her name.

Duke. Her fhould this Angelo have married ; was affianced to her by oath,⁵ and the nuptial appointed : between which time of the contract, and limit of

4 —— *he made trial of you only.*] That is, *he will fay* he made trial of you only.   M. MASON.

5 —— by *oath,*] *By* inferted by the editor of the fecond folio.
MALONE.

the folemnity,[6] her brother Frederick was wrecked at fea, having in that perifh'd veffel the dowry of his fifter. But mark, how heavily this befel to the poor gentlewoman: there fhe loft a noble and renowned brother, in his love toward her ever moft kind and natural; with him the portion and finew of her fortune, her marriage–dowry; with both, her combinate hufband,[7] this well–feeming Angelo.

Isab. Can this be fo? Did Angelo fo leave her?

Duke. Left her in her tears, and dry'd not one of them with his comfort; fwallowed his vows whole, pretending, in her, difcoveries of difhonour: in few, beftowed her on her own lamentation,[8] which fhe yet wears for his fake; and he, a marble to her tears, is wafhed with them, but relents not.

Isab. What a merit were it in death, to take this poor maid from the world! What corruption in this life, that it will let this man live!—But how out of this can fhe avail?

Duke. It is a rupture that you may eafily heal: and the cure of it not only faves your brother, but keeps you from difhonour in doing it.

Isab. Show me how, good father.

Duke. This fore–named maid hath yet in her the continuance of her firft affection; his unjuft unkind-nefs, that in all reafon fhould have quenched her love, hath, like an impediment in the current, made

[6] —— *and* limit *of the folemnity,*] So, in *King John:*
  " Prefcribes how long the virgin ftate fhall laft,——
  " Gives *limits* unto holy nuptial rites."
i. e. appointed times. *Malone.*

[7] —— *her* combinate *hufband,*] *Combinate* is *betrothed, fettled by contract.*
                                                                    Steevens.

[8] —— beftowed *her on her own lamentation,*] i. e. *left* her to her forrows.
                                                                    Malone.

Rather, as our author expreffes himfelf in *King Henry V.*—— " *gave* her up" to them. *Steevens.*

U 2

it more violent and unruly.   Go you to Angelo; anfwer his requiring with a plaufible obedience; agree with his demands to the point : only refer yourfelf to this advantage,⁹—firft, that your ftay with him may not be long; that the time may have all fhadow and filence in it ; and the place anfwer to convenience : this being granted in courfe, now follows all.   We fhall advife this wronged maid to ftead up your appointment, go in your place; if the encounter acknowledge itfelf hereafter, it may compel him to her recompenfe : and here, by this, is your brother faved, your honour untainted, the poor Mariana advantaged, and the corrupt deputy fcaled.ᵃ   The maid will I frame, and make fit for

---

9 ——— *only refer yourfelf to this advantage,*] This is fcarcely to be reconciled to any eftablifhed mode of fpeech.   We may read, *only re-ferve yourfelf to,* or *only* referve to *yourfelf this advantage.* JOHNSON.

Refer yourfelf to, merely fignifies—*have recourfe to, betake yourfelf to,* this advantage.   STEEVENS.

ᵃ ——— *the corrupt deputy* fcaled.]   *To* fcale *the deputy* may be, *to reach him, notwithftanding the elevation of his place ;* or it may be, *to ftrip him and difcover his nakednefs, though armed and concealed by the inveftments of authority.*   JOHNSON.

To *fcale,* as may be learned from a note to Coriolanus, Act I. fc. i. moft certainly means, to *diforder,* to *difconcert,* to *put to flight.*   An army routed is called by Holinfhed, an army *fcaled.*   The word fometimes fignifies to *diffufe* or difperfe ; at others, as I fup-pofe in the prefent inftance, to *put into confufion.*   STEEVENS.

To *fcale* is certainly to reach (as Dr. Johnfon explains it) as well as to *difperfe* or *fpread abroad,* and hence its application to a routed army which is *fcattered over the field.*   The Duke's meaning ap-pears to be, either that Angelo would be *over-reached,* as a town is by the fcalade, or that his true character would be *fpread* or *laid open,* fo that his vilenefs would become evident.   Dr. Warburton thinks it is *weighed,* a meaning which Dr. Johnfon affixes to the word in another place.   See *Coriolanus,* Act. I. fc. i.

Scaled, however, may mean—laid open, as a *corrupt fore* is by removing the flough that covers it.   The allufion is rendered lefs difgufting, by more elegant language, in *Hamlet :*

"   It will but *fkin* and *film* the *ulcerous place ;*
"   Whiles *rank corruption,* mining all within,
"   Infects unfeen."   RITSON.

his attempt. If you think well to carry this as you may, the doubleneſs of the benefit defends the deceit from reproof. What think you of it?

ISAB. The image of it gives me content already; and, I truſt, it will grow to a moſt proſperous perfection.

DUKE. It lies much in your holding up: Haſte you ſpeedily to Angelo; if for this night he entreat you to his bed, give him promiſe of ſatisfaction. I will preſently to St. Luke's; there, at the moated grange³ reſides this dejected Mariana: At that place call upon me; and diſpatch with Angelo, that it may be quickly.

ISAB. I thank you for this comfort: Fare you well, good father. *[Exeunt ſeverally.*

³ —— *the moated* grange——] A *grange* is a ſolitary farm-houſe. So, in *Othello:*
" —— this is Venice,
" My houſe is not a *grange.*" STEEVENS.

A *grange* implies ſome one particular houſe immediately inferior in rank to a *hall*, ſituated at a ſmall diſtance from the town or village from which it takes its name; as, *Hornby grange, Blackwell grange*; and is in the neighbourhood ſimply called *The Grange.* Originally, perhaps, theſe buildings were the lord's *granary* or ſtorehouſe, and the reſidence of his chief bailiff. (*Grange,* from *Granagium,* Lat.) RITSON.

A *grange,* in its original ſignification, meant a farm-houſe of a monaſtery (from *grana* gerendo), from which it was always at ſome little diſtance. One of the monks was uſually appointed to inſpect the accounts of the farm. He was called the Prior of the Grange; —in barbarous Latin, *Grangiarius.* Being placed at a diſtance from the monaſtery, and not connected with any other buildings, Shakſpeare, with his wonted licence, uſes it, both here and in *Othella,* in the ſenſe of a *ſolitary* farm-houſe.

I have ſince obſerved that the word was uſed in the ſame ſenſe by the contemporary writers. So, in Tarleton's *Newes out of Purgatory,* printed about the year 1590: " —— till my return I would have thee ſtay at our little *graunge* houſe in the country."
In Lincolnſhire they at this day call every lone houſe that is unconnected with others, a *grange.* MALONE.

U 3

SCENE II.

The Street before the Prison.

Enter DUKE as a Friar; to him ELBOW, Clown, and
Officers.

ELB. Nay, if there be no remedy for it, but that
you will needs buy and sell men and women like
beasts, we shall have all the world drink brown and
white bastard.[4]

DUKE. O, heavens! what stuff is here?

CLO. 'Twas never merry world, since, of two
usuries,[5] the merriest was put down, and the worser
allow'd by order of law a furr'd gown to keep him
warm; and furr'd with fox and lamb-skins too,[6] to

---

[4] —— bastard.] A kind of sweet wine, then much in vogue, from
the Italian bastardo. WARBURTON.

See a note on King Henry IV. Part I. Act II. sc. iv. STEEVENS.

Bastard was raisin-wine. See Minshieu's Dict. in v. and Cole's
Latin Dict. 1679. MALONE.

[5] —— since, of two usuries,] Here a satire on usury turns abruptly
to a satire on the person of the usurer, without any kind of preparation. We may be assured then, that a line or two, at least, have
been lost. The subject of which we may easily discover was a comparison between the two usurers; as, before, between the two usuries.
So that, for the future, the passage should be read with asterisks, thus—
by order of law, * * * a furr'd gown, &c. WARBURTON.

Sir Thomas Hanmer corrected this with less pomp, then since of
two usurers the merriest was put down, and the worser allowed, by order
of law, a furr'd gown, &c. His punctuation is right, but the alteration, small as it is, appears more than was wanted. Usury may
be used by an easy licence for the professors of usury. JOHNSON.

[6] —— and furr'd with fox and lamb-skins too, &c.] In this passage the foxes skins are supposed to denote craft, and the lamb-
skins innocence. It is evident therefore that we ought to read,
" furred with fox on lamb-skins," instead of " and lamb-skins;"
for otherwise, craft will not stand for the facing. M. MASON.

Fox-skins and lamb-skins were both used as facings to cloth in
Shakspeare's time. See the Statute of Apparel, 24 Henry VIII.

fignify, that craft, being richer than innocency, ftands for the facing.

Elb. Come your way, fir:——Blefs you, good father friar.

Duke. And you, good brother father: [7] What of-fence hath this man made you, fir?

Elb. Marry, fir, he hath offended the law; and, fir, we take him to be a thief too, fir; for we have found upon him, fir, a ftrange pick-lock, [8] which we have fent to the deputy.

Duke. Fie, firrah; a bawd, a wicked bawd!
The evil that thou caufeft to be done,
That is thy means to live: Do thou but think
What 'tis to cram a maw, or clothe a back,
From fuch a filthy vice: fay to thyfelf,——
From their abominable and beaftly touches

c. 13. Hence *fox-furr'd* flave is ufed as an opprobrious epithet in *Wily Beguiled*, 1606, and in other old comedies. See alfo *Cha-racterifmi, or Lenton's Leafures*, &c. 1631: "An *Ufurer* is an old *fox*, clad in *lamb-fkin*, who hath pray'd [prey'd] fo long abroad," &c.
MALONE.

7 —— *and you, good* brother father:] In return to Elbow's blundering addrefs of *good father friar*, i. e. *good father brother*, the Duke humouroufly calls him, in his own ftyle, *good brother father*. This would appear ftill clearer in French. *Dieu vous beniffe*, mon pere frere.——*Et vous auffi*, mon frere pere. There is no doubt that our *friar* is a corruption of the French *frere*. TYRWHITT.

Mr. Tyrwhitt's obfervation is confirmed by a paffage in *The Strangeft Adventure that ever happened*, &c. 4to. 1601:
"And I call to mind, that as the reverend *father brother*, Thomas Sequera, Superiour of Ebora, and mine auncient friend, came to vifite me," &c. STEEVENS.

8 —— *a ftrange* pick-lock,] As we hear no more of this charge, it is neceffary to prevent honeft Pompey from being taken for a houfe-breaker. The *locks* which he had occafion to *pick*, were by no means common, in this country at leaft. They were probably introduced, with *other Spanifh cuftoms*, during the reign of Philip and Mary; and were fo well known in Edinburgh, that in one of Sir David Lindfay's plays, reprefented to thoufands in the open air, fuch a *lock* is actually opened on the ftage. RITSON.

U 4

I drink, I eat, array myfelf, and live.[9]
Canft thou believe thy living is a life,
So ftinkingly depending? Go, mend, go, mend.

    Clo. Indeed, it does ftink in fome fort, fir; but
yet, fir, I would prove———

    Duke. Nay, if the devil have given thee proofs
            for fin,
Thou wilt prove his. Take him to prifon, officer;
Correction and inftruction muft both work,
Ere this rude beaft will profit.

    Elb. He muft before the deputy, fir; he has given
him warning: the deputy cannot abide a whore-
mafter: if he be a whoremonger, and comes before him, he were as good go a mile on his errand.

    Duke. That we were all, as fome would feem to be,
Free from our faults, as faults from feeming, free![2]

---

    [9] *I drink, I eat, array myfelf, and live.*] The old editions have,
        I drink, I eat away *myfelf, and live.*
This is one very excellent inftance of the fagacity of our editors,
and it were to be wifhed heartily, that they would have obliged
us with their phyfical folution, how a man can *eat* away himfelf,
and live. Mr. Bifhop gave me that moft certain emendation,
which I have fubftituted in the room of the former foolifh reading;
by the help whereof, we have this eafy fenfe: that the Clown fed
himfelf, and put cloaths on his back, by exercifing the vile trade
of a bawd. THEOBALD.

    [2] *That we were all, as fome would feem to be,*
        Free from our faults, as faults from feeming, *free!*] i. e. as
faults are deftitute of all comelinefs or *feeming.* The firft of thefe
lines refers to the deputy's fanctified hypocrify; the fecond to the
Clown's beaftly occupation. But the latter part is thus ill expreffed
for the fake of the rhime. WARBURTON.
    Sir Thomas Hanmer reads:
        Free from all faults, as from faults feeming free.
In the interpretation of Dr. Warburton, the fenfe is trifling, and
the expreffion harfh. To wifh *that men were as free from faults, as
faults are free from comelinefs,* [inftead of *void of comelinefs*] is a very
poor conceit. I once thought it fhould be read:
        O that all were, as all would feem to be,
        Free from all faults, or from falfe *feeming free.*

Enter LUCIO.

ELB. His neck will come to your waift, a cord, fir.[3]

So in this play:

"" O place, O, power—how doft thou
"" Wrench awe from fools, and tie the wifer fouls
"" To thy *falfe feeming!*"

But now I believe that a lefs alteration will ferve the turn:

Free from all faults, or *faults from feeming free.*
that men were really good, or that their faults were known, that men were free from faults, *or* faults from *hypocrify.* So Ifabella calls Angelo's hypocrify, *feeming, feeming.* JOHNSON,

I think we fhould read with Sir T. Hanmer:

Free from all faults, as from faults *feeming free.*

i. e. *I wifh we were all as good as we appear to be;* a fentiment very naturally prompted by his reflection on the behaviour of Angelo. Sir T. Hanmer has only tranfpofed a word to produce a convenient fenfe. STEEVENS.

Hanmer is right with refpect to the meaning of this paffage, but I think his tranfpofition unneceffary. The words, as they ftand, will exprefs the fame fenfe, if pointed thus:

Free from all faults, as, faults from, feeming free.

Nor is this conftruction more harfh than that of many other fentences in the play, which of all thofe which Shakfpeare has left us, is the moft defective in that refpect. M. MASON.

The original copy has not *Free* at the beginning of the line. It was added unneceffarily by the editor of the fecond folio, who did not perceive that *our,* like many words of the fame kind, was ufed by Shakfpeare as a diffyllable. The reading,—from *all* faults, which all the modern editors have adopted, (I think, improperly,) was firft introduced in the fourth folio. Dr. Johnfon's conjectural reading, *or,* appears to me very probable. The compofitor might have caught the word *as* from the preceding line. If *as* be right, Dr. Warburton's interpretation is perhaps the true one. Would we were all as free from faults, as faults are free from, or deftitute of comelinefs, or *feeming.* This line is rendered harfh and obfcure by the word *free* being dragged from its proper place for the fake of the rhyme. MALONE.

Till I meet with fome decifive inftance of the pronoun—*our,* ufed as a diffyllable, I read with the fecond folio, which I cannot fufpect of capricious alterations. STEEVENS.

[3] *His neck will come to your waift, a cord, fir.*] That is, his neck

Clo. I ſpy comfort; I cry, bail: Here's a gentleman, and a friend of mine.

Lucio. How now, noble Pompey? What, at the heels of Cæſar? Art thou led in triumph? What, is there none of Pygmalion's images, newly made woman,[4] to be had now, for putting the hand in the

---

will be tied, like your waiſt, with a rope.   The friars of the Franciſcan order, perhaps of all others, wear a hempen cord for a girdle.   Thus Buchanan:

  " *Fac gemant ſuis*
  " *Variata terga funibus.*"   JOHNSON.

[4] *Pygmalion's images, newly made woman,*] By *Pygmalion's images, newly made woman,* I believe Shakſpeare meant no more than——Have you no women now to recommend to your cuſtomers, as freſh and untouched as *Pygmalion's* ſtatue was, at the moment when it became fleſh and blood? The paſſage, may, however, contain ſome alluſion to a pamphlet printed in 1598, called, *The Metamorphoſis of Pygmalion's Image, and certain Satires.* I have never ſeen it, but it is mentioned by Ames, p. 568; and whatever its ſubject might be, we learn from an order ſigned by the Archbiſhop of Canterbury and the Biſhop of London, that this book was commanded to be burnt.   The order is inſerted at the end of the ſecond volume of the entries belonging to the Stationers' Company.
              STEEVENS.

If *Marſton's Metamorphoſis of Pygmalion's Image* be alluded to, I believe it muſt be in the *argument.*——" The *maide* (by the power of Venus) was metamorphoſed into a living *woman.*"
              FARMER.

There may, however, be an alluſion to a paſſage in Lylly's *Woman in the Moone,* 1597. The inhabitants of *Utopia* petition *Nature* for females, that they may, like other beings, propagate their ſpecies. *Nature* grants their requeſt, and " they draw the curtins from before *Nature's* ſhop, where ſtands an image clad, and ſome unclad, and they bring forth the cloathed image," &c.
              STEEVENS.

Perhaps the meaning is,——Is there no courtezan, who being *newly made woman,* i. e. *lately debauched,* ſtill retains the appearance of chaſtity, and looks as cold as a ſtatue, to be had, &c.

The following paſſage in *Blurt Maſter Conſtable,* a comedy, by Middleton, 1602, ſeems to authorize this interpretation:

" *Laz.* Are all theſe *women?*

" *Imp.* No, no, they are half men, and half women.

pocket and extracting it clutch'd? What reply? Ha?
What fay'ft thou to this tune, matter, and method?
Is't not drown'd i' the laft rain?[5] Ha? What fay'ft
thou, trot?[6] Is the world as it was, man? Which

"*Laæ.* You apprehend too faft. I mean by women, wives; for
wives are no maids, *nor are maids women.*"
Mulier in Latin had precifely the fame meaning. MALONE.

A pick-lock had juft been found upon the Clown, and therefore
without great offence to his morals, it may be prefumed that he was
likewife a pick-pocket; in which cafe *Pygmalion's images,* &c. may
mean new-coined money with the Queen's image upon it. DOUCE.

[5] *What fay'ft thou to this tune, matter, and method? Is't not
drown'd i' the laft rain?*] Lucio, a prating fop, meets his old friend
going to prifon, and pours out upon him his impertinent interrogatories, to which when the poor fellow makes no anfwer, he adds,
*What reply? ha? what fay'ft thou to this? tune, matter, and method,—
is't not? drown'd i' th' laft rain? ha? what fay'ft thou, trot?* &c.
It is a common phrafe ufed in low raillery of a man creft-fallen and
dejected, that *he looks like a drown'd puppy.* Lucio, therefore, afks
him, whether he was *drown'd in the laft rain,* and therefore cannot
fpeak. JOHNSON.

He rather afks him whether his *anfwer* was not drown'd in the
laft rain, for Pompey returns *no anfwer* to any of his queftions:
or, perhaps, he means to compare Pompey's miferable appearance to
a *drown'd moufe.* So, in *K. Henry VI.* Part I. Act I. fc. ii:
  " Or piteous they will look, like *drowned mice.*"
                                        STEEVENS.

[6] —— *what fay'ft thou, trot?*] It fhould be read, I think, *what
fay'ft thou* to't? the word *trot* being feldom, if ever, ufed to a
man.
Old *trot,* or *trat,* fignifies a decrepid old woman, or an old *drab.*
in this fenfe it is ufed by Gawin Douglas, *Virg. Æn.* B. IV:
  " Out on the old *trat,* aged dame or wyffe." GREY.

So, in *Wily Beguiled,* 1613: " Thou toothlefs old *trot* thou."
Again, in *The Wife Woman of Hogfden,* 1638:
  " What can this witch, this wizard, or old *trot.*"
Trot, however, fometimes fignifies a *bawd.* So, in Churchyard's
Tragicall Difcourfe of a dolorous Gentlewoman, 1593:
  " Awaie old *trots,* that fets young flefh to fale."
Pompey, it fhould be remembered, is of this profeffion.
                                        STEEVENS.

Trot, or as it is now often pronounced, honeft *trout,* is a familiar
addrefs to a man among the provincial vulgar. JOHNSON.

I

is the way?[7] Is it sad, and few words? Or how? The trick of it?

Duke. Still thus, and thus! still worse!

Lucio. How doth my dear morsel, thy mistress? Procures she still? Ha?

Clo. Troth, sir, she hath eaten up all her beef, and she is herself in the tub.[8]

Lucio. Why, 'tis good; it is the right of it; it must be so: Ever your fresh whore, and your pow-der'd bawd: An unshunn'd consequence; it must be so: Art going to prison, Pompey?

Clo. Yes, faith, sir.

Lucio. Why 'tis not amiss, Pompey: Farewell: Go; say, I sent thee thither.[9] For debt, Pompey? Or how?[2]

---

[7] *Which is the* way?] *What is the* mode *now?* JOHNSON.

[8] —— *in the* tub.] The method of cure for venereal complaints is grossly called the *powdering tub.* JOHNSON.

It was so called from the method of cure. See the notes on " —— the *tub-fast* and the *diet*"—in *Timon,* Act IV. STEEVENS.

[9] ——*say, I sent thee thither.*] Shakspeare seems here to allude to the words used by Glofter, in *K. Henry VI.* P. III. Act V. sc. vi:
" Down, down to hell; and *say—I sent thee thither.*"
REED.

[2] —— *Go; say, I sent thee thither. For debt, Pompey? or how?*] It should be pointed thus: *Go, say I sent thee thither for debt, Pompey; or how—* i. e. to hide the ignominy of thy case, say, I sent thee to prison for debt, or whatever other pretence thou fanciest better. The other humourously replies, *For being a bawd, for being a bawd,* i. e. the true cause is the most honourable. This is in character. WARBURTON.

I do not perceive any necessity for the alteration. Lucio first offers him the use of his name to hide the seeming ignominy of his case; and then very naturally desires to be informed of the true reason why he was ordered into confinement. STEEVENS.

Warburton has taken some pains to amend this passage, which does not require it; and Lucio's subsequent reply to Elbow, shows that his amendment cannot be right. When Lucio advises Pompey

ELB. For being a bawd, for being a bawd.

LUCIO. Well, then imprifon him: If Imprifonment be the due of a bawd, why, 'tis his right: Bawd is he, doubtlefs, and of antiquity too; bawdborn. Farewell, good Pompey: Commend me to the prifon, Pompey: You will turn good hufband now, Pompey; you will keep the houfe.[5]

CLO. I hope, fir, your good worfhip will be my bail.

LUCIO. No, indeed, will I not, Pompey; it is not the wear.[4] I will pray, Pompey, to increafe your bondage: if you take it not patiently, why, your mettle is the more: Adieu, trufty Pompey.—Blefs you, friar.

DUKE. And you.

LUCIO. Does Bridget paint ftill, Pompey? Ha?

ELB. Come your ways, fir; come.

CLO. You will not bail me then, fir?

LUCIO. Then, Pompey? nor now.[5]—What news abroad, friar? What news?

ELB. Come your ways, fir; come.

LUCIO. Go,—to kennel, Pompey, go:[6]
　　　　[*Exeunt* ELBOW, CLOWN, *and* Officers.
What news, friar, of the duke?

to fay he fent him to the prifon, and in his next fpeech defires him to commend him to the prifon, he fpeaks as one who had fome intereft there, and was well known to the keepers.　M. MASON.

[5] —— *You will turn good* hufband *now, Pompey; you will* keep *the* houfe.] Alluding to the etymology of the word *hufband.*
　　　　　　　　　　　　　　　　　　　MALONE.

[4] —— *it is not the* wear.] i. e. it is not the fafhion.　STEEVENS.

[5] *Then, Pompey? nor now.*] The meaning, I think, is: *I will neither bail thee* then, nor now. So again, in this play:
　　" *More, nor lefs* to others paying" ——.　MALONE.

[6] *Go,—to* kennel, *Pompey, go:*] It fhould be remembered, that *Pompey* is the common name of a dog, to which allufion is made in the mention of a *kennel.* JOHNSON.

Duke. I know none : Can you tell me of any ?

Lucio. Some fay, he is with the emperor of Ruf-fia ; other fome, he is in Rome : But where is he, think you ?

Duke. I know not where : But wherefoever, I wifh him well.

Lucio. It was a mad fantaftical trick of him, to fteal from the ftate, and ufurp the beggary he was never born to. Lord Angelo dukes it well in his abfence ; he puts tranfgreffion to't.

Duke. He does well in't.

Lucio. A little more lenity to lechery would do no harm in him : fomething too crabbed that way, friar.

Duke. It is too general a vice,⁷ and feverity muft cure it.

Lucio. Yes, in good footh, the vice is of a great kindred ; it is well ally'd : but it is impoffible to extirp it quite, friar, till eating and drinking be put down. They fay, this Angelo was not made by man and woman, after the downright way of creation : Is it true, think you ?

Duke. How fhould he be made then ?

Lucio. Some report, a fea-maid fpawn'd him :— Some, that he was begot between two ftock-fifhes : —But it is certain, that when he makes water, his urine is congeal'd ice ; that I know to be true : and he is a motion ungenerative, that's infallible.⁸

---

⁷ *It is too general a vice,*] *Yes,* replies Lucio, *the vice is of great kindred ; it is well ally'd :* &c. As much as to fay, Yes, truly, it is general ; for the greateft men have it as well as we little folks. A little lower he taxes the Duke perfonally with it. EDWARDS.

⁸ —— *and he is a motion* ungenerative, *that's infallible.*] In the former editions :—*and he is a motion* generative ; *that's infallible.*

Duke. You are pleafant, fir; and fpeak apace.

Lucio. Why, what a ruthlefs thing is this in him, for the rebellion of a cod-piece, to take away the life of a man? Would the duke, that is abfent, have done this? Ere he would have hang'd a man for the getting a hundred baftards, he would have paid for the nurfing a thoufand: He had fome feeling of the fport; he knew the fervice, and that inftructed him to mercy.

Duke. I never heard the abfent duke much detected for women;[9] he was not inclined that way.

This may be fenfe; and Lucio, perhaps, may mean, that though Angelo have the organs of generation, yet that he makes no more ufe of them, than if he were an inanimate puppet. But I rather think our author wrote,—*and be is a motion* ungenerative, becaufe Lucio again in this very fcene fays,—*this* ungenitured agent *will unpeople the province with continency.* THEOBALD.

A *motion generative* certainly means a *puppet of the mafculine gender*; a thing that appears to have thofe powers of which it is not in reality poffeffed. STEEVENS.

A *motion ungenerative* is a moving or animated body without the power of generation. RITSON.

[9] —— *much* detected *for women*;] This appears fo like the language of *Dogberry*, that at firft I thought the paffage corrupt, and wifhed to read *fufpected*. But perhaps *detected* had anciently the fame meaning. So in an old collection of Tales, entitled, *Wits, Fits, and Fancies*, 1595: "—— An officer whofe daughter was *detected* of difhoneftie, and generally fo reported."—— That *detected* is there ufed for *fufpected*, and not in the prefent fenfe of the word, appears, I think, from the words that follow—*and fo generally reported*, which feem to relate not to a *known* but *fufpected* fact.

MALONE.

In the Statute 3d Edward Firft, c. 15. the words gentz rettez de felonie are rendered perfons *detected* of felony, that is, as I conceive, *fufpected.* REED.

Again, in *Rich's Adventures of Simonides*, 1584, 4to: "—— all Rome, *detected* of inconftancie." HENDERSON.

Detected, however, may mean, *notoriufly charged*, or guilty. So, in North's tranflation of Plutarch: "—— he only of all other kings in his time was moft *detected* with this vice of leacherie."

Lucio. O, fir, you are deceived.

Duke. 'Tis not poffible.

Lucio. Who? not the duke? yes, your beggar of fifty;—and his ufe was, to put a ducat in her clack-difh:[2] the duke had crotchets in him: He would be drunk too; that let me inform you.

Duke. You do him wrong, furely.

Lucio. Sir, I was an inward of his:[3] A fhy fellow

Again, in Howe's Abridgment of Stowe's Chronicle, 1618, p. 363: "In the month of February divers traiterous perfons were apprehended, and *detected* of moft wicked confpiracie againft his majeftie:—the 7th of Sept. certaine of them wicked fubjeﬆs were indicted," &c. MALONE.

[2] —— *clack-difh:*] The beggars, two or three centuries ago, ufed to proclaim their want by a wooden-difh with a moveable cover, which they clacked, to fhow that their veﬀel was empty. This appears from a paﬀage quoted on another occafion by Dr. Grey.

Dr. Grey's aﬀertion may be fupported by the following paﬀage in an old comedy, called *The Family of Love,* 1608:

" Can you think I get my living by a bell and a *clack-difh?*"
" By a bell and a *clack-difh?* how's that?"
" Why, by begging, fir," &c.

Again, in Henderfon's Supplement to Chaucer's *Troilus and Creﬀeid:*

" Thus fhalt thou go a begging from hous to hous,
" With *cuppe* and *clappir* like a lazarous."

And by a ftage direction in the Second Part of *K. Edward IV.* 1619:

" Enter Mrs. Blague very poorly, begging with her bafket and a *clap-difh.*"

There is likewife an old proverb to be found in Ray's Collection, which alludes to the fame cuftom:

" He *claps his difh* at a wrong man's door." STEEVENS.

[3] —— *an inward of his:*] *Inward* is intimate. So, in Daniel's *Hymen's Triumph,* 1623:

" You two were wont to be moft *inward* friends."

Again, in *Marfton's Malcontent,* 1604:

" Come we muft be *inward,* thou and I all one."

STEEVENS.

was the duke: [4] and, I believe, I know the cause of his withdrawing.

Duke. What, I pr'ythee, might be the cause?

Lucio. No,—pardon;—'tis a secret must be lock'd within the teeth and the lips: but this I can let you understand,—The greater file of the subject [5] held the duke to be wise.

Duke. Wise? why, no question but he was.

Lucio. A very superficial, ignorant, unweighing [6] fellow.

Duke. Either this is envy in you, folly, or mistaking; the very stream of his life, and the business he hath helmed, [7] must, upon a warranted need, give him a better proclamation. Let him be but testimonied in his own bringings forth, and he shall appear to the envious, a scholar, a statesman, and a soldier: Therefore, you speak unskilfully; or, if your knowledge be more, it is much darken'd in your malice.

Lucio. Sir, I know him, and I love him.

Duke. Love talks with better knowledge, and knowledge with dearer love.

---

4 —— *A shy fellow was the duke:*] The meaning of this term may be best explained by the following lines in the fifth Act:
 " The wicked'st caitiff on the ground,
 " May seem as *shy*, as grave, as just, as absolute," &c.
 MALONE.

5 *The greater* file *of the subject* ——] The larger list, the greater number. JOHNSON.

So, in *Macbeth* :
 " —— the valued *file.*" STEEVENS.

6 —— *unweighing* ——] i. e. inconsiderate. So, in *The Merry Wives of Windsor:* " What an *unweighed* behaviour hath this Flemish drunkard pick'd out of my conversation," &c. STEEVENS.

7 —— *the business he hath* helmed,] *The difficulties he hath steer'd through.* A metaphor from navigation. STEEVENS.

VOL. IV. X

Lucio. Come, fir, I know what I know.

Duke. I can hardly believe that, fince you know not what you fpeak. But, if ever the duke return, (as our prayers are he may,) let me defire you to make your anfwer before him : If it be honeft you have fpoke, you have courage to maintain it : I am bound to call upon you ; and, I pray you, your name?

Lucio. Sir, my name is Lucio ; well known to the duke.

Duke. He fhall know you better, fir, if I may live to report you.

Lucio. I fear you not.

Duke. O, you hope the duke will return no more ; or you imagine me too unhurtful an oppo-fite.[6] But, indeed, I can do you little harm : you'll forfwear this again.

Lucio. I'll be hang'd firft : thou art deceived in me, friar. But no more of this : Canft thou tell, if Claudio die to-morrow, or no?

Duke. Why fhould he die, fir?

Lucio. Why? for filling a bottle with a tun-difh. I would, the duke, we talk of, were return'd again : this ungenitur'd agent [7] will unpeople the province with continency ; fparrows muft not build in his houfe-eaves, becaufe they are lecherous. The duke yet would have dark deeds darkly anfwer'd ; he would never bring them to light : would he were

[6] —— *oppofite.*] i. e. opponent, adverfary. So, in *King Lear :* —
" —— thou waft not bound to anfwer
" An unknown *oppofite.*" STEEVENS.

[7] ——ungenitur'd *agent*—] This word feems to be formed from *genitoirs,* a word which occurs in Holland's Pliny, tom. ii. p. 321, 560, 589, and comes from the French *genitoires,* the *genitals.*
TOLLET.

return'd! Marry, this Claudio is condemn'd for un-
truffing. Farewell, good friar; I pr'ythee, pray for
me. The duke, I fay to thee again, would eat mutton on Fridays.[8] He's now paft it; yet,[9] and I fay
to thee, he would mouth with a beggar, though fhe
fmelt brown bread and garlick:[2] fay, that I faid fo.
Farewell.   [*Exit.*

Duke. No might nor greatnefs in mortality
Can cenfure 'fcape; back-wounding calumny
The whiteft virtue ftrikes: What king fo ftrong,
Can tie the gall up in the flanderous tongue?
But who comes here?

Enter ESCALUS, Provoft, Bawd, *and* Officers.

Escal. Go, away with her to prifon.

Bawd. Good my lord, be good to me; your honour is accounted a merciful man: good my lord.

Escal. Double and treble admonition, and ftill

M. MASON.

...ve inferted Mr. M. Mafon's remark: and yet the old
...is, in my opinion, too intelligible to need explanation.
                                                    STEEVENS.
...*ough fhe* fmelt brown bread and garlick:] This was
...ogy of our author's time. In *The Merry Wives of*
...fter Fenton is faid to "*fmell April and May*," not " to
...c. MALONE.

forfeit [3] in the fame kind? This would make mercy fwear, and play the tyrant. [4]

Prov. A bawd of eleven years continuance, may it pleafe your honour.

Bawd. My lord, this is one Lucio's information againft me: miftrefs Kate Keep-down was with child by him in the duke's time, he promifed her marriage; his child is a year and a quarter old, come Philip and Jacob: I have kept it myfelf; and fee how he goes about to abufe me.

Escal. That fellow is a fellow of much licence:— let him be called before us.—Away with her to prifon: Go to; no more words. [*Exeunt* Bawd *and* Officers.] Provoft, my brother Angelo will not be alter'd, Claudio muft die to-morrow: let him be furnifhed with divines, and have all charitable preparation: if my brother wrought by my pity, it fhould not be fo with him.

Prov. So pleafe you, this friar hath been with him, and advifed him for the entertainment of death.

Escal. Good even, good father.

---

[3] ——*forfeit*—] i. e. tranfgrefs, offend; from the French *forfaire.*   STEEVENS.

[4] —— *mercy* fwear, *and play the tyrant.*] We fhould read *fwerve*, i. e. deviate from her nature. The common reading gives us the idea of a ranting whore.   WARBURTON.

There is furely no need of emendation. We fay at prefent, Such a thing *is enough to make a parfon fwear*, i. e. deviate from a proper refpect to decency, and the fanctity of his character. The idea of *fwearing* agrees very well with that of a *tyrant* in our ancient myfteries.   STEEVENS.

I do not much like *mercy fwear*, the old reading; or *mercy fwerve*, Dr. Warburton's correction. I believe it fhould be, *this would make mercy fevere.*   FARMER.

We ftill fay, *to fwear like an emperor*; and from fome old book, of which I unfortunately neglected to copy the title, I have noted— *to fwear like a tyrant. To fwear like a termagant* is quoted elfewhere.   RITSON.

Duke. Blifs and goodnefs on you!

Escal. Of whence are you?

Duke. Not of this country, though my chance is now

To ufe it for my time: I am a brother
Of gracious order, late come from the fee,[4]
In fpecial bufinefs from his holinefs.

Escal. What news abroad i' the world?

Duke. None, but that there is fo great a fever on goodnefs, that the diffolution of it muft cure it: novelty is only in requeft; and it is as dangerous to be aged in any kind of courfe, as it is virtuous to be conftant in any undertaking. There is fcarce truth enough alive, to make focieties fecure; but fecurity enough, to make fellowfhips accurs'd:[5] much upon this riddle runs the wifdom of the world. This news is old enough, yet it is every

---

[4] —— *from the* fee,] The folio reads:
—— *from the* fea. JOHNSON.

The emendation, which is undoutedly right, was made by Mr. Theobald. In Hall's Chronicle, *fea* is often written for *fee*.
MALONE.

[5] *There is fcarce truth enough alive, to make focieties fecure; but fecurity enough, to make fellowfhips accurs'd:*] The fpeaker here alludes to thofe legal fecurities into which "fellowfhip" leads men to enter for each other. So, in *King Henry IV.* Part II: " He would not take his bond and yours; he liked not the *fecurity*." Falftaff in the fame fcene, plays, like the Duke, on the fame word: " I had as lief they fhould put ratfbane in my mouth, as offer to ftop it with *fecurity*. I look'd he fhould have fent me two and twenty yards of fattin,—and he fends me *fecurity*. Well, he may fleep in *fecurity*," &c. MALONE.

The fenfe is, " There fcarcely exifts fufficient honefty in the world to make focial life fecure; but there are occafions enough where a man may be drawn in to become *furety*, which will make him pay dearly for his friendfhips." In excufe of this quibble, Shakfpeare may plead high authority.—" He that hateth *furetifhip is fure*." Prov. xi. 15. HOLT WHITE.

X 3

day's news. I pray you, fir, of what difpofition was the duke?

Escal. One, that, above all other ftrifes, contended efpecially to know himfelf.

Duke. What pleafure was he given to?

Escal. Rather rejoicing to fee another merry, than merry at any thing which profefs'd to make him rejoice: a gentleman of all temperance. But leave we him to his events, with a prayer they may prove profperous; and let me defire to know how you find Claudio prepared. I am made to underftand, that you have lent him vifitation.

Duke. He profeffes to have received no finifter meafure from his judge, but moft willingly humbles himfelf to the determination of juftice: yet had he framed to himfelf, by the inftruction of his frailty, many deceiving promifes of life; which I, by my good leifure, have difcredited to him, and now is he refolved[6] to die.

Escal. You have paid the heavens your function, and the prifoner the very debt of your calling. I have labour'd for the poor gentleman, to the extremeft fhore of my modefty; but my brother juftice have I found fo fevere, that he hath forced me to tell him, he is indeed—juftice.[7]

Duke. If his own life anfwer the ftraitnefs of his proceeding, it fhall become him well; wherein if he chance to fail, he hath fentenced himfelf.

Escal. I am going to vifit the prifoner: Fare you well.

[6] —— *refolved*—] i. e. fatisfied. So, in Middleton's *More Diffemblers befides Women*, Act I. fc. iii:
  " The bleffing of perfection to your thoughts lady;
  " For I'm *refolved* they are good ones." REED.

[7] —— *he is indeed*—juftice.] Summum jus, fumma injuria.
  STEEVENS.

DUKE. Peace be with you!

      [*Exeunt* ESCALUS *and* Provoſt.

He, who the ſword of heaven will bear,
Should be as holy as ſevere;
Pattern in himſelf to know,
Grace to ſtand, and virtue go; *

---

* *Pattern in himſelf to know,*
  Grace to ſtand, and virtue go;] Theſe lines I cannot underſtand, but believe that they ſhould be read thus:
   Patterning *himſelf to know,*
   In *grace to ſtand,* in *virtue go.*
To *pattern* is *to work after a pattern,* and, perhaps, in Shakſpeare's
licentious diction, ſimply to *work.* The ſenſe is, *he that bears the
ſword of heaven ſhould be holy as well as ſevere; one that after good
examples labours to know himſelf, to live with innocence, and to act
with virtue.* JOHNSON.

This paſſage is very obſcure, nor can be cleared without a more
licentious paraphraſe than any reader may be willing to allow. *He
that bears the ſword of heaven ſhould be not leſs holy than ſevere:
ſhould be able to diſcover in himſelf a pattern of ſuch grace as can
avoid temptation, together with ſuch virtue as dares venture abroad
into the world without danger of ſeduction.* STEEVENS.

 Grace to ſtand, and virtue go;] This laſt line is not intelligible
as it ſtands; but a very ſlight alteration, the addition of the word
in, at the beginning of it, which may refer to *virtue* as well as to
grace, will render the ſenſe of it clear. " Pattern in himſelf to
know," is to feel in his own breaſt that virtue which he makes
others practiſe. M. MASON.

 " *Pattern* in himſelf to know," is, to experience in his own boſom
an *original* principle of action, which, inſtead of being borrowed or
copied from others, might ſerve as a *pattern* to them. Our author,
in *The Winter's Tale,* has again uſed the ſame kind of imagery:
  " By the *pattern* of mine own thoughts I cut out
  " The purity of his."
In *The Comedy of Errors* he uſes an expreſſion equally hardy and
licentious:
  " And will have no *attorney* but *myſelf*;"
which is an abſolute catachreſis; an attorney importing preciſely a
perſon appointed to act for *another.* In *Every Woman in her Humour,*
1609, we find the ſame expreſſion:
  " —— he hath but ſhown
  " *A pattern in himſelf,* what thou ſhall find
  " In others." MALONE.

       X 4

More nor lefs to others paying,
Than by felf-offences weighing.
Shame to him, whofe cruel ftriking
Kills for faults of his own liking!
Twice treble fhame on Angelo,
To weed my vice, and let his grow! [9]
O, what may man within him hide,
Though angel on the outward fide! [2]

had not been guilty of any vice, but to any indefinite perfon. The meaning feems to be—*To deftroy by extirpation* (as it is expreffed in another place) a fault that I have committed, and to fuffer his own vices to grow to a rank and luxuriant height. The fpeaker, for the fake of argument, puts himfelf in the cafe of an offending perfon.　MALONE.

The Duke is plainly fpeaking in his own perfon. What he here terms " *my* vice," may be explained from his converfation in Act I. fc. iv. with Friar Thomas, and efpecially the following line :

" —— 'twas *my* fault to give the people fcope."
The *vice of Angelo* requires no explanation.　HENLEY.

[2] *Though* angel *on the outward fide !*] Here we fee what induced our author to give the outward-fainted deputy, the name of Angelo.
　　　　　　　　　　　　　　　　　　　　　　MALONE.

[3] *How may likenefs, made in crimes,*
Making practice on the times,
Draw with idle fpiders' ftrings,
Moft pond'rous and fubftantial things !] The old copy reads——
" To *draw with,*" &c.　STEEVENS.

Thus all the editions read corruptly; and fo have made an obfcure paffage in itfelf, quite unintelligible.　Shakfpeare wrote it thus :

Craft againſt vice I muſt apply:
With Angelo to-night ſhall lie

> *How may* that *likeneſs, made in crimes,*
> *Making practice on the times,*
> *Draw* ——

The ſenſe is this.   How much wickedneſs may a man hide *within,* though he appear angel *without.*   How may *that likeneſs made in crimes* i. e. by hypocriſy; [a pretty paradoxical expreſſion, *an angel made in crimes*] by impoſing upon the world [thus emphatically expreſſed, *making practice on the times*] draw with its falſe and feeble pretences [finely called *ſpiders' ſtrings*] the moſt pondrous and ſubſtantial matters of the world, as riches, honour, power, reputation, &c.   WARBURTON.

Likeneſs may mean *ſeemlineſs,* fair appearance, as we ſay, a *likely* man.

The *Reviſal* reads thus:

> *How may* ſuch *likeneſs* trade *in crimes,*
> *Making practice on the times,*
> To *draw with idle ſpider's ſtrings*
> *Moſt pond'rous and ſubſtantial things.*

Meaning by *pond'rous and ſubſtantial things,* pleaſure and wealth.
STEEVENS.

The old copy reads—*Making* practice, &c. which renders the paſſage ungrammatical, and unintelligible.   For the emendation now made, [*mocking*] I am anſwerable.   A line in *Macbeth* may add ſome ſupport to it:

> "Away, and *mock the time* with faireſt ſhow."

There is no one more convinced of the general propriety of adhering to old readings.   I have ſtrenuouſly followed the courſe which was pointed out and ſucceſsfully purſued by Dr. Farmer and Mr. Steevens, that of. elucidating and ſupporting our author's genuine text by illuſtrations drawn from the writings of his contemporaries.   But in ſome caſes alteration is a matter not of choice, but neceſſity; and ſurely the preſent is one of them.   Dr. Warburton, to obtain ſome ſenſe, omitted the word *To* in the third line; in which he was followed by all the ſubſequent editors. But omiſſion, in my apprehenſion, is, of all the modes of emendation, the moſt exceptionable.   In the paſſage before us, it is clear from the context, that ſome *verb* muſt have ſtood in either the firſt or ſecond of theſe lines.   Some years ago I conjectured that, inſtead of *made,* we ought to read *wade,* which was uſed in our author's time in the ſenſe of *to proceed.*   But having ſince had occaſion to obſerve how often the words *mock* and *make* have been confounded in theſe plays, I am now perſuaded that the ſingle error in the

His old betrothed, but despis'd;
So disguise shall, by the disguis'd,[4]
Pay with falshood false exacting,
And perform an old contracting.   [*Exit*

present passage is, the word *Making* having been printed instead of *Mocking*, a word of which our author has made very frequent use, and which exactly suits the context. In this very play we have had *make* instead of *mock*. [See my note on p. 209.] In the handwriting of that time, the small *c* was merely a straight line; so that if it happened to be subjoined and written very close to an *o*, the two letters might easily be taken for an *a*. Hence I suppose it was, that these words have been so often confounded. The aukwardness of the expression——"*Making* practice," of which I have met with no example, may be likewise urged in support of this emendation.

Likeness is here used for *specious* or *seeming* virtue. So, before: " O seeming, seeming!" The sense then of the passage is,——How may persons assuming the *likeness* or semblance of virtue, *while they are in fact guilty of the grossest crimes, impose with this counterfeit sanctity upon the world,* in order *to draw to themselves by the flimsiest pretensions the most solid advantages*; i. e. pleasure, honour, reputation, &c.

In *Much Ado about Nothing* we have a similar thought:
" O, what authority and show of truth
" Can cunning sin cover itself withal!"   MALONE.

I cannot admit that *make*, in the ancient copies of our author, has been so frequently printed instead of *mock*; for the passages in which the one is supposed to have been substituted for the other, are still unsettled.——But, be this as it may, I neither comprehend the drift of the lines before us as they stand in the old edition, or with the aid of any changes hitherto attempted; and must therefore bequeath them to the luckier efforts of future criticism.   STEEVENS.

By *made in crimes*, the Duke means, trained in iniquity, and perfect in it. Thus we say—a *made* horse; a *made* pointer; meaning one well trained.   M. MASON.

[4] *So disguise shall, by the disguis'd,*] So *disguise* shall by means of a person *disguised*, return an *injurious demand* with a *counterfeit person*.   JOHNSON.

ACT IV.   SCENE I.

A Room in MARIANA'S *House.*

MARIANA *discovered sitting; a Boy singing.*

S O N G.

Take, oh take those lips away,[5]
  That so sweetly were forsworn :
And those eyes, the break of day,
  Lights that do mislead the morn :
But my kisses bring again,
        bring again,
Seals of love, but seal'd in vain, .
        seal'd in vain.

[5] *Take, oh take, &c.*] This is part of a little song of Shakspeare's own writing, consisting of two stanzas, and so extremely sweet, that the reader won't be displeased to have the other :
  Hide, oh hide those hills of snow,
    Which thy frozen bosom bears,
  On whose tops the pinks that grow,
    Are of those that April wears.
  But first set my poor heart free,
  Bound in those icy chains by thee.   WARBURTON.

This song is entire in Beaumont's *Bloody Brother*, and in Shakspeare's Poems. The latter stanza is omitted by Mariana, as not suiting a female character. THEOBALD.

Though Sewell and Gildon have printed this among Shakspeare's Poems, they have done the same to so many other pieces, of which the real authors are since known, that their evidence is not to be depended on. It is not found in Jaggard's edition of our author's Sonnets, which was printed during his life-time.

Our poet, however, has introduced one of the same thoughts in his 142d Sonnet :
  " —— not from those lips of thine
  " That have prophan'd their scarlet ornaments,
  " And *seal'd false bonds of love,* as oft as mine." STEEVENS.

Again, in his *Venus and Adonis :*
  " Pure *lips,* sweet *seals* in my soft lips imprinted,
  " What bargains may I make, still to be sealing." MALONE.

MARI. Break off thy song, and haste thee quick
away;
Here comes a man of comfort, whose advice
Hath often still'd my brawling discontent.——

[Exit Boy.

Enter DUKE.

I cry you mercy, sir; and well could wish
You had not found me here so musical:
Let me excuse me, and believe me so,——
My mirth it much displeas'd, but pleas'd my woe.[6]

DUKE. 'Tis good: though musick oft hath such
a charm,
To make bad, good, and good provoke to harm.
I pray you, tell me, hath any body inquired for me
here to day? much upon this time have I promis'd
here to meet.

MARI. You have not been inquired after: I have
sat here all day.

Enter ISABELLA.

DUKE. I do constantly[7] believe you:——The time
is come, even now. I shall crave your forbearance a

The same image occurs also in the old black-letter Translation
of Amadis of Gaule, 4to. p. 171: " —— rather with *kisses* (which
are counted the *seales of Love*) they chose to confirm their unani-
mitie, than otherwise to offend a resolved pacience." REED.

This song is found entire in Shakspeare's Poems, printed in 1640;
but that is a book of no authority: Yet I believe that both these
stanzas were written by our author. MALONE.

[6] *My mirth it much displeas'd, but pleas'd my woe.*] Though the
musick soothed my sorrows, it had no tendency to produce light
merriment. JOHNSON.

[7] —— *constantly* ——] Certainly; without fluctuation of mind.
JOHNSON.

little; may be, I will call upon you anon, for some
advantage to yourself.

MARI. I am always bound to you.   [*Exit.*

DUKE. Very well met, and welcome.
What is the news from this good deputy?

ISAB. He hath a garden circummur'd with
      brick,[8]
Whose western side is with a vineyard back'd;
And to that vineyard is a planched gate,[9]
That makes his opening with this bigger key:
This other doth command a little door,
Which from the vineyard to the garden leads;
There have I made my promise to call on him,
Upon the heavy middle of the night.[2]

DUKE. But shall you on your knowledge find this
      way?

ISAB. I have ta'en a due and wary note upon't;
With whispering and most guilty diligence,

So, in *The Merchant of Venice:*
    " Could so much turn the constitution
    " Of any *constant* man." STEEVENS.

[8] —— circummur'd *with brick,*] *Circummured*, walled round.
" He caused the doors to be *mured* and cased up."
                        Painter's Palace of Pleasure. JOHNSON.

[9] —— *a* planched *gate,*] i. e. a gate made of boards. *Planche*, Fr.
A *plancher* is a plank. So, in Lyly's *Maid's Metamorphosis,*
1600:
    " —— upon the ground doth lie
    " A hollow *plancher.*"——
Again, in Sir *Arthur Gorges'* translation of Lucan, 1614:
    " Yet with his hoofes doth beat and rent
    " The *planched* floore, the barres and chaines."
                                STEEVENS.

[2] *There have I,* &c.] In the old copy the lines stand thus:
    There have I made my promise upon the
    Heavy middle of the night, to call upon him. STEEVENS.
The present regulation was made by Mr. Steevens. MALONE.

In action all of precept,[3] he did fhow me
The way twice o'er.

  DUKE.   Are there no other tokens
Between you 'greed, concerning her obfervance?

  ISAB. No, none, but only a repair i' the dark;
And that I have poffefs'd him,[4] my moft ftay
Can be but brief: for I have made him know,
I have a fervant comes with me along,
That ftays upon me;[5] whofe perfuafion is,
I come about my brother.

  DUKE.   'Tis well borne up.
I have not yet made known to Mariana
A word of this:——What, ho! within! come forth!

    Re-enter MARIANA.

I pray you, be acquainted with this maid;
She comes to do you good.

  ISAB.   I do defire the like.

  DUKE. Do you perfuade yourfelf that I refpect
    you?

  MARI. Good friar, I know you do; and have
    ·found it.

---

 [3] *In action all of precept,*] i. e. fhewing the feveral turnings of
the way with his hand; which action contained fo many precepts,
being given for my direction. WARBURTON.

 I rather think we fhould read,
   In precept of all action,——
that is, *in direction given not by words, but by mute figns.* JOHNSON.

 [4] —— *I have* poffefs'd *him,*] I have made him clearly and
ftrongly comprehend. JOHNSON.

 To *poffefs* had formerly the fenfe of *inform* or *acquaint.* As in
Every Man in his Humour, Act I. fc. v. Captain Bobadil fays:
"*Poffefs* no gentleman of our acquaintance with notice of my
lodging." REED.

 [5] *That* ftays upon *me;*] So, in *Macbeth:*
  " Worthy Macbeth, *we ftay upon* your leifure." STEEVENS.

I

Duke. Take then this your companion by the
      hand,
Who hath a ſtory ready for your ear:
I ſhall attend your leiſure; but make haſte;
The vaporous night approaches.

Mari.   Will't pleaſe you walk aſide?
            [*Exeunt* Mariana *and* Isabella.

Duke. O place and greatneſs,[6] millions of falſe
      eyes[7]
Are ſtuck upon thee! volumes of report
Run with theſe falſe and moſt contrarious queſts[8]

[6] *O place and greatneſs,*] It plainly appears that *this* fine ſpeech belongs to *that* which concludes the preceding ſcene between the Duke and Lucio. For they are abſolutely foreign to the ſubject of this, and are the natural reflections ariſing from that. Beſides, the very words,
    Run with theſe falſe and moſt contrarious queſts,
evidently refer to Lucio's ſcandals juſt preceding; which the Oxford editor, in his uſual way, has emended, by altering *theſe* to *their.* But that ſome time might be given to the two women to confer together, the players, I ſuppoſe, took part of the ſpeech, beginning at *No might nor greatneſs,* &c. and put it here, without troubling themſelves about its pertinency. However, we are obliged to them for not giving us their own impertinency, as they have frequently done in other places. Warburton.

I cannot agree that theſe lines are placed here by the players. The ſentiments are common, and ſuch as a prince, given to reflection, muſt have often preſent. There was a neceſſity to fill up the time in which the ladies converſe apart, and they muſt have quick tongues and ready apprehenſions, if they underſtood each other while this ſpeech was uttered. Johnson.

[7] —— *millions of falſe eyes* ——] That is, Eyes inſidious and traiterous. Johnson.

So, in Chaucer's *Sompnoures Tale,* Tyrwhitt's edit. v. 7633:
    " Ther is *ful many an eye,* and many an ere,
    " Awaiting on a lord," &c. Steevens.

[8] —— *contrarious queſts* ——] Different reports, *running counter* to each other. Johnson.

So, in *Othello:*
    " The ſenate has ſent out three ſeveral *queſts.*"

Upon thy doings! thousand 'scapes of wit'
Make thee the father of their idle dream,
And rack thee in their fancies! [8]——Welcome! How
     agreed?

     Re-enter MARIANA *and* ISABELLA.

  Isab. She'll take the enterprize upon her, father,
If you advise it.
  Duke.   It is not my consent,
But my intreaty too.
  Isab.   Little have you to say,
When you depart from him, but, soft and low,
Remember now my brother.
  Mari.   Fear me not.
  Duke. Nor, gentle daughter, fear you not at all:
He is your husband on a pre-contráct:

  In our author's *K. Richard III.* is a passage in some degree
similar to the foregoing:
     " My conscience hath a thousand several tongues,
     " And every tongue brings in a several tale,
     " And every tale condemns"—— STEEVENS.
  I incline to think that *quests* here means *inquisitions,* in which
sense the word was used in Shakspeare's time. See Minshieu's
Dict. in v. Cole in his Latin Dictionary, 1679, renders " A
quest," by " *examen, inquisitio.*" MALONE.
  False and contrarious quests in this place rather mean *lying and
contradictory messengers,* with whom *run volumes of report.* An explanation, which the line quoted by Mr. Steevens will serve to
confirm. RITSON.
  [7] —— 'scapes *of wit*——] i. e. sallies, irregularities. So, in
King John, Act III. sc. iv :
     " No *'scape* of nature, no distemper'd day." STEEVENS.
  [8] *And* rack *thee in their fancies !*] Though *rack,* in the present
instance, may signify *torture* or *mangle,* it might also mean *confuse;*
as the *rack,* i. e. fleeting cloud, renders the object behind it obscure,
and of undetermined form. So, in *Antony and Cleopatra :* ——
     " That which was now a horse, even with a thought,
     " The *rack* dislimns, and makes it indistinct,
     " As water is in water." STEEVENS.

To bring you thus together, 'tis no fin;
Sith that the juftice of your title to him
Doth flourifh the deceit.⁹   Come, let us go;
Our corn's to reap, for yet our tithe's to fow.²

[*Exeunt.*

⁹ *Doth* flourifh *the deceit.*]   A metaphor taken from embroidery, where a coarfe ground is filled up, and covered with figures of rich materials and elegant workmanfhip.   WARBURTON.

Flourifh is *ornament in general.*   So, in our author's *Twelfth Night:*

" ―――― empty trunks *o'erflourifh'd* by the devil."

STEEVENS.

Dr. Warburton's illuftration of the metaphor feems to be inaccurate.   The paffage from another of Shakfpeare's plays, quoted by Mr. Steevens, fuggefts to us the true one.

The term—*flourifh,* alludes to the flowers impreffed on the wafte printed paper and old books, with which trunks are commonly lined.   HENLEY.

When it is proved that the practice alluded to, was as ancient as the time of Shakfpeare, Mr. Henley's explanation may be admitted.

STEEVENS.

² ―――― *for yet our* tithe's *to fow.*]   As before, the blundering editors have made a *prince* of the *prieftly* Angelo, fo here they have made a *prieft* of the *prince.*   We fhould read *tilth,* i. e. our tillage is yet to make.   The grain from which we expect our harveft, is not yet put into the ground.   WARBURTON.

The reader is here attacked with a petty fophifm.   We fhould read *tilth,* i. e. our *tillage is to make.*   But in the text it is *to fow;* and who has ever faid that his *tillage* was to *fow?*   I believe *tythe* is right, and that the expreffion is proverbial, in which *tythe* is taken, by an eafy metonymy, for *harveft.*   JOHNSON.

Dr. Warburton did not do juftice to his own conjecture; and no wonder, therefore, that Dr. Johnfon has not.—*Tilth* is provincially ufed for *land till'd,* prepared for fowing.   Shakfpeare, however, has applied it before in its ufual acceptation.   FARMER.

Dr. Warburton's conjecture may be fupported by many inftances in Markham's *Englifh Hufbandman,* 1635: " After the beginning of March you fhall begin to fowe your barley upon that ground which the year before did lye fallow, and is commonly called your *tilth* or fallow field."   In p. 74 of this book, a corruption, like our author's, occurs.   " As before, I faid beginne to fallow your *tithe* field:" which is undoubtedly mifprinted for *tilth* field.

TOLLET.

S C E N E   II.

A Room in the Prison.

Enter Provost *and* Clown.

Prov. Come hither, firrah : Can you cut off a man's head ?

Clo. If the man be a bachelor, fir, I can : but if he be a married man, he is his wife's head, and I can never cut off a woman's head.

Prov. Come, fir, leave me your fnatches, and yield me a direct anfwer.   To-morrow morning are to die Claudio and Barnardine : Here is in our prifon a common executioner, who in his office lacks a helper : if you will take it on you to affift him, it fhall redeem you from your gyves ; if not, you fhall have your full time of imprifonment, and your deliverance with an unpitied whipping ;[a]   for you have been a notorious bawd.

Clo. Sir, I have been an unlawful bawd, time out of mind ; but yet I will be content to be a lawful hangman.   I would be glad to receive fome inftruction from my fellow partner.

Tilth is ufed for *crop*, or *harveft*, by Gower, *De Confeffione Amantis*, Lib. V. fol. 93. b :

"   To fowe cockill with the corne,
"   So that the *tilth* is nigh forlorne,
"   Which Chrift *few* firft his owne honde."

Shakfpeare ufes the word *tilth* in a former fcene of this play ; and, (as Dr. Farmer has obferved,) in its common acceptation :

"   —— her plenteous womb
"   Expreffeth its full *tilth* and hufbandry."

Again, in *The Tempeft* :

"   —— bound of land, *tilth*, vineyard, none."

but my quotation from Gower fhows that, to *fow tilth*, was a phrafe once in ufe.   STEEVENS.

This conjecture appears to me extremely probable.   MALONE.

[a]   —— *an* unpitied *whipping* ;] i. e. an unmerciful one.   STEEVENS.

Prov. What ho, Abhorſon! Where's Abhorſon, there?

Enter ABHORSON.

Abhor. Do you call, ſir?

Prov. Sirrah, here's a fellow will help you to-morrow in your execution: If you think it meet, compound with him by the year, and let him abide here with you; if not, uſe him for the preſent, and diſmiſs him: He cannot plead his eſtimation with you; he hath been a bawd.

Abhor. A bawd, ſir? Fie upon him, he will diſ-credit our myſtery.

Prov. Go to, ſir; you weigh equally; a feather will turn the ſcale.   [*Exit.*

Clo. Pray, ſir, by your good favour, (for, ſurely, ſir, a good favour[3] you have, but that you have a hanging look,) do you call, ſir, your occupation a myſtery?

Abhor. Ay, ſir; a myſtery.

Clo. Painting, ſir, I have heard ſay, is a myſtery; and your whores, ſir, being members of my occupa-tion, uſing painting, do prove my occupation a myſtery: but what myſtery there ſhould be in hang-ing, if I ſhould be hang'd, I cannot imagine.[4]

---

[3] —— *a good* favour —] *Favour* is countenance. So, in *Antony and Cleopatra*:

　　" —— why ſo tart a *favour*,
　　" To publiſh ſuch good tidings?" STEEVENS.

[4] —— *what myſtery,* &c.] Though I have adopted an emenda-tion independent of the following note, the omiſſion of it would have been unwarrantable. STEEVENS.

　—— *what miſtery there ſhould be in hanging, if I ſhould be hang'd, I cannot imagine.*
　Abhor. *Sir, it is a miſtery.*
　Clo. *Proof.*

ABHOR. Sir, it is a myſtery.

CLO. Proof.

Abhor. *Every true man's apparel fits your thief:*

Clo. *If it be too little for your thief, your true man thinks it big enough; if it be too big for your thief, your thief thinks it little enough: ſo every true man's apparel fits your thief.*] Thus it ſtood in all the editions till Mr. Theobald's, and was, methinks, not very difficult to be underſtood. The plain and humorous ſenſe of the ſpeech is this. Every true man's apparel, which the thief robs him of, fits the thief. Why? Becauſe, if it be too little for the thief, the true man thinks it big enough: i. e. a purchaſe too good for him. So that this fits the thief in the opinion of the true man. But if it be too big for the thief, yet the thief thinks it little enough: i. e. of value little enough. So that this fits the thief in his own opinion. Where we ſee, that the pleaſantry of the joke conſiſts in the equivocal ſenſe of *big enough*, and *little enough*. Yet Mr. Theobald ſays, he can ſee no ſenſe in all this, and therefore alters the whole thus:—

Abhor. *Every true man's apparel fits your thief.*

Clown. *If it be too little for your true man, your thief thinks it big enough: if it be too big for your true man, your thief thinks it little enough.*

And for his alteration gives this extraordinary reaſon.——*I am ſatisfied the poet intended a* regular ſyllogiſm; *and I ſubmit it to judgement, whether my regulation has not reſtored that wit and humour which was quite loſt in the depravation.*——But the place is corrupt, though Mr. Theobald could not find it out. Let us conſider it a little. The Hangman calls his trade a miſtery: the Clown cannot conceive it. The Hangman undertakes to prove it in theſe words, *Every true man's apparel,* &c. but this proves the *thief's* trade a miſtery, not the *hangman's*. Hence it appears, that the ſpeech, in which the Hangman proved his trade a miſtery, is loſt. The very words it is impoſſible to retrieve, but one may eaſily underſtand what medium he employed in proving it: without doubt, the very ſame the Clown employed to prove the thief's trade a miſtery; namely, *that all ſorts of clothes fitted the hangman.* The Clown, on hearing this argument, replied, I ſuppoſe, to this effect: *Why, by the ſame kind of reaſoning, I can prove the thief's trade too to be a miſtery.* The other aſks how, and the Clown goes on as above, *Every true man's apparel fits your thief; if it be too little,* &c. The jocular concluſion from the whole, being an inſinuation that *thief* and *hangman* were rogues alike. This conjecture gives a ſpirit and integrity to the dialogue, which, in its preſent mangled condition, is altogether wanting; and ſhews why the argument of *every true man's apparel,* &c. was in all

Abhor. Every true man's apparel fits your thief: [5]

editions given to the Clown, to whom indeed it belongs; and likewise that the present reading of that argument is the true. WARBURTON.

If Dr. Warburton had attended to the argument by which the Bawd proves his own profession to be a mystery, he would not have been driven to take refuge in the groundless supposition, "that part of the dialogue had been lost or dropped,"

The argument of the Hangman is exactly similar to that of the Bawd. As the latter puts in his claim to the whores, as members of his occupation, and, in virtue of their painting, would enroll his own fraternity in the mystery of painters; so the former equally lays claim to the thieves, as members of his occupation, and, in their right, endeavours to rank his brethren, the hangmen, under the mystery of fitters of apparel, or tailors. The reading of the old editions is therefore undoubtedly right; except that the last speech, which makes part of the Hangman's argument, is, by mistake, as the reader's own sagacity will readily perceive, given to the Clown or Bawd. I suppose, therefore the poet gave us the whole thus:

Abhor. *Sir, it is a mystery.*

Clown. *Proof.*

Abhor. *Every true man's apparel fits your thief: if it be too little for your thief, your true man thinks it big enough: if it be too big for your thief, your thief thinks it little enough; so every true man's apparel fits your thief.*

I must do Dr. Warburton the justice to acknowledge, that he hath rightly apprehended, and explained the force of the Hangman's argument. HEATH.

There can be no doubt but the word *Clown*, prefixed to the last sentence, *If it be too little,* &c. should be struck out. It makes part of Abhorson's argument, who has undertaken to prove that hanging was a mystery, and convinces the Clown of it by this very speech. M. MASON.

[5] *Every* true man's *apparel fits your thief:*] So, in *Promos and Cassandra,* 1578, the Hangman says:

"Here is nyne and twenty futes of apparell for my share." *True man,* in the language of ancient times, is always placed in opposition to *thief.*

So, in Churchyard's *Warning to Wanderers abroade,* 1593:

"The priuy *thiefe* that steales away our wealth,

"Is fore afraid a *true man's* steps to fee." STEEVENS.

Mr. Steevens seems to be mistaken in his assertion that *true man* in ancient times was always placed in opposition to *thief.* At least in the book of Genesis, there is one instance to the contrary, ch. xlii. v. 11:—"We are all one man's sons: we are all *true men;* thy servants are no *spies.*" HENLEY.

If it be too little for your thief, your true man thinks it big enough; if it be too big for your thief, your thief thinks it little enough: so every true man's apparel fits your thief.

Re-enter Provoſt.

Prov. Are you agreed?

Clo. Sir, I will ſerve him; for I do find, your hangman is a more penitent trade than your bawd; he doth oftner aſk forgiveneſs.[6]

Prov. You, ſirrah, provide your block and your axe, to-morrow four o'clock.

Abhor. Come on, bawd; I will inſtruct thee in my trade; follow.

Clo. I do deſire to learn, ſir; and, I hope, if you have occaſion to uſe me for your own turn, you ſhall find me yare:[7] for, truly ſir, for your kindneſs, I owe you a good turn.[8]

Prov. Call hither Barnardine and Claudio:
          [*Exeunt* Clown *and* Abhorson.
One has my pity; not a jot the other,
Being a murderer, though he were my brother.

Enter Claudio.

Look, here's the warrant, Claudio, for thy death:

---

[6] —— *aſk forgiveneſs.*] So, in *As you like it :*
  " —— The common executioner,
  " Whoſe heart the accuſtom'd ſight of death makes hard,
  " Falls not the axe upon the humbled neck,
  " But firſt *begs pardon.*" Steevens.

[7] —— *yare :*] i. e. handy, nimble in the execution of my office. So, in *Twelfth Night :* " —— diſmount thy tuck, be *yare* in thy preparation." Again, in *Antony and Cleopatra :*
  " His ſhips are *yare*, yours heavy. Steevens.

[8] —— *a good turn.*] i. e. a turn off the ladder. He quibbles on the phraſe according to its common acceptation. Farmer.

I

'Tis now dead midnight, and by eight to-morrow
Thou muft be made immortal. Where's Barnardine?

CLAUD. As faft lock'd up in fleep, as guiltlefs la-
bour
When it lies ftarkly⁹ in the traveller's bones:
He will not wake.

PROV. Who can do good on him?
Well, go, prepare yourfelf. But hark, what noife?
        [Knocking within.
Heaven give your fpirits comfort! [Exit CLAUDIO.]
   By and by :——
I hope it is fome pardon, or reprieve,
For the moft gentle Claudio.——Welcome, father.

     Enter DUKE.

DUKE. The beft and wholefomeft fpirits of the
night
Envelop you, good Provoft! Who call'd here of late?

PROV. None, fince the curfew rung.

DUKE.   Not Ifabel?

PROV. No,

DUKE.   They will then,² ere't be long.

PROV. What comfort is for Claudio?

DUKE.   There's fome in hope.

PROV. It is a bitter deputy.

⁹ ——ftarkly—] Stiffly. Thefe two lines afford a very pleafing
image. JOHNSON.

 So, in The Lege——
  " Leaft fla——

² They will the——
 The Duke expe——
fays:
  " —— N——

Duke. Not fo, not fo; his life is parallel'd
Even with the ftroke[3] and line of his great juftice,
He doth with holy abftinence fubdue
That in himfelf, which he fpurs on his power
To qualify[4] in others : were he meal'd[5]
With that which he corrects, then were he tyran-
            nous ;
But this being fo,[6] he's juft.——Now are they come.——
            [*Knocking within.*——Provoft *goes out.*
This is a gentle provoft : Seldom, when
The fteeled gaoler is the friend of men.——
How now ? What noife ? That fpirit's poffefs'd with
            hafte,
That wounds the unfifting poftern with thefe ftrokes.[7]

---

[3] *Even with the* ftroke——]   *Stroke* is here put for the *ftroke* of a
pen or a line.   JOHNSON.

[4] *To* qualify——]   To temper, to moderate, as we fay wine is
qualified with water.   JOHNSON.
    Thus before in this play :
        " So to enforce, or *qualify* the laws."
Again, in *Othello* :
    " I have drank but one cup to-night, and that was craftily
qualified too."   STEEVENS.

[5] ——— *were he* meal'd——]   Were he fprinkled ; were he defiled.
A figure of the fame kind our author ufes in *Macbeth* :
        " The *blood-bolter'd* Banquo."   JOHNSON.
More appofitely, in *The Philofophers Satires,* by Robert Anton :
        " As if their perriwigs to death they gave,
        " To *meale* them in fome gaftly dead man's grave."
                                STEEVENS.
    Mealed is mingled, compounded ; from the French *mefler.*
                                BLACKSTONE.

[6] *But this being fo,*]   The tenor of the argument feems to require——But this *not* being fo,———.   Perhaps, however, the author
meant only to fay——But, his life being paralleled, &c. he's juft.
                                MALONE.

[7] ——— *That fpirit's poffefs'd with hafte,*
    That wounds the unfifting poftern *with thefe ftrokes.*]   The line is
irregular, and the old reading, *unrefifting poftern,* fo ftrange an expreffion, that want of meafure, and want of fenfe, might juftly raife

V.
353.

[Provoſt *returns, ſpeaking to one at the door.*

PROV. There he muſt ſtay, until the officer
Ariſe to let him in; he is call'd up.

DUKE. Have you no countermand for Claudio yet,
But he muſt die to-morrow?

PROV.   None, ſir, none.

DUKE. As near the dawning, Provoſt, as it is,
You ſhall hear more ere morning.

PROV.   Happily,
You ſomething know; yet, I believe, there comes
No countermand; no ſuch example have we:
Beſides, upon the very ſiege of juſtice,[8]
Lord Angelo hath to the publick ear
Profeſs'd the contrary.

ſuſpicion of an error; yet none of the latter editors ſeem to have
ſuppoſed the place faulty, except Sir Thomas Hanmer, who reads:
            —— *the* unreſting *poſtern* ——
The three folios have it,
            —— unſiſting *poſtern* ——
out of which Mr. Rowe made *unreſiſting*, and the reſt followed
him. Sir Thomas Hanmer ſeems to have ſuppoſed *unreſiſting* the
word in the copies, from which he plauſibly enough extracted
unreſting; but he grounded his emendation on the very ſyllable that
wants authority. What can be made of *unſiſting* I know not; the
beſt that occurs to me is *unfeeling*. JOHNSON.

Unſiſting may ſignify " never at reſt," always opening.
                                          BLACKSTONE.

I ſhould think we might ſafely read:
            —— unliſt'ning *poſtern*, or unſhifting *poſtern*.
The meaſure requires it, and the ſenſe remains uninjured.
    Mr. M. Maſon would read *unliſting*, which means *unregarding*.
I have, however, inſerted Sir William Blackſtone's emendation in
the text. STEEVENS.

    [8] —— ſiege *of juſtice*,] i. e. *ſeat* of juſtice. *Siege*, French.
So, in *Othello*:
        " —— I fetch my birth
        " From men of royal *ſiege*." STEEVENS.

Enter a Meffenger.

Duke. This is his lordfhip's man.[8]

Prov. And here comes Claudio's pardon.[9]

Mess. My lord hath fent you this note; and by me this further charge, that you fwerve not from the fmalleft article of it, neither in time, matter, or other circumftance. Good morrow; for, as I take it, it is almoft day.

Prov. I fhall obey him.   [*Exit* Meffenger.

Duke. This is his pardon; purchas'd by fuch fin,
                                                [*Afide.*

For which the pardoner himfelf is in:
Hence hath offence his quick celerity,
When it is borne in high authority:

---

[8] *— This is his lord*ship's *man.*] The old copy has—his *lord's* man, Corrected by Mr. Pope. In the MS. plays of our author's time they often wrote *Lo.* for Lord, and *Lord.* for Lordfhip; and thefe contractions were fometimes improperly followed in the printed copies.
                                                MALONE.

[9] Enter a Meffenger.
     Duke. *This is his lordfhip's man.*
     Prov. *And here comes Claudio's pardon.*] The Provoft has juft declared a fixed opinion that the execution will not be counter-manded, and yet, upon the firft appearance of the Meffenger, he immediately gueffes that his errand is to bring Claudio's pardon. It is evident, I think, that the names of the fpeakers are mifplaced. If we fuppofe the Provoft to fay:
          This is his lordfhip's man,
it is very natural for the Duke to fubjoin,
          And here comes Claudio's pardon.
The Duke might believe, upon very reafonable grounds, that An-gelo had now fent the pardon. It appears that he did fo, from what he fays to himfelf, while the Provoft is reading the letter:
          This is his pardon; purchas'd by fuch fin.   TYRWHITT.

. When, immediately after the Duke had hinted his expectation of a pardon, the Provoft fees the Meffenger, he fuppofes the Duke to have *known fomething*, and changes his mind. Either reading may ferve equally well. JOHNSON.

When vice makes mercy, mercy's fo extended,
That for the fault's love, is the offender friended.——
Now, fir, what news?

Prov. I told you: Lord Angelo, be-like, thinking me remifs in mine office, awakens me with this
unwonted putting on:* methinks, ftrangely; for he
hath not ufed it before.

Duke. Pray you, let's hear.

Prov. [Reads.] *Whatfoever you may hear to the
contrary, let Claudio be executed by four of the clock;
and, in the afternoon, Barnardine: for my better fatif-
faction, let me have Claudio's head fent me by five. Let
this be duly perform'd; with a thought, that more depends on it than we muft yet deliver. Thus fail not to
do your office, as you will anfwer it at your peril.*
What fay you to this, fir?

Duke. What is that Barnardine, who is to be executed in the afternoon?

Prov. A Bohemian born; but here nurfed up and
bred: one that is a prifoner nine years old.*

Duke. How came it, that the abfent duke had not
either deliver'd him to his liberty, or executed him?
I have heard, it was ever his manner to do fo.

Prov. His friends ftill wrought reprieves for him:
And, indeed, his fact, till now in the government of
lord Angelo, came not to an undoubtful proof.

Duke. Is it now apparent?

Prov. Moft manifeft, and not denied by himfelf.

---

* ——*putting on*:] i. e. fpur, incitement. So, in *Macbeth,*
Act IV. fc. iii:
    " —— the powers above
    " *Put on* their inftruments." STEEVENS.

* ——*one that is a prifoner nine years old.*] i. e. That has been
confined thefe nine years. So, in *Hamlet:* " Ere we were two
days *old* at fea, a pirate of very warlike preparation," &c. MALONE.

Duke. Hath he borne himfelf penitently in prifon? How feems he to be touch'd?

Prov. A man that apprehends death no more dreadfully, but as a drunken fleep; carelefs, recklefs, and fearlefs of what's paft, prefent, or to come; infenfible of mortality, and defperately mortal.[2]

Duke. He wants advice.

Prov. He will hear none: he hath evermore had the liberty of the prifon; give him leave to efcape hence, he would not: drunk many times a day, if not many days entirely drunk. We have very often awaked him, as if to carry him to execution, and fhow'd him a feeming warrant for it: it hath not moved him at all.

Duke. More of him anon. There is written in your brow, Provoft, honefty and conftancy: if I read it not truly, my ancient fkill beguiles me; but in the boldnefs of my cunning,[3] I will lay myfelf in hazard. Claudio, whom here you have a warrant to execute, is no greater forfeit to the law than Angelo who hath fentenced him: To make you under-

---

[2] —— *defperately* mortal.] This expreffion is obfcure. Sir Thomas Hanmer reads, *mortally defperate.* *Mortally* is in low converfation ufed in this fenfe, but I know not whether it was ever written. I am inclined to believe, that *defperately mortal* means *defperately mifchievous.* Or *defperately mortal* may mean a man likely to die in a *defperate ftate,* without reflection or repentance. JOHNSON.

The word is often ufed by Shakfpeare in the fenfe firft affixed to it by Dr. Johnfon, which I believe to be the true one. So, in *Othello:* " And you, ye *mortal* engines," &c. MALONE.

As our author, in *The Tempeft,* feems to have written " harmonious charmingly," inftead of " harmonioufly charming," he may, in the prefent inftance, have given us " defperately mortal," for " mortally defperate:" i. e. defperate in the extreme.——In low provincial language,——*mortal* fick,——*mortal* bad,——*mortal* poor, is phrafeology of frequent occurrence. STEEVENS.

[3] —— *in the* boldnefs *of my* cunning,] i. e. in *confidence* of my *fagacity.* STEEVENS.

ftand this in a manifefted effect, I crave but four days refpite; for the which you are to do me both a prefent and a dangerous courtefy.

Prov. Pray, fir, in what?

Duke. In the delaying death.

Prov. Alack! how may I do it? having the hour limited; and an exprefs command, under penalty, to deliver his head in the view of Angelo? I may make my cafe as Claudio's, to crofs this in the fmalleft.

Duke. By the vow of mine order, I warrant you, if my inftructions may be your guide. Let this Barnardine be this morning executed, and his head borne to Angelo.

Prov. Angelo hath feen them both, and will dif_cover the favour.[4]

Duke. O, death's a great difguifer: and you may add to it. Shave the head, and tie the beard;[5] and fay, it was the defire of the penitent to be fo bared[6]

---

[4] —— *the favour.*] See note 3. p. 323.   STEEVENS.

[5] —— *and* tie *the beard*;] The *Revifal* recommends Mr. Simpfon's emendation, DIE *the beard*, but the prefent reading may ftand. Perhaps it was ufual to *tie* up the beard before decollation. Sir T. More is faid to have been ludicroufly careful about this ornament of his face. It fhould, however, be remembered, that it was alfo the cuftom *to die beards.*

So, in the old comedy of *Ram-Alley*, 1611:

    " What *colour'd beard* comes next by the window?

    " A black man's, I think.

    " I think, a *red*; for that is moft in fafhion."

Again, in *The Silent Woman:* " I have fitted my divine and canonift, *dyed their beards and all.*"

Again, in *The Alchemift:* " —— he had *dy'd his beard,* and all."
                      STEEVENS.

A beard *tied* would give a very new air to that face, which had never been feen but with the beard loofe, long, and fqualid.   JOHNSON.

[6] —— *to be fo* bared——] Thefe words relate to what has juft preceded—*fhave the head.* The modern editions following the fourth folio, read—to be fo *barb'd*; but the old copy is certainly right. So, in *All's well that ends well:* " I would the cutting of

before his death: You know, the courfe is common.[6] If any thing fall to you upon this, more than thanks and good fortune, by the faint whom I profefs, I will plead againft it with my life.

Prov. Pardon me, good father; it is againft my oath.

Duke. Were you fworn to the duke, or to the deputy?

Prov. To him, and to his fubftitutes.

Duke. You will think you have made no offence, if the duke avouch the juftice of your dealing?

Prov. But what likelihood is in that?

Duke. Not a refemblance, but a certainty. Yet fince I fee you fearful, that neither my coat, integrity, nor my perfuafion, can with eafe attempt you, I will go further than I meant, to pluck all fears out of you. Look you, fir, here is the hand and feal of the duke. You know the character, I doubt not; and the fignet is not ftrange to you.

Prov. I know them both.

Duke. The contents of this is the return of the duke; you fhall anon over-read it at your pleafure; where you fhall find, within thefe two days he will be here. This is a thing, that Angelo knows not: for he this very day receives letters of ftrange te-

---

my garments would ferve the turn, or the *baring* of my beard; and to fay it was in ftratagem." MALONE.

[6] —— *you know, the courfe is common.*] P. Mathieu, in his *Heroyke Life and deplorable Death of Henry the Fourth, of France,* fays, that Ravaillac, in the midft of his tortures, lifted up his head and fhook a fpark of fire from his *beard.* "This unprofitable care, (he adds) to fave it, being noted, afforded matter to divers to praife *the cuftome in Germany, Swifferland*, and divers other places, *to fhave off,* and then to burn all the haire from all parts of the bodies of thofe who are convicted for any notorious crimes." *Grimfton's Tranflation,* 4to. 1612. p. 181. REED.

This alludes to a practice frequent among Roman Catholicks, of defiring to receive the tonfure of the Monks before they die. — It cannot allude to the cuftom which Mr Reed tells us was eftablifhed in fome parts of Germany, that of criminals previous to their execution, as here the penitent is fuppofed to be bared at his own requeft. M. Mason.

nor; perchance, of the duke's death; perchance, entering into fome monaftery; but, by chance, nothing of what is writ.[7]   Look, the unfolding ftar calls up the fhepherd:[8] Put not yourfelf into amazement, how thefe things fhould be: all difficulties are but eafy when they are known.   Call your executioner, and off with Barnardine's head: I will give him a prefent fhrift, and advife him for a better place. Yet—————————————— ————— —— —— ——— this fhall abfo-lutely refolve ;
dawn.

Enter Clown.

CLO. I am as well acquainted here, as I was in our houfe of profeffion:[9] one would think, it were miftrefs Over-done's own houfe, for here be many of her old cuftomers.   Firft, here's young mafter Rafh;[2] he's in for a commodity of brown paper

---

[7] —— *nothing of what is writ.*] We fhould read—*here writ*—the Duke pointing to the letter in his hand.   WARBURTON.

[8] —— *the unfolding ftar calls up the fhepherd:*]
   " The ftar, that bids the fhepherd fold,
   " Now the top of heaven doth hold." *Milton's Comus.*
                                        STEEVENS.
   " So doth the evening ftar prefent itfelf
   " Unto the careful fhepherd's gladfome eyes,
   " By which unto the fold he leads his flock."
         Marfton's *Infatiate Countefs*, 1613.   MALONE.

[9] —— *in our houfe of* profeffion:] i. e. in my late miftrefs's houfe, which was a *profeffed*, a notorious bawdy-houfe. MALONE.

[2] *Firft, here's young mafter Rafh*; &c.] This enumeration of the inhabitants of the prifon affords a very ftriking view of the practices predominant in Shakfpeare's age.   Befides thofe whofe follies are common to all times, we have four fighting men and a traveller.

and old ginger,[3] ninescore and seventeen pounds; of which he made five marks, ready money: marry,

It is not unlikely that the originals of the pictures were then known. JOHNSON.

Rass was the name of some kind of stuff. So, in *An Aprill Shower, shed in abundance of teares, for the death and incomparable losse, &c. of Richard Sacvile, &c. Earl of Dorset, &c.* 1624:

" For with the plainest plaine yee saw him goe,
" In ciuill blacke of *Rass*, of Serge, or so;
" The liuerie of wise stayednesse"———. STEEVENS.

If this term alludes to the stuff so called, (which was probably one of the commodities fraudulently issued out by money-lenders) there is nevertheless a pun intended. So, in an old MS. poem, entitled, *The Description of Women*:

" Their head is made of *Rass*,
" Their tongues are made of Say." DOUCE.

All the names here mentioned are characteristical. *Rass* was a stuff formerly used. So, in *A Reply as true as Steele, to a rusty, rayling, ridiculous, lying Libell, which was lately written by an impudent unsoder'd* Ironmonger, *and called by the name of* an Answer to a foolish pamphlet entitled *A Swarme of Sectaries and Schismatiques. By* John Taylour, 1641:

" And with *mockado* suit, and judgement *rass*,
" And tongue of *saye*, thou'lt say all is but trash."

Sericum rasum. See Minsheu's Dict. in v. *Rass*, and Florio's Italian Dict. 1598, in v. *rascia, rascetta.* MALONE.

[3] ——— *a commodity of brown* paper *and old ginger*,] Thus the old copy. The modern editors read, *brown* pepper; but the following passage in *Michaelmas Term*, Com. 1607, will completely establish the original reading:

" I know some gentlemen in town have been glad, and are glad at this time, to take up commodities in hawk's-hoods and *brown paper*." Again, in *A New Trick to cheat the Devil*, 1636:

" ——— to have been so bit already
" With taking up *commodities of brown paper*,
" Buttons past fashion, silks, and sattins,
" Babies and children's fiddles, with like trash
" Took up at a dear rate, and sold for trifles."

Again, in Greene's *Quip for an Upstart Courtier*, 1620:

" For the merchant, he delivered the iron, tin, lead, hops, sugars, spices, oyls, *brown paper*, or whatever else, from six months to six months. Which when the poor gentleman came to sell again, he could not make three score and ten in the hundred besides the usury." Again, in Greene's *Defence of Coney-catching*, 1592:

then, ginger was not much in requeſt, for the old
women were all dead.[4] Then is there here one maſter
Caper, at the ſuit of maſter Three-pile the mercer,
for ſome four ſuits of peach-colour'd ſatin, which
now peaches him a beggar.   Then have we here

" —— ſo that if he borrow an hundred pound, he ſhall have forty
in ſilver, and threeſcore in wares ; as luteſtrings ; hobby-horſes, or
brown paper, or cloath," &c.
Again, in *The Spaniſh Curate* of Beaumont and Fletcher :
  " Commodities of pins, *brown papers*, packthread."
Again, in Gaſcoigne's *Steele Glaſſe* :
  " To teach young men the trade to ſell *browne paper*."
Again, in *Hall's Satires*, Lib. IV :
  " But Nummius eas'd the needy gallant's care,
  " With a baſe bargaine of his blowen ware,
  " Of fuſted hoppes now loſt for lacke of ſayle,
  " Or mol'd *browne-paper* that could nought auaile."
Again, in Decker's *Seven deadly Sinnes of London*, 4to. bl. l. 1606 :
" —— and theſe are uſurers who, for a little money, and a great
deale of traſh, (as fire-ſhouels, *browne paper*, motley cloake-bags,
&c.) bring yong nouices into a foole's paradice, till they have
ſealed the mortgage of their landes," &c.   STEEVENS.

A commodity of brown paper—] Mr. Steevens ſupports this rightly.
Fennor aſks, in his *Comptor's Commonwealth*, " ſuppoſe the *commodities* are delivered after Signior *Unthrift* and Maſter *Broaker*
have both ſealed the bonds, how muſt thoſe hobby-horſes, *reams of
brown paper*, Jewes trumpes and babies, babies and rattles, be
ſolde ?"   FARMER.

In a MS. letter from Sir John Hollis to Lord Burleigh, is the
following paſſage : " Your Lordſhip digged into my aunceſtors
graves, and pulling one up from his 70 yeares reſte, pronounced
him an abominable uſurer and merchante of *browne paper*, ſo
hatefull and contemptible that the players acted him before the
kinge with great applauſe."   And again : " Nevertheles I denye
that any of them were *merchantes of browne paper*, neither doe I
thinke any other but your Lordſhip's imagination ever ſawe or
hearde any of them playde upon a ſtage ; and that they were ſuch
uſurers I ſuppoſe your Lordſhip will want teſtimonye."
                                        DOUCE.

  [4] —— ginger *was not much in requeſt, for the* old women *were all
dead*.]   So, in *The Merchant of Venice* :——" I would, ſhe were
as lying a *goſſip* in that, as ever knapt *ginger*."   STEEVENS.

young Dizy,[3] and young master Deep-vow, and master
Copper-spur, and master Starve-lacky the rapier
and dagger-man, and young Drop-heir that kill'd
lusty Pudding, and master Forthright[4] the tilter,
and brave master Shoe-tye the great traveller,[5] and

---

[3] —— *young* Dizy,] The old copy has——Dizzy. This name,
like the rest, must have been designed to convey some meaning.
It might have been corrupted from *Dizzy*, i. e. giddy, thoughtless.
Thus Milton styles the people "——the *dizzy* multitude."
STEEVENS.

[4] —— *master* Forthright——] The old copy reads——Forthsight.
Dr. Johnson, however, proposes to read *Forthright*, alluding to the
line in which the thrust is made. Mr. Ritson defends the present
reading, by supposing the allusion to be to the fencers threat of
making the *light* shine through his antagonist. REED.

Had he produced any proof that such an expression was in use
in our author's time, his observation might have had some weight.
It is probably a phrase of the present century. MALONE.

Shakspeare uses the word *forthright* in *The Tempest*:
   "Through *forthrights* and meanders."
Again, in *Troilus and Cressida*, Act III. sc. iii:
   "Or hedge aside from the direct *forthright*." STEEVENS.

[5] —— *and* brave *master* Shoe-tye *the great traveller*,] The old
copy reads——Shooty; but as most of these are compound names, I
suspect that this was originally written as I have printed it. At
this time *Shoe-strings* were generally worn. So, in Decker's *Match
me in London*, 1631:
   "I think your wedding *shoes* have not been oft untied."
Again, in Randolph's *Muses' Looking Glass*, 1638:
   "Bending his supple hams, kissing his hands,
   "Honouring *shoe-strings*."
Again, in Marston's 8th Satire:
   "Sweet-faced Corinna, daine the *riband tie*
   "Of thy corke-*shooe*, or els thy slave will die."
As the person described was a traveller, it is not unlikely that he
might be solicitous about the minutiæ of dress; and the epithet
brave, i. e. *showy*, seems to countenance the supposition. STEEVENS.

Mr. Steevens's supposition is strengthened by Ben Jonson's Epi-
gram upon *English Monsieur*, Whalley's edit. Vol. VI. p. 253:
   "That so much scarf of France, and hat and feather,
   "And *shoe*, and *tye*, and garter, should come hither."
TOLLET.

1

wild Half-can that ſtabb'd Pots, and, I think, forty
more; all great doers in our trade,[6] and are now
for the Lord's ſake.[7]

The finery which induced our author to give his traveller the
name of *Shoe-tie*, was uſed on the ſtage in his time. " Would not
this, ſir, (ſays Hamlet) and a foreſt of feathers,—with two *Proven-
cial roſes* on my raz'd *ſhoes*, get me a fellowſhip in a cry of players,
ſir ?" MALONE.

The *roſes* mentioned in the foregoing inſtance, were not the
ligatures of the ſhoe, but the ornaments above them. STEEVENS.

[6] —— *all great* doers *in our trade.*] The word *doers* is here uſed
in a wanton ſenſe. See Mr. Collins's note, Act I. ſc. ii.
MALONE.

[7] —— *for the Lord's ſake.*] i. e. to beg for the reſt of their lives.
WARBURTON.

I rather think this expreſſion intended to ridicule the Puritans,
whoſe turbulence and indecency often brought them to priſon, and
who conſidered themſelves as ſuffering for religion.

It is not unlikely that men impriſoned for other crimes, might
repreſent themſelves to caſual enquirers, as ſuffering for pu-
ritaniſm, and that this might be the common cant of the priſons.
In Donne's time, every priſoner was brought to jail by ſuretiſhip.
JOHNSON.

The word *in* (now expunged in conſequence of a following and
appoſite quotation of Mr. Malone's) had been ſupplied by ſome of
the modern editors. The phraſe which Dr. Johnſon has juſtly
explained, is uſed in *A New Trick to cheat the Devil*, 1636: " —— I
held it, wife, a deed of charity, and did it *for the Lord's ſake.*"
STEEVENS.

I believe Dr. Warburton's explanation is right. It appears from
a poem entitled, *Paper's Complaint*, printed among Davies's
epigrams, [about the year 1611] that this was the language in
which priſoners who were confined for debt, addreſſed paſſengers :
" Good gentle writers, *for the Lord's ſake, for the Lord's ſake,*
" Like *Ludgate* priſoner, lo, I, *begging*, make
" My mone."

The meaning, however, may be, to beg or *borrow* for the reſt
of their lives. A paſſage in *Much Ado about Nothing* may countenance this interpretation : " he wears a key in his ear, and a lock
hanging to it, and *borrows* money in *God's name*, the which he hath
uſed ſo long, and never paid, that men grow hard-hearted, and
will lend nothing *for God's ſake.*"

Enter ABHORSON.

ABHOR. Sirrah, bring Barnardine hither.

CLO. Mafter Barnardine! you muft rife and be hang'd, mafter Barnardine!

ABHOR. What, ho, Barnardine!

BARNAR. [*Within*] A pox o' your throats! Who makes that noife there? What are you?

CLO. Your friends, fir; the hangman : You muft be fo good, fir, to rife and be put to death.

BARNAR. [*Within.*] Away, you rogue, away; I am fleepy.

ABHOR. Tell him, he muft awake, and that quickly too.

CLO. Pray, mafter Barnardine, awake till you are executed, and fleep afterwards.

ABHOR. Go in to him, and fetch him out.

CLO. He is coming, fir, he is coming; I hear his ftraw ruftle.

Enter BARNARDINE.

ABHOR. Is the axe upon the block, firrah?

CLO. Very ready, fir.

BARNAR. How now, Abhorfon? what's the news with you?

ABHOR. Truly, fir, I would defire you to clap into your prayers;[7] for, look you, the warrant's come.

Mr. Pope reads—and are now *in* for the Lord's fake. Perhaps unneceffarily. In *K. Henry IV.* P. I. Falftaff fays,—" there's not three of my hundred and fifty left alive; and *they are for* the town's end,—to beg during life." MALONE.

[7] —— *to* clap into *your prayers* ;] This cant phrafe occurs alfo in *As you Like it* : " Shall we *clap into't* roundly, without hawking or fpitting?" STEEVENS.

Barnar. You rogue, I have been drinking all night, I am not fitted for't.

Clo. O, the better, fir; for he that drinks all night, and is hang'd betimes in the morning, may fleep the founder all the next day.

Enter Duke.

Abhor. Look you, fir, here comes your ghoftly father; Do we jeft now, think you?

Duke. Sir, induced by my charity, and hearing how haftily you are to depart, I am come to advife you, comfort you, and pray with you.

Barnar. Friar, not I; I have been drinking hard all night, and I will have more time to prepare me, or they fhall beat out my brains with billets: I will not confent to die this day, that's certain.

Duke. O, fir, you muft: and therefore, I befeech you,
Look forward on the journey you fhall go.

Barnar. I fwear, I will not die to-day for any man's perfuafion.

Duke. But hear you,——

Barnar. Not a word; if you have any thing to fay to me, come to my ward; for thence will not I to-day. [*Exit,*

Enter Provoft.

Duke. Unfit to live, or die: O, gravel heart!—— After him, fellows; * bring him to the block. [*Exeunt* Abhorson *and* Clown.

* *After him, fellows;* Here is a line given to the Duke, which belongs to the Provoft. The Provoft, while the Duke is lamenting

Z 3

Prov. Now, fir, how do you find the prifoner?

Duke. A creature unprepar'd, unmeet for death;
And, to tranfport him [9] in the mind he is,
Were damnable.

Prov. Here in the prifon, father,
There died this morning of a cruel fever
One Ragozine, a moft notorious pirate,
A man of Claudio's years; his beard, and head,
Juft of his colour: What if we do omit
This reprobate, till he were well inclin'd;
And fatisfy the deputy with the vifage
Of Ragozine, more like to Claudio?

Duke. O, 'tis an accident that heaven provides!
Difpatch it prefently; the hour draws on
Prefix'd by Angelo: See, this be done,
And fent according to command; whiles I
Perfuade this rude wretch willingly to die.

Prov. This fhall be done, good father, prefently.
But Barnardine muft die this afternoon:
And how fhall we continue Claudio,
To fave me from the danger that might come,
If he were known alive?

Duke. Let this be done;—Put them in fecret
holds,
Both Barnardine and Claudio: Ere twice
The fun hath made his journal greeting to

the obduracy of the prifoner, cries out:
After him, fellows, &c.
and when they are gone out, turns again to the Duke. JOHNSON.

I do not fee why this line fhould be taken from the Duke, and
ftill lefs why it fhould be given to the Provoft, who, by his queftion to the Duke in the next line, appears to be ignorant of every
thing that has paffed between him and Barnardine. TYRWHITT.

9 —— *to tranfport him*—] To remove him from one world to
another. The French *trépas* affords a kindred fenfe. JOHNSON.

The under generation,* you shall find
Your safety manifested.

   PROV. I am your free dependant.

   DUKE.   Quick, despatch,
And send the head to Angelo.   [*Exit* Provost.
Now will I write letters to Angelo,—
The provost, he shall bear them,—whose contents
Shall witness to him, I am near at home;
And that, by great injunctions, I am bound
To enter publickly: him I'll desire
To meet me at the consecrated fount,
A league below the city; and from thence,

---

   * *The* under *generation*,] So Sir Thomas Hanmer, with true judgement. It was in all the former editions:
      To yonder————
*y*ᵉ *under* and *yonder* were confounded. JOHNSON.

   The old reading is not *yonder* but *yond*. STEEVENS,

   To yond *generation*,] Prisons are generally so constructed as not to admit the rays of the sun. Hence the Duke here speaks of its greeting only those *without* the doors of the jail, to which he must be supposed to point when he speaks these words. Sir T. Hanmer, I think without necessity, reads—To *the under* generation, which has been followed by the subsequent editors.
   Journal, in the preceding line, is *daily*. Journalier, Fr.
                           MALONE.

   Mr. Malone reads:
      To yond *generation, you shall find*——
But surely it is impossible that *yond* should be the true reading; for unless ge-ne-ra-ti-on were founded as a word of five syllables, (a practice from which every ear must revolt,) the metre would be defective. It reminds one too much of Peascod, in Gay's *What d'ye call it:*
     " The Pilgrim's Progress—eighth—e-di-ti-on,
     " Lon-don prin-ted for Ni-cho-las Bod-ding-ton."
By the *under generation* our poet means the *antipodes*. So, in *King Richard II:*
     " ———— when the searching eye of heaven is hid
     " Behind the globe, and lights the *lower world*."
                           STEEVENS.

               Z 4

*, in Chapman's version of the nineteenth Il.
we will see a ...... of th'un
in Fletcher's Two Noble Kinsmen:
     " —— clap their wings and sing
  " To all the under world —"

By cold gradation and weal-balanced form,[3]
We shall proceed, with Angelo.

Re-enter Provoſt.

Prov. Here is the head; I'll carry it myſelf.

Duke. Convenient is it: Make a ſwift return;
For I would commune with you of ſuch things,
That want no ear but yours.

Prov.　　　　　　　　　I'll make all ſpeed.
　　　　　　　　　　　　　　　　　　[*Exit.*

Isab. [*Within.*] Peace, ho, be here!

Duke. The tongue of Iſabel:—She's come to
　　　　　know,
If yet her brother's pardon be come hither:
But I will keep her ignorant of her good,
To make her heavenly comforts of deſpair,
When it is leaſt expected.[4]

Enter ISABELLA.

Isab. Ho, by your leave.

Duke. Good morning to you, fair and gracious
　　　　　daughter.

Isab. The better, given me by ſo holy a man.
Hath yet the deputy ſent my brother's pardon?

Duke. He hath releas'd him, Iſabel, from the
　　　　　world;
His head is off, and ſent to Angelo.

---

[3] —— weal-*balanced form,*] Thus the old copy. Mr. Heath
thinks that *well*-balanced is the true reading; and Hanmer was
of the ſame opinion. STEEVENS.

[4] *When it is leaſt expected.*} A better reaſon might have been
given. It was neceſſary to keep Iſabella in ignorance, that ſhe
might with more keenneſs accuſe the deputy. JOHNSON.

*In Milton's Ode on the Nativity we also
meet with the ſame compound epithet:
"and the well-balanc'd world on hinges hung*

Isab. Nay, but it is not fo.

Duke.   It is no other:
Show your wifdom, daughter, in your clofe patience.

Isab. O, I will to him, and pluck out his eyes.

Duke. You fhall not be admitted to his fight.

Isab. Unhappy Claudio! Wretched Ifabel!
Injurious world! Moft damned Angelo!

Duke. This nor hurts him, nor profits you a jot:
Forbear it therefore; give your caufe to heaven.
Mark what I fay; which you fhall find
By every fyllable, a faithful verity:
The duke comes home to-morrow;—nay, dry your
          eyes;
One of our convent, and his confeffor,
Gives me this inftance: Already he hath carried
Notice to Efcalus and Angelo;
Who do prepare to meet him at the gates,
There to give up their power. If you can, pace your
          wifdom
In that good path that I would wifh it go;
And you fhall have your bofom⁵ on this wretch,
Grace of the duke, revenges to your heart,
And general honour.

Isab.   I am directed by you.

Duke. This letter then to friar Peter give;
'Tis he that fent me of the duke's return;
Say, by this token, I defire his company
At Mariana's houfe to-night. Her caufe, and yours,
I'll perfect him withal; and he fhall bring you
Before the duke; and to the head of Angelo
Accufe him home, and home. For my poor felf,
I am combined by a facred vow.⁶

⁵ —— your bofom——] Your wifh; your heart's defire. JOHNSON.

⁶ —— combined by a facred vow,] I once thought this fhould be
—— but Shakfpeare ufes combine for to bind by a pact or agreement;
—— Angelo the combinate hufband of Mariana. JOHNSON.

[handwritten note:] This verb, to combine, appears to be as irregularly used by Chapman, in his verfion of the fixteenth book of Homer's Odyffey:
" —— as thou art mine,
" and as thy veins my own true blood combine
                                        Steev.

And shall be absent.   Wend you' with this letter:
Command these fretting waters from your eyes
With a light heart; trust not my holy order,
If I pervert your course.——Who's here?

Enter Lucio.

Lucio.   Good even!
Friar, where is the provost?

Duke.   Not within, sir.

Lucio. O, pretty Isabella, I am pale at mine
heart, to see thine eyes so red: thou must be patient:
I am fain to dine and sup with water and bran; I
dare not for my head fill my belly; one fruitful
meal would set me to't: But they say the duke will
be here to-morrow.   By my troth, Isabel, I lov'd
thy brother: if the old fantastical duke of dark
corners[8] had been at home, he had lived.

[*Exit* Isabella.

Duke. Sir, the duke is marvellous little beholden
to your reports; but the best is, he lives not in
them.[9]

---

[7] Wend *you*——] To *wend* is *to go.*——An obsolete word. So, in
The Comedy of Errors:
　　" Hopeless and helpless doth Ægeon *wend.*"
　Again, in *Orlando Furioso*, 1599:
　　" To let his daughter *wend* with us to France."
　　　　　　　　　　　　　　　　　　　　　Steevens.

[8] ——*if the* old, *&c.*] Sir Thomas Hanmer reads——*the* odd
fantastical duke; but *old* is a common word of aggravation in ludicrous language, as, *there was* old *revelling.*   Johnson.
　——*duke of dark* corners——] This duke who meets his mistresses
in by-places.   So, in *King Henry VIII*:
　　" There is nothing I have done yet, o' my conscience,
　　" Deserves a *corner.*"   Malone.

[9] ——*he* lives *not in them.*] i. e. his character depends not on
them.   So, in *Much ado about Nothing*:
　　" The practice of it *lives in* John the bastard."   Steevens.

Lucio. Friar, thou knoweft not the duke fo well as I do: he's a better woodman [a] than thou takeft him for.

Duke. Well, you'll anfwer this one day. Fare ye well.

Lucio. Nay, tarry; I'll go along with thee; I can tell thee pretty tales of the duke.

Duke. You have told me too many of him already, fir, if they be true; if not true, none were enough.

Lucio. I was once before him for getting a wench with child.

Duke. Did you fuch a thing?

Lucio. Yes, marry, did I: but was fain to for-fwear it; they would elfe have married me to the rotten medlar.

Duke. Sir, your company is fairer than honeft: Reft you well.

Lucio. By my troth, I'll go with thee to the lane's end: If bawdy talk offend you, we'll have very little of it: Nay, friar, I am a kind of burr, I fhall ftick.

[*Exeunt.*

---

[a] ——— *woodman* —] A *woodman* feems to have been an attendant or fervant to the Officer called *Forrefter*. See *Manwood on the Foreft Laws,* 4to. 1615. p. 46. It is here, however, ufed in a wanton fenfe, and was, probably, in our author's time generally fo received. In like manner in *The Chances,* Act I. fc. ix. the Landlady fays:

 "——— Well, well, fon John,
 " I fee you are a *woodman,* and can choofe
 " Your deer tho' it be i' th' dark." REED.

So, in *The Merry Wives of Windfor,* Falftaff afks his miftreffes:
 "——— Am I a *woodman?* Ha!" STEEVENS.

S C E N E   IV.

A Room in ANGELO'S *Houſe.*

Enter ANGELO *and* ESCALUS.

ESCAL. Every letter he hath writ hath diſvouch'd other.

ANG. In moſt uneven and diſtracted manner. His actions ſhow much like to madneſs : pray heaven, his wiſdom be not tainted! And why meet him at the gates, and re-deliver our authorities there?

ESCAL. I gueſs not.

ANG. And why ſhould we[*] proclaim it in an hour before his entering, that, if any crave redreſs of in-juſtice, they ſhould exhibit their petitions in the ſtreet?

ESCAL. He ſhows his reaſon for that : to have a diſpatch of complaints; and to deliver us from de-vices hereafter, which ſhall then have no power to ſtand againſt us.

ANG. Well, I beſeech you, let it be proclaim'd: Betimes i' the morn, I'll call you at your houſe;[*]

---

[*] Ang. *And why ſhould we,* &c.] It is the conſcious guilt of Angelo that prompts this queſtion. The reply of Eſcalus is ſuch as ariſes from an undiſturbed mind, that only conſiders the myſ-terious conduct of the Duke in a political point of view.
                                                    STEEVENS.

[*] —— *let it be proclaim'd :*
    Betimes i' the morn, &c.] Perhaps it ſhould be pointed thus :
        —— *let it be proclaim'd*
    Betimes i' the morn : I'll call you at your houſe.
So above :
"And why ſhould we *proclaim it an hour* before his entering?"
                                                    MALONE.

Give notice to such men of sort and suit,[4]
As are to meet him.

    Escal.   I shall, sir: fare you well.
                                    [*Exit.*

    Ang. Good night.——
This deed unshapes me quite, makes me unpregnant,[5]
And dull to all proceedings. A deflower'd maid!
And by an eminent body, that enforc'd
The law against it!—But that her tender shame
Will not proclaim against her maiden loss,
How might she tongue me? Yet reason dares her?
    —no:[6]

---

[4] *——sort and suit,*] Figure and rank. JOHNSON.

    Not so, as I imagine, in this passage. In the feudal times all vassals were bound to hold *suit* and *service* to their over-lord; that is, to be ready at all times to attend and serve him, either when summoned to his courts, or to his standard in war. *Such men of sort and suit as are to meet him,* I presume, means the Duke's vassals or tenants *in capite.*—Edinburgh Magazine, Nov. 1786.
                        STEEVENS.

[5] *—— makes me* unpregnant,] In the first scene the Duke says that *Escalus* is *pregnant,* i. e. ready in the forms of law. *Unpregnant* therefore, in the instance before us, is *unready, unprepared.*
                        STEEVENS.

[6] *—— Yet reason dares her?*—no:] The old folio impressions read:
    Yet reason dares her No.
And this is right. The meaning is, the circumstances of our case are such, that she will never venture to contradict me; *dares her* to reply *No* to me, whatever I say. WARBURTON.

    Mr. Theobald reads:
    —— Yet reason dares her note.
Sir Thomas Hanmer:
    —— Yet reason dares her : No.
Mr. Upton:
    —— Yet reason dares her——No.
which he explains thus: *Were it not for her maiden modesty, how might the lady proclaim my guilt? Yet (you'll say) she has reason on her side, and that will make her dare to do it. I think not; for my authority is of such weight,* &c. I am afraid *dare* has no such signification. I have nothing to offer worth insertion. JOHNSON.

For my authority bears a credent bulk,
That no particular scandal once can touch,

To *dare* has two significations; to *terrify*, as in *The Maid's Tragedy*:
" ——— those mad mischiefs
" Would *dare* a woman."
In *King Henry IV*. Part I. it means, to *challenge*, or *call forth*:
" Unless a brother should a brother *dare*
" To gentle exercise," &c.
I would therefore read:
——— *Yet reason dares her* not,
For my authority, &c.
Or perhaps, with only a slight transposition:
——— *yet no reason dares her*, &c.
The meaning will then be,—*Yet reason does not challenge, call forth, or incite her to appear against me, for my authority is above the reach of her accusation*. STEEVENS.

——— *Yet reason dares her No.*] Dr. Warburton is evidently right with respect to this reading, though wrong in his application. The expression is a provincial one, and very intelligible:
——— *But that her tender shame*
Will not proclaim against her maiden loss,
How might she tongue me ? Yet reason dares her No.
That is, reason dares her to do it, as by this means she would not only publish her " maiden loss," but also as she would certainly suffer from the imposing credit of his station and power, which would repel with disgrace any attack on his reputation:
For my authority bears a credent bulk,
That no particular scandal once can touch,
But it confounds the breather.——— HENLEY.

We think Mr. Henley rightly understands this passage, but has not sufficiently explained himself. Reason, or reflection, we conceive, personified by Shakspeare, and represented as *daring* or *ever-awing* Isabella, and crying *No* to her, whenever she finds herself prompted to " tongue" Angelo. *Dare* is often met with in this sense in Shakspeare. Beaumont and Fletcher have used the word *No* in a similar way in *The Chances*, Act III. sc. iv:
" I wear a sword to satisfy the world *no*."
Again, in *A Wife for a Month*, Act IV:
" I'm sure he did not, for I charg'd him *no*."
MONTHLY REVIEW.

——— *Yet reason dares her?* no:] Yet does not reason *challenge* or *incite her* to accuse me?—no, (answers the speaker) for my authority, &c. To *dare*, in this sense, is yet a school-phrase:

Again, in Chapman's Translation of the elev
ed. " ——— the wound did dare him sore."

But it confounds the breather.[7]   He fhould have
    liv'd,
Save that his riotous youth, with dangerous fenfe,
Might, in the times to come, have ta'en revenge,
By fo receiving a difhonour'd life,
With ranfom of fuch fhame.   'Would yet he had
    liv'd!
Alack, when once our grace we have forgot,
Nothing goes right; we would, and we would not.[8]
                    [*Exit.*

Shakfpeare probably learnt it there.   He has again ufed the word
in *King Henry VI.* Part II:
    " What dares not Warwick, if falfe Suffolk *dare him ?*"
                              MALONE.

[7] —— *my authority bears a* credent *bulk,*
    That no particular fcandal, &c.] *Credent* is *creditable, inforcing
credit, not queftionable.* The old Englifh writers often confound the
active and paffive adjectives.   So Shakfpeare, and Milton after
him, ufe *inexpreffive* for *inexpreffible.*
    Particular is *private,* a French fenfe.   No fcandal from any
private mouth can reach a man in my authority.   JOHNSON.

    The old copy reads—" bears *of* a credent bulk."   If *of* be any
thing more than a blunder, it muft mean—bears *off,* i. e. *carries
with it.*   As this monofyllable, however, does not improve our
author's fenfe, and clogs his metre, I have omitted it. STEEVENS.

    Perhaps Angelo means, that his authority will ward off or fet
afide the weightieft and moft probable charge that can be brought
againft him.   MALONE.

[8] —— *we would, and we would not.*]   Here undoubtedly the
act fhould end, and was ended by the poet; for here is properly
a ceffation of action, and a night intervenes, and the place
is changed, between the paffages of this fcene, and thofe of the
next.   The next act beginning with the following fcene, proceeds
without any interruption of time or change of place.   JOHNSON.

SCENE V.

Fields without the Town.

Enter DUKE *in his own habit, and Friar* PETER.

DUKE. Thefe letters[9] at fit time deliver me.
                              [*Giving letters.*
The provoft knows our purpofe, and our plot.
The matter being afoot, keep your inftruction,
And hold you ever to our fpecial drift ;
Though fometimes you do blench from this to that,[2]
As caufe doth minifter. Go, call at Flavius' houfe,
And tell him where I ftay : give the like notice,
To Valentinus, Rowland, and to Craffus,
And bid them bring the trumpets to the gate ;
But fend me Flavius firft.

F. PETER.   It fhall be fpeeded well.
                              [*Exit* Friar.

Enter VARRIUS.

DUKE. I thank thee, Varrius ; thou haft made good
          hafte :

[9] *Thefe letters ——*] Peter never delivers the letters, but tells his ftory without any credentials. The poet forgot the plot which he had formed. JOHNSON.

The firft claufe of this remark is undoubtedly juft ; but, refpecting the fecond, I wifh our readers to recollect that all the plays of Shakfpeare, before they reached the prefs, had paffed through a dangerous medium, and probably experienced the injudicious curtailments to which too many dramatic pieces are ftill expofed, from the ignorance, caprice, and prefumption of tranfcribers, players, and managers. STEEVENS.

[2] *—— you do* blench *from this to that,*] To *blench* is to ftart off, to fly off. So, in *Hamlet :*
    " ——————— if he but *blench,*
    " I know my courfe." STEEVENS.

Come, we will walk: There's other of our friends
Will greet us here anon, my gentle Varrius. [*Exeunt.*

SCENE VI.

Street near the City Gate.

Enter ISABELLA *and* MARIANA.

ISAB. To fpeak fo indirectly, I am loth;
I would fay the truth; but to accufe him fo,
That is your part: yet I'm advis'd to do it;
He fays, to veil full purpofe.[3]

MARI.   Be rul'd by him.

ISAB. Befides, he tells me, that, if peradventure
He fpeak againft me on the adverfe fide,

---

[3] *He fays, to* veil *full purpofe.*] Mr. Theobald alters it to,
     He fays, t' availful *purpofe;*
becaufe he has no idea of the common reading. A good reafon!
Yet the common reading is right. *Full* is ufed for *beneficial*; and
the meaning is, *He fays, it is to hide a beneficial purpofe, that muft
not yet be revealed.* WARBURTON.

To veil full purpofe, may, with very little force on the words,
mean, *to hide the whole extent of our defign,* and therefore the reading may ftand; yet I cannot but think Mr. Theobald's alteration
either lucky or ingenious. To interpret words with fuch laxity,
as to make *full* the fame with *beneficial*, is to put an end, at once,
to all neceffity of emendation, for any word may then ftand in
the place of another. JOHNSON.

I think Theobald's explanation right, but his amendment unneceffary. We need only read *vailful* as one word. Shakfpeare,
who fo frequently ufes *cite* for *excite*, *bate* for *abate*, *force* for
enforce, and many other abbreviations of a fimilar nature, may
well be fuppofed to ufe *vailful* for *availful*. M. MASON.

If Dr. Johnfon's explanation be right, (as I think it is,) the word
fhould be written—*veil*, as it is now printed in the text.

That *vail* was the old fpelling of *veil*, appears from a line in
The Merchant of Venice, folio, 1623:
     " *Vailing* an Indian beauty ———"
for which in the modern editions *veiling* has been rightly fubftituted. MALONE.

VOL. IV.   A a

I fhould not think it ftrange; for 'tis a phyfick,
That's bitter to fweet end.

    MARI. I would, friar Peter——

    ISAB.   O, peace; the friar is come.

Enter Friar PETER.[4]

    F. PETER. Come, I have found you out a ftand
               moft fit,
Where you may have fuch vantage on the duke,
He fhall not pafs you: Twice have the trumpets
      founded;
The generous[5] and graveft citizens
Have hent the gates,[6] and very near upon
The duke is ent'ring; therefore hence, away.
                                  [Exeunt.

---

[4] *Enter Friar* Peter.] This play has two friars, either of whom
might fingly have ferved. I fhould therefore imagine, that Friar
Thomas, in the firft act, might be changed, without any harm,
to Friar Peter; for why fhould the Duke unneceffarily truft two
in an affair which required only one? The name of Friar Thomas
is never mentioned in the dialogue, and therefore feems arbitrarily
placed at the head of the fcene. JOHNSON.

[5] *The* generous, *&c.*] i. e. the *moft noble*, &c. *Generous* is here
ufed in its Latin fenfe. "*Virgo* generofa *et nobilis.*" Cicero.
Shakfpeare ufes it again in *Othello* :
    "——— the *generous* iflanders
    " By you invited——" STEEVENS.

[6] *Have* hent *the gates,*] Have feized or taken poffeffion of the
gates. JOHNSON.
  So, in Sir A. Gorges' tranflation of the 4th book of Lucan :
    "——— did prevent
    " His foes, ere they the hills had *hent.*"
Again, in T. Heywood's Rape of Lucrece, 1630 :
    " Lament thee, Roman land,
    " The king is from thee *hent.*"
Again, in the black-letter Romance of *Syr Eglamoure of Artoys,*
no date :
    " But with the childe homeward gan ryde
    " That fro the gryffon was *hent.*"
      I

ACT V. SCENE I.

A publick Place near the City Gate.

MARIANA (*veil'd*) ISABELLA, *and* PETER, *at a dif-*
tance. Enter at oppofite doors, DUKE, VARRIUS,
Lords ; ANGELO, ESCALUS, LUCIO, Provoſt,
Officers, *and* Citizens.

DUKE. My very worthy coufin, fairly met :——
Our old and faithful friend, we are glad to fee you.

ANG. and ESCAL. Happy return be to your royal
  grace !

DUKE. Many and hearty thankings to you both.
We have made inquiry of you ; and we hear
Such goodnefs of your juſtice, that our foul
Cannot but yield you forth to public thanks,
Fore-running more requital.

ANG.   You make my bonds ſtill greater.

DUKE. O, your defert fpeaks loud ; and I fhould
  wrong it,
To lock it in the wards of covert bofom,
When it deferves with characters of brafs
A forted refidence, 'gainſt the tooth of time,
And razure of oblivion : Give me your hand,
And let the fubject fee, to make them know

Again, in the ancient metrical Romance of *Syr Gay of Warwick*,
b. l. no date :
  " Some by the arms *bent* good Guy," &c.
Again,
  " And fome by the bridle him *bent.*"
Spenfer often ufes the word *bend* for to *feize* or *take*, and *overbend*
for to *overtake.* STEEVENS.

  Hent, henten, hende, (fays Junius, in his *Etymologicon*,) *Chaucero*
eſt, capere, affequi, prehendere, arripere, ab A. S. hendan.
                                          MALONE.

A a 2

That outward courtefies would fain proclaim
Favours that keep within.——Come, Efcalus;
You muft walk by us on our other hand;——
And good fupporters are you.

PETER *and* ISABELLA *come forward.*

F. PETER. Now is your time; fpeak loud, and
    kneel before him.

ISAB. Juftice, O royal Duke! Vail your regard [7]
Upon a wrong'd, I'd fain have faid, a maid!
O worthy prince, difhonour not your eye
By throwing it on any other object,
Till you have heard me in my true complaint,
And given me juftice, juftice, juftice, juftice!

    DUKE. Relate your wrongs: In what? By whom?
        Be brief:
Here is lord Angelo fhall give you juftice;
Reveal yourfelf to him.

    ISAB.   O, worthy duke,
You bid me feek redemption of the devil:
Hear me yourfelf; for that which I muft fpeak
Muft either punifh me, not being believ'd,
Or wring redrefs from you: hear me, O, hear me,
    here.

---

[7] —— Vail *your regard*—] That is, withdraw your thoughts
from higher things, let your notice defcend upon a wronged
woman. To *vail* is to lower. JOHNSON.

    This is one of the few expreffions which might have been bor-
rowed from the old play of *Promos and Caffandra,* 1578:
    " —— *vail* thou thine ears."
So, in Stanyhurft's tranflation of the 4th Book of Virgil's *Æneid:*
    " —— *Phrygio liceat* fervire *marito.*"
    " Let Dido *vail* her heart to bed-fellow Trojan."
                        STEEVENS.
Thus alfo, in *Hamlet:*
    " Do not for ever, with thy *vailed lids*,
    " Seek for thy noble father in the duft." HENLEY.

Ang. My lord, her wits, I fear me, are not firm :
She hath been a fuitor to me for her brother,
Cut off by courfe of juftice.

Isab.   By courfe of juftice !

Ang. And fhe will fpeak moft bitterly, and ftrange.

Isab. Moft ftrange, but yet moft truly, will I fpeak :
That Angelo's forfworn ; is it not ftrange ?
That Angelo's a murderer ; is't not ftrange ?
That Angelo is an adulterous thief,
An hypocrite, a virgin-violator ;
Is it not ftrange, and ftrange ?

Duke.   Nay, it is ten times ftrange.

Isab. It is not truer he is Angelo,
Than this is all as true as it is ftrange :
Nay, it is ten times true ; for truth is truth
To the end of reckoning.[8]

Duke.   Away with her :——Poor foul,
She fpeaks this in the infirmity of fenfe.

Isab. O prince, I cónjure thee, as thou believ'ft
There is another comfort than this world,
That thou neglect me not, with that opinion
That I am touch'd with madnefs : make not impof-
          fible
That which but feems unlike : 'tis not impoffible,
But one, the wicked'ft caitiff on the ground,
May feem as fhy, as grave, as juft, as abfolute,[9]

---

[8] —————— *truth is truth*
To the end of reckoning.] That is, truth has no gradations ;
nothing which admits of encreafe can be fo much what it is, as
truth is truth. There may be a *ftrange* thing, and a thing *more
ftrange*, but if a propofition be *true*, there can be none *more true*.
                                                      JOHNSON.

[9] —————— *as fhy, as grave, as juft, as abfolute*,] *As fhy* ; as referved,
as abftracted : *as juft* ; as nice, as exact : *as abfolute* ; as complete
in all the round of duty. JOHNSON.

As Angelo; even so may Angelo,
In all his dreſſings,[2] characts,[3] titles, forms,
Be an arch-villain: believe it, royal prince,
If he be leſs, he's nothing; but he's more,
Had I more name for badneſs.

    Duke.   By mine honeſty,
If ſhe be mad, (as I believe no other,)
Her madneſs hath the oddeſt frame of ſenſe,
Such a dependency of thing on thing,
As e'er I heard in madneſs.[4]

    Isab.   O, gracious duke,
Harp not on that; nor do not baniſh reaſon
For inequality:[5] but let your reaſon ſerve

---

  [2] *In all his* dreſſings, &c.] In all his ſemblance of virtue, in all his habiliments of office. JOHNSON.

  [3] —— *characts*,] i. e. characters. See *Dugdale, Orig. Jurid.* p. 81 :—" That he uſe ne hide, no charme, ne *carecte.*"
                            TYRWHITT.

  So, in Gower, *De Confeſſione Amantis,* B. I :
    " With his *carecte* would him enchaunt."
Again, B. V. fol. 103 :
    " And read his *carecte* in the wife."
Again, B. VI. fol. 140 :
    " Through his *carectes* and figures."
Again :
    " And his *carecte* as he was taught,
    " He rad," &c. STEEVENS.

  Charact ſignifies an inſcription. The ſtat. 1 Edward VI. c. 2. directed the ſeals of office of every biſhop to have " certain *characts* under the king's arms, for the knowledge of the dioceſe." *Characters* are the letters in which the inſcription is written. *Charactery* is the materials of which characters are compoſed.
    " Fairies uſe flowers for their *charactery.*"
        Merry Wives of Windſor. BLACKSTONE.

  [4] *As e'er I heard,* &c.] I ſuppoſe Shakſpeare wrote :
    As ne'er *I heard in madneſs.* MALONE.

  [5] —— *do not baniſh* reaſon
  For inequality :] Let not the high quality of my adverſary prejudice you againſt me. JOHNSON.

To make the truth appear, where it seems hid;
And hide the false, seems true.[6]

DUKE.   Many that are not mad,
Have, sure, more lack of reason.—What would you
  say?

ISAB. I am the sister of one Claudio,
Condemn'd upon the act of fornication
To lose his head; condemn'd by Angelo:
I, in probation of a sisterhood,
Was sent to by my brother: One Lucio
As then the messenger;—

LUCIO.   That's I, an't like your grace:
I came to her from Claudio, and desir'd her
To try her gracious fortune with lord Angelo,
For her poor brother's pardon.

ISAB.   That's he, indeed.

DUKE. You were not bid to speak.

LUCIO.   No, my good lord;
Nor wish'd to hold my peace.

DUKE.   I wish you now then;
Pray you, take note of it: and when you have

Inequality appears to me to mean, in this place, *apparent incon-sistency*; and to have no reference to the high rank of Angelo, as Johnson supposes. M. MASON.

I imagine the meaning rather is—*Do not* suppose I am mad, because I speak passionately and *unequally.* MALONE.

[6] And hide *the false, seems true.*] And for ever *hide*, i. e. plunge into eternal darkness, the false *one*, i. e. Angelo, who now seems honest. Many other words would have expressed our poet's mean-ing better than *hide*; but he seems to have chosen it merely for the sake of opposition to the preceding line. Mr. Theobald unneces-sarily reads—*Not* hide the false,—which has been followed by the subsequent editors. MALONE.

I do not profess to understand these words; nor can I perceive how the meaning suggested by Mr. Malone is to be deduced from them. STEEVENS.

I agree with Theobald in reading,
Not hide the false seems true.
which requires no explanation. I cannot
receive how the word — hide, can mean to
lunge into eternal darkness, as Mr. Malone
does. M. Mason.

A bufinefs for yourfelf, pray heaven, you then
Be perfect.

 LUCIO. I warrant your honour.

 DUKE. The warrant's for yourfelf; take heed to it.

 ISAB. This gentleman told fomewhat of my tale.

 LUCIO. Right.

 DUKE. It may be right; but you are in the wrong
To fpeak before your time.——Proceed.

 ISAB.   I went
To this pernicious caitiff deputy.

 DUKE. That's fomewhat madly fpoken.

 ISAB.   Pardon it;
The phrafe is to the matter.

 DUKE. Mended again: the matter;——Proceed.

 ISAB. In brief,——to fet the needlefs procefs by,
How I perfuaded, how I pray'd, and kneel'd,
How he refell'd me,[7] and how I reply'd;
(For this was of much length,) the vile conclufion
I now begin with grief and fhame to utter:
He would not, but by gift of my chafte body
To his concupifcible intemperate luft,[8]
Releafe my brother; and, after much debatement,
My fifterly remorfe [9] confutes mine honour,

---

[7] *How he* refell'd *me*,] To *refel* is to refute.
 " Refellere *et coarguere mendacium.*" Cicero pro Ligario.
Ben Jonfon ufes the word:
 " Friends not to *refel* you,
 " Or any way quell you."
Again, in *The Second Part of Robert Earl of Huntington*, 1601:
 " Therefore go on, young Bruce, proceed, *refell*
 " The allegation."
The modern editors changed the word to *repel*. STEEVENS.

[8] *To his* concupifcible, *&c.*] Such is the old reading. The
modern editors unauthoritatively fubftitute *concupifcent*. STEEVENS.

[9] *My fifterly* remorfe—] i. e. *pity.* So, in *King Richard III*:
 " And gentle, kind, effeminate *remorfe.*" STEEVENS.

And I did yield to him : But the next morn betimes,
His purpofe furfeiting,[2] he fends a warrant
For my poor brother's head.

Duke.   This is moft likely!

Isab. O, that it were as like, as it is true![3]

Duke. By heaven, fond wretch,[4] thou know'ft not
                what thou fpeak'ft;
Or elfe thou art fuborn'd againft his honour,
In hateful practice:[5] Firft, his integrity
Stands without blemifh:—next, it imports no reafon,
That with fuch vehemency he fhould purfue
Faults proper to himfelf: if he had fo offended,
He would have weigh'd thy brother by himfelf,

---

[2] *His purpofe* furfeiting,] Thus the old copy. We might read *forfeiting*, but the former word is too much in the manner of Shakfpeare to be rejected. So, in *Othello*:
"—— my hopes not *furfeited* to death." STEEVENS.

[3] *O, that it were as* like, *as it is true!*] *Like* is not here ufed for *probable*, but for *feemly*. She catches at the Duke's word, and turns it into another fenfe; of which there are a great many examples in Shakfpeare, and the writers of that time. WARBURTON.

I do not fee why *like* may not ftand here for *probable*, or why the lady fhould not wifh, that fince her tale is true, it may obtain belief. If Dr. Warburton's explication be right, we fhould read:
O! *that it were as* likely, *as 'tis true!*
Likely I have never found for *feemly*. JOHNSON.

Though I concur in Dr. Johnfon's explanation, I cannot help obferving that *likely* is ufed by Shakfpeare himfelf for *feemly*. So, in *King Henry IV*. Part II. Act III. fc. ii : "Sir John, they are your *likelieft* men." STEEVENS.

The meaning, I think, is: O that it had as much of the *appearance*, as it has of the *reality*, of truth! MALONE.

[4] —— fond *wretch*,] *Fond* wretch is *foolifh* wretch. So, in *Coriolanus*, Act IV. fc. i :
"'Tis *fond* to wail inevitable ftrokes." STEEVENS.

[5] *In hateful* practice:] *Practice* was ufed by the old writers for any unlawful or infidious ftratagem. So again:
"This muft needs be *practice*."
And again:
"Let me have way to find this *practice* out." JOHNSON.

And not have cut him off: Some one hath set you on;
Confess the truth, and say by whose advice
Thou cam'st here to complain.

Isab.   And is this all?
Then, oh, you blessed ministers above,
Keep me in patience; and, with ripen'd time,
Unfold the evil which is here wrapt up
In countenance![6]——Heaven shield your grace from
          woe,
As I, thus wrong'd, hence unbelieved go!

Duke. I know, you'd fain be gone:——An officer!
To prison with her:——Shall we thus permit
A blasting and a scandalous breath to fall
On him so near us? This needs must be a practice.[7]
——Who knew of your intent, and coming hither?

Isab. One that I would were here, friar Lodowick.

Duke. A ghostly father, belike:——Who knows
          that Lodowick?

Lucio. My lord, I know him; 'tis a medling
          friar;
I do not like the man: had he been lay, my lord,
For certain words he spake against your grace
In your retirement, I had swing'd him soundly.

Duke. Words against me? This' a good friar, be-
          like!

---

[6] *In countenance!*] i. e. in partial favour. WARBURTON.

Countenance, in my opinion, does not mean partial favour, as
Warburton supposes, but *false appearance, hypocrisy.* Isabella does
not mean to accuse the Duke of partiality; but alludes to the
sanctified demeanour of Angelo, which, as she supposes, prevented
the Duke from believing her story. M. MASON.

[7] ——*practice.*] *Practice,* in Shakspeare, very often means
shameful artifice, unjustifiable stratagem. So, in *King Lear:*
          " —— This is *practice,* Gloster."
Again, in *King John:*
          " It is the shameful work of Hubert's hand,
          " The *practice* and the purpose of the king." STEEVENS.

And to fet on this wretched woman here
Againſt our ſubſtitute !—Let this friar be found.

Lucio. But yeſternight, my lord, ſhe and that friar
I ſaw them at the priſon : a ſawcy friar,
A very ſcurvy fellow.

F. Peter.   Bleſſed be your royal grace !
I have ſtood by, my lord, and I have heard
Your royal ear abus'd : Firſt, hath this woman
Moſt wrongfully accus'd your ſubſtitute ;
Who is as free from touch or ſoil with her,
As ſhe from one ungot.

Duke.   We did believe no leſs.
Know you that friar Lodowick, that ſhe ſpeaks of?

F. Peter. I know him for a man divine and holy ;
Not ſcurvy, nor a temporary medler,[8]
As he's reported by this gentleman ;
And, on my truſt, a man that never yet
Did, as he vouches, miſreport your grace.

Lucio. My lord, moſt villainouſly ; believe it.

F. Peter. Well, he in time may come to clear
          himſelf ;
But at this inſtant he is ſick, my lord,

---

[8] ——— *nor a* temporary *medler*,] It is hard to know what is
meant by a *temporary* medler. In its uſual ſenſe, as oppoſed to
perpetual, it cannot be uſed here. It may ſtand for *temporal :* the
ſenſe will then be, *I know him for a holy man, one that meddles not
with* ſecular *affairs.* It may mean *temporifing : I know him to be
a holy man, one who would not* temporiſe, *or take the opportunity of
your abſence to defame you.* Or we may read :
   Not ſcurvy, nor a tamperer *and medler :*
not one who would have *tampered* with this woman to make her a
falſe evidence againſt your deputy. Johnson.

   Peter here refers to what Lucio had before affirmed concerning
Friar Lodowick. Hence it is evident that the phraſe " *temporary
medler,*" was intended to ſignify *one who introduced himſelf*, as often
as he could find opportunity, *into other men's concerns.* See the
context. Henley.

Of a ftrange fever : Upon his mere requeft,[9]
(Being come to knowledge that there was complaint
Intended 'gainft lord Angelo,) came I hither,
To fpeak, as from his mouth, what he doth know
Is true, and falfe ; and what he with his oath,
And all probation, will make up full clear,
Whenfoever he's convented.[2] Firft, for this woman ;
(To juftify this worthy nobleman,
So vulgarly[3] and perfonally accus'd,)

[9] — *his* mere *requeft.*] i. e. his *abfolute requeft.* So, in *Julius Cæfar :*
" Some *mere* friends, fome honourable Romans."
Again, in *Othello :*
" The *mere* perdition of the Turkifh fleet." STEEVENS.

[2] *Whenfoever he's* convented.] The firft folio reads, *convented,*
and this is right: for to *convene* fignifies to affemble; but *convent,*
to cite, or fummons. Yet becaufe *convented* hurts the meafure,
the Oxford editor fticks to *conven'd,* though it be nonfenfe, and
fignifies, *Whenever he is affembled together.* But thus it will be,
when the author is thinking of one thing, and his critic of another.
The poet was attentive to his fenfe, and the editor quite throughout his performance, to nothing but the meafure ; which Shakfpeare having entirely neglected, like all the dramatic writers of
that age, he has fpruced him up with all the exactnefs of a modern
meafurer of fyllables. This being here taken notice of once for
all, fhall, for the future, be forgot, as if it had never been.
WARBURTON.

The foregoing account of the meafure of Shakfpeare, and his
contemporaries, ought indeed to be forgotten, becaufe it is untrue.
To *convent* is no uncommon word. So, in *Woman's a Weathercock,* 1612 :
" —— left my looks
" Should tell the company *convented* there," &c.
To *convent* and to *convene* are derived from the fame Latin verb,
and have exactly the fame meaning. STEEVENS.

[3] *So* vulgarly ——] Meaning either fo *grofly,* with fuch *indecency*
of invective, or by fo *mean* and inadequate witneffes. JOHNSON.

Vulgarly, I believe, means *publickly.* The *vulgar* are *the common
people.* Daniel ufes *vulgarly* for *among the common people :*
" —— and which pleafes *vulgarly.*" STEEVENS.

Mr. Steevens's interpretation is certainly the true one. So, in
The Comedy of Errors, Act III. fc. i :

Her fhall you hear difproved to her eyes,
Till fhe herfelf confefs it.

Duke.   Good friar, let's hear it.
[ISABELLA *is carried off, guarded; and* MARIANA
comes forward.
Do you not fmile at this, lord Angelo?——
O heaven! the vanity of wretched fools!——
Give us fome feats.——Come, coufin Angelo;
In this I'll be impartial; be you judge
Of your own caufe.⁴——Is this the witnefs, friar?
Firft, let her fhow her face;⁵ and, after, fpeak.

" A *vulgar* comment will be made of it;
" And that fuppofed by the *common rout*,——
" That may," &c.

Again, in *Twelfth Night:*
" ——— for 'tis a *vulgar* proof,
" That very oft we pity enemies." MALONE.

⁴ ——— *Come, coufin Angelo;*
   In this I'll be impartial; *be you judge*
  Of your own caufe.] Surely, fays Mr. Theobald, this duke had
odd notions of impartiality! He reads therefore,——*I will be
partial,* and all the editors follow him: even Mr. Heath declares
the obfervation unanfwerable. But fee the uncertainty of criticifm! *impartial* was fometimes ufed in the fenfe of *partial.* In
the old play of *Swetnam, the Woman Hater,* Atlanta cries out, when
the judges decree againft the women:
" You are *impartial,* and we do appeal
" From you to judges more indifferent." FARMER.

So, in Marfton's *Antonio and Mellida,* 2d Part, 1602:
" There's not a beauty lives,
" Hath that *impartial* predominance
" O'er my affects, as your enchanting graces."
Again, in *Romeo and Juliet,* 1597:
" Cruel, unjuft, *impartial* deftinies!"
Again:
" ——— this day, this unjuft, *impartial* day."
In the language of our author's time *im* was frequently ufed as
an augmentative or intenfive particle. MALONE.

⁵ ——— her *face;*] The original copy reads——*your* face. The
emendation was made by the editor of the fecond folio.
MALONE.

MARI. Pardon, my lord; I will not show my face,
Until my husband bid me.

DUKE.   What, are you married?

MARI. No, my lord.

DUKE.   Are you a maid?

MARI.   No, my lord.

DUKE. A widow then?

MARI.   Neither, my lord.

DUKE.   Why, you
Are nothing then :—Neither maid, widow, nor wife?[6]

LUCIO. My lord, she may be a punk ; for many
of them are neither maid, widow, nor wife.

DUKE. Silence that fellow : I would, he had some
            cause
To prattle for himself.

LUCIO. Well, my lord.

MARI. My lord, I do confess I ne'er was married;
And, I confess, besides, I am no maid :
I have known my husband ; yet my husband knows
            not,
That ever he knew me.

LUCIO. He was drunk then, my lord ; it can be
no better.

DUKE. For the benefit of silence, 'would thou
wert so too.

LUCIO. Well, my lord.

DUKE. This is no witness for lord Angelo.

MARI. Now I come to't, my lord :
She, that accuses him of fornication,

<hr>

[6] *Neither maid, widow, nor wife?*] This is a proverbial phrase,
to be found in Ray's Collection. STEEVENS.

In felf-fame manner doth accufe my hufband ;
And charges him, my lord, with fuch a time,
When I'll depofe I had him in mine arms,
With all the effect of love.

ANG. Charges fhe more than me?

MARI. Not that I know.

DUKE. No? you fay, your hufband.

MARI. Why, juft, my lord, and that is Angelo,
Who thinks, he knows, that he ne'er knew my body,
But knows, he thinks, that he knows Ifabel's.

ANG. This is a ftrange abufe :[7]—Let's fee thy face.

MARI. My hufband bids me; now I will unmafk.
[*Unveiling.*

This is that face, thou cruel Angelo,
Which, once thou fwor'ft, was worth the looking on :
This is the hand, which, with a vow'd contract,
Was faft belock'd in thine : this is the body
That took away the match from Ifabel,
And did fupply thee at thy garden-houfe,[8]
In her imagin'd perfon.

---

[7] *This is a ftrange* abufe :] *Abufe* ftands in this place for *deception* or *puzzle.* So, in *Macbeth :*
 " —— my ftrange and felf *abufe,"*
means, *this ftrange* deception *of myfelf.* JOHNSON.

[8] *And did fupply thee at thy* garden-houfe,] A *garden-houfe* in the time of our author was ufually appropriated to purpofes of intrigue. So, in SKIALETHIA, *or a fhadow of truth, in certain Epigrams and Satyres,* 1598 :
 " Who, coming from the CURTAIN, fneaketh in
 " To fome old *garden* noted *houfe* for fin."
Again, in *The London Prodigal,* a comedy, 1605 : " Sweet lady, if you have any friend, or *garden-houfe,* where you may employ a poor gentleman as your friend, I am yours to command in all fecret fervice." MALONE.

See alfo an extract from *Stubbes's Anatomie of Abufes,* 4to, 1597, p. 57; quoted in Vol. V. of *Dodfley's Old Plays,* edit. 1780, p. 74.
REED.

Duke.   Know you this woman?

Lucio. Carnally, she says.

Duke.   Sirrah, no more.

Lucio. Enough, my lord.

Ang. My lord, I must confess, I know this woman;
And, five years since, there was some speech of mar-
          riage
Betwixt myself and her : which was broke off,
Partly, for that her promised proportions
Came short of composition ;[9] but, in chief,
For that her reputation was disvalued
In levity : since which time, of five years,
I never spake with her, saw her, nor heard from her,
Upon my faith and honour.

Mari.   Noble prince,
As there comes light from heaven, and words from
          breath,
As there is sense in truth, and truth in virtue,
I am affianc'd this man's wife, as strongly
As words could make up vows : and, my good lord,
But Tuesday night last gone, in his garden-house,
He knew me as a wife : As this is true,
Let me in safety raise me from my knees ;
Or else for ever be confixed here,
A marble monument !

Ang.   I did but smile till now ;
Now, good my lord, give me the scope of justice ;
My patience here is touch'd : I do perceive,
These poor informal women[a] are no more

---

9 ―――― *her promised* proportions
  Came short of composition ;] Her fortune, which was promised
proportionate to mine, fell short of the *composition,* that is, contract
or bargain. JOHNSON.

a *These poor* informal *women* ――] *Informal* signifies *out of their*
senses. In *The Comedy of Errors,* we meet with these lines :

But inftruments of fome more mightier member,
That fets them on : Let me have way, my lord,
To find this practice out.

   Duke.   Ay, with my heart ;
And punifh them unto your height of pleafure.——
Thou foolifh friar ; and thou pernicious woman,
Compáct with her that's gone ! think'ft thou, thy
          oaths,
Though they would fwear down each particular
          faint,[3]
Were teftimonies againft his worth and credit,
That's feal'd in approbation ?[4]——You, lord Efcalus,
Sit with my coufin ; lend him your kind pains
To find out this abufe, whence 'tis deriv'd.——
There is another friar that fet them on ;
Let him be fent for.

  · *F. Peter.* Would he were here, my lord ; for he,
         indeed,
Hath fet the women on to this complaint :

       " —— I will not let him ftir,
       " Till I have us'd the approved means I have,
       " With wholefome fyrups, drugs, and holy prayers,
       " To make of him a *formal* man again."

Formal, in this paffage, evidently fignifies *in his fenfes.* The lines
are fpoken of Antipholis of Syracufe, who is behaving like a madman. Again, in *Antony and Cleopatra :*
       " Thou fhouldft come like a fury crown'd with fnakes,
       " Not like a *formal* man."   STEEVENS.

   [3] *Though they would fwear down each particular faint,*] So, in
Antony and Cleopatra, Act I. fc. iii :
       " Though you in fwearing fhake the throned gods."
                                      STEEVENS.

   [4] *That's feal'd in* approbation ?] When any thing fubject to
counterfeits is tried by the proper officers and approved, a ftamp
or *feal* is put upon it, as among us on plate, weights, and meafures.
So the Duke fays, that Angelo's faith has been tried, *approved*, and
feal'd in teftimony of that *approbation*, and, like other things fo
fealed, is no more to be called in queftion.   JOHNSON.

Your provost knows the place where he abides,
And he may fetch him.

Duke. Go, do it instantly.——   [*Exit* Provost.
And you, my noble and well-warranted cousin,
Whom it concerns to hear this matter forth,[4]
Do with your injuries as seems you best,
In any chastisement: I for a while
Will leave you; but stir not you, till you have well
Determined upon these slanderers.

Escal. My lord, we'll do it thoroughly.——[*Exit.*
Duke.] Signior Lucio, did not you say, you knew
that friar Lodowick to be a dishonest person?

Lucio. Cucullus non facit monachum: honest in nothing, but in his clothes; and one that hath spoke
most villainous speeches of the duke.

Escal. We shall entreat you to abide here till he
come, and enforce them against him: we shall find
this friar a notable fellow.

Lucio. As any in Vienna, on my word.

Escal. Call that same Isabel here once again;
[*To an Attendant.*] I would speak with her: Pray
you, my lord, give me leave to question; you shall
see how I'll handle her.

Lucio. Not better than he, by her own report.

Escal. Say you?

Lucio. Marry, sir, I think, if you handled her
privately, she would sooner confess; perchance,
publickly she'll be ashamed.

Re-enter Officers, *with* ISABELLA; *the* DUKE, *in the
Friar's habit, and* Provost.

Escal. I will go darkly to work with her.

4 ——— *to bear this matter forth,*] To hear it to the end; to
search it to the bottom. JOHNSON.

Lucio. That's the way; for women are light at midnight.[5]

Escal. Come on, miftrefs: [*To* Isabella.] here's a gentlewoman denies all that you have faid.

Lucio. My lord, here comes the rafcal I fpoke of; here with the provoft.

Escal. In very good time :——fpeak not you to him, till we call upon you.

Lucio. Mum.

Escal. Come, fir: Did you fet thefe women on to flander lord Angelo? they have confefs'd you did.

Duke. 'Tis falfe.

Escal. How! know you where you are?

Duke. Refpect to your great place! and let the devil
Be fometime honour'd for his burning throne :[6]——
Where is the duke? 'tis he fhould hear me fpeak.

Escal. The duke's in us, and we will hear you fpeak:
Look, you fpeak juftly.

Duke. Boldly, at leaft:——But, O, poor fouls,
Come you to feek the lamb here of the fox?
Good night to your redrefs. Is the duke gone?

---

5 ——— *are* light *at midnight.*] This is one of the words on which Shakfpeare chiefly delights to quibble. Thus, Portia in *The Merchant of Venice*, Act V. fc. i:
" Let me give *light*, but let me not be *light*." STEEVENS.

6 *Refpect to your great place! and let the devil*, &c.] I fufpect that a line preceding this has been loft. MALONE.

I fufpect no omiffion. *Great place* has reference to the preceding queftion——" know you *where* you are ?"

Shakfpeare was a reader of Philemon Holland's tranflation of Pliny; and in the fifth book and eighth chapter, might have met with his next idea : " The Augylæ *do no worfhip* to any but to the devils beneath." STEEVENS.

Then is your caufe gone too.   The duke's unjuft,
Thus to retort your manifeft appeal,[7]
And put your trial in the villain's mouth,
Which here you come to accufe.

   Lucio. This is the rafcal; this is he I fpoke of.

   Escal. Why, thou unreverend and unhallow'd
       friar!
Is't not enough, thou haft fuborn'd thefe women
To accufe this worthy man; but, in foul mouth,
And in the witnefs of his proper ear,
To call him villain?
And then to glance from him to the duke himfelf;
To tax him with injuftice?——Take him hence;
To the rack with him:——We'll touze you joint by
       joint,
But we will know this purpofe:[8]——What! unjuft?

   Duke. Be not fo hot; the duke
Dare no more ftretch this finger of mine, than he
Dare rack his own; his fubject am I not,
Nor here provincial:[9] My bufinefs in this ftate

---

   [7] —— *to retort your manifeft* appeal,] To *refer back* to Angelo
the caufe in which you *appealed* from Angelo to the Duke.
                                   JOHNSON.

   [8] —— this *purpofe:*] The old copy has—*bis* purpofe. The
emendation was made by Sir T. Hanmer. I believe the paffage has
been corrected in the wrong place; and would read:
     —— *We'll touze* him *joint by joint,*
   But we will know his *purpofe.* MALONE.

   [9] *Nor here* provincial:] Nor here *accountable.* The meaning
feems to be, I am not one of his natural fubjects, nor of any dependent province. JOHNSON.

   The different orders of monks have a chief, who is called the
General of the order; and they have alfo fuperiors, fubordinate to
the general, in the feveral provinces through which the order may
be difperfed. The Friar therefore means to fay, that the Duke
dares not touch a finger of his, for he could not punifh him by his
own authority, as be was not his fubject, nor through that of the
fuperior, as he was not of that province. M. MASON.

Made me a looker-on here in Vienna,
Where I have feen corruption boil and bubble,
Till it o'er-run the ftew :² laws, for all faults ;
But faults fo countenanc'd, that the ftrong ftatutes
Stand like the forfeits in a barber's fhop,³
As much in mock as mark.

² ————— boil and bubble,
Till it o'er-run the ftew :] I fear that, in the prefent inftance,
our author's metaphor is from the kitchen. So, in *Macbeth :*
  " Like a hell-*broth, boil and bubble.*" STEEVENS.

³ *Stand like the forfeits in a barber's fhop,*] Barbers' fhops were,
at all times, the refort of idle people :
  " *Tonftrina erat quædam : hic folebamus ferè*
  " *Plerumque eam opperiri"* ————.
which Donatus calls *apta fedes otiofis.* Formerly with us, the
better fort of people went to the barber's fhop to be trimmed; who
then practifed the under parts of furgery: fo that he had occafion
for numerous inftruments, which lay there ready for ufe; and the
idle people, with whom his fhop was generally crowded, would be
perpetually handling and mifufing them. To remedy which, I
fuppofe there was placed up againft the wall a table of forfeitures,
adapted to every offence of this kind; which, it is not likely, would
long preferve its authority. WARBURTON.

This explanation may ferve till a better is difcovered. But
whoever has feen the inftruments of a chirurgeon, knows that they
may be very eafily kept out of improper hands in a very fmall box,
or in his pocket. JOHNSON.

It was formerly part of a *barber's* occupation to *pick* the *teeth*
and *ears.* So, in the old play of *Herod* and *Antipater,* 1622, *Try-
phon* the *barber,* enters with a cafe of inftruments, to each of which
he addreffes himfelf feparately :
  " Toothpick, dear toothpick; earpick, both of you
  " Have been her fweet companions!—" &c.
I have converfed with feveral people who had repeatedly read the
lift of forfeits alluded to by Shakfpeare, but have failed in my
endeavours to procure a copy of it. The metrical one, publifhed
by the late Dr. Kenrick, was a forgery. STEEVENS.

I believe Dr. Warburton's explanation in the main to be right,
only that inftead of chirurgical inftruments, the barber's prohibited
implements were principally his razors; his whole ftock of which,
from the number and impatience of his cuftomers on a Saturday
night or a market morning, being neceffarily laid out for ufe, were

Escal. Slander to the ftate! Away with him to prifon.

Ang. What can you vouch againft him, fignior Lucio?
Is this the man, that you did tell us of?

Lucio. 'Tis he, my lord. Come hither, good-man bald-pate: Do you know me?

Duke. I remember you, fir, by the found of your voice: I met you at the prifon, in the abfence of the duke.

Lucio. O, did you fo? And do you remember what you faid of the duke?

Duke. Moft notedly, fir.

Lucio. Do you fo, fir? And was the duke a flefh-monger, a fool, and a coward,[3] as you then reported him to be?

Duke. You muft, fir, change perfons with me, ere you make that my report: you, indeed, fpoke fo of him; and much more, much worfe.

Lucio. O thou damnable fellow! Did not I pluck thee by the nofe, for thy fpeeches?

Duke. I proteft, I love the duke, as I love myfelf.

---

expofed to the idle fingers of the bye-ftanders, in waiting for fuc-ceffion to the chair.

Thefe forfeits were as much in *mock* as *mark*, both becaufe the barber had no authority of himfelf to enforce them, and alfo as they were of a ludicrous nature. I perfectly remember to have feen them in Devonfhire (printed like King Charles's Rules,) though I cannot recollect their contents. HENLEY.

[3] —— *and a* coward,] So again, afterwards:
  You, firrah, that know me for a fool, a coward,
  One all of luxury ——.
But Lucio had not, in the former converfation, mentioned cow-ardice among the faults of the Duke.—Such failures of memory are incident to writers more diligent than this poet. JOHNSON.

Ang. Hark! how the villain would clofe now, after his treafonable abufes.

Escal. Such a fellow is not to be talk'd withal :—— Away with him to prifon:——Where is the provoft? ——Away with him to prifon ; lay bolts enough upon him: let him fpeak no more:——Away with thofe giglots too,[4] and with the other confederate companion. [*The* Provoft *lays hands on the* Duke.

Duke. Stay, fir; ftay a while.

Ang. What! refifts he? Help him, Lucio.

Lucio. Come, fir; come, fir; come, fir; foh, fir: Why, you bald-pated, lying rafcal! you muft be hooded, muft you? Show your knave's vifage, with a pox to you! fhow your fheep-biting face, and be hang'd an hour! Will't not off?[5]

[*Pulls off the friar's hood, and difcovers the* Duke.

---

[4] ——— *thofe* giglots *too,*] A *giglot* is a wanton wench. So, in *K. Henry VI. P. I:*

" ——————young Talbot was not born
" To be the pillage of a *giglot* wench." Steevens.

[5] ——— *Show your fheep-biting face, and be hang'd* an hour! *Will't not off?*] This is intended to be the common language of vulgar indignation. Our phrafe on fuch occafions is fimply : *fhow your fheep-biting face and be hanged.* The words *an hour* have no particular ufe here, nor are authorifed by cuftom. I fuppofe it was written thus: *fhow your fheep-biting face, and be hanged—an how? will't not off?* In the midland counties, upon any unexpected obftruction or refiftance, it is common to exclaim *an' how?*
Johnson.

Dr. Johnfon's alteration is wrong. In *The Alchemift* we meet with " a man that has been *ftrangled an hour.*"

" What, Piper, ho! *be hang'd a-while,*" is a line of an old madrigal. Farmer.

A fimilar expreffion is found in Ben Jonfon's *Bartholomew Fair,* 1614:

" Leave the bottle behind you, and be *curft a-while.*"
Malone.

Dr. Johnfon is much too pofitive in afferting " that the words *an hour* have no particular ufe here, nor are authorifed by cuftom,"

Duke. Thou art the firſt knave, that e'er made
        a duke.———
Firſt, Provoſt, let me bail theſe gentle three:———
Sneak not away, ſir; [*To* Lucio.] for the friar and
        you
Muſt have a word anon:——lay hold on him.

   Lucio. This may prove worſe than hanging.

   Duke. What you have ſpoke, I pardon; ſit you
        down.———   [*To* Escalus.
We'll borrow place of him:——Sir, by your leave:
                            [*To* Angelo.
Haſt thou or word, or wit, or impudence,
That yet can do thee office?⁵ If thou haſt,
Rely upon it till my tale be heard,
And hold no longer out.

   Ang.   O my dread lord,
I ſhould be guiltier than my guiltineſs,
To think I can be undiſcernable,
When I perceive, your grace, like power divine,
Hath look'd upon my paſſes:⁶ Then, good prince,
No longer ſeſſion hold upon my ſhame,
But let my trial be mine own confeſſion;
Immediate ſentence then, and ſequent death,
Is all the grace I beg.

---

as Dr. Farmer has well proved. The poet evidently refers to the
ancient mode of puniſhing by colliſtrigium, or the original pillory,
made like that part of the pillory at preſent which receives the neck,
only it was placed horizontally, ſo that the culprit hung ſuſpended
in it by his chin, and the back of his head. A diſtinct account
of it may be found, if I miſtake not, in Mr. Barrington's *Obſerva-*
tions on the Statutes. Henley.

   ⁵ ——— *can do thee* office?] i. e. do thee ſervice. Steevens.

   ⁶ ——— *my* paſſes:] i. e. what has paſt in my adminiſtration.
"Not ſo; (ſays the *Edinburgh Magazine,* Nov. 1786.) *Paſſes* means
here *artful devices, deceitful contrivances. Tours de paſſe-paſſe,* in
French, are tricks of jugglery." Steevens.

Duke.   Come hither, Mariana :——
Say, waſt thou e'er contracted to this woman ?

Ang. I was, my lord.

Duke. Go take her hence, and marry her in-
    ſtantly.——
Do you the office, friar; which conſummate,[7]
Return him here again :——Go with him, Provoſt.

[*Exeunt* ANGELO, MARIANA, PETER, *and* Provoſt.

Escal. My lord, I am more amaz'd at his diſ-
    honour,
Than at the ſtrangeneſs of it.

Duke.   Come hither, Iſabel:
Your friar is now your prince : As I was then
Advértiſing, and holy[8] to your buſineſs,
Not changing heart with habit, I am ſtill
Attorney'd at your ſervice.

Isab.   O, give me pardon,
That I, your vaſſal, have employ'd and pain'd
Your unknown ſovereignty.

Duke.   You are pardon'd, Iſabel:
And now, dear maid, be you as free to us.[9]
Your brother's death, I know, ſits at your heart ;
And you may marvel, why I obſcur'd myſelf,
Labouring to ſave his life; and would not rather
Make raſh remonſtrance of my hidden power,[2]
Than let him ſo be loſt: O, moſt kind maid,
It was the ſwift celerity of his death,
Which I did think with ſlower foot came on,

---

7 —— *which* conſummate,] i. e. which *being* conſummated.
                                        MALONE.

8 *Advértiſing, and holy*——] Attentive and faithful. JOHNSON.

9 —— *be you as* free *to us.*] Be as *generous* to us ; pardon us as
we have pardoned you. JOHNSON.

2 *Make raſh remonſtrance of my hidden power,*] That is, *a pre-
mature diſcovery of it.* M. MASON.

That brain'd my purpofe:[2] But, peace be with him!
That life is better life, paft fearing death,
Than that which lives to fear: make it your com—
        fort,
So happy is your brother.

Re-enter ANGELO, MARIANA, PETER, *and* Provoſt.

   ISAB.   I do, my lord.
   DUKE. For this new-married man, approaching
        here,
Whoſe ſalt imagination yet hath wrong'd
Your well-defended honour, you muſt pardon
For Mariana's ſake: but as he adjudg'd your brother,
(Being criminal, in double violation
Of ſacred chaſtity, and of promiſe-breach,[3]
Thereon dependant, for your brother's life,)
The very mercy of the law cries out
Moſt audible, even from his proper tongue,[4]
An Angelo for Claudio, death for death.
Haſte ſtill pays haſte, and leiſure anſwers leiſure;

   [2] *That* brain'd *my purpoſe:*] We now uſe in converſation a like
phraſe: *This it was that knocked my deſign on the head.* Dr. Warburton reads:
       —— baned *my purpoſe.* JOHNSON.
   [3] —— *and of promiſe*-breach,] Our author ought to have
written—" in double violation of ſacred chaſtity, and of *promiſe,*"
inſtead of—promiſe-*breach.* Sir T. Hanmer reads—and *in* promiſe-
breach; but change is certainly here improper, Shakſpeare having
many ſimilar inaccuracies. *Double* indeed may refer to Angelo's
conduct to Mariana and Iſabel; yet ſtill ſome difficulty will remain: for then he will be ſaid to be " *criminal* [inſtead of *guilty*] *of*
promiſe-breach." MALONE.

   [4] —— *even from his* proper *tongue,*] Even from Angelo's *own*
tongue. So, above:
    " In the witneſs of his *proper* ear
    " To call him villain." JOHNSON.

Like doth quit like, and *Meafure* ftill *for Meafure*.[5]
Then, Angelo, thy fault's thus manifefted;
Which though thou would'ft deny, denies thee van-
     tage:[6]
We do condemn thee to the very block
Where Claudio ftoop'd to death, and with like
     hafte;—
Away with him.

   MARI.   O, my moft gracious lord,
I hope you will not mock me with a hufband!

    DUKE. It is your hufband mock'd you with a
     hufband:
Confenting to the fafeguard of your honour,
I thought your marriage fit; elfe imputation,
For that he knew you, might reproach your life,
And choke your good to come: for his poffeffions,
Although by confifcation they are ours,[7]

<hr>

[5] —— Meafure *ftill* for Meafure.] So, in the Third Part of
K. Henry VI:
    " *Meafure for Meafure* muft be anfwered." STEEVENS.
  Shakfpeare might have remembered thefe lines in *A Warning for
faire Women*, a tragedy, 1599 (but apparently written fome years
before):
    " The trial now remains, as fhall conclude
    " *Meafure for Meafure*, and loft blood for blood." MALONE.

[6] —— *denies thee* vantage:] Takes from thee all opportunity,
all expedient of denial. WARBURTON.
  Which though thou would'ft deny, denies thee vantage:] The denial
of which will avail thee nothing. So, in *The Winter's Tale:*
    " Which to deny, concerns more than avails." MALONE.

[7] *Although by* confifcation *they are ours,*] This reading was furnifhed by the editor of the fecond folio. The original copy has
confutation, which may be right:—by his being confuted, or proved
guilty of the fact which he had denied. This however being rather
harfh, I have followed all the modern editors in adopting the
emendation that has been made. MALONE.

  I cannot think it even *poffible* that *confutation* fhould be the true
reading. But the value of the fecond folio, it feems, muft on all
occafions be difputed. STEEVENS.

We do inftate and widow you withal,
To buy you a better hufband.

  Mari.   O, my dear lord,
I crave no other, nor no better man.

  Duke. Never crave him; we are definitive.

  Mari. Gentle, my liege,——   [*Kneeling.*

  Duke.   You do but lofe your labour;
Away with him to death.——Now, fir, [*To* Lucio.]
   to you.

  Mari. O, my good lord!——Sweet Ifabel, take my
   part;
Lend me your knees, and all my life to come
I'll lend you, all my life to do you fervice.

  Duke. Againft all fenfe you do impórtune her:[8]
Should fhe kneel down, in mercy of this fact,
Her brother's ghoft his paved bed would break,
And take her hence in horror.

  Mari.   Ifabel,
Sweet Ifabel, do yet but kneel by me;
Hold up your hands, fay nothing, I'll fpeak all.
They fay, beft men are moulded out of faults;
And, for the moft, become much more the better
For being a little bad: fo may my hufband.
O, Ifabel! will you not lend a knee?

  Duke. He dies for Claudio's death.

  Isab.   Moft bounteous fir,
           [*Kneeling.*
Look, if it pleafe you, on this man condemn'd,

---

 [8] *Againft all* fenfe *you do impórtune her:*] The meaning required
is, againft all reafon and natural affection; Shakfpeare, therefore,
judicioufly ufes a fingle word that implies both; *fenfe* fignifying
both reafon and affection. Johnson.

 The fame expreffion occurs in *The Tempeft*, Act II:
   " You cram thefe words into my ears, againft
   " The ftomach of my *fenfe*." Steevens.

As if my brother liv'd: I partly think,
A due fincerity govern'd his deeds,
Till he did look on me; [9] fince it is fo,
Let him not die: My brother had but juftice,
In that he did the thing for which he died:
For Angelo,
His act did not o'ertake his bad intent; [8]
And muft be buried but as an intent
That perifh'd by the way: [3] thoughts are no fubjects;
Intents but merely thoughts.

[9] *Till he did look on me;*] The Duke has juftly obferved, that Ifabel is *importuned againft all fenfe* to folicit for Angelo, yet here *againft all fenfe* fhe folicits for him. Her argument is extraordinary:

A due fincerity govern'd his deeds
Till he did look on me: fince it is fo,
Let him not die.

That Angelo had committed all the crimes charged againft him, as far as he could commit them, is evident. The only *intent* which *his act did not overtake*, was the defilement of Ifabel. Of this Angelo was only intentionally guilty.

Angelo's crimes were fuch, as muft fufficiently juftify punifh-ment, whether its end be to fecure the innocent from wrong, or to deter guilt by example; and I believe every reader feels fome indignation when he finds him fpared. From what extenuation of his crime, can Ifabel, who yet fuppofes her brother dead, form any plea in his favour? *Since he was good till he looked on me, let him not die.* I am afraid our varlet poet intended to inculcate, that women think ill of nothing that raifes the credit of their beauty, and are ready, however virtuous, to pardon any act which they think incited by their own charms. JOHNSON.

It is evident that Ifabella condefcends to Mariana's importunate folicitation, with great reluctance. Bad as her argument might be, it is the beft that the guilt of Angelo would admit. The facrifice that fhe makes of her revenge to her friendfhip, fcarcely merits to be confidered in fo harfh a light. RITSON.

[8] *His act did not o'ertake his bad intent;*] So, in *Macbeth*:
    " The flighty purpofe never is *o'ertook,*
    " Unlefs the *deed* go with it." STEEVENS.

[3] ——————— buried *but as an intent*
    That perifh'd by the way:] i. e. like the traveller, who dies on his journey, is obfcurely interred, and thought of no more:
    Illum expirantem ——————
    Obliti *ignoto camporum in pulvere linquunt.* STEEVENS.

Mari.   Merely, my lord.

Duke. Your fuit's unprofitable; ftand up, I fay.——
I have bethought me of another fault :——
Provoft, how came it, Claudio was beheaded
At an unufual hour?

Prov.   It was commanded fo.

Duke. Had you a fpecial warrant for the deed?

Prov. No, my good lord ; it was by private meffage.

Duke. For which I do difcharge you of your
office :
Give up your keys.

Prov.   Pardon me, noble lord :
I thought it was a fault, but knew it not ;
Yet did repent me, after more advice :³
For teftimony whereof, one in the prifon,
That fhould by private order elfe have died,
I have referv'd alive.

Duke.   What's he?

Prov.   His name is Barnardine.

Duke. I would thou had'ft done fo by Claudio.——
Go, fetch him hither; let me look upon him.
                              [*Exit* Provoft.

Escal. I am forry, one fo learned and fo wife
As you, lord Angelo, have ftill appear'd,
Should flip fo grofsly, both in the heat of blood,
And lack of temper'd judgement afterward.

Ang. I am forry, that fuch forrow I procure :
And fo deep fticks it in my penitent heart,
That I crave death more willingly than mercy ;
'Tis my deferving, and I do entreat it.

---

³ ——— *after more advice :*] i. e. after more mature confideration.
So, in *Titus Andronicus :*
        " The Greeks, upon *advice*, did bury Ajax." Steevens.

Re-enter Provoſt, BARNARDINE, CLAUDIO, *and*
JULIET.

DUKE. Which is that Barnardine?

PROV.   This, my lord.

DUKE. There was a friar told me of this man:——
Sirrah, thou art ſaid to have a ſtubborn ſoul,
That apprehends no further than this world,
And ſquar'ſt thy life according.   Thou'rt con-
          demn'd;
But, for thoſe earthly faults,[4] I quit them all;
And pray thee, take this mercy to provide
For better times to come:——Friar, adviſe him;
I leave him to your hand.——What muffled fellow's
          that?

PROV. This is another priſoner, that I ſav'd,
That ſhould have died when Claudio loſt his head;
As like almoſt to Claudio, as himſelf.

                    [*Unmuffles* CLAUDIO.

DUKE. If he be like your brother, [*To* ISABELLA.]
          for his ſake
Is he pardon'd; And, for your lovely ſake,
Give me your hand, and ſay you will be mine,
He is my brother too: But fitter time for that.
By this, lord Angelo perceives he's ſafe;[5]
Methinks, I ſee a quick'ning in his eye:——
Well, Angelo, your evil quits you well:[6]

---

[4] ——*for thoſe* earthly faults,] Thy faults, ſo far as they are
puniſhable on earth, ſo far as they are cogniſable by temporal
power, I forgive. JOHNSON.

[5] ——*perceives he's ſafe*;] It is ſomewhat ſtrange that Iſabel
is not made to expreſs either gratitude, wonder, or joy, at the ſight
of her brother. JOHNSON.

[6] ——*your evil* quits you *well:*] *Quits you*, recompenſes, re-
quites you. JOHNSON.

I

Look that you love your wife;[7] her worth, worth
        yours.[8]——
I find an apt remiffion in myfelf:
And yet here's one in place I cannot pardon;[9]——
You, firrah, [*To* Lucio.] that knew me for a fool,
      a coward,
One all of luxury,[2] an afs, a madman;
Wherein have I fo deferved of you,
That you extol me thus?

    Lucio. 'Faith, my lord, I fpoke it but according
to the trick:[3] If you will hang me for it, you may,

[7] *Look, that you love your wife;*] So, in *Promos,* &c.
    " Be loving to good Caffandra, thy wife." STEEVENS.

[8] —— *her worth, worth yours.*] Sir T. Hanmer reads,
    Her worth works *yours.*
This reading is adopted by Dr. Warburton, but for what reafon?
How does her *worth work Angelo's worth?* it has only contributed
to *work* his pardon. The words are, as they are too frequently,
an affected gingle; but the fenfe is plain. *Her worth, worth yours;*
that is, her value is equal to your value, the match is not unworthy
of you. JOHNSON.

[9] —— *here's one in place I cannot pardon;*] The Duke only means
to frighten *Lucio,* whofe final fentence is to marry the woman
whom he had wronged, on which all his other punifhments are
remitted. STEEVENS.

[2] *One all of* luxury,] *Luxury* means *incontinence.* So, in *King
Lear* :
    " To't, *luxury,* pellmell, for I lack foldiers."
                      STEEVENS.

[3] —— *according to the* trick :] To my cuftom, my habitual
practice. JOHNSON.
    Lucio does not fay *my* trick, but *the* trick; nor does he mean
to excufe himfelf by faying that he fpoke according to his ufual
practice, for that would be an aggravation to his guilt, but according to *the* trick and practice of the times. It was probably then
the practice, as it is at this day, for the diffipated and profligate,
to ridicule and flander perfons in high ftation, or of fuperior
virtue. M. MASON.
    According to the *trick,* is, according to the fafhion of thoughtlefs
youth. So, in *Love's Labour's Loft* : " —— yet I have a *trick* of

but I had rather it would pleafe you, I might be whip'd.

Duke. Whip'd firft, fir, and hang'd after.——
Proclaim it, provoft, round about the city;
If any woman's wrong'd by this lewd fellow,
(As I have heard him fwear himfelf, there's one
Whom he begot with child,) let her appear,
And he fhall marry her: the nuptial finifh'd,
Let him be whip'd and hang'd.

Lucio. I befeech your highnefs, do not marry me
to a whore! Your highnefs faid even now, I made
you a duke; good my lord, do not recompenfe me,
in making me a cuckold.

Duke. Upon mine honour, thou fhalt marry her.
Thy flanders I forgive; and therewithal
Remit thy other forfeits: [4]——Take him to prifon:
And fee our pleafure herein executed.

Lucio. Marrying a punk, my lord, is preffing to
death, whipping, and hanging.

Duke. Sland'ring a prince deferves it.——
She, Claudio, that you wrong'd, look you reftore.——
Joy to you, Mariana!—love her, Angelo;
I have confefs'd her, and I know her virtue.——

the old rage." Again, in a collection of epigrams, entitled *Wit's
Bedlam*, printed about the year 1615:
    " Carnus calls lechery a *trick* of youth;
    " So he grows old; but this trick hurts his growth."
                           MALONE.

4 ——'*thy other* forfeits:] Thy other punifhments.
                              JOHNSON.

  To *forfeit* anciently fignified to *commit a carnal offence*. So, in *The
Hiftory of Helyas, Knight of the Swanne*, b. l. no date: " — to
affirme by an untrue knight, that the noble queen Beatrice had
forfayted with a dogge." Again, in the 12th Pageant of the
Coventry Collection of Myfteries, the Virgin Mary tells Jofeph:
    " I dede nevyr *forfete* with man I wys."
MS. Cott. Vefp. D. viii. STEEVENS.

VOL. IV.   C c

Thanks, good friend Efcalus, for thy much good-
 nefs: [5]
There's more behind, that is more gratulate.[6]——
Thanks, Provoft, for thy care, and fecrecy;
We fhall employ thee in a worthier place:——
Forgive him, Angelo, that brought you home

[5] *Thanks, good friend Efcalus, for thy much goodnefs:*] I have
always thought that there is great confufion in this concluding
fpeech. If my criticifm would not be cenfured as too licentious,
I fhould regulate it thus:

 Thanks, good friend Efcalus, for thy much goodnefs,
 Thanks, Provoft, for thy care and fecrecy;
 We fhall employ thee in a worthier place.
 Forgive him, Angelo, that brought you home
 The head of Ragozine for Claudio's.
 Ang. The offence pardons itfelf.
 Duke. There's more behind
 That is more gratulate. Dear Ifabel,
 I have a motion, &c. JOHNSON.

[6] —— *that is more* gratulate.] i. e. *to be more rejoiced in*; meaning, I fuppofe, that there is another world, where he will find yet
greater reafon to rejoice in confequence of his upright miniftry.
Efcalus is reprefented as an ancient nobleman, who, in conjunction
with Angelo, had reached the higheft office of the ftate; and
therefore could not be fufficiently rewarded here; but is neceffarily referred to a future and more exalted recompenfe.
          STEEVENS.

 I cannot approve of Steevens's explanation of this paffage, which
is very far-fetched indeed. The Duke gives Efcalus thanks for
his much goodnefs, but tells him that he had fome other reward
in ftore for him, more acceptable than thanks; which agrees with
what he faid before, in the beginning of this act:

  " —— we hear
  " Such goodnefs of your juftice, that our foul
  " Cannot but yield you forth to public thanks,
  " Fore-running more requital." M. MASON.

Heywood alfo in his *Apology for Actors,* 1612, ufes to gratulate
in the fenfe of to *reward.* " I could not chufe but *gratulate* your
honeft endeavours with this remembrance." MALONE.

 Mr. M. Mafon's explanation may be right; but he forgets that
the fpeech he brings in fupport of it, was delivered before the
denouement of the fcene, and was, at that moment, as much addreffed to *Angelo* as to Efcalus; and for *Angelo* the Duke had other

The head of Ragozine for Claudio's;
The offence pardons itself.—Dear Isabel,
I have a motion much imports your good;
Whereto if you'll a willing ear incline,
What's mine is yours, and what is yours is mine:—
So, bring us to our palace; where we'll show
What's yet behind, that's meet you all should know.

                           [Exeunt.]

tainly no reward or honours, in store.—Besides, I cannot but regard the word—*requital* as an interpolation, because it destroys the measure, without improvement of the sense. " Fore-running more," therefore, would only signify—*preceding farther thanks.* STEEVENS.

  [7] I cannot help taking notice with how much judgement Shakspeare has given turns to this story from what he found it in Cynthio Giraldi's novel. In the first place, the brother is there actually executed, and the governour sends his head in a bravado to the sister, after he had debauched her on promise of marriage: a circumstance of too much horror and villainy for the stage. And, in the next place, the sister afterwards is, to folder up her disgrace, married to the governour, and begs his life of the emperour, though he had unjustly been the death of her brother. Both which absurdities the poet has avoided by the episode of Mariana, a creature purely of his own invention. The Duke's remaining incognito at home to supervise the conduct of his deputy, is also entirely our author's fiction.

  This story was attempted for the scene before our author was fourteen years old, by one George Whetstone, in *Two Comical Discourses,* as they are called, containing the right excellent and famous history of Promos and Cassandra, printed with the black letter, 1578. The author going that year with Sir Humphrey Gilbert to Norimbega, left them with his friends to publish.

                              THEOBALD.

  The novel of Cynthio Giraldi, from which Shakspeare is supposed to have borrowed this fable, may be read in *Shakspeare illustrated,* elegantly translated, with remarks which will assist the enquirer to discover how much absurdity Shakspeare has admitted or avoided.

  I cannot but suspect that some other had new-modelled the novel of Cynthio, or written a story which in some particulars resembled it, and that Cynthio was not the author whom Shakspeare immediately followed. The Emperor in Cynthio is named Maximine; the Duke, in Shakspeare's enumeration of the persons of the drama, is called Vincentio. This appears a very slight remark; but since

                        C c 2

the Duke has no name in the play, nor is ever mentioned but by his title, why should he be called Vincentio among the *persons*, but because the name was copied from the story, and placed superfluously at the head of the list by the mere habit of transcription? It is therefore likely that there was then a story of Vincentio Duke of Vienna, different from that of Maximine Emperor of the Romans.

Of this play the light or comic part is very natural and pleasing, but the grave scenes, if a few passages be excepted, have more labour than elegance. The plot is rather intricate than artful. The time of the action is indefinite; some time, we know not how much, must have elapsed between the recess of the Duke and the imprisonment of Claudio; for he must have learned the story of Mariana in his disguise, or he delegated his power to a man already known to be corrupted. The unities of action and place are sufficiently preserved. JOHNSON.

The duke probably had learnt the story of Mariana in some of his former retirements, " having ever loved the life removed." (Page 203) " And he had a suspicion that Angelo was but a *seemer*. (page 207) and therefore he stays to watch him." BLACKSTONE.

The Fable of Whetstone's *Promos and Cassandra*, 1578.

" The Argument of the whole *History*."

" In the cyttie of *Julio* (sometimes under the dominion of *Corvinus* kynge of *Hungarie* and *Bohemia*,) there was a law, that what man so ever committed adultery should lose his head, and the woman offender should weare some disguised apparel, during her life, to make her infamously noted. This severe lawe, by the favour of some mercifull magistrate, became little regarded, untill the time of lord *Promos*' auctority; who convicting a young gentleman named *Andrugio* of incontinency, condemned both him and his minion to the execution of this statute. *Andrugio* had a very virtuous and beautiful gentlewoman to his sister, named *Cassandra*: *Cassandra*, to enlarge her brother's life, submitted an humble petition to the lord *Promos*: *Promos* regarding her good behaviours, and fantasying her great beawtie, was much delighted with the sweete order of her talke; and doyng good, that evill might come thereof, for a time he repryved her brother: but wicked man, tourning his liking into unlawfull lust, he set downe the spoile of her honour, raunsome for her brother's life: chaste *Cassandra*, abhorring both him and his sute, by no persuasion would yeald to this raunsome. But in fine, wonne by the importunitye of hir brother (pleading for life), upon these conditions she agreed to *Promos*. First, that he should pardon her brother.

and after marry her. *Promos*, as feareles in promiffe, as careleffe in performance, with follemne vowe fygned her conditions; but worfe then any infydell, his will fatiffyed, he performed neither the one nor the other: for to keepe his auctoritye unfpotted with favour, and to prevent *Caffandra's* clamors, he commaunded the gayler fecretly, to prefent *Caffandra* with her brother's head. The gayler, [touched] with the outcryes of *Andrugio*, (abhorryng *Promos'* lewdenes) by the providence of God provided thus for his fafety. He prefented *Caffandra* with a felon's head newlie executed; who knew it not, being mangled, from her brother's (who was fet at libertie by the gayler). [She] was fo agreeved at this trecherye, that, at the point to kyl her felf, fhe fpared that ftroke, to be avenged of *Promos:* and devyfing a way, fhe concluded, to make her fortunes knowne unto the kinge. She, executing this refolution, was fo highly favoured of the king, that forthwith he hafted to do juftice on *Promos:* whofe judgment was, to marry *Caffandra*, to repaire her crafed honour; which donne, for his hainous offence, he fhould lofe his head. This maryage folempnifed, *Caffandra* tyed in the greateft bondes of affection to her hufband, became an earneft futer for his life: the kinge, tendringe the generall benefit of the comon weale before her fpecial cafe, although he favoured her much, would not graunt her fute. *Andrugio* (difguifed amonge the company) forrowing the griefe of his fifter, bewrayde his fafety, and craved pardon. The kinge, to renowne the vertues of *Caffandra*, pardoned both him and *Promos.* The circumftances of this rare hiftorye, in action livelye foloweth."

Whetftone, however, has not afforded a very correct analyfis of his play, which contains a mixture of comick fcenes, between a Bawd, a Pimp, Felons, &c. together with fome ferious fituations which are not defcribed. STEEVENS.

One paragraph of the foregoing narrative being ftrangely confufed in the old copy, by fome careleffnefs of the printer, I have endeavoured to rectify it, by tranfpofing a few words, and adding two others, which are included within crotchets. MALONE.

MUCH ADO

ABOUT

NOTHING.*

* MUCH ADO ABOUT NOTHING.] The ſtory is taken from Arioſto, Orl. Fur. B. V. POPE.

It is true, as Mr. Pope has obſerved, that ſomewhat reſembling the ſtory of this play is to be found in the fifth book of the Orlando Furioſo. In Spenſer's Faery Queen, B. II. c. iv. as remote an original may be traced. A novel, however, of Belleforeſt, copied from another of Bandello, ſeems to have furniſhed Shakſpeare with his fable, as it approaches nearer in all its particulars to the play before us, than any other performance known to be extant. I have ſeen ſo many verſions from this once popular collection, that I entertain no doubt but that a great majority of the tales it comprehends, have made their appearance in an Engliſh dreſs. Of that particular ſtory which I have juſt mentioned. viz. the 18th hiſtory in the third volume, no tranſlation has hitherto been met with.

This play was entered at Stationers' Hall, Aug. 23, 1600.

STEEVENS.

Arioſto is continually quoted for the fable of *Much ado about Nothing* ; but I ſuſpect our poet to have been ſatisfied with the *Geneura* of Turberville. " The tale (ſays Harington) is a pretie comical matter, and hath bin written in *Engliſh* verſe ſome few years paſt, learnedly and with good grace, by M. George Turbervil." *Arioſto*, fol. 1591, p. 39. FARMER.

I ſuppoſe this comedy to have been written in 1600, in which year it was printed. See *An Attempt to aſcertain the Order of Shakſpeare's Plays*, Vol. I. MALONE.

Persons reprefented.

Don Pedro, *Prince of* Arragon.
Don John, *his baftard brother.*
Claudio, *a young lord of* Florence, *favourite to Don*
Pedro.
Benedick, *a young lord of* Padua, *favoured likewife*
by Don Pedro.
Leonato, *governor of* Meffina.
Antonio, *his brother.*
Balthazar, *fervant to Don* Pedro.
Borachio, ⎱ *followers of Don* John.
Conrade, ⎰
Dogberry, ⎱ *two foolifh officers.*
Verges, ⎰
A Sexton.
A Friar.
A Boy.

Hero, *daughter to* Leonato.
Beatrice, *niece to* Leonato.
Margaret, ⎱ *gentlewomen attending on* Hero.
Urfula, ⎰

Meffengers, Watch, and Attendants.

SCENE, Meffina.

MUCH ADO

ABOUT

NOTHING.

ACT I.   SCENE I.

Before LEONATO's *Houſe.*

Enter LEONATO, HERO,[1] BEATRICE, *and Others,*
with a Meſſenger.

LEON. I learn in this letter, that Don Pedro of
Arragon comes this night to Meſſina.

MESS. He is very near by this; he was not three
leagues off when I left him.

LEON. How many gentlemen have you loſt in this
action?

[1] *Innogen,* (the mother of Hero,) in the old quarto that I have
ſeen of this play, printed in 1600, is mentioned to enter in two
ſeveral ſcenes.   The ſucceeding editions have all continued her
name in the Dramatis Perſonæ.   But I have ventured to expunge
it; there being no mention of her through the play, no one ſpeech
addreſs'd to her, nor one ſyllable ſpoken by her.   Neither is there
any one paſſage, from which we have any reaſon to determine that
Hero's mother was living.   It ſeems as if the poet had in his
firſt plan deſigned ſuch a character: which, on a ſurvey of it, he
found would be ſuperfluous; and therefore he left it out.
                                                    THEOBALD.

The name of Hero's mother occurs alſo in the firſt folio. "Enter
Leonato governor of Meſſina, *Innogen his wife,*" &c. STEEVENS.

Mess. But few of any fort,[3] and none of name.

Leon. A victory is twice itfelf, when the atchiever brings home full numbers. I find here, that Don Pedro hath beftowed much honour on a young Florentine, called Claudio.

Mess. Much deferved on his part, and equally remember'd by Don Pedro: He hath borne himfelf beyond the promife of his age; doing, in the figure of a lamb, the feats of a lion: he hath, indeed, better better'd expectation, than you muft expect of me to tell you how.

Leon. He hath an uncle here in Meffina will be very much glad of it.

Mess. I have already delivered him letters, and there appears much joy in him; even fo much, that joy could not fhow itfelf modeft enough, without a badge of bitternefs.[4]

---

[3] —— *of any* fort,] *Sort* is rank, diftinction. So, in Chapman's verfion of the 16th Book of *Homer's Odyffey* :

" A fhip, and in her many a man of *fort.*"

I incline, however, to Mr. M. Mafon's eafier explanation. Of any *fort*, fays he, means of any kind whatfoever. *There were but few killed of any kind, and none of rank.* STEEVENS.

[4] —— *joy could not fhow itfelf* modeft *enough, without a* badge *of bitternefs.*] This is judicioufly expreffed. Of all the tranfports of joy, that which is attended with tears is leaft offenfive; becaufe, carrying with it this mark of pain, it allays the envy that ufually attends another's happinefs. This he finely calls a *modeft* joy, fuch a one as did not infult the obferver by an indication of happinefs unmixed with pain. WARBURTON.

A fomewhat fimilar expreffion occurs in Chapman's verfion of the 10th Book of the *Odyffey* :

" —————— our eyes wore
" The fame wet *badge* of weak humanity."

This is an idea which Shakfpeare feems to have been delighted to introduce. It occurs again in *Macbeth* :

" —— my plenteous joys,
" Wanton in fullnefs, feek to hide themfelves
" In drops of forrow." STEEVENS.

A *badge* being the diftinguifhing *mark* worn in our author's time by the fervants of noblemen, &c. on the fleeve of their liveries, with

Leon. Did he break out into tears?

Mess. In great meafure.[5]

Leon. A kind overflow of kindnefs: There are no faces truer [6] than thofe that are fo wafhed. How much better is it to weep at joy, than to joy at weeping?

Beat. I pray you, is fignior Montanto returned [7] from the wars, or no?

Mess. I know none of that name, lady; there was none fuch in the army of any fort.[8]

Leon. What is he that you afk for, niece?

Hero. My coufin means fignior Benedick of Padua.

Mess. O, he is returned; and as pleafant as ever he was.

Beat. He fet up his bills here in Meffina,[9] and

his ufual licence he employs the word to fignify a *mark* or *token* in general. So, in *Macbeth:*
"Their hands and faces were all *badg'd* with blood." MALONE.

[5] *In great meafure.*] i. e. in abundance. STEEVENS.

[6] —— *no faces* truer—] That is, none *honefter*, none *more fincere.* JOHNSON.

[7] ——*is fignior* Montanto *returned*—] *Montante*, in Spanifh, is a *huge two-banded fword*, [a title] given, with much humour, to one [whom] the fpeaker would reprefent as a boafter or bravado. WARBURTON.
Montanto was one of the ancient terms of the fencing-fchool. So, in *Every Man in his Humour:* "—— your punto, your reverfo, your ftoccata, your imbrocata, your paffada, your *montanto,*" &c. Again, in *The Merry Wives of Windfor:*
"—— thy reverfe, thy diftance, thy *montant.*" STEEVENS.

[8] —— *there was none fuch in the army of any* fort.] Not meaning there was none fuch of *any order or degree whatever,* but that there was none fuch of *any quality above the common.* WARBURTON.

[9] *He fet up his bills,* &c.] So, in B. Jonfon's *Every Man out of his Humour,* Shift fays:
"This is rare, I have *fet up* my *bills* without difcovery."
Again, in *Swetnam Arraign'd,* 1620:
"I have bought foils already, *fet up bills,*
"Hung up my two-hand fword," &c.

challenged Cupid at the flight:[9] and my uncle's
fool, reading the challenge, subscribed for Cupid,

Again, in Nash's *Have with you to Saffron Walden*, &c. 1596:
"——*setting up bills*, like a bearward or fencer, what fights
we shall have, and what weapons she will meet me at."
The following account of one of these challenges, taken from
an ancient MS. of which further mention is made in a note on
The Merry Wives of Windsor, Act I. sc. i. may not be unac-
ceptable to the inquisitive reader. "Item a challenge playde
before the King's majestie (Edward VI.) at Westminster, by three
maisters, Willyam Pascall, Robert Greene, and W. Browne, at
seven kynde of weapons. That is to saye, the axe, the pike, the
rapier and target, the rapier and cloke, and with two swords,
agaynst all alyens and strangers being borne without the King's
dominions, of what countrie so ever he or they were, geving them
warning by theyr *bills set up* by the three maisters, the space of
eight weeks before the sayd challenge was playde; and it was
holden four severall Sundayes one after another." It appears from
the same work, that all challenges "to any maister within the
realme of Englande being an Englishe man," were against the
statutes of the "Noble science of Defence."
Beatrice means, that Benedick published a general challenge,
like a prize-fighter. STEEVENS.

9 ——*challenged Cupid at the* flight:] *Flight* (as Mr. Douce
observes to me) does not here mean an *arrow*, but a sort of shooting
called *roving*, or shooting at long lengths. The arrows used at
this sport are called *flight*-arrows; as were those used in battle for
great distances. So, in Beaumont and Fletcher's *Bonduca*:
"—— not the quick rack swifter;
"The virgin from the hated ravisher
"Not half so fearful: not a *flight* drawn home,
"A round stone from a sling,——."
Again, in *A Woman kill'd with Kindness*, 1617:
"We have tied our geldings to a tree, two *flight-shot* off."
Again, in Middleton's *Game of Chess*:
"Who, as they say, discharg'd it like a *flight*."
Again, in *The Entertainment at Causome House*, &c. 1613:
"—— it being from the park about two *flight-shots* in length."
Again, in *The Civil Wars* of Daniel, B. VIII. st. 15:
"—— and assign'd
"The archers their *flight*-shafts to shoot away;
"Which th' adverse side (with fleet and dimness blind,
"Mistaken in the distance of the way,)
"Answer with their *sheaf-arrows*, that came short
"Of their intended aim, and did no hurt."

and challenged him at the bird-bolt.[2]—I pray you,
how many hath he killed and eaten in thefe wars?

Holinfhed makes the fame diftinction in his account of the fame
occurrence, and adds, that thefe *flights* were provided on purpofe.
Again, in Holinfhed, p. 649: " He caufed the foldiers to fhoot
their *flights* towards the lord Audlies company."
    Mr. Tollet obferves, that the length of a *flight-foot* feems afcer-
tained by a paffage in Leland's Itinerary, 1769, Vol. IV. p. 44:
" The paffage into it at ful fe is a *flite-foot* over, as much as the
Tamife is above the bridge."—It were eafy to know the length
of London-bridge, and Stowe's Survey may inform the curious
reader whether the river has been narrowed by embanking fince
the days of Leland.
    Mr. Douce, however, obferves, that as the length of the fhot
depended on the ftrength and fkill of the archer, nothing can with
certainty be determined by the paffage quoted from Leland.
                                                    STEEVENS.

    The *flight* was an arrow of a particular kind:—In the Harleian
Catalogue of MSS. Vol. I. n. 69. is " a challenge of the lady
Maiee's fervants to all comers, to be performed at *Greenwiche*—to
fhoot ftandart arrow, or *flight.*" I find the title-page of an old
pamphlet ftill more explicit—" A new *poft*—a marke exceeding
neceffary for all men's arrows: whether the great man's *flight,* the
gallant's *rover,* the wife man's *pricke-fhaft,* the poor man's *but-
fhaft,* or the fool's *bird-bolt.*" FARMER.

    [2] —— *at the* bird-bolt.] The *bird-bolt* is a fhort thick arrow
without a point, and fpreading at the extremity fo much, as to
leave a flat furface, about the breadth of a fhilling. Such are to
this day in ufe to kill rooks with, and are fhot from a crofs-
bow. So, in Marfton's *What You Will,* 1607:
    " —— ignorance fhould fhoot
    " His grofs-knobb'd *bird-bolt* ——.''
Again, in *Love in a Maze,* 1632:
    " —— Cupid,
    " Pox of his *bird-bolt!* Venus,
    " Speak to thy boy to fetch his *arrow* back,
    " Or ftrike her with a *fharp one!*" STEEVENS.

    The meaning of the whole is—Benedick, from a vain conceit of
his influence over women, challenged Cupid at *roving* (a particular
kind of archery, in which *flight*-arrows are ufed.) In other words,
he challenged him *to fhoot at hearts.* The fool, to ridicule this
piece of vanity, in his turn challenged Benedick to fhoot at crows
with the crofs-bow and bird-bolt; an inferior kind of archery

I

But how many hath he killed? ~~for indeed, I~~ pro-

:too
: it

efe

lp
th

~~good foldier to a lady;~~
is he to a lord?

   Mess. A lord to a lord, a man to a man, ~~stuffed~~
with all honourable virtues.[3]

   Beat. It is fo, indeed; he is no lefs than a ſtuffed
man: but for the ſtuffing,—Well, we are all mortal.[4]

ufed by Fools, who, for obvious reafons, were not permitted to ſhoot
with pointed arrows: Whence the proverb—" A fool's bolt is foon
ſhot."   D o u c e.

   [2] —— *he'll be* meet *with you,*]   This is a very common expreffion in the midland counties, and fignifies *he'll be your match,
he'll be even with you.*

   So, in ΤΕΧΝΟΓΑΜΙΑ, by B. Holiday, 1618:
       " Go meet her, or elfe ſhe'll *be meet* with me." [o]

   [3] —— ſtuffed *with all honourable virtues*—
inſtance, has no ridiculous meaning.   Mr.
Mede in his *Difcourfes on Scripture,* ſpea[k]
" —— he whom God had *ſtuffed* with fo
Edwards's MS.

   Again, in *The Winter's Tale:*
       " —— whom you know
       " Of *ſtuff'd* fufficiency."
Un homme bien *etoffé,* fignifies, in Fre[nch] —— *man in good cir-
cumſtances.*   S t e e v e n s.

   [4] —— *he is no lefs than a* ſtuffed *man: but for the* ſtuffing,—*Well,
we are all mortal.*]   Mr. Theobald plumed himfelf much on the

Leon. You muſt not, ſir, miſtake my niece: there is a kind of merry war betwixt ſignior Benedick and her: they never meet, but there is a ſkirmiſh of wit between them.

Beat. Alas, he gets nothing by that. In our laſt conflict, four of his five wits ⁵ went halting off, and now is the whole man governed with one: ſo that if he have wit enough to keep himſelf warm, let him bear it for a difference between himſelf and his horſe; ⁶ for it is all the wealth that he hath left, to

---

pointing of this paſſage; which, by the way, he might learn from D'Avenant: but he ſays not a word, nor any one elſe that I know of, about the reaſon of this abruption. The truth is, Beatrice ſtarts an idea at the words *ſtuff'd man*; and prudently checks her-ſelf in the purſuit of it. A *ſtuff'd man* was one of the many cant phraſes for a *cuckold*. In *Lily's Midas,* we have an inventory of *Motto's moveables:* " Item, ſays Petulus, one paire of hornes in the bride-chamber on the *bed's head.*—The *beaſt's* head, obſerves Licio; for *Motto is ſtuff'd in the head,* and theſe are among *un-moveable goods.*" FARMER.

⁵ ——*four of his five* wits—] In our author's time *wit* was the general term for intellectual powers. So, *Davies on the Soul:*
   " *Wit,* ſeeking truth from cauſe to cauſe aſcends,
      " And never reſts till it the firſt attain;
   " *Will,* ſeeking good, finds many middle ends,
      " But never ſtays till it the laſt do gain."
And, in another part:
   " But if a phrenzy do poſſeſs the brain,
      " It ſo diſturbs and blots the forms of things,
   " As fantaſy proves altogether vain,
      " And to the *wit* no true relation brings.
   " Then doth the *wit,* admitting all for true,
      " Build fond concluſions on thoſe idle grounds;"——
The *wits* ſeem to have been reckoned five, by analogy to the five ſenſes, or the five inlets of ideas. JOHNSON.

⁶ —— *if he have* wit enough to keep himſelf warm, *let him bear it for a* difference, *&c.*] *Such a one has wit enough to keep himſelf warm,* is a proverbial expreſſion. So in *The Wiſe Woman of Hogſden,* 1638: " You are the wiſe woman, are you? and have *wit to keep yourſelf warm* enough, I warrant you." Again, in *Cynthia's Revels,* by Ben Jonſon:

in Haywood's Epigrams on Proverbs:
   "wit kept by warmth."
u art wiſe inough if thou keepe thee warme,
it the leaſt colde that cumeth, kilth thy wit by h

be known a reasonable creature.——Who is his companion now? He hath every month a new sworn brother.[6]

Mess. Is it possible?

Beat. Very easily possible: he wears his faith[7] but as the fashion of his hat, it ever changes with the next block.[8]

Mess. I see, lady, the gentleman is not in your books.[9]

" —— your whole self cannot but be perfectly wise; for your hands have *wit enough to keep themselves warm.*"

To bear any thing for a *difference*, is a term in heraldry. So, in *Hamlet*, Ophelia says:

" —— you may wear your rue with a *difference.*"

STEEVENS.

[6] ——*sworn brother.*] i. e. one with whom he hath *sworn* (as was anciently the custom among adventurers) to share fortunes. See Mr. Whalley's note on—" we'll be all three *sworn-brothers* to France," in *King Henry V.* Act II. sc. i. STEEVENS.

[7] —— *he wears his* faith ——] Not religious profession, but *profession of friendship*; for the speaker gives it as the reason of her asking, *who was now his companion?* that *he had every month a new sworn brother.* WARBURTON.

[8] —— *with the next* block.] A *block* is the mould on which a hat is formed. So, in Decker's *Satiromastix*:

" Of what fashion is this knight's wit? of what *block?*

See a note on *K. Lear*, Act IV. sc. vi.

The old writers sometimes use the word *block*, for the hat itself.

STEEVENS.

[9] —— *the gentleman is not* in your books.] This is a phrase used, I believe, by more than understand it. *To be in one's books is to be in one's* codicils *or* will, *to be among friends set down for legacies.*

JOHNSON.

I rather think that the *books* alluded to, are memorandum-books, like the visiting books of the present age. So, in Decker's *Honest Whore*, Part II. 1630:

" I am sure her name was in my *table-book* once."

Or, perhaps the allusion is to matriculation at the University. So, in *Aristippus*, or *The Jovial Philosopher*, 1630:

" You must be matriculated, and have your name recorded in *Albo Academiæ.*"

I

Beat. No: an he were, I would burn my study. But, I pray you, who is his companion? Is there no

Again: "What have you enrolled him in *albo?* Have you fully admitted him into the society?—to be a member of the body academic?"

Again: "And if I be not entred, and have my name admitted into some of their *books,* let," &c.

And yet I think the following passage in *The Maid's Revenge,* by Shirley, 1639, will sufficiently support my first supposition:

"Pox of your compliment, you were best not write in her *table-books.*"

It appears to have been anciently the custom to *chronicle the small beer* of every occurrence, whether literary or domestic, in *table-books.*

So, in the play last quoted:

"Devolve itself!—that word is not in my *table-books.*"

Hamlet likewise has,—"my *tables,*" &c.

Again, in *The Whore of Babylon,* 1607:

"—— Campeius!—Babylon

"His name hath *in her tables.*"

Again, in *Acolastus,* a comedy, 1540:

"—— We weyl haunse thee, or set thy name into our *felowship boke,* with clappynge of handes," &c.

I know not exactly to what custom this last quoted passage refers, unless to the *album:* for just after, the same expression occurs again: that "—from henceforthe thou may'st have a place worthy for thee in our *whyte:* from hence thou may'st have thy name written in our *boke.*"

It should seem from the following passage in *The Taming of a Shrew,* that this phrase might have originated from the *Herald's Office:*

"A herald, Kate! oh, put me *in thy books!*"

After all, the following note in one of the Harleian MSS. No. 847, may be the best illustration:

"W. C. to Henry Fradsham, Gent. the owner of this book:

"Some write their fantasies in verse

"*In theire bookes* where they friendshippe shewe,

"Wherein oft tymes they doe rehearse

"The great good will that they do owe," &c. STEEVENS.

This phrase has not been exactly interpreted. *To be in a man's books,* originally meant to be in the list of his *retainers.* Sir John Mandeville tells us, "alle the mynstrelles that comen before the great Chan ben witholden with him, as of his houshold, and entred in his *bookes,* as for his own men." FARMER.

A *servant* and a *lover* were in Cupid's Vocabulary, synonymous.

young fquarer [a] now, that will make a voyage with him to the devil?

Mess. He is moft in the company of the right noble Claudio.

Beat. O Lord! he will hang upon him like a difeafe : he is fooner caught than the peftilence, and the taker runs prefently mad. God help the noble Claudio! if he have caught the Benedick, it will coft him a thoufand pound ere he be cured.

Mess. I will hold friends with you, lady.

Beat. Do, good friend.

Leon. You will never run mad, niece.

Beat. No, not till a hot January.

Mess. Don Pedro is approach'd.

Enter Don PEDRO, *attended by* BALTHAZAR *and others;* Don JOHN, CLAUDIO, *and* BENEDICK.

D. Pedro. Good fignior Leonato, you are come to meet your trouble : the fashion of the world is to avoid coft, and you encounter it.

Leon. Never came trouble to my houfe in the likenefs of your grace : for trouble being gone, comfort fhould remain; but, when you depart from me, forrow abides, and happinefs takes his leave.

Hence perhaps the phrafe—*to be in a perfon's books*—was applied equally to the *lover* and the *menial attendant.* MALONE.

There is a MS. of Lord Burleigh's, in the Marquis of Lanf-downe's library, wherein, among many other houfehold concerns, he has entered the names of all his fervants, &c. DOUCE.

[a] ———*young* fquarer——] A *fquarer* I take to be a cholerick, quarrelfome fellow, for in this fenfe Shakfpeare ufes the word to *fquare.* So, in *A Midfummer Night's Dream,* it is faid of Oberon and Titania, that *they never meet but they* fquare. So the fenfe may be, *Is there no* hot-blooded *youth that will keep him company through all his mad pranks?* JOHNSON.

D. Pedro. You embrace your charge [3] too willingly.—I think, this is your daughter.

Leon. Her mother hath many times told me fo.

Bene. Were you in doubt, fir, that you afk'd
her?

Leon. Signior Benedick, no; for then were you
a child.

D. Pedro. You have it full, Benedick: we may
guefs by this what you are, being a man. Truly,
the lady fathers herfelf:—Be happy, lady! for you
are like an honourable father.

Bene. If fignior Leonato be her father, fhe would
not have his head on her fhoulders, for all Meffina,
as like him as fhe is.

Beat. I wonder, that you will ftill be talking,
fignior Benedick; no body marks you.

Bene. What, my dear lady Difdain! are you yet
living?

Beat. Is it poffible, difdain fhould die, while fhe
hath fuch meet food to feed it, as fignior Benedick? [4]
Courtefy itfelf muft convert to difdain, if you come
in her prefence.

Bene. Then is courtefy a turn-coat:—But it is
certain, I am loved of all ladies, only you excepted:
and I would I could find in my heart that I had not
a hard heart; for, truly, I love none.

---

[3] ——*your* charge—] That is, your *burden*, your *incumbrance.*
                                                        JOHNSON.
Charge does not mean, as Dr. Johnfon explains it, *burden, in-*
cumbrance, but " the perfon committed to your care." So it is
ufed in the relationfhip between guardian and ward. DOUCE.

[4] ——*fuch meet food to feed it, as fignior Benedick?*] A kindred
thought occurs in *Coriolanus,* Act II. fc. i:
" Our very priefts muft become *mockers,* if they encounter fuch
ridiculous fubjects as you are." STEEVENS.

Vol VI.
C-17.

BEAT. A dear happiness to women; they would elfe have been troubled with a pernicious fuitor. I thank God, and my cold blood, I am of your humour for that; I had rather hear my dog bark at a crow, than a man fwear he loves me.

BENE. God keep your ladyfhip ftill in that mind! fo fome gentleman or other fhall 'fcape a predeftinate fcratched face.

BEAT. Scratching could not make it worfe, an 'twere fuch a face as yours were.

BENE. Well, you are a rare parrot-teacher.

BEAT. A bird of my tongue, is better than a beaft of yours.

BENE. I would, my horfe had the fpeed of your tongue; and fo good a continuer: But keep your way o' God's name; I have done.

BEAT. You always end with a jade's trick; I know you of old.

D. PEDRO. This is the fum of all: Leonato,—fignior Claudio, and fignior Benedick,—my dear friend Leonato, hath invited you all. I tell him, we fhall ftay here at the leaft a month; and he heartily prays, fome occafion may detain us longer: I dare fwear he is no hypocrite, but prays from his heart.

LEON. If you fwear, my lord, you fhall not be forfworn.—Let me bid you welcome, my lord: being reconciled to the prince your brother, I owe you all duty.

D. JOHN. I thank you: [5] I am not of many words, but I thank you.

LEON. Pleafe it your grace lead on?

---

[5] *I thank you:*] The poet has judicioufly marked the gloominefs of Don John's character, by making him averfe to the common forms of civility. SIR J. HAWKINS.

D. Pedro. Your hand, Leonato; we will go together.

[*Exeunt all but* BENEDICK *and* CLAUDIO.

Claud. Benedick, didſt thou note the daughter
of ſignior Leonato?

Bene. I noted her not; but I looked on her.

Claud. Is ſhe not a modeſt young lady?

Bene. Do you queſtion me, as an honeſt man
ſhould do, for my ſimple true judgement? or would
you have me ſpeak after my cuſtom, as being a pro-
feſſed tyrant to their ſex?

Claud. No, I pray thee, ſpeak in ſober judgement.

Bene. Why, i'faith, methinks ſhe is too low for
a high praiſe, too brown for a fair praiſe, and too
little for a great praiſe: only this commendation I
can afford her; that were ſhe other than ſhe is, ſhe
were unhandſome; and being no other but as ſhe is,
I do not like her.

Claud. Thou thinkeſt, I am in ſport; I pray
thee, tell me truly how thou likeſt her.

Bene. Would you buy her, that you inquire after
her?

Claud. Can the world buy ſuch a jewel?

Bene. Yea, and a caſe to put it into. But ſpeak
you this with a ſad brow? or do you play the flouting Jack; [6] to tell us Cupid is a good hare-finder,

---

[6] —— *the flouting* Jack;] *Jack,* in our author's time, I know
not why, was a term of contempt. So, in *King Henry IV.* P. I.
Act III: " —— the prince is a *Jack,* a ſneak-cup."
   Again, in *The Taming of the Shrew:*
      " —— raſcal fidler,
      " And twangling *Jack,* with twenty ſuch vile terms," &c.
   See in *Minſheu's Dict.* 1617: " A *Jack* ſauce, or ſaucie *Jack.*"
See alſo Chaucer's *Cant. Tales,* ver. 14816, and the note, edit,
Tyrwhitt. MALONE.

and Vulcan a rare carpenter? ⁷ Come, in what key
ſhall a man take you, to go in the ſong? ⁸

CLAUD. In mine eye, ſhe is the ſweeteſt lady that
ever I looked on.

BENE. I can ſee yet without ſpectacles, and I ſee
no ſuch matter : there's her couſin, an ſhe were not
poſſeſſed with a fury, exceeds her as much in beauty, as the firſt of May doth the laſt of December.
But I hope, you have no intent to turn huſband;
have you?

⁷ —— *to tell us Cupid is a good hare-finder*, &c.] I know not
whether I conceive the jeſt here intended. Claudio hints his
love of Hero. Benedick aſks, whether he is ſerious, or whether
he only means to jeſt, and to tell them that *Cupid is a good hare-*
finder, and Vulcan a rare carpenter. A man praiſing a pretty lady
in jeſt, may ſhow the quick ſight of Cupid, but what has it to do
with the *carpentry* of Vulcan? Perhaps the thought lies no deeper
than this, *Do you mean to tell us as new what we all know already?*
                                             JOHNSON.

I believe no more is meant by thoſe ludicrous expreſſions than
this.—Do you mean, ſays Benedick, to amuſe us with improbable
ſtories?

An ingenious correſpondent, whoſe ſignature is R. W. explains
the paſſage in the ſame ſenſe, but more amply. " Do you mean
to tell us that love is not blind, and that fire will not conſume
what is combuſtible?"—for both theſe propoſitions are implied in
making Cupid *a good hare-finder*, and Vulcan (the God of fire)
a good carpenter. In other words, *would you convince me, whoſe*
opinion on this head is well known, that you can be in love without
being blind, and can play with the flame of beauty without being
ſcorched. STEEVENS.

I explain the paſſage thus : *Do you ſcoff and mock in telling us*
that Cupid, who is blind, is a good hare-finder, which requires a
quick eye-ſight ; and that Vulcan, a blackſmith, is a rare carpenter?
                                             TOLLET.

After ſuch attempts at decent illuſtration, I am afraid that he
who wiſhes to know why Cupid is a good *hare-finder*, muſt diſcover
it by the aſſiſtance of many quibbling alluſions of the ſame ſort,
about *hair* and *boar*, in Mercutio's ſong in the ſecond Act of *Romeo*
and Juliet. COLLINS.

⁸ —— to go *in the ſong?*] i. e. to join with you in your ſong—
to ſtrike in with you in the ſong. STEEVENS.

CLAUD. I would scarce trust myself, though I had sworn the contrary, if Hero would be my wife.

BENE. Is it come to this, i'faith? Hath not the world one man, but he will wear his cap with suspicion?[9] Shall I never see a bachelor of threescore again? Go to, i'faith; an thou wilt needs thrust thy neck into a yoke, wear the print of it, and sigh away Sundays.[2] Look, Don Pedro is returned to seek you.

Re-enter Don PEDRO.

D. PEDRO. What secret hath held you here, that you followed not to Leonato's?

9 —— *wear his* cap *with suspicion?*] That is, subject his head to the disquiet of jealousy. JOHNSON.

In Painter's *Palace of Pleasure*, p. 233, we have the following passage: " All they that *weare hornes* be pardoned to weare their *cappes* upon their heads." HENDERSON.

In our author's time none but the inferior classes wore caps, and such persons were termed in contempt *flat-caps*. All gentlemen wore *hats*. Perhaps therefore the meaning is,—Is there not one man in the world prudent enough to keep out of that state where he must live in apprehension that his *night-cap* will be worn occasionally by another. So, in *Othello:*
   " For I *fear* Cassio with my *night-cap* too." MALONE.

If this remark on the disuse of *caps* among people of higher rank be accurate, Sir Christopher Hatton, and other worthies of the court of Elizabeth, have been injuriously treated; for the painters of their time exhibit several of them with *caps* on their heads.—It should be remembered that there was a material distinction between the *plain statute-caps* of citizens, and the *ornamented ones* worn by gentlemen. STEEVENS.

2 —— *sigh away Sundays.*] A proverbial expression to signify that a man has no rest at all; when Sunday, a day formerly of ease and diversion, was passed so uncomfortably. WARBURTON.

I cannot find this *proverbial* expression in any ancient book whatever. I am apt to believe that the learned commentator has mistaken the drift of it, and that it most probably alludes to the strict manner in which the sabbath was observed by the *Puritans*, who usually spent that day in *sighs* and *gruntings*, and other hypocritical marks of devotion. STEEVENS.

BENE. I would, your grace would conſtrain me to tell.

D. PEDRO. I charge thee on thy allegiance.

BENE. You hear, Count Claudio: I can be ſecret as a dumb man, I would have you think ſo; but on my allegiance,——mark you this, on my allegiance:——He is in love. With who?——now that is your grace's part.——Mark, how ſhort his anſwer is:——With Hero, Leonato's ſhort daughter.

CLAUD. If this were ſo, ſo were it uttered.[2]

BENE. Like the old tale, my lord: it is not ſo, nor 'twas not ſo; but, indeed, God forbid it ſhould be ſo.

CLAUD. If my paſſion change not ſhortly, God forbid it ſhould be otherwiſe.

D. PEDRO. Amen, if you love her; for the lady is very well worthy.

CLAUD. You ſpeak this to fetch me in, my lord.

D. PEDRO. By my troth, I ſpeak my thought.

CLAUD. And, in faith, my lord, I ſpoke mine.

BENE. And, by my two faiths and troths, my lord, I ſpoke mine.[3]

---

[2] Claud. *If this were ſo, ſo were it uttered.*] This and the three next ſpeeches I do not well underſtand; there ſeems ſomething omitted relating to Hero's conſent, or to Claudio's marriage, elſe I know not what Claudio can wiſh *not to be otherwiſe.* The copies all read alike. Perhaps it may be better thus:

Claud. *If this were ſo, ſo were it.*
Bene. *Uttered like the old tale,* &c.
Claudio gives a ſullen anſwer, *if it is ſo, ſo it is.* Still there ſeems ſomething omitted which Claudio and Pedro concur in wiſhing. JOHNSON.

Claudio, evading at firſt a confeſſion of his paſſion, ſays; if I had really confided ſuch a ſecret to him, yet he would have blabbed it in this manner. In his next ſpeech, he thinks proper to avow his love; and when Benedick ſays, *God forbid it ſhould be ſo,* i. e. God forbid he ſhould even wiſh to marry her; Claudio replies, God forbid I ſhould not wiſh it. STEEVENS.

[3] ——*I* ſpoke *mine.*] Thus the quarto, 1600. The folio reads——

CLAUD. That I love her, I feel.

D. PEDRO. That she is worthy, I know.

BENE. That I neither feel how she should be loved, nor know how she should be worthy, is the opinion that fire cannot melt out of me; I will die in it at the stake.

D. PEDRO. Thou wast ever an obstinate heretick in the despite of beauty.

CLAUD. And never could maintain his part, but in the force of his will.[4]

BENE. That a woman conceived me, I thank her; that she brought me up, I likewise give her most humble thanks: but that I will have a recheat winded in my forehead,[5] or hang my bugle in an

---

" I *speak* mine." But the former is right. Benedick means, that he *spoke* his mind when he said—" God forbid it should be so;" i. e. that Claudio should be in love, and marry in consequence of his passion. STEEVENS.

[4] —— *but in the force of his will.*] Alluding to the definition of a heretick in the schools. WARBURTON.

[5] ——*but that I will have a* recheat *winded in my forehead,*] That is, *I will wear a horn on my forehead which the huntsman may blow.* A *recheate* is the sound by which dogs are called back. Shakspeare had no mercy upon the poor cuckold, his *horn* is an inexhaustible subject of merriment. JOHNSON.

So, in *The Return from Parnassus:* " —— When you blow the death of your fox in the field or covert, then you must sound three notes, with three winds; and *recheat,* mark you, sir, upon the same three winds."

" Now, sir, when you come to your stately gate, as you sounded the *recheat* before, so now you must sound the relief three times."

Again, in *The Book of Huntynge,* &c. bl. l. no date : " Blow the whole *rechate* with three wyndes, the first wynde one longe and six shorte. The seconde wynde two shorte and one longe. The thred wynde one longe and two shorte."

Among Bagford's Collections relative to Typography, in the British Museum, 1044, II. C. is an engraved half sheet, containing the ancient Hunting Notes of England, &c. Among these, I find,

invifible baldrick,[6] all women fhall pardon me:
Becaufe I will not do them the wrong to miftruft
any, I will do myfelf the right to truft none; and the
fine is, (for the which I may go the finer,) I will
live a bachelor.

D. Pedro. I fhall fee thee, ere I die, look pale
with love.

Bene. With anger, with ficknefs, or with hunger, my lord; not with love: prove, that ever I lofe
more blood with love, than I will get again with
drinking, pick out mine eyes with a ballad-maker's
pen, and hang me up at the door of a brothel-houfe,
for the fign of blind Cupid.

D. Pedro. Well, if ever thou doft fall from this
faith, thou wilt prove a notable argument.[7]

Bene. If I do, hang me in a bottle like a cat,[8]

Single, Double, and Treble *Recheats,* Running *Recheat,* Warbling
Recheat, another *Recheat* with the tongue very hard, another fmoother
Recheat, and another warbling *Recheat.* The mufical notes are
affixed to them all.   Steevens.

A *recheate* is a particular leffon upon the horn, to call dogs back
from the fcent: from the old French word *recet,* which was ufed
in the fame fenfe as *retraite.*   Hanmer.

[6] —— *hang my* bugle *in an invifible baldrick,*] *Bugle,* i. e. bugle-
horn, hunting-horn.   The meaning feems to be——or that I fhould
be compelled to carry a horn on my forehead where there is nothing
vifible to fupport it.   So, in John Alday's tranflation of Pierre
Boifteau's *Theatrum Mundi,* &c. bl. l. no date: "——Beholde the
hazard wherin thou art (fayth William de la Perriere) that thy
round head become not forked, which were a fearfull fight *if it
were vifible and apparent.*"
It is ftill faid of the mercenary cuckold, that he *carries his horns
in his pockets.*   Steevens.

[7] —— *notable argument.*] An eminent fubject for fatire.
                                                   Johnson.

[8] —— *in a bottle like a cat,*] As to *the cat and bottle,* I can
procure no better information than the following.
In fome counties in England, a cat was formerly clofed up with
a quantity of foot in a wooden bottle, (fuch as that in which

and shoot at me; and he that hits me, let him be
clapped on the shoulder, and call'd Adam.[9]

shepherds carry their liquor,) and was suspended on a line. He
who beat out the bottom as he ran under it, and was nimble enough
to escape its contents, was regarded as the hero of this inhuman
diversion.

Again, in *Warres, or the Peace is broken*, bl. l.—" arrowes flew
faster than they did at a *catte in a basket*, when Prince Arthur, or
the Duke of Shordich, strucke up the drumme in the field."

In a Poem, however, called *Cornu-copiæ, or Pasquil's Night-cap,
or an Antidote to the Head ache*, 1623, p. 48, the following passage
occurs :

  " Fairer than any stake in Greys-inn field, &c.
  " Guarded with gunners, bill-men, and a rout
  " Of bow-men bold, which *at a cat do shoot.*"

Again, *ibid:*

  " Nor at the top a *cat-a-mount* was fram'd,
  " Or some wilde beast that ne'er before was tam'd;
  " Made at the charges of some archer stout,
  " To have his name canoniz'd in the clout."

The foregoing quotations may serve to throw some light on
Benedick's allusion. They prove, however, that it was the custom
to shoot at factitious as well as real cats. STEEVENS.

This practice is still kept up at Kelso, in Scotland, where it is
called—*Cat-in-barrel.* See a description of the whole ceremony in
a little account of the town of Kelso, published in 1789, by one
Ebenezer Lazarus, a silly Methodist, who has interlarded his book
with scraps of pious and other poetry. Speaking of this sport, he
says :

  " The *cat in the barrel* exhibits such a farce,
  " That he who can relish it is worse than an ass." DOUCE.

9 ———*and he that hits me, let him be clapped on the shoulder, and
call'd* Adam.] But why should he therefore be called *Adam?*
Perhaps, by a quotation or two we may be able to trace the poet's
allusion here. In *Law-Tricks,* or, *Who would have thought it,*
(a comedy written by John Day, and printed in 1608,) I find this
speech: " Adam Bell, a substantial outlaw, and a passing good
archer, yet no tobacconist." By this it appears, that Adam Bell
at that time of day was of reputation for his skill at the bow. I
find him again mentioned in a burlesque poem of Sir William
D'Avenant's, called *The long Vacation in London.* THEOBALD.

- Adam Bel, Clym of the Cloughe, and Wyllyam of Cloudesle,
were, says Dr. Percy, three noted outlaws, whose skill in Archery,
rendered them formerly as famous in the North of England, as

D. Pedro. Well, as time fhall try :
In time the favage bull doth bear the yoke.[2]

Bene. The favage bull may ; but if ever the fenfible Benedick bear it, pluck off the bull's horns,
and fet them in my forehead : and let me be vilely
painted ; and in fuch great letters as they write,
Here is good horfe to hire, let them fignify under my
fign,——*Here you may fee Benedick the married man.*

Claud. If this fhould ever happen, thou would'ft
be horn-mad.

D. Pedro. Nay, if Cupid have not fpent all his
quiver in Venice,[3] thou wilt quake for this fhortly.

Bene. I look for an earthquake too then.

D. Pedro. Well, you will temporize with the
hours. In the mean time, good fignior Benedick,
repair to Leonato's ; commend me to him, and tell
him, I will not fail him at fupper ; for, indeed, he
hath made great preparation.

Robin Hood and his fellows were in the midland counties. Their
place of refidence was in the foreft of Englewood, not far from
Carlifle. At what time they lived does not appear. The author
of the common ballads on *The Pedigree, Education, and Marriage
of Robin Hood*, makes them contemporary with Robin Hood's
father, in order to give him the honour of beating them. See
celebrated *Reliques of Ancient Englifh Poetry*, Vol. I. p. 143, where the ballad
outlaws is preferved. Steevens.

[2] *In time the favage bull doth bear the yoke.*] This line is from
The Spanifh Tragedy, or *Hieronymo*, &c. and occurs alfo, with a
flight variation, in Watfon's Sonnets, 4to. bl. l. printed in 1581.
See note on the laft edition of Dodfley's Old Plays, Vol. XII.
p. 387. Steevens.

The Spanifh Tragedy was printed and acted before 1593. Malone.

It may be proved that *The Spanifh Tragedy* had at leaft been
written before 1562. Steevens.

[3] ——*if Cupid have not fpent all his quiver in* Venice,] All
modern writers agree in reprefenting Venice in the fame light as
the ancients did Cyprus. And it is this character of the people that
is here alluded to. Warburton.

Bene. I have almoſt matter enough in me for ſuch an embaſſage ; and ſo I commit you——

Claud. To the tuition of God : From my houſe, (if I had it,)——

D. Pedro. The ſixth of July : Your loving friend, Benedick.

Bene. Nay, mock not, mock not : The body of your diſcourſe is ſometime guarded with fragments,[4] and the guards are but ſlightly baſted on neither : ere you flout old ends any further,[5] examine your conſcience ; and ſo I leave you.   [*Exit* BENEDICK.

---

[4] —— guarded *with fragments*,] *Guards* were ornamental lace or borders.   So, in *The Merchant of Venice :*
   " —— give him a livery
   " More *guarded* than his fellows."
Again, in *Henry IV.* Part I:
   " —— velvet *guards*, and Sunday citizens." STEEVENS.

[5] —— *ere you flout* old ends, &c.] *Before you endeavour to diſtinguiſh yourſelf any more by antiquated alluſions, examine whether you can fairly claim them for your own.* This, I think is the meaning ; or it may be underſtood in another ſenſe, *examine, if your ſarcaſms do not touch yourſelf.* JOHNSON.

The ridicule here is to the formal concluſions of Epiſtles dedicatory and Letters.   Barnaby Googe thus ends his dedication to the firſt edition of Palingenius, 12mo. 1560: "And thus *committyng* your Ladiſhip with all yours to the *tuicion* of the moſte mercifull *God*, I ende.   From Staple Inne at London, the eighte and twenty of March."   The practice had however become obſolete in Shakſpeare's time.   In *A Poſte with a Packet of mad Letters*, by Nicholas Breton, 4to. 1607 ; I find a Letter ending in this manner, entitled, "A letter to laugh at after the *old faſhion* of love to a Maide."   REED.

Dr. Johnſon's latter explanation is, I believe, the true one.   By *old ends* the ſpeaker may mean the concluſion of letters commonly uſed in Shakſpeare's time ; "From my houſe this fixth of July," &c. So, in the concluſion of a letter which our author ſuppoſes Lucrece to write :
   "So I *commend* me *from our houſe* in grief ;
   "My woes are tedious, though my words are brief."
See *The Rape of Lucrece*, p. 547, edit. 1780, and the note there.

CLAUD. My liege, your highnefs now may do me good.

D. PEDRO. My love is thine to teach; teach it but how,
And thou fhalt fee how apt it is to learn
Any hard leffon that may do thee good.

CLAUD. Hath Leonato any fon, my lord?

D. PEDRO. No child but Hero, fhe's his only heir:
Doft thou affect her, Claudio?

CLAUD. O my lord,
When you went onward on this ended action,
I look'd upon her with a foldier's eye,
That lik'd, but had a rougher tafk in hand
Than to drive liking to the name of love:
But now I am return'd, and that war-thoughts
Have left their places vacant, in their rooms
Come thronging foft and delicate defires,
All prompting me how fair young Hero is,
Saying, I lik'd her ere I went to wars.

D. PEDRO. Thou wilt be like a lover prefently,
And tire the hearer with a book of words:
If thou doft love fair Hero, cherifh it;
And I will break with her, and with her father,

Old ends, however, may refer to the quotation that D. Pedro had made from *The Spanifh Tragedy.* "Ere you attack me on the fubject of love, with fragments of old plays, examine whether you are yourfelf free from its power." So, *King Richard:*
"With odd *old ends*, ftol'n forth of holy writ."
This kind of conclufion to letters was not obfolete in our author's time, as has been fuggefted. Michael Drayton concludes one of his letters to Drummond of Hawthornden, in 1619, thus: "And fo wifhing you all happinefs, I *commend you to God's tuition*, and reft your affured friend." So alfo Lord Salifbury concludes a letter to Sir Ralph Winwood, April 7th, 1610: " — And fo I commit you to God's protection."
Winwood's *Memorials*, III. 147. MALONE.

And thou fhalt have her: Was't not to this end,
That thou began'ft to twift fo fine a ftory?

CLAUD. How fweetly do you minifter to love,
That know love's grief by his complexion!
But left my liking might too fudden feem,.
I would have falv'd it with a longer treatife.

D. PEDRO. What need the bridge much broader
            than the flood?
The faireft grant is the neceffity:[6]
Look, what will ferve, is fit: 'tis once, thou lov'ft;[7]
And I will fit thee with the remedy.
I know, we fhall have revelling to-night;
I will affume thy part in fome difguife,
And tell fair Hero I am Claudio;
And in her bofom I'll unclafp my heart,
And take her hearing prifoner with the force
And ftrong encounter of my amorous tale:
Then, after, to her father will I break;

[6] *The faireft grant is the neceffity:*] i. e. no one can have a better
reafon for granting a requeft than the neceffity of its being granted.
                                                    WARBURTON.

Mr. Hayley with great acutenefs propofes to read,
    The faireft grant is to neceffity. STEEVENS.

    Thefe words cannot imply the fenfe that Warburton contends
for; but if we fuppofe that *grant* means *conceffion,* the fenfe is
obvious; and that is no uncommon acceptation of that word.
                                                    M. MASON.

[7] —— 'tis once, *thou lov'ft;*] This phrafe, with concomitant
obfcurity, appears in other dramas of our author, viz. *The Merry
Wives of Windfor,* and *K. Henry VIII.* In *The Comedy of Errors,*
it ftands as follows:
    "*Once this*—Your long experience of her wifdom," &c.
Balthafar is fpeaking to the Ephefian Antipholis.
    Once may therefore mean " *once* for all,"—" 'tis enough to
fay at *once.*" STEEVENS.

    Once has here, I believe, the force of—*once for all.* So, in
Coriolanus: " *Once,* if he do require our voices, we ought not
to deny him." MALONE.

[handwritten marginal note: i.e. "necessitas quod cogit defend"]

And, the conclusion is, she shall be thine :
In practice let us put it presently.   [*Exeunt.*

SCENE II.

A Room in LEONATO'S *House.*

Enter LEONATO *and* ANTONIO.

LEON. How now, brother? Where is my cousin, your son? Hath he provided this musick?

ANT. He is very busy about it. But, brother, I can tell you strange news [7] that you yet dream'd not of.

LEON. Are they good?

ANT. As the event stamps them ; but they have a good cover, they show well outward. The prince and Count Claudio, walking in a thick-pleached alley [8] in my orchard, were thus much overheard by a man of mine : The prince discovered to Claudio, that he loved my niece your daughter, and meant to acknowledge it this night in a dance ; and, if he found her accordant, he meant to take the present time by the top, and instantly break with you of it.

LEON. Hath the fellow any wit, that told you this?

ANT. A good sharp fellow ; I will send for him, and question him yourself.

LEON. No, no ; we will hold it as a dream, till it appear itself :——but I will acquaint my daughter withal, that she may be the better prepared for an

---

[7] —— strange *news* —] Thus the quarto, 1600. The folio omits the epithet, which indeed is of little value. STEEVENS.

[8] —— a thick-pleached *alley* —] *Thick-pleached* is thickly interwoven. So afterwards, Act III. sc. i :
     " —— bid her steal into the *pleached bower.*"
Again, in *King Henry V :*
     " —— her hedges even-*pleach'd*——." STEEVENS.

I

anfwer, if peradventure this be true. Go you, and tell her of it. [*Several perfons crofs the ftage.*] Coufins, you know[9] what you have to do.—O, I cry you mercy, friend; go you with me, and I will ufe your fkill :—Good coufins, have a care this bufy time.

[*Exeunt.*

SCENE III.

Another Room in LEONATO'S *Houfe.*

Enter Don JOHN *and* CONRADE.

Con. What the goujere,[2] my lord! why are you thus out of meafure fad?

D. John. There is no meafure in the occafion that breeds it, therefore the fadnefs is without limit.

Con. You fhould hear reafon.

D. John. And when I have heard it, what bleffing bringeth it?

Con. If not a prefent remedy, yet a patient fufferance.

D. John. I wonder, that thou being (as thou fay'ft thou art) born under Saturn, goeft about to apply a moral medicine to a mortifying mifchief. I cannot hide what I am:[3] I muft be fad when I have

---

[9] *Coufins*, you know —]—and afterwards,—*good coufins.*] *Coufins* were anciently enrolled among the dependants, if not the domefticks, of great families, fuch as that of Leonato. Petruchio, while intent on the fubjection of Katharine, calls out, in terms imperative, for his *coufin Ferdinand.* STEEVENS.

[2] *What the* goujere,] i. e. *morbus Gallicus.* The old copy corruptly reads, "good-year." The fame expreffion occurs again in *K. Lear,* Act V. fc. iii:

"The *goujeres* fhall devour them, flefh and fell."
See note on this paffage. STEEVENS.

[3] *I cannot hide what I am :*] This is one of our author's natural touches. An envious and unfocial mind, too proud to give

E c 2

caufe, and fmile at no man's jefts; eat when I have
ftomach, and wait for no man's leifure; fleep when
I am drowfy, and tend on no man's bufinefs; laugh
when I am merry, and claw no man in his humour.[4]

Con. Yea, but you muft not make the full fhow
of this, till you may do it without controlment.
You have of late ftood out againft your brother, and
he hath ta'en you newly into his grace; where it is
impoffible you fhould take true root, but by the fair
weather that you make yourfelf: it is needful that
you frame the feafon for your own harveft.

D. JOHN. I had rather be a canker in a hedge,
than a rofe in his grace; [5] and it better fits my blood

pleafure, and too fullen to receive it, always endeavours to hide
its malignity from the world and from itfelf, under the plainnefs
of fimple honefty, or the dignity of haughty independence.

JOHNSON.

[4] —— claw *no man in his humour.*] To *claw* is to flatter. So
the pope's claw-backs, in Bifhop Jewel, are the pope's *flatterers.*
The fenfe is the fame in the proverb, *Mulus mulum fcabit.*

JOHNSON.

So, in *Albion's England,* 1597, p. 125:

" The overweening of thy wits doth make thy foes to fmile,
" Thy friends to weepe, and *claw-backs* thee with foothings
to beguile."

Again, in *Wylfon on Ufury,* 1571, p. 141: " —— therefore I will
clawe him, and faye well might he fare, and godds bleffing have
he too. For the more he fpeaketh, the better it itcheth, and
maketh better for me." REED.

[5] *I had rather be a* canker *in a hedge, than a* rofe *in his grace;*]
A *canker* is the *canker*-rofe, *dog-rofe, cynofbatus,* or *hip.* The fenfe
is, I would rather live in obfcurity the wild life of nature, than
owe dignity or eftimation to my brother. He ftill continues his
wifh of gloomy independence. But what is the meaning of the
expreffion, *a rofe in his grace?* If he was a *rofe* of himfelf, his
brother's *grace* or *favour* could not degrade him. I once read
thus: *I had rather be a canker in a hedge, than a rofe in his* garden:
that is, I had rather be what nature makes me, however mean,
than owe any exaltation or improvement to my brother's kindnefs
or cultivation. But a lefs change will be fufficient: I think it

to be difdain'd of all, than to fafhion a carriage to rob love from any: in this, though I cannot be faid to be a flattering honeft man, it muft not be denied but I am a plain-dealing villain. I am trufted with a muzzle, and enfranchifed with a clog; therefore I have decreed not to fing in my cage: If I had my mouth, I would bite; if I had my liberty, I would do my liking: in the mean time, let me be that I am, and feek not to alter me.

Con. Can you make no ufe of your difcontent?

D. John. I make all ufe of it, for I ufe it only.[6] Who comes here? What news, Borachio?

Enter BORACHIO.

Bora. I came yonder from a great fupper; the prince, your brother, is royally entertain'd by Leo-

---

fhould be read, *I had rather be a canker in a hedge, than a rofe* by *his grace.* JOHNSON.

The *canker* is a term often fubftituted for the *canker-rofe.* Heywood, in his *Love's Miftrefs,* 1636, calls it the " *canker-flower.*" Again, in Shakfpeare's 54th Sonnet:

" The *canker* blooms have full as deep a die
" As the perfumed tincture of the *rofe.*"

I think no change is neceffary. The fenfe is,—I had rather be a neglected dog-rofe in a hedge, than a garden-flower of the fame fpecies, if it profited by his culture. STEEVENS.

The latter words are intended as an anfwer to what Conrade has juft faid—" he hath ta'en you newly into his *grace,* where it is impoffible you fhould take true *root,*" &c. In *Macbeth* we have a kindred expreffion:

" —— Welcome hither:
" I have begun to *plant* thee, and will labour
" To make thee full of *growing.*"

Again, in *K. Henry VI.* P. III:

" I'll *plant* Plantagenet, *root* him up who dares."

MALONE.

6 ——*for I ufe it* only.] i. e. for I make nothing elfe my counfellor. STEEVENS.

nato; and I can give you intelligence of an intended marriage.

D. John. Will it ferve for any model to build mifchief on? What is he for a fool, that betroths himfelf to unquietnefs?

Bora. Marry, it is your brother's right hand.

D. John. Who? the moft exquifite Claudio?

Bora. Even he.

D. John. A proper fquire! And who, and who? which way looks he?

Bora. Marry, on Hero, the daughter and heir of Leonato.

D. John. A very forward March-chick! How came you to this?

———— a non *Jure* and firm-fet earth———." STEEVENS.

were of my mind!——Shall we go prove what's to be done?

Bora. We'll wait upon your lordship. [*Exeunt.*

ACT II. SCENE I.

A Hall in LEONATO'S *House.*

Enter LEONATO, ANTONIO, HERO, BEATRICE, *and Others.*

Leon. Was not count John here at supper?

Ant. I saw him not.

Beat. How tartly that gentleman looks! I never can see him, but I am heart-burn'd an hour after.[9]

Hero. He is of a very melancholy disposition.

Beat. He were an excellent man, that were made ft in the mid-way between him and Benedick: e one is too like an image, and says nothing; and e other, too like my lady's eldest son, evermore tling.

Leon. Then half signior Benedick's tongue in nt John's mouth, and half count John's melanoly in signior Benedick's face,——

Beat. With a good leg, and a good foot, uncle, money enough in his purse, such a man would any woman in the world,——if he could get her d will.

Leon. By my troth, niece, thou wilt never get a husband, if thou be so shrewd of thy tongue.

Ant. In faith, she is too curst.

—— heart-burn'd *an hour after.*] The pain commonly called *heart-burn,* proceeds from an *acid* humour in the stomach, and therefore properly enough imputed to *tart* looks. JOHNSON.

Beat. Too curſt is more than curſt: I ſhall leſſen God's ſending that way: for it is ſaid, *God ſends a curſt cow ſhort horns*; but to a cow too curſt he ſends none.

Leon. So, by being too curſt, God will ſend you no horns.

Beat. Juſt, if he ſend me no huſband; for the which bleſſing, I am at him upon my knees every morning and evening: Lord! I could not endure a huſband with a beard on his face; I had rather lie in the woollen.[2]

Leon. You may light upon a huſband, that hath no beard.

Beat. What ſhould I do with him? dreſs him in my apparel, and make him my waiting-gentle-woman? He that hath a beard, is more than a youth; and he that hath no beard, is leſs than a man: and he that is more than a youth, is not for me; and he that is leſs than a man, I am not for him: There-fore I will even take ſix-pence in earneſt of the bear-herd, and lead his apes into hell.

Leo. Well then, go you into hell?[3]

Beat. No; but to the gate: and there will the devil meet me, like an old cuckold, with horns on his head, and ſay, *Get you to heaven, Beatrice, get you to heaven; here's no place for you maids:* ſo de—

---

[2] —— *in the* woollen.] I ſuppoſe ſhe means—between blankets, without ſheets. STEEVENS.

[3] *Well then*, &c.] Of the two next ſpeeches Dr. Warburton ſays, *All this impious nonſenſe thrown to the bottom, is the players', and foiſted in without rhyme or reaſon.* He therefore puts them in the margin. They do not deſerve indeed ſo honourable a place; yet I am afraid they are too much in the manner of our author, who is ſometimes trying to purchaſe merriment at too dear a rate. JOHNSON.

I have reſtored the lines omitted. STEEVENS.

liver I up my apes, and away to Saint Peter for the heavens; he shows me where the bachelors sit, and there live we as merry as the day is long.

Ant. Well, niece, [*To* Hero] I trust, you will be ruled by your father.

Beat. Yes, faith; it is my cousin's duty to make courtesy, and say, *Father, as it please you :*—but yet for all that, cousin, let him be a handsome fellow, or else make another courtesy, and say, *Father, as it please me.*

Leon. Well, niece, I hope to see you one day fitted with a husband.

Beat. Not till God make men of some other metal than earth. Would it not grieve a woman to be over-master'd with a piece of valiant dust? to make an account of her life to a clod of wayward marl? No, uncle, I'll none: Adam's sons are my brethren; and truly, I hold it a sin to match in my kindred.

Leon. Daughter, remember, what I told you : if the prince do solicit you in that kind, you know your answer.

Beat. The fault will be in the musick, cousin, if you be not woo'd in good time : if the prince be too important,⁴ tell him, there is measure in every thing,⁵ and so dance out the answer. For hear me, Hero;

---

⁴ —— *if the prince be too* important,] *Important* here, and in many other places, is *importunate.* JOHNSON.

So, in *King Lear*, Act IV. sc. iv:
"—— great France
"My mourning, and *important* tears hath pitied." STEEVENS.

⁵ —— *there is* measure *in every thing,*] A *measure* in old language, beside its ordinary meaning, signified also a *dance.* MALONE.

So, in *King Richard II :*
"My legs can keep no *measure* in delight, ·
"When my poor heart no *measure* keeps in grief." STEEVENS.

Wooing, wedding, and repenting, is as a Scotch jig, a measure, and a cinque-pace: the first suit is hot and hasty, like a Scotch jig, and full as fantastical; the wedding, mannerly-modest, as a measure full of state and ancientry; and then comes repentance, and, with his bad legs, falls into the cinque-pace faster and faster, till he sink into his grave.

Leon. Cousin, you apprehend passing shrewdly.

Beat. I have a good eye, uncle; I can see a church by day-light.

Leon. The revellers are entering; brother, make good room.

Enter Don PEDRO, CLAUDIO, BENEDICK, BALTHAZAR; [6] *Don* JOHN, BORACHIO, MARGARET, URSULA, *and others, mask'd.*

D. Pedro, Lady, will you walk about with your friend? [7]

Hero. So you walk softly, and look sweetly, and say nothing, I am yours for the walk; and, especially, when I walk away.

---

[6] —— *Balthazar;*] The quarto and folio add—*or dumb John.* STEEVENS.

Here is another proof that when the first copies of our author's plays were prepared for the press, the transcript was made out by the ear. If the MS. had lain before the transcriber, it is very unlikely that he should have mistaken *Don* for *dumb:* but, by an inarticulate speaker, or inattentive hearer, they might easily be confounded. MALONE.

Don John's taciturnity has been already noticed. It seems therefore not improbable that the author himself might have occasionally applied the epithet *dumb* to him. REED.

[7] —— *your* friend?] *Friend,* in our author's time, was the common term for a *lover.* So also in French and Italian. MALONE.

Mr. Malone might have added, that this term was equally applicable to both sexes; for, in *Measure for Measure,* Lucio tells Isabella that her brother had " got his *friend* with child." STEEVENS

D. Pedro. With me in your company?

Hero. I may fay fo, when I pleafe.

D. Pedro. And when pleafe you to fay fo?

Hero. Whe
the lute fhoul

D. Pedro.
the houfe is J

Hero. Why

D. Pedro.

Bene. Wel

Marg. So
I have many i

---

² —— *the* lute
be as homely and

⁹ *My vifor is* Ph
firft folio has—*Love*; the quarto, 1600—*Iove*; fo that here Mr.
Theobald might have found the very reading which, in the following note, he reprefents as a conjecture of his own. STEEVENS.

'Tis plain, the poet alludes to the ftory of Baucis and Philemon
from Ovid: and this old couple, as the Roman poet defcribes it,
lived in a thatch'd cottage:

" —— *ftipulis & canna tecta paluftri.*"

But why, *within this houfe is* love? Though this old pair lived in
a cottage, this cottage received two ftraggling Gods, (Jupiter and
Mercury) under its roof. So, Don Pedro is a prince; and though
his vifor is but ordinary, he would infinuate to Hero, that he has
fomething *godlike* within: alluding either to his dignity or the
qualities of his mind and perfon. By thefe circumftances, I am
fure, the thought is mended: as, I think verily, the text is too,
by the addition of a fingle letter—*within the houfe is* Jove. Nor
is this emendation a little confirmed by another paffage in our
author, in which he plainly alludes to the fame ftory. *As you like it:*

" Jaques. O, *knowledge ill inhabited, worfe than* Jove *in a
thatched houfe!*" THEOBALD.

The line of Ovid above quoted is thus tranflated by Golding,
1587:

" The *roofe* thereof was *thatched* all with ftraw and fennifh
reede." MALONE.

Bene. Which is one?

Marg. I fay my prayers aloud.

Bene. I love you the better; the hearers may cry, amen.

Marg. God match me with a good dancer!

Balth. Amen.

Marg. And God keep him out of my fight, when the dance is done!—Anfwer, clerk.

Balth. No more words; the clerk is anfwer'd.

Urs. I know you well enough; you are fignior Antonio.

Ant. At a word, I am not.

Urs. I know you by the waggling of your head.

Ant. To tell you true, I counterfeit him.

Urs. You could never do him fo ill-well,[2] unlefs you were the very man: Here's his dry hand[3] up and down; you are he, you are he.

Ant. At a word, I am not.

Urs. Come, come; do you think I do not know you by your excellent wit? Can virtue hide itfelf? Go to, mum, you are he: graces will appear, and there's an end.

Beat. Will you not tell me who told you fo?

Bene. No, you fhall pardon me.

Beat. Nor will you not tell me who you are?

Bene. Not now.

---

[2] *You could never do him fo* ill-well,] A fimilar phrafe occurs in *The Merchant of Venice :*
"He hath a *better bad* habit of frowning, than the Count Palatine." STEEVENS.

[3] —— *his* dry *hand*——] A *dry* hand was anciently regarded as the fign of a cold conftitution. To this, Maria, in *Twelfth-Night,* alludes, Act I. fc. iii. STEEVENS.

Beat. That I was difdainful,—and that I had my good wit out of the *Hundred merry Tales*; [4]—Well, this was fignior Benedick that faid fo.

Bene. What's he?

Beat. I am fure, you know him well enough.

---

[4] *Hundred merry Tales*;] The book, to which Shakfpeare alludes, might be an old tranflation of *Les cent Nouvelles Nouvelles.* The original was publifhed at Paris, in the black letter, before the year 1500, and is faid to have been written by fome of the royal family of France. Ames mentions a tranflation of it prior to the time of Shakfpeare.

In *The London Chaunticleres*, 1659, this work, among others, is cried for fale by a ballad-man. "The Seven Wife Men of Gotham; a *Hundred merry Tales*; Scoggin's Jefts," &c. Again, in *The Nice Valour*, &c. by Beaumont and Fletcher:

"—— the Almanacs,

" The *Hundred Novels*, and the Books of Cookery."

Of this collection there are frequent entries in the regifter of the Stationers' Company. The firft I met with was in Jan. 1581.

STEEVENS.

This book was certainly printed before the year 1575, and in much repute, as appears from the mention of it in Laneham's Letter concerning the entertainment at Kenelworth - Caftle. Again, in *The Englifh Courtier and the Cuntrey Gentleman*, bl. l. 1586. fig. H 4: "—— wee want not alfo pleafant mad headed knaves that bee properly learned and well reade in diverfe pleafant bookes and good authors. As Sir Guy of Warwicke, the Foure Sonnes of Aymon, the Ship of Fooles, the Budget of Demaundes, *the Hundredth merry Tales*, the Booke of Ryddles, and many other excellent writers both witty and pleafaunt." It has been fuggefted to me that there is no other reafon than the word *hundred* to fuppofe this book a tranflation of the *Cent Nouvelles Nouvelles*. I have now but little doubt that Boccace's *Decameron* was the book here alluded to. It contains juft one hundred Novels. So, in *Guazzo's Civile Converfation*, 1586, p. 158: "—— we do but give them occafion to turne over the *Hundred Novelles* of Boccace, and to write amorous and lafcivious letters."

REED.

The Hundred merry Tales can never have been a tranflation of *Les cent Nouvelles Nouvelles*, many of which are very tragical relations, and none of them calculated to furnifh a lady with *good wit*. It fhould feem rather to have been a fort of jeft-book.

RITSON.

Bene. Not I, believe me.

Beat. Did he never make you laugh?

Bene. I pray you, what is he?

Beat. Why, he is the prince's jester: a very dull fool; only his gift is in devising impossible slanders:[5] none but libertines delight in him; and the commendation is not in his wit, but in his villainy;[6] for he both pleaseth men, and angers them, and then they laugh at him, and beat him: I am sure, he is in the fleet; I would he had boarded me.

Bene. When I know the gentleman, I'll tell him what you say.

Beat. Do, do: he'll but break a comparison or two on me; which, peradventure, not mark'd, or not laugh'd at, strikes him into melancholy; and then there's a partridge' wing saved, for the fool will eat no supper that night. [*Musick within.*] We must follow the leaders.

Bene. In every good thing.

Beat. Nay, if they lead to any ill, I will leave them at the next turning. [*Dance. Then exeunt all but Don* John, Borachio, *and* Claudio.

---

[5] —— *his gift is in devising* impossible *slanders:*] We should read *impassible*, i. e. slanders so ill invented, that they will pass upon no body. Warburton.

Impossible slanders are, I suppose, such slanders as, from their absurdity and impossibility, bring their own confutation with them. Johnson.

Johnson's explanation appears to be right. Ford says, in *The Merry Wives of Windsor*, that he shall search for Falstaff in " *impossible* places." The word *impossible* is also used in a similar sense in Jonson's *Sejanus*, where Silius accuses Afer of
" Malicious and manifold applying,
" Foul wresting, and *impossible* construction." M. Mason.

[6] —— *his* villainy;] By which she means his malice and impiety. By his impious jests, she insinuates, he *pleased* libertines; and by his *devising slanders* of them, he angered them. Warburton.

D. John. Sure, my brother is amorous on Hero, and hath withdrawn her father to break with him about it: The ladies follow her, and but one visor remains.

Bora. And that is Claudio: I know him by his bearing.[7]

D. John. Are not you signior Benedick?

Claud. You know me well; I am he.

D. John. Signior, you are very near my brother in his love: he is enamoured on Hero; I pray you, dissuade him from her, she is no equal for his birth: you may do the part of an honest man in it.

Claud. How know you he loves her?

D. John. I heard him swear his affection.

Bora. So did I too; and he swore he would marry her to-night.

D. John. Come, let us to the banquet.

             [*Exeunt Don* John *and* Borachio.

Claud. Thus answer I in name of Benedick,
But hear these ill news with the ears of Claudio.——
'Tis certain so;—the prince wooes for himself.
Friendship is constant in all other things,
Save in the office and affairs of love:
Therefore,[8] all hearts in love use their own tongues;
Let every eye negotiate for itself,
And trust no agent: for beauty is a witch,
Against whose charms faith melteth into blood.[9]

---

7 —— *his* bearing.] i. e. his carriage, his demeanour. So, in *Measure for Measure:*
    " How I may formally in person *bear* me." STEEVENS.

8 *Therefore.* &c.] *Let,* which is found in the next line, is understood here. MALONE.

9 —— *beauty is a witch,*
   Against whose charms faith melteth into blood.] i. e. as wax

This is an accident of hourly proof,
Which I miftrufted not : Farewell therefore, Hero!

Re-enter BENEDICK.

BENE. Count Claudio?

CLAUD. Yea, the fame.

BENE. Come, will you go with me?

CLAUD. Whither?

BENE. Even to the next willow, about your own bufinefs, count. What fafhion will you wear the garland of? About your neck, like an ufurer's chain?[2] or under your arm, like a lieutenant's fcarf?

when oppofed to the fire kindled by a witch, no longer preferves the figure of the perfon whom it was defigned to reprefent, but flows into a fhapelefs lump; fo fidelity, when confronted with beauty, diffolves into our ruling paffion, and is loft there like a drop of water in the fea.

That *blood* fignifies (as Mr. Malone has alfo obferved) *amorous heat*, will appear from the following paffage in *All's well that ends well*, Act III. fc. vii:

　　" Now his important *blood* will nought deny
　　" That fhe'll demand."　STEEVENS.

[2] ———— *ufurer's* chain?] *Chains* of gold, of confiderable value, were in our author's time, ufually worn by wealthy citizens, and others, in the fame manner as they now are, on publick occafions, by the Aldermen of London. See *The Puritan, or the Widow of Watling-Street*, Act III. fc. iii. *Albumazar*, Act I. fc. vii. and other pieces. REED.

Ufury feems about this time to have been a common topic of invective. I have three or four dialogues, pafquils, and difcourfes on the fubject, printed before the year 1600. From every one of thefe it appears, that the merchants were the chief ufurers of the age. STEEVENS.

So, in *The Choice of Change, containing the triplicitie of Divinitie, Philofophie, and Poetrie*, by S. R. Gent. 4to. 1598 : " Three fortes of people, in refpect of ufe in neceffitie, may be accounted good :— *Merchantes*, for they may play the *ufurers*, inftead of the Jewes." Again, *ibid:* " There is a fcarcitie of Jewes, becaufe Chriftians make an occupation of *ufurie*." MALONE.

You muſt wear it one way, for the prince hath got your Hero.

CLAUD. I wiſh him joy of her.

BENE. Why, that's ſpoken like an honeſt drover; ſo they ſell bullocks. But did you think, the prince would have ſerved you thus?

CLAUD. I pray you, leave me.

BENE. Ho! now you ſtrike like the blind man; 'twas the boy that ſtole your meat, and you'll beat the poſt.

CLAUD. If it will not be, I'll leave you. [*Exit.*

BENE. Alas, poor hurt fowl! Now will he creep into ſedges.——But, that my lady Beatrice ſhould know me, and not know me! The prince's fool!—Ha! it may be, I go under that title, becauſe I am merry.—Yea; but ſo; I am apt to do myſelf wrong: I am not ſo reputed: it is the baſe, the bitter diſpoſition of Beatrice, that puts the world into her perſon,' and ſo gives me out. Well, I'll be revenged as I may.

Re-enter Don PEDRO, HERO, *and* LEONATO.

... Now, ſignior, where's the count?
...?

... y lord, I have play'd the part of ... nd him here as melancholy as a

... the *bitter diſpoſition of Beatrice, that puts* ...,] That is, *It is the diſpoſition of Beatrice, perſonate the world, and therefore repreſents t ſhe only ſays herſelf.*

—*baſe*, though *bitter :* but I do not underſtand ... inconſiſtent, or why what is *bitter* ſhould ..., we may ſafely read,——*It is the baſe,* the how *buy* ... not be *baſe* ... ... ISON. *bitter diſpoſition.*

I have adopted Dr. Johnſon's emendation, though I once thought it unneceſſary. STEEVENS.

VOL. IV. F f

lodge in a warren; [4] I told him, and, I think, I told him true, that your grace had got the good will of this young lady; [5] and I offered him my company to a willow tree, either to make him a garland, as being forsaken, or to bind him up a rod, as being worthy to be whipped.

D. Pedro. To be whipped! What's his fault?

Bene. The flat transgression of a school-boy; who, being overjoy'd with finding a bird's nest, shows it his companion, and he steals it.

D. Pedro. Wilt thou make a trust a transgression? The transgression is in the stealer.

Bene. Yet it had not been amiss, the rod had been made, and the garland too; for the garland he might have worn himself; and the rod he might have bestow'd on you, who, as I take it, have stol'n his bird's nest.

D. Pedro. I will but teach them to sing, and restore them to the owner.

Bene. If their singing answer your saying, by my faith, you say honestly.

[4] —— *as melancholy as a* lodge *in a warren;*] A parallel thought occurs in the first chapter of *Isaiah,* where the prophet, describing the desolation of Judah, says: "The daughter of Zion is left as a cottage in a vineyard, as a *lodge* in a garden of cucumbers," &c. I am informed, that near Aleppo, these lonely buildings are still made use of, it being necessary, that the fields where watermelons, cucumbers, &c. are raised, should be regularly watched. I learn from Tho. Newton's *Herball to the Bible,* 8vo. 1587, that "so soone as the cucumbers, &c. be gathered, these lodges are abandoned of the watchmen and keepers, and no more frequented." From these forsaken buildings, it should seem, the prophet takes his comparison. STEEVENS.

[5] —— *of this young lady;*] Benedick speaks of Hero as if she were on the stage. Perhaps, both she and Leonato, were meant to make their entrance with Don Pedro. When Beatrice enters, she is spoken of as coming in with only Claudio. STEEVENS.

I have regulated the entries accordingly. MALONE.

I

D. Pedro. The lady Beatrice hath a quarrel to
you; the gentleman, that danced with her, told her,
she is much wrong'd by you.

Bene. O, she misused me past the endurance of a
block; an oak, but with one green leaf on it, would
have answer'd her; my very visor began to assume
life, and scold with her: She told me, not thinking
I had been myself, that I was the prince's jester;
that I was duller than a great thaw; huddling jest
upon jest, with such impossible conveyance,[6] upon
me, that I stood like a man at a mark, with a whole

---

[6] ——*such* impossible *conveyance,*] Dr. Warburton reads *impassable*: Sir Tho. Hanmer *impetuous*, and Dr. Johnson *importable*,
which, says he, is used by Spenser, in a sense very congruous to
this passage, for *insupportable, or not to be sustained.* Also by the last
translators of the Apocrypha; and therefore such a word as
Shakspeare may be supposed to have written. REED.

Importable is very often used by Lidgate in his Prologue to the
translation of *The Tragedies gathered by Jhon Bochas,* &c. as well as
by Holinshed.

Impossible may be licentiously used for *unaccountable.* Beatrice
has already said, that Benedick invents *impossible* slanders.

So, in *The Fair Maid of the Inn,* by Beaumont and Fletcher:

" You would look for some most *impossible* antick."

Again, in *The Roman Actor,* by Massinger:

" ——to lose

" Ourselves, by building on *impossible* hopes." STEEVENS.

Impossible may have been what Shakspeare wrote, and be used in
the sense of *incredible* or *inconceivable,* both here and in the beginning
of the scene, where Beatrice speaks of *impossible* slanders. M. MASON.

I believe the meaning is—*with a rapidity equal to that of* jugglers,
who appear to perform impossibilities. We have the same epithet
again in *Twelfth-Night:* " There is no Christian can ever believe
such *impossible* passages of grossness." So Ford says in *The Merry
Wives of Windsor,*—" I will examine *impossible* places." Again,
in *Julius Cæsar:*

" —— Now bid me run,

" And I will strive with *things impossible,*

" And get the better of them."

Conveyance was the common term in our author's time for *sleight
of hand.* MALONE.

Ff 2

my visor began to assume life, and scold —]
is comical, that a similar thought should have
end in the tenth Thebaid of Statius, v. 658
——ipsa insanire videtur
whynx galea custos —— Steevens

army fhooting at me: She fpeaks poniards,[6] and
every word ftabs: if her breath were as terrible as
her terminations, there were no living near her, fhe
would infect to the north ftar. I would not marry
her, though fhe were endowed with all that Adam
had left him before he tranfgrefs'd: fhe would have
made Hercules have turn'd fpit; yea, and have cleft
his club to make the fire too. Come, talk not of
her; you fhall find her the infernal Até in good
apparel.[7] I would to God, fome fcholar would
conjure her;[8] for, certainly, while fhe is here, a
man may live as quiet in hell, as in a fanctuary;
and people fin upon purpofe, becaufe they would
go thither; fo, indeed, all difquiet, horror, and per-
turbation follows her.

Re-enter CLAUDIO, and BEATRICE.

D. PEDRO. Look, here fhe comes.

BENE. Will your grace command me any fervice
to the world's end? I will go on the flighteft errand now to the Antipodes, that you can devife to
fend me on; I will fetch you a toothpicker now
from the fartheft inch of Afia; bring you the length
of Prefter John's foot; fetch you a hair off the great
Cham's beard;[9] do you any embaffage to the Pig-

6 —— She fpeaks poniards,] So, in Hamlet:
"I'll fpeak daggers to her"——. STEEVENS.
7 —— the infernal Até in good apparel.] This is a pleafant allufion to the cuftom of ancient poets and painters, who reprefent
the Furies in rags. WARBURTON.
Até is not one of the Furies, but the Goddefs of Revenge, or
Difcord. STEEVENS.
8 —— fome fcholar would conjure her;] As Shakfpeare always
attributes to his exorcifts the power of raifing fpirits, he gives his
conjurer, in this place, the power of laying them. M. MASON.
9 —— bring you the length of Prefter John's foot; fetch you a hair
off the great Cham's beard;] i. e. I will undertake the hardeft talk,

mies, rather than hold three words' conference with this harpy: You have no employment for me?

D. Pedro. None, but to defire your good company.

Bene. O God, fir, here's a difh I love not; I cannot endure my lady Tongue.[2]   [*Exit.*

D. Pedro. Come, lady, come; you have loft the heart of fignior Benedick.

Beat. Indeed, my lord, he lent it me a while; and I gave him ufe for it,[3] a double heart for his fingle one: marry, once before, he won it of me with falfe dice, therefore your grace may well fay, I have loft it.

D. Pedro. You have put him down, lady, you have put him down.

Beat. So I would not he fhould do me, my lord, left I fhould prove the mother of fools. I have brought count Claudio, whom you fent me to feek.

---

rather than have any converfation with lady Beatrice. Alluding to the difficulty of accefs to either of thofe monarchs, but more particularly to the former.

So, Cartwright, in his comedy called *The Siege, or Love's Convert,* 1651:

" —— bid me take the Parthian king by the beard; or draw an eye-tooth from the jaw royal of the Perfian monarch."

Such an achievement, however, *Huon of Bourdeaux* was fent to perform, and performed it. See chap. 46, edit. 1601: " he opened his mouth, and tooke out his foure great teeth, and then cut off his beard, and tooke thereof as much as pleafed him." STEEVENS.

" Thou muft goe to the citie of Babylon to the Admiral Gaudiffe, to bring me thy hand full of the heare of his beard, and foure of his greateft teeth. Alas, my lord, (quoth the Barrons) we fee well you defire greatly his death, when you charge him with fuch a meffage." *Huon of Bourdeaux,* ch. 17. BOWLE.

[2] —— my *lady Tongue.*] Thus the quarto, 1600. The folio reads—*this* lady Tongue. STEEVENS.

[3] —— *I gave him ufe for it,*] *Ufe,* in our author's time, meant *intereft* of money. MALONE.

F f 3

D. Pedro. Why, how now, count? wherefore are you fad?

Claud. Not fad, my lord.

D. Pedro. How then? Sick?

Claud. Neither, my lord.

Beat. The count is neither fad, nor fick, nor merry, nor well: but civil, count; civil as an orange,[4] and fomething of that jealous complexion.[5]

D. Pedro. I'faith, lady, I think your blazon to be true; though, I'll be fworn, if he be fo, his conceit is falfe. Here, Claudio, I have wooed in thy name, and fair Hero is won; I have broke with her father, and his good will obtained: name the day of marriage, and God give thee joy!

Leon. Count, take of me my daughter, and with her my fortunes: his grace hath made the match, and all grace fay Amen to it!

Beat. Speak, count, 'tis your cue.

Claud. Silence is the perfecteft herald of joy: I were but little happy, if I could fay how much.— Lady, as you are mine, I am yours: I give away myfelf for you, and dote upon the exchange.

Beat. Speak, coufin; or, if you cannot, ftop his mouth with a kifs, and let not him fpeak, neither.

D. Pedro. In faith, lady, you have a merry heart.

Beat. Yea, my lord; I thank it, poor fool,[3] it keeps on the windy fide of care:——My coufin tells him in his ear, that he is in her heart.

---

[4] ——*civil* as an *orange*,] This conceit occurs likewife in *Nafhe's four Letters confuted*, 1592: " For the order of my life, it is as *civil as an orange*." Steevens.

[5] —— *of* that *jealous complexion*.] Thus the quarto, 1600. The folio reads, *of a jealous complexion.* Steevens.

[3] —*poor fool*,] This was formerly an expreffion of tendernefs. See *King Lear*, laft fcene: " And my *poor fool* is hang'd." Malone.

Claud. And so she doth, cousin.

Beat. Good lord, for alliance![6]—Thus goes every one to the world but I, and I am sun-burn'd;[7] I may sit in a corner, and cry, heigh ho! for a husband.

D. Pedro. Lady Beatrice, I will get you one.

Beat. I would rather have one of your father's getting: Hath your grace ne'er a brother like you? Your father got excellent husbands, if a maid could come by them.

D. Pedro. Will you have me, lady?

Beat. No, my lord, unless I might have another for working-days; your grace is too costly to wear every day:—But, I beseech your grace, pardon me; I was born to speak all mirth, and no matter.

D. Pedro. Your silence most offends me, and to be merry best becomes you; for, out of question, you were born in a merry hour.

---

⁶ *Good lord, for* alliance!] Claudio has just called Beatrice *cousin.* I suppose, therefore, the meaning is,—Good Lord, here have I got a new kinsman by marriage. MALONE.

I cannot understand these words, unless they imply a wish for the speaker's *alliance* with a husband. STEEVENS.

⁷ *Thus goes every one to the* world *but I, and I am* sun-burn'd;] What is it, *to go to the world?* perhaps, to enter by marriage into a settled state; but why is the unmarried lady *sun-burnt?* I believe we should read,—*Thus goes every one to the* wood *but I, and I am sun-burnt.* Thus does every one but I find a shelter, and I am left exposed to wind and *sun. The nearest way to the* wood, is a phrase for the readiest means to any end. It is said of a woman, who accepts a worse match than those which she had refused, that she has passed through the *wood,* and at last taken a crooked stick. But conjectural criticism has always something to abate its confidence. Shakspeare, in *All's well that Ends well,* uses the phrase, *to go to the world,* for *marriage.* So that my emendation depends only on the opposition of *wood* to *sun-burnt.* JOHNSON.

I am *sun-burnt* may mean, I have lost my beauty, and am consequently no longer such an object as can tempt a man to marry. STEEVENS.

Beat. No, fure, my lord, my mother cry'd; but then there was a ftar danced, and under that was I born.——Coufins, God give you joy!

Leon. Niece, will you look to thofe things I told you of?

Beat. I cry you mercy, uncle.——By your grace's pardon.   [*Exit* Beatrice.

D. Pedro. By my troth, a pleafant-fpirited lady.

Leon. There's little of the melancholy element in her,[8] my lord: fhe is never fad, but when fhe fleeps; and not ever fad then; for I have heard my daughter fay, fhe hath often dream'd of unhappinefs,[9] and waked herfelf with laughing.

D. Pedro. She cannot endure to hear tell of a hufband.

Leon. O, by no means; fhe mocks all her wooers out of fuit.

D. Pedro. She were an excellent wife for Benedick.

Leon. O Lord, my lord, if they were but a week married, they would talk themfelves mad.

D. Pedro. Count Claudio, when mean you to go to church?

---

[8] *There's little of the* melancholy element *in her.*] " Does not our life confift of the *four elements?*" fays Sir Toby, in *Twelfth Night.* So, alfo in *King Henry V:* " He is pure air and fire, and the *dull elements* of *earth* and *water* never appear in him."

MALONE.

[9] ——*fhe hath often dream'd of* unhappinefs.] So all the editions; but Mr. Theobald alters it to, *an happinefs,* having no conception that *unhappinefs* meant any thing but misfortune, and that, he thinks, fhe could not laugh at. He had never heard that it fignified a wild, wanton unlucky trick. Thus Beaumont and Fletcher, in their comedy of *The Maid of the Mill:*

   " —— My *dreams* are like my thoughts, honeft and innocent:
   " Yours are *unhappy.*" WARBURTON.

CLAUD. To-morrow, my lord: Time goes on crutches, till love have all his rites.

LEON. Not till Monday, my dear fon, which is hence a juft fevennight; and a time too brief too, to have all things anfwer my mind.

D. PEDRO. Come, you fhake the head at fo long a breathing; but, I warrant thee, Claudio, the time fhall not go dully by us; I will, in the interim, undertake one of Hercules' labours; which is, to bring fignior Benedick, and the lady Beatrice into a mountain of affection, the one with the other.² I would fain have it a match; and I doubt not but to fafhion it, if you three will but minifter fuch affiftance as I fhall give you direction.

---

² —— *into a* mountain *of affection, the one with the other.*] *A mountain of affection with one another* is a ftrange expreffion, yet I know not well how to change it. Perhaps it was originally written *to bring Benedick and Beatrice into a* mooting *of affection*; to bring them not to any more *mootings* of contention, but to a *mooting* or converfation of love. This reading is confirmed by the prepofition *with*; *a mountain* with *each other*, or *affection* with *each other*, cannot be ufed, but *a mooting* with *each other* is proper and regular.
                                                        JOHNSON.

Uncommon as the word propofed by Dr. Johnfon may appear, it is ufed in feveral of the old plays. So, in *Glapthorne's Wit in a Conftable*, 1639:
"—— one who never
"Had *mooted* in the hall, or feen the revels
"Kept in the houfe at Chriftmas."
Again, in *The Return from Parnaffus*, 1606:
"It is a plain cafe, whereon I *mooted* in our temple."
Again:
"—— at a *mooting* in our temple." *Ibid.*
And yet, all that I believe is meant by a *mountain of affection* is, *a great deal of affection*.
In one of Stanyhurft's poems is the following phrafe to denote a large quantity of love:
"*Lumps* of love promift, nothing perform'd," &c.
Again, in *The Renegado*, by Maffinger:
"—— 'tis but parting with
"*A mountain* of vexation."

Leon. My lord, I am for you, though it coft me ten nights' watchings.

Claud. And I, my lord.

D. Pedro. And you too, gentle Hero?

Hero. I will do any modeft office, my lord, to help my coufin to a good hufband.

D. Pedro. And Benedick is not the unhopefulleft hufband that I know : thus far can I praife him ; he is of a noble ftrain,² of approved valour, and confirm'd honefty. I will teach you how to humour your coufin, that fhe fhall fall in love with Bene- dick :—and I, with your two helps, will fo practice on Benedick, that, in defpite of his quick wit and his queafy ftomach,³ he fhall fall in love with

---

Thus, alfo in *K. Henry VIII* : we find " a *fea* of glory." In *Hamlet :* " a *fea* of troubles." Again, in Howel's *Hiftory of Venice :* " though they fee *mountains* of miferies heaped on one's back." Again, in Bacon's *Hiftory of K. Henry VII* : " Perkin fought to corrupt the fervants to the lieutenant of the tower by *mountains* of promifes." Again, in *The Comedy of Errors* : " — the *mountain* of mad flefh that claims marriage of me." Little can be inferred from the prefent offence againft grammar ; an offence which may not ftrictly be im- putable to Shakſpeare, but rather to the negligence or ignorance of his tranfcribers or printers. STEEVENS.

Shakſpeare has many phrafes equally harfh. He who would hazard fuch expreffions as *a ftorm of fortune*, a *vale of years*, and *a tempeft of provocation*, would not fcruple to write *a mountain of affection.*"
MALONE.

² —— a noble *ftrain*,] i. e. defcent, lineage. So in *The Faery Queen*, B. IV. C. viii. S. 33 :
"Sprung from the auncient ftocke of prince's *ftraine :*"
Again, B. V. C. ix. S. 32 :
" Sate goodly temperaunce in garments clene,
" And facred reverence yborn of heavenly ~~ftrene.~~" R—so.
Again, in *King Lear*, Act V. fc. iii :
" Sir, you have fhown to-day your valiant *ftrain.*" STEEVENS.

³ ——*queafy* ftomach,] i. e. fqueamifh. So, in *Antony and Cleopatra :*
" Who *queafy* with his infolence already"—— STEEVENS.

⁴ *It was used in the same sense by Shadwell in Virtuoso as " — Gentlemen care not upon what strain they get their sons* Reed

Beatrice. If we can do this, Cupid is no longer an archer; his glory fhall be ours, for we are the only love-gods.   Go in with me, and I will tell you my drift.   [*Exeunt.*

S C E N E   II.

Another Room in LEONATO'S *Houfe.*

Enter Don JOHN *and* BORACHIO.

D. JOHN. It is fo; the count Claudio fhall marry the daughter of Leonato.

BORA. Yea, my lord; but I can crofs it.

D. JOHN. Any bar, any crofs, any impediment will be medicinable to me: I am fick in difpleafure to him; and whatfoever comes athwart his affection, ranges evenly with mine.   How canft thou crofs this marriage?

BORA. Not honeftly, my lord; but fo covertly that no difhonefty fhall appear in me.

D. JOHN. Show me briefly how.

BORA. I think, I told your lordfhip, a year fince, how much I am in the favour of Margaret, the waiting-gentlewoman to Hero.

D. JOHN. I remember.

BORA. I can, at any unfeafonable inftant of the night, appoint her to look out at her lady's chamber-window.

D. JOHN. What life is in that, to be the death of this marriage?

BORA. The poifon of that lies in you to temper. Go you to the prince your brother; fpare not to tell him, that he hath wrong'd his honour in marrying the renowned Claudio (whofe eftimation do you mightily hold up) to a contaminated ftale, fuch a one as Hero.

D. John. What proof fhall I make of that?

Bora. Proof enough to mifufe the prince, to vex Claudio, to undo Hero, and kill Leonato: Look you for any other iffue?

D. John. Only to defpite them, I will endeavour any thing.

⁴*Bora.* Go then, find me a meet hour to draw

---

⁴ Bora. *Go then, find me a meet hour to draw Don Pedro and the count Claudio, alone: tell them, that you know that Hero loves me;——offer them inftances; which fhall bear no lefs likelihood, than to fee me at her chamber-window; bear me call Margaret, Hero; bear Margaret term me* Claudio; *and bring them to fee this, the very night before the intended wedding:*] Thus the whole ftream of the editions from the firft quarto downwards. I am obliged here to give a fhort account of the plot depending, that the emendation I have made may appear the more clear and unqueftionable. The bufinefs ftands thus: Claudio, a favourite of the Arragon prince, is, by his interceffions with her father, to be married to fair Hero; Don John, natural brother of the prince, and a hater of Claudio, is in his fpleen zealous to difappoint the match. Borachio, a rafcally dependant on Don John, offers his affiftance, and engages to break off the marriage by this ftratagem. " Tell the prince and Claudio (fays he) that Hero is in love with *me*; they won't believe it: offer them proofs, as, that they fhall fee me converfe with her in her chamber-window. I am in the good graces of her waiting-woman, Margaret; and I'll prevail with Margaret, at a dead hour of night, to perfonate her miftrefs Hero; do you then bring the prince and Claudio to overhear our difcourfe; and they fhall have the torment to hear *me* addrefs Margaret by the name of Hero, and her fay fweet things to me by the name of Claudio."——This is the fubftance of Borachio's device to make Hero fufpected of difloyalty, and to break off her match with Claudio. But, in the name of common fenfe, could it difpleafe Claudio, to hear his miftrefs making ufe of *his* name tenderly? If he faw another man with her, and heard her call him Claudio, he might reafonably think her betrayed, but not have the fame reafon to accufe her of difloyalty. Befides, how could her naming Claudio, make the prince and Claudio believe that fhe loved Borachio, as he defires Don John to infinuate to them that fhe did? The circum-

Don Pedro and the count Claudio, alone: tell them,
that you know that Hero loves me; intend a kind of
zeal [5] both to the prince and Claudio, as—in love of
your brother's honour who hath made this match;
and his friend's reputation, who is thus like to be
cozen'd with the semblance of a maid,—that you
have discover'd thus. They will scarcely believe
this without trial: offer them instances; which shall
bear no less likelihood, than to see me at her
chamber-window; hear me call Margaret, Hero;
hear Margaret term me Borachio; and bring them
to see this, the very night before the intended wedding: for, in the mean time, I will so fashion the

stances weighed, there is no doubt but the passage ought to be
reformed, as I have settled in the text—*hear me call Margaret,
Hero; hear Margaret term me,* Borachio. THEOBALD.

Though I have followed Mr. Theobald's direction, I am not
convinced that this change of names is absolutely necessary. *Claudio*
would naturally resent the circumstance of hearing another called
by his own name; because, in that case, baseness of treachery
would appear to be aggravated by wantonness of insult; and, at
the same time he would imagine the person so distinguished
to be *Borachio,* because *Don John* was previously to have informed
both him and *Don Pedro,* that *Borachio* was the favoured lover.
STEEVENS.

We should surely read *Borachio* instead of *Claudio.*—There could
be no reason why Margaret should call him *Claudio;* and that
would ill agree with what Borachio says in the last Act, where he
declares that Margaret knew not what she did when she spoke to
him. M. MASON.

Claudio would naturally be enraged to find his mistress, Hero,
(for such he would imagine Margaret to be,) address Borachio, or
any other man, by his name, as he might suppose that she called
him by the name of Claudio in consequence of a secret agreement
between them, as a cover, in case she were overheard; and *he*
would know, without a possibility of error, that it was not Claudio,
with whom in fact she conversed. MALONE.

5 ——intend *a kind of zeal*—] i. e. *pretend.* So, in *King
Richard III :*
 " *Intending* deep suspicion." STEEVENS.

matter, that Hero shall be absent; and there shall appear such seeming truth of Hero's disloyalty, that jealousy shall be call'd assurance, and all the pre-paration overthrown.

D. John. Grow this to what adverse issue it can, I will put it in practice: Be cunning in the work-ing this, and thy fee is a thousand ducats.

Bora. Be you constant in the accusation, and my cunning shall not shame me.

D. John. I will presently go learn their day of marriage.   [*Exeunt.*

S C E N E   III.

Leonato's *Garden.*

Enter *Benedick and a Boy.*

Bene. Boy,——

Boy. Signior.

Bene. In my chamber-window lies a book; bring it hither to me in the orchard.[6]

Boy. I am here already, sir.

Bene. I know that;——but I would have thee hence, and here again.   [*Exit Boy.*]——I do much wonder, that one man, seeing how much another man is a fool when he dedicates his behaviours to love, will, after he hath laugh'd at such shallow fol-lies in others, become the argument of his own scorn, by falling in love: And such a man is Claudio. I have known, when there was no musick with him

---

[6] —— *in the* orchard.] Gardens were anciently called *orchards.* So, in *Romeo and Juliet :*
    " The *orchard* walls are high, and hard to climb."
                                                        Steevens.

but the drum and the fife; and now had he rather
hear the tabor and the pipe: I have known, when he
would have walk'd ten mile afoot, to fee a good armour; and now will he lie ten nights awake, carving
the fashion of a new doublet.[7] He was wont to
fpeak plain, and to the purpofe, like an honeft man,
and a foldier; and now is he turn'd orthographer;[8]
his words are a very fantaftical banquet, juft fo many
ftrange difhes. May I be fo converted, and fee
with thefe eyes? I cannot tell; I think not: I will
not be fworn, but love may transform me to an
oyfter; but I'll take my oath on it, till he have
made an oyfter of me, he fhall never make me fuch
a fool. One woman is fair; yet I am well; ano-

---

[7] —— *carving the fashion of a new doublet.*] This folly, fo con-
fpicuous in the gallants of former ages, is laughed at by all our
comic writers. So, in Greene's *Fare well to Folly*, 1617: " —— We
are almoft as fantaftic as the Englifh gentleman that is painted
naked, with a pair of fheers in his hand, as not being refolved
after what fafhion to have his coat cut." STEEVENS.

The Englifh gentleman in the above extract alludes to a plate
in Borde's *Introduction of Knowledge*. In Barnaby Riche's *Faults
and nothing but Faults*, 4to. 1606, p. 6, we have the following
account of a *Fafhionmonger*: " —— here comes firft the Fafhionmonger that fpends his time in the contemplation of futes. Alas!
good gentleman, there is fomething amiffe with him. I perceive it
by his fad and heavie countenance: for my life his tailer and he
are at fome fquare about the making of his new fute; he hath cut
it after the old ftampe of fome ftale fafhion that is at the leaft of
a whole fortnight's ftanding." REED.

The Englifh gentleman is reprefented [by Borde] naked, with a
pair of tailor's fheers in one hand, and a piece of cloth on his
arm, with the following verfes:
    " I am an Englifhman, and naked I ftand here,
    " Mufing in my mynde what rayment I fhall were,
    " For now I will ware this, and now I will were that,
    " Now I will were I cannot tell what," &c.
See Camden's *Remaines*, 1614, p. 17. MALONE.

[8] —— *orthographer*;] The old copies read—*orthography*. Corrected by Mr. Pope. STEEVENS.

ther is wife; yet I am well: another virtuous; yet
I am well: but till all graces be in one woman, one
woman fhall not come in my grace.   Rich fhe fhall
be, that's certain; wife, or I'll none; virtuous, or
I'll never cheapen her; fair, or I'll never look on
her; mild, or come not near me; noble, or not I
for an angel; of good difcourfe, an excellent mufician, and her hair fhall be of what colour it pleafe
God." Ha! the prince and monfieur Love! I will
hide me in the arbour.   [*Withdraws.*

9 ——— *and her* hair *fhall be of what* colour *it pleafe God.*]   Perhaps *Benedick* alludes to a fafhion, very common in the time of
Shakfpeare, that of *dying the hair.*

Stubbes, in his *Anatomy of Abufes,* 1595, fpeaking of the attires
of women's heads, fays: "If any have haire of her owne naturall growing, which is not faire ynough, then will they *die* it in
divers colours." STEEVENS.

The practice of dying the hair was one of thofe fafhions fo frequent before and in Queen Elizabeth's time, as to be thought worthy
of particular animadverfion from the pulpit.   In the Homily againft
excefs of apparel, b. l. 1547, after mentioning the common excufes
of fome nice and vain women for painting their faces, *dying their
hair,* &c. the preacher breaks out into the following invective:
"Who can paynt her face, and curle her heere, and *change it
into an unnaturall coloure,* but therein doth worke reprofe to her
maker who made her? as thoughe fhe coulde make herfelfe more
comelye than God hath appoynted the meafure of her beautie.
What do thefe women but go about to refourme that which God
hath made? not knowyng that all thynges naturall is the worke of
God: and thynges difguyfed and unnatural be the workes of the
devyll," &c.   REED.

Or he may allude to the fafhion of wearing *falfe hair,* "of whatever colour it pleafed God."   So, in a fubfequent fcene: "I like
the new tire within, if the *hair* were a thought browner."   Fines
Moryfon, defcribing the drefs of the ladies of Shakfpeare's time,
fays, "Gentlewomen virgins weare gownes clofe to the body, and
aprons of fine linnen, and go bareheaded, with their hair curioufly
knotted, and raifed at the forehead, but *many* (againft the cold, as
they fay,) weare caps of hair that *is not their own."*   See *The Two
Gentlemen of Verona.*   MALONE.

The practice of colouring the hair in Shakfpeare's time, receives confiderable illuftration from *Maria Magdalene her Life and*

Enter Don PEDRO, LEONATO, *and* CLAUDIO.

D. PEDRO. Come, fhall we hear this mufick?

CLAUD. Yea, my good lord :——How ftill the evening is,
As hufh'd on purpofe to grace harmony !

D. PEDRO. See you where Benedick hath hid himfelf?

CLAUD. O, very well, my lord : the mufick ended,
We'll fit the kid-fox with a penny-worth.[2]

Repentance, 1567, where *Infidelitie* (the Vice) recommends her to a goldfmith to die her hair yellow with fome preparation, when it fhould fade ; and *Carnal Concupifcence* tells her likewife that there was " other geare befides goldfmith's water," for the purpofe.
DOUCE.

[2] Pedro. *See you where Benedick hath hid himfelf?*
Claudio. *O, very well, my lord : the mufick ended,*
We'll fit the kid-fox *with a penny-worth.*] i. e. we will be even with the fox now difcovered. So the word *kid*, or *kidde*, fignifies in Chaucer :

" The foothfaftnefs that now is hid,
" Without coverture fhall be *kid*,
" When I undoen have this dreming."
Romaunt of the Rofe, 2171, &c.

" Perceiv'd or fhew'd.
" He *kidde* anon his bone was not broken."
Troilus and Creffeide, lib. i. 208.

" With that anon fterte out daungere,
" Out of the place where he was hidde ;
" His malice in his cheere was *kidde*."
Romaunt of the Rofe, 2130. GREY.

It is not impoffible but that Shakfpeare chofe on this occafion to employ an antiquated word ; and yet if any future editor fhould choofe to read—*bid* fox, he may obferve that Hamlet has faid— " *Hide* fox and all after." STEEVENS.

Dr. Warburton reads as Mr. Steevens propofes. MALONE.

A *kid-fox* feems to be no more than a *young fox* or cub. In *As you Like it*, we have the expreffion of—" two *dog-apes*."
RITSON.

Enter BALTHAZAR, *with mufick.*[9]

D. PEDRO. Come, Balthazar, we'll hear that fong
     again.[2]

BALTH. O good my lord, tax not fo bad a voice
To flander mufick any more than once.

D. PEDRO. It is the witnefs ftill of excellency,
To put a ftrange face on his own perfection:—
I pray thee, fing, and let me woo no more.

BALTH. Becaufe you talk of wooing, I will fing:
Since many a wooer doth commence his fuit
To her he thinks not worthy; yet he wooes;
Yet will he fwear, he loves.

D. PEDRO.   Nay, pray thee, come:
Or, if thou wilt hold longer argument,
Do it in notes.

BALTH.   Note this before my notes,
There's not a note of mine that's worth the noting.

D. PEDRO. Why thefe are very crotchets that he
          fpeaks;
Note, notes, forfooth, and noting![3]   [*Mufick.*

BENE. Now, *Divine air!* now is his foul ravifh'd!—
Is it not ftrange, that fheeps' guts fhould hale fouls
out of men's bodies?—Well, a horn for my money,
when all's done.

---

[9] —— *with mufick.*] I am not fure that this ftage-direction
(taken from the quarto, 1600) is proper. Balthazar might have
been defigned at once for a vocal and an inftrumental performer.
Shakfpeare's orcheftra was hardly numerous; and the firft folio,
inftead of Balthazar, only gives us *Jacke Wilfon*, the name of the
actor who reprefented him. STEEVENS.

[2] *Come,* Balthazar, *we'll hear that fong again.*] *Balthazar*, the
mufician and fervant to Don Pedro, was perhaps thus named from
the celebrated Baltazarini, called *De Beaujoyeux*, an Italian performer
on the violin, who was in the higheft fame and favour at the court
of Henry II. of France, 1577. BURNEY.

[3] —— *and* noting!] The old copies—*nothing.* The correction
was made by Mr. Theobald. MALONE.

BALTHAZAR *sings.*

I.

BALTH. *Sigh no more, ladies, sigh no more,*[4]
Men were deceivers ever;
One foot in sea, and one on shore;
To one thing constant never:
Then sigh not so,
But let them go,
And be you blith and bonny;
Converting all your sounds of woe
Into, Hey nonny, nonny.

II.

Sing no more ditties, sing no mo
Of dumps so dull and heavy;
The fraud of men was ever so,
Since summer first was leavy.
Then sigh not so, &c.

D. PEDRO. By my troth, a good song.

BALTH. And an ill singer, my lord.

D. PEDRO. Ha? no; no, faith; thou sing'st well
enough for a shift.

BENE. [*Aside.*] An he had been a dog, that should
have howl'd thus, they would have hang'd him: and,
I pray God, his bad voice bode no mischief! I had
as lief have heard the night-raven,[5] come what
plague could have come after it.

---

[4] *Sigh no more, ladies, sigh no more,*]
    " Weep no more, woful shepherds, weep no more."
                            Milton's *Lycidas.* STEEVENS.

[5] ——*I pray God, his bad voice* bode no mischief! *I had as lief*
have heard the night-raven,] i. e. the owl; νυκτικόραξ. So, in *King*
Henry VI. P. III. sc. vi:
    " The *night-crow* cried, *aboding luckless time."* STEEVENS.
Thus also, Milton, in *L'Allegro:*
    " And the *night-raven* sings." DOUCE.

D. Pedro. Yea, marry; [*To* Claudio.]—Doſt thou hear, Balthazar? I pray thee, get us ſome excellent muſick; for to-morrow night we would have it at the lady Hero's chamber-window.

Balth. The beſt I can, my lord.

D. Pedro. Do ſo: farewell. [*Exeunt* Balthazar *and muſick.*] Come hither, Leonato: What was it you told me of to-day? that your niece Beatrice was in love with ſignior Benedick?

Claud. O, ay:——Stalk on, ſtalk on; the fowl ſits.[6] [*Aſide to* Pedro.] I did never think that lady would have loved any man.

Leon. No, nor I neither; but moſt wonderful, that ſhe ſhould ſo dote on ſignior Benedick, whom ſhe hath in all outward behaviours ſeem'd ever to abhor.

---

[6] ——— *Stalk on, ſtalk on; the fowl ſits.*] This is an alluſion to the *ſtalking-horſe*; a horſe either real or factitious, by which the fowler anciently ſheltered himſelf from the ſight of the game.
So, in *The Honeſt Lawyer*, 1616:
    " Lye there, thou happy warranted caſe
    " Of any villain. Thou haſt been my *ſtalking-horſe*
    " Now theſe ten months."
Again, in the 25th Song of Drayton's *Polyolbion:*
    " One underneath his *horſe* to get a ſhoot doth *ſtalk.*"
Again, in his *Muſes' Elyſium :*
    " Then underneath my horſe, I *ſtalk* my game to ſtrike."
                     Steevens.
Again, in *New Shreds of the Old Snare*, by John Gee, quarto, p. 23:
" ——— Methinks I behold the cunning fowler, ſuch as I have knowne in the fenne countries and els-where, that doe ſhoot at woodcockes, ſnipes, and wilde fowle, by ſneaking behind a painted cloth which they carrey before them, having pictured in it the *ſhape of a horſe*; which while the ſilly fowle gazeth on, it is knockt downe with hale ſhot, and ſo put in the fowler's budget." Reed.
A *ſtalking-bull*, with a cloth thrown over him, was ſometimes uſed for deceiving the game; as may be ſeen from a very elegant cut in *Loniceri Venatus et Aucupium.* Francofurti, 1582, 4to. and from a print by F. Valeggio, with the motto——
    " *Veſte boves operit, dum ſturnos fallit edaces.*" Douce.

BENE. Is't poffible? Sits the wind in that corner?
[*Afide.*

LEON. By my troth, my lord, I cannot tell what to think of it; but that fhe loves him with an enraged affection,—it is paft the infinite of thought.[7]

D. PEDRO. May be, fhe doth but counterfeit.

CLAUD. 'Faith, like enough.

LEON. O God! counterfeit! There never was

---

[7] *—— but that fhe loves him with an enraged affection,—it is paft the* infinite *of thought.*] It is impoffible to make fenfe and grammar of this fpeech. And the reafon is, that the two beginnings of two different fentences are jumbled together and made one. For— *but that fhe loves him with an enraged affection,* is only part of a fentence, which fhould conclude thus,—*is moft certain.* But a new idea ftriking the fpeaker, he leaves his fentence unfinifhed, and turns to another,—*It is paft the infinite of thought,*—which is like-wife left unfinifhed; for it fhould conclude thus—*to fay how great that affection is.* Thofe broken disjointed fentences are ufual in converfation. However, there is one word wrong, which yet per-plexes the fenfe; and that is *infinite.* Human thought cannot furely be called *infinite* with any kind of figurative propriety. I fuppofe the true reading was *definite.* 'This makes the paffage intelligible. *It is paft the* definite *of thought,*—i. e. it *cannot be defined* or con-ceived how great that affection is. Shakfpeare ufes the word again in the fame fenfe in *Cymbeline :*

" For ideots, in this cafe of favour, would
" Be wifely *definite.*——"

i. e. could tell how to pronounce or determine in the cafe.
WARBURTON.

Here are difficulties raifed only to fhow how eafily they can be removed. The plain fenfe is, *I know not what to think otherwife, but that fhe loves him with an* enraged *affection: It* (this affection) *is paft the infinite of thought.* Here are no abrupt ftops, or im-perfect fentences. *Infinite* may well enough ftand; it is ufed by more careful writers for *indefinite :* and the fpeaker only means, that *thought,* though in itfelf *unbounded,* cannot reach or eftimate the degree of her paffion. JOHNSON.

The meaning I think, is,—*but with what an enraged affection fhe loves him, it is beyond the power of thought to conceive.* MALONE.

Shakfpeare has a fimilar expreffion in *King John :*
" Beyond the *infinite* and boundlefs reach
" Of mercy"——. STEEVENS.

G g 3

counterfeit of paſſion came ſo near the life of paſſion, as ſhe diſcovers it.

D. Pedro. Why, what effects of paſſion ſhows ſhe?

Claud. Bait the hook well; this fiſh will bite.
            [*Aſide.*

Leon. What effects, my lord! She will ſit you,—
You heard my daughter tell you how.

Claud. She did, indeed.

D. Pedro. How, how, I pray you? You amaze
me: I would have thought her ſpirit had been in-
vincible againſt all aſſaults of affection.

Leon. I would have ſworn it had, my lord; eſpe-
cially againſt Benedick.

Bene. [*Aſide.*] I ſhould think this a gull, but that
the white-bearded fellow ſpeaks it: knavery cannot, ſure, hide himſelf in ſuch reverence.

Claud. He hath ta'en the infection; hold it up.
            [*Aſide.*

D. Pedro. Hath ſhe made her affection known
to Benedick?

Leon. No; and ſwears ſhe never will: that's
her torment.

Claud. 'Tis true, indeed; ſo your daughter ſays:
Shall I, ſays ſhe, *that have ſo oft encounter'd him with
ſcorn, write to him that I love him?*

Leon. This ſays ſhe now when ſhe is beginning
to write to him: for ſhe'll be up twenty times a
night; and there will ſhe ſit in her ſmock, till ſhe
have writ a ſheet of paper: *——my daughter tells us all.

---

 * *This ſays ſhe now when ſhe is beginning to write to him: for
ſhe'll be up twenty times a night; and there will ſhe ſit in her ſmock, till
ſhe have writ a ſheet of paper:*] Shakſpeare has more than once
availed himſelf of ſuch incidents as occurred to him from hiſtory,
&c. to compliment the princes before whom his pieces were performed. A ſtriking inſtance of flattery to James occurs in
 I

CLAUD. Now you talk of a sheet of paper, I remember a pretty jest your daughter told us of.

LEON. O!—When she had writ it, and was reading it over, she found Benedick and Beatrice between
the sheet?—

CLAUD. That.

LEON. O! she tore the letter into a thousand half-
pence

model

her:

should

bim,

Macbeth
Elizabe
of the
Bothwe
" I
scribble
I am n
to the

Mr.

every edition of Mary's letter which

hi

A

th
"

A *farthing*, and perhaps a *halfpenny*, was used to signify any small
particle or division. So, in the character of the *Prioress* in *Chaucer*:

" That in hire cuppe was no *ferthing* sene
" Of grese, whan she dronken hadde hire draught."
Prol. to the Cant. Tales, Tyrwhitt's edit. v. 135. STEEVENS.

See *Mortimeriados,* by Michael Drayton, 4to. 1596:

" She now begins to write unto her lover,—
" Then turning back to read what she had writ,
" She teyrs the paper, and condemns her wit." MALONE.

CLAUD. Then down upon her knees she falls, weeps, sobs, beats her heart, tears her hair, prays, curses;—*O sweet Benedick! God give me patience!*

LEON. She doth indeed; my daughter says so: and the ecstasy[a] hath so much overborne her, that my daughter is sometime afraid she will do a desperate outrage to herself; It is very true.

D. PEDRO. It were good, that Benedick knew of it by some other, if she will not discover it.

CLAUD. To what end? He would but make a sport of it, and torment the poor lady worse.

D. PEDRO. An he should, it were an alms to hang him: She's an excellent sweet lady; and, out of all suspicion, she is virtuous.

CLAUD. And she is exceeding wise.

D. PEDRO. In every thing, but in loving Benedick.

LEON. O my lord, wisdom and blood[3] combating in so tender a body, we have ten proofs to one, that blood hath the victory. I am sorry for her, as I have just cause, being her uncle and her guardian.

D. PEDRO. I would, she had bestowed this dotage on me; I would have daff'd[4] all other respects, and

---

[a] —— *and the* ecstasy——] i. e. alienation of mind. So, in *The Tempest,* Act III. sc. iii:——" Hinder them from what this *ecstasy* may now provoke them to." STEEVENS.

[3] —— *and* blood——] I suppose *blood,* in this instance, to mean *nature,* or disposition. So, in *The Yorkshire Tragedy:*
" For 'tis our *blood* to love what we're forbidden."A
STEEVENS.

Blood is here as in many other places used by our author in the sense of *passion,* or rather *temperament of body.* MALONE.

[4] —— *have* daff'd——] To *daff* is the same as to *doff,* to *do off,* to put aside. So, in *Macbeth:*
" —— to *doff* their dire distresses." STEEVENS.

made her half myfelf: I pray you, tell Benedick of it, and hear what he will fay.

LEON. Were it good, think you?

CLAUD. Hero thinks furely, fhe will die: for fhe fays, fhe will die if he love her not; and fhe will die ere fhe make her love known; and fhe will die if he woo her, rather than fhe will 'bate one breath of her accuftom'd croffnefs.

D. PEDRO. She doth well: if fhe fhould make tender of her love, 'tis very poffible he'll fcorn it; for the man, as you know all, hath a contemptible fpirit.[5]

CLAUD. He is a very proper man.[6]

D. PEDRO. He hath, indeed, a good outward hap-pinefs.

CLAUD. 'Fore God, and in my mind, very wife.

D. PEDRO. He doth, indeed, fhow fome fparks that are like wit.

LEON. And I take him to be valiant.

D. PEDRO. As Hector, I affure you: and in the

---

[5] —— contemptible *fpirit.*] That is, a temper inclined to fcorn and contempt. It has been before remarked, that our author ufes his verbal adjectives with great licence. There is therefore no need of changing the word with Sir Thomas Hanmer to *contemptuous.*
JOHNSON.

In the *argument* to *Darius*, a tragedy, by Lord Sterline, 1603, it is faid, that Darius wrote to Alexander " in a proud and *contemptible* manner." In this place *contemptible* certainly means *contemptuous.*
Again, Drayton, in the 24th Song of his *Polyolbion*, fpeaking in praife of a hermit, fays, that he,
" The mad tumultuous world *contemptibly* forfook,
" And to his quiet cell by Crowland him betook."
STEEVENS.

[6] —— *a very* proper man.] i. e. a very handfome one. So, in *Othello* :
" This Ludovico is a *proper man.*" STEEVENS.

managing of quarrels you may fay he is wife; for either he avoids them with great difcretion, or undertakes them with a moft chriftian-like fear.

Leon. If he do fear God, he muft neceffarily keep peace; if he break the peace, he ought to enter into a quarrel with fear and trembling.

D. Pedro. And fo will he do; for the man doth fear God, howfoever it feems not in him, by fome large jefts he will make. Well, I am forry for your niece: Shall we go feek Benedick, and tell him of her love?

Claud. Never tell him, my lord; let her wear it out with good counfel.

Leon. Nay, that's impoffible; fhe may wear her heart out firft.

D. Pedro. Well, we'll hear further of it by your daughter; let it cool the while. I love Benedick well; and I could wifh he would modeftly examine himfelf, to fee how much he is unworthy fo good a lady.[6]

Leon. My lord, will you walk? dinner is ready.

Claud. If he do not dote on her upon this, I will never truft my expectation.   [*Afide.*

D. Pedro. Let there be the fame net fpread for her; and that muft your daughter and her gentlewomen carry. The fport will be, when they hold one an opinion of another's dotage, and no fuch matter; that's the fcene that I would fee, which will be merely a dumb fhow. Let us fend her to call him in to dinner.   [*Afide.*]

          [*Exeunt Don* Pedro, Claudio, *and* Leonato.

[6] ——— *unworthy fo good a lady.*] Thus the quarto, 1600. "The firft folio unneceffarily reads—" unworthy *to have* fo good a lady."
          Steevens.

BENEDICK *advances from the Arbour.*

BENE. This can be no trick : The conference was sadly borne.[7]—They have the truth of this from Hero. They seem to pity the lady; it seems, her affections have their full bent.[8] Love me! why, it must be requited. I hear how I am censured : they say, I will bear myself proudly, if I perceive the love come from her; they say too, that she will rather die than give any sign of affection.—I did never think to marry :—I must not seem proud :—Happy are they that hear their detractions, and can put them to mending. They say, the lady is fair; 'tis a truth, I can bear them witness : and virtuous ;—'tis so, I cannot reprove it : and wise, but for loving me :—By my troth, it is no addition to her wit ;—nor no great argument of her folly, for I will be horribly in love with her.—I may chance have some odd quirks and remnants of wit broken on me, because I have rail'd so long against marriage : But doth not the appetite alter? A man loves the meat in his youth, that he cannot endure in his age : Shall quips, and sentences, and these paper bullets of the brain, awe a man from the career of his humour? No : The world must be peopled. When I said, I would die a bachelor, I did not think I should live till I were married.—Here comes Beatrice : By this day, she's a fair lady : I do spy some marks of love in her.

---

7 —— *was sadly borne.*] i. e. was seriously carried on.
STEEVENS.

8 —— *have their* full bent.] Metaphor from the exercise of the bow. So, in *Hamlet* :
  " And here give up ourselves in the *full bent*,
  " To lay our service freely at your feet."
The first folio reads—" *the* full bent." I have followed the quarto, 1600. STEEVENS.

Enter BEATRICE.

BEAT. Againſt my will, I am ſent to bid you come in to dinner.

BENE. Fair Beatrice, I thank you for your pains.

BEAT. I took no more pains for thoſe thanks, than you take pains to thank me; if it had been painful, I would not have come.

BENE. You take pleaſure then in the meſſage?

BEAT. Yea, juſt ſo much as you may take upon a knife's point, and choke a daw withal:——You have no ſtomach, ſignior; fare you well.   [*Exit.*

BENE. Ha! *Againſt my will I am ſent to bid you come in to dinner*—there's a double meaning in that. *I took no more pains for thoſe thanks, than you took pains to thank me*—that's as much as to ſay, Any pains that I take for you is as eaſy as thanks:——If I do not take pity of her, I am a villain; if I do not love her, I am a Jew: I will go get her picture.   [*Exit.*

A C T   III.   S C E N E   I.

LEONATO'S *Garden.*

Enter HERO, MARGARET, *and* URSULA.

HERO. Good Margaret, run thee into the parlour;
There ſhalt thou find my couſin Beatrice
Propoſing with the Prince and Claudio:[9]
Whiſper her ear, and tell her, I and Urſula
Walk in the orchard, and our whole diſcourſe
Is all of her; ſay, that thou overheard'ſt us;

[9] Propoſing *with the Prince and Claudio :*] *Propoſing* is converſing, from the French word—*propos*, diſcourſe, talk. STEEVENS.

And bid her steal into the pleached bower,
Where honey-suckles, ripen'd by the sun,
Forbid the sun to enter;—like favourites,
Made proud by princes, that advance their pride
Against that power that bred it :—there will she
      hide her,
To listen our propose :[2] This is thy office,
Bear thee well in it, and leave us alone.

    Marg. I'll make her come, I warrant you, pre-
      sently.   [*Exit.*

    Hero. Now, Ursula, when Beatrice doth come,
As we do trace this alley up and down,
Our talk must only be of Benedick :
When I do name him, let it be thy part
To praise him more than ever man did merit :
My talk to thee must be, how Benedick
Is sick in love with Beatrice : Of this matter
Is little Cupid's crafty arrow made,
That only wounds by hearsay.   Now begin;

        Enter BEATRICE, *behind.*

For look where Beatrice, like a lapwing, runs
Close by the ground, to hear our conference.

    Urs. The pleasant'st angling is to see the fish
Cut with her golden oars the silver stream,
And greedily devour the treacherous bait :
So angle we for Beatrice; who even now

---

    [2] —— *our* propose :] Thus the quarto. The folio reads—our
purpose. Propose is right. See the preceding note. STEEVENS.

    Purpose, however, may be equally right. It depends only on the
manner of accenting the word, which, in Shakspeare's time, was
often used in the same sense as *propose.* Thus, in *Knox's History of
the Reformation in Scotland,* p. 72 : " —— with him six persons;
and getting entrie, held *purpose* with the porter." Again, p. 54,
" After supper he held comfortable *purpose* of God's chosen children." REED.

Is couched in the woodbine coverture :
Fear you not my part of the dialogue.

    HERO. Then go we near her, that her ear lose no-
              thing
Of the false sweet bait that we lay for it.——
             [*They advance to the bower.*
No, truly, Ursula, she is too disdainful ;
I know, her spirits are as coy and wild
As haggards of the rock.[3]

    URS.   But are you sure,
That Benedick loves Beatrice so entirely ?

    HERO. So says the prince, and my new-trothed lord.

    URS. And did they bid you tell her of it, madam ?

    HERO. They did intreat me to acquaint her of it :
But I persuaded them, if they lov'd Benedick,
To wish him [4] wrestle with affection,
And never to let Beatrice know of it.

    URS. Why did you so ? Doth not the gentleman
Deserve as full, as fortunate a bed,[5]
As ever Beatrice shall couch upon ?

    [3] *As* haggards *of the rock.*] Turbervile, in his book of *Falconry,*
1575, tells us, that " the *haggard* doth come from foreign parts
a stranger and a passenger ;" and Latham, who wrote after him,
says, that, " she keeps in subjection the most part of all the fowl
that fly, insomuch, that the tassel gentle, her natural and chiefest
companion, dares not come near that coast where she useth, nor fit
by the place where she standeth. Such is the greatness of her spirit,
she will not admit of any society, until such a time as nature worketh," &c. So, in *The tragical History of Didaco and Violenta,* 1576 :
      " Perchaunce she's not of *haggard's* kind,
      " Nor heart so hard to bend," &c.   STEEVENS.

    [4] *To wish* him——] i. e. *recommend* or *desire.* So, in *The Honest
Whore,* 1604 :
      " Go *wish* the surgeon to have great respect," &c.
Again, in *The Hog hath lost his Pearl,* 1614 : " But lady mine that shall
be, your father, hath *wish'd* me to appoint the day with you." REED.

    [5] —— *as* full, *&c.*] So in *Othello :*
      " What a *full* fortune doth the thick-lips owe ?" &c.

Hero. Then go we near her, that her ear lose
     nothing
Of the false sweet bait that we lay for it.——
          [*They advance to the bower.*
No, truly, Ursula, she is too disdainful ;
I know, her spirits are as coy and wild
As haggards of the rock.⁵

  Urs.   But are you sure,
That Benedick loves Beatrice so entirely ?

  Hero. So says the prince, and my new-trothed
     lord.

  Urs. And did they bid you tell her of it, ma-
     dam ?

  Hero. They did intreat me to acquaint her of it :
But I persuaded them, if they lov'd Benedick,
To wish him⁶ wrestle with affection,
And never to let Beatrice know of it.

  Urs. Why did you so ? Doth not the gentleman

---

⁵ *As haggards of the rock.*] Turberville, in his book of *Falconry,* 1575, tells us, that " the haggard doth come from foreign
parts a stranger and a passenger;" and Latham, who wrote after
him, says, that, " she keeps in subjection the most part of all
the fowl that fly, insomuch, that the tassel gentle, her natural
and chiefest companion, dares not come near that coast where
she useth, nor sit by the place where she standeth. Such is the
greatness of her spirit, *she will not admit of any society,* until
such a time as nature worketh," &c. So, in *The tragical History
of Didaco and Violenta,* 1576 :
    " Perchaunce she's not of haggard's kind,
    " Nor heart so hard to bend," &c. STEEVENS.

⁶ *To wish him*—] i. e. *recommend* or *desire.* So, in *The
Honest Whore,* 1604 :
    " Go *wish* the surgeon to have great respect," &c.
Again, in *The Hog hath lost his Pearl,* 1614 : " But lady mine
that shall be, your father, hath *wish'd* me to appoint the day
with you." REED.

Deferve as full, as fortunate a bed,[7]
As ever Beatrice fhall couch upon ?

Hero. O God of love! I know, he doth deferve
As much as may be yielded to a man :
But nature never fram'd a woman's heart
Of prouder ftuff than that of Beatrice :
Difdain and fcorn ride fparkling in her eyes,
Mifprifing [8] what they look on ; and her wit
Values itfelf fo highly, that to her
All matter elfe feems weak : [9] fhe cannot love,
Nor take no fhape nor project of affection,
She is fo felf-endeared.

Urs.   Sure, I think fo ;
And therefore, certainly, it were not good
She knew his love, left fhe make fport at it.

Hero. Why, you fpeak truth : I never yet faw
                man,
How wife, how noble, young, how rarely featur'd,
But fhe would fpell him backward : [1] if fair-faced,

[7] —— *as* full, *&c.*] So in *Othello* :
    " What a *full* fortune doth the thick-lips owe ?" &c.
Mr. M. Mafon very juftly obferves, that what Urfula means
to fay is, " that he is as deferving of complete happinefs in the
marriage ftate, as Beatrice herfelf." STEEVENS.

[8] *Mifprifing*—] Defpifing, contemning. JOHNSON.
    To *mifprife* is to *undervalue*, or take in a wrong light. So,
in *Troilus and Creffida* :
    " —— a great deal *mifprifing*
    " The knight oppos'd." STEEVENS.

[9] ——*that to her*
All matter elfe feems weak !] So, in *Love's Labour's Loft* :
    " —— to your huge ftore
    " Wife things *feem foolifh*, and rich things but poor."
                STEEVENS.

[1] ——*fpell him* backward:] Alluding to the practice of
witches in uttering prayers.

She'd fwear, the gentleman fhould be her fifter ;
If black, why, nature, drawing of an antick,
Made a foul blot : [2] if tall, a lance ill-headed ;

The following paffages containing a fimilar train of thought,
are from Lyly's *Anatomy of Wit*, 1581 :
" If one be hard in conceiving, they pronounce him a dowlte :
if given to ftudy, they proclaim him a dunce : if merry, a
jefter : if fad, a faint : if full of words, a fot : if without
fpeech, a cypher : if one argue with him boldly, then is he
impudent : if coldly, an innocent : if there be reafoning of
divinitie, they cry, *Quæ fupra nos, nihil ad nos :* if of huma-
nite, *fententias loquitur carnifex.*"
Again, p. 44, b : " ———— if he be cleanly, they [women]
term him proude : if meene in apparel, a floven : if tall, a
lungis : if fhort, a dwarf : if bold, blunt : if fhamefaft, a cow-
arde," &c. P. 55 : " If fhe be well fet, then call her a boffe :
if flender, a bafill twig : if nut brown, black as a coal : if
well colour'd, a painted wall : if fhe be pleafant, then is fhe
wanton : if fullen, a clowne : if honeft, then is fhe coye."
STEEVENS.

[2] *If* black, *why, nature, drawing of an* antick,
Made a foul blot :] The *antick* was a buffoon character in
the old Englifh farces, with a *blacked face,* and a *patch-work
habit.* What I would obferve from hence is, that the name of
antick or *antique,* given to this character, fhows that the people
had fome traditional ideas of its being borrowed from the *ancient
mimes,* who are thus defcribed by Apuleius : " *mimi centunculo,
uligine faciem obducti.*" WARBURTON.

I believe what is here faid of the old Englifh farces, is faid at
random. Dr. Warburton was thinking, I imagine, of the
modern Harlequin. I have met with no proof that the face of
the antick or Vice of the old Englifh comedy was blackened.
By the word *black* in the text, is only meant, as I conceive,
fwarthy, or dark brown. MALONE.

A *black man* means a man with a dark or thick beard, not a
fwarthy or dark-brown complexion, as Mr. Malone conceives.
DOUCE.

When Hero fays, that—" nature *drawing* of an *antick,* made
a foul *blot,*" fhe only alludes to *a drop* of *ink* that may cafually
fall out of a pen, and fpoil a *grotefque drawing.* STEEVENS.

If low, an agate very vilely cut : [3]   *c v.*

[3] *If low, an* agate *very vilely cut :*]   But why an *agate*, if low ?   For what likenefs between a *little man* and an *agate ?* The ancients, indeed, ufed this ftone to cut upon ; but very exquifitely.   I make no queftion but the poet wrote :

    —— an aglet *very vilely cut :*

An *aglet* was a tag of thofe points, formerly fo much in fafhion. Thefe tags were either of gold, filver, or brafs, according to the quality of the wearer ; and were commonly in the fhape of little images ; or at leaft had a head cut at the extremity.   The French call them, *aiguillettes.*   Mezeray, fpeaking of Henry the Third's forrow for the death of the princefs of Conti, fays, " *——portant meme fur les* aiguillettes *des petites tetes de mort.*" And as a *tall* man is before compared to a *lance ill-headed* ; fo, by the fame figure, a *little man* is very aptly liken'd to an *aglet ill-cut.*   WARBURTON.

The old reading is, I believe, the true one.   *Vilely cut* may not only mean aukwardly out by a tool into fhape, but grotefquely veined by nature as it grew.   To this circumftance, I fuppofe, Drayton alludes in his *Mufes' Elizium :*

    " With th' *agate,* very oft that is
    " *Cut ftrangely* in the quarry ;
    " As nature meant to fhow in this
    " How fhe herfelf can vary."

Pliny mentions that the fhapes of various beings are to be difcovered in *agates* ; and Mr. Addifon has very elegantly compared Shakfpeare, who was born with all the feeds of poetry, to the *agate* in the ring of Pyrrhus, which, as Pliny tells us, had the figure of Apollo and the nine Mufes in the veins of it, produced by the fpontaneous hand of nature, without any help from art.   STEEVENS.

Dr. Warburton reads *aglet,* which was adopted, I think, too haftily by the fubfequent editors.   I fee no reafon for departing from the old copy.   Shakfpeare's comparifons fcarcely ever anfwer completely on both fides.   Dr. Warburton afks, " What likenefs is there between a little man and an *agate ?*"   No other than that both are *fmall.*   Our author has himfelf, in another place, compared a *very little man* to an *agate.*   " Thou whorfon mandrake, (fays Falftaff to his *page,*) thou art fitter to be worn in my cap, than to wait at my heels.   I was never fo *man'd* with an *agate* till now."   Hero means no more than this : " If a man be low, Beatrice will fay that he is as diminutive and unhappily formed as an ill-cut agate."

If fpeaking, why, a vane blown with all winds;[2]

The old reading is, I believe, the true one. *Vilely cut* may not only mean aukwardly worked by a tool into fhape, but grotefquely veined by nature as it grew. To this circumftance, I fuppofe, *Drayton* alludes in his *Mufes' Elizium:*

"With th' *agate*, very oft that is
"*Cut ftrangely* in the quarry;
"As nature meant to fhow in this
"How fhe herfelf can vary."

Pliny mentions that the fhapes of various beings are to be dif-covered in *agates*; and Mr. Addifon has very elegantly compared Shakfpeare, who was born with all the feeds of poetry, to the *agate* in the ring of Pyrrhus, which, as Pliny tells us, had the figure of Apollo and the nine Mufes in the veins of it, produced by the fpontaneous hand of nature, without any help from art.

STEEVENS.

Dr. Warburton reads *aglet*, which was adopted, I think, too haftily by the fubfequent editors. I fee no reafon for departing from the old copy. Shakfpeare's comparifons fcarcely ever anfwer completely on both fides. Dr. Warburton afks, "What likenefs is there between a little man and an *agate?*" No other than that both are *fmall.* Our author has himfelf in another place compared a *very little man* to an *agate.* "Thou whorfon mandrake, (fays Falftaff to his page,) thou art fitter to be worn in my cap, than to wait at my heels. I was never fo *man'd* with an *agate* till now." Hero means no more than this: "If a man be low, Beatrice will fay that he is as diminutive and unhappily formed as an ill-cut agate."

It appears both from the paffage juft quoted, and from one of Sir John Harrington's epigrams, 4to. 1618, that agates were com-monly worn in Shakfpeare's time:

" *The author to a daughter nine years old.*

"Though pride in damfels is a hateful vice,
"Yet could I like a noble-minded girl,
"That would demand me things of coftly price,
"Rich velvet gowns, pendents, and chains of pearle,
"Cark'nets of *agats, cut* with *rare device,*" &c.

Thefe lines, at the fame time that they add fupport to the old reading, fhew, I think, that the words "vilely *cut*," are to be underftood in their ufual fenfe, when applied to precious ftones, *viz. awkwardly wrought by a tool,* and not, as Mr. Steevens fup-pofes, *grotefquely veined* by nature. MALONE.

[2] —— *a vane blown with all winds;*] This comparifon might

If filent, why, a block moved with none.
So turns fhe every man the wrong fide out;
And never gives to truth and virtue, thát
Which fimplenefs and merit purchafeth.

    Urs. Sure, fure, fuch carping is not commend-
        able.

    Hero. No: not to be fo odd, and from all fafhions,
As Beatrice is, cannot be commendable:
But who dare tell her fo? If I fhould fpeak,
She'd mock me into air; O, fhe would laugh me
Out of myfelf, prefs me to death with wit.[3]
Therefore let Benedick, like cover'd fire,
Confume away in fighs, wafte inwardly:
It were a better death than die with mocks;
Which is as bad as die with tickling.[4]

    Urs. Yet tell her of it; hear what fhe will fay.

    Hero. No; rather I will go to Benedick,
And counfel him to fight againft his paffion:
And, truly, I'll devife fome honeft flanders
To ftain my coufin with: One doth not know,
How much an ill word may empoifon liking.

have been borrowed from an ancient black-letter ballad, entitled
A Comparifon of the Life of Man:
      " I may compare a *man* againe,
      " Even like unto a *twining vane,*
      " That changeth even as doth the wind;
      " Indeed fo is man's fickle mind." STEEVENS.

    [3] —— *prefs me to death* —] The allufion is to an ancient punifh-
ment of our law, called *peine fort et dure,* which was formerly inflicted on thofe perfons, who, being indicted, refufed to plead.
In confequence of their filence, they were preffed to death by an
heavy weight laid upon their ftomach. This punifhment the good
fenfe and humanity of the legiflature have within thefe few years
abolifhed. MALONE.

    [4] *Which is as bad as die with* tickling.] The author meant that
tickling fhould be pronounced as a triffyllable; *tickeling.* So, in
Spenfer, B. II. Canto xii:
      " —— a ftrange kind of harmony;
      " Which Guyon's fenfes foftly *tickeled,*" &c. MALONE.

to be fo odd &c] I fhould read
— to be fo odd &c
           M. Mason

Urs. O, do not do your cousin such a wrong.
She cannot be so much without true judgement,
(Having so swift and excellent a wit,[5]
As she is priz'd to have,) as to refuse
So rare a gentleman as signior Benedick.

Hero. He is the only man of Italy,
Always excepted my dear Claudio.

Urs. I pray you, be not angry with me, madam,
Speaking my fancy; signior Benedick,
For shape, for bearing, argument,[6] and valour,
Goes foremost in report through Italy.

Hero. Indeed, he hath an excellent good name.

Urs. His excellence did earn it, ere he had it.——
When are you married, madam?

Hero. Why, every day;——to-morrow: Come, go in;
I'll show thee some attires; and have thy counsel,
Which is the best to furnish me to-morrow.

Urs. She's lim'd[7] I warrant you; we have caught
her, madam.

Hero. If it prove so, then loving goes by haps:
Some Cupid kills with arrows, some with traps.
[*Exeunt* Hero *and* Ursula.

---

[5] ——*so swift and excellent a wit,*] *Swift* means *ready.* So,
in *As you Like it,* Act V. sc. iv:
" He is very *swift* and sententious." Steevens.

[6] —— *argument,*] This word seems here to signify *discourse,* or,
the *powers* of reasoning. Johnson.

Argument, in the present instance, certainly means *conversation.*
So, in *King Henry IV.* P. 1: " — It would be *argument* for a
week, laughter for a month, and a good jest for ever." Steevens.

[7] *She's* lim'd——] She is ensnared and entangled as a sparrow
with *birdlime.* Johnson.

So, in *The Spanish Tragedy:*
" Which sweet conceits are *lim'd* with sly deceits."
The folio reads—She's *ta'en.* Steevens.

BEATRICE *advances.*

BEAT. What fire is in mine ears?[7] Can this be true?
    Stand I condemn'd for pride and fcorn fo much?
Contempt, farewell! and maiden pride, adieu!
    No glory lives behind the back of fuch.
And, Benedick, love on, I will requite thee;
    Taming my wild heart to thy loving hand;[8]
If thou doft love, my kindnefs fhall incite thee
    To bind our loves up in a holy band:
For others fay, thou doft deferve; and I
Believe it better than reportingly.   [*Exit.*

SCENE II.

A Room in LEONATO'S *Houfe.*

Enter Don PEDRO, CLAUDIO, BENEDICK, *and*
LEONATO.

D. PEDRO. I do but ftay till ~~marriage~~ be

bmen has transplanted this very
ssion of the 22d Iliad :
    " ——— *Now burns my ominous*
respiring, Hector's selfe conceit hath cast a
his la
    Steevens

D. Pedro. Nay, that would be as great a foil in the new glofs of your marriage, as to fhow a child his new coat, and forbid him to wear it.[9]   I will only be bold with Benedick for his company ; for, from the crown of his head to the fole of his foot, he is all mirth ; he hath twice or thrice cut Cupid's bow-ftring, and the little hangman dare not fhoot at him :[2] he hath a heart as found as a bell, and his tongue is the clapper ; for what his heart thinks, his tongue fpeaks.[3]

Bene. Gallants, I am not as I have been.

Leon. So fay I ; methinks, you are fadder,

Claud. I hope, he be in love.

D. Pedro. Hang him, truant ; there's no true drop of blood in him, to be truly touch'd with love : if he be fad, he wants money.

Bene. I have the tooth-ach.

D. Pedro. Draw it.

Bene. Hang it !

---

[9] —— *as to fhow a child his new coat, and forbid him to wear it.*] ; in *Romeo and Juliet* :
"" As is the night before fome feftival,
"" To an impatient child, that hath new robes,
"" And may not wear them." STEEVENS.

[2] —— *the little* hangman *dare not fhoot at him :*] This character Cupid came from the *Arcadia* of Sir Philip Sidney :
"" Millions of yeares this old drivell Cupid lives ;
"" While ftill more wretch, more wicked he doth prove :
"" Till now at length that Jove him office gives,
"" (At Juno's fuite, who much did Argus love,)
"" In this our world a *hangman* for to be
"" Of all thofe fooles that will have all they fee."
B. II. ch. xiv. FARMER.

—— *as a bell, and his tongue is the clapper ;* &c.] A covert alon to the old proverb :
"" As the fool thinketh
"" So the bell clinketh." STEEVENS.

CLAUD. You muft hang it firft, and draw it after-wards.

D. PEDRO. What? figh for the tooth-ach?

LEON. Where is but a humour, or a worm?

BENE. Well, Every one can mafter a grief,[3] but he that has it.

CLAUD. Yet fay I, he is in love.

D. PEDRO. There is no appearance of fancy in him, unlefs it be a fancy that he hath to ftrange dif-guifes;[4] as, to be a Dutch-man to-day; a French-man to-morrow; or in the fhape of two countries at once,[5] as, a German from the waift downward, all flops;[6] and a Spaniard from the hip upward, no

---

[3] —— can *mafter a grief,*] The old copies read corruptly—*can-not.* The correction was made by Mr. Pope. MALONE.

[4] *There is no appearance of* fancy, *&c.*] Here is a play upon the word *fancy*, which Shakfpeare ufes for *love* as well as for *humour*, *caprice*, or *affectation.* JOHNSON.

[5] —— *or in the fhape of two countries at once, &c.*] So, in *The Seven deadly Sinnes of London*, by Tho. Dekker, 1606, 4to. bl. L. "For an Englifhman's fute is like a traitor's bodie that hath been hanged, drawne, and quartered, and is fet up in feverall places: his codpiece is in Denmarke; the collor of his dublet and the belly, in France: the wing and narrow fleeve, in Italy: the fhort wafte hangs ouer a Dutch botcher's ftall in Utrich: his huge floppes fpeaks Spanifh: Polonia gives him the bootes, &c.——and thus we mocke euerie nation, for keeping one fafhion, yet fteale patches from euerie one of them, to peece out our pride; and are now laugh-ing-ftocks to them, becaufe their cut fo fcurvily becomes us." STEEVENS.

[6] —— *all* flops;] *Slops* are large loofe *breeches*, or *trowfers*, worn only by failors at prefent. They are mentioned by Jonfon, in his *Alchymift:*

"—— fix great *flops*
"Bigger than three Dutch hoys."

Again, in *Ram Alley, or Merry Tricks*, 1611:

"—— three pounds in gold
"Thefe *flops* contain." STEEVENS.

Hence evidently the term *flop-feller*, for the venders of ready made clothes. NICHOLS.

doublet:[7] Unless he have a fancy to this foolery, as it appears he hath, he is no fool for fancy, as you would have it appear he is.[8]

Claud. If he be not in love with some woman, there is no believing old signs: he brushes his hat o' mornings; What should that bode?

D. Pedro. Hath any man seen him at the barber's?

Claud. No, but the barber's man hath been seen with him; and the old ornament of his cheek hath already stuffed tennis-balls.[9]

Leon. Indeed, he looks younger than he did, by the loss of a beard.

D. Pedro. Nay, he rubs himself with civet: Can you smell him out by that?

Claud. That's as much as to say, The sweet youth's in love.

---

[9] —— *a Spaniard from the hip upward, no doublet:*] There can be no doubt but we should read, *all* doublet, which corresponds with the actual dress of the old Spaniards. As the passage now stands, it is a negative description, which is in truth no description at all. M. Mason.

—— *no doublet:*] or, in other words, *all cloak.* The words—"Or in the shape of two countries," &c. to "no doublet," were omitted in the folio, probably to avoid giving any offence to the Spaniards, with whom James became a friend in 1604. Malone.

[8] —— *have it appear he is.*] Thus the quarto, 1600. The folio, 1623, reads—"have it to appear," &c. Steevens.

[9] —— *and the old ornament of his cheek hath already* stuff'd tennis-balls.] So, in *A wonderful, strange, and miraculous astrological Prognostication for this Year of our Lord* 1591; written by Nashe, in ridicule of Richard Harvey: "——they may sell their haire by the pound, to stuffe tennice balles." Steevens.

Again, in *Ram Alley, or Merry Tricks,* 1611:
"Thy *beard* shall serve to *stuff* those *balls* by which I get me heat at tenice."
Again, in *The Gentle Craft,* 1600:
"He'll shave it off, and *stuffe tenice balls* with it." Henderson.

H h 4

D. PEDRO. The greateft note of it is his melancholy.

CLAUD. And when was he wont to wafh his face?

D. PEDRO. Yea, or to paint himfelf? for the which, I hear what they fay of him.

CLAUD. Nay, but his jefting fpirit; which is now crept into a luteftring,[9] and now governed by ftops.

D. PEDRO. Indeed, that tells a heavy tale for him: Conclude, conclude, he is in love.

CLAUD. Nay, but I know who loves him.

D. PEDRO. That would I know too; I warrant, one that knows him not.

CLAUD. Yes, and his ill conditions; and, in defpite of all, dies for him.

D. PEDRO. She fhall be buried with her face upwards.[2]

---

[9] *——crept into a* luteftring,] *Love*-fongs in our author's time were generally fung to the mufick of the lute. So, in *K. Henry IV.* P. I: " — as melancholy as an old lion, or a *lover's lute.*" MALONE.

[2] *She fhall be buried with her* face *upwards.*] Thus the whole fet of editions: but what is there any way particular in this? Are not all men and women buried fo? Sure, the poet means, in oppofition to the general rule, and by way of diftinction, with her *heels* upwards, or *face* downwards. I have chofen the firft reading, becaufe I find it the expreffion in vogue in our author's time. THEOBALD.

This emendation, which appears to me very fpecious, is rejected by Dr. Warburton. The meaning feems to be, that fhe who acted upon principles contrary to others, fhould be buried with the fame contrariety. JOHNSON.

Mr. Theobald quite miftakes the fcope of the poet, who prepares the reader to expect fomewhat uncommon or extraordinary; and the humour confifts in the difappointment of that expectation, as at the end of Iago's poetry in *Othello*:

" She was a wight, (if ever fuch wight were)——
" To fuckle fools, and chronicle fmall beer." HEATH.

Theobald's conjecture may, however, be fupported by a paffage in *The Wild Goofe Chafe* of Beaumont and Fletcher:

Bene. Yet is this no charm for the tooth-ach.——
Old fignior, walk afide with me; I have ftudied

> " ——— love cannot ftarve me;
> " For if I die o'th' firft fit, I am unhappy,
> " And worthy to be *buried with my heels upwards.*"

Dr. Johnfon's explanation may likewife be countenanced by a
paffage in an old black letter book, without date, intitled, *A merye
Jeft of a man that was called* Howleglas, &c. " How *Howleglas*
was buried."—" Thus as *Howleglas* was deade, than they brought
him to be buryed.   And as they would have put the coffyn into
the pytte with 11 cordes, the corde at the fete brake, fo that
the fote of the coffyn fell into the botome of the pyt, and the
coffyn ftood bolt upryght in the middes of the grave.   Then defired the people that ftode about the grave that tyme, to let the
coffyn to ftand bolt upryght.   For in his lyfe tyme he was a very
marvelous man, &c. and fhall be buryed as marvailoufly; and in
this maner they left *Howleglafs*," &c.

That this book was once popular, may be inferred from *Ben
Jonfon's* frequent allufions to it in his *Poetafter:*

> " What do you laugh, *Owleglas?*"

Again, in *The Fortunate Ifles,* a Mafque:

> " ——— What do you think of *Owlglas,*
> " Inftead of him?"

And again, in *The Sad Shepherd.*   This hiftory was originally
written in Dutch.   The hero is there called *Uyle-fpegel.*   Under
this title he is likewife introduced by *Ben Jonfon* in his *Alchymift,*
and the *Mafque* and Paftoral already quoted.   *Menage* fpeaks of
Ulefpeigle as a man famous for *tromperies ingenienfes*; adds that his
Life was tranflated into French; and quotes the title-page of it.
I have another copy publifhed *A Troyes,* in 1714, the title of
which differs from that fet down by *Menage.*

The paffage indeed, may mean only—*She fhall be buried in her
lover's arms.*   So, in *The Winter's Tale:*

> " *Flo.* What? like a corfe?
> " *Per.* No, like a bank for love to lie and play on;
> " Not like a corfe:——or if,—not to be *buried,*
> " But *quick and in my arms.*"

On the whole, however, I prefer Mr. Theobald's conjecture to my
own explanation.   Steevens.

This laft is, I believe, the true interpretation.   Our author often
quotes Lilly's Grammar; and here perhaps he remembered a phrafe
that occurs in that book, p. 59, and is thus interpreted:—" Tu
cubas fupinus, thou lieft *in bed with thy face upwards.*"   *Heels* and

eight or nine wife words to fpeak to you, which thefe hobby-horfes muft not hear.

        [Exeunt BENEDICK *and* LEONATO.

D. PEDRO. For my life, to break with him about Beatrice.

CLAUD. 'Tis even fo : Hero and Margaret have by this play'd their parts with Beatrice; and then the two bears will not bite one another, when they meet.

Enter Don JOHN.

D. JOHN. My lord and brother, God fave you.

D. PEDRO. Good den, brother.

D. JOHN. If your leifure ferv'd, I would fpeak with you.

D. PEDRO. In private?

D. JOHN. If it pleafe you;—yet count Claudio may hear; for what I would fpeak of, concerns him.

D. PEDRO. What's the matter?

D. JOHN. Means your lordfhip to be married to-morrow?   *[To* CLAUDIO.

D. PEDRO. You know, he does.

D. JOHN. I know not that, when he knows what I know.

CLAUD. If there be any impediment, I pray you, difcover it.

---

face never could have been confounded by either the eye or the ear.

    Befides; Don Pedro is evidently playing on the word *dies* in Claudio's fpeech, which Claudio ufes metaphorically, and of which Don Pedro avails himfelf to introduce an allufion to that confummation which he fuppofes Beatrice was *dying* for.

                                MALONE.

D. John. You may think, I love you not; let that appear hereafter, and aim better at me by that I now will manifest: For my brother, I think, he holds you well; and in dearness of heart hath holp to effect your ensuing marriage: surely, suit ill spent, and labour ill bestowed!

D. Pedro. Why, what's the matter?

D. John. I came hither to tell you; and, circumstances shorten'd, (for she hath been too long a talking of,) the lady is disloyal.

Claud. Who? Hero?

D. John. Even she; Leonato's Hero, your Hero, every man's Hero.[3]

Claud. Disloyal?

D. John. The word is too good to paint out her wickedness; I could say, she were worse; think you of a worse title, and I will fit her to it. Wonder not till further warrant: go but with me tonight, you shall see her chamber-window enter'd; even the night before her wedding day: if you love her then, to-morrow wed her; but it would better fit your honour to change your mind.

Claud. May this be so?

D. Pedro. I will not think it.

D. John. If you dare not trust that you see, confess not that you know: if you will follow me, I will show you enough; and when you have seen more, and heard more, proceed accordingly.

Claud. If I see any thing to-night why I should not marry her to-morrow; in the congregation, where I should wed, there will I shame her.

---

[3] —— *Leonato's Hero, your Hero, every man's Hero.*] Dryden has transplanted this sarcasm into his *All for Love:*

"Your Cleopatra; Dolabella's Cleopatra; every man's Cleopatra." Steevens,

D. Pedro. And, as I wooed for thee to obtain her, I will join with thee to difgrace her.

D. John. I will difparage her no farther, till you are my witneffes: bear it coldly but till midnight, and let the iffue fhow itfelf.

D. Pedro. O day untowardly turned!

Claud. O mifchief ftrangely thwarting!

D. John. O plague right well prevented! So will you fay, when you have feen the fequel.

[*Exeunt.*

S C E N E   III.

A Street.

Enter Dogberry *and* Verges,[4] *with the* Watch.

Dogb. Are you good men and true?

Verg. Yea, or elfe it were pity but they fhould fuffer falvation, body and foul.

Dogb. Nay, that were a punifhment too good for them, if they fhould have any allegiance in them, being chofen for the prince's watch.

Verg. Well, give them their charge,[5] neighbour Dogberry.

Dogb. Firft, who think you the moft defartlefs man to be conftable?

---

[4] ———— Dogberry *and* Verges,] The firft of thefe worthies had his name from the *Dog-berry,* i. e. the female cornel, a fhrub that grows in the hedges in every county of England.

Verges is only the provincial pronunciation of *Verjuice.*

STEEVENS.

[5] *Well, give them their* charge,] To *charge* his fellows, feems to have been a regular part of the duty of the conftable of the Watch. So, in *A New Trick to cheat the Devil,* 1639: "My watch is fet—*charge given*—and all at peace." Again, in *The Infatiate Countefs,* by Marfton, 1603: "Come on; my hearts; we are the city's fecurity—I'll give you your *charge.*" MALONE.

1 Watch. Hugh Oatcake, fir, or George Sea-coal; for they can write and read.

Dogb. Come hither, neighbour Seacoal : God hath bleſſed you with a good name : to be a well-favoured man is the gift of fortune; but to write and read comes by nature.

2 Watch. Both which, maſter conſtable,——

Dogb. You have; I knew it would be your anſwer. Well, for your favour, fir, why, give God thanks, and make no boaſt of it ; and for your writing and reading, let that appear when there is no need of ſuch vanity. You are thought here to be the moſt ſenſeleſs and fit man for the conſtable of the watch ; therefore bear you the lantern : This is your charge ; You ſhall comprehend all vagrom men; you are to bid any man ſtand, in the prince's name.

2 Watch. How if he will not ſtand?

Dogb. Why then, take no note of him, but let him go; and preſently call the reſt of the watch together, and thank God you are rid of a knave.

Verg. If he will not ſtand when he is bidden, he is none of the prince's ſubjects.

Dogb. True, and they are to meddle with none but the prince's ſubjects:——You ſhall alſo make no noiſe in the ſtreets; for, for the watch to babble and to talk, is moſt tolerable and not to be endured.

2 Watch. We will rather ſleep than talk; we know what belongs to a watch.

Dogb. Why, you ſpeak like an ancient and moſt quiet watchman; for I cannot ſee how ſleeping ſhould offend : only, have a care that your bills be not ſtolen :⁶——Well, you are to call at all the ale-

---

⁶ —— bills *be not ſtolen* :] A *bill* is ſtill carried by the watchmen at Litchfield. It was the old weapon of Engliſh infantry, which, ſays Temple, *gave the moſt ghaſtly and deplorable wounds.* It may be called *ſecuris falcata.* JOHNSON.

houfes, and bid thofe that are drunk [6] get them to bed.

About Shakfpeare's time *halberds* were the weapons borne by the watchmen, as appears from Blount's *Voyage to the Levant:* " ——— certaine Janizaries, who with great ftaves guard each ftreet, as our night watchmen with *halberds* in London." REED.

The weapons to which the care of Dogberry extends, are mentioned in Glapthorne's *Wit in a Conftable,* 1639:

      " ———— Well faid, neighbours ;
      " You're chatting wifely o'er your *bills* and-lanthorns,
      " As becomes watchmen of difcretion."

Again, in *Arden of Feverfham,* 1592 :

      " ————— the watch
      " Are coming tow'rd our houfe with glaives and *bills.*"

The following reprefentation of a *watchman,* with his *bill* on his fhoulder, is copied from the title-page to Decker's *O per fe O,* &c. 4to. 1612 :

STEEVENS.

[6] ——— *bid* thofe *that are drunk*——] Thus the quarto, 1600. The folio, 1623, reads—" bid *them* that," &c.   STEEVENS.

2 *Watch*. How if they will not?

Dogb. Why then, let them alone till they are fober; if they make you not then the better anfwer, you may fay, they are not the men you took them for.

2 *Watch*. Well, fir.

Dogb. If you meet a thief, you may fufpect him, by virtue of your office, to be no true man: and, for fuch kind of men, the lefs you meddle or make with them, why, the more is for your honefty.

2 *Watch*. If we know him to be a thief, fhall we not lay hands on him?

Dogb. Truly, by your office, you may; but, I think, they that touch pitch will be defiled: the moft peaceable way for you, if you do take a thief, is, to let him fhow himfelf what he is, and fteal out of your company.

Verg. You have been always called a merciful man, partner.

Dogb. Truly, I would not hang a dog by my will; much more a man who hath any honefty in him.

Verg. If you hear a child cry in the night, you muft call to the nurfe, and bid her ftill it.[7]

---

[7] *If you hear a child cry*, &c.] It is not impoffible but that part of this fcene was intended as a burlefque on *The Statutes of the Streets*, imprinted by Wolfe, in 1595. Among thefe I find the following:

22. " No man fhall blowe any horne in the night, within this citie, or whiftle after the houre of nyne of the clock in the night, under paine of imprifonment.

23. " No man fhall ufe to go with vifoures, or difguifed by night, under like paine of imprifonment.

24. " Made th : night-walkers, and evifdroppers, like punifhment.

25. " No hammer-man, as a fmith, a pewterer, a founder, and all artificers making great found, fhall not worke after the houre of nyne at night, &c.

4

2 *Watch.* How if the nurfe be afleep, and will not hear us?

Dogb. Why then, depart in peace, and let the child wake her with crying: for the ewe that will not hear her lamb when it baes, will never anfwer a calf when he bleats.

Verg. 'Tis very true.

Dogb. This is the end of the charge. You, con-ftable, are to prefent the prince's own perfon; if you meet the prince in the night, you may ftay him.

Verg. Nay by'r lady, that, I think, he cannot.

Dogb. Five fhillings to one on't, with any man that knows the ftatues,[7] he may ftay him: marry, not without the prince be willing: for, indeed, the watch ought to offend no man; and it is an offence to ftay a man againft his will.

Verg. By'r lady, I think, it be fo.

Dogb. Ha, ha, ha! Well, mafters, good night; an there be any matter of weight chances, call up

30. "No man fhall, after the houre of nyne at night, keepe any rule, whereby any fuch fuddaine outcry be made in the ftill of the night, as making any affray, or beating his wyfe, or fervant, or finging, or revylling in his houfe, to the difturbaunce of his neigh-bours, under payne of iii s. iiii d." &c. &c.

Ben Jonfon, however, appears to have ridiculed this fcene in the Induction to his *Bartholomew-Fair*:

"And then a fubftantial *watch* to have ftole in upon 'em, and taken them away with *miftaking words*, as the fafhion is in the ftage practice." Steevens.

Mr. Steevens obferves, and I believe juftly, that Ben Jonfon intended to ridicule this fcene in his Induction to *Bartholomew-Fair*; yet in his *Tale of a Tub*, he makes his wife men of Finfbury fpeak juft in the fame ftyle, and blunder in the fame manner, without any fuch intention. M. Mason.

7 ——— *the* ftatues,] Thus the folio, 1623. The quarto, 1600, reads—"the ftatures." But whether the blunder was defigned by the poet, or created by the printer, muft be left to the confideration of our readers. Steevens.

me : keep your fellows' counfels and your own,[8] and good night.—Come, neighbour.

2 *WATCH*. Well, mafters, we hear our charge : let us go fit here upon the church-bench till two, and then all to-bed.

DOGB. One word more, honeft neighbours : I pray you, watch about fignior Leonato's door ; for the wedding being there to-morrow, there is a great coil to-night : Adieu, be vigitant, I befeech you.

[*Exeunt* DOGBERRY *and* VERGES.

Enter BORACHIO *and* CONRADE.

BORA. What ! Conrade,—

WATCH. Peace, ftir not.   [*Afide.*

BORA. Conrade, I fay !

CON. Here, man, I am at thy elbow.

BORA. Mafs, and my elbow itch'd ; I thought, there would a fcab follow.

CON. I will owe thee an anfwer for that ; and now forward with thy tale.

BORA. Stand thee clofe then under this penthoufe, for it drizzles rain ; and I will, like a true drunkard,[9] utter all to thee.

WATCH. [*Afide.*] Some treafon, mafters ; yet ftand clofe.

BORA. Therefore know, I have earned of Don John a thoufand ducats.

---

[8] —— *keep your fellows' counfels and your own,*] This is part of the oath of a grand juryman ; and is one of many proofs of Shakfpeare's having been very converfant, at fome period of his life, with legal proceedings and courts of juftice. MALONE.

[9] —— *like a true* drunkard,] I fuppofe, it was on this account that Shakfpeare called him *Borachio*, from *Boraccho*, Spanifh, a drunkard ; or *Borracha*, a leathern receptacle for wine. STEEVENS.

VOL. IV.   I i

Con. Is it possible that any villainy should be so dear?

Bora. Thou should'st rather ask, if it were possible any villainy should be so rich;[9] for when rich villains have need of poor ones, poor ones may make what price they will.

Con. I wonder at it.

Bora. That shows, thou art unconfirm'd :[2] Thou knowest, that the fashion of a doublet, or a hat, or a cloak, is nothing to a man.

Con. Yes, it is apparel.

Bora. I mean, the fashion.

Con. Yes, the fashion is the fashion.

Bora. Tush! I may as well say, the fool's the fool. But see'st thou not what a deformed thief this fashion is?

Watch. I know that Deformed; he has been a vile thief this seven year; he goes up and down like a gentleman: I remember his name.

Bora. Didst thou not hear somebody?

Con. No; 'twas the vane on the house.

Bora. Seest thou not, I say, what a deformed thief this fashion is? how giddily he turns about all the hot bloods, between fourteen and five and thirty? sometime, fashioning them like Pharaoh's soldiers in the reechy painting;[3] sometime, like god

---

9 —— *any* villainy *should be so rich*;] The sense absolutely requires us to read, *villain*. WARBURTON.

The old reading may stand. STEEVENS.

2 —— *thou art* unconfirm'd :] i. e. unpractised in the ways of the world. WARBURTON.

3 —— reechy *painting*;] Is painting discoloured by smoke. So, in *Hans Beer Pot's Invisible Comedy*, 1618 :

   " —————— he look'd so *reechily*,

   " Like bacon hanging on the chimney's roof."

from Recan, Anglo-Saxon, to *reek*, *fumare*. STEEVENS.

Bel's priests [4] in the old church window ; sometime,
like the shaven Hercules [5] in the smirch'd [6] worm-
eaten tapestry, where his codpiece seems as massy
as his club?

Con. All this I see ; and see, that the fashion
wears out more apparel than the man : But art not
thou thyself giddy with the fashion too, that thou
hast shifted out of thy tale into telling me of the
fashion ?

[4] —— *like god Bel's priests* ——] Alluding to some aukward representation of the story of *Bel and the Dragon*, as related in the
Apocrypha. STEEVENS.

[5] —— *sometime, like the shaven Hercules*, &c.] By the *shaven
Hercules* is meant *Sampson*, the usual subject of old tapestry. In
this ridicule on the fashion, the poet has not unartfully given a
stroke at the barbarous workmanship of the common tapestry hang-
ings, then so much in use. The same kind of raillery Cervantes
has employed on the like occasion, when he brings his knight and
'squire to an inn, where they found the story of Dido and Æneas
represented in bad tapestry. On Sancho's seeing the tears fall
from the eyes of the forsaken queen as big as walnuts, he hopes
that when their atchievements became the general subject for these
sorts of works, that fortune will send them a better artist.——What
authorised the poet to give this name to Sampson was the folly of
certain Christian mythologists, who pretend that the Grecian Hercules was the Jewish Sampson. The retenue of our author is to
be commended : The sober audience of that time would have been
offended with the mention of a venerable name on so light an occasion. Shakspeare is indeed sometimes licentious in these matters :
But to do him justice, he generally seems to have a sense of religion, and to be under its influence. What Pedro says of Benedick,
in this comedy, may be well enough applied to him : *The man doth
fear God, however it seems not to be in him by some large jests he will
make.* WARBURTON.

I believe that Shakspeare knew nothing of these Christian
mythologists, and by *the shaven Hercules* meant only *Hercules when
shaved to make him look like a woman*, while he remained in the service of Omphale, his Lydian mistress. Had *the shaven Hercules*
been meant to represent Sampson, he would probably have been
equipped with a *jaw bone* instead of a *club*. STEEVENS.

[6] —— *smirch'd* ——] Smirch'd is soiled, obscured. So, in *As you
Like it*, Act I. sc. iii:
     " And with a kind of umber *smirch* my face." STEEVENS.

Bora. Not so neither : but know, that I have to-
night wooed Margaret, the lady Hero's gentlewoman, by the name of Hero ; she leans me out at
her mistress' chamber-window, bids me a thousand
times good night,——I tell this tale vilely :—— I should
first tell thee, how the prince, Claudio, and my
master, planted, and placed, and possessed by my
master Don John, saw afar off in the orchard this
amiable encounter.

Con. And thought they, Margaret was Hero?

Bora. Two of them did, the prince and Claudio ;
but the devil my master knew she was Margaret ;
and partly by his oaths, which first possessed them,
partly by the dark night, which did deceive them,
but chiefly by my villainy, which did confirm any
slander that Don John had made, away went Claudio enraged ; swore he would meet her as he was
appointed, next morning at the temple, and there,
before the whole congregation, shame her with what
he saw over-night, and send her home again without
a husband.

1 *Watch.* We charge you in the prince's name,
stand.

2 *Watch.* Call up the right master constable:
We have here recovered the most dangerous piece
of lechery that ever was known in the commonwealth.

1 *Watch.* And one Deformed is one of them ; I
know him, he wears a lock.[6]

Con. Masters, masters,[7]——

---

[6] ——*wears a lock.*] So, in *The Return from Parnassus*, 1606 :
　　" He whose thin fire dwells in a smoky roofe,
　　" Must take tobacco, and must wear *a lock.*"
See Dr. Warburton's note, Act V. sc. i. Steevens.

[7] Con. *Masters, masters, &c.*] In former copies :
Con. *Masters.*

2 *WATCH.* You'll be made bring Deformed forth, I warrant you.

CON. Mafters,——

1 *WATCH.* Never fpeak; we charge you, let us obey you to go with us.

BORA. We are like to prove a goodly commodity, being taken up of thefe men's bills.[8]

Con. A commodity in queftion,[9] I warrant you. Come, we'll obey you.   [*Exeunt.*

SCENE IV.

A Room in LEONATO'S *Houfe.*

Enter HERO, MARGARET, *and* URSULA.

HERO. Good Urfula, wake my coufin Beatrice, and defire her to rife.

URS. I will, lady.

2 Watch. *You'll be made bring Deformed forth, I warrant you.*
Con. *Mafters never fpeak, we charge you, let us obey you to go with us.*
The regulation which I have made in this laft fpeech, though againft the authority of all the printed copies, I flatter myfelf, carries its proof with it. Conrade and Borachio are not defigned to talk abfurd nonfenfe. It is evident therefore, that Conrade is attempting his own juftification; but is interrupted in it by the impertinence of the men in office. THEOBALD.

[8] —— *a goodly* commodity, *being* taken up *of thefe men's* bills.] Here is a clufter of conceits. *Commodity* was formerly as now, the ufual term for an article of merchandife. To *take up*, befides its common meaning, (*to apprehend*,) was the phrafe for obtaining goods on credit. " If a man is thorough with them in honeft *taking up*, (fays Falftaff,) then they muft ftand upon fecurity." *Bill* was the term both for a fingle bond, and a halberd.
We have the fame conceit in *King Henry VI. P. II*: " My lord, When fhall we go to Cheapfide, and *take up commodities* upon our *bills*?" MALONE.

[9] *A commodity in* queftion,] i. e. a commodity fubject to judicial trial or examination. Thus Hooker: " Whofoever be found guilty, the communion book hath deferved leaft to be called *in queftion* for this fault." STEEVENS.

Hero. And bid her come hither.

Urs. Well.   [*Exit* Ursula.

Marg. Troth, I think, your other rabato[9] were better.

Hero. No, pray thee, good Meg, I'll wear this.

Marg. By my troth, it's not so good ; and I warrant, your cousin will say so.

Hero. My cousin's a fool, and thou art another ; I'll wear none but this.

Marg. I like the new tire within excellently, if the hair were a thought browner :[2] and your gown's a most rare fashion, i'faith. I saw the duchess of Milan's gown, that they praise so.

Hero. O, that exceeds, they say.

Marg. By my troth it's but a night-gown in re-

---

9 —— *rabato*—] An ornament for the neck, a collar-band or kind of ruff. Fr. *Rabat.* Menage saith it comes from *rabattre*, to put back, because it was at first nothing but the collar of the shirt or shift turn'd back towards the shoulders.   T. Hawkins.

This article of dress is frequently mentioned by our ancient comic writers.

So, in the comedy of *Law Tricks*, &c. 1608 :
      " Broke broad jests upon her narrow heel,
      " Pok'd her *rabatoes*, and survey'd her *steel*."

Again, in Decker's *Guls Hornbook*, 1609 :—" Your stiff-necked *rebatoes* (that have more arches for pride to row under, than can stand under five London-bridges) durst not then," &c.

Again, in Decker's *Untrussing the Humorous Poet* : " What miserable thing is

fpect of yours: Cloth of gold, and cuts, and laced with filver; fet with pearls, down fleeves, fide-fleeves,[2] and fkirts round, underborne with a bluifh tinfel: but for a fine, quaint, graceful, and excellent fafhion, yours is worth ten on't.

[2] —— fide-fleeves,] Side-fleeves, I believe, mean *long* ones. So, in *Greene's Farewell to Follie*, 1617: " As great felfe-love lurketh in a *fide-gowne*, as in a *fhort* armour." Again, in Laneham's Account of Queen Elizabeth's entertainment at Kenelworth-Caftle, 1575, the minftrel's " gown had *fide*-fleeves down to the midleg." Clement Pafton (See *Pafton Letters*, Vol. I. p. 145, 2nd edit.} had " a *fhort* blue gown that was made of a *fide*-gown." i. e. of a *long* one. Again, in *The laft Voyage of Captaine Frobifher*, by Dionyfe Settle, 12mo. bl. l. 1577 : " They make their apparell with hoodes and tailes, &c. The men have them not fo *fyde* as the women."

Such long fleeves, within my memory, were worn by children, and were called *hanging-fleeves*; a term which is preferved in a line, I think, of Dryden:
" And mifs in *hanging-fleeves* now fhakes the dice."
Side or *fyde* in the North of England, and in Scotland, is ufed for *long* when applied to a garment, and the word has the fame fignification in the Anglo-Saxon and Danifh. Vide Gloffary to Gawaine Douglas's Virgil. To remove an appearance of tautology; as *down-fleeves* may feem fynonymous with *fide-fleeves*, a comma muft be taken out, and the paffage printed thus— " Set with pearls down fleeves, or down *th'* fleeves." The fecond paragraph of this note is copied from the *Edinburgh Magazine*, for Nov. 1786. STEEVENS.

Side-fleeves were certainly *long*-fleeves, as will appear from the following inftances. *Stowe's Chronicle*, p. 327, tempore Hen. IV: " This time was ufed exceeding pride in garments, gownes with deepe and broad fleeves commonly called poke fleeves, the fervants ware them as well as their mafters, which might well have been called the receptacles of the devil, for what they ftole they hid in their fleeves; whereof fome hung downe to the feete, and at leaft fo the knees, full of cuts and jagges, whereupon were made thefe verfes: [i. e. by Tho. Hoccleve.]
" Now hath this land little neede of broomes
" To fweepe away the filth out of the ftreete,
" Sen *fide-fleeves* of pennilefe groomes
" Will it up licke be it drie or weete."
Again, in *Fitzherbert's Book of Hufbandry:* " Theyr cotes be fo *fyde* that they be fayne to tucke them up whan they ride, as women do theyr kyrtels whan they go to the market," &c. REED.

I i 4

also A. Wyntown's Cronykil, B. IX. ch. viii v. 120.
and for the hete tuk on syd gownys"]

Hero. God give me joy to wear it, for my heart is exceeding heavy!

Marg. 'Twill be heavier foon, by the weight of a man.[3]

Hero. Fie upon thee! art not afhamed?

Marg. Of what, lady? of fpeaking honourably? Is not marriage honourable in a beggar? Is not your lord honourable without marriage? I think, you would have me fay, faving your reverence,— *a hufband:* an bad thinking do not wreft true fpeaking, I'll offend no body: Is there any harm in —*the heavier for a hufband?* None, I think, an it be the right hufband, and the right wife; otherwife 'tis light, and not heavy: Afk my lady Beatrice elfe, here fhe comes.

Enter BEATRICE.

Hero. Good morrow, coz.

Beat. Good morrow, fweet Hero.

Hero. Why, how now! do you fpeak in the fick tune?

Beat. I am out of all other tune, methinks.

Marg. Clap us into—*Light o' love*;[4] that goes without a burden; do you fing it, and I'll dance it.

---

[3] *"Twill be* heavier *foon, by the weight of a man.*] So, in *Troilus and Creffida :*
"   ——— the *heavier* for a whore." STEEVENS.

[4] ——— *Light o' love*;] This tune is alluded to in Fletcher's *Two Noble Kinfmen.* The gaoler's daughter, fpeaking of a horfe, fays:
"   He gallops to the tune of *Light o' love.*"
It is mentioned again in *The Two Gentlemen of Verona :*
"   Beft fing it to the tune of *Light o' love.*"
And in *The Noble Gentleman* of Beaumont and Fletcher. Again, in *A Gorgious Gallery of gallant Inventions,* &c. 4to. 1578: " The lover exhorteth his lady to be conftant to the tune of
"   Attend go play thee——
"   Not *Light of love*, lady," &c. STEEVENS.

BEAT. Yea, *Light o' love,* with your heels !—then if your hufband have ftables enough, you'll fee he fhall lack no barns.[5]

MARG. O illegitimate conftruction ! I fcorn that with my heels.

BEAT. 'Tis almoft five o'clock, coufin; 'tis time you were ready. By my troth I am exceeding ill :— hey ho !

MARG. For a hawk, a horfe, or a hufband ? [6]

BEAT. For the letter that begins them all, H.[7]

This is the name of an old dance tune which has occurred already in *The Two Gentlemen of Verona.* I have lately recovered it from an ancient MS. and it is as follows :

SIR J. HAWKINS.

[5] —— *no* barns.] A quibble between *barns,* repofitories of corn, and *bairns,* the old word for children. JOHNSON.

So, in *The Winter's Tale :*
"Mercy on us, a *barn!* a very pretty *barn!*" STEEVENS.

[6] ——————— hey ho !
Marg. For *a hawk, a horfe, or a* hufband?] "*Heigh ho for a hufband,* or the willing maid's wants made known," is the title of an old ballad in the Pepyfian Collection, in Magdalen College, Cambridge. MALONE.

[7] *For the letter that begins them all,* H.] This is a poor jeft, fomewhat obfcured, and not worth the trouble of elucidation.

Margaret afks Beatrice for what fhe cries, *hey ho;* Beatrice anfwers, for an *H,* that is for an *ache,* or *pain.* JOHNSON.

MARG. Well, an you be not turn'd Turk,[*] there's no more sailing by the star.

BEAT. What means the fool, trow?[9]

MARG. Nothing I; but God send every one their heart's desire!

HERO. These gloves the count sent me, they are an excellent perfume.

BEAT. I am stuff'd, cousin, I cannot smell.

MARG. A maid, and stuff'd! there's goodly catching of cold.

BEAT. O, God help me! God help me! how long have you profess'd apprehension?

MARG. Ever since you left it: Doth not my wit become me rarely?

BEAT. It is not seen enough, you should wear it in your cap.——By my troth, I am sick.

Heywood, among his Epigrams, published in 1566, has one on the letter H:

    " H is worst among letters in the cross-row;
    " For if thou find him either in thine elbow,
    " In thine arm, or leg, in any degree;
    " In thine head, or teeth, or toe, or knee;
    " Into what place soever H may pike him,
    " Wherever thou find *ache* thou shalt not like him."
                              STEEVENS.

[*] *——turn'd Turk,*] i. e. taken captive by love, and turned a renegado to his religion. WARBURTON.

This interpretation is somewhat far-fetched, yet, perhaps, it is right. JOHNSON.

Hamlet uses the same expression, and talks of his *fortune's turning Turk.* *To turn Turk,* was a common phrase for a change of condition or opinion. So, in *The Honest Whore,* by Decker, 1616:
    " If you *turn Turk* again," &c. STEEVENS.

[9] *What means the fool,* trow?] This obsolete exclamation of enquiry, is corrupted from *I trow,* or *trow you,* and occurs again in *The Merry Wives of Windsor:* " Who's there, *trow?*" To *trow* is to *imagine,* to *conceive.* So, in *Romeo and Juliet,* the Nurse says: " 'Twas no need, I *trow,* to bid me trudge." STEEVENS.

Marg. Get you some of this diſtill'd Carduus Benedictus,[2] and lay it to your heart; it is the only thing for a qualm.

Hero. There thou prick'ſt her with a thiſtle.

Beat. Benedictus! why Benedictus? you have ſome moral[3] in this Benedictus.

Marg. Moral? no, by my troth, I have no moral meaning; I meant, plain holy-thiſtle. You may think, perchance, that I think you are in love: nay, by'r lady, I am not ſuch a fool to think what I liſt; nor I liſt not to think what I can; nor, indeed, I cannot think, if I would think my heart out of thinking, that you are in love, or that you will be in love, or that you can be in love: yet Benedick was ſuch another, and now is he become a man: he ſwore he would never marry; and yet now, in deſpite of his heart, he eats his meat without grudging:[4] and

---

[2] —— *Carduus Benedictus,*] " *Carduus Benedictus,* or bleſſed thiſtle (ſays Cogan in his *Haven of Health,* 1595) ſo worthily named for the ſingular virtues that it hath."——" This herbe may worthily be called *Benedictus,* or *Omnimorbia, that* is, a ſalve for every ſore, not knowen to phyſitians of old time, but lately revealed by the ſpeciall providence of Almighty God." STEEVENS.

[3] —— *ſome moral* —] That is, ſome ſecret meaning, like the *moral* of a fable. JOHNSON.

Dr. Johnſon's explanation is certainly the true one, though it has been doubted. In *The Rape of Lucrece* our author uſes the verb to *moralize* in the ſame ſenſe:

" Nor could ſhe *moralize* his wanton ſight."

i. e. inveſtigate the *latent meaning* of his looks.

Again, in *The Taming of the Shrew:* " —— and has left me here behind, to expound the meaning or *moral* of his ſigns and tokens." MALONE.

Moralizations (for ſo they were called) are ſubjoined to many of our ancient Tales, reducing them into Chriſtian or moral leſſons. See the *Geſta Romanorum,* &c. STEEVENS.

[4] —— *he eats his meat without grudging:*] I do not ſee how this is a proof of Benedick's change of mind. It would afford more proof of amorouſneſs to ſay, *he eats* not *his meat without grudging;* but it is impoſſible to fix the meaning of proverbial expreſſions:

how you may be converted, I know not; but methinks, you look with your eyes as other women do.[1]

BEAT. What pace is this that thy tongue keeps?

MARG. Not a falfe gallop.

Re-enter URSULA:

URS. Madam, withdraw; the prince, the count,
fignior Benedick, Don John, and all the gallants of
the town, are come to fetch you to church.

HERO. Help to drefs me, good coz, good Meg,
good Urfula.   [*Exeunt.*

S C E N E V.

Another Room in LEONATO'S *Houfe.*

Enter LEONATO, *with* DOGBERRY *and* VERGES.

LEON. What would you with me, honeft neighbour?

DOGB. Marry, fir, I would have fome confidence
with you, that decerns you nearly.

LEON. Brief, I pray you; for you fee, 'tis a bufy
time with me.

DOGB. Marry, this it is, fir.

VERG. Yes, in truth it is, fir.

LEON. What is it, my good friends?

---

perhaps, *to eat meat without grudging,* was the fame as, *to do as other
do,* and the meaning is, *he is content to live by eating like other mortals,
and will be content, notwithftanding his boafts, like other mortals, to
have a wife.* JOHNSON.

Johnfon confiders this paffage too literally. The meaning of it
is, that Benedick *is in love, and takes kindly to it.* M. MASON.

The meaning, I think, is, " and yet now, in fpite of his refolution to the contrary, he *feeds* on *love,* and likes his food." MALONE.

[3] —— *you look with your eyes as other women do.*] i. e. you direct
your eyes toward the fame object; viz. a hufband. STEEVENS.

Dogb. Goodman Verges, fir, fpeaks a little off the matter: an old man, fir, and his wits are not fo blunt, as, God help, I would defire they were; but, in faith, honeft, as the fkin between his brows.[4]

Verg. Yes, I thank God, I am as honeft as any man living, that is an old man, and no honefter than I.[5]

Dogb. Comparifons are odorous: *palabras*,[6] neighbour Verges.

Leon. Neighbours, you are tedious.

Dogb. It pleafes your worfhip to fay fo, but we are the poor duke's officers;[7] but, truly, for mine own part, if I were as tedious as a king, I could find in my heart to beftow it all of your worfhip.

---

[4] —— *honeft, as the fkin between his brows.*] This is a proverbial expreffion. STEEVENS.
So, in *Gammar Gurton's Needle*, 1575:
" I am as true, I would thou knew, as *fkin betwene thy brows.*"
Again, in *Cartwright's Ordinary*, Act V. fc. ii:
" I am as *honeft as the fkin that is between thy brows.*"
REED.

[5] *I am as honeft as any man living; that is an old man, and no honefter than I.*] There is much humour, and extreme good fenfe under the covering of this blundering expreffion. It is a fly infinuation, that length of years, and the being much *backnied in the ways of men*, as Shakfpeare expreffes it, take off the glofs of virtue, and bring much defilement on the manners. For, as a great wit [Swift] fays, *Youth is the feafon of virtue: corruptions grow with years, and I believe the oldeft rogue in England is the greateft.*
WARBURTON.

Much of this is true, but I believe Shakfpeare did not intend to beftow all this reflection on the fpeaker. JOHNSON.

[6] —— *palabras.*] So, in *The Taming of the Shrew*, the Tinker fays, *pocas pallabras*, i. e. few words. A fcrap of Spanifh, which might once have been current among the vulgar, and had appeared,
as
mi

ha
El
co

LEON. All thy tedioufnefs on me! ha!

DOGB. Yea, and 'twere a thoufand times more than 'tis: for I hear as good exclamation on your worfhip, as of any man in the city; and though I be but a poor man, I am glad to hear it.

VERG. And fo am I.

LEON. I would fain know what you have to fay.

VERG. Marry, fir, our watch to-night, excepting your worfhip's prefence, have ta'en a couple of as arrant knaves as any in Meffina.

DOGB. A good old man, fir; he will be talking; as they fay, When the age is in, the wit is out; God help us! it is a world to fee![7]—Well faid, i'faith, neighbour Verges:—well, God's a good man;[8] An two men ride of a horfe, one muft ride

---

[7] —— *it is a world to fee!*] i. e. it is wonderful to fee. So, in *All for Money*, an old morality, 1594: " *It is a world to fee how* greedy they be of money." The fame phrafe often occurs, with the fame meaning, in Holinfhed. STEEVENS.

Again, in a letter from the Earl of Worcefter to the Earl of Salifbury, 1609: " While this tragedee was acting *yt was a world* to heare the reports heare."

            Lodge's Illuftrations, Vol. III. p. 380. REED.

Rather, *it is worth feeing.* Barret in his *Alvearie*, 1580, explains " It is a world to heare," by *it is a thing worthie the hearing.* Audire eft operæ pretium. *Horat.*

And in *The Myrrour of good manners compyled in latyn by Do-mynike Mancyn and tranflate into englyfhe by Alexander Bercley preft.* Imprynted by Rychard Kynfon, bl. l. no date, the line " *Eft operæ pretium* doctos fpectare colonos"—is rendered " *A world it is to fe* wyfe tyllers of the grounde." HOLT WHITE.

[8] —— *well,* God's a good man;] So, in the old Morality or Interlude of *Lufty Juventus* :
     " He wyl fay, that *God is a good Man,*
     " He can make him no better, and fay the beft he can."
Again, in *A mery Gefte of Robin Hoode*, bl. l. no date:
     " For God is bold a ~~right wife~~ *righteous* man,
     " And fo is his dame," &c. STEEVENS.

again, in Burton's Anatomy of Melancholy edit 163 p. 670. "God is a good man, y will doe no harme, &

behind : [9]—An honeſt ſoul, i'faith, ſir; by my troth he is, as ever broke bread : but, God is to be worſhipp'd : All men are not alike; alas good neighbour!

Leon. Indeed, neighbour, he comes too ſhort of you.

Dogb. Gifts, that God gives.

Leon. I muſt leave you.

Dogb. One word, ſir : our watch, ſir, have, indeed, comprehended two aſpicious perſons, and we would have them this morning examined before your worſhip.

Leon. Take their examination yourſelf, and bring it me; I am now in great haſte, as it may appear unto you.

Dogb. It ſhall be ſuffigance.

Leon. Drink ſome wine ere you go : fare you well.

Enter a Meſſenger.

Mess. My lord, they ſtay for you to give your daughter to her huſband.

Leon. I will wait upon them; I am ready.
[*Exeunt* LEONATO *and* Meſſenger.

Dogb. Go, good partner, go, get you to Francis Seacoal, bid him bring his pen and inkhorn to the gaol; we are now to examination theſe men.

---

9 —— *An two men ride,* &c.] This is not out of place, or without meaning. Dogberry, in his vanity of ſuperior parts, apologizing for his neighbour, obſerves, that *of two men on an horſe, one muſt ride behind.* The *firſt* place of rank or underſtanding can belong but to *one,* and that happy *one* ought not to deſpiſe his inferiour. JOHNSON.

Verg. And we muſt do it wiſely.

Dogb. We will ſpare for no wit, I warrant you; here's that [*Touching his forehead.*] ſhall drive ſome of them to a *non com:* [2] only get the learned writer to ſet down our excommunication, and meet me at the gaol. [*Exeunt.*

ACT IV.   SCENE I.

The inſide of a Church.

Enter Don PEDRO, *Don* JOHN, LEONATO, Friar, CLAUDIO, BENEDICK, HERO, *and* BEATRICE, *&c.*

Leon. Come, friar Francis, be brief; only to the plain form of marriage, and you ſhall recount their particular duties afterwards.

Friar. You come hither, my lord, to marry this lady?

Claud. No.

Leon. To be married to her, friar; you come to marry her.

Friar. Lady, you come hither to be married to this count?

Hero. I do.

Friar. If either of you know any inward im—pediment [3] why you ſhould not be conjoined, I charge you, on your ſouls, to utter it.

---

[2] —— *to a* non com:] i. e. to a *non compos mentis*; put them out of their wits:——or perhaps he confounds the term with *non-plus*.
MALONE.

[3] *If either of you know any inward impediment,* &c.] This is bor—rowed from our Marriage Ceremony, which (with a few ſlight changes in phraſeology) is the ſame as was uſed in the time of Shakſpeare.
DOUCE.

Claud. Know you any, Hero?

Hero. None, my lord.

Friar. Know you any, count?

Leon. I dare make his anſwer, none.

Claud. O, what men dare do! what men may do! what men daily do! not knowing what they do!

Bene. How now! Interjections? Why, then ſome be of laughing,[4] as, ha! ha! he!

Claud. Stand thee by, friar:——Father, by your leave;
Will you with free and unconſtrained ſoul
Give me this maid, your daughter?

Leon. As freely, ſon, as God did give her me.

Claud. And what have I to give you back, whoſe worth
May counterpoiſe this rich and precious gift?

D. Pedro. Nothing, unleſs you render her again.

Claud. Sweet prince, you learn me noble thank-
fulneſs.——
There, Leonato, take her back again;
Give not this rotten orange to your friend;
She's but the ſign and ſemblance of her honour:——
Behold, how like a maid ſhe bluſhes here:
O, what authority and ſhow of truth
Can cunning ſin cover itſelf withal!
Comes not that blood, as modeſt evidence,
To witneſs ſimple virtue? Would you not ſwear,
All you that ſee her, that ſhe were a maid,
By theſe exterior ſhows? But ſhe is none:

---

4 ——*ſome be of laughing*.] This is a quotation from the *Accidence.* Johnson.

VOL. IV.   K k

She knows the heat of a luxurious bed : [5]
Her blush is guiltiness, not modesty.

 LEON. What do you mean, my lord ?

 CLAUD.   Not to be married,
Not knit my soul [6] to an approved wanton.

 LEON. Dear my lord, if you, in your own proof [7]
Have vanquish'd the resistance of her youth,
And made defeat of her virginity,———

 CLAUD. I know what you would say ; If I have
    known her,
You'll say, she did embrace me as a husband,
And so extenuate the 'forehand sin :
No, Leonato,
I never tempted her with word too large ; [8]
But, as a brother to his sister, show'd
Bashful sincerity, and comely love.

 HERO. And seem'd I ever otherwise to you ?

 CLAUD. Out on thy seeming ! [9] I will write against
    it : [2]

---

[5] ———luxurious *bed:*] That is, *lascivious.* LUXURY is the confessor's term for unlawful pleasures of the sex. JOHNSON.

 Thus Pistol, in *King Henry V.* calls Fluellen a
  " ——— damned and *luxurious* mountain goat." STEEVENS.

 Again, in *The Life and Death of Edward II.* p. 129 :
  " *Luxurious* Queene, this is thy foule desire." REED.

[6] Not knit *my soul*, &c.] The old copies read, injuriously to metre,—Not *to* knit, &c. I suspect, however, that our author wrote—*Nor* knit, &c. STEEVENS.

[7] Dear *my lord, if you, in your own* proof—] In *your own proof* may signify *in your own trial of her.* TYRWHITT.

 Dear like *door, fire, hour*, and many similar words, is here used as a dissyllable. MALONE.

[8] ——— *word too* large ;] So he uses *large jests* in this play, for *licentious, not restrained within due bounds.* JOHNSON.

[9] ———thy *seeming !*] The old copies have *thee.* The emendation is Mr. Pope's. In the next line Shakspeare probably wrote— *seem'd.* MALONE.

 I

You seem to me as Dian in her orb;
As chaste as is the bud ' ere it be blown;
But you are more intemperate in your blood
Than Venus, or those pamper'd animals
That rage in savage sensuality.

HERO. Is my lord well, that he doth speak so
wide? [4]

LEON. Sweet prince, why speak not you?

D. PEDRO. What should I speak?
I stand dishonour'd, that have gone about
To link my dear friend to a common stale.

LEON. Are these things spoken? or do I but
dream? [5]

D. JOHN. Sir, they are spoken, and these things
are true.

BENE. This looks not like a nuptial.

HERO. True, O God!

CLAUD. Leonato, stand I here?
Is this the prince? Is this the prince's brother?
Is this face Hero's? Are our eyes our own?

LEON. All this is so; But what of this, my lord?

---

[2] —— *I will* write against it :] So, in *Cymbeline*, Posthumus
speaking of women, says,
" —— I'll *write against them*,
" Detest them, curse them." STEEVENS.

[3] —— *chaste as is the bud*—] Before the air has tasted its sweet-
ness. JOHNSON.

[4] —— *that he doth speak so* wide?] i. e. so remotely from the
present business. So, in *Troilus and Cressida* :—" No, no ; no such
matter, you are *wide*." Again, in *The Merry Wives of Windsor* :
" I never heard a man of his place, gravity, and learning, *so wide*
of his own respect." STEEVENS.

[5] *Are these things spoken? or do I but dream?*] So, in *Macbeth* :
" Were such things here, as we do speak about?
" Or have we," &c. STEEVENS.

K k 2

CLAUD. Let me but move one queſtion to your
           daughter ;
And, by that fatherly and kindly power ³
That you have in her, bid her anſwer truly.

LEON. I charge thee do ſo, as thou art my child.

HERO. O God defend me! how am I beſet!——
What kind of catechizing call you this ?

CLAUD. To make you anſwer truly to your name.

HERO. Is it not Hero? Who can blot that name
With any juſt reproach ?

CLAUD.   Marry, that can Hero ;
Hero itſelf can blot out Hero's virtue.
What man was he talk'd with you yeſternight
Out at your window, betwixt twelve and one ?
Now, if you are a maid, anſwer to this.

HERO. I talk'd with no man at that hour, my lord.

D. PEDRO. Why, then are you no maiden.——
           Leonato,
I am ſorry you muſt hear ; Upon mine honour,
Myſelf, my brother, and this grieved count,
Did ſee her, hear her, at that hour laſt night,
Talk with a ruffian at her chamber-window ;
Who hath, indeed, moſt like a liberal villain, ⁴

---

³ —— kindly *power*—] That is, *natural power.* **Kind** is
nature. JOHNSON.
    Thus, in the Introduction to *The Taming of the Shrew ;*
       " This do, and do it *kindly,* gentle ſirs."
i. e. *naturally.* STEEVENS.

⁴ —— liberal *villain,*] *Liberal* here, as in many places of theſe
plays, means *frank beyond honeſty,* or *decency. Free of tongue.*
Dr. Warburton unneceſſarily reads, *illiberal.* JOHNSON.
    So, in *The Fair Maid of Briſtow,* 1605 :
       " But Vallinger, moſt like a *liberal* villain
       " Did give her ſcandalous ignoble terms."
Again, in *The Captain,* by Beaumont and Fletcher :
       " And give allowance to your *liberál* jeſts
       " Upon his perſon." STEEVENS.

Confefs'd the vile encounters they have had
A thoufand times in fecret.

  D. John.   Fie, fie! they are
Not to be nam'd, my lord, not to be fpoke of;
There is not chaftity enough in language,
Without offence, to utter them : Thus, pretty lady,
I am forry for thy much mifgovernment.

  Claud. O Hero! what a Hero hadft thou been,[5]
If half thy outward graces had been placed
About thy thoughts, and counfels of thy heart!
But, fare thee well, moft foul, moft fair! farewell,
Thou pure impiety, and impious purity!
For thee I'll lock up all the gates of love,
And on my eye-lids fhall conjecture[6] hang,
To turn all beauty into thoughts of harm,
And never fhall it more be gracious.[7]

  Leon. Hath no man's dagger here a point for
    me?[8]   [Hero *fwoons.*

  Beat. Why, how now, coufin? wherefore fink
    you down?

 This fenfe of the word *liberal* is not peculiar to Shakfpeare. John Taylor, in his *Suite concerning Players,* complains of the " many afperfions very *liberally,* unmannerly, and ingratefully beftowed upon him." Farmer.

 [5] —— *what a Hero had'ft thou been,*] I am afraid here is intended a poor conceit upon the word *Hero.* Johnson.

 [6] —— *conjecture* —] Conjecture is here ufed for fufpicion.
               Malone.

 [7] *And never fhall it more be* gracious.] i. e. lovely, attractive.
               Malone.

So, in *King John :*
  " There was not fuch a *gracious* creature born." Steevens.

 [8] *Hath no man's dagger here a point for me?*] So, in *Venice Preferv'd:*
  " A thoufand daggers, all in honeft hands!
  " And have not I a friend to ftick one here?" Steevens.

D. John. Come, let us go: thefe things, come
       thus to light,
Smother her fpirits up.

    [*Exeunt Don* PEDRO, *Don* JOHN, *and* CLAUDIO.

Bene. How doth the lady?

Beat.   Dead, I think;—Help, uncle;—
Hero! why, Hero!—Uncle!—Signior Benedick!—
       friar!

Leon. O fate, take not away thy heavy hand!
Death is the faireft cover for her fhame,
That may be wifh'd for.

Beat.   How now, coufin Hero?

Friar. Have comfort, lady.

Leon.   Doft thou look up?[*]

Friar.   Yea; Wherefore fhould fhe not?

Leon. Wherefore? Why, doth not every earthly
       thing
Cry fhame upon her? Could fhe here deny
The ftory that is printed in her blood?[9]—
Do not live, Hero; do not ope thine eyes:
For did I think thou would'ft not quickly die,
Thought I thy fpirits were ftronger than thy fhames,
Myfelf would, on the rearward of reproaches,
Strike at thy life. Griev'd I, I had but one?
Chid I for that at frugal nature's frame?[*]

---

  [*] *Doft thou look up?*] The metre is here imperfect. Perhaps our
author wrote—*Doft thou* ftill *look up?* STEEVENS.

  [9] *The ftory that is printed in her blood?*] That is, *the ftory which
her blufhes difcover to be true.* JOHNSON.

  [*] *Chid I for that at frugal nature's* frame?] *Frame* is contrivance,
order, difpofition of things. So, in *The Death of Robert Earl of
Huntington,* 1603:
     " And therefore feek to fet each thing in *frame.*"
  Again, in Holinfhed's *Chronicle,* p. 555: " —— there was no
man that ftudied to bring the unrulie to *frame.*"

O, one too much by thee! Why had I one?
Why ever waſt thou lovely in my eyes?
Why had I not, with charitable hand,
Took up a beggar's iſſue at my gates;
Who ſmirched thus,[3] and mired with infamy,
I might have ſaid, *No part of it is mine,*
This ſhame derives itſelf from unknown loins?
But mine, and mine I lov'd, and mine I prais'd,
And mine that I was proud on;[4] mine ſo much,

Again, in Daniel's *Verſes on Montaigne:*
"——— extracts of men,
"Though in a troubled *frame* confus'dly ſet."
Again, in this play:
"Whoſe ſpirits toil in *frame* of villainies." STEEVENS.

It ſeems to me, that by *frugal nature's frame,* Leonato alludes to the particular formation of himſelf, or of Hero's mother, rather than to the univerſal ſyſtem of things. *Frame* means here *framing,* as it does where Benedick ſays of John, that
"His ſpirits toil in *frame* of villainies."
Thus Richard ſays of Prince Edward, that he was
"*Fram'd* in the prodigality of nature."
And, in *All's well that ends well,* the King ſays to Bertram:
"Frank nature, rather curious than in haſte,
"Hath well *compos'd* thee."
But Leonato, diſſatisfied with his own *frame,* was wont to complain of the *frugality of nature.* M. MASON.

The meaning, I think, is,——Grieved I at nature's being ſo *frugal* as to have *framed* for me only one child? MALONE.

[3] *Who* ſmirched *thus,* &c.] Thus the quarto, 1600. The folio reads—
"ſmeared." To *ſmirch* is to *daub,* to ſully. So, in *King Henry V:*
"Our gayneſs and our gilt are all *beſmirch'd.*" &c. STEEVENS.

[4] *But mine,* and *mine I lov'd, and mine I prais'd,*
And *mine that I was proud on;*] The ſenſe requires that we ſhould read, *as* in theſe three places. The reaſoning of the ſpeaker ſtands thus——*Had this been my adopted child, her ſhame would not have rebounded on me. But this child was mine, as mine I lov'd her, praiſed her, was proud of her: conſequently, as I claimed the glory, I muſt needs be ſubject to the ſhame,* &c. WARBURTON.

Even of this ſmall alteration there is no need. The ſpeaker utters his emotion abruptly. But *mine, and mine that I lov'd,* &c. by an ellipſis frequent, perhaps too frequent, both in verſe and proſe. JOHNSON.

K k 4

That I myſelf was to myſelf not mine,
Valuing of her; why, ſhe—O, ſhe is fallen
Into a pit of ink! that the wide ſea
Hath drops too few to waſh her clean again;[2]
And ſalt too little, which may ſeaſon give
To her foul tainted fleſh![3]

    Bene.   Sir, ſir, be patient:
For my part, I am ſo attir'd in wonder,
I know not what to ſay.

    Beat. O, on my ſoul, my couſin is belied!

    Bene. Lady, were you her bedfellow laſt night?

    Beat. No, truly, not; although, until laſt night,
I have this twelvemonth been her bedfellow.

    Leon. Confirm'd, confirm'd! O, that is ſtronger
              made,
Which was before barr'd up with ribs of iron!
Would the two princes lie? and Claudio lie?
Who lov'd her ſo, that, ſpeaking of her foulneſs,
Waſh'd it with tears? Hence from her; let her die.

    Friar. Hear me a little;
For I have only been ſilent ſo long,
And given way unto this courſe of fortune,
By noting of the lady: I have mark'd
A thouſand bluſhing apparitions ſtart
Into her face; a thouſand innocent ſhames
In angel whiteneſs bear away thoſe bluſhes;

        ———— *the wide ſea*
    Hath drops too few to waſh her clean again;] The ſame thought
is repeated in *Macbeth*:
      " Will all great Neptune's *ocean waſh* this blood
      " *Clean* from my hand?" STEEVENS.

    [3] ———— *which may ſeaſon give*
    To her foul tainted fleſh!] The ſame metaphor from the kitchen
occurs in *Twelfth Night*:
      " ———— all this to *ſeaſon*
      " A brother's dead love." STEEVENS.

And in her eye there hath appear'd a fire,
To burn the errors [4] that thefe princes hold
Againft her maiden truth :——Call me a fool ;
Truft not my reading, nor my obfervations,
Which with experimental feal doth warrant
The tenour of my book ; [5] truft not my age,
My reverence, calling, nor divinity,
If this fweet lady lie not guiltlefs here
Under fome biting error.

    LEON.   Friar, it cannot be :
Thou feeft, that all the grace that fhe hath left,
Is, that fhe will not add to her damnation
A fin of perjury ; fhe not denies it :
Why feek'ft thou then to cover with excufe
That which appears in proper nakednefs ?

    FRIAR. Lady, what man is he you are accus'd of? [6]

    HERO. They know, that do accufe me ; I know
        none :
If I know more of any man alive,

---

  [4] *To* burn *the* errors—} The fame idea occurs in *Romeo and Juliet :*

     " Tranfparent *hereticks* be *burnt* for liars." STEEVENS.

  [5] ——*of my* book ;} i. e. of what I have read. MALONE.

  [6] Friar. ——*what man is he you are accus'd of?*] The friar had juft before boafted his great fkill in fifhing out the truth. And, indeed, he appears by this queftion to be no fool. He was by, all the while at the accufation, and heard no name mentioned. Why then fhould he afk her what man fhe was accufed of? But in this lay the fubtilty of his examination. For, had Hero been guilty, it was very probable that in that hurry and confufion of fpirits, into which the terrible infult of her lover had thrown her, fhe would never have obferved that the man's name was not mentioned ; and fo, on this queftion, have betrayed herfelf by naming the perfon fhe was confcious of an affair with. The Friar obferved this, and fo concluded, that were fhe guilty, fhe would probably fall into the trap he laid for her.—I only take notice of this to fhow how admirably well Shakfpeare knew how to fuftain his characters. WARBURTON.

Than that which maiden modesty doth warrant,
Let all my sins lack mercy!—O my father,
Prove you that any man with me convers'd
At hours unmeet, or that I yesternight
Maintain'd the change of words with any creature,
Refuse me, hate me, torture me to death.

 FRIAR. There is some strange misprision in the
   princes.

 BENE. Two of them have the very bent of ho-
   nour;[6]
And if their wisdoms be misled in this,
The practice of it lives in John the bastard,
Whose spirits toil in frame of villainies.

 LEON. I know not; If they speak but truth of her,
These hands shall tear her; if they wrong her ho-
   nour,
The proudest of them shall well hear of it.
Time hath not yet so dried this blood of mine,
Nor age so eat up my invention,
Nor fortune made such havock of my means,
Nor my bad life reft me so much of friends,
But they shall find, awak'd in such a kind,
Both strength of limb, and policy of mind,
Ability in means, and choice of friends,
To quit me of them throughly.

 FRIAR.   Pause a while,
And let my counsel sway you in this case.
Your daughter here the princes left for dead;[7]

---

 [6] —— bent *of honour*;] *Bent* is used by our author for the
utmost degree of any passion, or mental quality. In this play before, Benedick says of Beatrice, *her affection has its full bent.* The
expression is derived from archery; the bow has its *bent,* when it
is drawn as far as it can be. JOHNSON.

 [7] *Your daughter here the princes left for dead;*] In former copies
   Your daughter here the princess (*left for dead*;)
But how comes Hero to start up a princess here? We have no in-

Let her awhile be fecretly kept in,
And publifh it, that fhe is dead indeed:
Maintain a mourning oftentation;[8]
And on your family's old monument
Hang mournful epitaphs, and do all rites
That appertain unto a burial.

  Leon. What fhall become of this? What will
    this do?

  Friar. Marry, this, well carried, fhall on her
    behalf
Change flander to remorfe; that is fome good:
But not for that, dream I on this ftrange courfe,
But on this travail look for greater birth.
She dying, as it muft be fo maintain'd,
Upon the inftant that fhe was accus'd,
Shall be lamented, pitied and excus'd,
Of every hearer: For it fo falls out,
That what we have we prize not to the worth,
Whiles we enjoy it; but being lack'd and loft,
Why, then we rack the value;[9] then we find
The virtue, that poffeffion would not fhow us
Whiles it was ours:——So will it fare with Claudio:
When he fhall hear fhe died upon his words,[2]

---

timation of her father being a prince; and this is the firft and only
time fhe is complimented with this dignity. The remotion of a
fingle letter, and of the parenthefis, will bring her to her own
rank, and the place to its true meaning:
  Your daughter here the princes *left for dead*;
i. e. Dòn Pedro, prince of Arragon; and his baftard brother, who
is likewife called a prince. THEOBALD.

  [8] ——*oftentation*;] Show, appearance. JOHNSON.

  [9] ——*we* rack *the value*;] i. e. we exaggerate the value. The
allufion is to *rack-rents.* The fame kind of thought occurs in
Antony and Cleopatra:
   " What our contempts do often hurl from us,
   " We wifh it ours again." STEEVENS.

  [2] ——*died* upon *his words*,] i. e. died *by* them. So, in *A
Midfummer Night's Dream:*
   " To die *upon* the hand I love fo well." STEEVENS.

The idea of her life fhall fweetly creep
Into his ftudy of imagination ;
And every lovely organ of her life
Shall come apparel'd in more precious habit,
More moving-delicate, and full of life,
Into the eye and profpect of his foul,
Than when fhe liv'd indeed :—then fhall he mourn,
(If ever love had intereft in his liver,²)
And wifh he had not fo accufed her ;
No, though he thought his accufation true.
Let this be fo, and doubt not but fuccefs
Will fafhion the event in better fhape
Than I can lay it down in likelihood.
But if all aim but this be levell'd falfe,
The fuppofition of the lady's death
Will quench the wonder of her infamy :
And, if it fort not well, you may conceal her
(As beft befits her wounded reputation,)
In fome reclufive and religious life,
Out of all eyes, tongues, minds, and injuries.

    Bene. Signior Leonato, let the friar advife you :
And though, you know, my inwardnefs³ and love
Is very much unto the prince and Claudio,
Yet, by mine honour, I will deal in this
As fecretly, and juftly, as your foul
Should with your body.

    Leon.   Being that I flow in grief,
The fmalleft twine may lead me.⁴

---

   ² *If ever* love *had intereft in his* liver,] The liver, in conformity
to ancient fuppofition, is frequently mentioned by Shakfpeare as
the feat of love.   Thus Piftol reprefents Falftaff as loving Mrs.
Ford—" with *liver* burning hot." STEEVENS.

   ³ ——— *my* inwardnefs—] i. e. intimacy.   Thus Lucio, in *Meafure for Meafure*, fpeaking of the Duke, fays—" I was an *inward*
of his."   Again, in *King Richard III :*
      " Who is moft *inward* with the noble duke ?" STEEVENS.

   ⁴ *The fmalleft twine may lead me.*] This is one of our author's
obfervations upon life.   Men overpowered with diftrefs, eagerly

Friar. 'Tis well confented; prefently away;
    For to ftrange fores ftrangely they ftrain the
       cure.——
Come, lady, die to live: this wedding day,
    Perhaps, is but prolong'd; have patience, and
       endure.

          [*Exeunt* FRIAR, HERO, *and* LEONATO.

Bene. Lady Beatrice,[5] have you wept all this
    while?

Beat. Yea, and I will weep a while longer.

Bene. I will not defire that.

Beat. You have no reafon, I do it freely.

Bene. Surely, I do believe your fair coufin is
    wrong'd.

Beat. Ah, how much might the man deferve
of me, that would right her!

Bene. Is there any way to fhow fuch friendfhip?

Beat. A very even way, but no fuch friend.

Bene. May a man do it?

---

liften to the firft offers of relief, clofe with every fcheme, and believe every promife.   He that has no longer any confidence in
himfelf, is glad to repofe his truft in any other that will undertake
to guide him.   JOHNSON.

   5 *Lady Beatrice,* &c.]   The poet, in my opinion, has fhown
a great deal of addrefs in this fcene.   Beatrice here engages her
lover to revenge the injury done her coufin Hero: and without
this very natural incident, confidering the character of Beatrice,
and that the ftory of her paffion for Benedick was all a fable, fhe
could never have been eafily or naturally brought to confefs fhe
loved him, notwithftanding all the foregoing preparation.   And
yet, on this confeffion, in this very place, depended the whole
fuccefs of the plot upon her and Benedick.   For had fhe not owned
her love here, they muft have foon found out the trick, and then
the defign of bringing them together had been defeated; and fhe
would never have owned a paffion fhe had been only tricked into,
had not her defire of revenging her coufin's wrong made her drop
her capricious humour at once.   WARBURTON.

Beat. It is a man's office, but not yours.

Bene. I do love nothing in the world so well as you; Is not that strange?

Beat. As strange as the thing I know not: It were as possible for me to say, I loved nothing so well as you: but believe me not; and yet I lie not; I confess nothing, nor I deny nothing:—I am sorry for my cousin.

Bene. By my sword, Beatrice, thou lovest me.

Beat. Do not swear by it, and eat it.

Bene. I will swear by it, that you love me; and I will make him eat it, that says, I love not you.

Beat. Will you not eat your word?

Bene. With no sauce that can be devised to it: I protest, I love thee.

Beat. Why then, God forgive me!

Bene. What offence, sweet Beatrice?

Beat. You have staid me in a happy hour; I was about to protest, I loved you.

Bene. And do it with all thy heart.

Beat. I love you with so much of my heart, that none is left to protest.

Bene. Come, bid me do any thing for thee.

Beat. Kill Claudio.

Bene. Ha! not for the wide world.

Beat. You kill me to deny it: Farewell.

Bene. Tarry, sweet Beatrice.

Beat. I am gone, though I am here;⁴—There is no love in you:—Nay, I pray you, let me go.

---

⁴ *I am gone, though I am here;*] i. e. I am out of your mind already, though I remain here in person before you. STEEVENS.

I cannot approve of Steevens's explanation of these words, and

Bene. Beatrice,——

Beat. In faith, I will go.

Bene. We'll be friends firſt.

Beat. You dare eaſier be friends with me, than

to eate

woul

B

B

per

B

B

der'

B

B

believe Beatrice means to ſay, " I am gone," that is, " I am loſt to you, though I am here." In this ſenſe Benedick takes them, and deſires to be friends with her. M. MASON.

Or, perhaps, my affection is withdrawn from you, though I am yet here. MALONE.

⁵ —— *in the* height *a villain*,] So, in *King Henry VIII*:
" He's a traitor to the *height*."
" *In præcipiti* vitium ſtetit." Juv. I. 149. STEEVENS.

⁶ —— *bear her in hand*—] i. e. delude her by fair promiſes. So, in *Macbeth*:
" How you were *borne in hand*, how croſs'd," &c.
STEEVENS.

⁷ —— *and* counties!] *County* was the ancient general term for a *nobleman*. See a note on the *County* Paris in *Romeo and Juliet*.
STEEVENS.

teftimony, a goodly count-confect; [7] a fweet gallant, furely! O that I were a man for his fake! or that I had any friend would be a man for my fake! But manhood is melted into courtefies, [8] valour into compliment, and men are only turned into tongue, and trim ones too: [9] he is now as valiant as Hercules, that only tells a lie, and fwears it :——I cannot be a man with wifhing, therefore I will die a woman with grieving.

Bene. Tarry, good Beatrice: By this hand, I love thee.

Beat. Ufe it for my love fome other way than fwearing by it.

Bene. Think you in your foul, the count Claudio hath wrong'd Hero?

Beat. Yea, as fure as I have a thought, or a foul.

Bene. Enough, I am engaged, I will challenge him; I will kifs your hand, and fo leave you: By this hand, Claudio fhall render me a dear account: As you hear of me, fo think of me. Go, comfort your coufin: I muft fay, fhe is dead; and fo, farewell.   [*Exeunt.*

---

[7] —— *a goodly* count-confect;] i. e. a fpecious nobleman made out of fugar. STEEVENS.

[8] —— *into* courtefies,] i. e. into ceremonious obeifance, like the *courtefies* dropped by women. Thus, in *Othello:*
"Very good; well kifs'd! an excellent *courtefy!*"
Again, in *King Richard III:*
"Duck with French nods, and apifh *courtefy.*" STEEVENS.

[9] —— *and men are only turned into* tongue, *and trim ones too:*] Mr. Heath would read *tongues,* but he miftakes the conftruction of the fentence, which is——not only men but trim ones, are turned into tongue, i. e. not only *common,* but *clever* men, &c.
                                              STEEVENS.

S C E N E   II.[2]

A Prifon.

Enter Dogberry, Verges, *and* Sexton, *in gowns;*[3] *and the* Watch, *with* Conrade *and* Borachio.

Dogb. Is our whole diffembly appear'd?

---

[2] *Scene II.*] The perfons, throughout this fcene, have been ftrangely confounded in the modern editions. The firft error has been the introduction of a *Town-Clerk*, who is, indeed, mentioned in the ftage-direction, prefixed to this fcene in the old editions, (*Enter the Conftables, Borachio, and the Towne-Clerke, in gownes,*) but no where elfe; nor is there a fingle fpeech afcribed to him in thofe editions. The part, which he might reafonably have been expected to take upon this occafion, is performed by *the Sexton;* who affifts at, or rather directs, the examinations; fets them down in writing, and reports them to Leonato. It is probable, therefore, I think, that *the Sexton* has been ftyled *the Town-Clerk*, in the ftage-direction above-mentioned, from his doing the duty of fuch an officer. But the editors, having brought *both Sexton and Town-Clerk* upon the ftage, were unwilling, as it feems, that the latter fhould be a mute perfonage; and therefore they have put into his mouth *almoft all the abfurdities* which the poet certainly intended for his ignorant *conftable.* To rectify this confufion, little more is neceffary than to go back to the old editions, remembering that the names of *Kempe* and *Cowley*, two celebrated actors of the time, are put in this fcene, for the names of the perfons reprefented; viz. *Kempe* for *Dogberry*, and *Cowley* for *Verges.* Tyrwhitt.

I have followed Mr. Tyrwhitt's regulation, which is undoubtedly juft; but have left Mr. Theobald's notes as I found them.

Steevens.

[3] —— *in gowns;*] It appears from *The Black Book*, 4to. 1604, that this was the drefs of a conftable in our author's time: "—— when they'mift their *conftable*, and fawe the *black gowne* of his office lye full in a puddle——."

The Sexton (as Mr. Tyrwhitt obferved) is ftyled in this ftage-direction, in the old copies, *the Town-Clerk*, "probably from his doing the duty of fuch an officer." But this error has only happened here; for throughout the fcene itfelf he is defcribed by his proper title. By miftake alfo in the quarto, and the folio, which

VERG. O, a ftool and a cufhion for the fexton! [3]

SEXTON. Which be the malefactors?

DOGB. Marry, that am I and my partner.

VERG. Nay, that's certain; we have the exhibition to examine. [4]

SEXTON. But which are the offenders that are to be examined? let them come before mafter conftable.

DOGB. Yea, marry, let them come before me.—What is your name, friend?

BORA. Borachio.

DOGB. Pray write down—Borachio.——Yours, firrah?

CON. I am a gentleman, fir, and my name is Conrade.

DOGB. Write down—mafter gentleman Conrade.—Mafters, do you ferve God?

CON. BORA. Yea, fir, we hope.

DOGB. Write down—that they hope they ferve God:—and write God firft; for God defend but God fhould go before fuch villains! [4]—Mafters, it is

appears to have been printed from it, the name of Kempe (an actor in our author's theatre) throughout this fcene is prefixed to the fpeeches of Dogberry, and that of Cowley to thofe of Verges, except in two or three inftances, where either *Conftable* or *Andrew* are fubftituted for Kempe. MALONE.

[3] *O, a ftool and a cufhion for the Sexton!*] Perhaps a ridicule was here aimed at *The Spanifh Tragedy* :

" *Hieron.* What, are you ready?

" *Balth.* Bring a *chaire and a cufhion* for the king."

MALONE.

[4] Con. Bora. *Yea, fir, we hope.*

Dogb. *Write down—that they hope they ferve God:—and write God firft; for God defend but God fhould go before fuch villains!*] This fhort paffage, which is truly humorous and in character, I have added from the old quarto. Befides, it fupplies a defect:

‡ — *we have the exhibition to examine.*] Blunder for — *examination to exhibit. See p. 495. " Take their examination yourfelf and —ing it me."* STEEVENS.

proved already that you are little better than falfe knaves; and it will go near to be thought fo fhortly. How anfwer you for yourfelves?

Con. Marry, fir, we fay we are none.

Dogb. A marvellous witty fellow, I affure you; but I will go about with him.——Come you hither, firrah; a word in your ear, fir; I fay to you, it is thought you are falfe knaves.

Bora. Sir, I fay to you, we are none.

Dogb. Well, ftand afide.——'Fore God, they are both in a tale:[5] Have you writ down—that they are none?

Sexton. Mafter conftable, you go not the way to examine; you muft call forth the watch that are their accufers.

Dogb. Yea, marry, that's the efteft way:[6]—Let the watch come forth:—Mafters, I charge you, in the prince's name, accufe thefe men.

---

for without it, the Town-Clerk afks a queftion of the prifoners, and goes on without ftaying for any anfwer to it. THEOBALD.

The omiffion of this paffage fince the edition of 1600, may be accounted for from the ftat. 3 Jac. I. c. 21. the facred name being jeftingly ufed four times in one line. BLACKSTONE.

5 *'Fore God, they are both in a tale:*] This is an admirable ftroke of humour: *Dogberry* fays of the prifoners that they are falfe knaves; and from that denial of the charge, which one in his wits could not but be fuppofed to make, he infers a communion of counfels, and records it in the examination as an evidence of their guilt. SIR J. HAWKINS.

If the learned annotator will amend his comment by omitting the word *guilt*, and inferting the word *innocence*, it will (except as to the fuppofed inference of a communication of counfels, which fhould likewife be omitted or corrected) be a juft and pertinent remark. RITSON.

6 *Yea, marry, that's the efteft way:*] Our modern editors, who were at a lofs to make out the corrupted reading of the old copies, read *eafieft*. The quarto, in 1600, and the firft and fecond editions in folio,

1 *WATCH.* This man faid, fir, that Don John, the prince's brother, was a villain.

DOGB. Write down—prince John a villain :— Why this is flat perjury, to call a prince's brother—villain.

BORA. Mafter conftable,—

DOGB. Pray thee, fellow, peace; I do not like thy look, I promife thee.

SEXTON. What heard you him fay elfe?

2 *WATCH.* Marry, that he had received a thoufand ducats of Don John, for accufing the lady Hero wrongfully.

DOGB. Flat burglary, as ever was committed.

VERG. Yea, by the mafs, that it is.

SEXTON. What elfe, fellow?

1 *WATCH.* And that count Claudio did mean, upon his words, to difgrace Hero before the whole affembly, and not marry her.

DOGB. O villain! thou wilt be condemned into everlafting redemption for this.

SEXTON. What elfe?

2 *WATCH.* This is all.

all concur in reading—*Yea, marry, that's the* efteft *way,* &c. A letter happened to flip out at prefs in the firft edition; and 'twas too hard a tafk for the fubfequent editors to put it in, or guefs at the word under this accidental depravation. There is no doubt but the author wrote, as I have reftored the text—*Yea, marry, that's the* defteft *way,* i. e. the *readieft,* moft *commodious* way. The word is pure Saxon. Dea*rlice, debite, congrue,* duely, fitly, Gebæche, *opportune, commode,* fitly, conveniently, feafonably, in good time, commodioufly. Vide *Spelman's Saxon Gloff.* THEOBALD.

Mr. Theobald might have recollected the word *deftly* in *Macbeth:*
 "Thyfelf and office *deftly* fhow."
Shakfpeare, I fuppofe, defigned Dogberry to corrupt this word as well as many others. STEEVENS.

SEXTON. And this is more, masters, than you can deny. Prince John is this morning secretly stolen away; Hero was in this manner accused, in this very manner refused, and upon the grief of this, suddenly died.—Master constable, let these men be bound, and brought to Leonato's; I will go before, and show him their examination.   [*Exit.*

DOGB. Come, let them be opinion'd.

VERG. Let them be in band.

CON. Off, coxcomb!⁷

---

⁷ Verg. *Let them be in* band.
  Con. *Off, coxcomb!*] The old copies read,
    " Let them be in the hands *of coxcomb.*"   STEEVENS.

Mr. Theobald gives these words to Conrade, and says—*But why the Sexton should be so pert upon his brother officers, there seems no reason from any superior qualifications in him; or any suspicion he shows of knowing their ignorance.* This is strange. The Sexton through-out shows as good sense in their examination as any judge upon the bench could do. And as to *his suspicion of their ignorance,* he tells the Town-Clerk, *That he goes not the way to examine.* The mean-ness of his name hindered our editor from seeing the goodness of his sense. But this Sexton was an ecclesiastic of one of the inferior orders called the *sacristan,* and not a *brother officer,* as the editor calls him. I suppose the book from whence the poet took his subject, was some old English novel translated from the Italian, where the word *sagristano* was rendered *sexton.* As in Fairfax's *Godfrey of Boulogne:*
    " When Phœbus next unclos'd his wakeful eye,
    " Up rose the *Sexton* of that place prophane."
The passage then in question is to be read thus :
    Sexton. *Let them be in band.*   [*Exit.*
    Con. *Off, coxcomb!*
Dogberry would have them pinion'd. The Sexton says, it was sufficient if they were kept in safe custody, and then goes out. When one of the watchmen comes up to bind them, Conrade says, *Off, coxcomb!* as he says afterwards to the constable, *Away! you are an ass.*—But the editor adds, *The old quarto gave me the first umbrage for placing it to Conrade.* What these words mean I don't know : but I suspect the old quarto divides the passage as I have done. WARBURTON.

Theobald has fairly given the reading of the quarto.

L l 3

Dogb. God's my life! where's the fexton? let him write down——the prince's officer, coxcomb.—— Come, bind them :——Thou naughty varlet!

Con. Away! you are an afs, you are an afs.

Dogb. Doft thou not fufpect my place? Doft thou not fufpect my years?—O that he were here to write

Dr. Warburton's affertion, as to the dignity of a *fexton* or *facriftan*, may be fupported by the following paffage in Stanyhurft's *Verfion of the fourth Book of the Æneid*, where he calls the Maffylian prieftefs :
" —— in foil Maffyla begotten,
" *Sexten* of Hefperides finagog." STEEVENS.

Let them be in band.] I had conjectured that thefe words fhould be given to *Verges*, and read thus—*Let them bind their hands.* I am ftill of opinion that the paffage belongs to *Verges*; but, for the true reading of it, I fhould wifh to adopt a much neater emendation, which has fince been fuggefted to me in converfation by Mr. Steevens—*Let them be in band.* Shakfpeare, as he obferved to me, commonly ufes *band* for *bond.* TYRWHITT.

It is plain that they were *bound* from a fubfequent fpeech of Pedro : " Whom have you offended, mafters, that you are thus *bound* to your anfwer?" STEEVENS.

Off, coxcomb!] The old copies read—*of*, and thefe words make a part of the laft fpeech, " Let them be in the hands *of coxcomb.*" The prefent regulation was made by Dr. Warburton, and has been adopted by the fubfequent editors. *Off* was formerly fpelt *of.* In the early editions of thefe plays a broken fentence (like that before us,—*Let them be in the hands*—) is almoft always corrupted by being tacked, through the ignorance of the tranfcriber or printer, to the fubfequent words. So, in *Coriolanus*, inftead of
" You fhames of Rome! you herd of—Boils and plagues
" Plaifter you o'er!"
we have in the folio, 1623, and the fubfequent copies,
" You fhames of Rome, you! Herd of boils and plagues," &c.
See alfo *Meafure for Meafure.*

Perhaps, however, we fhould read and regulate the paffage thus:
Ver. *Let them be in the hands of*—[the law, *he might have intended to fay.*]
Con. *Coxcomb!* MALONE.

There is nothing in the old quarto different in this fcene from the common copies, except that the names of two actors, *Kempe* and *Cowley*, are placed at the beginning of the fpeeches, inftead of the proper words. JOHNSON.

I

me down—an afs!—but, mafters, remember, that I
am an afs; though it be not written down, yet
forget not that I am an afs:—No, thou villain, thou
art full of piety, as fhall be proved upon thee by
good witnefs. I am a wife fellow; and, which is
more, an officer; and, which is more, a houfholder;
and, which is more, as pretty a piece of flefh as any
is in Meffina; and one that knows the law, go to;
and a rich fellow enough, go to; and a fellow that
hath had loffes; and one that hath two gowns,
and every thing handfome about him:—Bring him
away. O, that I had been writ down—an afs!

[*Exeunt.*

ACT V.   SCENE I.

Before LEONATO's *Houfe.*

Enter LEONATO *and* ANTONIO.

ANT. If you go on thus, you will kill yourfelf;
And 'tis not wifdom, thus to fecond grief
Againft yourfelf.

LEON.   I pray thee, ceafe thy counfel,
Which falls into mine ears as profitlefs
As water in a fieve: give not me counfel;
Nor let no comforter delight mine ear,
But fuch a one whofe wrongs do fuit with mine.
Bring me a father, that fo lov'd his child,
Whofe joy of her is overwhelm'd like mine,
And bid him fpeak of patience;[2]

---

[2] *And bid him fpeak of patience;*] Read—
    " And bid him fpeak *to me* of patience." RITSON.

Meafure his woe the length and breadth of mine,
And let it anfwer every ftrain for ftrain;
As thus for thus, and fuch a grief for fuch,
In every lineament, branch, fhape, and form:
If fuch a one will fmile, and ftroke his beard;
Cry—forrow, wag! and hem, when he fhould groan;[*]

9 *Cry—forrow, wag! and hem, when he fhould groan*;] The quarto 1600 and folio 1623, read—
      " And *forrow, wagge*, cry hem," &c.
Mr. Rowe and Mr. Pope—
      " And *hallow*, wag," &c.
Mr. Theobald—
      " And forrow *wage*," &c.
Sir Tho. Hanmer and Dr. Warburton—
      " And forrow *waive*," &c.
Mr. Tyrwhitt—
      " And forrow *gagge*," &c.
Mr. Heath and Mr. T. Warton—
      " And *forrowing* cry hem," &c.
I had inadvertently offered—
      " And, *forry* wag!" &c.
Mr. Ritfon—
      " And forrow *waggery*," &c.
Mr. Malone—
      " *In* forrow wag," &c.
But I am perfuaded that Dr. Johnfon's explanation as well as arrangement of the original words, is appofite and juft: " I cannot (fays he) but think the true meaning nearer than it is imagined.
    If fuch a one will fmile, and ftroke his beard,
     And, forrow, wag! cry; hem, when he fhould groan, &c.
That is, ' If he will fmile, and cry *forrow be gone!* and hem inftead of groaning.' The order in which *and* and *cry* are placed, is harfh, and this harfhnefs made the fenfe miftaken. Range the words in the common order, and my reading will be free from all difficulty.
    If fuch a one will fmile, and ftroke his beard,
     Cry, forrow, wag! and hem when he fhould groan —"
Thus far Dr. Johnfon; and in my opinion he has left fucceeding criticks nothing to do refpecting the paffage before us. Let me, however, claim the honour of fupporting his opinion.
    To cry—*Care away!* was once an expreffion of triumph. So, in *Acolaftus*, a comedy, 1540: " ———— I may now fay, *Care awaye!*"

Patch grief with proverbs ; make misfortune drunk
With candle-wasters ;[2] bring him yet to me,
And I of him will gather patience.

Again, *ibidem:* " —— Now grievous *sorrowe and care away!*"
Again, at the conclusion of Barnaby Googe's third *Eglog:*
  " Som cheftnuts have I there in ftore,
   " With cheefe and pleafaunt whaye ;
  " God fends me vittayles for my nede,
   " And I fynge *Care awaye!*"
 Again, as Dr. Farmer obferves to me, in George Withers's
Philarete, 1622 :
  " Why fhould we grieve or pine at that?
  " *Hang forrow!* care will kill a cat."
 Sorrow go by! is alfo (as I am affured) a common exclamation of
hilarity even at this time, in Scotland. *Sorrow wag!* might have
been juft fuch another. The verb, to *wag,* is feveral times ufed
by our author in the fenfe of to *go,* or *pack off.*
 The Prince, in the Firft Part of *King Henry IV.* Act II. fc. iv.
fays—" They cry *hem!* and bid you play it off." And Mr. M.
Mafon obferves that this expreffion alfo occurs in *As you Like it,*
where Rofalind fays—" Thefe burs are in my heart ;" and Celia
replies—" *Hem* them away." The foregoing examples fufficiently
prove the exclamation *hem,* to have been of a comic turn.
             STEEVENS.

 [2] —— *make misfortune drunk*
 With candle-wafters ;] This may mean, either wafh away his
forrow among thofe who fit up all night to drink, and in that fenfe
may be ftyled *wafters of candles;* or overpower his misfortunes by
fwallowing flap-dragons in his glafs, which are defcribed by
Falftaff as made of *candles' ends.* STEEVENS.

 This is a very difficult paffage, and hath not, I think, been
fatisfactorily cleared up. The explanation I fhall offer, will give,
I believe, as little fatisfaction ; but I will, however, venture it.
Candle-wafters is a term of contempt for fcholars : thus Jonfon,
in *Cynthia's Revels,* Act III. fc. ii : " —— fpoiled by a whorefon
book-worm, a *candle-wafter.*" In *The Antiquary,* Act III. is a
like term of ridicule : " He fhould more catch your delicate court-
ear, than all your head-fcratchers, thumb-biters, *lamp-wafters* of
them all." The fenfe then, which I would affign to Shakfpeare,
is this : " If fuch a one will patch grief with proverbs,—*cafe or
cover the wounds of his grief with proverbial fayings ;*—make misfortune drunk with candle-wafters,—*ftupify misfortune, or render
himfelf infenfible to the ftrokes of it, by the converfation or lucu-
brations of fcholars ; the production of the* lamp, *but not fitted to*

But there is no such man : For, brother, men
Can counsel, and speak comfort to that grief
Which they themselves not feel ; but, tasting it,
Their counsel turns to passion, which before
Would give preceptial medicine to rage,
Fetter strong madness in a silken thread,
Charm ach with air, and agony with words :
No, no ; 'tis all men's office to speak patience
To those that wring under the load of sorrow ;
But no man's virtue, nor sufficiency,
To be so moral, when he shall endure
The like himself : therefore give me no counsel :
My griefs cry louder than advertisement.[3]

Ant. Therein do men from children nothing differ.

Leon. I pray thee, peace ; I will be flesh and blood ;
For there was never yet philosopher,
That could endure the tooth-ach patiently ;
However they have writ the style of gods,[4]

human nature." *Patch*, in the sense of mending a defect or breach,
occurs in *Hamlet*, Act V. sc. i :

" O, that that earth, which kept the world in awe,
" Should *patch* a wall, to expel the winter's flaw."

WHALLEY.

[3] ———— *than* advertisement.] That is, than *admonition*, than *moral*
instruction. JOHNSON.

[4] *However they have writ* the style of gods,] This alludes to
the extravagant titles the Stoics gave their wise men. *Sapiens ille*
cum Diis, *ex pari, vivit.* Senec. Ep. 59. *Jupiter quo antecedit vi-*
rum bonum ? diutius bonus est. Sapiens *nihilo se minoris æstimat.——*
Deus *non vincit* sapientem *felicitate.* Ep. 73. WARBURTON.

Shakspeare might have used this expression, without any acquaintance with the hyperboles of stoicism. By the *style of gods,*
he meant an exalted language ; such as we may suppose would be
written by beings superior to human calamities, and therefore regarding them with neglect and coldness.

Beaumont and Fletcher have the same expression in the first of
their *Four Plays in One :*

" Athens doth make women philosophers,
" And sure their children chat *the talk of gods.*" STEEVENS.

And made a pifh at chance and fufferance.⁵

ANT. Yet bend not all the harm upon yourfelf;
Make thofe, that do offend you, fuffer too.

LEON. There thou fpeak'ft reafon: nay, I will
   do fo :
My foul doth tell me, Hero is bely'd;
And that fhall Claudio know, fo fhall the prince,
And all of them, that thus difhonour her.

Enter Don PEDRO *and* CLAUDIO.

ANT. Here comes the prince, and Claudio, haftily.

D. PEDRO. Good den, good den.

CLAUD.   Good day to both of you.

LEON. Hear you, my lords,——

D. PEDRO.   We have fome hafte, Leonato.

LEON. Some hafte, my lord!——well, fare you well,
   my lord :——
Are you fo hafty now?——well, all is one.

D. PEDRO. Nay, do not quarrel with us, good old
   man.

ANT. If he could right himfelf with quarreling,
Some of us would lie low.

CLAUD.   Who wrongs him?

LEON.   Marry,
Thou, thou⁶ doft wrong me; thou diffembler,
   thou :——
Nay, never lay thy hand upon thy fword,
I fear thee not.

---

⁵ *And made a pifb at* chance and fufferance.] Alludes to their
famous *apathy.* WARBURTON.

 The old copies read—*pufb.* Corrected by Mr. Pope. MALONE.

 ⁶ *Thou,* thou —] I have repeated the word—*thou,* for the fake
of meafure. STEEVENS.

CLAUD.　　　Marry, befhrew my hand,
If it fhould give your age fuch caufe of fear :
In faith, my hand meant nothing to my fword.

LEON. Tufh, tufh, man, never fleer and jeft at
　　　me :
I fpeak not like a dotard, nor a fool;
As, under privilege of age, to brag
What I have done being young, or what would do,
Were I not old: Know, Claudio, to thy head,
Thou haft fo wrong'd mine innocent child and me,
That I am forc'd to lay my reverence by;
And, with grey hairs, and bruife of many days,
Do challenge thee to trial of a man.
I fay, thou haft bely'd mine innocent child;
Thy flander hath gone through and through her
　　　heart,
And fhe lyes buried with her anceftors :
O! in a tomb where never fcandal flept,
Save this of her's, fram'd by thy villainy.

CLAUD. My villainy!

LEON.　　　　　　　Thine, Claudio; thine I fay.

D. PEDRO. You fay not right, old man.

LEON.　　　　　　　　　My lord, my lord,
I'll prove it on his body, if he dare;
Defpite his nice fence,[5] and his active practice,
His May of youth, and bloom of luftyhood.

CLAUD. Away, I will not have to do with you.

LEON. Canft thou fo daff me?[6] Thou haft kill'd
　　　my child;
If thou kill'ft me, boy, thou fhalt kill a man.

―――――

⁵ *Defpite his nice* fence,] i. e. defence, or fkill in the fcience of
fencing, or defence.　Douce.

⁶ *Can'ft thou fo* daff *me?*] This is a country word, Mr. Pope
tells us, fignifying, *damn*. It may be fo; but that is not the
expofition here: To *daff* and *doff* are fynonymous terms, that

Ant. He fhall kill two of us, and men indeed:[7]
But that's no matter; let him kill one firft;——
Win me and wear me,—let him anfwer me:——
Come, follow me, boy; come, boy, follow me:[8]
Sir boy, I'll whip you from your foining fence;[9]
Nay, as I am a gentleman, I will.

    Leon. Brother,——

    Ant. Content yourfelf: God knows, I lov'd my
        niece;

mean to *put off*: which is the very fenfe required here, and what
Leonato would reply, upon Claudio's faying, he would have nothing
to do with him. THEOBALD.

    Theobald has well interpreted the word. Shakfpeare ufes it
more than once. Thus, in *K. Henry IV.* P. I:
        " The nimble-footed mad-cap Prince of Wales,
        " And his comrades, that *daff'd* the world afide."
Again, in the comedy before us:
        " I would have *daff'd* all other refpefts," &c.
Again, in *The Lover's Complaint*:
        " There my white ftole of chaftity I *daff'd*."
    It is, perhaps, of Scottifh origin, as I find it in *Ane verie excellent
and delectabill Treatife intitulit* PHILOTUS, &c. Edinburgh, 1603:
        " Their *daffing* does us fo undo." STEEVENS.

    [7] Ant. *He fhall kill two of us*, &c.] This *brother Antony* is the
trueft picture imaginable of human nature. He had affumed the
character of a fage to comfort his brother, overwhelmed with grief
for his only daughter's affront and difhonour; and had feverely
reproved him for not commanding his paffion better on fo trying
an occafion. Yet, immediately after this, no fooner does he begin
to fufpect that his *age* and *valour* are flighted, but he falls into
the moft intemperate fit of rage himfelf: and all he can do or fay
is not of power to pacify him. This is copying nature with a
penetration and exactnefs of judgement peculiar to Shakfpeare.
As to the expreffion, too, of his paffion, nothing can be more highly
painted. WARBURTON.

    [8] ——*come, boy, follow me:*] Here the old copies deftroy the
meafure by reading—
        " —— come, *fir* boy, *come*, follow me:"
I have omitted the unneceffary words. STEEVENS.

    [9] —— foining *fence*;] *Foining* is a term in fencing, and means
thrufting. DOUCE.

And she is dead, slander'd to death by villains ;
That dare as well answer a man, indeed,
As I dare take a serpent by the tongue :
Boys, apes, braggarts, Jacks, milksops !——

LEON.   Brother Antony,——

ANT. Hold you content ; What, man ! I know
       them, yea,
And what they weigh, even to the utmost scruple :
Scambling,[2] out-facing, fashion-mong'ring boys,
That lie, and cog, and flout, deprave and slander,
Go antickly, and show outward hideousness,[3]
And speak off half a dozen dangerous words,
How they might hurt their enemies, if they durst,
And this is all.

LEON. But, brother Antony,——

ANT.   Come, 'tis no matter ;
Do not you meddle, let me deal in this.

D. PEDRO. Gentlemen both, we will not wake
       your patience.[4]

---

[2] *Scambling,*] i. e. *scrambling.* The word is more than once
used by Shakspeare. See Dr. Percy's note on the first speech of
the play of *K. Henry V.* and likewise the Scots proverb, " It is
well ken'd your father's son was never a *scambler.*" A *scambler* in
its literal sense, is one who goes about among his friends to get a
dinner, by the Irish called a *cosherer.* STEEVENS.

[3] —— *show* outward hideousness,] i. e. what in *King Henry V.*
Act III. sc. vi. is called——
     " —— a *horrid suit* of the camp." STEEVENS.

[4] —— *we will not* wake *your patience.*] This conveys a sentiment that the speaker would by no means have implied,——That
the patience of the two old men was not exercised, but asleep,
which upbraids them for insensibility under their wrong. Shakspeare must have wrote :
     —— *we will not* wrack——
i. e. destroy your patience by tantalizing you. WARBURTON.

This emendation is very specious, and perhaps is right ; yet the
present reading may admit a congruous meaning with less difficulty
than many other of Shakspeare's expressions.

My heart is forry for your daughter's death ;
But, on my honour, fhe was charg'd with nothing
But what was true, and very full of proof.

Leon. My lord, my lord,——

D. Pedro.   I will not hear you.

Leon.   No?

Brother, away : '——I will be heard ;——

Ant.   And fhall,
Or fome of us will fmart for it.
                [*Exeunt* Leonato *and* Antonio.

Enter Benedick.

D. Pedro. See, fee ; here comes the man we went
to feek.

Claud. Now, fignior ! what news !

Bene. Good day, my lord.

D. Pedro. Welcome, fignior : You are almoft
come to part almoft ' a fray.

The old men have been both very angry and outrageous ; the
prince tells them that he and Claudio *will not* wake *their patience* ;
will not any longer force them to *endure* the prefence of thofe
whom, though they look on them as enemies, they cannot refift.
                                                    Johnson.

Wake, I believe, is the original word. The ferocity of wild
beafts is overcome by not fuffering them to fleep. *We will not*
wake *your patience,* therefore means, we will forbear any further
provocation.   Henley.

The fame phrafe occurs in *Othello :*
        " Thou hadft been better have been born a dog,
        " Than anfwer my *wak'd* wrath."   Steevens.

 ⁵ *Brother, away :*—] The old copies, without regard to metre,
read—
        Come, *brother, away,* &c.
I have omitted the ufelefs and redundant word—*come.* Steevens.

 ⁶ —— *to part* almoft—] This fecond *almoft* appears like a cafual
infertion of the compofitor. As the fenfe is complete without it,
I wifh the omiffion of it had been licenfed by either of the ancient
copies.   Steevens.

Claud. We had like to have had our two nofes fnapped off with two old men without teeth.

D. Pedro. Leonato and his brother: What think'ft thou? Had we fought, I doubt, we fhould have been too young for them.

Bene. In a falfe quarrel there is no true valour. I came to feek you both.

Claud. We have been up and down to feek thee; for we are high-proof melancholy, and would fain have it beaten away: Wilt thou ufe thy wit?

Bene. It is in my fcabbard; Shall I draw it?

D. Pedro. Doft thou wear thy wit by thy fide?

Claud. Never any did fo, though very many have been befide their wit.—I will bid thee draw, as we do the minftrels; 5 draw, to pleafure us.

D. Pedro. As I am an honeft man, he looks pale:—Art thou fick, or angry?

Claud. What! courage, man! What though care kill'd a cat,6 thou haft mettle enough in thee to kill care.

Bene. Sir, I fhall meet your wit in the career, an you charge it againft me:—I pray you, choofe another fubject.

Claud. Nay, then give him another ftaff; this laft was broke crofs.7

---

5 *I will bid thee* draw, *as we do the* minftrels;] An allufion perhaps to the itinerant *fword-dancers.* In what low eftimation *minftrels* were held in the reign of Elizabeth, may be feen from Stat. Eliz. 39. C. iv. and the term was probably ufed to denote any fort of vagabonds who amufed the people at particular feafons.
                                                            Douce.

6 *What though* care kill'd a cat,] This is a proverbial expreffion. See *Ray's Proverbs.* Douce.

7 *Nay, then give him another ftaff*; &c.] An allufion to *tilting.* See note, *As you Like it*, Act III. fc. iv. Warburton.

D. Pedro. By this light, he changes more and more ; I think, he be angry indeed.

Claud. If he be, he knows how to turn his gir-dle.[8]

Bene. Shall I fpeak a word in your ear?

Claud. God blefs me from a challenge!

Bene. You are a villain ;—I jeft not :—I will make it good how you dare, with what you dare, and when you dare :—Do me right,[9] or I will pro-teft your cowardice. You have kill'd a fweet lady,

---

[8] —— *to turn his girdle.*] We have a proverbial fpeech, *If be be angry, let him turn the buckle of his girdle.* But I do not know its original or meaning. JOHNSON.

A correfponding expreffion is to this day ufed in Ireland—*If he be angry, let him tie up his brogues.* Neither proverb, I believe, has any other meaning than this: If he is in a bad humour, let him employ himfelf till he is in a better.

Dr. Farmer furnifhes me with an inftance of this proverbial expreffion as ufed by Claudio, from *Winwood's Memorials*, fol. edit. 1725. Vol. I. p. 453. See letter from Winwood to Cecyll, from Paris, 1602, about an affront he received there from *an Englifhman :* " I faid what I fpake was not to make *him* angry. He replied, if I were angry, *I might turn the buckle of my girdle behind me.*" So likewife, Cowley *On the Government of Oliver Cromwell :* " —— The next month he fwears by the living God, that he will turn them out of doors, and he does fo in his princely way of threatening, bidding them *turne the buckles of their girdles* behind them." STEEVENS.

Again, in *Knavery in all Trades, or the Coffee Houfe,* 1664. fign. E : " Nay, if the gentleman be angry, let him turn *the buckles of his girdle behind him.*" REED.

Large belts were worn with the buckle before, but for wreftling the buckle was turned behind, to give the adverfary a fairer grafp at the girdle. To turn the buckle behind, therefore, was a challenge. HOLT WHITE.

[9] *Do me right,*] This phrafe occurs in Juftice Silence's fong in *King Henry IV.* P. II. Act V. fc. iii. and was the ufual form of challenge to pledge a bumper toaft in a bumper. See note on the foregoing paffage. STEEVENS.

VOL. IV.   M m

and her death fhall fall heavy on you : Let me hear from you.

CLAUD. Well, I will meet you, fo I may have good cheer.

D. PEDRO. What, a feaft? a feaft?

CLAUD. I'faith, I thank him; he hath bid⁹ me to a calf's-head and a capon; the which if I do not carve moft curioufly, fay, my knife's naught.——Shall I not find a woodcock too?ª

BENE. Sir, your wit ambles well; it goes eafily.

D. PEDRO. I'll tell thee how Beatrice prais'd thy wit the other day : I faid, thou hadft a fine wit; *True,* fays fhe, *a fine little one: No,* faid I, *a great wit; Right,* fays fhe, *a great grofs one: Nay,* faid I, *a good wit; Juft,* faid fhe, *it hurts no body: Nay,* faid I, *the gentleman is wife; Certain,* faid fhe, *a wife gentleman:*ª *Nay,* faid I, *he hath the tongues; That I believe,* faid fhe, *for he fwore a thing to me on Mon-*

---

⁹ ——— *bid*——] i. e. invited. So, in *Titus Andronicus,* Act I. fc. ii :

    " I am not *bid* to wait upon this bride."——— REED.

ª *Shall I not find a* woodcock *too?*] A *woodcock,* being fuppofed to have no brains, was a proverbial term for a foolifh fellow. See *The London Prodigal,* 1605, and other comedies. MALONE.

A *woodcock,* means one caught in a fpringe; alluding to the plot againft Benedick. So, in *Hamlet,* fc. ult.

    " Why, as a *woodcock* to my own fpringe, Ofrick."

Again, in *Love's Labour's Loft,* Act IV. fc. iii. Biron fays— " four *woodcocks* in a difh." DOUCE.

ª ——— *a wife gentleman:*] This jeft depending on the colloquial ufe of words is now obfcure; perhaps we fhould read—*a wife gentleman,* or *a man wife enough to be a coward.* Perhaps *wife gentleman* was in that age ufed ironically, and always ftood for *filly fellow.* JOHNSON.

We ftill ludicroufly call a man deficient in underftanding—*a wife-acre.* STEEVENS.

*day night, which he forfwore on Tuefday morning;
there's a double tongue, there's two tongues.* Thus did
fhe, an hour together, tranf-fhape thy particular
virtues ; yet, at laft, fhe concluded with a figh, thou
waft the propereft man in Italy.

CLAUD. For the which fhe wept heartily, and faid,
fhe cared not.

D. PEDRO. Yea, that fhe did ; but yet, for all
that, an if fhe did not hate him deadly, fhe would
love him dearly : the old man's daughter told us
all.

CLAUD. All, all ; and moreover, *God faw him
when he was hid in the garden.*

D. PEDRO. But when fhall we fet the favage bull's
horns on the fenfible Benedick's head ?

CLAUD. Yea, and text underneath, *Here dwells
Benedick the married man ?*

BENE. Fare you well, boy ; you know my mind ;
I will leave you now to your goffip-like humour :
you break jefts as braggarts do their blades, which,
God be thanked, hurt not.——My lord, for your
many courtefies I thank you : I muft difcontinue
your company : your brother, the baftard, is fled
from Meffina : you have, among you, kill'd a fweet
and innocent lady : For my lord Lack-beard, there,
he and I fhall meet ; and till then, peace be with
him.　　　　　　　　　　　　　[*Exit* BENEDICK.

D. PEDRO. He is in earneft.

CLAUD. In moft profound earneft ; and, I'll warrant you, for the love of Beatrice.

D. PEDRO. And hath challeng'd thee ?

CLAUD. Moft fincerely.

D. PEDRO. What a pretty thing man is, when he

goes in his doublet and hose, and leaves off his wit!⁴

Enter DOGBERRY, VERGES, *and the Watch, with* CONRADE *and* BORACHIO.

CLAUD. He is then a giant to an ape: but then is an ape a doctor to such a man.

D. PEDRO. But, soft you, let be;⁵ pluck up, my

---

⁴ *What a pretty thing man is, when he goes in his doublet and hose, and leaves off his wit!*] It was esteemed a mark of levity and want of becoming gravity, at that time, *to go in the doublet and hose, and leave off the cloak,* to which this well-turned *expression* alludes. The *thought* is, that love makes a man as ridiculous, and exposes him as naked as being in the doublet and hose without a cloak. WARBURTON.

I doubt much concerning this interpretation, yet am by no means confident that my own is right. I believe, however, these words refer to what Don Pedro had said just before—" And hath *challenged* thee?"—and that the meaning is, What a pretty thing a man is, when he is silly enough to throw off his cloak, and go in his doublet and hose, to *fight* for a woman? In *The Merry Wives of Windsor,* when Sir Hugh is going to engage with Dr. Caius, he walks about in his doublet and hose: " *Page.* And youthful still in your *doublet and hose,* this raw rheumatick day!"—" ——— There is reasons and causes for it," says Sir Hugh, alluding to the duel he was going to fight.—I am aware that there was a particular species of single combat called *Rapier and cloak*; but I suppose, nevertheless, that when the small sword came into common use, the cloak was generally laid aside in duels, as tending to embarrass the combatants. MALONE.

Perhaps the whole meaning of the passage is this:—What an inconsistent fool is man, when he covers his body with clothes, and at the same time divests himself of his understanding!
STEEVENS.

⁵ *But, soft you,* let be;] The quarto and first folio read corruptly—*let me be,* which the editor of the second folio, in order to obtain some sense, converted to—*let me see.* I was once idle enough to suppose that copy was of some authority; but a minute examination of it has shewn me that all the alterations made in it

heart, and be fad![6] Did he not fay, my brother was fled ?

Dogb. Come, you, fir; if juftice cannot tame you, fhe fhall ne'er weigh more reafons in her balance:[7] nay, an you be a curfing hypocrite once, you muft be look'd to.

D. Pedro. How now, two of my brother's men bound ! Borachio, one !

Claud. Hearken after their offence, my lord !

D. Pedro. Officers, what offence have thefe men done ?

Dogb. Marry, fir, they have committed falfe report; moreover, they have fpoken untruths; fecondarily, they are flanders; fixth and laftly, they have bely'd a lady ; thirdly, they have verified unjuft things : and, to conclude, they are lying knaves.

D. Pedro. Firft, I afk thee what they have done; thirdly, I afk thee what's their offence ; fixth and laftly, why they are committed ; and, to conclude, what you lay to their charge.

---

were merely arbitrary, and generally very injudicious. *Let be* were without doubt the author's words. The fame expreffion occurs again in *Antony and Cleopatra*, Act IV. fc. iv :
   " What's this for? Ah, *let be, let be.*" Malone.

If *let be*, is the true reading, it muft mean, *let things remain as they are.* I have heard the phrafe ufed by Dr. Johnfon himfelf. Mr. Henley obferves, that the fame expreffion occurs in *St. Matt.* xxvii. 49.

   So, in

      "
      "

Again, in
be, let be."

   6 ———
heart, and

   7 ——— *n*
between *req*

Claud. Rightly reafoned, and in his own divifion ; and, by my troth, there's one meaning well fuited.[8]

D. Pedro. Who have you offended, mafters, that you are thus bound to your anfwer? this learned conftable is too cunning to be underftood: What's your offence?

Bora. Sweet prince, let me go no further to mine anfwer; do you hear me, and let this count kill me. I have deceived even your very eyes: what your wifdoms could not difcover, thefe fhallow fools have brought to light; who, in the night, overheard me confeffing to this man, how Don John your brother incenfed me to flander[9] the lady Hero; how you were brought into the orchard, and faw me court Margaret in Hero's garments; how you difgraced her, when you fhould marry her: my villainy they have upon record; which I had rather feal with my death, than repeat over to my fhame: the lady is dead upon mine and my mafter's falfe accufation; and, briefly, I defire nothing but the reward of a villain.

D. Pedro. Runs not this fpeech like iron through your blood?

Claud. I have drunk poifon, whiles he utter'd it.

D. Pedro. But did my brother fet thee on to this?

Bora. Yea, and paid me richly for the practice of it.

***

[8] —— *one meaning well fuited.*] That is, *one meaning is put into many different dreffes*; the prince having afked the fame queftion in four modes of fpeech.   Johnson.

[9] —— incens'd *me to flander*, &c.] That is, incited me.   The word is ufed in the fame fenfe in *Richard III.* and *Henry VIII.*
M. Mason.

See Minfheu's Dict in v.   Malone.
I

D. Pedro. He is compos'd and fram'd of trea-
      chery:——
And fled he is upon this villainy.

Claud. Sweet Hero! now thy image doth ap-
      pear
In the rare femblance that I lov'd it firft.

Dogb. Come, bring away the plaintiffs; by this
time our Sexton hath reform'd fignior Leonato of
the matter: And mafters, do not forget to fpecify,
when time and place fhall ferve, that I am an
afs.

Verg. Here, here comes mafter fignior Leonato,
and the Sexton too.

Re-enter Leonato *and* Antonio, *with the* Sexton.

Leon. Which is the villain? Let me fee his eyes;
That when I note another man like him,
I may avoid him: Which of thefe is he?

Bora. If you would know your wronger, look on
      me.

Leon. Art thou the flave, that with thy breath
      haft kill'd
Mine innocent child?

Bora.   Yea, even I alone.

Leon. No, not fo, villain; thou bely'ft thyfelf;
Here ftand a pair of honourable men,
A third is fled, that had a hand in it:——
I thank you, princes, for my daughter's death;
Record it with your high and worthy deeds;
'Twas bravely done, if you bethink you of it.

Claud. I know not how to pray your patience,
Yet I muft fpeak: Choofe your revenge yourfelf;

Impofe me to what penance [2] your invention
Can lay upon my fin : yet finn'd I not,
But in miftaking.

    D. Pedro.   By my foul, nor I;
And yet, to fatisfy this good old man,
I would bend under any heavy weight
That he'll enjoin me to.

    Leon. I cannot bid you bid my daughter live,
That were impoffible; but, I pray you both,
Poffefs the people [3] in Meffina here
How innocent fhe died : and, if your love
Can labour aught in fad invention,
Hang her an epitaph upon her tomb,
And fing it to her bones; fing it to night :——
To-morrow morning come you to my houfe;
And fince you could not be my fon-in-law,
Be yet my nephew : my brother hath a daughter,
Almoft the copy of my child that's dead,
And fhe alone is heir to both of us; [4]
Give her the right you fhould have given her coufin,
And fo dies my revenge.

    Claud.   O, noble fir,

---

  [2] Impofe *me to what penance*—] i. e. *command* me to undergo
whatever penance, &c. A tafk or exercife prefcribed by way of
punifhment for a fault committed at the Univerfities, is yet called
(as Mr. Steevens has obferved in a former note) an *impofition.*
                                          Malone.

  [3] Poffefs *the people,* &c.] To *poffefs,* in ancient language, fignifies,
to *inform,* to make acquainted with. So, in *The Merchant of
Venice :*
     " Is he yet *poffefs'd* how much you would ?"
Again, *ibid :*
     " I have *poffefs'd* your grace of what I purpofe."
                                          Steevens.

  [4] *And fhe alone is heir to both of us* ;] Shakfpeare feems to have
forgot what he had made Leonato fay, in the fifth fcene of the firft
Act to Antonio, " How now, brother; where is my coufin your
fon? hath he provided the mufick?" Anonymous.

Your over-kindnefs doth wring tears from me!
I do embrace your offer; and difpofe
For henceforth of poor Claudio.

 Leon. To-morrow then I will expect your com-
   ing;
To-night I take my leave.——This naughty man
Shall face to face be brought to Margaret,
Who, I believe, was pack'd in all this wrong,[5]
Hir'd to it by your brother.

 Bora.   No, by my foul, fhe was not;
Nor knew not what fhe did, when fhe fpoke to me;
But always hath been juft and virtuous,
In any thing that I do know by her.

 Dogb. Moreover, fir, (which, indeed, is not under white and black,) this plaintiff here, the offender, did call me afs: I befeech you, let it be
remembered in his punifhment: And alfo, the watch
heard them talk of one Deformed: they fay, he
wears a key in his ear, and a lock hanging by it;[6]

---

 [5] *Who, I believe, was* pack'd *in all this wrong,*] i. e. combined;
an accomplice. So, in Lord Bacon's Works, Vol. IV. p. 269.
edit. 1740: " If the iffue fhall be this, that whatever fhall be done
for him, fhall be thought done for a number of perfons that fhall
be laboured and *packed*——." Malone.

 So, in *King Lear:*
   " —— fnuffs and *packings* of the dukes." Steevens.

 Again, in *Melvill's Memoirs,* p. 90: " —— he was a fpecial
inftrument of helping my Lord of Murray and Secretary Lidington
to *pack* up the firft friendfhip betwixt the two queens," &c.
              Reed.

 [6] —— *he wears a* key *in his ear, and a* lock *hanging by it*;]
There could not be a pleafanter ridicule on the fafhion, than the
conftable's defcant on his own blunder. They heard the con-
fpirators fatirize the *fafhion*; whom they took to be a man fur-
named *Deformed.* This the conftable applies with exquifite
humour to the courtiers, in a defcription of one of the moft
fantaftical fafhions of that time, the men's wearing rings in their
ears, and indulging a favourite lock of hair which was brought

and borrows money in God's name;' the which he hath ufed fo long, and never paid, that now men grow hard-hearted, and will lend nothing for God's fake : Pray you, examine him upon that point.

LEON. I thank thee for thy care and honeft pains.'

DOGB. Your worſhip ſpeaks like a moſt thankful and reverend youth ; and I praiſe God for you.

before, and tied with ribbons, and called a *love-lock*. Againſt this faſhion William Prynne wrote his treatiſe, called, *The Unlovelyneſs of Love-Locks*. To this fantaſtick mode Fletcher alludes in his *Cupid's Revenge*: " This morning I brought him a new perriwig with *a lock at it*—And yonder's a fellow come has *bored a hole in his ear*." And again, in his *Woman-Hater*: " —If I could endure an ear with a *hole* in it, or a platted *lock*," &c.
WARBURTON.

Dr. Warburton, I believe, has here (as he frequently does,) refined a little too much. There is no alluſion, I conceive, to the faſhion of wearing rings in the ears (a faſhion which our author himſelf followed). The pleaſantry ſeems to conſiſt in Dogberry's ſuppoſing that the *lock* which DEFORMED wore, muſt have a key to it.

Fynes Moryſon in a very particular account that he has given of the dreſs of Lord Montjoy, (the rival, and afterwards the friend of Robert, Earl of Eſſex,) ſays, that his hair was " thinne on the head, where he wore it ſhort, except a *lock under his left eare*, which he nouriſhed the time of this warre, [the Iriſh War, in 1599,] and being woven up, hid it in his neck under his ruffe." ITINERARY, P. II. p. 45. When he was not on ſervice, he probably wore it in a different faſhion. The portrait of Sir Edward Sackville, Earl of Dorſet, painted by Vandyck, (now at Knowle,) exhibits this lock with a large knotted ribband at the end of it. It hangs under the ear on the left ſide, and reaches as low as where the ſtar is now worn by the knights of the garter.

The ſame faſhion is alluded to in an epigram already quoted :
" Or what he doth with ſuch a horſe-tail-*lock*," &c.
MALONE.

⁸ —— *and* borrows *money in* God's name;] i. e. is a common beggar. This alludes, with too much levity, to the 17th verſe of the xixth chapter of *Proverbs:* " He that giveth to the poor, lendeth unto the Lord." STEEVENS.

LEON. There's for thy pains.

DOGB. God save the foundation! [9]

LEON. Go, I discharge thee of thy prisoner, and I thank thee.

DOGB. I leave an arrant knave with your worship; which, I beseech your worship, to correct yourself, for the example of others. God keep your worship; I wish your worship well; God restore you to health: I humbly give you leave to depart; and if a merry meeting may be wish'd, God prohibit it.—Come, neighbour.

[*Exeunt* DOGBERRY, VERGES, *and* Watch.

LEON. Until to-morrow morning, lords, farewell.

ANT. Farewell, my lords; we look for you to-morrow.

D. PEDRO. We will not fail.

CLAUD. 'To-night I'll mourn with Hero.

[*Exeunt* D. PEDRO *and* CLAUDIO.

LEON. Bring you these fellows on; we'll talk with Margaret,

How her acquaintance grew with this lewd fellow.[2]

[*Exeunt.*

---

[9] *God save the* foundation!] Such was the customary phrase employed by those who received alms at the gates of religious houses. Dogberry, however, in the present instance, might have designed to say—" God save the *founder!*" STEEVENS.

[2] —— lewd *fellow.*] *Lewd,* in this, and several other instances, has not its common meaning, but merely signifies—idle. *ignorant* So, in *King Richard III.* Act I. sc. iii:

" But you must trouble him with *lewd* complaints."

STEEVENS.

again, in the ancient metrical romance of the Sowdon of Babyloyne, &c:

" That writnessith both lerned and lewde."

again, ibid.

" He spared nither lewde nor clerke."

SCENE II.

LEONATO's *Garden.*

Enter BENEDICK *and* MARGARET, *meeting.*

BENE. Pray thee, fweet miftrefs Margaret, de-ferve well at my hands, by helping me to the fpeech of Beatrice.

MARG. Will you then write me a fonnet in praife of my beauty?

BENE. In fo high a ftyle, Margaret, that no man living fhall come over it; for, in moft comely truth, thou deferveft it.

MARG. To have no man come over me? why, fhall I always keep below ftairs?[3]

BENE. Thy wit is as quick as the greyhound's mouth, it catches.

---

[3] *To have no man come* over *me? why, fhall I always keep* below *ftairs?*] I fuppofe, every reader will find the meaning.
JOHNSON.

Left he fhould not, the following inftance from Sir Afton's Cockayne's *Poems* is at his fervice:

"But to prove rather he was not beguil'd,
"Her he *o'er-came*, for he got her with child."

And another, more appofite, from Marfton's *Infatiate Countefs,* 1613:

"Alas! when we are once o'the falling hand,
"A, man may eafily *come over* us."   COLLINS.

Mr. Theobald, to procure an obvious fenfe, would read—*above* ftairs. But there is danger in any attempt to reform a joke two hundred years old.

The fenfe, however, for which Mr. Theobald contends, may be reftored by fuppofing the lofs of a word; and that our author wrote—"Why, fhall I always keep *men* below ftairs?" i. e. never fuffer them to come up into my bed-chamber, for the purpofes of love. STEEVENS.

MARG. And your's as blunt as the fencer's foils, which hit, but hurt not.

BENE. A moſt manly wit, Margaret, it will not hurt a woman; and ſo, I pray thee, call Beatrice: I give thee the bucklers.[4]

MARG. Give us the ſwords, we have bucklers of our own.

BENE. If you uſe them, Margaret, you muſt put in the pikes with a vice; and they are dangerous weapons for maids.

MARG. Well, I will call Beatrice to you, who, I think, hath legs.   [*Exit* MARGARET.

BENE. And therefore will come.

> *The god of love,*   [Singing.]
> *That ſits above,[5]*
> *And knows me, and knows me,*
> *How pitiful I deſerve,——*

---

[4] *—— I give thee the bucklers.*] I ſuppoſe that *to give the bucklers* is, *to yield,* or to *lay by all thoughts of defence,* ſo *clypeum abjicere.* The reſt deſerves no comment. JOHNSON.

Greene, in his Second Part of *Coney-Catching,* 1592, uſes the ſame expreſſion: " At this his maſter laught, and was glad, for further advantage, to *yield the bucklers* to his prentiſe."

Again, in *A Woman never Vex'd,* a comedy by Rowley, 1632: " —into whoſe hands ſhe thruſts the weapons firſt, let him *take up the bucklers.*"

Again, in Decker's *Satiromaſtix*:
" Charge one of them to *take up the bucklers* againſt that hair-monger Horace."

Again, in Chapman's *May-day,* 1611:
" And now I lay *the bucklers* at your feet."

Again, in *Every Woman in her Humour,* 1609:
" —if you lay down *the bucklers,* you loſe the victory."

Again, in P. Holland's tranſlation of Pliny's *Natural Hiſtory,* B. X. Ch. xxi: " —— it goeth againſt his ſtomach (the cock's) to yeeld the gantlet and *give the bucklers.*" STEEVENS.

[5] *The god of love,* &c.] This was the beginning of an old ſong,

I mean, in finging; but in loving,——Leander the good fwimmer, Troilus the firft employer of pandars, and a whole book full of thefe quondam carpet-mongers, whofe names yet run fmoothly in the even road of a blank verfe, why, they were never fo truly turn'd over and over as my poor felf, in love: Marry, I cannot fhow it in rhime; I have try'd; I can find out no rhime to *lady* but *baby*, an innocent rhime; for *fcorn*, *born*, a hard rhime; for *fchool*, *fool*, a babbling rhime; very ominous endings: No, I was not born under a rhiming planet, nor I cannot woo in feftival terms.[6]——

Enter BEATRICE.

Sweet Beatrice, would'ft thou come when I called thee?

BEAT. Yea, fignior, and depart when you bid me.

BENE. O, ftay but till then!

BEAT. Then, is fpoken; fare you well now:——and yet, ere I go, let me go with that I came for,[7] which

by W. E. (William Elderton) a puritanical parody of which, by one W. Birch, under the title of *The complaint of a Sinner, &c.* *Imprinted at London, by Alexander Lacy for Richard Applow,* is ftill extant.   The words in this moralifed copy are as follows:
    " *The god of love, that fits above,*
    " *Doth know us, doth know us,*
    " *How finful that we be.*"   RITSON.

In *Bacchus' Bountie,* &c. 4to. bl. l. 1593, is a fong, beginning——
    " The Gods of love
    " Which raigne above."   STEEVENS.

[6] —— *in* feftival terms.] i. e. in fplendid phrafeology, fuch as differs from common language, as holidays from common days. Thus, Hotfpur, in *K. Henry IV.* P. I:
    " With many *holiday* and lady *terms.*"   STEEVENS.

[7] —— *with that I came* for,] *For,* which is wanting in the old copy, was inferted by Mr. Rowe.   MALONE.

is, with knowing what hath paffed between you and Claudio.

Bene. Only foul words; and thereupon I will kifs thee.

Beat. Foul words is but foul wind, and foul wind is but foul breath, and foul breath is noifome; therefore I will depart unkifs'd.

Bene. Thou haft frighted the word out of his right fenfe, fo forcible is thy wit: But, I muft tell thee plainly, Claudio undergoes my challenge;[8] and either I muft fhortly hear from him, or I will fubfcribe him a coward. And, I pray thee now, tell me, for which of my bad parts didft thou firft fall in love with me?

Beat. For them all together; which maintain'd fo politick a ftate of evil, that they will not admit any good part to intermingle with them. But for which of my good parts did you firft fuffer love for me?

Bene. *Suffer love*; a good epithet! I do fuffer love, indeed, for I love thee againft my will.

Beat. In fpite of your heart, I think; alas! poor heart! If you fpite it for my fake, I will fpite it for yours; for I will never love that which my friend hates.

Bene. Thou and I are too wife to woo peaceably.

Beat. It appears not in this confeffion: there's not one wife man among twenty, that will praife himfelf.

Bene. An old, an old inftance, Beatrice, that

---

[8] —— undergoes *my challenge*;] i. e. is fubject to it. So, in *Cymbeline*, Act III. fc. v: " —— *undergo* thofe employments, wherein I fhould have caufe to ufe thee." STEEVENS.

lived in the time of good neighbours:[9] if a man do not erect in this age his own tomb ere he dies, he shall live no longer in monument, than the bell rings, and the widow weeps.

Beat. And how long is that, think you?

Bene. Question?——Why, an hour in clamour, and a quarter in rheum:[2] Therefore it is most expedient for the wife, (if Don Worm, his conscience, find no impediment to the contrary,) to be the trumpet of his own virtues, as I am to myself: So much for praising myself, (who, I myself will bear witness, is praise-worthy,) and now tell me, How doth your cousin?

Beat. Very ill.

Bene. And how do you?

Beat. Very ill too.

Bene. Serve God, love me, and mend: there will I leave you too, for here comes one in haste.

Enter URSULA.

Urs. Madam, you must come to your uncle; yonder's old coil at home:[3] it is proved, my lady

---

[9] —— *in the time of good neighbours:*] i. e. when men were not envious, but every one gave another his due. The reply is extremely humourous. WARBURTON.

[2] *Question?——Why, an hour, &c.*] i. e. What a question's there, or what a foolish question do you ask? But the Oxford editor, not understanding this phrase, contracted into a single word, (of which we have many instances in English) has fairly struck it out.
WARBURTON.

The phrase occurs frequently in Shakspeare, and means no more than—*you ask a question,* or *that is the question.* RITSON.

[3] —— old coil *at home:*] So, in *King Henry IV.* P. II. Act II. sc. iv: " By the mass, here will be *old* Utis." See note on this

Hero hath been falfely accufed, the prince and Claudio mightily abufed; and Don John is the author of all, who is fled and gone: Will you come prefently?

BEAT. Will you go hear this news, fignior?

BENE. I will live in thy heart, die in thy lap, and be buried in thy eyes; and, moreover, I will go with thee to thy uncle's.   [*Exeunt.*

S C E N E   III.

The infide of a Church.

Enter Don PEDRO, CLAUDIO, *and Attendants with muſick and tapers.*

CLAUD. Is this the monument of Leonato?

ATTEN. It is, my lord.

CLAUD. [*Reads from a ſcroll.*]

> *Done to death* [4] *by ſlanderous tongues*
> *Was the Hero that here lies:*
> *Death, in guerdon* [5] *of her wrongs,*
> *Gives her fame which never dies:*

paffage.   *Old,* (I know not why) was anciently a common augmentative in familiar language.

Coil is buftle, ftir.   So, in *King John:*

" I am not worth this *coil* that's made for me." STEEVENS.

[4] *Done to death* —] This obfolete phrafe occurs frequently in our ancient writers.   Thus, in Marlowe's *Luſt's Dominion,* 1657:

" __
" __

'To *do to* __
Faire mourn __

[5] —— i__

Coftard's u__

The verb, __

*King Henr*__

VOL. __

So the life, that died with shame,
Lives in death with glorious fame.

Hang thou there upon the tomb,   [affixing it.
Praising her when I am dumb.——

Now, musick, sound, and sing your solemn hymn.

S O N G.

Pardon, Goddess of the night,
Those that slew thy virgin knight ; [6]

[6] *Those that slew thy virgin* knight ;] *Knight*, in its original signification, means *follower*, or *pupil*, and in this sense may be feminine. Helena, in *All's well that ends well*, uses *knight* in the same signification. JOHNSON.

Virgin *knight* is virgin hero. In the times of chivalry, a *virgin knight* was one who had as yet atchieved no adventure. Hero had as yet atchieved no matrimonial one. It may be added, that a *virgin knight* wore no device on his shield, having no right to any till he had deserved it.

So, in *The History of Clyomon, Knight of the Golden Shield*, &c. 1599:

    " Then as thou seem'st in thy attire a *virgin knight* to be,

    " Take thou this *shield* likewise *of white*," &c.

It appears, however, from several passages in Spenser's *Faerie Queen*, B. I. c. vii. that an *ideal order* of this name was supposed, as a compliment to Queen Elizabeth's virginity :

    " Of doughtie knights whom faery land did raise

    " That noble order hight of *maidenhed*."

Again, B. II. c. ii :

    " Order of *maidenhed* the most renown'd."

Again, B. II. c. ix :

    " And numbred be mongst knights of *maidenhed*."

On the books of the Stationers' Company in the year 1594, is entered, " ——Pheander the *mayden knight*." STEEVENS.

I do not believe that any allusion was here intended to Hero's having yet atchieved " no matrimonial adventure." *Diana's knight* or *Virgin knight*, was the common poetical appellation of virgins, in Shakspeare's time.

So, in *The Two Noble Kinsmen*, 1634:

    " O sacred, shadowy, cold and constant queen,

    " ——————— who to thy *female knights*

3

For the which, with fongs of woe,
Round about her tomb they go.
Midnight, affift our moan ;
Help us to figh and groan,
Heavily, heavily :
Graves, yawn, and yield your dead,
Till death be uttered,[7]
Heavily, heavily.

CLAUD. Now, unto thy bones good night !
Yearly will I do this rite.

D. PEDRO. Good morrow, mafters; put your
torches out :
The wolves have prey'd; and look, the gentle
y,
Before the wheels of Phœbus, round about
Dapples the drowfy eaft with fpots of grey :
Thanks to you all, and leave us; fare you well.

CLAUD. Good morrow, mafters ; each his feveral
way.

" Allow'ft no more blood than will make a blufh,
" Which is their order's robe,———."
Again, more appofitely in Spenfer's *Faery Queene,* B. III. c. xii :
" Soon as that *virgin knight* he faw in place,
" His wicked bookes in haft he overthrew."
MALONE.

This laft inftance will by no means apply; for the *virgin knight*
is the maiden Britomart, who appeared in the accoutrements of a
knight, and from that circumftance was fo denominated.
STEEVENS.

[7] *Till death be uttered,*] I do not profefs to underftand this line,
which to me appears both defective in fenfe and metre. I fuppofe
two words have been omitted, which perhaps were——
Till fongs of *death be uttered,* &c.
So, in *King Richard III :*
" Out on you, owls! nothing but *fongs of death?*"
STEEVENS.

D. Pedro. Come, let us hence, and put on other
       weeds;
And then to Leonato's we will go.
    Claud. And, Hymen, now with luckier issue
       speed's,
Than this, for whom we render'd up this woe![*]
                           [*Exeunt.*

SCENE IV.

A Room in Leonato's *House.*

Enter Leonato, Antonio, Benedick, Beatrice,
    Ursula, Friar, *and* Hero.

    Friar. Did I not tell you she was innocent?
    Leon. So are the prince and Claudio, who ac-
       cus'd her,
Upon the error that you heard debated:
But Margaret was in some fault for this;
Although against her will, as it appears
In the true course of all the question.
    Ant. Well, I am glad that all things sort so
       well.
    Bene. And so am I, being else by faith enforc'd
To call young Claudio to a reckoning for it.

---

[*] *And, Hymen, now with luckier issue* speed's,
    Than this, for whom we render'd up this woe!] The old copy
has—*speeds.* Steevens.
    Claudio could not know, without being a prophet, that this new
proposed match should have any luckier event than that designed
with Hero. Certainly, therefore, this should be a wish in Claudio;
and, to this end, the poet might have wrote, *speed's;* i. e. *speed us:*
and so it becomes a prayer to Hymen. Thirlby.
    The contraction introduced is so extremely harsh, that I doubt
whether it was intended by the author. However I have followed
former editors in adopting it. Malone.

Leon. Well, daughter, and you gentlewomen all,
Withdraw into a chamber by yourſelves;
And, when I ſend for you, come hither maſk'd:
The prince and Claudio promis'd by, this hour
To viſit me:——You know your office, brother;
You muſt be father to your brother's daughter,
And give her to young Claudio. *[Exeunt Ladies.*

Ant. Which I will do with confirm'd countenance.

Bene. Friar, I muſt entreat your pains, I think.

Friar. To do what, ſignior?

Bene. To bind me, or undo me, one of them.——
Signior Leonato, truth it is, good ſignior,
Your niece regards me with an eye of favour.

Leon. That eye my daughter lent her; 'Tis
moſt true.

Bene. And I do with an eye of love requite her.

Leon. The ſight whereof, I think, you had from
me,
From Claudio, and the prince; But what's your will?

Bene. Your anſwer, ſir, is enigmatical:
But, for my will, my will is, your good will
May ſtand with ours, this day to be conjoin'd
In the ſtate of honourable marriage; [9]——
In which, good friar, I ſhall deſire your help.

Leon. My heart is with your liking.

Friar. And my help.
Here comes the prince, and Claudio.

---

[9] *In the ſtate of honourable* marriage;] *Marriage,* in this inſtance,
is uſed as a triſyllable. So, in *The Taming of the Shrew,* Act III.
ſc. ii:

     " 'Twere good, methinks, to ſteal our *marriage.*"
                           STEEVENS.

Enter Don PEDRO *and* CLAUDIO, *with Attendants.*

D. PEDRO. Good morrow to this fair affembly.

LEON. Good morrow, prince ; good morrow,
   Claudio ;
We here attend you ; Are you yet determin'd
To-day to marry with my brother's daughter?

CLAUD. I'll hold my mind, were fhe an Ethiop.

LEON. Call her forth, brother, here's the friar
   ready.   [*Exit* ANTONIO.

D. PEDRO. Good morrow, Benedick : Why, what's
   the matter,
That you have fuch a February face,
So full of froft, of ftorm, and cloudinefs?

 CLAUD. I think, he thinks upon the favage bull : [2]——
Tufh, fear not, man, we'll tip thy horns with gold,
And all Europa fhall rejoice at thee ; [3]
As once Europa did at lufty Jove,
When he would play the noble beaft in love.

BENE. Bull Jove, fir, had an amiable low ;
And fome fuch ftrange bull leap'd your father's cow,
And got a calf in that fame noble feat,
Much like to you, for you have juft his bleat.

Re-enter ANTONIO, *with the Ladies mafk'd.*

CLAUD. For this I owe you : here come other
   reckonings.
Which is the lady I muft feize upon?

[2] —— *the* favage bull :] Still alluding to the paffage quoted in
a former fcene from Kyd's *Hieronymo.* STEEVENS.

[3] *And all* Europa *fhall*, &c.] I have no doubt but that our
author wrote——
  And all our *Europe,* &c.
So, in *King Richard II :*
  " As were *our* England in reverfion his." STEEVENS.

Ant. This fame is fhe,[4] and I do give you her.

Claud. Why, then fhe's mine: Sweet, let me
    fee your face.

Leon. No, that you fhall not, till you take her
    hand
Before this friar, and fwear to marry her.

Claud. Give me your hand before this holy
    friar;
I am your hufband, if you like of me.

Hero. And when I liv'd, I was your other wife:
                         [Unmafking.
And when you lov'd, you were my other hufband.

Claud. Another Hero?

Hero.   Nothing certainer:
One Hero died defil'd; but I do live,
And, furely as I live, I am a maid.

D. Pedro. The former Hero! Hero that is dead!

Leon. She died, my lord, but whiles her flander
    liv'd.

Friar. All this amazement can I qualify;
When, after that the holy rites are ended,
I'll tell you largely of fair Hero's death:
Mean time, let wonder feem familiar,
And to the chapel let us prefently.

Bene. Soft and fair, friar.——Which is Beatrice?

Beat. I anfwer to that name; [*Unmafking*] What
    is your will?

Bene. Do not you love me?

---

4 Ant. *This fame,* &c.] This fpeech is in the old copies given
to Leonato. Mr. Theobald firft affigned it to the right owner.
Leonato has in a former part of this fcene told Antonio,——that *he*
" muft be father to his brother's daughter, and *give her* to young
Claudio." Malone.

BEAT.   No, no more than reason.[5]

BENE. Why, then your uncle, and the prince,
        and Claudio,
Have been deceived; for they swore you did.[6]

BEAT. Do not you love me?

BENE.   No, no more than reason.[7]

BEAT. Why, then my cousin, Margaret, and
        Ursula,
Are much deceiv'd; for they did swear, you did.

BENE. They swore that you were almost sick for
        me.

BEAT. They swore that you were well-nigh dead
        for me.

BENE. 'Tis no such matter :—Then, you do not
        love me?

BEAT. No, truly, but in friendly recompence.

LEON. Come, cousin, I am sure you love the gen-
        tleman.

CLAUD. And I'll be sworn upon't, that he loves
        her;
For here's a paper, written in his hand,
A halting sonnet of his own pure brain,
Fashion'd to Beatrice.

HERO.   And here's another,

---

[5] *No, no more than reason.*] The old copies, injuriously to metre,
read—*Why*, no, &c. It should seem that the compositor's eye
had caught the here unnecessary adverb from the following speech.
                                        STEEVENS.

[6] —— for *they swore you did.*] *For*, which both the sense and
metre require, was inserted by Sir Thomas Hanmer. So, below :
    " Are much deceiv'd; *for* they did swear you did."
                                        MALONE.

[7] *No, no more than reason.*] Here again the metre, in the old
copies, is overloaded by reading—Troth, *no, no more*, &c.
                                        STEEVENS.

Writ in my coufin's hand, ftolen from her pocket,
Containing her affection unto Benedick.

Bene. A miracle! here's our own hands againft
our hearts!—Come, I will have thee; but, by this
light, I take thee for pity.

Beat. I would not deny you;—but, by this good
day, I yield upon great perfuafion; and, partly, to
fave your life, for I was told you were in a con-
fumption.

Bene. Peace, I will ftop your mouth.

[*Kiffing her.*

D. Pedro. How doft thou, Benedick the married man?

Bene. I'll tell thee what, prince; a college of
wit-crackers cannot flout me out of my humour:

---

8   *I would* not *deny you;* &c.] Mr. Theobald fays, *is not this
mock-reafoning? She would not deny him, but that fhe yields upon
great perfuafion. In changing the negative, I make no doubt but I
have retrieved the poet's humour:* and fo changes *not* into *yet.* But
is not this a *mock-critic?* who could not fee that the plain obvious
fenfe of the common reading was this, I cannot find in my heart
to deny you, but for all that I yield, after having ftood out great
perfuafions to fubmiffion. He had faid—*I take thee for pity,* fhe
replies—*I would not deny thee,* i. e. I take thee for pity too: but
as I live, I am won to this compliance by importunity of friends.
Mr. Theobald, by altering *not* to *yet,* makes it fuppofed that *he*
had been importunate, and that *fhe* had often denied, which was
not the cafe.   WARBURTON.

9   *Bene. Peace, I will ftop your mouth.* [Kiffing her.] In former
copies:
    Leon. *Peace, I will ftop your mouth.*
What can Leonato mean by this? " Nay, pray, peace, niece!
don't keep up this obftinacy of profeffions, for I have proofs to
ftop your mouth." The ingenious Dr. Thirlby agreed with me,
that this ought to be given to Benedick, who, upon faying it,
kiffes Beatrice; and this being done before the whole company,
how natural is the reply which the prince makes upon it?
    How doft thou, Benedick the married man?
Befides, this mode of fpeech, preparatory to a falute, is familiar
to our poet in common with other ftage-writers.   THEOBALD.

Doſt thou think, I care for a ſatire, or an epigram?
No: if a man will be beaten with brains, he ſhall
wear nothing handſome about him: In brief, ſince
I do purpoſe to marry, I will think nothing to any
purpoſe that the world can ſay againſt it; and
therefore never flout at me for what I have ſaid
againſt it; for man is a giddy thing, and this is my
concluſion.——For thy part, Claudio, I did think
to have beaten thee; but in that[8] thou art like to
be my kinſman, live unbruis'd, and love my couſin.

CLAUD. I had well hoped, thou wouldſt have denied Beatrice, that I might have cudgell'd thee out
of thy ſingle life, to make thee a double dealer;
which, out of queſtion, thou wilt be, if my couſin
do not look exceeding narrowly to thee.

BENE. Come, come, we are friends:——let's have
a dance ere we are married, that we may lighten
our own hearts, and our wives' heels.

LEON. We'll have dancing afterwards.

BENE. Firſt, o' my word; therefore, play, muſick.——

Prince, thou art ſad; get thee a wife, get thee a
wife: there is no ſtaff more reverend than one
tipp'd with horn.[9]

---

[8] ——*in that*—] i. e. becauſe. So, Hooker: "Things are
preached not *in that* they are taught, but *in that* they are publiſhed." STEEVENS.

[9] ——*no* ſtaff *more reverend than one* tipp'd with horn.] This
paſſage may admit of ſome explanation that I am unable to furniſh.
By accident I loſt ſeveral inſtances I had collected for the purpoſe
of throwing light on it. The following, however, may aſſiſt the
future commentator.

MS. Sloan, 1691.

" THAT   A   FELLON   MAY   WAGE   BATTAILE,   WITH   THE
ORDER   THEREOF.

" ——by order of the lawe both the parties muſt at their owne
charge be armed withoute any yron or long armoure, and their

Enter a Meſſenger.

Mess. My lord, your brother John is ta'en in
           flight,
And brought with armed men back to Meſſina.

Bene. Think not on him till to-morrow; I'll
deviſe thee brave puniſhments for him.——Strike up,
pipers.   [*Dance.*
                                                [*Exeunt.*

heades bare, and bare-handed and bare-footed, every one of them
having a *baſton horned* at ech ende, of one length," &c.

Again, in Stowe's *Chronicle*, edit. 1615, p. 669: "—— his
baſton a *ſtaffe* of an elle long, made taper-wiſe, *tipt with horne,*
&c. was borne after him." Steevens.

Again, *Britton, Pleas of the Crown*, c. xxvii. f. 18: " Next let
them go to combat armed without iron and without linnen armour,
their heads uncovered and their hands naked, and on foot, with
two baſtons tipped with horn of equal length, and each of them a
target of four corners, without any other armour, whereby any of
them may annoy the other; and if either of them have any other
weapon concealed about him, and therewith annoy his adverſary,
let it be done as ſhall be mentioned amongſt combats in a plea of
land." Reed.

Mr. Steevens's explanation is undoubtedly the true one. The
alluſion is certainly to the ancient trial by *wager of battel,* in ſuits
both criminal and civil. The quotation above given recites the
form in the former caſe,——viz. an appeal of felony. The practice
was nearly ſimilar in civil caſes, upon iſſue joined in a writ of
right. Of the laſt trial of this kind in England, (which was in
the thirteenth year of Queen Elizabeth,) our author might have
read a particular account in Stowe's *Annales.* Henry Nailor,
maſter of defence, was champion for the demandants, Simon Low
and John Kyme; and George Thorne for the tenant, (or defendant,)
Thomas Paramoure. The combat was appointed to be fought in
Tuthill-fields, and the Judges of the Common Pleas and Serjeants
at law attended. But a compromiſe was entered into between the
parties, the evening before the appointed day, and they only went
through the forms, for the greater ſecurity of the tenant. Among
other ceremonies Stowe mentions, that " the gauntlet that was caſt
down by George Thorne was borne before the ſayd Nailor, in his
paſſage through London, upon a ſword's point, and his baſton (a

*inſtrument is also mentioned in the
naire's Tale of Chaucer:
is felow had a staf tipped with horne."*

ſtaff of an ell long, made taper-wiſe, *tipt with horn*,) with his ſhield of hard leather, was borne after him," &c. See alſo Minſheu's Dict. 1617, in v. *Combat*; from which it appears that Naylor on this occaſion was introduced to the Judges, with " *three ſolemn congees*," by a very *reverend* perſon, " Sir Jerome Bowes, ambaſſador from Queen Elizabeth into Ruſſia, who carried a red *baſton* of an ell long, *tipped with horne*."—In a very ancient law-book entitled *Britton*, the manner in which the combatants are to be armed is particularly mentioned. The quotation from the Sloanian MS. is a tranſlation from thence. By a ridiculous miſtake the words, " ſauns lōge arme," are rendered in the modern tranſlation of that book, printed a few years ago, " without *linnen armour*;" and " a mains nues and pies" [bare-handed and bare-footed] is tranſlated, " and their hands naked, and *on foot*. MALONE.

This play may be juſtly ſaid to contain two of the moſt ſprightly characters that Shakſpeare ever drew. The wit, the humouriſt, the gentleman, and the ſoldier, are combined in Benedick. It is to be lamented, indeed, that the firſt and moſt ſplendid of theſe diſtinctions, is diſgraced by unneceſſary profaneneſs; for the goodneſs of his heart is hardly ſufficient to atone for the licence of his tongue. The too ſarcaſtic levity, which flaſhes out in the converſation of Beatrice, may be excuſed on account of the ſteadineſs and friendſhip ſo apparent in her behaviour, when ſhe urges her lover to riſque his life by a challenge to Claudio. In the conduct of the fable, however, there is an imperfection ſimilar to that which Dr. Johnſon has pointed out in *The Merry Wives of Windſor* :—the ſecond contrivance is leſs ingenious than the firſt:—or, to ſpeak more plainly, the ſame incident is become ſtale by repetition. I wiſh ſome other method had been found to entrap Beatrice, than that very one which before had been ſucceſsfully practiſed on Benedick.

Much ado about Nothing, (as I underſtand from one of Mr. Vertue's MSS.) formerly paſſed under the title of *Benedick and Beatrix*. Heming the player received, on the 20th of May, 1613, the ſum of forty pounds, and twenty pounds more as his Majeſty's gratuity, for exhibiting ſix plays at Hampton-Court, among which was this comedy. STEEVENS.

THE END OF THE FOURTH VOLUME.

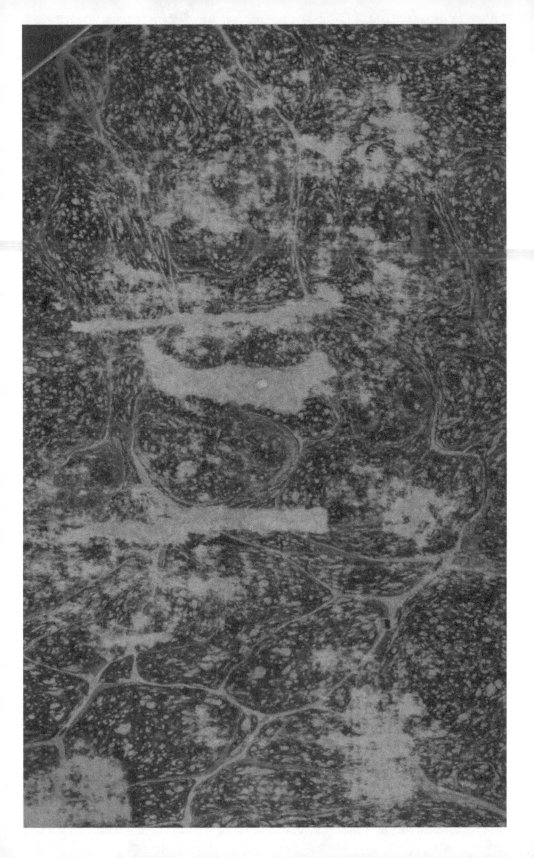

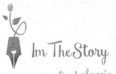

Im TheStory

personalised classic books

"Beautiful gift.. lovely finish.
My Niece loves it, so precious!"

Helen R Brumfieldon

★★★★★

UNIQUE GIFT

FOR KIDS, PARTNERS
AND FRIENDS

Timeless books such as:

Kids

Alice in Wonderland · The Jungle Book · The Wonderful Wizard of Oz
Peter and Wendy · Robin Hood · The Prince and The Pauper
The Railway Children · Treasure Island · A Christmas Carol

Adults

Romeo and Juliet · Dracula

Highly Customizable **Change** Books Title **Replace** Characters Names with yours **Upload** Photo not inside page **Add** Inscriptions

Visit
Im TheStory .com
and order yours today!

CPSIA information can be obtained
at www.ICGtesting.com
Printed in the USA
BVHW082121250819
556756BV00010B/847/P